Twelfth Edition

Accounting

What the Numbers Mean

David H. Marshall, MBA, CPA, CMA

Wayne W. McManus, LLM, JD, MS, MBA, CFA, CPA, CMA, CIA
Professor of Accounting and Law
International College of the Cayman Islands

Daniel F. Viele, MS, CPA, CMA
Professor of Accounting
Dean, School of Adult & Online Education
Maryville University

Mc
Graw
Hill
Education

ACCOUNTING: WHAT THE NUMBERS MEAN, TWELFTH EDITION

Published by McGraw-Hill Education, 2 Penn Plaza, New York, NY 10121. Copyright © 2020 by McGraw-Hill Education. All rights reserved. Printed in the United States of America. Previous editions © 2017, 2014, and 2011. No part of this publication may be reproduced or distributed in any form or by any means, or stored in a database or retrieval system, without the prior written consent of McGraw-Hill Education, including, but not limited to, in any network or other electronic storage or transmission, or broadcast for distance learning.

Some ancillaries, including electronic and print components, may not be available to customers outside the United States.

This book is printed on acid-free paper.

1 2 3 4 5 6 7 8 9 LWI 21 20 19

ISBN 978-1-259-96952-2
MHID 1-259-96952-5 (bound edition)

ISBN 978-1-260-48069-6 (loose-leaf edition)
MHID 1-260-48069-0 (loose-leaf edition)

Portfolio Manager: *Steve Schuetz*
Product Developers: *Jaroslaw Szymanski / Michael McCormick*
Marketing Manager: Michelle Williams
Lead Content Project Managers: *Dana M. Pauley / Brian Nacik*
Senior Buyer: *Sandy Ludovissy*
Design: *Jessica Cuevas*
Content Licensing Specialist: *Beth Cray*
Cover Image: *©Ingram Publishing*
Compositor: *SPi Global*

All credits appearing on page or at the end of the book are considered to be an extension of the copyright page.

Library of Congress Cataloging-in-Publication Data

Names: Marshall, David H., author. | McManus, Wayne W., author. | Viele, Daniel F., author.
Title: Accounting : what the numbers mean / David H. Marshall, MBA, CPA, CMA,
Professor of Accounting Emeritus, Millikin University, Wayne W. McManus,
LLM, JD, MS, MBA, CFA, CPA, CMA, CIA, Professor of Accounting and Law,
International College of the Cayman Islands, Daniel F. Viele, MS, CPA,
CMA, Professor of Accounting, Dean, School of Adult & Online Education,
Maryville University.
Description: Twelfth edition. | New York, NY : McGraw-Hill Education, [2020]
Identifiers: LCCN 2018043223 | ISBN 9781259969522 (alk. paper)
Subjects: LCSH: Accounting. | Managerial accounting.
Classification: LCC HF5636 .M37 2020 | DDC 657—dc23
LC record available at https://lccn.loc.gov/2018043223

The Internet addresses listed in the text were accurate at the time of publication. The inclusion of a website does not indicate an endorsement by the authors or McGraw-Hill Education, and McGraw-Hill Education does not guarantee the accuracy of the information presented at these sites.

mheducation.com/highered

Meet the Authors

David H. Marshall (1933–2018) was Professor of Accounting Emeritus at Millikin University. He taught at Millikin, a small, independent university located in Decatur, Illinois, for 25 years. He taught courses in accounting, finance, computer information systems, and business policy, and was recognized as an outstanding teacher. The draft manuscript of this book was written in 1986 and used in a one-semester course that was developed for the nonbusiness major. Subsequently supplemented with cases, it was used in the business core accounting principles and managerial accounting courses. Concurrently, a one-credit-hour accounting laboratory taught potential accounting majors the mechanics of the accounting process. Prior to his teaching career, Marshall worked in public accounting and industry and he earned an MBA from Northwestern University. Professor Marshall's interests outside academia included community service, woodturning, sailing, and travel. It is with great sadness that we announce his passing on April 17, 2018.

Courtesy of David H. Marshall

Wayne W. McManus makes his home in Grand Cayman, Cayman Islands, BWI, where he worked in the private banking sector for several years and is now a semiretired consultant. He maintains an ongoing relationship with the International College of the Cayman Islands as an adjunct Professor of Accounting and Law and is the Chair of the College's Board of Trustees. McManus offers the Cayman CPA Review course through the Financial Education Institute Ltd. and several professional development courses through the Chamber of Commerce. He earned an MS in accounting from Illinois State University, an MBA from the University of Kansas, a law degree from Northern Illinois University, and a master's of law in taxation from the University of Missouri–Kansas City. He serves as an independent director and chairman of the audit committee for Endeavour Mining Corp. (EDV on the TSX exchange). He is a member of the Cayman Islands Institute of Professional Accountants and the local chapter of the CFA Institute. Professor McManus volunteers as a "professional" Santa each December, enjoys travel, golf, and scuba diving, and is an audio/video enthusiast.

Courtesy of Wayne W. MacManus

Daniel F. Viele is Professor of Accounting and currently serves as Dean of the School of Adult and Online Education and directs the Office of Strategic Information at Maryville University of Saint Louis. He has taught courses in financial, managerial, and cost accounting, as well as accounting information systems. Prior to joining Maryville, Professor Viele's previous teaching experience includes 15 years at Webster University and 10 years at Millikin University with Professor Marshall. He has also served as a systems consultant to the graphics arts industry. Professor Viele has developed and taught numerous online graduate courses, and for his leadership role in pioneering online teaching and learning, he was presented a Presidential Recognition Award. His students and colleagues have also cited his dedication to teaching and innovative use of technology for which Webster awarded him its highest honor—the Kemper Award for Teaching Excellence. Professor Viele holds an MS in accounting from Colorado State University and has completed the Information Systems Faculty Development Institute at the University of Minnesota and the Advanced Information Systems Faculty Development Institute at Indiana University. He is a member of the American Accounting Association and the Institute of Management Accountants, where he has served as president of the Sangamon Valley Chapter and as a member of the National Board of Directors. Professor Viele enjoys sports of all kinds, boating, and a good book.

Courtesy of Daniel F. Viele

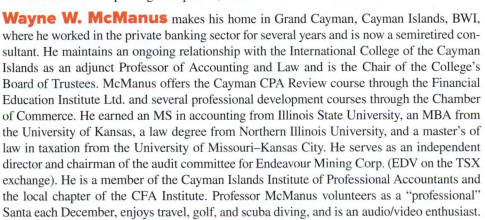

In Loving Memory

of

David H. Marshall
March 12, 1933 - April 17, 2018

David was our colleague, mentor, and friend. The marks that he left on each of our lives are indelible and will never be forgotten. Words simply cannot describe what a good man that he was.

"Write down what you know, and solve for the difference."

Wayne and Dan

Named

Named after a Chinese word meaning "sparrow," mah-jongg is a centuries-old game of skill. The object of the game is to collect different tiles; players win points by accumulating different combinations of pieces and creating patterns. We've chosen mah-jongg tiles as our cover image for the twelfth edition of *Accounting: What the Numbers Mean* because the text is designed to show students how to put the pieces together and understand their relationship to one another to see the larger pattern.

Accounting has become known as the language of business. Financial statements result from the accounting process and are used by owners/investors, employees, creditors, and regulators in their planning, controlling, and decision-making activities as they evaluate the achievement of an organization's objectives.

Accounting: What the Numbers Mean takes the user through the basics: what accounting information is, how it is developed, how it is used, and what it means. Financial statements are examined to learn what they do and do not communicate, enhancing the student's decision-making and problem-solving abilities from a user perspective. Achieving expertise in the preparation of financial statements is not an objective of this text. Instead, we have designed these materials to assist those who wish to learn "what the numbers mean" in a clear, concise, and conceptual manner, without focusing on the mechanical aspects of the accounting process.

The user-oriented approach taken by this text will benefit a variety of non-accounting majors, including students focusing on other areas of business or nonbusiness programs such as engineering, behavioral sciences, public administration, or prelaw. Aspiring MBA and other graduate management or administration students who do not have an undergraduate business degree will likewise benefit from a course using this text.

Best wishes for successful use of the information presented here.

David H. Marshall

Wayne W. McManus

Daniel F. Viele

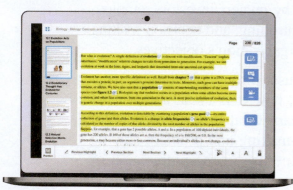
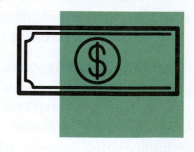
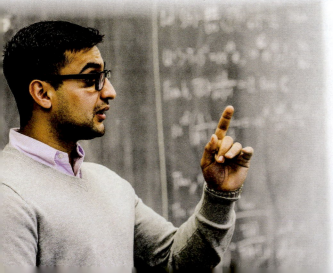

Effective, efficient studying.

Connect helps you be more productive with your study time and get better grades using tools like SmartBook, which highlights key concepts and creates a personalized study plan. Connect sets you up for success, so you walk into class with confidence and walk out with better grades.

©Shutterstock/wavebreakmedia

> " I really liked this app—it made it easy to study when you don't have your textbook in front of you. "
>
> - Jordan Cunningham, Eastern Washington University

Study anytime, anywhere.

Download the free ReadAnywhere app and access your online eBook when it's convenient, even if you're offline. And since the app automatically syncs with your eBook in Connect, all of your notes are available every time you open it. Find out more at **www.mheducation.com/readanywhere**

No surprises.

The Connect Calendar and Reports tools keep you on track with the work you need to get done and your assignment scores. Life gets busy; Connect tools help you keep learning through it all.

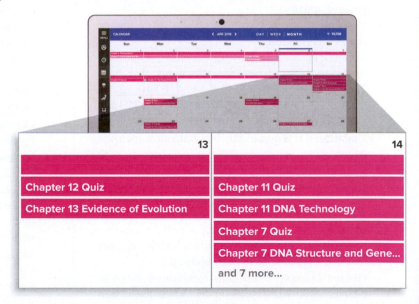

13	14
Chapter 12 Quiz	Chapter 11 Quiz
Chapter 13 Evidence of Evolution	Chapter 11 DNA Technology
	Chapter 7 Quiz
	Chapter 7 DNA Structure and Gene...
	and 7 more...

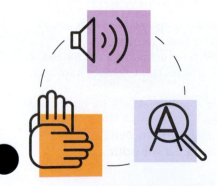

Learning for everyone.

McGraw-Hill works directly with Accessibility Services Departments and faculty to meet the learning needs of all students. Please contact your Accessibility Services office and ask them to email accessibility@mheducation.com, or visit **www.mheducation.com/about/accessibility.html** for more information.

Enhancements for This Edition

Chapter 1
- SmartBook assessments within each chapter learning objective have been updated.
- Overall chapter content revisions for clarity and general updates, including an updated discussion of international financial reporting issues.
- Updated references to Campbell's 2017 annual report information.
- Update and revision of the Test Bank.
- Update and revision of the PowerPoints.

Chapter 2
- SmartBook assessments within each chapter learning objective have been updated.
- Guided example video demonstrations for end of chapter Mini-Exercises and Exercises have been updated.
- Overall chapter content revisions for clarity and general updates.
- Updated references to Campbell's 2017 annual report information.
- General update of all Mini-Exercises, Exercises, Problems, and Cases. Specific items that have been refreshed include: M2.2, M2.4, E2.10, E2.12, E2.14, P2.16, P2.18, P2.22, P2.24, P2.25, and P2.26.
- Update and revision of the Test Bank now includes quantitative multiple-choice questions, with 10 percent new multiple-choice questions added.
- Update and revision of the PowerPoints and Demonstration Problem PowerPoints.

Chapter 3
- SmartBook assessments within each chapter learning objective have been updated.
- Guided example video demonstrations for end of chapter Mini-Exercises and Exercises have been updated.
- Overall chapter content revisions for clarity and general updates.
- Reintegrated Campbell's 2017 annual report information for the financial and graphical analysis of liquidity and profitability trends.
- General update of all Mini-Exercises, Exercises, Problems, and Cases. Specific items that have been refreshed include: M3.2, M3.4, M3.6, E3.7, E3.8, E3.10, E3.12, E3.14, E3.16, E3.17, P3.20, P3.22, and C3.24.
- Update and revision of the Test Bank now includes quantitative multiple-choice questions, with 50 percent new multiple-choice questions added.
- Update and revision of the PowerPoints and Demonstration Problem PowerPoints.

Chapter 4
- SmartBook assessments within each chapter learning objective have been updated.
- Guided example video demonstrations for end of chapter Mini-Exercises and Exercises have been updated.
- Overall chapter content revisions for clarity and general updates. Specific rewrites or enhancements to add clarity or visualization of concepts have been added for the following content items: the adjustments section of the chapter, the Business in Practice Box on Bookkeeping Language In Everyday English, and the flowchart illustrating the bookkeeping process.
- A Study Suggestion has been added to explain that adjustments are necessitated by cash leads and cash lags.
- General update of all Mini-Exercises, Exercises, Problems, and Cases. Specific items that have been refreshed include: M4.4, E4.6, E4.8, E4.10, E4.12, E4.14, E4.16, E4.18, E4.20, P4.24, P4.26, P4.27, and C4.30.
- Update and revision of the Test Bank now includes quantitative multiple-choice questions, with 10 percent new multiple-choice questions added.
- Update and revision of the PowerPoints and Demonstration Problem PowerPoints.

Chapter 5
- SmartBook assessments within each chapter learning objective have been updated.
- Guided example video demonstrations for end of chapter Mini-Exercises and Exercises have been updated.
- Overall chapter content revisions for clarity and general updates.

- Updated discussion and analysis of Campbell's 2017 annual report information for the accounting and presentation of current assets, including cash, accounts receivable, and inventories.
- General update of all Mini-Exercises, Exercises, Problems, and Cases. Specific items that have been refreshed include: M5.1, M5.2, M5.3, M5.4, M5.6, E5.8. E5.10, E5.12, E5.16, E5.20, E5.22, E5.24, P5.26, P5.27, P5.28, P5.30, P5.32, P5.34, and P5.36. Note also that C5.38 has been deleted.
- Update and revision of the Test Bank now includes quantitative multiple-choice questions, with 19 percent new multiple-choice questions added.
- Update and revision of the PowerPoints and Demonstration Problem PowerPoints.

Chapter 6
- SmartBook assessments within each chapter learning objective have been updated.
- Guided example video demonstrations for end of chapter Mini-Exercises and Exercises have been updated.
- Overall chapter content revisions for clarity and general updates. The Accounting for Leases section of the chapter was significantly rewritten to reflect recent accounting standards updates.
- Updated discussion and analysis of Campbell's 2017 annual report information for the accounting and presentation of property, plant, and equipment, and other noncurrent assets.
- General update of all Mini-Exercises, Exercises, Problems, and Cases. Specific items that have been refreshed include: M6.2, M6.3, M6.4, M6.6, E6.8, E6.14, E6.16, E6.18, E6.20, P6.22, P6.24, P6.26, P6.28, P6.29, P6.30, P6.32, and C6.34.
- Update and revision of the Test Bank now includes quantitative multiple-choice questions, with 17 percent new multiple-choice questions added.
- Update and revision of the PowerPoints and Demonstration Problem PowerPoints.

Chapter 7
- SmartBook assessments within each chapter learning objective have been updated.
- Guided example video demonstrations for end of chapter Mini-Exercises and Exercises have been updated.

- Overall chapter content revisions for clarity and general updates.
- Updated discussion and analysis of Campbell's 2017 annual report information for the accounting and presentation of liabilities.
- General update of all Mini-Exercises, Exercises, Problems, and Cases. Specific items that have been refreshed include: M7.2, M7.4, E7.6, E7.8, E7.10, E7.12, E7.14, E7.16, E7.18, E7.22, E7.24, P7.25, P7.26, P7.28, P7.30, and P7.32.
- Update and revision of the Test Bank now includes quantitative multiple-choice questions, with 13 percent new multiple-choice questions added.
- Update and revision of the PowerPoints and Demonstration Problem PowerPoints.

Chapter 8
- SmartBook assessments within each chapter learning objective have been updated.
- Guided example video demonstrations for end of chapter Mini-Exercises and Exercises have been updated.
- Overall chapter content revisions for clarity and general updates, with a specific rewrite of the accumulated other comprehensive income section.
- Updated discussion and analysis of Campbell's 2017 annual report information for the accounting and presentation of stockholders' equity.
- General update of all Mini-Exercises, Exercises, Problems, and Cases. Specific items that have been refreshed include: M8.2, M8.4, E8.6, E8.8, E8.10, E8.12, E8.14, E8.18, E8.20, E8.22, P8.24, P8.26, P8.28, P8.30, P8.32, C8.34, C8.35, and C8.36.
- Update and revision of the Test Bank now includes quantitative multiple-choice questions, with 30 percent new multiple-choice questions added.
- Update and revision of the PowerPoints and Demonstration Problem PowerPoints.

Chapter 9
- SmartBook assessments within each chapter learning objective have been updated.
- Guided example video demonstrations for end of chapter Mini-Exercises and Exercises have been updated.

- Overall chapter content revisions for clarity and general updates.
- Updated discussion and analysis of Campbell's 2017 annual report information for the presentation and disclosure of income statement and statement of cash flows data.
- General update of all Mini-Exercises, Exercises, Problems, and Cases. Specific items that have been refreshed include: M9.2, M9.4, E9.6, E9.8, E9.9. E9.10. E9.12, E9.13, E9.16, E9.18. P9.20. P9.22, P9.24, P9.26, and C9.33.
- Update and revision of the Test Bank now includes quantitative multiple-choice questions, with 54 percent new multiple-choice questions added.
- Update and revision of the PowerPoints and Demonstration Problem PowerPoints.

Chapter 10

- SmartBook assessments within each chapter learning objective have been updated.
- Guided example video demonstrations for end of chapter Mini-Exercises and Exercises have been updated.
- Overall chapter content revisions for clarity and general updates. Specific rewrites have been added for the following content items: mention of the impact of the *Internal Control - Integrated Framework* (2013) issued by the Committee of Sponsoring Organizations of the Treadway Commission (COSO) and the Tax Cuts and Jobs Act of 2017; updates to the "general organization of the notes" with more detail regarding the types of financial statements presented, and the order in which they usually appear; new discussion of "Big R" and "little r" financial statement restatements and the recent trends observed in each category.
- Updated discussion and analysis of Campbell's 2017 annual report information for the Notes to the Financial Statements section of the chapter.
- General update of all Mini-Exercises, Exercises, Problems, and Cases. Specific items that have been refreshed include: M10.2, E10.3, E10.8, E10.10, P10.11, P10.12, and C10.14.
- Update and revision of the Test Bank.
- Update and revision of the PowerPoints and Demonstration Problem PowerPoints.

Chapter 11

- SmartBook assessments within each chapter learning objective have been updated.
- Guided example video demonstrations for end of chapter Mini-Exercises and Exercises have been updated.
- Overall chapter content revisions for clarity and general updates.
- Updated discussion of Campbell's 2017 annual report information for the performance of financial ratio analysis.
- General update of all Mini-Exercises, Exercises, Problems, and Cases. Specific items that have been refreshed include: M11.2, M11.4, P11.9, P11.10, P11.14, C11.16, and C11.18.
- Update and revision of the Test Bank now includes quantitative multiple-choice questions, with 64 percent new multiple-choice questions added.
- Update and revision of the PowerPoints and Demonstration Problem PowerPoints.

Chapter 12

- SmartBook assessments within each chapter learning objective have been updated.
- Guided example video demonstrations for new end of chapter Mini-Exercises have been added.
- Overall chapter content revisions for clarity and general updates. Specific rewrites or enhancements to add clarity or visualization of concepts have been added for the following content items: the management control process, the relevant range assumption, expressing fixed costs per unit, the cost formula, the contribution margin ratio, and interpreting a break-even chart.
- Chapter Study Suggestion, FYI, and Business in Practice boxes updated or replaced.
- General update of all Mini-Exercises, Exercises, Problems, and Cases. New Mini-exercises M12.6 and M12.7 have been added. Specific items that have been refreshed include: M12.2, M12.4, M12.8, E12.10, E12.12, E12.14, E12.16, E12.18, P12.20, P12.22, P12.24, P12.26, P12.28, P12.30, and P12.34.
- Update and revision of the Test Bank now includes quantitative multiple-choice questions, with 14 percent new multiple-choice questions added.

- Update and revision of the PowerPoints and Demonstration Problem PowerPoints.

Chapter 13

- SmartBook assessments within each chapter learning objective have been updated.
- Guided example video demonstrations for new end of chapter Mini-Exercises have been added.
- Overall chapter content revisions for clarity and general updates. Specific rewrites or enhancements to add clarity or visualization of concepts have been added for the following content items: chapter introduction, the value chain, manufacturing inventory accounts, product costing process steps, Campbell Soup discussion, process costing and equivalent units of production, and reporting differences using absorption vs. direct costing. New section headings for Product Costing and Statement of Cost of Goods Manufactured have also been added.
- Chapter Study Suggestion, FYI, and Business in Practice boxes updated or replaced.
- General update of all Mini-Exercises, Exercises, Problems, and Cases. New Mini-exercises M13.5 and M13.7 have been added. Specific items that have been refreshed include: M13.2, M13.4, M13.8, E13.10, E13.12, E13.14, E13.16, E13.18, E13.20, E13.22, P13.24, P13.26, P13.28, P13.30, and C13.33.
- Update and revision of the Test Bank now includes quantitative multiple-choice questions, with 22 percent new multiple-choice questions added.
- Update and revision of the PowerPoints and Demonstration Problem PowerPoints.

Chapter 14

- SmartBook assessments within each chapter learning objective have been updated.
- Guided example video demonstrations for new end of chapter Mini-Exercises have been added.
- Overall chapter content revisions for clarity and general updates. Specific rewrites or enhancements to add clarity or visualization of concepts have been added for the following content items: management's approach to the budgeting process, using the model for purchases/production budgets,

and behavioral implications of standard setting strategy.

- Chapter Study Suggestion, FYI, and Business in Practice boxes updated or replaced.
- General update of all Mini-Exercises, Exercises, Problems, and Cases. New Mini-exercises M14.1 and M14.6 have been added. Specific items that have been refreshed include: M14.3, M14.5, M14.7, M14.8, E14.10, E14.12, E14.14, E14.16, E14.18, P14.20, P14.24, P14.26, and C14.28.
- Update and revision of the Test Bank now includes quantitative multiple-choice questions, with 18 percent new multiple-choice questions added.
- Update and revision of the PowerPoints and Demonstration Problem PowerPoints.

Chapter 15

- SmartBook assessments within each chapter learning objective have been updated.
- Guided example video demonstrations for new end of chapter Mini-Exercises have been added.
- Overall chapter content revisions for clarity and general updates. Specific rewrites or enhancements to add clarity or visualization of concepts have been added for the following content items: understanding favorable and unfavorable variances, the design of performance reports, discussion of Exhibit 15-3, direct and common fixed expenses, and the transfer pricing discussion.
- Chapter Study Suggestion, FYI, and Business in Practice boxes updated or replaced.
- General update of all Mini-Exercises, Exercises, Problems, and Cases. New Mini-exercises M15.7 and M15.8 have been added. Specific items that have been refreshed include: M15.1, M15.2, M15.3, M15.4, M15.5, E15.10, M15.12, M15.14, M15.16, M15.18, M15.20, P15.22, P15.24, P15.26, and C15.34.
- Update and revision of the Test Bank now includes quantitative multiple-choice questions, with 26 percent new multiple-choice questions added.
- Update and revision of the PowerPoints and Demonstration Problem PowerPoints.

Chapter 16

- SmartBook assessments within each chapter learning objective have been updated.

- Guided example video demonstrations for new end of chapter Mini-Exercises have been added.
- Overall chapter content revisions for clarity and general updates. Specific rewrites or enhancements to add clarity or visualization of concepts have been added for the following content items: relevant costs, introduction for analytical considerations for NPV model, new graphic presentation of payback period, and new graphic IRR using Excel.
- Chapter Study Suggestion, FYI, and Business in Practice boxes updated or replaced.
- General update of all Mini-Exercises, Exercises, Problems, and Cases. New Mini-exercises M16.4 and M16.5 have been added. Specific items that have been refreshed include: M16.2, M16.6, M16.8, E16.12, E16.14, E16.16, E16.18, E16.20, E16.22, E16.24, E16.26, E16.28, P16.30, P16.32, P16.34, P16.36, P16.38, C16.40, and C16.41.
- Update and revision of the Test Bank now includes quantitative multiple-choice questions, with 15 percent new multiple-choice questions added.

- Update and revision of the PowerPoints and Demonstration Problem PowerPoints.

Epilogue:
- Overall content revisions for clarity and general updates. Specific rewrites or enhancements to add clarity or visualization of concepts have been added for the following content items: welcome section and scandals discussion, ethics compliance and corporate progress, IFRS adoption and reporting in the U.S., data warehousing, data mining, big data, predictive analytics, prescriptive analytics, and artificial intelligence.
- New infographic added reporting ethics and compliance data in large corporations and new graphic added for IFRS adoption status in the U.S.
- Updated or added FYI box information for the following items: worst corporate scandals, CPA Vision Project and Horizons 2025 Report, and information resources for big data and artificial intelligence.

Acknowledgments

The task of creating and revising a textbook is not accomplished by the work of the authors alone. Thoughtful feedback from reviewers is integral to the development process and gratitude is extended to all who have participated in earlier reviews of *Accounting: What the Numbers Mean* as well as to our most recent panel of reviewers. Your help in identifying strengths to further develop and areas of weakness to improve was invaluable to us. We are grateful to the following for their comments and constructive criticisms that helped us with development of the twelfth edition, and previous editions:

Janet Adeyiga, *Hampton University*
Gary Adna Ames, *Brigham Young University–Idaho*
Sharon Agee, *Rollins College*
Vernon Allen, *Central Florida Community College*
Tim Alzheimer, *Montana State University*
David Anderson, *Louisiana State University*
Susan Anderson, *North Carolina A&T State University*
Florence Atiase, *University of Texas–Austin*
Benjamin Bae, *Virginia Commonwealth University*
Linda T. Bartlett, *Bessemer State Technical College*
Jean Beaulieu, *Westminster College*
Robert Beebe, *Morrisville State College*
Jekabs Bikis, *Dallas Baptist University*
David Bilker, *Temple University*
Scott Butler, *Dominican University of California*
Marci L. Butterfield, *University of Utah*
Sandra Byrd, *Southwest Missouri State University*
Harlow Callander, *University of St. Thomas*
John Callister, *Cornell University*
Sharon Campbell, *University of North Alabama*
Elizabeth D. Capener, *Dominican University of CA*
Kay Carnes, *Gonzaga University*
Thomas J. Casey, *DeVry University*
Royce E. Chaffin, *University of West Georgia*
James Crockett, *University of Southern Mississippi*
Alan B. Czyzewski, *Indiana State University*
Weldon Terry Dancer, *Arkansas State University*
Thomas D'Arrigo, *Manhattan College*
Patricia Davis, *Keystone College*
Francis Dong, *DeVry University*
Martha Doran, *San Diego State University*
Robert Dunn, *Columbus State University*
Marthanne Edwards, *Colorado State University*
Craig Ehlert, *Montana State University–Bozeman*
John A. Elfrink, *Central Missouri State University*

Robert C. Elmore, *Tennessee Tech University*
Leslie Fletcher, *Georgia Southern University*
Norman Foy, *Mercy College*
Randy Frye, *Saint Francis University*
Harry E. Gallatin, *Indiana State University*
Regan Garey, *Immaculata University*
Terrie Gehman, *Elizabethtown College*
Daniel Gibbons, *Waubonsee Community College*
Louis Gingerella, *Rensselaer–Hartford*
Dan Goldzband, *University of California–San Diego*
Kyle L. Grazier, *University of Michigan*
Alice M. Handlang, *Southern Christian University*
Betty S. Harper, *Middle Tennessee State University*
Elaine Henry, *Rutgers University*
William Hood, *Central Michigan University*
Fred Hughes, *Faulkner University*
Kim Hurt, *Central Community College*
Lori Jacobson, *North Idaho College*
Linda L. Kadlecek, *Central Arizona College*
Zulfiqar Khan, *Benedictine University*
Charles Kile, *Middle Tennessee State University*
Nancy Kelly, *Middlesex Community College*
Ronald W. Kilgore, *University of Tennessee*
Bert Luken, *Wilmington College–Cincinnati*
Anna Lusher, *West Liberty State College*
Suneel Maheshwari, *Marshall University*
Gwen McFadden, *North Carolina A&T State University*
Tammy Metzke, *Milwaukee Area Technical College*
Melanie Middlemist, *Colorado State University*
Richard Monbrod, *DeVry University*
Murat Neset Tanju, *University of Alabama–Birmingham*
Eugene D. O'Donnell, *Harcum College*
William A. O'Toole, *Defiance College*
Sandra Owen, *Indiana University–Bloomington*

Carol Pace, *Grayson County College*
Robert Patterson, *Penn State–Erie*
Robert M. Peevy, *Tarleton State University*
Craig Pence, *Highland Community College*
Candace Person, *University of California–San Diego Extension*
David H. Peters, *Southeastern University*
Ronald Picker, *St. Mary of the Woods College*
Martha Pointer, *East Tennessee State University*
James Pofal, *University of Wisconsin–Oshkosh*
Shirley Powell, *Arkansas State University–Beebe*
Barbara Powers-Ingram, *Wytheville Community College*
M. Jeff Quinlan, *Madison College*
John Rush, *Illinois College*
Robert W. Rutledge, *Texas State University*
Robert E. Rosacker, *The University of South Dakota*
Paul Schwin, *Tiffin University*
Raymond Shaffer, *Youngstown State University*
Erin Sims, *DeVry University*
Forest E. Stegelin, *University of Georgia*
Mark Steadman, *East Tennessee State University*
Charles Smith, *Iowa Western Community College*
Ray Sturm, *University of Central Florida*
John Suroviak, *Pacific University*
Linda Tarrago, *Hillsborough Community College*
Judith A. Toland, *Bucks County Community College*
Catherine Traynor, *Northern Illinois University*
Michael Vasilou, *DeVry University*
David Verduzco, *University of Texas–Austin*
Joseph Vesci, *Immaculata University*
William Ward, *Mid-Continent University*
Kortney White, *Arkansas State University*
Dennis Wooten, *Erie Community College–North*

We Are Grateful . . . Although the approach to the material and the scope of coverage in this text are the results of our own conclusions, truly new ideas are rare. The authors whose textbooks we have used in the past have influenced many of our ideas for particular accounting and financial management explanations. Likewise, students and colleagues through the years have helped us clarify illustrations and teaching techniques. Many of the users of the first 11 editions—both teachers and students—have offered comments and constructive criticisms that have been encouraging and helpful. All this input is greatly appreciated.

We extend special thanks to Robert Picard of Idaho State University, for his careful accuracy check of the text manuscript and solutions manual and ancillaries, and to April L. Mohr of Jefferson Community and Technical College, SW, in Louisville, Kentucky, for her invaluable assistance and guidance in the development of our text's LearnSmart content.

We also wish to thank our many colleagues at McGraw-Hill, who, for more than 25 years, have provided exceptional editorial assistance and product development guidance. Your collective efforts have helped to shape every aspect of this text, and it continues to be a pleasure to work with such a fine group of publishing professionals.

Finally, we wish to thank David H. Marshall for making this text possible, and for his many years of guidance, kindness, and deep and abiding friendship. Were it not for his insight, vision, and determination, this book would have forever remained a dream. Thank you, David. We are proud to carry on your legacy through our work on *Accounting: What the Numbers Mean*.

Wayne W. McManus   Daniel F. Viele

Brief Contents

Contents

1

Accounting— Present and Past

The worldwide financial and credit crisis that came to a head in the fall of 2008 was precipitated by many factors. Not the least of these factors were greed, inadequate market regulatory supervision, and an excess of "financial engineering" involved in the creation of financial instruments that almost defied understanding even by sophisticated investors. This crisis was preceded in the first decade of the century by the bankruptcy filings of two large, publicly owned corporations, which resulted in billions of dollars of losses by thousands of stockholders. In 2001, it had been Enron Corporation, and a few months later, WorldCom Inc. In each case, a number of factors caused the precipitous fall in the value of the firms' stock. The most significant factor was probably the loss of investor confidence in each company's financial reports and other disclosures reported to stockholders and regulatory bodies, including the Securities and Exchange Commission (SEC).

The Enron and WorldCom debacles, and other widely publicized breakdowns of corporate financial reporting, resulted in close scrutiny of such reporting by the accounting profession itself and also by the U.S. Congress and other governing bodies. The accounting practices that were criticized generally involved complex transactions.

Also contributing to the issue were aggressive attempts by some executives to avoid the spirit of sound accounting, even though many of the financial reporting practices in question were not specifically forbidden by existing accounting pronouncements at that time. To be sure, the financial reporting requirements faced by companies whose securities are publicly traded have since become more strenuously scrutinized under the Sarbanes–Oxley Act of 2002 (SOX) and the watchful eye of the Public Company Accounting Oversight Board (PCAOB), which is the regulatory body created under SOX to oversee the activities of the auditing profession and further protect the public interest. These enhanced regulatory efforts have helped to increase the transparency of the financial reporting process and the understandability of financial statements. Although the financial crisis that disrupted the financial world in 2008 was not directly blamed on financial accounting or auditing weaknesses, some accounting and financial reporting practices that existed at that time were severely criticized. This book briefly addresses some of the more troublesome technical issues still faced by the accounting profession today, but the elaborate attempts to embellish the financial image of those companies in question certainly went beyond the fundamentals described in the following pages.

The objective of this text is to present enough of the fundamentals of accounting to permit the nonaccountant to understand the financial statements of an organization operating in our society and to understand how financial information can be used in the management planning, control, and decision-making processes. Although usually expressed in the context of profit-seeking business enterprises, most of the material presented here is equally applicable to not-for-profit social service and governmental organizations.

Accounting is sometimes called the *language of business,* and it is appropriate for people who are involved in the economic activities of our society—and that is just about everyone—to know at least enough of this language to be able to make decisions and informed judgments about those economic activities.

LEARNING OBJECTIVES (LO)

After studying this chapter, you should understand and be able to

LO 1-1   Explain the definition of *accounting.*

LO 1-2   Identify who the users of accounting information are and explain why they find accounting information useful.

LO 1-3   Identify the variety of professional services that accountants provide.

LO 1-4   Summarize the development of accounting from a broad historical perspective.

LO 1-5   Explain the role that the FASB plays in the development of financial accounting standards.

LO 1-6   Generalize about how financial reporting standards evolve.

LO 1-7   Identify the key elements of ethical behavior for a professional accountant.

LO 1-8   Summarize the reasons for the FASB's Conceptual Framework project.

LO 1-9   Summarize the objective of general-purpose financial reporting.

LO 1-10   Describe the plan of the book.

What Is Accounting?

In a broad sense, **accounting** is the process of identifying, measuring, and communicating economic information about an organization for the purpose of making decisions and informed judgments. (Accountants frequently use the term **entity** instead of *organization* because it is more inclusive.)

This definition of accounting can be expressed schematically as follows:

Accounting is the process of

$$\left.\begin{array}{l} \text{Identifying} \\ \text{Measuring} \\ \text{Communicating} \end{array}\right\} \quad \begin{array}{c} \text{Economic information} \\ \text{about an entity} \end{array} \quad \rightarrow \quad \begin{array}{c} \text{For decisions and} \\ \text{informed judgments} \end{array}$$

LO 1
Explain the definition of *accounting.*

Exhibit 1-1

Users and Uses of
Accounting Information

LO 2

Identify who the users
of accounting informa-
tion are and explain why
they find accounting
information useful.

User	Decision/Informed Judgment Made
Management	When performing its functions of planning, directing, and controlling, management makes many decisions and informed judgments. For example, when considering the expansion of a product line, planning involves identifying and measuring costs and benefits; directing involves communicating the strategies selected; and controlling involves identifying, measuring, and communicating the results of the product line expansion during and after its implementation.
Investors/ shareholders	When considering whether to invest in the common stock of a company, **investors** use accounting information to help assess the amounts, timing, and uncertainty of future cash returns on their investment.
Creditors/ suppliers	When determining how much merchandise to ship to a customer before receiving payment, **creditors** assess the probability of collection and the risks of late (or non-) payment. Banks also become creditors when they make loans and thus have similar needs for accounting information.
Employees	When planning for retirement, employees assess the company's ability to offer long-term job prospects and an attractive retirement benefits package.
SEC (Securities and Exchange Commission)	When reviewing for compliance with SEC regulations, analysts determine whether financial statements issued to investors fully disclose all required information.

Who makes these decisions and informed judgments? Users of accounting information include the management of the entity or organization; the owners of the organization (who are frequently not involved in the management process); potential investors in and creditors of the organization; employees; and various federal, state, and local governmental agencies that are concerned with regulatory and tax matters. Exhibit 1-1 describes some of the users and uses of accounting information. Pause, and try to think of at least one other decision or informed judgment that each of these users might make from the economic information that could be communicated about an entity.

Accounting information is required for just about every kind of organization. When accounting is mentioned, most people initially think of the information needs and reporting requirements of business firms, but not-for-profit social service organizations, governmental units, educational institutions, social clubs, political committees, and other groups all require accounting for their economic activities as well.

Accounting is frequently perceived as something that others who are good with numbers do, rather than as the process of providing information that supports decisions and informed judgments. Relatively few people become accountants, but almost all people use accounting information. The principal objective of this text is to help you become an informed user of accounting information, rather than to prepare you to become an accountant. However, the essence of this user orientation provides a solid foundation for students who choose to seek a career in accounting.

If you haven't already experienced the lack of understanding or confusion that results from looking at a set of financial statements, you have been spared one of life's frustrations. Certainly during your formal business education and early during your employment experience, you will be presented with financial data. Being an informed user means knowing how to use those data as information.

The following sections introduce the major areas of practice within the accounting discipline and will help you understand the types of work done by professional accountants within each of these broad categories. In a similar way, the accompanying Business in Practice discussion highlights career opportunities in accounting.

1. What does it mean to state that the accounting process should support decisions and informed judgments?

What Does It Mean?
Answer on page 27

Business in Practice

Career Opportunities in Accounting

Because accounting is a profession, most entry-level positions require at least a bachelor's degree with a major in accounting. Individuals are encouraged to achieve Certified Public Accountant (CPA) licensure as quickly as feasible and/or to attend graduate school to pursue an area of specialization. Persons who work hard and smart can expect to attain high professional levels in their careers. The major employers of accountants include public accounting firms, industrial firms, government, and not-for-profit organizations.

Public Accounting

The work done by public accountants varies significantly depending on whether they are employed by a local, regional, or international CPA firm. Small local firms concentrate on the bookkeeping, accounting, tax return, and financial planning needs of individuals and small businesses. These firms need generalists who can adequately serve in a variety of capacities. The somewhat larger, regional firms offer a broad range of professional services but concentrate on the performance of audits (frequently referred to as *attestation* or *compliance services*), corporate tax returns, and management advisory services. They often hire experienced financial and industry specialists to serve particular client needs, in addition to recruiting well-qualified recent graduates.

The large, international CPA firms also perform auditing, tax, and consulting services. Their principal clients are large domestic and international corporations. The "Big 4" CPA firms are Deloitte Touche Tohmatsu (Deloitte), PricewaterhouseCoopers (known as PwC), EY (formerly Ernst & Young), and KPMG International (KPMG). These firms dominate the market in terms of total revenues; number of corporate audit clients; and the number of offices, partners, and staff members. The Big 4 international firms generally recruit outstanding graduates and highly experienced CPAs and encourage the development of specialized skills by their personnel. (*Visit any of the Big 4 websites for detailed information regarding career opportunities in public accounting:* deloitte.com, pwc.com, ey.com, or kpmg.com.)

Industrial Accounting

More accountants are employed in industry than in public accounting because of the vast number of manufacturing, merchandising, and service firms of all sizes. In addition to using the services of public accounting firms, these firms employ cost and management accountants, as well as financial accountants. Many accountants in industry start working in this environment right out of school; others get their start in public accounting as auditors but move to industry after getting at least a couple of years of experience.

Government and Not-for-Profit Accounting

Opportunities for accounting professionals in the governmental and not-for-profit sectors of the economy are constantly increasing. In the United States, literally thousands of state and local government reporting entities touch the lives of every citizen. Likewise, accounting specialists are employed by colleges and universities, hospitals, and voluntary health and welfare organizations such as the American Red Cross, United Way, and Greenpeace.

Financial Accounting

LO 3

Identify the variety of professional services that accountants provide.

Financial accounting generally refers to the process that results in the preparation and reporting of financial statements for an entity. As will be explained in more detail, financial statements present the financial position of an entity at a point in time, the results of the entity's operations for some period of time, the **cash flow** activities for the same period, and other information (the notes to the financial statements or financial review) about the entity's financial resources, obligations, owners'/stockholders' interests, and operations.

Financial accounting is primarily oriented toward the external user. The financial statements are directed to individuals who are not in a position to be aware of the day-to-day financial and operating activities of the entity. Financial accounting is also primarily concerned with the historical results of an entity's performance. Financial statements reflect what has happened in the past. Although readers may want to project past activities and their results into future performance, financial statements are not a crystal ball. Many corporate annual reports refer to the historical nature of financial accounting information to emphasize that users must make their own judgments about a firm's future prospects.

Bookkeeping procedures are used to accumulate the financial results of many of an entity's activities, and these procedures are part of the financial accounting process. Bookkeeping procedures have been thoroughly systematized using manual, mechanical, and computer techniques. Although these procedures support the financial accounting and reporting process, they are only a part of the process.

Financial accounting is done by accounting professionals who have generally earned a bachelor's degree with a major in accounting. The financial accountant is employed by an entity to use her or his expertise, analytical skills, and judgment in the many activities that are necessary for the preparation of financial statements. The title **controller** is used to designate the chief accounting officer of a corporation. The controller is usually responsible for both the financial and managerial accounting functions of the organization (as discussed later). Sometimes the title *comptroller* (the Old English spelling) is used for this position.

An individual earns the **Certified Public Accountant (CPA)** professional designation by fulfilling certain education and experience requirements and passing a comprehensive four-part examination. A uniform CPA exam is given nationally, although it is administered by individual states.[1] Some states require that candidates have accounting work experience before sitting for the exam. A total of 54 of the 55 U.S. jurisdictions, including all 50 states, have now enacted legislation increasing the educational requirements for CPA candidates from 120 semester hours of college study, or a bachelor's degree, to a minimum of 150 semester hours of college study to be granted licensure as a CPA.[2] Thirty-two of these states allow candidates to sit for the CPA exam with 120 hours, but require 150 hours for certification.[3] The American Institute of Certified Public Accountants (AICPA), the national professional organization of CPAs, has also endorsed this movement by requiring that an individual CPA wanting to become

---

[1] Since 2004, CPA candidates have been allowed to schedule their own exam dates; they may sit for one part at a time because the examination is now computer-based. The former "pencil and paper" CPA exam has become a relic of the past.

[2] The U.S. Virgin Islands is the only jurisdiction that has not enacted the 150-hour education requirement as this text goes to print.

[3] See becker.com/cpa-review/resources/about-exam/requirements for the exam requirements of your state.

a member must have met the 150-hour requirement. This increase in the educational requirements for becoming a CPA and for joining the AICPA reflects the increasing demands placed on accounting professionals to be both broadly educated and technically competent. Practicing CPAs work in all types of organizations, but as explained later, a CPA who expresses an auditor's opinion about an entity's financial statements must be licensed by the jurisdiction/state in which she or he performs the auditing service.

Managerial Accounting/Cost Accounting

Managerial accounting is concerned with the use of economic and financial information to plan and control many activities of the entity and to support the management decision-making process. **Cost accounting** is a subset of managerial accounting that relates to the determination and accumulation of product, process, or service costs. Managerial accounting and cost accounting have primarily an internal orientation, in contrast to the primarily external orientation of financial accounting. Many of the same data used in or generated by the financial accounting process are used in managerial and cost accounting, but the data are more likely to be used in a future-oriented way, such as in the preparation of budgets. A detailed discussion of the similarities and differences between financial and managerial accounting is provided in Chapter 12 and highlighted in Exhibit 12-1.

Managerial accountants and cost accountants are professionals who have usually earned a bachelor's degree with a major in accounting. Their work frequently involves close coordination with the production, marketing, and finance functions of the entity. The **Certified Management Accountant (CMA)** designation can be earned by a management accountant or cost accountant by passing a broad two-part examination. Each part of the CMA examination is given in a computer-based format and consists of three hours of descriptive (multiple-choice) questions and two 30-minute essay questions.

Auditing—Public Accounting

Many entities have their financial statements reviewed or examined by an independent third party. In most cases, an audit (examination) is required by securities laws if the stock or bonds of a company are owned and publicly traded by investors. **Public accounting** firms and individual CPAs provide this **auditing** service, which constitutes an important part of the accounting profession.

The result of an audit is the **independent auditor's report.** The report usually has four relatively brief paragraphs. The first paragraph identifies the financial statements that were audited, explains that the statements are the responsibility of the company's management, and states that the auditor's responsibility is to express an opinion about the financial statements. The second paragraph explains that the audit was conducted "in accordance with the standards of the Public Company Accounting Oversight Board (United States)" and describes briefly what those standards require and what work is involved in performing an audit. (In effect, they require the application of **generally accepted auditing standards, or GAAS.**) The third paragraph contains the auditor's opinion, which is usually that the named statements "present fairly, in all material respects" the financial position of the entity and the results of its operations and cash flows for the identified periods "in conformity with U.S. generally accepted accounting principles." This is an unqualified, or "clean," opinion. Occasionally the opinion will be qualified with respect to fair presentation, departure from **generally accepted accounting principles (GAAP),** or the auditor's inability to perform certain auditing procedures. Similarly, an explanatory paragraph may be added to an unqualified opinion regarding the firm's ability to continue as a going concern (that is, as a viable economic entity) when substantial doubt exists. An unqualified opinion is not a clean bill of health about either the current financial condition or the future prospects of the entity. Readers must reach their own judgments about these and other matters after studying the **annual report,** which includes the financial statements and the notes to the financial statements, as well as management's extensive discussion and analysis. A final paragraph makes reference to the auditors' opinion about the effectiveness of the company's internal control over financial reporting. The entire auditors' report is further discussed in Chapter 10.

Auditors who work in public accounting are professional accountants who usually have earned at least a bachelor's degree with a major in accounting. The auditor may work for a public accounting firm (a few firms have several thousand partners and professional staff) or as an individual practitioner. Most auditors seek and earn the CPA designation; the firm partner or individual practitioner who signs the audit opinion must be a licensed CPA in the state in which she or he practices. To be licensed, the CPA must satisfy the character, education, examination, and experience requirements of the state or other jurisdiction.

Campbell's

To see an example of the independent auditors' report, refer to page 75 in the 2017 annual report of Campbell Soup Company, which is reproduced in the appendix.

What Does It Mean?
Answers on page 27

2. What does it mean to work in public accounting?
3. What does it mean to be a CPA?

Internal Auditing

Organizations with many plant locations or activities involving many financial transactions employ professional accountants to do **internal auditing.** In many cases, the internal auditor performs functions much like those of the external auditor/public accountant, but perhaps on a smaller scale. For example, internal auditors may be responsible for reviewing the financial statements of a single plant or for analyzing the operating efficiency of an entity's activities. The qualifications of an internal auditor are similar to those of any other professional accountant. In addition to having the CPA and the CMA designation, the internal auditor may have also passed the examination to become a Certified Internal Auditor (CIA).

Governmental and Not-for-Profit Accounting

Governmental units at the municipal, state, and federal levels and not-for-profit entities, such as colleges and universities, hospitals, and voluntary health and welfare organizations, require the same accounting functions to be performed as do other accounting entities. Religious organizations, labor unions, trade associations, performing arts organizations, political parties, libraries, museums, country clubs, and many other not-for-profit organizations employ accountants with similar educational qualifications as those employed in business and public accounting.

Income Tax Accounting

The growing complexity of federal, state, municipal, and foreign income tax laws has led to a demand for professional accountants who are specialists in various aspects of taxation. Tax practitioners often develop specialties in the taxation of individuals, partnerships, corporations, trusts and estates, or in international tax law issues. These accountants work for corporations, public accounting firms, governmental units, and other entities. Many tax accountants have bachelor's degrees and are CPAs; some have a master's degree in accounting or taxation or are attorneys as well.

How Has Accounting Developed?

Accounting has developed over time in response to the needs of users of financial statements for financial information to support decisions and informed judgments such as those mentioned in Exhibit 1-1 and others that you were challenged to identify. Even though an aura of exactness is conveyed by the numbers in financial statements, a great deal of judgment and approximation is involved in determining the numbers to be reported. Although broad, generally accepted principles of accounting exist, different accountants may reach different but often equally legitimate conclusions about how to account for a particular transaction or event. A brief review of the history of the development of accounting principles may make this often confusing state of affairs a little easier to understand.

LO 4
Summarize the development of accounting from a broad historical perspective.

Early History

It is not surprising that evidence of record keeping for economic events has been found in the earliest civilizations. Dating back to the clay tablets used by Mesopotamians in about 3000 B.C. to record tax receipts, accounting has responded to the information needs of users. In 1494, Luca Pacioli, a Franciscan monk and mathematics professor, published the first known text to describe a comprehensive double-entry bookkeeping system. Modern bookkeeping systems (as discussed in Chapter 4) have evolved directly from Pacioli's "method of Venice" system, which was developed in response to the needs of the Italian mercantile trading practices in that period.

The Industrial Revolution generated the need for large amounts of capital to finance the enterprises that supplanted individual craftsmen. This need resulted in the corporate form of organization marked by absentee owners, or investors, who entrusted their money to managers. It followed that investors required reports from the corporate managers showing the entity's financial position and results of operations. In mid-19th-century England, the independent (external) audit function added credence to financial reports. As British capital was invested in a growing U.S. economy in the late 19th century, British-chartered accountants and accounting methods came to the United States. However, no group was legally authorized to establish financial reporting standards. This led to alternative methods of reporting financial condition and results of operations, which resulted in confusion and, in some cases, outright fraud.

The Accounting Profession in the United States

Accounting professionals in this country organized themselves in the early 1900s and worked hard to establish certification laws, standardized audit procedures, and other attributes of a profession. However, not until 1932–1934 did the American Institute of Accountants (predecessor of today's American Institute of Certified Public

Accountants—AICPA) and the New York Stock Exchange agree on five broad principles of accounting. This was the first formal accounting standard-setting activity. The accounting, financial reporting, and auditing weaknesses related to the 1929 stock market crash gave impetus to this effort.

The Securities Act of 1933 and the Securities Exchange Act of 1934 apply to securities offered for sale in interstate commerce. These laws had a significant effect on the standard-setting process because they gave the **Securities and Exchange Commission (SEC)** the authority to establish accounting principles to be followed by companies whose securities had to be registered with the SEC. The SEC still has this authority, but the standard-setting process has been delegated to other organizations over the years. Between 1939 and 1959, the Committee on Accounting Procedure of the American Institute of Accountants issued 51 *Accounting Research Bulletins* that dealt with accounting principles. This work was done without a common conceptual framework for financial reporting. Each bulletin dealt with a specific issue in a relatively narrow context, and alternative methods of reporting the results of similar transactions remained.

In 1959, the Accounting Principles Board (APB) replaced the Committee on Accounting Procedure as the standard-setting body. The APB was an arm of the AICPA, and although it was given resources and directed to engage in more research than its predecessor, its early efforts intensified the controversies that existed. The APB issued 39 *Opinions* on serious accounting issues, but it failed to develop a conceptual underpinning for accounting and financial reporting.

Financial Accounting Standard Setting at the Present Time

LO 5

Explain the role that the FASB plays in the development of financial accounting standards.

In 1973, as a result of congressional and other criticism of the accounting standard-setting process being performed by an arm of the AICPA, the **Financial Accounting Foundation (FAF)** was created as a more independent entity. The foundation established the **Financial Accounting Standards Board (FASB)** as the authoritative standard-setting body within the accounting profession. The FASB embarked on a project called the Conceptual Framework of Financial Accounting and Reporting and issued eight *Statements of Financial Accounting Concepts* by February 2018.

Concurrently with its Conceptual Framework project, the FASB issued 168 *Statements of Financial Accounting Standards* (**SFAS**) that established standards of accounting and reporting for particular issues, much as its predecessors did. Effective in July 2009, however, all such FASB standards were superseded by the *FASB Accounting Standards Codification* (**FASB Codification**). Essentially, the FASB Codification reorganized divergent sources of U.S. GAAP in a more accessible and researchable format. The FASB Codification now represents a single source of U.S. GAAP. Changes to the Codification are communicated through an *Accounting Standards Update* (**Update or ASU**), regardless of the form in which such guidance may have been issued prior to the release of the FASB Codification. Although such Updates do in fact amend the FASB Codification, the FASB does not consider ASUs as authoritative in their own right. A total of 148 ASUs had been issued by February 2018.

Alternative ways of accounting for and reporting the effects of similar transactions still exist. In many aspects of financial reporting, the accountant still must use judgment in selecting between equally acceptable alternatives. To make sense of financial statements, one must understand the impact of the accounting methods used by a firm, relative to alternative methods that were not selected. Subsequent chapters describe many of these alternatives and the impact that various accounting choices have on financial statements. For example, Chapter 5 discusses the effects of the first-in, first-out inventory cost flow assumption in comparison to the last-in, first-out and the weighted-average assumptions. Chapter 6 discusses the difference between the straight-line and accelerated methods of depreciating long-lived assets. Although such terminology may not be meaningful to you at this time, you should understand that the FASB has sanctioned each of these alternative methods of accounting for inventory and depreciation, and that the methods selected can significantly affect a firm's reported profits.

The FASB does not set standards in a vacuum. An open, due process procedure is followed. The FASB invites input from any individual or organization who cares to provide ideas and viewpoints about the particular standard under consideration. Among the many professional accounting and financial organizations that regularly present suggestions to the FASB, in addition to the AICPA and the SEC, are the **International Accounting Standards Board (IASB),** the American Accounting Association, the Institute of Management Accountants, Financial Executives International, and the Chartered Financial Analysts (CFA) Institute.

The accounting and auditing standard-setting processes were heavily criticized as a result of the Enron and WorldCom collapses and the accounting and reporting problems of other companies that came to light in 2001 and early 2002. In July 2002, President George W. Bush signed into law the most significant legislation affecting the accounting profession since 1933: the Sarbanes–Oxley Act (SOX) of 2002. Essentially, the act created a five-member **Public Company Accounting Oversight Board (PCAOB),** which has the authority to set and enforce auditing, attestation, quality control, and ethics (including independence) standards for public companies. It is also empowered to inspect the auditing operations of public accounting firms that audit public companies and impose disciplinary sanctions for violations of the Board's rules, securities laws, and professional auditing standards. The impact of SOX on financial reporting has been far reaching and will be explored in some detail in Chapter 10, which addresses corporate governance and disclosure issues.

The point of this discussion is to emphasize that financial accounting and reporting practices are not based on a set of inflexible rules to be mastered and blindly followed. The reality is that financial reporting practices have evolved over time in response to the changing needs of society, and they are still evolving. In recent years, financial instruments and business transactions have become increasingly complex and are now being used with greater frequency by firms of all sizes. The FASB has thus been hard pressed to develop appropriate standards to adequately address emerging accounting issues in a timely manner. Moreover, many recent ASUs appear to be more like rules than the judgmental application of fair guidelines. Don't worry about any critical reviews you may read concerning new FASB Codification updates; instead, keep your eye on the big picture. Your objective is to learn enough about the fundamentals of financial accounting and reporting practices to be neither awed nor confounded by the overall presentation of financial data.

LO 6
Generalize about how financial reporting standards evolve.

---

4. What does it mean to state that generally accepted accounting principles are not a set of rules to be blindly followed?
5. What does it mean when the Financial Accounting Standards Board issues a new *Accounting Standards Update*?

What Does It Mean?
Answers on page 27

Standards for Other Types of Accounting

Because managerial/cost accounting is oriented primarily to internal use, it is presumed that internal users will know about the accounting practices being followed by their firms. As a result, the accounting profession has not regarded the development of internal reporting standards for use by management as an important issue. Instead, individual companies are generally allowed to self-regulate with respect to internal reporting matters. One significant exception is accounting for the cost of work done under government contracts. Over the years, various governmental agencies have issued directives prescribing the procedures to be followed by government contractors. During the 1970–1980 period, the **Cost Accounting Standards Board (CASB)** operated as a governmental body to establish standards applicable to government contracts. Congress abolished the CASB in 1981, although its standards remained in effect. In 1988, Congress reestablished the CASB as an independent body within the Office of Federal Procurement Policy. The CASB now has authority to establish cost-accounting standards for government contracts in excess of $750,000, provided that the contractor or subcontractor is performing a total of $7.5 million or more in all such contracts. Since 1995, CASB standards also have applied to colleges and universities that receive major federal research funds.

In the auditing/public accounting area, auditing, attestation, and quality control standards are established by the Auditing Standards Board, a technical committee of the AICPA, unless superseded or amended by the PCAOB. The SEC has had input into this process, and over the years a number of auditing standards and procedures have been issued. One of the most important of these standards requires the auditor to be *independent* of the client whose financial statements are being audited. Yet the auditor's judgment is still very important in the auditing process. Because of this, critics of the accounting profession often raise questions concerning the independence of CPA firms in the auditing process (see Business in Practice—Auditor Independence). It is worth repeating here that an unqualified auditor's opinion does not constitute a clean bill of health about either the current financial condition of or the future prospects for the entity. It is up to the readers of the financial statements to reach their own judgments about these and other matters after studying the firm's annual report, which includes the financial statements and notes to the financial statements.

In 1984, the **Governmental Accounting Standards Board (GASB)** was established to develop guidelines for financial accounting and reporting by state and local governmental units. The GASB operates under the auspices of the Financial Accounting Foundation, which is also the parent organization of the FASB. The GASB is attempting to unify practices of the nation's many state and municipal entities, thus providing investors and taxpayers with a better means of comparing financial data of the issuers of state and municipal securities. In the absence of a GASB standard for a particular activity or transaction occurring in both the public and private sectors, governmental entities will continue to use FASB standards for guidance. The GASB had issued 87 standards and 6 concepts statements by February 2018.

The U.S. Internal Revenue Code and related regulations and the various state and local tax laws specify the rules to be followed in determining an entity's income tax liability. Although quite specific and complicated, the code and regulations provide rules of law to be followed. In income tax matters, accountants use their judgment and expertise to design transactions so that the entity's overall income tax liability is minimized. In addition, accountants prepare or help prepare tax returns and may represent clients whose returns are being reviewed or challenged by taxing authorities.

Auditor Independence

Business in
Practice

Certified public accountants have traditionally provided auditing, tax, and consulting services designed to meet a broad range of client needs. In recent years, the consultancy area of practice has expanded considerably, especially among the Big 4 international CPA firms. Consulting services commonly offered include financial advisory services, assurance (risk management) services, and information systems design and installation services. Until recent years, it was not unusual for a CPA firm to provide such services to its audit clients.

In the opinion of some observers, including the SEC, having the auditing firm involved in the development of information and accounting systems raises the possibility and appearance of a conflict of interest. Such a conflict might arise if the auditors are reluctant to challenge the results of a system from which the amounts shown on an audit client's financial statements were derived. The appearance of independence could be further affected by the fact that consulting fees frequently exceed the auditing fees generated from many corporate clients.

For several years prior to the Enron case, the SEC and the AICPA discussed the impact of auditors' consulting practices on auditor independence. To help achieve independence in fact and in appearance, several auditing firms split off their consulting practices, thus making them separate entities. However, when it was learned that Arthur Andersen had earned considerably more in consulting fees from Enron than it had earned in auditing fees, and that this situation prevailed for many auditing firms, there was strong pressure to require all auditing firms to divest their consulting practices. As discussed in Chapter 10, SOX now prohibits auditors from performing a variety of nonaudit services for financial statement audit clients. Clearly, the issue of auditor independence continues to have a "hot button" status, and it is likely to remain under close scrutiny for the foreseeable future.

International Accounting Standards

Accounting standards in individual countries have evolved in response to the unique user needs and cultural attributes of each country. Thus, despite the development of a global marketplace, accounting standards in one country may differ significantly from those in another country. In 1973, the International Accounting Standards Committee (IASC) was formed by accountancy bodies in Australia, Canada, France, Germany, Japan, Mexico, the Netherlands, the United Kingdom and Ireland, and the United States to create and promote worldwide acceptance and observation of accounting and financial reporting standards. In 2001, the International Accounting Standards Board (IASB) was formed in a restructuring effort and has since assumed all responsibilities previously carried out by the IASC, which was disbanded at that time. The IFRS Foundation, based in London, is the legal entity under which the IASB operates as an independent, not-for-profit private sector organization.

The goal of the IASB is to develop a single set of high-quality, understandable, enforceable, and globally accepted financial reporting standards based on clearly articulated principles. The IASB and its predecessor organization had issued 41 International Accounting Standards (IAS) and 17 **International Financial Reporting Standards (IFRS)** by February 2018, with much of this progress coming in recent years. As a result, all major nations except the United States have now established timelines to converge with or adopt IFRS standards in the near future.

The IASB and the FASB have been working together since 2002 to achieve convergence of IFRS and U.S. GAAP. The principal difference between IFRS and U.S.

GAAP is that U.S. financial reporting standards have been increasingly based on detailed rules, whereas IFRS standards require companies to follow broad principles, which can result in "situational" accounting that can lead to financial reporting differences between companies having similar transactions. With this in mind, the boards agreed on a Memorandum of Understanding in 2006 (updated in 2008 and again in 2010) that identified several short-term and longer-term convergence projects that would bring the most significant improvements to IFRS and U.S. GAAP. Through these ongoing projects—some covering major components of the financial statements, such as leases, impairment of financial instruments, and insurance contracts—the boards intend to improve financial reporting to investors while also aligning U.S. and international standards.

In November 2008, the SEC issued a "Roadmap" discussion paper for a possible path to the adoption of IFRS standards in the United States. In May 2011, the SEC released a more detailed proposal for the FASB to change U.S. GAAP over a defined period of perhaps five to seven years by endorsing, and thereby incorporating, individual IFRS standards into U.S. GAAP. Under this proposal, the FASB would have continued as the U.S. standard setter, and would have participated in the development of new standards, but the nature of its role would have changed significantly. Rather than acting as the principal standard setter for new standards, the FASB would have provided input and support to the IASB in its mission to develop high-quality, global standards.

In more recent years, however, the FASB and IASB have backed away almost completely from the goal of a single global accounting language because of a lack of interest in accounting convergence on the part of U.S. investors and corporations. Yet, the boards did manage to agree as recently as January 2016 on another key area—lease accounting, which along with a revenue recognition standard issued in May 2014, is thought to be one of the crowning achievements of their mutual efforts in the ongoing convergence era. Moreover, the major goals of the highly successful convergence project clearly have been achieved, with substantially improved and fully aligned U.S. and international financial reporting for business combinations, segment reporting, stock compensation, fair value measurements, borrowing costs, and noncontrolling interests, as well as leases and revenue recognition. But at its core, the fatal flaw in the U.S. side of the complete convergence plan was the huge switching cost that domestic companies and auditors would have to pay for changing their reporting language from U.S. GAAP to IFRS. Thus, it would appear the U.S. GAAP and IFRS will continue to peacefully coexist indefinitely.

Although it is appropriate to follow the progress of these convergence developments, this text explains and illustrates only those current U.S. financial accounting and reporting standards that are necessary for you to gain a comprehension of the "big picture"—what the numbers mean from the perspective of financial statement users. However, where appropriate, IFRS standards currently in effect and under development are identified in text boxes titled "The IFRS Approach." These text boxes contain brief explanations of the relevant international standards, particularly where they differ significantly from their corresponding U.S. standards. A variety of hot topic issues affecting the accounting profession, such as those mentioned here, are discussed further in the Epilogue, "Accounting—The Future."

Exhibit 1-2 lists the website addresses of various accounting organizations. You are encouraged to visit these sites for more information about each one.

The IFRS Approach

Exhibit 1-2

Websites for Accounting Organizations

American Institute of Certified Public Accountants: aicpa.org

Financial Accounting Standards Board: fasb.org

Government Accounting Standards Board: gasb.org

Institute of Internal Auditors: theiia.org

Institute of Management Accountants: imanet.org

IFRS Foundation and the International Accounting Standards Board: ifrs.org

Public Company Accounting Oversight Board: pcaob.org

Securities and Exchange Commission: sec.gov

6. What does it mean that the FASB and IASB have been working together to achieve convergence?

What Does It Mean?

Answer on page 27

Ethics and the Accounting Profession

One characteristic frequently associated with any profession is that those practicing the profession acknowledge the importance of an ethical code. This is especially important in the accounting profession because so much of an accountant's work involves providing information to support the decisions and informed judgments made by users of accounting information.

LO 7

Identify the key elements of ethical behavior for a professional accountant.

The American Institute of Certified Public Accountants (AICPA) and the Institute of Management Accountants (IMA) both have published ethics codes. The *Code of Professional Conduct,* most recently amended in 2014, was adopted by the membership of the AICPA. The organization's bylaws state that members shall conform to the rules of the Code or be subject to disciplinary action by the AICPA. Although it doesn't have the same enforcement mechanism, the IMA's *Statement of Ethical Professional Practice* calls on management accountants to maintain the highest standards of ethical conduct as they fulfill their obligations to the organizations they serve, their profession, the public, and themselves.

Both codes of conduct identify integrity and objectivity as two key elements of ethical behavior for a professional accountant. Having **integrity** means being honest and forthright in dealings and communications with others; **objectivity** means impartiality and freedom from conflict of interest. An accountant who lacks integrity and/or objectivity cannot be relied on to produce complete and relevant information with which to make a decision or informed judgment.

Other elements of ethical behavior include independence, competence, and acceptance of an obligation to serve the best interests of the employer, the client, and the public. **Independence** is related to objectivity and is especially important to the auditor, who must be independent both in appearance and in fact. Having competence means having the knowledge and professional skills to adequately perform the work assigned. Accountants should recognize that the nature of their work requires an understanding of the obligation to serve those who will use the information communicated by them.

In the recent past, incidents involving allegations that accountants have violated their ethical codes by being dishonest, biased, and/or incompetent have been highly publicized.

That some of these allegations have been proved true should not be used to condemn all accountants. The profession has used these rare circumstances to reaffirm that the public and the profession expect accountants to exhibit a very high level of ethical behavior. In this sense, are accountants really any different from those involved in any other endeavor?

What Does It Mean?

Answer on page 27

7. What does it mean to state that ethical behavior includes being objective and independent?

The Conceptual Framework

LO 8

Summarize the reasons for the FASB's Conceptual Framework project.

Various accounting standards have existed for many years. But it wasn't until the mid-1970s that the FASB began the process of identifying a structure or framework of financial accounting concepts. New users of financial statements can benefit from an overview of these concepts because they provide the foundation for understanding financial accounting reports. The FASB issued eight *Statements of Financial Accounting Concepts* through February 2018, the first six of which were issued between 1978 and 1985. These statements represented a great deal of effort by the FASB, and progress made on this project did not come easily.

In concert with their efforts to converge U.S. and international accounting standards, the FASB and IASB have undertaken a project to improve and converge their respective Conceptual Frameworks as well. In September 2010, *FASB Concepts Statement No. 8,* "Conceptual Framework for Financial Reporting," was issued; it included two chapters of the new Conceptual Framework and superseded *FASB Concepts Statements No. 1* and *No. 2.* In *Concepts Statement No. 8,* the FASB made the following assertions:[4]

> Concepts Statements are not part of the *FASB Accounting Standards Codification,* which is the source of authoritative GAAP recognized by the FASB to be applied by nongovernmental entities. Rather, Concepts Statements describe concepts that will underlie guidance on future accounting practices and in due course will serve as a basis for evaluating existing guidance and practices.
>
> Establishment of objectives and identification of fundamental concepts will not directly solve accounting and reporting problems. Rather, objectives give direction, and concepts are tools for solving problems.
>
> The Board itself is likely to be the most direct beneficiary of the guidance provided by Concepts Statements. They will guide the Board in developing accounting and reporting guidance by providing the Board with a common foundation and basic reasoning on which to consider merits of alternatives.[5]

Summary of *Concepts Statement No. 8,* Chapter 1: "The Objective of General Purpose Financial Reporting"

LO 9

Summarize the objective of general-purpose financial reporting.

To set the stage more completely for your study of financial accounting, it is appropriate to have an overview of the foundational building blocks of financial reporting, as expressed in Chapter 1 of *Concepts Statement No. 8.* (To gain a comprehensive

---

[4] Source: FASB, *Statement of Financial Accounting Concepts No. 8,* Preface.
[5] Source: FASB, Statement of Financial Accounting Concepts No. 8, Preface.

Business Ethics

Events like the 2008–2009 global economic crisis highlight the necessity of sound ethical practices across the business world. An indication of the breadth of this concern is the development of the term *stakeholder* to refer to the many entities—owners/stockholders, managers, employees, customers, suppliers, communities, and even competitors—who have a stake in the way an organization conducts its activities. Another indicator of this concern is that business ethics and corporate social responsibility issues are merging into a single broad area of interest.

This concern is international in scope and is attracting political attention. In 2017, the Caux Round Table (CRT) celebrated its 23rd year of leadership in corporate business ethics after publishing its *Principles for Business* in 1994, which attempts to express a worldwide standard for ethical and socially responsible corporate behavior. Another influential organization is Business for Social Responsibility (BSR), a U.S.-based global resource for companies seeking to sustain their commercial success in ways that demonstrate respect for ethical values and for people, communities, and the environment. For more information, visit cauxroundtable.org or bsr.org.

The Foreign Corrupt Practices Act of 1977, as amended by the International Anti-Bribery and Fair Competition Act of 1998, has certainly contributed to a management focus on ethical behavior—although government regulation, in and of itself, tends to curtail only the most abusive ethical violations. As early as 1987, a private-sector commission was convened in response to perceived weaknesses in corporate financial reporting practices. This resulted in a series of recommendations to the SEC that publicly owned corporations include in their annual reports disclosures about how the company fulfills its responsibilities for achieving a broadly defined set of internal control objectives related to safeguarding assets, authorizing transactions, and reporting properly. (See the Business in Practice discussion of internal control in Chapter 5.) Section 404 of the Sarbanes–Oxley Act of 2002 requires all SEC-regulated companies to include in their annual reports a report by management on the effectiveness of the company's internal control over financial reporting. The auditor that audits the company's financial statements included in the annual report is also required to attest to and report on management's assessment of internal controls. Many companies provide further disclosures in their annual reports concerning their corporate code of conduct or ethics and whistle-blowing systems. Within the accounting profession, it is generally accepted that an organization's integrity and ethical values bear directly on the effectiveness of its internal control system.

Researchers have demonstrated that well-constructed ethical and social programs can contribute to profitability by helping to attract customers, raise employee morale and productivity, and strengthen trust relationships within the organization. Indeed, organizations that are committed to ethical quality often institute structures and procedures (such as codes of conduct) to encourage decency. Ethics codes vary from generalized value statements and credos to detailed discussions of global ethical policy. Johnson & Johnson's "Our Credo" is perhaps the most frequently cited corporate ethics statement, and rightfully so (see jnj.com).

For a list of the 100 Best Corporate Citizens as determined by one observer of the corporate scene, see thecro.com. Incidentally, Campbell's was ranked fifth on the 2017 list, which also included Hasbro, Intel, Microsoft, Cisco Systems, Hormel Foods, and Lockheed Martin in the top 10.

For additional guidance, check out US SIF (The Forum for Sustainable and Responsible Investment), which offers comprehensive information, contacts, and resources on socially responsible investing (see ussif.org).

It is never too early to understand and refine your own value system and to sharpen your awareness of the ethical dimensions of your activities, and don't be surprised if you are asked to literally "sign on" to an employer's code of conduct.

The following websites reference other sites dealing with business ethics:

scu.edu/ethics (then click *Business Ethics*)

ethics.org

Campbell's

understanding of the author summary that follows, you may want to download the full text of *Concepts Statement No. 8* from the FASB's website.)

Financial reporting is done for individual firms, or entities, rather than for industries or the economy as a whole. It is aimed primarily at meeting the needs of external users of accounting information who would not otherwise have access to the firm's records. Investors, creditors, and financial advisers are the primary users who create the demand for accounting information. Financial reporting is designed to meet the needs of users by providing information that is relevant to making rational investment and credit decisions and other informed judgments. The users of accounting information are assumed to be reasonably astute in business and financial reporting practices. However, each user reads the financial statements with her or his own judgment and biases and must be willing to take responsibility for her or his own decision making.

Most users are on the outside looking in. For its own use, management can prescribe the information it wants. Reporting for *internal* planning, control, and decision making need not be constrained by financial reporting requirements—thus the Concepts Statements are not directed at internal (i.e., managerial) uses of accounting information.

Financial accounting is historical scorekeeping; it is not future oriented. Although the future is unknown, it is likely to be influenced by the past. To the extent that accounting information provides a fair basis for the evaluation of past performance, it may be helpful in assessing an entity's future prospects. However, financial reports are not the sole source of information about an entity. For example, a potential employee might want to know about employee turnover rates, which are not disclosed in the financial reporting process. The information reported in financial accounting relates primarily to past transactions and events that can be measured in dollars and cents.

Financial accounting information is developed and used at a cost, and the benefit to the user of accounting information should exceed the cost of providing it.

Many of the objectives of financial reporting relate to the presentation of earnings and cash flow information. Investors and creditors are interested in making judgments about the firm's profitability and whether they are likely to receive payment of amounts owed to them. The user may ask, "How much profit did the firm earn during the year ended December 31, 2019?" or "What was the net cash inflow from operating the firm for the year?" Users understand that cash has to be received from somewhere before the firm can pay principal and interest to its creditors or dividends to its investors. A primary objective of financial reporting is to provide timely information about a firm's earnings and cash flow.

Financial reporting includes detailed notes and other disclosures.

Accrual accounting—to be explained in more detail later—involves accounting for the effect of an economic activity, or transaction, on an entity when the activity has occurred, rather than when the cash receipt or payment takes place. Thus, the company you work for reports a cost for your wages in the month in which you do the work, even though you may not be paid until the next month. Earnings information is reported on the accrual basis rather than the cash basis because past performance can be measured more accurately under accrual accounting. In the process of measuring a firm's accrual accounting earnings, some costs applicable to one year's results of operations may have to be estimated; for example, product warranty costs applicable to 2019 may not be finally determined until 2020. Reporting an approximately correct amount in 2019 is obviously preferable to recording nothing at all until 2020, when the precise amount is known.

In addition to providing information about earnings and cash flows, financial reporting should provide information to help users assess the relative strengths and weaknesses of a firm's financial position. The user may ask, "What economic resources does the firm own? How much does the firm owe? What caused these amounts to change over time?" Financial accounting does not attempt to directly measure the value of a firm, although it can be used to facilitate the efforts of those attempting to achieve such an objective. The numbers reported in a firm's financial statements do not change just because the market price of its stock changes.

Financial accounting standards are still evolving; with each new update to the FASB Codification, accounting procedures are modified to mirror new developments in the business world as well as current views and theories of financial reporting. At times, the FASB finds it difficult to keep pace with the ever-changing economic activities addressed by its ASUs. Fortunately, however, such efforts have resulted in improved financial reporting practices each step along the way.

Students of accounting should be aware that the how-to aspects of accounting are not static; the accounting discipline is relatively young in comparison to other professions and is in constant motion. Perhaps the most important outcome of the conceptual framework project is the sense that the profession now has a blueprint in place that will carry financial reporting into the future.

---

8. What does it mean to state that the objectives of financial reporting given in *Statement of Financial Accounting Concepts No. 8* provide a framework for this text?

What Does It Mean?

Answer on page 27

Objectives of Financial Reporting for Nonbusiness Organizations

At the outset of this chapter, it was stated that the material to be presented, although usually to be expressed in the context of profit-seeking business enterprises, would also be applicable to not-for-profit social service and governmental organizations. The FASB's "Highlights" of *Concepts Statement No. 4,* "Objectives of Financial Reporting by Nonbusiness Organizations," states, "Based on its study, the Board believes that the objectives of general-purpose external financial reporting for government-sponsored entities (e.g., hospitals, universities, or utilities) engaged in activities that are not unique to government should be similar to those of business enterprises or other nonbusiness organizations engaged in similar activities."[6] *Statement 6* amended *Statement 2*

---

[6] Source: FASB, Statement of Financial Accounting Concepts No. 4.

by affirming that the qualitative characteristics described in *Statement 2* apply to the information about both business enterprises and not-for-profit organizations.

The objectives of financial reporting for nonbusiness organizations focus on providing information for resource providers (such as taxpayers to governmental entities and donors to charitable organizations), rather than investors. Information is provided about the economic resources, obligations, net resources, and performance of an organization during a period of time. Thus, even though nonbusiness organizations have unique characteristics that distinguish them from profit-oriented businesses, the information characteristics of the financial reporting process for each type of organization are similar.

It will be appropriate to remember the gist of the preceding objectives as individual accounting and financial statement issues are encountered in subsequent chapters and are related to real-world situations.

Plan of the Book

LO 10

Describe the plan of the book.

This text is divided into two main parts. Chapters 2 through 11, which compose the first part of the book, are devoted to financial accounting topics. The remaining chapters, Chapters 12 through 16, provide an in-depth look at managerial accounting.

As you study the topics that lie ahead, the authors believe it will be to your advantage to be aware of the organizational strategy that we followed in writing this book. In general, the coverage of each topic begins with a "big picture" designed to put the topic in perspective relative to its role in financial accounting and reporting (Chapters 2 through 11) and managerial analysis and decision making (Chapters 12 through 16). The text coverage is limited in detail and is designed to provide a broad "high spot" understanding of the material and a foundation for further learning in a more advanced academic environment or experiential setting. You are quite likely to encounter certain situations in practice that do not follow exactly this textbook's descriptions of accounting practices. Yet we are confident that your own thoughtful study, and practical input from others who do accounting-related work and use its results, will permit you to refine your knowledge and use this material effectively.

Chapter 2, which kicks off our discussion of financial accounting, describes financial statements, presents a model of how they are interrelated, and briefly summarizes key accounting concepts and principles. This is a "big picture" chapter; later chapters elaborate on most of the material introduced here. This chapter also includes four Business in Practice features. As you have seen from the features in this chapter, these are brief explanations of business practices that make some of the ideas covered in the text easier to understand.

Chapter 3 describes some of the basic analytical tools that allow financial statement users to make fundamental interpretations of a company's financial position and results of operations. This is a "big picture" chapter that just scratches the surface of financial statement analysis; a more complete explanation of the key financial statement relationships is presented in subsequent chapters. Understanding the basic relationships presented here permits a better comprehension of the impact of alternative accounting methods discussed in Chapters 4 through 10. However, because Chapter 11 presents a more comprehensive treatment of financial statement analysis, some instructors may prefer to cover the Chapter 3 material with that of Chapter 11.

Chapter 4 describes the bookkeeping process and presents a powerful transaction analysis model. Using this model, the financial statement user can understand the effect of any transaction on the statements, and many of the judgments based on the statements. You will not be asked to learn bookkeeping in this chapter.

Chapters 5 through 9 examine specific financial statement elements. Chapter 5 describes the accounting for short-term *(current)* assets, including cash, accounts and notes receivable, inventory, and prepaid items. Chapter 6 describes the accounting for long-term assets—including land, buildings and equipment—and a variety of intangible assets and natural resources. Chapter 7 discusses the accounting issues related to current and long-term liabilities, including accounts and notes payable, bonds payable, and deferred income taxes. Chapter 8 deals with the components of stockholders' equity, including common stock, preferred stock, retained earnings, and treasury stock. Chapter 9 presents a comprehensive view of the income statement and the statement of cash flows.

Chapter 10 covers corporate governance issues as well as the notes to the financial statements, and Chapter 11 concludes our look at financial accounting with a detailed discussion of financial statement analysis. The financial accounting chapters frequently make reference to Campbell Soup Company's 2017 annual report, appropriate elements of which are reproduced in the appendix. You should refer to those financial statements and notes, as well as other company financial reports you may have, to get acquainted with actual applications of the issues being discussed in the text.

Following Chapter 11, we turn our focus to managerial accounting topics. Chapter 12 presents the "big picture" of managerial accounting. It contrasts financial and managerial accounting; introduces key managerial accounting terminology; and illustrates cost behavior patterns by describing various applications of cost–volume–profit analysis, including the calculation of a firm's breakeven point in units and sales dollars. Chapter 13 describes the principal cost accounting systems used in business today, with emphasis on the cost accumulation and assignment activities carried out by most firms. Chapter 14 illustrates many aspects of a typical firm's operating budget, including the sales forecast, production and purchases budgets, and the cash budget, as well as the development and use of standard costs for planning purposes. Chapter 15 concentrates on cost analysis for control; it highlights a number of performance reporting techniques and describes the analysis of variances for raw materials, direct labor, and manufacturing overhead. Chapter 16 concludes our discussion of managerial accounting with an overview of short-run versus long-run decision making, including a demonstration of the payback, net present value, and internal rate of return techniques used to support capital budgeting decisions.

An epilogue titled "Accounting—The Future" (with no homework problems!) reemphasizes the evolutionary nature of the accounting discipline and the relationships between financial and managerial accounting, and calls students' attention to a world of possibilities that remains to be explored in the future.

Use each chapter's learning objectives, "What Does It Mean?" questions, summary, and glossary of key terms and concepts to help manage your learning. With reasonable effort, you will achieve your objective of becoming an effective user of accounting information to support the related decisions and informed judgments you will make throughout your life.

Campbell's

Summary

Accounting is the process of identifying, measuring, and communicating economic information about an entity for the purpose of making decisions and informed judgments. **(LO 1)**

Users of financial statements include management, investors, creditors, employees, and government agencies. Decisions made by users relate to, among other things, entity operating results, investment and credit questions, employment characteristics, and compliance with laws. Financial statements support these decisions because they communicate important financial information about the entity. **(LO 2)**

The major classifications of accounting include financial accounting, managerial accounting/cost accounting, auditing/public accounting, internal auditing, governmental and not-for-profit accounting, and income tax accounting. **(LO 3)**

Accounting has developed over time in response to the information needs of users of financial statements. Financial accounting standards have been established by different organizations over the years. These standards have become increasingly complex in recent decades and, in some cases, are now extremely specific almost to the point of being statute-like. As a result, interest in converging U.S. financial reporting standards with International Financial Reporting Standards, which are more general and flow from broad principles, increased greatly beginning in the late 1990s. The Securities and Exchange Commission, the Financial Accounting Standards Board, and the International Accounting Standards Board have made substantial progress on the so-called convergence project that promises to make the existing financial reporting standards fully compatible as soon as possible. Currently in the United States, the FASB is the standard-setting body for financial accounting and is likely to remain so indefinitely. Other organizations are involved in establishing standards for cost accounting, auditing, governmental accounting, and income tax accounting. **(LO 4, 5, 6)**

Integrity, objectivity, independence, and competence are several characteristics of ethical behavior required of a professional accountant. High standards of ethical conduct are appropriate for all people, but professional accountants have a special responsibility because so many people make decisions and informed judgments using information provided by the accounting process. **(LO 7)**

The Financial Accounting Standards Board has issued several *Statements of Financial Accounting Concepts* resulting from the Conceptual Framework project that began in the late 1970s and still receives attention today. These statements describe concepts and relations that will underlie future financial accounting standards and practices and will in due course serve as a basis for evaluating existing standards and practices. Efforts are under way to ensure that the FASB and IASB Conceptual Frameworks will be converged similarly to the way in which their respective accounting standards have been converged. **(LO 8)**

Highlights of the Concepts Statement dealing with the objectives of financial reporting provide that financial information should be useful to investor and creditor concerns about the cash flows of the enterprise, the resources and obligations of the enterprise, and the profit of the enterprise. Financial accounting is not designed to directly measure the value of a business enterprise. **(LO 9)**

The objectives of financial reporting for nonbusiness enterprises are not significantly different from those for business enterprises, except that resource providers, rather than investors, are concerned about performance results, rather than profit.

The book starts with the big picture of financial accounting and then moves to some of the basic financial interpretations made from accounting data. An overview of the bookkeeping process is followed by a discussion of specific financial statement elements and notes to the financial statements. The financial accounting material ends with a chapter focusing on financial statement analysis and use of the data developed from analysis. The managerial accounting chapters focus on the development and use of financial information for managerial planning, control, and decision making. **(LO 10)**

Key Terms and Concepts

accounting (p. 3)   The process of identifying, measuring, and communicating economic information about an organization for the purpose of making decisions and informed judgments.

Accounting Standards Update **(Update or ASU) (p. 10)**   A transient document that communicates the details of specific amendments to the FASB Codification and explains the basis for the Board's decisions. Although ASUs update the FASB Codification, the FASB does not consider Updates as authoritative in their own right.

accrual accounting (p. 18)   Accounting that recognizes revenues and expenses as they occur, even though the cash receipt from the revenue or the cash disbursement related to the expense may occur before or after the event that causes revenue or expense recognition.

annual report (p. 8)   A document distributed to shareholders and other interested parties that contains the financial statements, notes to the financial statements, and management's discussion and analysis of financial and operating factors that affected the firm together with the report of the external auditor's examination of the financial statements.

auditing (p. 7)   The process of examining the financial statements of an entity by an independent third party with the objective of expressing an opinion about the fairness of the presentation of the entity's financial position, results of operations, changes in financial position, and cash flows. The practice of auditing is less precisely referred to as *public accounting.*

bookkeeping (p. 6)   Procedures that are used to keep track of financial transactions and accumulate the results of an entity's financial activities.

cash flow (p. 6)   Cash receipts or disbursements of an entity.

Certified Management Accountant (CMA) (p. 7)   Professional designation earned by passing a broad, two-part examination and meeting certain experience requirements. Examination topics include budgeting, performance management, cost management, financial statement analysis, corporate finance, decision analysis, and professional ethics.

Certified Public Accountant (CPA) (p. 6)   A professional designation earned by fulfilling certain education and experience requirements, in addition to passing a comprehensive, four-part examination. Examination topics include financial accounting theory and practice, income tax accounting, managerial accounting, governmental and not-for-profit accounting, auditing, business law, and other aspects of the business environment.

controller (p. 6)   The job title of the person who is the chief accounting officer of an organization. The controller is usually responsible for both the financial and managerial accounting functions. Sometimes referred to as *comptroller.*

cost accounting (p. 7)   A subset of managerial accounting that relates to the determination and accumulation of product, process, or service costs.

Cost Accounting Standards Board (CASB) (p. 12)   A group authorized by the U.S. Congress to establish cost accounting standards for government contractors.

creditor (p. 4)   An organization or individual who lends to the entity. Examples include suppliers who ship merchandise to the entity prior to receiving payment for their goods and banks that lend cash to the entity.

entity (p. 3)   An organization, individual, or a group of organizations or individuals for which accounting services are performed.

FASB Accounting Standards Codification (**FASB Codification**) (**p. 10**)   An advanced user-accessible computer application that systemized and reorganized many divergent elements of U.S. GAAP into one composite structure permitting users to review, study, and research topics. The Codification presents U.S. GAAP in a uniform and logical order, with approximately 90 major accounting topics. Since July 2009, the FASB Codification has represented a single source of all U.S. GAAP.

financial accounting (p. 6)   Accounting that focuses on reporting an entity's financial position at a point in time and/or its results of operations and cash flows for a period of time.

Financial Accounting Foundation (FAF) (p. 10)   An organization composed of people from the public accounting profession, businesses, and the public that is responsible for the funding of and appointing members to the Financial Accounting Standards Board and the Governmental Accounting Standards Board.

Financial Accounting Standards Board (FASB) (p. 10)   The body responsible for establishing U.S. generally accepted accounting principles.

generally accepted accounting principles (GAAP) (p. 7)   Pronouncements of the Financial Accounting Standards Board (FASB) and its predecessors that constitute appropriate accounting for various transactions used for reporting financial position and results of operations to investors and creditors. Since July 2009, the FASB Codification has represented a single source of U.S. GAAP.

generally accepted auditing standards (GAAS) (p. 7)   Standards for auditing that are established by the Auditing Standards Board of the American Institute of Certified Public Accountants unless superseded or amended by the PCAOB.

Governmental Accounting Standards Board (GASB) (p. 12)   Established by the Financial Accounting Foundation to develop guidelines for financial accounting and reporting by state and local governmental units.

independence (p. 15)   The personal characteristic of an accountant, especially an auditor, that refers to both appearing and in fact being objective and impartial.

independent auditor's report (p. 7)   The report accompanying audited financial statements that explains briefly the auditor's responsibility and the extent of work performed. The report includes an opinion about whether the information contained in the financial statements is presented fairly in accordance with generally accepted accounting principles.

integrity (p. 15)   The personal characteristic of honesty, including being forthright in dealings and communications with others.

internal auditing (p. 8)   The practice of auditing within a company by employees of the company.

International Accounting Standards Board (IASB) (p. 11)   Standard-setting body responsible for the development of International Financial Reporting Standards (IFRS) permitted or required by more than 100 countries.

International Financial Reporting Standards (IFRS) (p. 13)   Pronouncements of the International Accounting Standards Board that are considered to be a "principles-based" set of standards in that they establish broad rules as well as dictate specific treatments. Many of the standards forming part of IFRS are known by the older name of International Accounting Standards (IAS).

investor (p. 4)   An organization or individual who has an ownership interest in the firm. For corporations, referred to as *stockholder* or *shareholder*.

managerial accounting (p. 7)   Accounting that is concerned with the internal use of economic and financial information to plan and control many of the activities of an entity and to support the management decision-making process.

objectivity (p. 15)   The personal characteristic of impartiality, including freedom from conflict of interest.

public accounting (p. 7)   The segment of the accounting profession that provides auditing, income tax accounting, and management consulting services to clients.

Public Company Accounting Oversight Board (p. 11)   Established in 2002 with authority to set and enforce auditing and ethics standards for public companies and their auditing firms; affiliated with the SEC.

Securities and Exchange Commission (SEC) (p. 10)   A unit of the federal government that is responsible for establishing regulations and ensuring full disclosure to investors about companies and their securities that are traded in interstate commerce.

***Statements of Financial Accounting Standards* (SFAS) (p. 10)**   Pronouncements of the Financial Accounting Standards Board that formerly constituted generally accepted accounting principles. Effective in July 2009, the SFAS series was superseded by the *FASB Accounting Standards Codification.*

Exercises   connect

Obtain an annual report. Throughout this course, you will be asked to relate the material being studied to actual financial statements. After you complete this course, you will be able to use an organization's financial statements to make decisions and informed judgments about that organization. The purpose of this assignment is to provide the experience of obtaining a company's annual report. You may want to refer to the financial statements in the report during the rest of the course.

Exercise 1.1

Required:
Obtain the most recently issued annual report of a publicly owned manufacturing or merchandising corporation of your choice. Do not select a bank, insurance company, financial institution, or public utility. It would be appropriate to select a firm that you know something about or have an interest in.

Type www.firmname.com or use a search engine to locate your chosen company's website and then scan your firm's home page for information about annual report ordering. If you don't see a direct link to *Investor Relations* or *Investors* on the home page, look for links such as *Our Company, About Us,* or *Site Map* that may lead you to *SEC Filings, Financial Information,* or *Annual Reports.* Most companies allow you to save or print an Adobe Acrobat version of their annual reports.

Read and outline an article. The accounting profession is frequently in the news, not always in the most positive light. The purpose of this assignment is to increase your awareness of an issue facing the profession.

Exercise 1.2
LO 4

Required:
Find, read, outline, and prepare to discuss a brief article from a general audience or business audience publication about accounting and/or the accounting profession. The article should have been published within the past eight months and should relate to accounting or the accounting profession in general; it should *not* be about some technical accounting issue. The appropriate search terms to use are "accountants," "accounting," and/or "accounting (specific topic)."

Your ideas about accounting. Write a paragraph describing your perceptions of what accounting is all about and the work that accountants do.

Exercise 1.3
LO 3

Exercise 1.4
LO 10

Your expectations for this course. Write a statement identifying the expectations you have for this course.

Exercise 1.5
LO 7

Identify factors in an ethical decision. Jim Sandrolini is an accountant for a local manufacturing company. Jim's good friend, Dan Carruthers, has been operating a retail sporting goods store for about a year. The store has been moderately successful, and Dan needs a bank loan to help finance the next stage of his store's growth. He has asked Jim to prepare financial statements that the banker will use to help decide whether to grant the loan. Dan has proposed that the fee he will pay for Jim's accounting work should be contingent upon his receiving the loan.

Required:
What factors should Jim consider when making his decision about whether to prepare the financial statements for Dan's store?

Exercise 1.6
LO 2

Identify information used in making an informed decision. Chris and Tiasha Hirst have owned and operated a retail furniture store for more than 30 years. They have employed an independent CPA during this time to prepare various sales tax, payroll tax, and income tax returns, as well as financial statements for themselves and the bank from which they have borrowed money from time to time. They are considering selling the store but are uncertain about how to establish an asking price.

Required:
What type of information is likely to be included in the material prepared by the CPA that may help Mr. and Mrs. Hirst establish an asking price for the store?

Exercise 1.7
LO 6

Auditor independence. Using the search engine you are most comfortable with, identify at least five sources concerning the general topic of auditor independence. Write a brief memo to provide an update on the current status of the auditor independence standard-setting process. The Business in Practice box on auditor independence should serve as the starting point for this exercise. (*Note:* You might find it useful to contrast the opinions expressed by any of the Big 4 accounting firms to those expressed by nonaccounting professionals.)

Exercise 1.8

Find financial information. From the set of financial statements acquired for E1.1, determine the following:

a. Who is the chief financial officer?
b. What are the names of the directors?
c. Which firm conducted the audit? Have the auditors reviewed the entire report?
d. What are the names of the financial statements provided?
e. How many pages of notes accompany the financial statements?
f. In addition to the financial statements, are there other reports? If so, what are they?

1. It means that accounting is a service activity that helps many different users of accounting information who use the information in many ways.

2. It means to perform professional services for clients principally in the areas of auditing, income taxes, management consulting, and/or accounting systems evaluation and development.

3. It means that the individual has met the educational requirements and has passed the uniform examination. Subsequently, the individual has met the experience requirements and has applied for and been issued a license by a state board of accountancy granting the individual the right to practice as a Certified Public Accountant.

4. It means that generally accepted accounting principles sometimes permit alternative ways of accounting for identical transactions, thus requiring professional judgment, and that these principles are still evolving.

5. It means that the FASB has completed an extensive process of research and development, including receiving input from interested individuals and organizations, and has made an authoritative pronouncement (i.e., an Update to the FASB Codification) that defines accounting and reporting for a specific activity or transaction and becomes a generally accepted accounting principle.

6. It means that the FASB is committed to working with the IASB to ensure that a solution can be reached whereby U.S. accounting standards will eventually be merged with international accounting standards to the greatest extent possible.

7. It means that the individual is impartial, free from conflict of interest, and will not receive a personal gain from the activity in which she or he is involved.

8. It means that the accounting and financial reporting topics explained in the financial accounting part of this text should:

   a. Relate to external financial reporting.

   b. Support business and economic decisions.

   c. Provide information about cash flows.

   d. Focus on earnings based on accrual accounting.

   e. Not seek to directly measure the value of a business enterprise.

   f. Report information that is subject to evaluation by individual financial statement users.

2

Financial Statements and Accounting Concepts/Principles

Financial statements are the product of the financial accounting process. They are the means of communicating economic information about the entity to individuals who want to make decisions and informed judgments about the entity's financial position, results of operations, and cash flows. Although each of the four principal financial statements has a unique purpose, they are interrelated; to get a complete financial picture of the reporting entity, all must be considered.

Users cannot make meaningful interpretations of financial statement data without understanding the concepts and principles that relate to the entire financial accounting process. It is also important for users to understand that these concepts and principles are broad in nature; they do not constitute an inflexible set of rules, but serve as guidelines for the development of sound financial reporting practices.

LEARNING OBJECTIVES (LO)

After studying this chapter, you should understand and be able to

LO 2-1   Explain what transactions are.

LO 2-2   Identify and explain the kind of information reported in each financial statement and describe how financial statements are related to each other.

LO 2-3   Explain the meaning and usefulness of the accounting equation.

LO 2-4   Explain the meaning of each of the captions on the financial statements illustrated in this chapter.

LO 2-5   Identify and explain the broad, generally accepted concepts and principles that apply to the accounting process.

LO 2-6   Discuss why investors must carefully consider cash flow information in conjunction with accrual accounting results.

LO 2-7   Identify and explain several limitations of financial statements.

LO 2-8   Describe what a corporation's annual report is and why it is issued.

Financial Statements

From Transactions to Financial Statements

An entity's financial statements are the end product of a process that starts with **transactions** between the entity and other organizations and individuals. Transactions are economic interchanges between entities: for example, a sale/purchase, or a receipt of cash by a borrower and the payment of cash by a lender. The flow from transactions to financial statements can be illustrated as follows:

LO 1

Explain what transactions are.

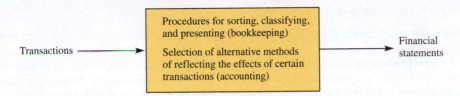

---

1. What does it mean to say that there has been an accounting transaction between you and your school? Give an example of such a transaction.

What Does It Mean?

Answer on page 66

Transactions are summarized in **accounts,** and accounts are further summarized in the financial statements. In this sense, transactions can be seen as the bricks that build the financial statements. By learning about the form, content, and relationships among financial statements in this chapter, you will better understand the process of building those results—bookkeeping and transaction analysis—described in Chapter 4 and subsequent chapters.

Current generally accepted accounting principles and auditing standards require that the financial statements of an entity show the following for the reporting period:

Financial position at the end of the period.

Earnings for the period.

Cash flows during the period.

Investments by and distributions to owners (i.e., stockholders) during the period.

The financial statements that satisfy these requirements are, respectively, the:

Balance sheet (or statement of financial position).

Income statement (or statement of earnings, or profit and loss statement, or statement of operations).

Statement of cash flows.

Statement of changes in stockholders' equity (or statement of stockholders' equity, or statement of equity, or statement of changes in capital stock, or statement of changes in retained earnings).

In addition to the financial statements themselves, the annual report will probably include several accompanying notes (sometimes called the financial review) that include explanations of the accounting policies and detailed information about many of the amounts and captions shown on the financial statements. These notes are designed to assist the reader of the financial statements by disclosing as much relevant supplementary information as the company and its auditors deem necessary and appropriate. For Campbell Soup Company, the notes to the 2017 financial statements are shown in the "Notes to Consolidated Financial Statements" section of the annual report in the appendix. One of this text's objectives is to enable you to read, interpret, and understand financial statement notes. Chapter 10 describes the notes to the financial statements in detail.

Business in
Practice

Organizing a Business

There are three principal forms of business organization: proprietorship, partnership, and corporation.

A **proprietorship** is an activity conducted by an individual. Operating as a proprietorship is the easiest way to get started in a business activity. Other than the possibility of needing a local license, there aren't any formal prerequisites to beginning operations. Besides being easy to start, a proprietorship has the advantage, according to many people, that the owner is his or her own boss. A principal disadvantage of the proprietorship is that the owner's liability for business debts is not limited by the assets of the business. For example, if the business fails, and if, after all available business assets have been used to pay business debts, the business creditors are still owed money, the owner's personal assets can be claimed by business creditors. Another disadvantage is that the individual proprietor may have difficulty raising the money needed to provide the capital base that will be required if the business is to grow substantially. Because of the ease of getting started, every year many business activities begin as proprietorships.

The **partnership** is essentially a group of proprietors who have banded together. The unlimited liability characteristic of the proprietorship still exists, but with several partners the ability of the firm to raise capital may be improved. Income earned from partnership activities is taxed at the individual partner level; the partnership itself is not a tax-paying entity. Accountants, attorneys, and other professionals frequently operate their firms as partnerships. In recent years, many large professional partnerships, including the Big 4 accounting firms, have been operating under *limited liability partnership* (LLP) rules, which shield individual partners from unlimited personal liability.

Most large businesses, and many new businesses, use the corporate form of organization. Note that "Inc." in the name of our example business, Main Street Stores Inc., is an abbreviation for *incorporated* and means that the firm was legally organized as a corporation. The owners of the corporation are called **stockholders** (or shareholders). They have invested funds in the corporation and received shares of **stock** as evidence of their ownership. Stockholders' liability is limited to the amount invested; creditors cannot seek recovery of losses from the personal assets of stockholders. Large amounts of capital can frequently be raised by selling shares of stock to many individuals. It is also possible for all of the stock of a corporation to be owned by a single individual. A stockholder can usually sell his or her shares to other investors or buy more shares from other stockholders if a change in ownership interest is desired. A **corporation** is formed by having a charter and bylaws prepared and registered with the appropriate office in 1 of the 50 states. The cost of forming a corporation is usually greater than that of starting a proprietorship or forming a partnership. A major disadvantage of the corporate form of business is that corporations are tax-paying entities. Thus, any income distributed to stockholders has been taxed first as income of the corporation and then is taxed a second time as income of the individual stockholders.

A form of organization that has now been authorized in all states and the District of Columbia is the *limited liability company* (LLC). For accounting and legal purposes, this type of organization is treated as a corporation even though some of the formalities of the corporate form of organization are not present. Stockholders of small corporations may find that banks and major creditors usually require the personal guarantees of the principal stockholders as a condition for granting credit to the corporation. Therefore, the limited liability of the corporate form may be, in the case of small corporations, more theoretical than real.

Fiscal Year

A firm's **fiscal year** is the annual period used for reporting to owners, the government, and others. Many firms select the calendar year as their fiscal year, but other 12-month periods can also be selected. Some firms select a reporting period ending on a date when inventories will be relatively low or business activity will be slow, because this facilitates the process of preparing financial statements.

Many firms select fiscal periods that relate to the pace of their business activity. Food retailers, for example, have a weekly operating cycle, and many of these firms select a 52-week fiscal year (with a 53-week fiscal year every five or six years so their year-end remains near to the same date every year). Campbell Soup Company has adopted this strategy; note, in the appendix, that Campbell's fiscal year ends on the Sunday nearest July 31 each year. (There were 52 weeks in 2017, 2016, and 2015; the last fiscal year with 53 weeks was 2014.)

For internal reporting purposes, many firms use periods other than the month (e.g., 13 four-week periods). Such firms want to maintain the same number of operating days in each period so that comparisons between the same periods of different years can be made without having to consider differences in the number of operating days in the respective periods.

Financial Statements Illustrated

To illustrate financial statements, we present an example of what they might look like for a simple retail business. Main Street Store Inc. was organized as a corporation and began business during September 2019 (see Business in Practice—Organizing a Business). The company buys clothing and accessories from distributors and manufacturers and sells these items from a rented building. The financial statements of Main Street Store Inc. at August 31, 2020, and for the fiscal year (see Business in Practice—Fiscal Year) ended on that date are presented in Exhibits 2-1, 2-2, 2-3, and 2-4.

As you look at these financial statements, you will probably have several questions concerning the nature of specific accounts and how the numbers are computed. For now, concentrate on the explanations and definitions that are appropriate and inescapable, and notice especially the characteristics of each financial statement. Many of your questions about specific accounts will be answered in subsequent chapters that explain in detail the individual statements and their components.

LO 2
Identify and explain the kind of information reported in each financial statement and describe how the statements are related to each other.

Explanations and Definitions

Balance Sheet The **balance sheet** is a listing of the organization's assets, liabilities, and stockholders' equity (often referred to simply as *owners' equity*) *at a point in time*. In this sense, the balance sheet is like a snapshot of the organization's financial position, frozen at a specific point in time. The balance sheet is sometimes called the **statement of financial position** because it summarizes the entity's resources (assets), obligations (liabilities), and owners' claims (stockholders' equity). The balance sheet for Main Street Store Inc. at August 31, 2020, the end of the firm's first year of operations, is illustrated in Exhibit 2-1.

Notice the two principal sections of the balance sheet that are shown side by side: (1) assets and (2) liabilities and stockholders' equity. Observe that the dollar total of $320,000 is the same for each side. This equality is sometimes referred to as the

LO 3
Explain the meaning and usefulness of the accounting equation.

Exhibit 2-1

Balance Sheet

MAIN STREET STORE INC. Balance Sheet August 31, 2020			
Assets		**Liabilities and Stockholders' Equity**	
Current assets:		Current liabilities:	
Cash	$ 34,000	Accounts payable	$ 35,000
Accounts receivable	80,000	Other accrued liabilities	12,000
Merchandise inventory	170,000	Short-term debt	20,000
Total current assets	$284,000	Total current liabilities	$ 67,000
Plant and equipment:		Long-term debt	50,000
Equipment	40,000	Total liabilities	$117,000
Less: Accumulated depreciation	(4,000)	Stockholders' equity	203,000
Total assets	$320,000	Total liabilities and stockholders' equity	$320,000

accounting equation or the **balance sheet equation.** It is the equality, or balance, of these two amounts from which the term *balance sheet* is derived.

$$\text{Assets} = \text{Liabilities} + \text{Stockholders' equity}$$
$$\$320,000 = \$117,000 + \$203,000$$

Now we will provide some of those appropriate and inescapable definitions and explanations:

"**Assets** are probable future economic benefits obtained or controlled by a particular entity as a result of past transactions or events."[1] In brief, assets represent the amount of resources controlled (which ordinarily means owned) by the entity. Assets are often tangible; they can be seen and handled (such as cash, merchandise inventory, or equipment), or evidence of their existence can be observed (such as a customer's acknowledgment of receipt of merchandise and the implied promise to pay the amount due when agreed upon—an account receivable).

"**Liabilities** are probable future sacrifices of economic benefits arising from present obligations of a particular entity to transfer assets or provide services to other entities in the future as a result of past transactions or events."[2] In brief, liabilities are amounts *owed* to other entities. For example, the accounts payable arose because suppliers shipped merchandise to Main Street Store Inc., and this merchandise will be paid for at some point in the future. In other words, the supplier has a "claim" against the firm for the amount Main Street Store Inc. has agreed to pay for the merchandise until the day it is paid for and, thus has, become a creditor of the firm by supplying merchandise on account.

Stockholders' equity (often referred to as **owners' equity**) is the ownership right of the stockholder(s) of the entity in the assets that remain after deducting the liabilities. (A car or house owner refers to his or her **equity** as the market value of the car or

---

[1] Source: FASB, Statement of Financial Accounting Concepts No. 6, "Elements of Financial Statements."
[2] Source: FASB, Statement of Financial Accounting Concepts No. 6, "Elements of Financial Statements."

house less the loan or mortgage balance.) Stockholders' equity is sometimes referred to as **net assets.** This can be shown by rearranging the basic accounting equation:

$$\text{Assets} - \text{Liabilities} = \text{Stockholders' equity}$$
$$\text{Net assets} = \text{Stockholders' equity}$$

Another term sometimes used when referring to stockholders' equity is **net worth.** However, this term is misleading because it implies that the net assets are "worth" the amount reported on the balance sheet as stockholders' equity. *Financial statements prepared in accordance with generally accepted accounting principles do not purport to show the current market value of the entity's assets, except in a few restricted cases.*

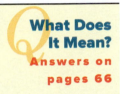

2. What does it mean to refer to a balance sheet for the year ended August 31, 2020?

3. What does it mean when a balance sheet has been prepared for an organization?

What Does It Mean?

Answers on pages 66

Each of the individual assets and liabilities reported by Main Street Store Inc. warrants a brief explanation. Each account (*caption* in the financial statements) is discussed in more detail in later chapters. Your task at this point is to achieve a broad understanding of each account and to make sense of its classification as an asset or liability.

Cash represents cash on hand and in the bank or banks used by Main Street Store Inc. If the firm had made any temporary cash investments to earn interest, these marketable securities probably would be shown as a separate asset because these funds are not as readily available as cash.

Accounts receivable represent amounts due from customers who have purchased merchandise on credit and who have agreed to pay within a specified period or when billed by Main Street Store Inc.

Merchandise inventory represents the cost to Main Street Store Inc. of the merchandise that it has acquired but not yet sold.

Equipment represents the cost to Main Street Store Inc. of the display cases, racks, shelving, and other store equipment purchased and installed in the rented building in which it operates. The building is not shown as an asset because Main Street Store Inc. does not own it.

Accumulated depreciation represents the portion of the cost of the equipment that is estimated to have been used up in the process of operating the business. Note that one-tenth ($4,000/$40,000) of the cost of the equipment has been depreciated. From this relationship, one might assume that the equipment is estimated to have a useful life of 10 years because this is the balance sheet at the end of the firm's first year of operations. **Depreciation** in accounting is the process of spreading the cost of an asset over its useful life to the entity—it is *not* an attempt to recognize the economic loss in value of an asset because of its age or use.

Accounts payable represent amounts owed to suppliers of merchandise inventory that was purchased on credit and will be paid within a specific period of time.

Other **accrued liabilities** represent amounts owed to various creditors, including any wages owed to employees for services provided to Main Street Store Inc. through August 31, 2020, the balance sheet date.

LO 4
Explain the meaning of each of the captions on the financial statements illustrated in this chapter.

Short-term debt represents amounts borrowed, probably from banks, that will be repaid within one year of the balance sheet date.

Long-term debt represents amounts borrowed from banks or others that will not be repaid within one year from the balance sheet date.

Stockholders' equity, shown as a single amount in Exhibit 2-1, is explained in more detail later in this chapter in the discussion of the statement of changes in stockholders' equity.

Notice that in Exhibit 2-1 some assets and liabilities are classified as "current." **Current assets** are cash and other assets that are likely to be converted into cash or used to benefit the entity within one year, and **current liabilities** are those liabilities that are likely to be paid with cash within one year of the balance sheet date. In this example, it is expected that the accounts receivable from the customers of Main Street Store Inc. will be collected within a year and that the merchandise inventory will be sold within a year of the balance sheet date. This time-frame classification is important and, as explained later, is used in assessing the entity's ability to pay its obligations when they come due.

To summarize, the balance sheet is a listing of the entity's assets, liabilities, and stockholders' equity. A balance sheet can be prepared as of any date but is most frequently prepared as of the end of a fiscal reporting period (e.g., month-end or year-end). The balance sheet as of the end of one period is the balance sheet as of the beginning of the next period. This can be illustrated on a timeline as follows:

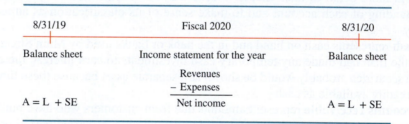

8/31/19	Fiscal 2020	8/31/20
Balance sheet	Income statement for the year	Balance sheet
	Revenues	
	− Expenses	
A = L + SE	Net income	A = L + SE

On the timeline, Fiscal 2020 refers to the 12 months during which the entity carried out its economic activities.

Income Statement   The principal purpose of the **income statement,** or **statement of earnings,** or **profit and loss statement,** or **statement of operations,** is to answer the question "Did the entity operate at a **profit** for the period of time under consideration?" The question is answered by first reporting **revenues** from the entity's operating activities (such as selling merchandise) and then subtracting the **expenses** incurred in generating those revenues and operating the entity. **Gains** and **losses** are also reported on the income statement. Gains and losses result from nonoperating activities, rather than from the day-to-day operating activities that generate revenues and expenses. The income statement reports results for *a period of time,* in contrast to the balance sheet focus on a single date. In this sense, the income statement is more like a movie than a snapshot; it depicts the results of activities that have occurred during a period of time.

The income statement for Main Street Store, Inc., for the year ended August 31, 2020, is presented in Exhibit 2-2. Notice that the statement starts with **net sales** (which are revenues) and that the various expenses are subtracted to arrive at **net income** in total and per share of common stock outstanding. Net income is the profit for the period; if expenses exceed net sales, a net loss results. The reasons for reporting earnings per share of common stock outstanding, and the calculation of this amount, are explained in Chapter 9.

MAIN STREET STORE INC. Income Statement For the Year Ended August 31, 2020	
Net sales	$1,200,000
Cost of goods sold	850,000
Gross profit	$ 350,000
Selling, general, and administrative expenses	311,000
Income from operations	$ 39,000
Interest expense	9,000
Income before taxes	$ 30,000
Income taxes	12,000
Net income	$ 18,000
Earnings per share of common stock outstanding	$ 1.80

Exhibit 2-2

Income Statement

Now look at the individual captions on the income statement. Each warrants a brief explanation, which will be expanded in subsequent chapters. Your task at this point is to make sense of how each item influences the determination of net income.

Net sales represent the amount of sales of merchandise to customers, less the amount of sales originally recorded but canceled because the merchandise was subsequently returned by customers for various reasons (wrong size, spouse didn't want it, and so on). The sales amount is frequently called *sales revenue,* or just *revenue.* Revenue results from selling a product or providing a service to a customer.

Cost of goods sold represents the total cost of merchandise removed from inventory and delivered to customers as a result of sales. This is shown as a separate expense because of its significance and because of the desire to show gross profit as a separate subtotal on the income statement. Frequently used synonyms are *cost of sales* and *cost of products sold.*

Gross profit is the difference between net sales and cost of goods sold and represents the seller's maximum amount of "cushion" from which all other expenses of operating the business must be met before it is possible to have net income. Gross profit (sometimes referred to as *gross margin*) is shown as a separate subtotal because it is significant to both management and nonmanagement readers of the income statement. The uses made of this amount will be explained in subsequent chapters.

Selling, general, and administrative expenses represent the operating expenses of the entity. In some income statements, these expenses will not be lumped together as in Exhibit 2-2 but will be reported separately for each of several operating expense categories, such as wages, advertising, and depreciation.

Income from operations represents one of the most important measures of the firm's activities. Income from operations (or *operating income* or *earnings from operations*) can be related to the assets available to the firm to obtain a useful measure of management's performance. A method of doing this is explained in Chapter 3.

Interest expense represents the cost of using borrowed funds. This item is reported separately because it is a function of how assets are financed, not how assets are used.

Income taxes are shown after all the other income statement items have been reported, because income taxes (often captioned as *income tax expense* or *provision for income taxes*) are a function of the firm's income before taxes.

Earnings per share of common stock outstanding is reported as a separate item at the bottom of the income statement because of its significance in evaluating the market value of a share of common stock. This measure, which is often referred to simply as *EPS,* is explained in more detail in Chapter 9.

To review, the income statement summarizes the entity's income- (or loss-) producing activities *for a period of time.* Transactions that affect the income statement also affect the balance sheet. For example, a sale made for cash increases sales revenue on the income statement and increases cash, an asset on the balance sheet. Likewise, wages earned by employees during the last week of the current year to be paid early in the next year are an expense of the current year. These wages will be deducted from revenues in the income statement and are considered a liability reported on the balance sheet at the end of the year. Thus, the income statement is a link between the balance sheets at the beginning and end of the year. How this link is made is explained in the next section, which describes the statement of changes in stockholders' equity. The timeline presented earlier can be expanded as follows:

8/31/19	Fiscal 2020	8/31/20
Balance sheet	Income statement for the year	Balance sheet
	Revenues	
	– Expenses	
A = L + SE	Net income	A = L + SE

Statement of Changes in Stockholders' Equity   The **statement of changes in stockholders' equity** (sometimes called the *statement of changes in owners' equity*), or **statement of changes in capital stock,** or **statement of changes in retained earnings,** or **statement of stockholders' equity,** or **statement of equity,** like the income statement, has a *period of time* orientation. This statement shows the detail of stockholders' equity and explains the changes that occurred in the components of stockholders' equity during the year.

Exhibit 2-3 illustrates this statement for Main Street Store Inc. for the year ended August 31, 2020. Remember that these are the results of Main Street Store's first year

Exhibit 2-3

Statement of Changes in Stockholders' Equity

MAIN STREET STORE INC. Statement of Changes in Stockholders' Equity For the Year Ended August 31, 2020	
Paid-In Capital:	
Beginning balance	$ –0–
Common stock, par value, $10; 50,000 shares authorized, 10,000 shares issued and outstanding	100,000
Additional paid-in capital	90,000
Balance, August 31, 2020	$190,000
Retained Earnings:	
Beginning balance	$ –0–
Net income for the year	18,000
Less: Cash dividends of $.50 per share	(5,000)
Balance, August 31, 2020	$ 13,000
Total stockholders' equity	$203,000

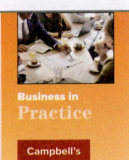

of operations, so the beginning-of-the-year balances are zero. On subsequent years' statements, the beginning-of-the-year amount is the ending balance from the prior year.

Notice in Exhibit 2-3 that stockholders' equity is made up of two principal components: **paid-in capital** and **retained earnings.** These items are briefly explained here and are discussed in more detail in Chapter 8.

Paid-in capital represents the total amount invested in the entity by the owners— in this case, the stockholders. When the stock issued to the owners has a **par value** (see Business in Practice—Par Value), there will usually be two categories of paid-in capital: common stock and additional paid-in capital.

Common stock reflects the number of shares authorized by the corporation's charter, the number of shares that have been issued to stockholders, and the number of shares that are held by the stockholders. When the common stock has a par value or stated value, the amount shown for common stock in the financial statements will always be the par value or stated value multiplied by the number of shares issued. If the common stock does not have a par value or stated value, the amount shown for common stock in the financial statements will be the total amount invested by the stockholders.

Additional paid-in capital is the difference between the total amount invested by the stockholders and the par value or stated value of the stock. (If no-par-value stock without a stated value is issued, there won't be any additional paid-in capital because the total amount paid in, or invested, by the stockholders will be shown as common stock.)

Retained earnings is the second principal category of stockholders' equity, and it represents the cumulative net income of the entity that has been retained for use in the business. **Dividends** are distributions of earnings that have been made to the stockholders, so these reduce retained earnings. If retained earnings has a negative balance because cumulative losses and dividends have exceeded cumulative net income, this part of stockholders' equity is referred to as an *accumulated deficit,* or simply *deficit.*

Note that net income of $18,000, as reported in Exhibit 2-2, is added to the beginning retained earnings of $0 in Exhibit 2-3, and cash dividends paid for the year of $5,000 are subtracted in arriving at the $13,000 ending retained earnings balance. The retained earnings section of the statement of changes in stockholders' equity is where the link (known as *articulation*) between the balance sheet and income statement is made. The timeline model is thus expanded and modified as follows:

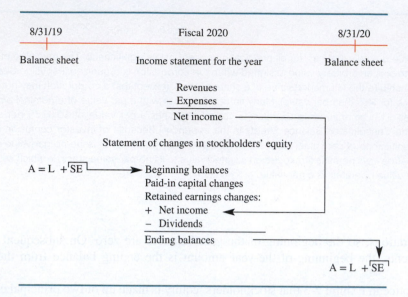

Notice that the total stockholders' equity reported in Exhibit 2-3 agrees with the stockholders' equity shown on the balance sheet in Exhibit 2-1. Most balance sheets include the amount of common stock, additional paid-in capital, and retained earnings within the stockholders' equity section. Changes that occur in these components of stockholders' equity are likely to be shown in a separate statement so that users of the financial statements can learn what caused these important balance sheet elements to change.

Statement of Cash Flows   The purpose of the **statement of cash flows** is to identify the sources and uses of cash during the year. This objective is accomplished by reporting the changes in all the other balance sheet items. Because of the equality that exists between assets and liabilities plus stockholders' equity, the total of the changes in every other asset and each liability and element of stockholders' equity will equal the change in cash. The statement of cash flows is described in detail in Chapter 9. For now, make sense of the three principal activity groups that cause cash to change, and see how the amounts on this statement relate to the balance sheet in Exhibit 2-1.

The statement of cash flows for Main Street Store Inc. for the year ended August 31, 2020, is illustrated in Exhibit 2-4. Notice that this statement, like the income statement and statement of changes in stockholders' equity, is *for a period of time.* Notice also the three activity categories: operating activities, investing activities, and financing activities.

Cash flows from operating activities are shown first, and net income is the starting point for this measure of cash flow. Using net income also directly relates the income statement (see Exhibit 2-2) to the statement of cash flows. Next, reconciling items are considered (i.e., items that must be added to or subtracted from net income to arrive at cash flows from operating activities).

Depreciation expense is added back to net income because, even though it was deducted as an expense in determining net income, *depreciation expense did not*

MAIN STREET STORE INC. Statement of Cash Flows For the Year Ended August 31, 2020	
Cash Flows from Operating Activities:	
Net income	$ 18,000
Add (deduct) items not affecting cash:	
Depreciation expense	4,000
Increase in accounts receivable	(80,000)
Increase in merchandise inventory	(170,000)
Increase in current liabilities	67,000
Net cash used by operating activities	$(161,000)
Cash Flows from Investing Activities:	
Cash paid for equipment	$ (40,000)
Cash Flows from Financing Activities:	
Cash received from issue of long-term debt	$ 50,000
Cash received from sale of common stock	190,000
Payment of cash dividend on common stock	(5,000)
Net cash provided by financing activities	$ 235,000
Net increase in cash for the year	$ 34,000

Exhibit 2-4

Statement of Cash Flows

require the use of cash. Remember—depreciation is the accounting process of spreading the cost of an asset over its estimated useful life.

The increase in accounts receivable is deducted because this reflects sales revenues, included in net income, that have not yet been collected in cash.

The increase in merchandise inventory is deducted because cash was spent to acquire the increase in inventory.

The increase in current liabilities is added because cash has not yet been paid for this amount of products and services that have been received during the current fiscal period.

Cash flows from investing activities show the cash used to purchase long-lived assets. You should find the increase in equipment in the balance sheet (Exhibit 2-1), which shows the cost of the equipment owned at August 31, 2020. Because this is the first year of the firm's operations, the equipment purchase required the use of $40,000 of cash during the year.

Cash flows from financing activities include amounts raised from the sale of long-term debt and common stock, and dividends paid on common stock. You should find each of these financing amounts in the balance sheet (Exhibit 2-1) or the statement of changes in stockholders' equity (Exhibit 2-3). For example, the $190,000 received from the sale of common stock is shown on the statement of changes in stockholders' equity (Exhibit 2-3) as the increase in paid-in capital during the year.

The net increase in cash for the year of $34,000 is the amount of cash in the August 31, 2020, balance sheet. Check this out. This should make sense because the firm started its business during September 2019, so it had no cash to begin with.

The statement of cash flows results in a further expansion and modification of the timeline model:

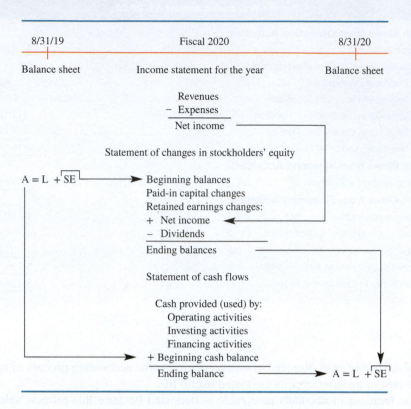

8/31/19	Fiscal 2020	8/31/20
Balance sheet	Income statement for the year	Balance sheet

Revenues
− Expenses
Net income

Statement of changes in stockholders' equity

A = L + SE → Beginning balances
Paid-in capital changes
Retained earnings changes:
+ Net income
− Dividends
Ending balances

Statement of cash flows

Cash provided (used) by:
Operating activities
Investing activities
Financing activities
+ Beginning cash balance
Ending balance → A = L + SE

What Does It Mean?

Answers on page 66

4. What does it mean when a stockholder says that she needs to look at her firm's set of four financial statements to fully understand its financial position and results of operations?

5. What does it mean when a company that has a high net income doesn't have enough cash to pay its bills?

Comparative Statements in Subsequent Years

The financial statements just presented for Main Street Store Inc. show data as of August 31, 2020, and for the year then ended. Because this was the first year of the firm's operations, comparative financial statements are not possible. In subsequent years, however, comparative statements for the current year and the prior year should be presented so that users of the data can more easily spot changes in the firm's financial position and in its results of operations. Some companies present data for two prior years in their financial statements. Most companies will include selected data from their balance sheets and income statements for at least five years, and sometimes for up to 25 years, as supplementary information in their annual report to stockholders. Campbell Soup Company's five-year selected financial data, which appear in the appendix, illustrate the firm's consistency and financial stability.

Campbell's

Illustration of Financial Statement Relationships

Exhibit 2-5 uses the financial statements of Main Street Store Inc. to illustrate the financial statement relationships just discussed. Note that in Exhibit 2-5, the August 31, 2019, balance sheet has no amounts because Main Street Store Inc. started business in September 2019. As you study this exhibit, note especially that net income for the year was an increase in retained earnings and is one of the reasons retained earnings changed during the year.

In subsequent chapters, the relationship between the balance sheet and income statement will be presented using the following diagram:

Balance Sheet	Income Statement
Assets = Liabilities + Stockholders' equity	← Net Income = Revenues − Expenses

The arrow from net income in the income statement to stockholders' equity in the balance sheet indicates that net income affects retained earnings, which is a component of stockholders' equity.

The following examples also illustrate the relationships within and between the principal financial statements. Using the August 31, 2020, Main Street Store Inc. data for assets and liabilities in the balance sheet equation of $A = L + SE$, stockholders' equity at August 31, 2020, can be calculated:

$$
\begin{aligned}
A &= L + SE \\
\$320{,}000 &= \$117{,}000 + SE \\
\$203{,}000 &= SE
\end{aligned}
$$

Remember, other terms for stockholders' equity are *owners' equity* and *net assets*. This is shown clearly in the previous calculation because stockholders' equity is the difference between assets and liabilities.

Now suppose that during the year ended August 31, 2021, total assets increased $10,000, and total liabilities decreased $3,000. What was stockholders' equity at the end of the year? There are two ways of solving the problem. First, focus on the changes in the elements of the balance sheet equation:

$$
\begin{aligned}
A &= L + SE \\
\text{Change: } + \$10{,}000 &= -\$3{,}000 + \text{?}
\end{aligned}
$$

It is clear that for the equation to stay in balance, stockholders' equity must have increased by $13,000. Because stockholders' equity was $203,000 at the beginning of the year, it must have been $216,000 at the end of the year.

The second approach to solving the problem is to calculate the amount of assets and liabilities at the end of the year and then solve for stockholders' equity at the end of the year, as follows:

$$
\begin{array}{lrcl}
 & A & = & L + SE \\
\text{Beginning:} & \$320{,}000 & = & \$117{,}000 + \$203{,}000 \\
\text{Change:} & +\$10{,}000 & = & -\$3{,}000 + \quad ? \\
\text{End:} & \$330{,}000 & = & \$114{,}000 + \quad ?
\end{array}
$$

The ending stockholders' equity or net assets is $330,000 − $114,000 = $216,000. Because ending stockholders' equity is $216,000, it increased by $13,000 during the year from August 31, 2020, to August 31, 2021.

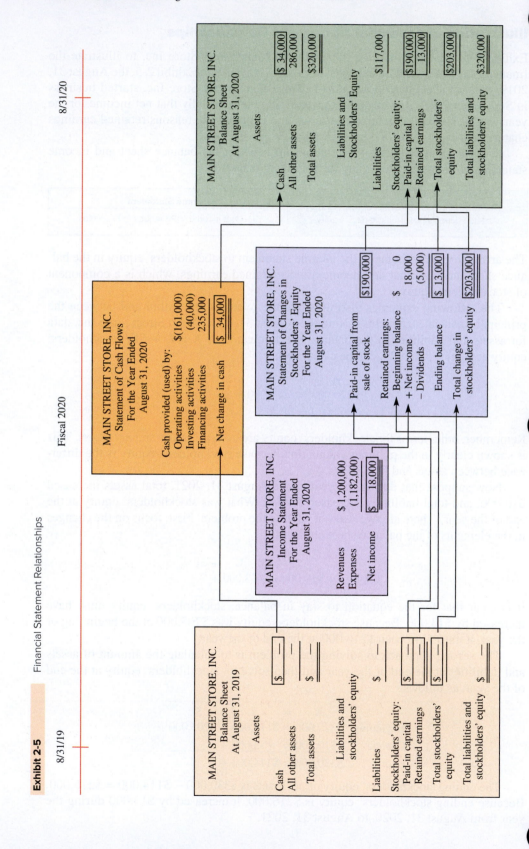

Exhibit 2-5   Financial Statement Relationships

8/31/19

Fiscal 2020

8/31/20

MAIN STREET STORE, INC.
Balance Sheet
At August 31, 2019

Assets

Cash $ —
All other assets   —
Total assets $ ——

Liabilities and
stockholders' equity

Liabilities $ —

Stockholders' equity:
Paid-in capital $ —
Retained earnings   —

Total stockholders'
equity $ ——

Total liabilities and
stockholders' equity $ ——

MAIN STREET STORE, INC.
Income Statement
For the Year Ended
August 31, 2020

Revenues $ 1,200,000
Expenses   (1,182,000)

Net income $ 18,000

MAIN STREET STORE, INC.
Statement of Cash Flows
For the Year Ended
August 31, 2020

Cash provided (used) by:
Operating activities $(161,000)
Investing activities   (40,000)
Financing activities   235,000

Net change in cash $ 34,000

MAIN STREET STORE, INC.
Statement of Changes in
Stockholders' Equity
For the Year Ended
August 31, 2020

Paid-in capital from
sale of stock $190,000

Retained earnings:
Beginning balance $ 0
+ Net income   18,000
– Dividends   (5,000)

Ending balance $ 13,000

Total change in
stockholders' equity $203,000

MAIN STREET STORE, INC.
Balance Sheet
At August 31, 2020

Assets

Cash $ 34,000
All other assets   286,000
Total assets $320,000

Liabilities and
Stockholders' Equity

Liabilities $117,000

Stockholders' equity:
Paid-in capital $190,000
Retained earnings   13,000

Total stockholders'
equity $203,000

Total liabilities and
stockholders' equity $320,000

Assume that during the year ended August 31, 2021, the stockholders invested an additional $8,000 in the firm and that dividends of $6,000 were declared. How much net income did the firm have for the year ended August 31, 2021? Recall that net income is one of the items that affects the retained earnings component of stockholders' equity. What else affects retained earnings? That's right—dividends. Because stockholders' equity increased from $203,000 to $216,000 during the year, and the items causing that change were net income, dividends, and the additional investment by the stockholders, the amount of net income can be calculated as follows:

Stockholders' equity, beginning of year	$203,000
Increase in paid-in capital from additional investment by stockholders	8,000
Net income	?
Dividends	−6,000
Stockholders' equity, end of year	$216,000

Solving for the unknown shows that net income was equal to $11,000.

An alternative solution to determine net income for the year involves focusing on just the *changes* in stockholders' equity during the year, as follows:

Increase in paid-in capital from additional investment by stockholders	$ 8,000
Net income	?
Dividends	−6,000
Change in stockholders' equity for the year	$13,000

Again, solving for the unknown, we find that net income was equal to $11,000. The important points to remember here are as follows:

- The balance sheet shows the amounts of assets, liabilities, and stockholders' equity at a point in time.
- The balance sheet equation must always be in balance.
- The income statement shows net income for a period of time.
- The retained earnings component of stockholders' equity changes over a period of time as a result of the firm's net income (or loss) and dividends for that period of time.

---

6. What does it mean to say that the balance sheet must be in balance after every transaction even though a lot of transactions affect the income statement?

What Does It Mean?

Answer on page 66

Accounting Concepts and Principles

To understand the kinds of decisions and informed judgments that can be made from the financial statements, it is appropriate to understand some of the broad concepts and principles of accounting that have become generally accepted for financial accounting and reporting purposes. The terms *concepts* and *principles* are used interchangeably here. Some of these ideas relate directly to the financial accounting concepts introduced in Chapter 1, and others relate to the broader notion of generally accepted accounting principles. Again, it is important to recognize that these concepts and principles are more like practices that have been generally agreed upon over time than hard-and-fast rules or basic laws such as those encountered in the physical sciences.

These concepts and principles can be related to the basic model of the flow of data from transactions to financial statements illustrated earlier and shown here:

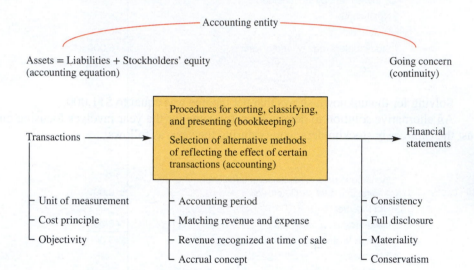

Concepts/Principles Related to the Entire Model

The basic accounting equation described earlier in this chapter is the mechanical key to the entire financial accounting process because the equation must be in balance after every transaction has been recorded in the accounting records. The method for recording transactions and maintaining this balance will be illustrated in Chapter 4.

Study
Suggestion

This chapter, titled "Financial Statements and Accounting Concepts/Principles," presents two sets of interrelated topics that are themselves related. As illustrated in Exhibit 2-5, individual financial statements are most meaningful when considered as part of an integrated set of financial statements presented by a firm. Likewise, the individual concepts and principles discussed in this section of the chapter are most meaningful when considered in relation to each other. The challenge that lies ahead (in the financial accounting part of this book) is for you to see logical connections between the end-product financial statements and the underlying concepts and principles upon which they are based. Our suggestion? Bookmark Exhibit 2-5 on page 42 and the concepts/principles model shown here. Learn the terminology presented in each of these illustrations, and refer back to these pages as you encounter difficulties in subsequent chapters. You will be surprised at how far this basic knowledge will carry you.

Parent and Subsidiary Corporations

Business in
Practice

It is not unusual for a corporation that wants to expand its operations to form a separate corporation to carry out its plans. In such a case, the original corporation owns all of the stock of the new corporation; it has become the "parent" of a **subsidiary.** One parent may have several subsidiaries, and the subsidiaries themselves may be parents of subsidiaries. It is not necessary for the parent to own 100 percent of the stock of another corporation for the parent–subsidiary relationship to exist. If one corporation owns more than half of the stock of another, it is presumed that the majority owner can exercise enough control to create a parent–subsidiary relationship. When a subsidiary is not wholly owned, the other stockholders of the subsidiary are referred to as *minority* (or *noncontrolling*) *stockholders,* and their ownership rights are referred to as the *noncontrolling interest.*

In most instances, the financial statements issued by the parent corporation will include the assets, liabilities, revenues, expenses, and gains and losses of the subsidiaries. Financial statements that reflect the financial position, results of operations, and cash flows of a parent and one or more subsidiaries are called *consolidated financial statements.*

The fact that one corporation is a subsidiary of another is frequently transparent to the general public. For example, Frito-Lay Inc., Quaker Oats Limited, and Tropicana Products Inc., are all subsidiaries of PepsiCo Inc., but that relationship is usually irrelevant to consumers of each company's products.

Accounting entity refers to the entity for which the financial statements are being prepared. The entity can be a proprietorship, partnership, corporation, or even a group of corporations (see Business in Practice—Parent and Subsidiary Corporations). The entity for which the accounting is being done is defined by the accountant; even though the entities may be related (such as an individual and the business she owns), the accounting is done for the defined entity.

The **going concern concept** refers to the presumption that the entity will continue to operate in the future—that it is not being liquidated. This continuity assumption is necessary because the amounts shown on the balance sheet for various assets do not reflect the liquidation value of those assets.

Concepts/Principles Related to Transactions

In the United States, the dollar is the *unit of measurement* for all transactions. No adjustment is made for changes in the purchasing power of the dollar. No attempt is made to reflect qualitative economic factors in the measurement of transactions.

The *cost principle* refers to the fact that transactions are recorded at their original (historical) cost to the entity as measured in dollars. For example, if a parcel of land were purchased by a firm for $8,600 even though an appraisal showed the land to be worth $10,000, the purchase transaction would be reflected in the accounting records and financial statements at its cost of $8,600. If the land is still owned and being used 15 years later, even though its market value has increased to $80,000, it continues to be reported in the balance sheet at its original cost of $8,600.

Objectivity refers to accountants' desire to have a given transaction recorded the same way in all situations. This objective is facilitated by using the dollar as the unit of measurement and by applying the cost principle. As previously stressed, there are transactions for which the exercise of professional judgment could result in alternative recording results. These alternatives will be illustrated in subsequent chapters.

Concepts/Principles Related to Bookkeeping Procedures and the Accounting Process

These concepts/principles relate to the *accounting period*—that is, the period of time selected for reporting results of operations and changes in financial position. Financial position will be reported at the end of this period (and the balance sheet at the beginning of the period will probably be included with the financial statements). For most entities, the accounting period will be one year in length.

Matching revenue and expense is necessary if the results of the firm's operations are to reflect accurately its economic activities during the period. The **matching concept** does not mean that revenues and expenses for a period are equal. Revenue is not earned without effort (businesses do not receive birthday gifts), and expenses are the measure of the economic efforts exerted to generate revenues. A fair presentation of the results of a firm's operations during a period of time requires that all expenses incurred in generating that period's revenues be deducted from the revenues earned. This results in an accurate measure of the net income or net loss for the period. This seems like common sense, but as we shall see, there are alternative methods of determining some of the expenses to be recognized in any given period. This concept of matching revenue and expense is of central importance to the accounting model and will be referred to again and again as accounting practices are discussed in the following chapters.

Revenue is recognized at the time of sale, which is when title to the product being sold passes from the seller to the buyer or when the services involved in the transaction have been performed. Passing of legal ownership (title) is the critical event, not the cash payment from buyer to seller.

LO 6
Discuss why investors must carefully consider cash flow information in conjunction with accrual accounting results.

Accrual accounting uses the *accrual concept* and results in recognizing revenue at the point of sale and recognizing expenses as they are incurred, even though the cash receipt or payment occurs at another time or in another accounting period. Thus, many activities of the firm will involve two transactions: one that recognizes the revenue or expense and the other that reflects the receipt or payment of cash. The use of accrual procedures accomplishes much of the matching of revenues and expenses because most transactions between business firms (and between many firms and individuals) involve purchase/sale at one point in time and cash payment/receipt at some other point.

The financial statement user relies on these concepts and principles related to the accounting period when making decisions and informed judgments about an entity's financial position and results of operations.

What Does It Mean?
Answers on page 67

7. What does matching of revenue and expense in the income statement mean?
8. What does the accrual concept mean?

Concepts/Principles Related to Financial Statements

Consistency in financial reporting is essential if meaningful trend comparisons are to be made using an entity's financial statements for several years. It is inappropriate to change from one generally accepted alternative of accounting for a particular type of transaction to another generally accepted method, unless both the fact that the change has been made and the effect of the change on the financial statements are explicitly described in the financial statements or the accompanying notes to the financial statements.

Full disclosure means that the financial statements and notes should include all necessary information to prevent a reasonably astute user of the financial statements from being misled. This is a tall order—one that the Securities and Exchange Commission (SEC) has helped to define over the years. This requirement for full disclosure is one reason that the notes to the financial statements are usually considered an integral part of the financial statements.

Materiality means that absolute exactness, even if that idea could be defined, is not necessary in the amounts shown in the financial statements. Because of the numerous estimates involved in accounting, amounts reported in financial statements may be approximate, but they will not be "wrong" enough to be misleading. The financial statements of publicly owned corporations usually show amounts rounded to the nearest thousand, hundred thousand, or even million dollars. This rounding does not impair the informational content of the financial statements and probably makes them easier to read. A management concept related to materiality is the cost–benefit relationship. Just as a manager would not spend $500 to get $300 worth of information, the incremental benefit of increased accuracy in accounting estimates is frequently not worth the cost of achieving the increased accuracy.

Conservatism in accounting relates to making judgments and estimates that result in lower profits and asset valuation estimates rather than higher profits and asset valuation estimates. Accountants try to avoid wishful thinking or pie-in-the-sky estimates that could result in overstating profits for a current period. This is not to say that accountants always look at issues from a gloom-and-doom viewpoint; rather, they seek to be realistic but are conservative when in doubt.

Limitations of Financial Statements

Financial statements report quantitative economic information; they do not reflect qualitative economic variables. Thus, the value to the firm of a management team or of the morale of the workforce is not included as a balance sheet asset because it cannot be objectively measured. Such qualitative attributes of the firm are frequently relevant to the decisions and informed judgments that the financial statement user is making, but they are not communicated in the financial statements. It's unfortunate that the accounting process does not capture these kinds of data because often a company's human resources and information resources are its most valuable assets. Many highly valued Internet and high-tech companies have little, if any, fixed assets or inventory—sometimes the "product" they intend to offer comes in the form of a service that has not yet made it through the research, design, and testing phases. In fact, a common saying about such companies is that their most valuable assets "walk out the door every night." The accounting profession is not yet comfortable with the idea of trying to measure these kinds of intangible assets, even though fairly reliable appraisal techniques are available, such as those endorsed in the Uniform Standards of Professional Appraisal Practice (USPAP).

As already emphasized, the cost principle requires assets to be recorded at their original cost. The balance sheet does not generally show the current market value or the replacement cost of the assets. Some assets are reported at the lower of their cost or market value—and, in some cases, market value may be reported parenthetically—but

LO 7

Identify and explain several limitations of financial statements.

asset values are not generally increased to reflect current value. For example, the trademark of a firm has virtually no cost; its value has developed over the years as the firm has successfully met customers' needs. Thus, trademarks usually are excluded from the balance sheet listing of assets even though they clearly have economic value to the firm.

Estimates are used in many areas of accounting; when the estimate is made, about the only fact known is that the estimate is probably not equal to the "true" amount. It is hoped that the estimate is near the true amount (the concept of materiality); it usually is. For example, recognizing depreciation expense involves estimating both the useful life to the entity of the asset being depreciated and the probable salvage value of the asset to the entity when it is disposed of. The original cost minus the salvage value is the amount to be depreciated or recognized as expense over the asset's life. Estimates also must be made to determine pension expense, warranty costs, and numerous other expense and revenue items to be reflected in the current year's income statement because they relate to the economic activity of the current year. These estimates also affect balance sheet accounts. So even though the balance sheet balances to the penny, do not be misled by this aura of exactness. Accountants do their best to make their estimates as accurate as possible, but estimates are still estimates.

The principle of consistency suggests that an entity should not change from one generally accepted method of accounting for a particular item to another generally accepted method of accounting for the same item, but it is possible that two firms operating in the same industry may follow different methods. This means that *comparability* between firms may not be appropriate, or if comparisons are made, the effects of any differences between the accounting methods followed by the firms must be understood.

Related to the use of the original cost principle is the fact that financial statements are not adjusted to show the impact of inflation. Land acquired by a firm 50 years ago is still reported at its original cost, even though it may have a significantly higher current value because of inflation. Likewise, depreciation expense and the cost of goods sold—both significant expense elements of the income statement of many firms—reflect original cost, not replacement cost. This weakness is not significant when the rate of inflation is low, but the usefulness of financial statements is seriously impaired when the inflation rate rises to double digits.

Financial statements do not reflect **opportunity cost,** which is an economic concept relating to income forgone because an opportunity to earn income was not pursued. For example, if an individual or organization maintains a non-interest-bearing checking account balance that is $3,000 more than that required to avoid any service charges, the opportunity cost associated with that $3,000 is the interest that could otherwise be earned on the money if it had been invested. Financial accounting does not give formal recognition to opportunity cost; however, financial managers should be aware of the concept as they plan the utilization of the firm's resources.

What Does It Mean?

Answer on page 67

9. What does it mean when some investors state that a corporation's published financial statements don't tell the whole story about a firm's financial position and results of operations?

The Corporation's Annual Report

The annual report is the document distributed (or made available electronically) to shareholders that contains the reporting firm's financial statements for the fiscal year, together with the report of the external auditor's examination of the financial statements. The annual report document can be as simple as a transmittal letter from the president or chair of the board of directors along with the financial statements, or as fancy as a glossy, 150-page booklet that showcases the firm's products, services, and personnel, as well as its financial results.

In addition to the financial statements described here and the notes to the financial statements described more fully in Chapter 10, some other financial data are usually included in the annual report. Highlights for the year, including net revenues, diluted earnings per share, and return on average stockholders' equity, often appear inside the front cover or elsewhere toward the front of the report. Most firms also include a historical summary of certain financial data for at least the past five years. This summary usually is located near the back of the annual report.

The vast majority of U.S. publicly traded companies now include within their annual reports the entire 10-K report that is filed with the SEC each year. As a result, the appendix material for Campbell Soup Company's 2017 annual report excludes certain disclosures that are not heavily referenced in this text, such as the Management's Discussion and Analysis section. To obtain a complete copy of Campbell's current annual report, please visit campbellsoup.com. Click "Connect" in the upper-right side the home page and then click "Investors," "Financial Information," and "Annual Reports" to reach the relevant Adobe Acrobat files that can be saved and/or printed. Many specific aspects of Campbell's annual report will be referred to in subsequent chapters.

LO 8
Describe what a corporation's annual report is and why it is issued.

Campbell's

Demonstration Problem

The Demonstration Problem walkthrough for this chapter is available in *Connect.*

Summary

Financial statements communicate economic information that helps individuals make decisions and informed judgments.

The bookkeeping and accounting processes result in an entity's numerous transactions with other entities being reflected in the financial statements. The financial statements presented by an entity are the balance sheet, income statement, statement of changes in stockholders' equity, and statement of cash flows. **(LO 1, 2)**

The balance sheet is a listing of the entity's assets, liabilities, and stockholders' equity at a point in time. Assets are probable future economic benefits (things or claims against others) controlled by the entity. Liabilities are amounts owed by the entity. An entity's stockholders' equity is the difference between its assets and liabilities. This relationship is known as the *accounting equation.* Current assets are cash and those assets likely to be converted to cash or used to benefit the entity within one year of the balance sheet date, such as accounts receivable and inventories. Current liabilities are expected to be paid or otherwise satisfied within one year of the balance sheet date. The balance sheet as of the end of a fiscal period is also the balance sheet as of the beginning of the next fiscal period. **(LO 2, 3)**

The income statement reports the results of an entity's operating activities for a period of time. Revenues are reported first, and expenses are subtracted to arrive at net income or net loss for the period. **(LO 3)**

The statement of changes in stockholders' equity describes changes in paid-in capital and retained earnings during the period. Retained earnings are increased by the amount of net income and decreased by dividends to stockholders (and by any net loss for the period). It is through retained earnings that the income statement is linked to the balance sheet. **(LO 3, 4)**

The statement of cash flows summarizes the impact on cash of the entity's operating, investing, and financing activities during the period. The bottom line of this financial statement is the change in cash from the amount shown in the balance sheet at the beginning of the period (e.g., fiscal year) to that shown in the balance sheet at the end of the period. **(LO 3, 4)**

Financial statements usually are presented on a comparative basis so users can easily spot significant changes in an entity's financial position (balance sheet) and results of operations (income statement). **(LO 4)**

The financial statements are interrelated. Net income for the period (from the income statement) is added to retained earnings, a part of stockholders' equity (in the balance sheet). The statement of changes in stockholders' equity explains the difference between the amounts of stockholders' equity at the beginning and the end of the fiscal period. The statement of cash flows explains the change in the amount of cash from the beginning to the end of the fiscal period. **(LO 4)**

Accounting concepts and principles reflect generally accepted practices that have evolved over time. They can be related to a schematic model of the flow of data from transactions to the financial statements. Pertaining to the entire model are the accounting entity concept, the accounting equation, and the going concern concept. **(LO 5)**

Transactions are recorded in currency units (e.g., the U.S. dollar) without regard to purchasing power changes. Thus, transactions are recorded at an objectively determinable original cost amount. **(LO 5)**

The concepts and principles for the accounting period involve recognizing revenue when a sale of a product or service is made and then relating to that revenue all the expenses incurred in generating the revenue of the period. This matching of revenues and expenses is a crucial and fundamental concept to understand if accounting itself is to be understood. The accrual concept is used to implement the matching concept by recognizing revenues when earned and expenses when incurred, regardless of whether cash is received or paid in the same fiscal period. **(LO 5, 6)**

The concepts of consistency, full disclosure, materiality, and conservatism relate primarily to financial statement presentation. **(LO 5)**

There are limitations to the information presented in financial statements. These limitations are related to the concepts and principles that have become generally accepted. Thus, subjective qualitative factors, current values, the impact of inflation, and opportunity cost are not usually reflected in financial statements. In addition, many financial statement amounts involve the use of estimates. Permissible alternative accounting practices may mean that interfirm comparisons are not appropriate. **(LO 7)**

Corporations and other organizations include financial statements in an annual report made available to stockholders, employees, potential investors, and others interested in the entity. Refer to the financial statements of the Campbell Soup Company annual report in the appendix, as well as to the financial statements of other annual reports, to see how the material discussed in this chapter applies to real companies. **(LO 8)**

Campbell's

Key Terms and Concepts

account (p. 29)   A record in which transactions affecting individual assets, liabilities, stockholders' equity, revenues, and expenses are recorded.

accounting equation (p. 32)   Assets = Liabilities + Stockholders' equity (A = L + SE). The fundamental relationship represented by the balance sheet and the foundation of the bookkeeping process.

accounts payable (p. 33)   A liability representing an amount payable to another entity, usually because of the purchase of merchandise or services on credit.

accounts receivable (p. 33)   An asset representing a claim against another entity, usually arising from selling goods or services on credit.

accrual accounting (p. 46)   Accounting that recognizes revenues and expenses as they occur, even though the cash receipt from the revenue or the cash disbursement related to the expense may occur before or after the event that causes revenue or expense recognition.

accrued liabilities (p. 33)   Amounts that are owed by an entity on the balance sheet date.

accumulated depreciation (p. 33)   The sum of the depreciation expense that has been recognized over time. Accumulated depreciation is a contra asset—an amount that is subtracted from the cost of the related asset on the balance sheet.

additional paid-in capital (p. 37)   The excess of the amount received from the sale of stock over the par value of the shares sold.

assets (p. 32)   Probable future economic benefits obtained or controlled by an entity as a result of past transactions or events.

balance sheet (p. 31)   The financial statement that is a listing of the entity's assets, liabilities, and stockholders' equity at a point in time. Sometimes this statement is called the *statement of financial position*.

balance sheet equation (p. 32)   Another term for *accounting equation*.

cash (p. 33)   An asset on the balance sheet that represents the amount of cash on hand and balances in bank accounts maintained by the entity.

common stock (p. 37)   The class of stock that represents residual ownership of the corporation.

corporation (p. 30)   A form of organization in which ownership is evidenced by shares of stock owned by stockholders; its features, such as limited liability of the stockholders, make this the principal form of organization for most business activity.

cost of goods sold (p. 35)   Cost of merchandise sold during the period; an expense deducted from net sales to arrive at gross profit. Frequently used synonyms are *cost of sales* and *cost of products sold*.

current assets (p. 34)   Cash and those assets that are likely to be converted to cash or used to benefit the entity within one year of the balance sheet date.

current liabilities (p. 34)   Those liabilities due to be paid within one year of the balance sheet date.

depreciation (p. 33)   The accounting process of recognizing the cost of an asset that is used up over its useful life to the entity.

depreciation expense (p. 38)   The expense recognized in a fiscal period for the depreciation of an asset.

dividend (p. 37)   A distribution of earnings to the stockholders of a corporation.

earnings per share of common stock outstanding (p. 35)   Net income available to the common stockholders divided by the average number of shares of common stock outstanding during the period. Usually referred to simply as *EPS*.

equity (p. 32)   The ownership right associated with an asset. See *stockholders' equity*.

expenses (p. 34)   Outflows or other using up of assets or incurring a liability during a period from delivering or producing goods, rendering services, or carrying out other activities that constitute the entity's major operations.

fiscal year (p. 31)   The annual period used for reporting to owners.

gains (p. 34)   Increases in net assets from incidental transactions that are not revenues or investments by owners.

going concern concept (p. 45)   A presumption that the entity will continue in existence for the indefinite future.

gross profit (p. 35)   Net sales less cost of goods sold. Sometimes called *gross margin.*

income from operations (p. 35)   The difference between gross profit and operating expenses. Also referred to as *operating income.*

income statement (p. 34)   The financial statement that summarizes the entity's revenues, expenses, gains, and losses for a period of time and thereby reports the entity's results of operations for that period of time.

liabilities (p. 32)   Probable future sacrifices of economic benefits arising from present obligations of a particular entity to transfer assets or provide services to other entities in the future as a result of past transactions or events.

losses (p. 34)   Decreases in net assets from incidental transactions that are not expenses or distributions to owners.

matching concept (p. 46)   The concept that expenses incurred in generating revenues should be deducted from revenues earned during the period for which results are being reported.

merchandise inventory (p. 33)   Items held by an entity for sale to customers in the normal course of business.

net assets (p. 33)   The difference between assets and liabilities; also referred to as *stockholders' equity* or *owners' equity.*

net income (p. 34)   The excess of revenues and gains over expenses and losses for a fiscal period.

net sales (p. 34)   Gross sales, less sales discounts and sales returns and allowances.

net worth (p. 33)   Another term for *net assets* or *stockholders' equity* or *owners' equity,* but not as appropriate because the term *worth* may be misleading.

opportunity cost (p. 48)   An economic concept relating to income forgone because an opportunity to earn income was not pursued.

owners' equity (p. 32)   Another term for *stockholders' equity.* The owners' claim in the assets of the entity. Sometimes called *net assets;* the difference between assets and liabilities.

paid-in capital (p. 37)   The amount invested in the entity by the stockholders.

par value (p. 37)   An arbitrary value assigned to a share of stock when the corporation is organized. Sometimes used to refer to the stated value or face amount of a security.

partnership (p. 30)   A form of organization indicating ownership by two or more individuals or corporations without the limited liability and other features of a corporation.

profit (p. 34)   The excess of revenues and gains over expenses and losses for a fiscal period; another term for *net income.*

profit and loss statement (p. 34)   Another term for *income statement.*

proprietorship (p. 30)   A form of organization indicating individual ownership without the limited liability and other features of a corporation.

retained earnings (p. 37) Cumulative net income that has not been distributed to the stockholders of a corporation as dividends.

revenues (p. 34) Inflows of cash or increases in other assets, or the settlement of liabilities during a period, from delivering or producing goods, rendering services, or performing other activities that constitute the entity's major operations.

statement of cash flows (p. 38) The financial statement that explains why cash changed during a fiscal period. Cash flows from operating, investing, and financing activities are shown.

statement of changes in capital stock (p. 36) The financial statement that summarizes changes during a fiscal period in capital stock and additional paid-in capital. This information may be included in the statement of changes in stockholders' equity.

statement of changes in retained earnings (p. 36) The financial statement that summarizes the changes during a fiscal period in retained earnings. This information may be included in the statement of changes in stockholders' equity.

statement of changes in stockholders' equity (p. 36) The financial statement that summarizes the changes during a fiscal period in capital stock, additional paid-in capital, retained earnings, and other elements of stockholders' equity.

statement of earnings (p. 34) Another term for *income statement;* it shows the revenues, expenses, gains, and losses for a period of time and thereby the entity's results of operations for that period of time.

statement of equity (p. 36) Another term for *statement of changes in stockholders' equity;* a description used for this financial statement primarily by large, publicly-traded companies, which are required to report changes in the equity of both the controlling (parent company) interests and noncontrolling (minority) interests.

statement of financial position (p. 31) Another term for *balance sheet;* a listing of the entity's assets, liabilities, and stockholders' equity at a point in time.

statement of operations (p. 34) Another term for *income statement.*

statement of stockholders' equity (p. 36) Another term for *statement of changes in stockholders' equity.*

stock (p. 30) The evidence of ownership of a corporation.

stockholders (p. 30) The owners of a corporation's stock; sometimes called *shareholders.*

stockholders' equity (p. 32) The stockholders' claim in the assets of the entity. Sometimes called *owners' equity* or *net assets;* the difference between assets and liabilities.

subsidiary (p. 45) A corporation whose stock is more than 50 percent owned by another corporation.

transactions (p. 29) Economic interchanges between entities that are accounted for and reflected in financial statements.

Mini-Exercises

All applicable Mini-Exercises are available in *Connect*.

Understanding financial statement relationships Total assets were $96,000 and total liabilities were $54,000 at the beginning of the year. Net income for the year was $16,000, and dividends of $4,000 were declared and paid during the year.

Mini-Exercise 2.1
LO 2, 3

Required:
Calculate total stockholders' equity at the end of the year.

Understanding financial statement relationships Stockholders' equity totaled $246,000 at the beginning of the year. During the year, net income was $36,000, dividends of $9,000 were declared and paid, and $30,000 of common stock was issued at par value.

Mini-Exercise 2.2
LO 2, 3

Required:
Calculate total stockholders' equity at the end of the year.

**Mini-Exercise
2.3
LO 2, 3**

Understanding income statement relationships During the year, net sales were $250,000; gross profit was $100,000; net income was $40,000; income tax expense was $10,000; and selling, general, and administrative expenses were $44,000.

Required:
Calculate cost of goods sold, income from operations, income before taxes, and interest expense. (*Hint:* Exhibit 2-2 may be used as a solution model.)

**Mini-Exercise
2.4
LO 2, 3**

Understanding income statement relationships During the year, cost of goods sold was $120,000; income from operations was $114,000; income tax expense was $24,000; interest expense was $18,000; and selling, general, and administrative expenses were $66,000.

Required:
Calculate net sales, gross profit, income before taxes, and net income. (*Hint:* Exhibit 2-2 may be used as a solution model.)

**Mini-Exercise
2.5
LO 2, 4**

Identify accounts by category Listed here are a number of accounts: Land, Common stock, Merchandise inventory, Equipment, Cost of goods sold, Accounts receivable, Interest expense, Supplies, Long-term debt, Cash, Sales, Accounts payable, Buildings, Retained earnings.

Required:
Which of the accounts listed above are not assets? How would you categorize each of these nonasset accounts?

**Mini-Exercise
2.6
LO 2, 4**

Identify accounts by statement Listed here are a number of accounts: Income tax expense, Accumulated depreciation, Notes payable, Land, Sales, Common stock, Cost of goods sold, Equipment, Accounts receivable, Rent expense, Supplies, Buildings, Service revenue, Cash.

Required:
Which of the accounts listed above would appear on a company's income statement?

---

connect **Exercises**

All applicable Exercises are available in *Connect*.

**Exercise 2.7
LO 2, 4**

Identify accounts by category and financial statement(s) Listed here are a number of financial statement captions. Indicate in the spaces to the right of each caption the category of each item and the financial statement(s) on which the item can usually be found. Use the following abbreviations:

Category		Financial Statement	
Asset	A	Balance sheet	BS
Liability	L	Income statement	IS
Stockholders' equity	SE		
Revenue	R		
Expense	E		
Gain	G		
Loss	LS		
Cash		_____	_____
Accounts payable		_____	_____
Common stock		_____	_____
Depreciation expense		_____	_____
Net sales		_____	_____
Income tax expense		_____	_____
Short-term investments		_____	_____
Gain on sale of land		_____	_____
Retained earnings		_____	_____
Dividends payable		_____	_____
Accounts receivable		_____	_____
Short-term debt		_____	_____

Identify accounts by category and financial statement(s) Listed here are a number of financial statement captions. Indicate in the spaces to the right of each caption the category of each item and the financial statement(s) on which the item can usually be found. Use the following abbreviations:

Exercise 2.8
LO 2, 4

Category		Financial Statement	
Asset	A	Balance sheet	BS
Liability	L	Income statement	IS
Stockholders' equity	SE		
Revenue	R		
Expense	E		
Gain	G		
Loss	LS		
Accumulated depreciation		_____	_____
Long-term debt		_____	_____
Equipment		_____	_____
Loss on sale of short-term investments		_____	_____
Net income		_____	_____
Merchandise inventory		_____	_____
Other accrued liabilities		_____	_____
Dividends paid		_____	_____
Cost of goods sold		_____	_____
Additional paid-in capital		_____	_____
Interest income		_____	_____
Selling expenses		_____	_____

Exercise 2.9

LO 2, 3

Understanding financial statement relationships The information presented here represents selected data from the December 31, 2019, balance sheets and income statements for the year then ended for three firms:

	Firm A	Firm B	Firm C
Total assets, 12/31/19	$210,000	$270,000	$162,000
Total liabilities, 12/31/19	108,000	72,000	?
Paid-in capital, 12/31/19	37,000	?	20,000
Retained earnings, 12/31/19	?	155,000	?
Net income for 2019	?	41,000	56,000
Dividends declared and paid during 2019	25,000	9,000	32,000
Retained earnings, 1/1/19	39,000	?	21,000

Required:
Calculate the missing amounts for each firm.

Exercise 2.10

LO 2, 3

Understanding financial statement relationships The information presented here represents selected data from the December 31, 2019, balance sheets and income statements for the year then ended for three firms:

	Firm A	Firm B	Firm C
Total assets, 12/31/19	?	$870,000	$310,000
Total liabilities, 12/31/19	$160,000	?	150,000
Paid-in capital, 12/31/19	110,000	118,000	90,000
Retained earnings, 12/31/19	?	372,000	?
Net income for 2019	136,000	220,000	50,000
Dividends declared and paid during 2019	24,000	?	32,000
Retained earnings, 1/1/19	100,000	248,000	?

Required:
Calculate the missing amounts for each firm.

Exercise 2.11

LO 2, 3

Calculate retained earnings From the following data, calculate the retained earnings balance as of December 31, 2019:

Retained earnings, December 31, 2018	$623,600
Cost of equipment purchased during 2019	64,800
Net loss for the year ended December 31, 2019	9,400
Dividends declared and paid in 2019	37,000
Decrease in cash balance from January 1, 2019 to December 31, 2019	27,200
Decrease in long-term debt in 2019	29,600

Exercise 2.12
LO 2, 3

Calculate retained earnings From the following data, calculate the retained earnings balance as of December 31, 2018:

Retained earnings, December 31, 2019	$630,900
Decrease in total liabilities during 2019	137,400
Gain on the sale of buildings during 2019	48,300
Dividends declared and paid in 2019	13,500
Proceeds from sale of common stock in 2019	148,200
Net income for the year ended December 31, 2019	67,800

Exercise 2.13
LO 2, 3

Calculate dividends using the accounting equation At the beginning of its current fiscal year, Willie Corp.'s balance sheet showed assets of $37,200 and liabilities of $21,000. During the year, liabilities decreased by $3,600. Net income for the year was $9,000, and net assets at the end of the year were $18,000. There were no changes in paid-in capital during the year.

Required:
Calculate the dividends, if any, declared during the year.
(*Hint:* Set up an accounting equation for the beginning of the year, changes during the year, and at the end of the year. Enter known data and solve for the unknowns.)
Here is a possible worksheet format:

$$
\begin{array}{ccccccc}
 & & & & & \text{SE} & \\
 & A & = & L & + & \overline{\text{PIC} \; + \; \text{RE}} & \\
\text{Beginning:} & \_\_ & = & \_\_ & + & \_\_ & + & \_\_ \\
\text{Changes:} & \_\_ & = & \_\_ & + & \_\_ & + & \_\_ \\
\text{Ending:} & \_\_ & = & \_\_ & + & \_\_ & + & \_\_ \\
\end{array}
$$

Exercise 2.14
LO 2, 3

Calculate net income (or loss) using the accounting equation At the beginning of the current fiscal year, the balance sheet for Davis Co. showed liabilities of $160,000. During the year, liabilities decreased by $9,000, assets increased by $33,000, and paid-in capital increased from $15,000 to $96,000. Dividends declared and paid during the year were $12,000. At the end of the year, stockholders' equity totaled $215,000.

Required:
Calculate net income (or loss) for the year.
(*Hint:* Set up an accounting equation for the beginning of the year, changes during the year, and at the end of the year. Enter known data and solve for the unknowns. Remember, net income [or loss] may not be the only item affecting retained earnings.)

Problems

All applicable Problems are available in *Connect*.

Problem 2.15

LO 2, 3, 6

Calculate cash available upon liquidation of business Circle-Square Ltd. is in the process of liquidating and going out of business. The firm's balance sheet shows $45,600 in cash, accounts receivable of $228,400, inventory totaling $122,800, plant and equipment of $530,000, and total liabilities of $611,200. It is estimated that the inventory can be disposed of in a liquidation sale for 80 percent of its cost, all but 5 percent of the accounts receivable can be collected, and plant and equipment can be sold for $380,000.

Required:

Calculate the amount of cash that would be available to the owners if the accounts receivable are collected, the other assets are sold as described, and the liabilities are paid off in full.

Problem 2.16

LO 2, 3, 6

Calculate cash available upon liquidation of business Kimber Co. is in the process of liquidating and going out of business. The firm's accountant has provided the following balance sheet and additional information:

Assets		
Cash	$ 30,000	
Accounts receivable	90,000	
Merchandise inventory	150,000	
Total current assets		$270,000
Land	$ 50,000	
Buildings and equipment	400,000	
Less: Accumulated depreciation	(120,000)	
Total land, buildings, and equipment		330,000
Total assets		$600,000
Liabilities and Stockholders' Equity		
Accounts payable	$ 80,000	
Notes payable	110,000	
Total current liabilities		$190,000
Long-term debt		130,000
Total liabilities		$320,000
Stockholders' Equity:		
Common stock, no par	$ 100,000	
Retained earnings	180,000	
Total stockholders' equity		280,000
Total liabilities and stockholders' equity		$600,000

It is estimated that all but 20 percent of the accounts receivable can be collected, and that the merchandise inventory can be disposed of in a liquidation sale for 70 percent of its cost. Buildings and equipment can be sold at $60,000 above book value (the difference between original cost and accumulated depreciation shown on the balance sheet), and the land can be sold at its current appraisal value of $85,000. In addition to the liabilities included in the balance sheet, $5,000 is owed to employees for their work since the last pay period, and interest of $10,000 has accrued on notes payable and long-term debt.

Required:

a. Calculate the amount of cash that will be available to the stockholders if the accounts receivable are collected, the other assets are sold as described, and all liabilities and other claims are paid in full.

b. Briefly explain why the amount of cash available to stockholders (computed in part **a**) is different from the amount of total stockholders' equity shown in the balance sheet.

Understanding and analyzing financial statement relationships—sales/ service organization Pope's Garage had the following accounts and amounts in its financial statements on December 31, 2019. Assume that all balance sheet items reflect account balances at December 31, 2019, and that all income statement items reflect activities that occurred during the year then ended.

Problem 2.17

LO 2, 3, 4

Accounts receivable	$ 99,000
Depreciation expense	36,000
Land	81,000
Cost of goods sold	270,000
Retained earnings	177,000
Cash	27,000
Equipment	213,000
Supplies	18,000
Accounts payable	69,000
Service revenue	60,000
Interest expense	12,000
Common stock	30,000
Income tax expense	36,000
Accumulated depreciation	135,000
Long-term debt	120,000
Supplies expense	42,000
Merchandise inventory	93,000
Net sales	420,000

Required:

a. Calculate the total current assets at December 31, 2019.

b. Calculate the total liabilities and stockholders' equity at December 31, 2019.

c. Calculate the earnings from operations (operating income) for the year ended December 31, 2019.

d. Calculate the net income (or loss) for the year ended December 31, 2019.

e. What was the average income tax rate for Pope's Garage for 2019?

f. If $48,000 of dividends had been declared and paid during the year, what was the January 1, 2019, balance of retained earnings?

Understanding and analyzing financial statement relationships—merchandising organization Gary's TV had the following accounts and amounts in its financial statements on December 31, 2019. Assume that all balance sheet items reflect account balances at December 31, 2019, and that all income statement items reflect activities that occurred during the year then ended.

Problem 2.18

LO 2, 3, 4

Interest expense	$ 4,500
Paid-in capital	10,000
Accumulated depreciation	3,000
Notes payable (long-term)	35,000
Rent expense	9,000
Merchandise inventory	106,000
Accounts receivable	28,000
Depreciation expense	1,500
Land	19,000
Retained earnings	122,000
Cash	20,000
Cost of goods sold	220,000
Equipment	10,000
Income tax expense	30,000
Accounts payable	13,000
Net sales	310,000

Required:

a. Calculate the difference between current assets and current liabilities for Gary's TV at December 31, 2019.

b. Calculate the total assets at December 31, 2019.

c. Calculate the earnings from operations (operating income) for the year ended December 31, 2019.

d. Calculate the net income (or loss) for the year ended December 31, 2019.

e. What was the average income tax rate for Gary's TV for 2019?

f. If $32,000 of dividends had been declared and paid during the year, what was the January 1, 2019, balance of retained earnings?

Problem 2.19
LO 2, 3, 4

Prepare an income statement, balance sheet, and statement of changes in stockholders' equity; analyze results The information on the following page was obtained from the records of Breanna Inc.:

Accounts receivable	$ 40,000
Accumulated depreciation	208,000
Cost of goods sold	512,000
Income tax expense	32,000
Cash	260,000
Net sales	800,000
Equipment	480,000
Selling, general, and administrative expenses	136,000
Common stock (36,000 shares)	360,000
Accounts payable	60,000
Retained earnings, 1/1/19	92,000
Interest expense	24,000
Merchandise inventory	148,000
Long-term debt	160,000
Dividends declared and paid during 2019	48,000

Except as otherwise indicated, assume that all balance sheet items reflect account balances at December 31, 2019, and that all income statement items reflect activities that occurred during the year ended December 31, 2019. There were no changes in paid-in capital during the year.

Required:

a. Prepare an income statement and statement of changes in stockholders' equity for the year ended December 31, 2019, and a balance sheet at December 31, 2019, for Breanna Inc.

     Based on the financial statements that you have prepared for part **a,** answer the questions in parts **b–e.** Provide brief explanations for each of your answers and state any assumptions you believe are necessary to ensure that your answers are correct.

b. What is the company's average income tax rate?

c. What interest rate is charged on long-term debt?

d. What is the par value per share of common stock?

e. What is the company's dividend policy (i.e., what proportion of the company's earnings are used for dividends)?

Prepare an income statement, balance sheet, and statement of changes in stockholders' equity; analyze results The following information was obtained from the records of Shae Inc.:

Problem 2.20
LO 2, 3, 4

Merchandise inventory	$ 88,000
Notes payable (long-term)	100,000
Net sales	300,000
Buildings and equipment	168,000
Selling, general, and administrative expenses	24,000
Accounts receivable	40,000
Common stock (14,000 shares)	70,000
Income tax expense	28,000
Cash	64,000
Retained earnings, 1/1/19	43,000
Accrued liabilities	6,000
Cost of goods sold	180,000
Accumulated depreciation	72,000
Interest expense	16,000
Accounts payable	30,000
Dividends declared and paid during 2019	13,000

Except as otherwise indicated, assume that all balance sheet items reflect account balances at December 31, 2019, and that all income statement items reflect activities that occurred during the year ended December 31, 2019. There were no changes in paid-in capital during the year.

Required:

a. Prepare an income statement and statement of changes in stockholders' equity for the year ended December 31, 2019, and a balance sheet at December 31, 2019, for Shae Inc.

     Based on the financial statements that you have prepared for part **a,** answer the questions in parts **b–e.** Provide brief explanations for each of your answers and state any assumptions you believe are necessary to ensure that your answers are correct.

b. What is the company's average income tax rate?

c. What interest rate is charged on long-term debt?

d. What is the par value per share of common stock?

e. What is the company's dividend policy (i.e., what proportion of the company's earnings is used for dividends)?

Problem 2.21

LO 2, 3

Transaction analysis—nonquantitative Indicate the effect of each of the following transactions on total assets, total liabilities, and total stockholders' equity. Use + for increase, − for decrease, and (NE) for no effect. The first transaction is provided as an illustration.

		Assets	Liabilities	Stockholders' Equity
a.	Borrowed cash on a bank loan	+	+	NE
b.	Paid an account payable			
c.	Sold common stock			
d.	Purchased merchandise inventory on account			
e.	Declared and paid dividends			
f.	Collected an account receivable			
g.	Sold merchandise inventory on account at a profit			
h.	Paid operating expenses in cash			
i.	Repaid principal and interest on a bank loan			

Problem 2.22

LO 2, 3, 6

Transaction analysis—quantitative; analyze results Rudy Gandolfi owns and operates Rudy's Furniture Emporium Inc. The balance sheet totals for assets, liabilities, and stockholders' equity at August 1, 2019, are as indicated. Described here are several transactions entered into by the company throughout the month of August.

Required:

a. Indicate the amount and effect (+ or −) of each transaction on total assets, total liabilities, and total stockholders' equity, and then compute the new totals for each category. The first transaction is provided as an illustration.

	Assets	=	Liabilities	+	Stockholder's Equity
August 1, 2019, totals	$700,000		$500,000		$200,000
August 3, borrowed $50,000 in cash from the bank	+ 50,000		+ 50,000		_____
New totals	$750,000		$550,000		$200,000
August 7, bought merchandise inventory valued at $75,000 on account	_____		_____		_____
New totals					
August 10, paid $25,000 cash for operating expenses. .	_____		_____		_____
New totals					
August 14, received $120,000 in cash from sales of merchandise that had cost $72,000	_____		_____		_____
New totals					
August 17, paid $60,000 owed on accounts payable . . .	_____		_____		_____
New totals					
August 21, collected $44,000 of accounts receivable . . .	_____		_____		_____
New totals					
August 24, repaid $30,000 to the bank plus $1,000 interest	_____		_____		_____
New totals					
August 29, paid Rudy Gandolfi a cash dividend of $15,000	_____		_____		_____
New totals					

b. What was the amount of net income (or loss) during August? How much were total revenues and total expenses during August?

c. What were the net changes during the month of August in total assets, total liabilities, and total stockholders' equity?

d. Explain to Rudy Gandolfi which transactions caused the net change in his stockholders' equity during August.

e. Explain why dividend payments are not an expense, but interest is an expense.

f. Explain why the money borrowed from the bank increased assets but did not increase net income.

g. Explain why paying off accounts payable and collecting accounts receivable do not affect net income.

Complete the balance sheet A partially completed balance sheet for Blue Co. Inc. as of October 31, 2019, is presented. Where amounts are shown for various items, the amounts are correct.

Problem 2.23
LO 2, 3, 5

Assets		Liabilities and Stockholders' Equity	
Cash	$3,500	Note payable	$ _____
Accounts receivable	_____	Accounts payable	16,000
Land	_____		
Automobile	$ _____	Total liabilities	$ _____
Less: Accumulated		Stockholders' equity:	
depreciation	_____	Common stock	$ 40,000
		Retained earnings	_____
		Total stockholders' equity	$ _____
Total assets	$ _____	Total liabilities and stockholders' equity	$ _____

Required:

Using the following data, complete the balance sheet.

a. Blue Co.'s records show that current and former customers owe the firm a total of $20,000; $3,000 of this amount has been due for more than a year from two customers who are now bankrupt.

b. The automobile, which is still being used in the business, cost $90,000 new; a used car dealer's Blue Book shows that it is now worth $50,000. Management estimates that the car has been used for one-third of its total potential use.

c. The land cost Blue Co. $55,000; it was recently assessed for real estate tax purposes at a value of $75,000.

d. Blue Co.'s president isn't sure of the amount of the note payable, but he does know that he signed a note.

e. Since Blue Co. was formed, net income has totaled $165,000, and dividends to stockholders have totaled $97,500.

Problem 2.24
LO 2, 3, 5, 6

Complete the balance sheet using cash flow data Following is a partially completed balance sheet for Epsico Inc. at December 31, 2019, together with comparative data for the year ended December 31, 2018. From the statement of cash flows for the year ended December 31, 2019, you determine the following (amounts in thousands of dollars):

> Net income for the year ended December 31, 2019, was $312.
>
> Dividends paid during the year ended December 31, 2019, were $96.
>
> Cash increased $96 during the year ended December 31, 2019.
>
> The cost of new equipment acquired during 2019 was $180; no equipment was disposed of.
>
> There were no transactions affecting the land account during 2019, but it is estimated that the fair market value of the land at December 31, 2019, is $480.

Required:
Complete the balance sheet at December 31, 2019.

EPSICO INC.
Balance Sheets
December 31, 2019 and 2018

	2019	2018		2019	2018
Assets			**Liabilities**		
Current assets:			Current liabilities:		
Cash	$	$ 360	Note payable	$ 588	$ 480
Accounts receivable	1,512	1,440	Accounts payable	1,476	1,320
Inventory	2,892	2,760			
Total current assets	$	$4,560	Total current liabilities	$2,064	$1,800
			Long-term debt		960
Land	$	$ 300	Total liabilities	$	$2,760
Equipment		4,500	**Stockholders' Equity**		
Less: Accumulated			Common stock	$2,400	$2,400
depreciation	(2,160)	(1,920)	Retained earnings		2,280
Total land & equipment	$	$2,880	Total stockholders' equity	$	$4,680
			Total liabilities and		
Total assets	$	$7,440	stockholders' equity	$	$7,440

Problem 2.25
LO 2, 4

Understanding income statement relationships—Levi Strauss & Co. The following selected data are adapted from the November 26, 2017, and November 27, 2016, consolidated balance sheets and income statements for the years then ended for Levi Strauss & Co. and Subsidiaries. All amounts are reported in thousands.

	2017	2016
Net revenues	$4,904,030	$?
Cost of goods sold	?	2,223,727
Gross profit	2,562,729	2,329,012
Selling, general, and administrative expenses	?	1,866,805
Operating income	?	?
Interest expense, and other expenses and losses, net	118,388	54,947
Income before income taxes	348,781	?
Income tax expense	?	
Net income	$ 284,556	$ 291,209
As at November 26 and 27, respectively:		
Total assets	$3,354,692	$?
Total liabilities	2,525,269	2,395,975
Total stockholders' equity	?	591,121

Required:

Calculate the missing amounts for each year.

Understanding income statement relationships—Apple Inc. Selected data from the September 30, 2017, and September 24, 2016, consolidated balance sheets and income statements for the years then ended for Apple Inc. follow. All amounts are reported in millions.

Problem 2.26
LO 2, 4

	2017	2016
Net sales	$229,234	$215,639
Cost of sales	141,048	131,376
Research and development expenses	11,581	10,045
Selling, general, and administrative expenses	15,261	14,194
Operating income	?	?
Other income, net	?	1,348
Provision for income taxes	15,738	?
Net income	$ 48,351	$ 45,687

Required:

a. Calculate the amount of Apple's gross profit for each year. Has gross profit as a percentage of sales changed significantly during the past year?

b. Calculate the amount of Apple's operating income for each year. Has operating income as a percentage of sales changed significantly during the past year?

c. After completing parts **a** and **b,** calculate the other missing amounts for each year.

Case

All applicable Cases are available in *Connect*.

Case 2.27

LO 2, 4, 6, 7

Prepare a personal balance sheet and projected income statement; explain financial statement relationships.

Required:

a. Prepare a personal balance sheet for yourself as of today. Work at identifying your assets and liabilities; use rough estimates for amounts.

b. Prepare a projected income statement for yourself for the current semester. Work at identifying your revenues and expenses, again using rough estimates for amounts.

c. Explain how your projected income statement for the semester is likely to impact your financial position (i.e., balance sheet) at the end of the semester. (*Note:* You are not required to prepare a projected balance sheet.)

d. Identify the major sources (and uses) of cash that you expect to receive (and spend) this semester. (*Note:* You are not required to prepare a projected statement of cash flows.)

e. Give three possible explanations why a full-time college student might incur a substantial net loss during the fall semester of her junior year, yet have more cash at the end of the semester than she had at the beginning.

ANSWERS TO What Does It Mean?

1. It means that there has been some sort of economic interchange; for example, you have agreed to pay tuition in exchange for classes.

2. It means the person doing this is really mixed up because the balance sheet presents data as of a point in time. It's a balance sheet as of August 31, 2020 and shows balances at that specific point in time rather than for a period of time.

3. It means that the organization's financial position at a point in time has been determined and summarized.

4. It means that each financial statement provides unique information but focuses on only a part of the big picture, so all four statements need to be reviewed to achieve a full understanding of the firm's financial position and results of operations.

5. It means that revenues have been earned from selling products or providing services but that the accounts receivable from those revenues have not yet been collected—or if the receivables have been collected, the cash has been used for some purpose other than paying bills.

6. It means that transactions affecting the income statement also affect the stockholders' equity section of the balance sheet as well as the asset and/or liability sections of the balance sheet.

7. It means that all expenses incurred in generating revenue for the period are subtracted from those revenues to determine net income for that period. Matching does not mean that revenues equal expenses.

8. It means that revenues and expenses are recognized in the accounting period in which they are earned or incurred, even though the related cash may be received or paid in a different accounting period.

9. It means that there may be both qualitative (e.g., workforce morale) and quantitative (e.g., opportunity cost) factors that are not reflected in the financial statements.

3

Fundamental Interpretations Made from Financial Statement Data

Chapter 2 presented an overview of the financial statements that result from the financial accounting process. It is now appropriate to preview some of the interpretations made by financial statement users to support their decisions and informed judgments. Understanding the uses of accounting information will make development of that information more meaningful. Current and potential stockholders are interested in making their own assessments of management's stewardship of the resources made available by the owners. For example, judgments about profitability will affect the investment decision. Creditors assess the entity's ability to repay loans and pay for products and services. These assessments of profitability and debt-paying ability involve interpreting the relationships among amounts reported in the financial statements. Most of these relationships will be referred to in subsequent chapters. They are introduced now to illustrate how management's financial objectives for the firm are quantified so that you may begin to understand what the numbers mean. Likewise, these concepts will prepare you to better understand the impact of alternative accounting methods on financial statements when accounting alternatives are explained in subsequent chapters.

This chapter introduces some fundamental financial statement analysis concepts and tools. Chapter 11 is a comprehensive explanation of how to use financial statement data to analyze a firm's financial condition and results of operations. You will better understand topics in that chapter after you have studied the financial accounting material in Chapters 5, 6, 7, 8, 9, and 10.

LEARNING OBJECTIVES (LO)

After studying this chapter, you should understand and be able to

LO 3-1   Discuss why financial statement ratios are important.

LO 3-2   Explain the importance and show the calculation of return on investment.

LO 3-3   Illustrate how to calculate and interpret margin and turnover using the DuPont model.

LO 3-4   Explain the importance and show the calculation of return on equity.

LO 3-5   Explain the meaning of liquidity and discuss why it is important.

LO 3-6   Discuss the significance and calculation of working capital, the current ratio, and the acid-test ratio.

LO 3-7   Generalize about how trend analysis can be used most effectively.

Study
Suggestion

The authors have found that learning about the basics of profitability and liquidity measures in this chapter is important for several reasons. (1) It introduces you to the "big picture" of real-world financial reporting before getting into the accounting details presented in subsequent chapters, (2) it demonstrates the relevance of studying financial accounting, (3) it encourages you to think about the impact of transactions on the financial statements, and (4) it provides a perspective that you can use in the homework assignments for Chapters 4, 5, 6, 7, 8, 9, 10, and 11. It is important that you attempt to understand the *business implications* of ROI, ROE, and the current ratio in particular.

Keep in mind that there are no singular, unchangeable rules that universally apply to the definitions of the data used in financial ratio analysis. Although the illustrations presented in this text endeavor to use the most commonly applied financial statement components, individual firms and financial analysts may define certain ratio components in a slightly (or even dramatically) different manner than is illustrated here. Presumably, sound and logical reasons exist for any such variations that you may encounter in practice. As a user of financial statement data, you should understand the reasons for those variations and the effects that any unique definition may have on ratio results relative to a more traditional definition for that same ratio.

Financial Ratios and Trend Analysis

The large dollar amounts reported in the financial statements of many companies, and the varying sizes of companies, make ratio analysis the only sensible method of evaluating various financial characteristics of a company. Students frequently are awed by the number of ratio measurements commonly used in financial management and sometimes are intimidated by the mere thought of calculating a ratio. Be neither awed nor intimidated! A ratio is simply the relationship between two numbers; the name of virtually every financial ratio describes the numbers to be related and usually how the ratio is calculated. As you study this material, concentrate on understanding why the ratio is considered important and work to understand the meaning of the ratio. If you do these things, you should avoid much of the stress associated with understanding financial ratios.

In most cases, a single ratio does not describe very much about the company whose statements are being studied. Much more meaningful analysis is accomplished when the *trend* of a particular ratio over several time periods is examined. However, consistency in financial reporting and in defining the ratio components is crucial if the trend is to be meaningful.

Most industry and trade associations publish industry average ratios based on aggregated data compiled by the associations from reports submitted by association members. Comparison of an individual company's ratio with the comparable industry ratio is frequently made as a means of assessing a company's relative standing in its industry. However, a comparison of a company with its industry that is based on a single observation may not be very meaningful because the company may use a financial accounting alternative that is different from that used by the rest of the industry.

LO 1
Discuss why financial statement ratios are important.

Trend analysis results in a much more meaningful comparison because even though the data used in the ratio may have been developed under different financial accounting alternatives, internal consistency within each of the trends will permit useful trend comparisons.

Trend analysis is described later in this chapter, but this brief example illustrates the process: Suppose a student's grade point average for last semester was 3.5 on a 4.0 scale. That GPA may be interesting, but it says little about the student's work. However, suppose you learn that this student's GPA was 1.9 four semesters ago, 2.7 three semesters ago, and 3.0 two semesters ago. The upward trend of grades suggests that the student is working "smarter and harder." This conclusion would be reinforced if you knew that the average GPA for all students in this person's class was 2.9 for each of the four semesters. You still don't know everything about the individual student's academic performance, but the comparative trend data let you make a more informed judgment than was possible with the grades from only one semester.

What Does It Mean?

Answer on page 93

1. What does it mean to state that the trend of data is frequently more important than the data themselves?

Return on Investment

LO 2

Explain the importance and show the calculation of return on investment.

Imagine that you are presented with two investment alternatives. Each investment will be made for one year, and each investment is equally risky. At the end of the year you will get your original investment back, plus income of $75 from investment A and $90 from investment B. Which investment alternative would you choose? The answer seems so obvious that you believe the question is loaded, so you hesitate to answer—a sensible response. But why is this a trick question? A little thought should make you think of a question to which you need an answer before you can select between investment A and investment B. Your question? "How much money would I have to invest in either alternative?" If the amount to be invested is the same—for example, $1,000— then clearly you would select investment B because your income would be greater than that earned on investment A for the same amount invested. If the amount to be invested in investment B is more than that required for investment A, you would have to calculate the **rate of return** on each investment to choose the more profitable alternative.

Rate of return is calculated by dividing the amount of return (the income of $75 or $90 in the preceding example) by the amount of the investment. For example, use an investment of $1,000 for each alternative:

Investment A:

$$\text{Rate of return} = \frac{\text{Amount of return}}{\text{Amount invested}} = \frac{\$75}{\$1,000} = 7.5\%$$

Investment B:

$$\text{Rate of return} = \frac{\text{Amount of return}}{\text{Amount invested}} = \frac{\$90}{\$1,000} = 9\%$$

Your intuitive selection of investment B as the better investment is confirmed by the fact that its rate of return is higher than that of investment A.

The example situation assumed that each of the investments would be made for one year. Remember that unless otherwise specified, rate of return calculations assume that the time period of the investment and return is one year.

The rate of return calculation is derived from the interest calculation you probably learned many years ago. Recall that

$$\text{Interest} = \text{Principal} \times \text{Rate} \times \text{Time}$$

Interest is the income or expense from investing or borrowing money.

Principal is the amount invested or borrowed.

Rate is the **interest rate** per year expressed as a percentage.

Time is the length of time the funds are invested or borrowed, expressed in years.

Note that when time is assumed to be one year, that term of the equation becomes 1/1 or 1, and it disappears. Thus, the rate of return calculation is simply a rearranged interest calculation that solves for the annual interest rate.

Return to the example situation and assume that the amounts required to be invested are $500 for investment A and $600 for investment B. Now which alternative would you select on the basis of rate of return? You should have made these calculations:

Investment A:

$$\text{Rate of return} = \frac{\text{Amount of return}}{\text{Amount invested}} = \frac{\$75}{\$500} = 15\%$$

Investment B:

$$\text{Rate of return} = \frac{\text{Amount of return}}{\text{Amount invested}} = \frac{\$90}{\$600} = 15\%$$

All other things being equal (and they seldom are except in textbook illustrations), you would be indifferent with respect to the alternatives available to you because each has a rate of return of 15% (per year).

Rate of return and riskiness related to an investment go hand in hand. **Risk** relates to the range of possible outcomes from an activity. The wider the range of possible outcomes, the greater the risk. An investment in a bank savings account is less risky than an investment in the stock of a corporation because the investor is virtually assured of receiving her or his principal and interest from the savings account, but the market value of stock may fluctuate widely even over a short period. Thus, the investor anticipates a higher rate of return from the stock investment than from the savings account as compensation for taking on additional risk. Yet the greater risk of the stock investment means that the actual rate of return earned could be considerably less (even negative) or much greater than the interest earned on the savings account. Market prices for products and commodities, as well as stock prices, reflect this basic risk–reward relationship. For now, understand that the higher the rate of return of one investment relative to another, the greater the risk associated with the higher return investment.

Rate of return is a universally accepted measure of profitability. Because it is a ratio, profitability of unequal investments can be compared, and risk–reward relationships can be evaluated. Bank advertisements for certificates of deposit feature the interest rate, or rate of return, that will be earned by the depositor. All investors evaluate the profitability of an investment by making a rate of return calculation.

Return on investment (ROI) is the label usually assigned to the rate of return calculation made using data from financial statements. This ratio is sometimes referred to as the **return on assets (ROA).** There are many ways of defining both the amount of return and the amount invested. For now, we use net income as the amount of return and use average total assets during the year as the amount invested. It is not appropriate to use total assets as reported on a single year-end balance sheet because that is the total at one point in time: the balance sheet date. Net income was earned during the entire fiscal year, so it should be related to the assets that were used during the entire year. Average assets used during the year usually are estimated by averaging the assets reported at the beginning of the year (the prior year-end balance sheet total) and assets reported at the end of the year. Recall from Chapter 2 that the income statement for the year is the link between the beginning and ending balance sheets. If seasonal fluctuations in total assets are significant (the materiality concept) and if quarter-end or month-end balance sheets are available, a more refined average asset calculation may be made.

The ROI of a firm is significant to most financial statement readers because it describes the rate of return that management was able to earn on the assets it had available to use during the year. Investors especially will make decisions and informed judgments about the quality of management and the relative profitability of a company based on ROI. Many financial analysts (these authors included) believe that ROI is the most meaningful measure of a company's profitability. Knowing net income alone is not enough; *an informed judgment about the firm's profitability requires relating net income to the assets used to generate that net income.*

The condensed balance sheets and income statement of Cruisers Inc., a hypothetical company, are presented in Exhibit 3-1. Using these data, the company's ROI calculation is illustrated here:

From the firm's balance sheets:	
Total assets, September 30, 2019	$364,720
Total assets, September 30, 2020	$402,654
From the firm's income statement for the year ended September 30, 2020:	
Net income	$ 34,910

$$\text{Return on investment} = \frac{\text{Net income}}{\text{Average total assets}}$$

$$= \frac{\$34,910}{(\$364,720 + \$402,654)/2} = 9.1\%$$

Some financial analysts prefer to use income from operations (or earnings before interest and income taxes) and average operating assets in the ROI calculation. They believe that excluding interest expense, income taxes, and assets not used in operations provides a better measure of the operating results of the firm. With these refinements, the ROI formula would be:

$$\text{Return on investment} = \frac{\text{Operating income}}{\text{Average operating assets}}$$

Condensed Balance Sheets and Income Statement of Cruisers Inc.   **Exhibit 3-1**

CRUISERS INC. Comparative Condensed Balance Sheets September 30, 2020 and 2019			CRUISERS INC. Condensed Income Statement For the Year Ended September 30, 2020	
	2020	**2019**		
Current assets:				
Cash and marketable securities	$ 22,286	$ 16,996	Net sales	$611,873
Accounts receivable	42,317	39,620	Cost of goods sold	428,354
Inventories	53,716	48,201	Gross margin	$183,519
Total current assets	$118,319	$104,817	Operating expenses............	122,183
Other assets	284,335	259,903	Income from operations	$ 61,336
Total assets	$402,654	$364,720	Interest expense	6,400
Current liabilities.....................	$ 57,424	$ 51,400	Income before taxes	$ 54,936
Other liabilities	80,000	83,000	Income taxes	20,026
Total liabilities	$137,424	$134,400		
Stockholders' equity	265,230	230,320	Net income	$ 34,910
Total liabilities and stockholders' equity	$402,654	$364,720	Earnings per share	$ 1.21

Other analysts will make similar adjustments to arrive at the amounts used in the ROI calculation. Consistency in the definition of terms is more important than the definition itself because the trend of ROI will be more significant for decision making than the absolute result of the ROI calculation for any one year. However, it is appropriate to understand the definitions used in any ROI results you see.

2. What does it mean to express economic performance as a rate of return?
3. What does it mean to say that return on investment (ROI) is one of the most meaningful measures of financial performance?

What Does It Mean?
Answer on page 93

The DuPont Model: An Expansion of the ROI Calculation

Financial analysts at E.I. DuPont de Nemours & Co. are credited with developing the **DuPont model,** an expansion of the basic ROI calculation, in the late 1930s. They reasoned that profitability from sales and utilization of assets to generate sales revenue were both important factors to be considered when evaluating a company's overall profitability. One popular adaptation of their model introduces total sales revenue into the ROI calculation as follows:

LO 3
Illustrate how to calculate and interpret margin and turnover using the DuPont model.

$$\text{Return on investment} = \frac{\text{Net income}}{\text{Sales}} \times \frac{\text{Sales}}{\text{Average total assets}}$$

The first term, net income/sales, is **margin.** The second term, sales/average total assets, is **asset turnover,** or simply **turnover.** Of course, the sales quantities cancel out algebraically, but they are introduced to this version of the ROI model because of their significance. *Margin* emphasizes that from every dollar of sales revenue, some amount must work its way to the bottom line (net income) if the company is to be profitable. *Turnover* relates to the efficiency with which the firm's assets are used in the revenue-generating process.

Another quick quiz will illustrate the significance of turnover. Many of us look forward to a 40-hour-per-week job, generally thought of as five 8-hour days. Imagine a company's factory operating on such a schedule—one shift per day, five days per week. What percentage of the available time is that factory operating? You may have answered 33 percent, or one-third of the time, because eight hours is one-third of a day. But what about Saturday and Sunday? In fact, there are 21 shifts available in a week (7 days × 3 shifts per day), so a factory operating five shifts per week is being used only 5/21 of the time—less than 25%. The factory is idle more than 75% of the time! As you can imagine, many of the occupancy costs (real estate taxes, utilities, insurance) are incurred whether or not the plant is in use. This explains why many firms operate their plants on a two-shift, three-shift, or even a seven-day basis rather than building additional plants—it allows them to increase their level of production and thereby expand sales volume without expanding their investment in assets. The higher costs associated with multiple-shift operations (such as late-shift premiums for workers and additional shipping costs relative to shipping from multiple locations closer to customers) will increase the company's operating expenses, thereby lowering net income and decreasing margin. Yet the multiple-shift company's overall ROI will be higher if turnover is increased proportionately more than margin is reduced, which is likely to be the case.

Calculation of ROI using the DuPont model is illustrated here, using data from the financial statements of Cruisers in Exhibit 3-1:

From the firm's balance sheets:	
Total assets, September 30, 2019	$364,720
Total assets, September 30, 2020	$402,654
From the firm's income statement for the year ended September 30, 2020:	
Net sales	$611,873
Net income	$ 34,910

$$\text{Return on investment} = \text{Margin} \times \text{Turnover}$$

$$= \frac{\text{Net income}}{\text{Sales}} \times \frac{\text{Sales}}{\text{Average total assets}}$$

$$= \frac{\$34,910}{\$611,873} \times \frac{\$611,873}{(\$364,720 + \$402,654)/2}$$

$$= 5.7\% \times 1.6$$

$$= 9.1\%$$

The significance of the DuPont model is that it has led top management in many organizations to consider utilization of assets, including keeping investment in assets as low as feasible, to be just as important to overall performance as generating profit from sales.

A rule of thumb useful for putting ROI in perspective is that for most American merchandising and manufacturing companies, average ROI based on net income normally ranges between 8 percent and 12 percent during stable economic times. Average ROI based on operating income (earnings before interest and taxes) for the same set of firms is typically between 10 percent and 15 percent. Average margin, based on net income, ranges from about 5 percent to 10 percent. Using operating income, average margin tends to range from 10 percent to 15 percent. Asset turnover is usually about 1.0 to 1.5 but often ranges as high as 3.0, depending on the operating characteristics of the firm and its industry. The ranges given here are rather wide and are intended to suggest only that a firm with ROI and component values consistently beyond these ranges is exceptional.

4. What does it mean when the straightforward ROI calculation is expanded by using margin and turnover?

What Does It Mean?

Answer on page 93

Return on Equity

Recall that the balance sheet equation is:

$$\text{Assets} = \text{Liabilities} + \text{Stockholders' equity}$$

The return on investment calculation relates net income (perhaps adjusted for interest, income taxes, or other items) to assets. Assets (perhaps adjusted to exclude nonoperating assets or other items) represent the amount invested to generate earnings. As the balance sheet equation indicates, the investment in assets can result from either amounts borrowed from creditors (liabilities) or amounts invested by the owners. Stockholders (and others) are interested in expressing the profits of the firm as a rate of return on the amount of stockholders' equity; this is called **return on equity (ROE),** and it is calculated as follows:

$$\text{Return on equity} = \frac{\text{Net income}}{\text{Average stockholders' equity}}$$

Return on equity usually is calculated using average stockholders' equity during the period for which the net income was earned for the same reason that average assets

LO 4
Explain the importance and show the calculation of return on equity.

is used in the ROI calculation; net income is earned over a period of time, so it should be related to the stockholders' equity over that same period.

Calculation of ROE is illustrated here using data from the financial statements of Cruisers in Exhibit 3-1:

From the firm's balance sheets:	
Total stockholders' equity, September 30, 2019	$230,320
Total stockholders' equity, September 30, 2020	$265,230
From the firm's income statement for the year ended September 30, 2020:	
Net income	$ 34,910

$$\text{Return on equity} = \frac{\text{Net income}}{\text{Average stockholders' equity}}$$

$$= \frac{\$34,910}{(\$230,320 + \$265,230)/2}$$

$$= \$34,910 / \$247,775$$

$$= 14.1\%$$

A rule of thumb for putting ROE in perspective is that average ROE for most American merchandising and manufacturing companies has historically ranged from 12 percent to 18 percent.

Keep in mind that return on equity is a special application of the rate of return concept. ROE is important to current stockholders and prospective investors because it relates earnings to stockholders' investment—that is, the stockholders' equity in the assets of the entity. Adjustments to both net income and average stockholders' equity are sometimes made in an effort to improve the comparability of ROE results between firms, and some of these will be explained later in the text. For now, you should understand that both return on investment and return on equity are fundamental measures of the profitability of a firm and that the data for making these calculations come from the firm's financial statements.

What Does It Mean?

Answer on page 93

5. What does it mean when return on equity is used to evaluate a firm's financial performance?

Working Capital and Measures of Liquidity

LO 5

Explain the meaning of liquidity and discuss why it is important.

Liquidity refers to a firm's ability to meet its current obligations and is measured by relating its current assets and current liabilities as reported on the balance sheet. **Working capital** is the excess of a firm's current assets over its current liabilities. Current assets are cash and other assets that are likely to be converted to cash within a year (principally accounts receivable and merchandise inventories). Current liabilities are obligations that are expected to be paid within a year, including loans, accounts payable, and other accrued liabilities (such as wages payable, interest payable, and rent payable). Most financially healthy firms have positive working capital. Even though a firm is not likely to have cash on hand at any point in time equal to its current liabilities, it will expect to collect accounts receivable or sell merchandise inventory and then collect the resulting accounts receivable in time to pay the liabilities when they are scheduled for payment. Of course, in the process of converting inventories to cash, the firm will be purchasing additional merchandise for its inventory, and the suppliers will want to be assured of collecting the amounts due according to the previously agreed provisions for when payment is due.

Liquidity is measured in three principal ways:

$$\text{Working capital} = \text{Current assets} - \text{Current liabilities}$$

$$\text{Current ratio} = \frac{\text{Current assets}}{\text{Current liabilities}}$$

$$\text{Acid-test ratio} = \frac{\text{Cash (including temporary cash investments)} + \text{Accounts receivable}}{\text{Current liabilities}}$$

The dollar amount of a firm's working capital is not as significant as the ratio of its current assets to current liabilities because the amount can be misleading unless it is related to another quantity (how large is large?). Therefore, the *trend* of a company's **current ratio** is most useful in judging its current bill-paying ability. The **acid-test ratio,** also known as the *quick ratio,* is a more conservative short-term measure of liquidity because merchandise inventories are excluded from the computation. This ratio provides information about an almost worst-case situation—the firm's ability to meet its current obligations even if none of the inventory can be sold.

The liquidity measure calculations shown here use September 30, 2020, data from the balance sheet of Cruisers in Exhibit 3-1:

$$\text{Working capital} = \text{Current assets} - \text{Current liabilities}$$
$$= \$118,319 - \$57,424$$
$$= \$60,895$$

$$\text{Current ratio} = \frac{\text{Current assets}}{\text{Current liabilities}} = \frac{\$118,319}{\$57,424} = 2.1$$

$$\text{Acid-test ratio} = \frac{\text{Cash (including temporary cash investments)} + \text{Accounts receivable}}{\text{Current liabilities}}$$
$$= \frac{\$22,286 + \$42,317}{\$57,424}$$
$$= 1.1$$

LO 6

Discuss the significance and calculation of working capital, the current ratio, and the acid-test ratio.

As a general rule, a current ratio of 2.0 and an acid-test ratio of 1.0 are considered indicative of adequate liquidity. From these data, it can be concluded that Cruisers Inc. has a high degree of liquidity; it should not have any trouble meeting its current obligations as they become due.

In terms of debt-paying ability, the higher the current ratio, the better. Yet an overly high current ratio sometimes can be a sign that the company has not made the most productive use of its assets. In recent years, many large, well-managed corporations have made efforts to streamline operations by reducing their current ratios to the 1.0–1.5 range or even lower, with corresponding reductions in their acid-test ratios. So what motivates this practice? It's clear that investments in cash, accounts receivable, and inventories are being minimized because these current assets tend to be the least productive assets employed by the company. For example, what kind of ROI is earned on accounts receivable or inventory? Very little, if any. Funds freed up by reducing a company's investment in working capital items can be used to purchase new production equipment or to expand marketing efforts for existing product lines.

Remember, however, that judgments based on the results of any of these calculations using data from a single balance sheet are not as meaningful as the trend of the results over several periods. It is also important to note the composition of working capital and to understand the impact on the ratios of equal changes in current assets and current liabilities. As the following illustration shows, if a short-term bank loan were repaid just before the balance sheet date, working capital would not change (because current assets and current liabilities would each decrease by the same amount), but the current ratio (and the acid-test ratio) would change:

	Before Loan Repayment	After $20,000 Loan Repaid
Current assets	$200,000	$180,000
Current liabilities	100,000	80,000
Working capital	$100,000	$100,000
Current ratio	2.0	2.25

If a new loan for $20,000 were then taken out just after the balance sheet date, the level of the firm's liquidity at the balance sheet date as expressed by the current ratio would have been overstated. Thus, liquidity measures should be viewed with a healthy

Business in
Practice

Establishing a Credit Relationship

Most transactions between businesses, and many transactions between individuals and businesses, are credit transactions. That is, the sale of products or provision of services is completed sometime before payment is made by the purchaser. Usually, before delivering the products or services, the seller wants to have some assurance that the bill will be paid when due. This involves determining that the buyer is a good **credit risk**.

Individuals usually establish credit by submitting to the potential creditor a completed credit application, which includes information about employment, salary, bank accounts, liabilities, and other credit relationships (such as charge accounts) established. Most credit grantors are looking for a good record of timely payments on existing credit accounts; this is why an individual's first credit account is usually the most difficult to obtain. Potential credit grantors also may check an individual's credit record as maintained by one or more of the three national credit bureaus in the United States (Equifax, Experion, and TransUnion). Note that individual consumers are entitled to a free annual credit report from each of these three nationwide consumer reporting agencies. (See annualcreditreport.com for more information.)

Businesses seeking credit may follow a procedure similar to that used by individuals. Alternatively, they may provide financial statements and names of firms with which a credit relationship has been established. A newly organized firm may have to pay for its purchases in advance or on delivery **(COD)** until it has been in operation for several months, and then the seller may set a relatively low credit limit for sales on credit. After a consistent record is established of having paid bills when due, the credit limit will be raised. After a firm has been in operation for a year or more, its credit history may be reported by the Dun & Bradstreet credit reporting service—a type of national credit bureau to which many companies subscribe. Even after a credit relationship has been established, it is not unusual for a firm to continue providing financial statements to its principal creditors.

dose of skepticism because the timing of short-term borrowings and repayments is entirely within the control of management.

Measures of liquidity are used primarily by potential creditors who are seeking to judge their prospects of being paid promptly if they enter a creditor relationship with the firm whose liquidity is being analyzed (see Business in Practice—Establishing a Credit Relationship).

The statement of cash flows also is useful in assessing the reasons for a firm's liquidity (or illiquidity). Recall that this financial statement identifies the reasons for the change in a firm's cash during the period (usually a year) by reporting the changes during the period in noncash balance sheet items.

---

6. What does it mean to say that the financial position of a firm is liquid?

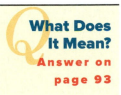
What Does It Mean?
Answer on page 93

Illustration of Trend Analysis

Trend analysis of return on investment, return on equity, and working capital and liquidity measures is illustrated in the following tables and exhibits. The data in these illustrations come primarily from the financial statements in the 2017 annual report of Campbell Soup Company, reproduced in the appendix.

The data in Table 3-1 come from the five-year "selected financial data" of Campbell's 2017 annual report (see the appendix) and from balance sheets of prior annual reports. The data in Table 3-1 are presented graphically in Exhibits 3-2, 3-3 and 3-4. Note that the sequence of the years in the table is opposite from that of the years in the graphs. Tabular data are frequently presented so the most recent year is closest to the captions of the table. Graphs of time series data usually flow from left to right. In any event, it is necessary to notice and understand the captions of both tables and graphs.

LO 7
Generalize about how trend analysis can be used most effectively.

Campbell's

Campbell Soup Company (Profitability* and Liquidity Data,[†] 2013–2017)   **Table 3-1**

	2017	2016	2015	2014	2013
Margin (net earnings[‡]/net sales)	11.2	7.1	8.2	10.5	8.8
Turnover (net sales/average total assets)	1.01	1.00	1.00	1.01	1.09
ROI (net earnings/average total assets)	11.4	7.1	8.2	10.6	9.6
ROE (net earnings/average total equity)	55.8	38.7	44.7	62.0	67.8
Year-end position (in millions):					
Current assets	$1,900	$1,908	$2,093	$2,100	$2,221
Current liabilities	2,395	2,555	2,806	2,989	3,282
Working capital	(495)	(647)	(713)	(889)	(1,061)
Current ratio	0.79	0.75	0.75	0.70	0.68

* Profitability calculations were made from the data presented in the five-year selected financial data.

[†] Liquidity calculations were made from the data presented in the balance sheets of this and prior annual reports.

[‡] Based on "Net Earnings Attributable to Campbell Soup Company," which was identical to "Net Earnings" in all years except 2014 and 2013, when these amounts were slightly higher than "Net Earnings." The slight differences are due to net losses attributed to the noncontrolling (outside) shareholders of Campbell's subsidiary companies.

Source: Campbell Soup Company, 2017 Annual Report, pp. 13, 33, 35.

Exhibit 3-2   Campbell Soup Company, Return on Investment (ROI) and Return on Equity (ROE), 2013–2017

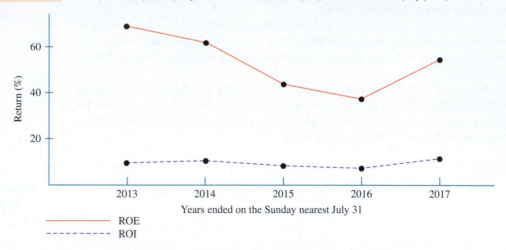

The graph in Exhibit 3-2 illustrates that Campbell's ROI and ROE results were generally downward trending during the five-year period presented, although 2017 was certainly an encouraging year. Scanning the graph from left to right reveals that ROE fell slightly while ROI rose slightly during the year ended July 31, 2014, then fell for both measures during 2015 and 2016, before rising significantly for both ROE and ROI in 2017. Although the overall trend in the profitability data presented is obviously downward sloping during the five-year period presented, it is difficult to meaningfully interpret company-specific results without understanding more about the company's core operations and any particular industry-based challenges they may have faced in recent years.

Campbell's

As the graphs in Exhibit 3-2 illustrate, Campbell's ROI trend was clearly more stable than its ROE trend during the five-year period from 2013 to 2017, as is typically the case for many companies. A firm's asset growth from year to year tends to be well planned and thus is likely to generate more consistency in the ROI results than would equity growth, which is much harder to predict and control. In recent years, Campbell's total assets have been approximately 5 to 7 times larger than the company's total equity due to the presence of substantial amounts of debt on the company's balance sheet. As a direct result of Campbell's aggressive use of *financial leverage* (i.e., taking the risk of borrowing funds from creditors on a long-term basis to enhance the return to stockholders), ROE ranged from an astonishing 38.7 percent to 67.8 percent during the five-year period depicted in the graph. Suffice it to say, stockholder returns of this magnitude are highly unusual for a mature company such as Campbell's, although competitive consumer goods companies such as Hershey's and Kellogg's have recently reported unusually high ROE results as well.

Not only do these ROE results represent a staggering five-year return to Campbell's stockholders, but they also present some difficulties in making meaningful comparisons of the company's ROI and ROE trends. In Exhibit 3-2, the vertical scale spans a range from 7.1 percent (ROI for 2016) to the high data point of 67.8 percent (ROE for 2013). By using such a heavily compressed vertical scale, the variation of the actual data points for ROI (from 7.1 percent to 11.4 percent) becomes lost in the flattened-out graphical representation. Yet the "big picture" is that Campbell's has consistently provided a satisfying ROI to all resource providers while also providing abnormally high returns to its stockholders.

Campbell Soup Company, Margin and Turnover, 2013–2017   **Exhibit 3-3**

Years ended on the Sunday nearest July 31

——————— Turnover
-- -- -- -- -- Margin

Exhibit 3-3 illustrates that Campbell's turnover has been remarkably stable in recent years, although slightly downward trending; this suggests that the company has had a relatively flat or even falling sales growth trend and that total asset growth has been minimal as well. Note that the range of turnover results during this period, 1.00–1.09, is not significant in absolute terms and is graphically depicted as a virtual flat-line representation.

The trend in margin is more difficult to interpret than the trend in turnover. Margin rose in 2014, and then fell in 2015 and 2016 before recovering to a more normal, or expected, level in 2017. Note that turnover was flat from 2014 through 2017, so the variations seen in Campbell Soup Company's ROI during those years had everything to do with the variations in margin (profitability per sales dollar) from year to year and nothing to do with turnover (which is a measure of the efficiency of asset utilization). Campbell's margin was within a healthy and relatively narrow range of 7.1 percent to 11.4 percent for all years presented; thus, the overall trend suggests that the company is able to generate modest but consistent profits.

Campbell's

The overall trend in Campbell's liquidity during this period is not difficult to determine, although it is perhaps somewhat difficult to understand. As illustrated in Exhibit 3-4, Campbell's maintained a highly consistent current ratio in the range of 0.68–0.79 throughout the five-year period, meaning that current liabilities exceeded current assets by substantial amounts in all years presented. Working capital peaked at ($495) million in 2017 after having reached a low point of ($1,061) million in 2013, meaning that current liabilities exceeded current asset by more than $1 billion at that point in time. Yet it is highly unlikely that Campbell Soup Company has ever failed to meet any significant debt obligation in a timely manner. The tight manner in which the working capital and current ratio graphs mimic each other's progress suggests that Campbell's keeps a very close eye on these important relationships.

Campbell's clearly adheres to contemporary working capital management techniques, which suggest that investments in current assets (especially cash, accounts receivable, and inventories) ought to be minimized to the greatest extent possible. Likewise, management appears to take a similar view that it is perfectly acceptable to carry significant levels of current liabilities, as long as cash is readily available to pay all obligations as they fall due. As discussed earlier in this chapter, funds freed up by reducing one's

Exhibit 3-4   Campbell Soup Company, Working Capital and Current Ratio, 2013–2017

investment in working capital items can be used, for example, to purchase new production equipment or to expand marketing efforts for existing product lines.

Large-scale multinational corporations often invest significant time and resources to develop sophisticated cash management systems that will help to facilitate the timely movement of funds and ensure that the company maximizes the utilization of its cash resources. Lines of credit are often arranged with major banks throughout the world as well, to provide for emergency cash needs. Although Campbell Soup Company may appear to be on the verge of a cash crisis, it's more likely that its working capital management team has carefully guided the company at every step along the way. To gain a better understanding of Campbell's working capital and current ratio trends, it would be helpful to add several more years of data to the analysis. Changes in the acid-test ratio also would be considered in evaluating the firm's overall liquidity position.

All of the graphs presented in this chapter use an arithmetic vertical scale, although in some cases, the vertical scale has been truncated to highlight only the key data ranges being depicted. For example, the scale for margin shown in Exhibit 3-3 highlights the data range from 6 percent to 12 percent while implicitly cutting out an unspecified portion of the nonrelevant data range from 0 percent to 6 percent. This graphing technique eliminates the need to include unnecessary white space in the presentation of data that may otherwise distract from the relationships being highlighted, but it likewise skews the perspective and sense of scale of the absolute data values. Note also that with arithmetic vertical scales, the distance between values shown on the vertical axis will always be uniform. So if the data being plotted increase at a constant rate over the period of time shown on the horizontal scale, the plot will be a line that curves upward more and more steeply.

Many analysts instead prefer to plot data that will change significantly over time (such as a company's sales data) on a graph that uses a logarithmic vertical scale. This is called a **semilogarithmic graph** because the horizontal scale is still arithmetic; the intervals between years, for example, are equal. The primary advantage of a semilogarithmic presentation is that a constant rate of growth will result in a straight-line plot. Extensive use of semilog graphs is made for data presented in the financial press, such as *The Wall Street Journal, The Financial Times, Fortune,* and *Bloomberg Businessweek,* so the key is to always carefully consider the scale being used in graphical presentations such that you can accurately interpret the data.

Demonstration Problem

The **Demonstration Problem** walkthrough for this chapter is available in *Connect*.

Summary

Financial statement users express financial statement data in ratio format to facilitate making decisions and informed judgments. Users are especially interested in the trend of a company's ratios over time and the comparison of the company's ratio trends with those of its industry as a whole. **(LO 1)**

The rate of return on investment is a universally accepted measure of profitability. Rate of return is calculated by dividing the amount of return, or profit, by the amount invested. Rate of return is expressed as an annual percentage rate.

Return on investment (ROI) is one of the most important measures of profitability because it relates the income earned during a period to the assets that were invested to generate those earnings. The DuPont model for calculating ROI expands the basic model by introducing sales to calculate margin (net income/sales) and asset turnover (sales/average assets); ROI equals margin × turnover. *Margin* describes the profit from each dollar of sales, and *turnover* expresses the sales-generating capacity (utilization efficiency) of the firm's assets. This financial ratio is often referred to as *return on assets (ROA)*. **(LO 2, 3)**

Return on equity (ROE) relates net income earned for the year to the average stockholders' equity for the year. This rate of return measure is important to current and prospective owners/stockholders because it relates earnings to the stockholders' investment. **(LO 4)**

Creditors are interested in an entity's liquidity—that is, its ability to pay its liabilities when due. The amount of working capital, the current ratio, and the acid-test ratio are measures of liquidity. These calculations are made using the amounts of current assets and current liabilities reported in the balance sheet. **(LO 5, 6)**

When ratio trend data are plotted graphically, it is easy to determine the significance of ratio changes and to evaluate a firm's performance. However, it is necessary to pay attention to how graphs are constructed because the visual image presented can be influenced by the scales used. **(LO 7)**

Key Terms and Concepts

acid-test ratio (p. 77) The ratio of the sum of cash (including temporary cash investments) and accounts receivable to current liabilities. A primary measure of a firm's liquidity.

asset turnover (p. 74) The quotient of sales divided by average assets for the year or other fiscal period.

COD (p. 78) Cash on delivery, or collect on delivery.

credit risk (p. 78) The risk that an entity to which credit has been extended will not pay the amount due on the date set for payment.

current ratio (p. 77)   The ratio of current assets to current liabilities. A primary measure of a firm's liquidity.

DuPont model (p. 73)   An expansion of the return on investment calculation to margin × turnover.

interest (p. 71)   The income or expense from investing or borrowing money.

interest rate (p. 71)   The percentage amount used, together with principal and time, to calculate interest.

liquidity (p. 76)   Refers to a firm's ability to meet its current financial obligations.

margin (p. 74)   The percentage of net income to net sales. Sometimes margin is calculated using operating income or other intermediate subtotals of the income statement. The term also can refer to the *amount* of gross profit, operating income, or net income.

principal (p. 71)   The amount of money invested or borrowed.

rate of return (p. 70)   A percentage calculated by dividing the amount of return on an investment for a period of time by the average amount invested for the period. A primary measure of profitability.

return on assets (ROA) (p. 72)   A synonym for *return on investment (ROI)*.

return on equity (ROE) (p. 75)   The percentage of net income divided by average stockholders' equity for the fiscal period in which the net income was earned; frequently referred to as *ROE*. A primary measure of a firm's profitability.

return on investment (ROI) (p. 72)   The rate of return on an investment; frequently referred to as *ROI*. Sometimes referred to as *return on assets* or *ROA*. A primary measure of a firm's profitability.

risk (p. 71)   A concept that describes the range of possible outcomes from an action. The greater the range of possible outcomes, the greater the risk.

semilogarithmic graph (p. 82)   A graph format in which the vertical axis is a logarithmic scale.

trend analysis (p. 70)   Evaluation of the trend of data over time.

turnover (p. 74)   The quotient of sales divided by the average assets for the year or some other fiscal period. A descriptor, such as total asset, inventory, or plant and equipment, usually precedes the turnover term. A measure of the efficiency with which assets are used to generate sales.

working capital (p. 76)   The difference between current assets and current liabilities. A measure of a firm's liquidity.

connect   Mini-Exercises

All applicable Mini-Exercises are available in *Connect*.

**Mini-Exercise
3.1**

LO 3

ROI analysis using the DuPont model   Firm J has net income of $76,800, sales of $480,000, and average total assets of $400,000.

Required:
Calculate Firm J's margin, turnover, and return on investment (ROI).

**Mini-Exercise
3.2**

LO 3

ROI analysis using the DuPont model   Firm K has a margin of 9%, turnover of 1.6, and sales of $4,000,000.

Required:
Calculate Firm K's net income, average total assets, and return on investment (ROI).

**Mini-Exercise
3.3**

LO 4

Calculate ROE   Firm L had net assets at the end of the year of $730,000. The only transactions affecting stockholders' equity during the year were net income of $154,000 and dividends of $94,000.

Required:

Calculate Firm L's average stockholders' equity and return on equity (ROE).

Calculate average total assets, net income, ROI, and ROE Firm M has a margin of 11%, turnover of 1.4, sales of $840,000, and average stockholders' equity of $400,000.

Mini-Exercise 3.4

LO 3, 4

Required:

Calculate Firm M's average total assets, net income, return on investment (ROI), and return on equity (ROE).

Calculate current liabilities and working capital Firm N has a current ratio of 1.7 and current assets of $141,100.

Mini-Exercise 3.5

LO 6

Required:

Calculate Firm N's current liabilities and working capital.

Calculate working capital and current ratio Firm O has accounts receivable of $20,100, cash of $18,400, property, plant, and equipment of $340,000, merchandise inventory of $21,500, accounts payable of $31,300, other accrued liabilities of $18,700, common stock of $300,000, and retained earnings of $50,000.

Mini-Exercise 3.6

LO 6

Required:

Calculate Firm N's working capital and current ratio.

Exercises

Ⓜ connect

All applicable Exercises are available in *Connect*.

Compare investment alternatives Two acquaintances have approached you about investing in business activities in which each is involved. Simone is seeking $8,000, and Riley needs $6,000. One year from now, your original investment will be returned, along with $920 income from Simone or $750 income from Riley. You can make only one investment.

Exercise 3.7

LO 2

Required:

a. Which investment would you prefer? Why? Round your percentage answer to two decimal places.

b. What other factors should you consider before making either investment?

Compare investment alternatives A friend has $5,000 that he has saved from his part-time job. He will need his money, plus any interest earned on it, in six months and has asked for your help in deciding whether to put the money in a bank savings account at 3% interest or to lend it to Victor. Victor has promised to repay $5,300 after six months.

Exercise 3.8

LO 2

Required:

a. Calculate the interest earned on the savings account for six months.

b. Calculate the rate of return if the money is lent to Victor. Round your percentage answer to two decimal places.

c. Which alternative would you recommend? Explain your answer.

Exercise 3.9

LO 2

Compare investment alternatives You have two investment opportunities. One will have an 8% rate of return on an investment of $10,000; the other will have a 10% rate of return on principal of $14,000. You would like to take advantage of the higher-yielding investment but have only $10,000 available.

Required:
What is the maximum rate of interest that you would pay to borrow the $4,000 needed to take advantage of the higher yield?

Exercise 3.10

LO 2

Compare investment alternatives You have accumulated $25,000 and are looking for the best rate of return that can be earned over the next year. A bank savings account will pay 3%. A one-year bank certificate of deposit will pay 6%, but the minimum investment is $30,000.

Required:
a. Calculate the amount of return you would earn if the $25,000 were invested for one year at 3%.
b. Calculate the net amount of return you would earn if $5,000 were borrowed at a cost of 12%, and then $30,000 were invested for one year at 6%.
c. Calculate the net rate of return on your investment of $25,000 if you accept the strategy of part **b.**
d. In addition to the amount of investment required and the rate of return offered, what other factors would you normally consider before making an investment decision such as the one described in this exercise?

Exercise 3.11

LO 3

ROI analysis using the DuPont model

a. Firm A has a margin of 8%, sales of $630,000, and ROI of 16.8%. Calculate the firm's average total assets.
b. Firm B has net income of $246,400, turnover of 1.1, and average total assets of $1,600,000. Calculate the firm's sales, margin, and ROI. Round your percentage answer to one decimal place.
c. Firm C has net income of $43,500, turnover of 2.9, and ROI of 23.2%. Calculate the firm's margin, sales, and average total assets. Round your percentage answer to one decimal place.

Exercise 3.12

LO 3

ROI analysis using the DuPont model

a. Firm D has net income of $54,000, sales of $1,200,000, and average total assets of $750,000. Calculate the firm's margin, turnover, and ROI.
b. Firm E has net income of $132,000, sales of $2,200,000, and ROI of 9.6%. Calculate the firm's turnover and average total assets.
c. Firm F has ROI of 12%, average total assets of $1,500,000, and turnover of 0.8. Calculate the firm's sales, margin, and net income. Round your answers to the nearest whole numbers.

Exercise 3.13

LO 4

Calculate ROE At the beginning of the year, the net assets of Shannon Co. were $617,900. The only transactions affecting stockholders' equity during the year were net income of $60,800 and dividends of $16,600.

Required:

Calculate Shannon Co.'s return on equity (ROE) for the year. Round your percentage answer to one decimal place.

Calculate margin, net income, and ROE For the year ended December 31, 2019, Settles Inc. earned an ROI of 12.6%. Sales for the year were $120 million, and average asset turnover was 2.8. Average stockholders' equity was $25 million.

Exercise 3.14
LO 3, 4

Required:

a. Calculate Settles Inc.'s margin and net income.

b. Calculate Settles Inc.'s return on equity.

Effect of transactions on working capital and current ratio Jay Oullette, CEO of Bumper to Bumper Inc., anticipates that his company's year-end balance sheet will show current assets of $180,000 and current liabilities of $100,000. Oullette has asked your advice concerning a possible early payment of $20,000 of accounts payable before year-end, even though payment isn't due until later.

Exercise 3.15
LO 6

Required:

a. Calculate the firm's working capital and current ratio under each situation. Would you recommend early payment of the accounts payable? Why? Round your current ratio answer to one decimal place.

b. Assume that Bumper to Bumper had negotiated a short-term bank loan of $60,000 that can be drawn down either before or after the end of the year. Calculate working capital and the current ratio at year-end under each situation, assuming that early payment of accounts payable is not made. When would you recommend that the loan be taken? Why? Round your current ratio answer to one decimal place.

Effect of transactions on working capital and current ratio Evans Inc. had current liabilities at April 30 of $275,000. The firm's current ratio at that date was 2.1.

Exercise 3.16
LO 6

Required:

a. Calculate the firm's current assets and working capital at April 30.

b. Assume that management paid $27,500 of accounts payable on April 29. Calculate the current ratio and working capital at April 30 as if the April 29 payment had not been made. Round your current ratio answer to two decimal places.

c. Explain the changes, if any, to working capital and the current ratio that would be caused by the April 29 payment.

Problems

McGraw Hill connect

All applicable Problems are available in *Connect*.

Calculate profitability measures using annual report data Using data from the financial statements of Campbell Soup Company in the appendix, calculate the following:

Problem 3.17
LO 3, 4, 6

Campbell's

a. ROI for 2017. Round your percentage answer to one decimal place.

b. ROE for 2017. Round your percentage answer to one decimal place.

c. Working capital at July 30, 2017, and July 31, 2016.

d. Current ratio at July 30, 2017, and July 31, 2016. Round your answers to two decimal places.

e. Acid-test ratio at July 30, 2017, and July 31, 2016. Round your answers to two decimal places.

Note: Visit campbellsoup.com to update this problem with data from the most recent annual report.

Problem 3.18
LO 3, 4, 6

Calculate profitability and liquidity measures Presented here are the comparative balance sheets of Hames Inc. at December 31, 2020 and 2019. Sales for the year ended December 31, 2020, totaled $1,700,000.

HAMES INC. Balance Sheets December 31, 2020 and 2019	2020	2019
Assets		
Cash	$ 63,000	$ 57,000
Accounts receivable	285,000	266,000
Merchandise inventory	261,000	247,000
Total current assets	$609,000	$570,000
Land	109,000	82,000
Plant and equipment	375,000	330,000
Less: Accumulated depreciation	(195,000)	(180,000)
Total assets	$898,000	$802,000
Liabilities		
Short-term debt	$ 54,000	$ 51,000
Accounts payable	168,000	144,000
Other accrued liabilities	68,000	54,000
Total current liabilities	$290,000	$249,000
Long-term debt	56,000	105,000
Total liabilities	$346,000	$354,000
Stockholders' Equity		
Common stock, no par, 200,000 shares authorized, 80,000 and 50,000 shares issued, respectively	$224,000	$162,000
Retained earnings:		
Beginning balance	$286,000	$217,000
Net income for the year	102,000	84,000
Dividends for the year	(60,000)	(15,000)
Ending balance	$328,000	$286,000
Total stockholders' equity	$552,000	$448,000
Total liabilities and stockholders' equity	$898,000	$802,000

Required:

a. Calculate ROI for 2020. Round your percentage answer to two decimal places.
b. Calculate ROE for 2020. Round your percentage answer to one decimal place.
c. Calculate working capital at December 31, 2020.
d. Calculate the current ratio at December 31, 2020. Round your answer to two decimal places.
e. Calculate the acid-test ratio at December 31, 2020. Round your answer to two decimal places.
f. Assume that on December 31, 2020, the treasurer of Hames decided to pay $50,000 of accounts payable. Explain what impact, if any, this payment will have on the answers you calculated for parts a–d (increase, decrease, or no effect).
g. Assume that instead of paying $50,000 of accounts payable on December 31, 2020, Hames collected $50,000 of accounts receivable. Explain what impact, if any, this receipt will have on the answers you calculated for parts a–d (increase, decrease, or no effect).

Calculate and analyze liquidity measures Following are the current asset and current liability sections of the balance sheets for Freedom Inc. at January 31, 2020 and 2019 (in millions):

Problem 3.19
LO 6

	January 31, 2020	January 31, 2019
Current Assets		
Cash	$15	$ 6
Accounts receivable	9	14
Inventories	18	24
Total current assets	$42	$44
Current Liabilities		
Note payable	$ 9	$ 9
Accounts payable	15	5
Other accrued liabilities	6	6
Total current liabilities	$30	$20

Required:

a. Calculate the working capital and current ratio at each balance sheet date. Round your current ratio answers to one decimal place.
b. Evaluate the firm's liquidity at each balance sheet date.
c. Assume that the firm operated at a loss during the year ended January 31, 2020. How could cash have increased during the year?

Calculate and analyze liquidity measures Following are the current asset and current liability sections of the balance sheets for Aroundsquare Inc. at August 31, 2020 and 2019 (in millions):

Problem 3.20
LO 6

	August 31, 2020	August 31, 2019
Current Assets		
Cash	$51	$12
Marketable securities	72	34
Accounts receivable	35	58
Inventories	94	169
Total current assets	$252	$273
Current Liabilities		
Note payable	$ 70	$ 59
Accounts payable	62	40
Other accrued liabilities	48	31
Total current liabilities	$180	$130

Required:

a. Calculate the working capital and current ratio at each balance sheet date. Round your current ratio answers to one decimal place.
b. Describe the change in the firm's liquidity from 2019 to 2020.

Problem 3.21

LO 3

Applications of ROI using the DuPont model; manufacturing versus service firm Mindspin Labs Inc. is a manufacturing firm that has experienced strong competition in its traditional business. Management is considering joining the trend to the "service economy" by eliminating its manufacturing operations and concentrating on providing specialized maintenance services to other manufacturers. Management of Mindspin Labs has had a target ROI of 18% on an asset base that has averaged $7 million. To achieve this ROI, average total asset turnover of 3.0 was required. If the company shifts its operations from manufacturing to providing maintenance services, it is estimated that average total assets will decrease to $2 million.

Required:

a. Calculate net income, margin, and sales required for Mindspin Labs to achieve its target ROI as a manufacturing firm.
b. Assume that the average margin of maintenance service firms is 2.5%, and that the average ROI for such firms is also 18%. Calculate the net income, sales, and total asset turnover that Mindspin Labs will have if the change to services is made and the firm is able to earn an average margin and achieve an 18% ROI.

Problem 3.22

LO 3

ROI analysis using the DuPont model Charlie's Furniture Store has been in business for several years. The firm's owners have described the store as a "high-price, high-service" operation that provides lots of assistance to its customers. Margin has averaged a relatively high 40% per year for several years, but turnover has been a relatively low 0.6 based on average total assets of $3,000,000. A discount furniture store is about to open in the area served by Charlie's, and management is considering lowering prices to compete effectively.

Required:

a. Calculate current sales and ROI for Charlie's Furniture Store.

b. Assuming that the new strategy would reduce margin to 30%, and assuming that average total assets would stay the same, calculate the sales that would be required to have the same ROI as Charlie's currently earns.

c. Suppose you presented the results of your analysis in parts **a** and **b** of this problem to Charlie, and he replied, "What are you telling me? If I reduce my prices as planned, then I have to increase my sales volume by 50% to earn the same return?" Given the results of your analysis, how would you react to Charlie?

d. Now suppose Charlie says, "You know, I'm not convinced that lowering prices is my only option in staying competitive. What if I were to increase my marketing effort? I'm thinking about kicking off a new advertising campaign after conducting more extensive market research to better identify who my target customer groups are." In general, explain to Charlie what the likely impact of a successful strategy of this nature would be on margin, turnover, and ROI.

e. Think of an alternative strategy that might help Charlie maintain the competitiveness of his business. Explain the strategy, and then describe the likely impact of this strategy on margin, turnover, and ROI.

Cases

All applicable Cases are available in *Connect*.

Focus company—analysis of liquidity and profitability measures In Exercise 1-1, you were asked to obtain a recent annual report of a company that you were interested in reviewing throughout this term.

Case 3.23
LO 3, 4, 6, 7

Required:

a. Please locate the five-year (or longer) selected financial data (usually in the management discussion and analysis section of the annual report), or use your focus company's income statement and balance sheet data to calculate as many of the following ratios and results as possible:

1. Working capital	4. Turnover
2. Current ratio	5. ROI
3. Margin	6. ROE

b. Briefly describe your perception of your focus company's liquidity and profitability based on your calculation and review of these ratios and results.

Analysis of liquidity and profitability measures of Apple Inc. The following summarized data (amounts in millions) are taken from the September 30, 2017, and September 24, 2016, comparative financial statements of Apple Inc., a company that designs, manufactures, and markets mobile communication and media devices and personal computers; sells a variety of related software, services, accessories, networking solutions, and offers third-party digital content and applications:

Case 3.24
LO 3, 4, 6, 7

(Amounts Expressed in Millions) For the Fiscal Years Ended September 30 and September 24, respectively:	2017	2016
Net sales	$229,234	$215,639
Costs of sales	114,048	131,376
Operating income	61,344	60,024
Net income	$ 48,351	$ 45,687
At Year End:		
Assets		
Current assets:		
Cash and cash equivalents	$ 20,289	$ 20,484
Short-term marketable securities	53,892	46,671
Accounts receivable, less allowances of $58 and		
$53, respectively	17,874	15,754
Inventories	4,855	2,132
Vendor nontrade receivables	17,799	13,545
Other current assets	13,936	8,283
Total current assets	128,645	106,869
Long-term marketable securities	194,714	170,430
Property, plant, and equipment, net	33,783	27,010
Goodwill	5,717	5,414
Acquired intangible assets, net	2,298	3,206
Other assets	10,162	8,757
Total assets	$375,319	$321,686
Liabilities and Shareholders' Equity		
Current liabilities:		
Accounts payable	$ 49,049	$ 37,294
Accrued expenses	25,744	22,027
Deferred revenue	7,548	8,080
Commercial paper	11,977	8,105
Current portion of long-term debt	6,496	3,500
Total current liabilities	100,814	79,006
Deferred revenue—noncurrent	2,836	2,930
Long-term debt	97,207	75,427
Other noncurrent liabilities	40,415	36,074
Total liabilities	241,272	193,437
Shareholders' equity:		

Common stock and additional paid-in capital, $0.00001 par value:
  12,600,000 shares authorized; 5,126,201 and 5,336,166 shares
  issued and outstanding, respectively
	35,867	31,251

Retained earnings	98,330	96,364
Accumulated other comprehensive income (loss)	(150)	634
Total shareholders' equity	134,047	128,249
Total liabilities and shareholders' equity	$375,319	$321,686

At September 26, 2015, total assets were $290,345 and total shareholders' equity was $119,355.

Required:

a.   Calculate Apple Inc.'s working capital, current ratio, and acid-test ratio at September 30, 2017, and September 24, 2016. Round your ratio answers to two decimal places.

b.   Calculate Apple's ROE for the years ended September 30, 2017, and September 24, 2016. Round your percentage answers to one decimal place.

c. Calculate Apple's ROI, showing margin and turnover, for the years ended September 30, 2017, and September 24, 2016. Round your turnover calculations to two decimal places. Round your margin and ROI percentages to one decimal place.

d. Evaluate the company's overall liquidity and profitability.

Optional continuation of Case 3.24—trend analysis

The following historical data were derived from Apple Inc.'s consolidated financial statements (in millions):

Note: Past data are not necessarily indicative of the results of future operations.

	2017	2016	2015	2014	2013
Net sales	$229,234	$215,639	$233,715	$182,795	$170,910
Net income	48,351	45,687	53,394	39,510	37,037
Cash, cash equivalents, and marketable securities	268,895	237,585	205,666	155,239	146,761
Total assets	375,319	321,686	290,345	231,839	207,000
Total term debt*	103,703	78,927	55,829	28,987	16,960
Other long-term obligations** ...	40,415	36,074	33,427	24,826	20,208
Total shareholders' equity	134,047	128,249	119,355	111,547	123,549

* Includes current and long-term portions of term debt.

**Excludes noncurrent deferred revenue.

e. Calculate Apple Inc.'s total liabilities for each year presented above.

f. Are the trends expressed in these data generally consistent with each other?

g. In your opinion, which of these trends would be most meaningful to a potential investor in common stock of Apple Inc.? Which trend would be least meaningful?

h. What other data (trend or otherwise) would you like to have access to before making an investment in Apple Inc.?

1. It means that almost everything is relative, so comparison of an individual firm's ratio results to the industry trends is important when making judgments about performance.

2. It means that the economic outcome (the amount of return) is related to the input (the investment) utilized to produce the return.

3. It means that investors and others can evaluate the economic performance of a firm, and make comparisons between firms, by using this ratio.

4. It means that a better understanding of ROI is achieved by knowing about the profitability from sales (margin) and the efficiency with which assets have been used (turnover) to generate sales.

5. It means that the focus is changed from return on total assets to return on the portion of total assets (sometimes referred to as capital) provided by the stockholders of the firm.

6. It means that the firm has enough cash, or is likely to soon collect enough cash, to pay its liabilities that are now, or soon will be, due for payment.

ANSWERS TO
What Does It Mean?

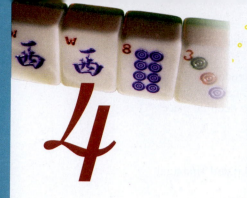

4

The Bookkeeping Process and Transaction Analysis

To understand how different transactions affect the financial statements and, in turn, make sense of the information in the financial statements, it is necessary to understand the mechanical operation of the bookkeeping process. The principal objectives of this chapter are to explain this mechanical process and to introduce a method of analyzing the effects of a transaction on the financial statements.

LEARNING OBJECTIVES (LO)

After studying this chapter, you should understand and be able to

LO 4-1   Illustrate the expansion of the basic accounting equation to include revenues and expenses.

LO 4-2   Describe how the expanded accounting equation stays in balance after every transaction.

LO 4-3   Describe how the income statement is linked to the balance sheet through stockholders' equity.

LO 4-4   Explain the meaning of the bookkeeping terms *journal, ledger, T-account, account balance, debit, credit,* and *closing the books.*

LO 4-5   Explain why the bookkeeping system is a mechanical adaptation of the expanded accounting equation.

LO 4-6   Analyze a transaction, prepare a journal entry, and determine the effects of the transaction on the financial statements.

LO 4-7   Apply the five questions of transaction analysis.

The Bookkeeping/Accounting Process

The bookkeeping/accounting process begins with **transactions** (economic inter-changes between entities that are accounted for and reflected in financial statements) and culminates in the financial statements. This flow was illustrated in Chapter 2 as follows:

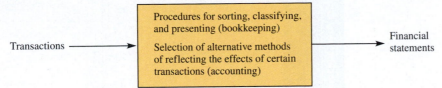

This chapter presents an overview of bookkeeping procedures. Your objective is not to become a bookkeeper but to learn enough about the mechanical process of bookkeeping so you will be able to determine the effects of any transaction on the financial statements. This ability is crucial to the process of making decisions and informed judgments from the financial statements. Bookkeepers (and accountants) use some special terms to describe the bookkeeping process, and you will have to learn these terms. When you understand the language of bookkeeping, you will see that the process is quite straightforward.

The Balance Sheet Equation—A Mechanical Key

You now know that the balance sheet equation expresses the equality between an enti-ty's assets and the claims to those assets:

$$Assets = Liabilities + Stockholders' \ equity$$

For present illustration purposes, let us consider a firm without liabilities. What do you suppose happens to the amounts in the equation if the entity operates at a profit? Assets (perhaps cash) increase, and if the equation is to balance (and it must), then clearly stockholders' equity must also increase. Yes, profits increase stockholders' equity, and to keep the equation in balance, assets will increase and/or liabilities will decrease. Every financial transaction that is accounted for will cause a change somewhere in the balance sheet equation, and the equation will remain in balance after every transaction.

You have already seen that a firm's net income (profit) or loss is the difference between the revenues and expenses reported on its income statement (Exhibit 2-2). Likewise, you have seen that net income from the income statement is reported as one of the factors causing a change in the retained earnings part of the statement of changes in stockholders' equity (Exhibit 2-3). The other principal element of stock-holders' equity is the amount of capital invested by the owners/stockholders—that is, the paid-in capital of Exhibit 2-3. Given these components of stockholders' equity, it is possible to modify the basic balance sheet equation as follows:

LO 1

Illustrate the expansion of the basic accounting equation to include revenues and expenses.

$$Assets = Liabilities + Stockholders' \ equity$$
$$Assets = Liabilities + Paid\text{-}in \ capital + Retained \ earnings$$
$$Assets = Liabilities + Paid\text{-}in \ capital + \begin{matrix} Retained \\ earnings \\ (beginning \\ of \ period) \end{matrix} + \begin{matrix} Revenues \\ (during \ the \\ period) \end{matrix} - \begin{matrix} Expenses \\ (during \ the \\ period) \end{matrix}$$

To illustrate the operation of this equation and the effect of several transactions, study how the following transactions are reflected in Exhibit 4-1. Note that in the

Exhibit 4-1 Transaction Summary (in thousands)

| | Assets | | | | = | Liabilities | | | + | Stockholders' Equity | | |
	Cash +	Accounts Receivable +	Merchandise Inventory +	Equipment =	=	Notes Payable +	Accounts Payable +	Paid-In Capital +		Retained Earnings +	Revenue −	Expenses
Transaction												
1.	+30							+30				
2.	−25			+25								
3.	+15					+15						
4.	−10		+20				+10					
5.	+2	+5		−7								
6.	+5	−5										
Total	17 +	0 +	20 +	18	=	15 +	10 +	30				
7. Revenues		+20									+20	
7. Expenses			−12									−12
8.							+3					−3
Total	17 +	20 +	8 +	18	=	15 +	13 +	30		+5	+20	−15

exhibit, some specific assets and liabilities have been identified within those general categories, and a column has been established for each. All dollar amounts are expressed in thousands.

Transactions

1. Investors organized the firm and invested $30, thus becoming the initial group of stockholders. (In this example, the broad category *Paid-In Capital* is used rather than *Common Stock* and, possibly, *Additional Paid-In Capital.* There isn't any beginning balance in Retained Earnings because the firm is just getting started.)
2. Equipment costing $25 was purchased for cash.
3. The firm borrowed $15 from a bank.
4. Merchandise costing $20 was purchased for inventory; $10 cash was paid, and $10 of the cost was charged on account.
5. Equipment that cost $7 was sold for $7; $2 was received in cash, and $5 will be received later.
6. The $5 account receivable from the sale of equipment was collected.

Each column of the exhibit has been totaled after transaction 6. Does the total of all the asset columns equal the total of all the liability and stockholders' equity columns? (They'd better be equal!)

The firm hasn't had any revenue or expense transactions yet, and it's hard to make a profit without them, so the transactions continue:

7. The firm sold merchandise inventory that had cost $12 for a selling price of $20; the sale was made **on account** (i.e., on credit), and the customer will pay later. Notice that in Exhibit 4-1, this transaction is shown on two lines; one reflects the revenue of $20 and the other reflects the expense, or cost of the merchandise sold, of $12.
8. Wages of $3 earned by the firm's employees are accrued. This means that the expense is recorded even though it has not yet been paid. The wages have been earned by employees (the expense has been incurred) and are owed but have not yet been paid; they will be paid in the next accounting period. The accrual is made in this period so that revenues and expenses of the current period will be matched (the matching concept), and net income will reflect the economic results of this period's activities.

Again, each column of the exhibit has been totaled, and the total of all the asset columns equals the total of all the liability and stockholders' equity columns. If the accounting period were to end after transaction 8, the income statement would report net income of $5, and the balance sheet would show total stockholders' equity of $35. Simplified financial statements for Exhibit 4-1 data after transaction 8 are presented in Exhibit 4-2.

LO 2
Describe how the expanded accounting equation stays in balance after every transaction.

---

1. What does it mean to determine "what kind of account" an account is?

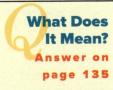

What Does It Mean?

Answer on page 135

Exhibit 4-2

Financial Statements
for Exhibit 4-1 Data
(in thousands)

Exhibit 4-1 Data Income Statement for Transactions 1 through 8		Exhibit 4-1 Data Statement of Changes in Retained Earnings	
Revenues	$20	Beginning balance	$ 0
Expenses	(15)	Net income	5
		Dividends	(0)
Net income	$ 5	Ending balance	$ 5

Exhibit 4-1 Data Balance Sheet after Transaction (8)			
Assets		**Liabilities**	
Cash	$17	Notes payable	$15
Accounts receivable	20	Accounts payable	13
Merchandise inventory	8	Total liabilities	$28
Total current assets	$45	**Stockholders' Equity**	
Equipment	18	Paid-in capital	$30
		Retained earnings	5
		Total stockholders' equity	$35
		Total liabilities and stockholders'	
Total assets	$63	equity	$63

LO 3

Describe how the
income statement is
linked to the balance
sheet through stock-
holders' equity.

Notice especially in Exhibit 4-2 how net income on the income statement gets into the balance sheet via the retained earnings section of stockholders' equity. In the equation of Exhibit 4-1, revenues and expenses were treated as a part of stockholders' equity to keep the equation in balance. For financial reporting purposes, however, revenues and expenses are shown in the income statement. In order to have the balance sheet balance, it is necessary that net income be reflected in the balance sheet, and this is done in retained earnings. If any retained earnings are distributed to the stockholders as a dividend, the dividend does not show on the income statement but is a deduction from retained earnings, shown in the statement of changes in retained earnings. This is so because a dividend is not an expense (it is not incurred in the process of generating revenue). A *dividend* is a distribution of earnings to the stockholders of the firm.

What you have just learned is the essence of the bookkeeping process. Transactions are analyzed to determine which asset, liability, or stockholders' equity category is affected and how each is affected. The amount of the effect is recorded, the amounts are totaled, and financial statements are prepared.

Bookkeeping Jargon and Procedures

LO 4

Explain the meaning
of the bookkeeping
terms *journal, ledger,*
T-account, account
balance, debit, credit,
and *closing the books.*

Because of the complexity of most business operations, and the frequent need to refer to past transactions, a bookkeeping system has evolved to facilitate the record-keeping process. Nearly all bookkeeping systems are now computerized, although manual systems still exist for some small businesses; the general features of each are virtually the same.

Transactions are initially recorded in a **journal.** A journal (derived from the French word *jour,* meaning *day*) is a day-by-day, or chronological, record of transactions. Transactions are then recorded in—**posted** to—a **ledger.** The ledger serves the

Bookkeeping Language in Everyday English

Always remember that in bookkeeping and accounting, *debit* and *credit* mean left and right, respectively, and nothing more. Debit means left. Credit means right. That's it; there is nothing more to it. Yet, many bookkeeping and accounting terms have found their way into the language, especially in the business context. *Debit* and *credit* are no exceptions to this, and some brief examples may stress the left–right definition.

The terms *debit* and *credit* are used by banks to describe additions to or subtractions from an individual's checking account. For example, your account is credited for interest earned and is debited for a service charge or for the cost of checks that are furnished to you. From the bank's perspective, your account is a liability; the bank owes you the balance in your account. Interest earned by your account increases that liability of the bank; hence, the interest is credited to your account. Service charges reduce your claim on the bank—its liability to you—so those transactions are referred to as debits from the bank's perspective. Perhaps because of these effects on a checking or savings account balance, many people think that *debit* is a synonym for *bad* (you now have less money in your account) and that *credit* means *good* (your account balance has increased). In certain contexts, these synonyms may be appropriate, but they do not apply in accounting. In fact, if you, as the account holder, were to describe these same transactions from your perspective, the opposite would be true. You would say that your account (which is an asset since it represents cash in the bank) was debited (it increased) by the amount of interest earned. Likewise, you would record the service charges as a credit (decrease) to your account when doing your own bookkeeping.

As another example, a synonym for *debit* that is used in accounting is the term *charge*. To **charge** an account is to make a debit entry to the account. This usage carries over from the terminology used when merchandise or services were purchased on credit from local merchants who personally knew and trusted their customers. Such customers would receive the goods or services now and make their payments later. This arrangement is frequently called a *charge account* because from the seller's perspective, an asset (accounts receivable) is increasing as a result of the transaction, and assets increase with a debit entry.

As a final example, the fact that a credit card is used as a form of payment to a merchant and that such a transaction is called a *credit transaction* refers to the increase in the purchaser's liability to the credit card company.

The key point of learning is of course that the terms debit and credit have simple meanings (left and right, respectively). The way in which many business transactions have been described historically is a reflection of perspective and language usage, but does not change this fundamental rule.

function of Exhibit 4-1, but rather than having a large sheet with a column for each asset, liability, and stockholders' equity category, there is an account for each category. In a manual bookkeeping system, each account is a separate page in a book, much like a loose-leaf binder. Accounts are arranged in a sequence to facilitate the posting process. Usually the sequence is assets, liabilities, stockholders' equity, revenues, and expenses. A **chart of accounts** serves as an index to the ledger, and each account is numbered to facilitate the frequent written references that are made to it.

The account format that has been used for several hundred years looks like a "T." (In the nearby illustration, notice the T under the captions for Assets, Liabilities, and Stockholders' Equity.) On one side of the T, additions to the account are recorded, and on the other side of the T, subtractions are recorded. The **account balance** at any point in time is the arithmetic difference between the prior balance and the additions and subtractions. This is the same as in Exhibit 4-1, where the account balance shown after transactions 6 and 8 is the sum of the prior balance, plus the additions, minus the subtractions.

To facilitate making reference to account entries and **balances** (and to confuse neophytes), the left side of a **T-account** is called the *debit* side, and the right side of a T-account is called the *credit* side. In bookkeeping and accounting, **debit** and **credit** mean left and right, respectively, and nothing more (see Business in Practice—Bookkeeping Language in Everyday English). A record of a transaction involving a posting to the left side of an account is called a *debit entry.* An account that has a balance on its right side is said to have a *credit balance.*

LO 5

Explain why the bookkeeping system is a mechanical adaptation of the expanded accounting equation.

The beauty of the bookkeeping system is that debit and credit entries to accounts, and account balances, are set up so that if debits equal credits, the balance sheet equation will remain in balance. The key to this is that asset accounts will normally have a debit balance: Increases in assets are recorded as debit entries to these accounts, and decreases in assets are recorded as credit entries to these accounts. For liabilities and stockholders' equity accounts, the opposite will be true:

Assets			Liabilities			Stockholders' Equity	
Debit Increases + Normal balance	*Credit* Decreases −	=	*Debit* Decreases −	*Credit* Increases + Normal balance	+	*Debit* Decreases −	*Credit* Increases + Normal balance

It is no coincidence that the debit and credit system of normal balances coincides with the balance sheet presentation illustrated earlier. In fact, most of the balance sheets illustrated so far have been presented in what is known as the *account format.* An alternative approach is to use the *report format,* in which assets are shown above liabilities and stockholders' equity.

Entries to revenue and expense accounts follow a pattern that is consistent with entries to other stockholders' equity accounts. Revenues are increases in stockholders' equity, so revenue accounts normally will have a credit balance and will increase with credit entries. Expenses are decreases in stockholders' equity, so expense accounts normally will have a debit balance and will increase with debit entries. Gains and losses are recorded like revenues and expenses, respectively.

The debit or credit behavior of accounts for assets, liabilities, stockholders' equity, revenues, and expenses is summarized in the following illustration:

Account Name	
Debit side	*Credit* side
Normal balance for:	Normal balance for:
Assets	Liabilities
Expenses	Stockholders' equity
	Revenues
Debit entries increase:	Credit entries increase:
Assets	Liabilities
Expenses	Stockholders' equity
	Revenues
Debit entries decrease:	Credit entries decrease:
Liabilities	Assets
Stockholders' equity	Expenses
Revenues	

Referring to the transactions that were illustrated in Exhibit 4-1, a bookkeeper would say that in transaction 1, which was the investment of $30 in the firm by the stockholders, Cash was debited—it increased—and Paid-In Capital was credited, each for $30. Transaction 2, the purchase of equipment for $25 cash, would be described as a $25 debit to Equipment and a $25 credit to Cash. Pretend that you are a bookkeeper and describe the remaining transactions of that illustration.

The bookkeeper would say, after transaction 8 has been recorded, that the Cash account has a debit balance of $17, the Notes Payable account has a credit balance of $15, and the Expense account has a debit balance of $15. (There was only one expense account in the example; usually there will be a separate account for each category of expense and each category of revenue.) What kind of balances (debit or credit) do the other accounts have after transaction 8?

The journal was identified earlier as the chronological record of the firm's transactions. The journal is also the place where transactions are first recorded, and it is sometimes referred to as the *book of original entry*. The **journal entry** format is a useful and convenient way of describing the effect of a transaction on the accounts involved, and will be used in subsequent chapters of this text, so it is introduced now and is worth learning now.

The general format of the journal entry is:

Date	Dr. Account Name	Amount	
	Cr. Account Name		Amount

Notice these characteristics of the journal entry:

- The date is recorded to provide a cross-reference to the transaction. In many of our textbook examples, however, a transaction number will be used instead of a date to provide this same cross-referencing function.
- The name (or names) of the account(s) to be debited are always listed first and shown to the left, while the name (or names) of the account(s) to be credited are indented and shown to the right. Likewise the debit amount(s) are shown to the left of the credit amount(s). Remember, debit means *left* and credit means *right*.
- The abbreviations *Dr.* and *Cr.* are used for debit and credit, respectively. These identifiers are frequently omitted from the journal entry to reduce writing time and because the indenting practice is universally followed and understood.

As alluded to earlier, it is possible for a journal entry to have more than one debit account and amount and/or more than one credit account and amount. The only requirement of a journal entry is that the total of the debit amounts equal the total of the credit amounts. Frequently, there will be a brief explanation of the transaction beneath the journal entry, especially if the **entry** is not self-explanatory.

The journal entry for transaction 1 of Exhibit 4-1 would appear as follows:

(1)	Dr. Cash	30	
	Cr. Paid-In Capital		30
	To record an investment in the firm by the stockholders.		

Technically, the journal entry procedure illustrated here is a *general journal entry*. Most bookkeeping systems also use specialized journals, but they are still books of original entry, recording transactions chronologically, involving various accounts, and resulting in entries in which debits equal credits. If you understand the basic general journal entry just illustrated, you will be able to understand a specialized journal if you ever see one.

Transactions generate **source documents,** such as an invoice from a supplier, a copy of a credit purchase made by a customer, a check stub, or a tape printout of the totals from a cash register's activity for a period. These source documents are the raw materials used in the bookkeeping process and support the journal entry.

The following flowchart illustrates the bookkeeping process that we have explored:

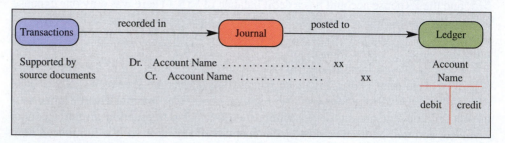

Although information systems technology has made it financially feasible for virtually all businesses to automate their accounting functions (see Business in Practice—Accounting Information Systems and Data Protection), many small firms continue to rely on manual processing techniques. Understanding basic bookkeeping terminology and appreciating how transactions are recorded will help you understand any accounting software you may encounter.

**What Does
It Mean?**
**Answer on
page 135**

2. What does it mean when an account has a debit balance?

3. What does it mean to say that asset and expense accounts normally have debit balances?

4. What does it mean when a liability, stockholders' equity, or revenue account is credited?

Understanding the Effects of Transactions on the Financial Statements

LO 6
Analyze a transaction, prepare a journal entry, and determine the effects of the transaction on the financial statements.

T-accounts and journal entries are models used by accountants to explain and understand the effects of transactions on the financial statements. These models are frequently difficult for a nonaccountant to use because one must know what kind of account (asset, liability, stockholders' equity, revenue, or expense) is involved, where in the financial statements (balance sheet or income statement) the account is found, and how the account is affected by the debit or credit characteristic of the transaction.

An alternative to the T-account and journal entry models that should be useful to you is the horizontal financial statement relationship model first introduced in Chapter 2. The **horizontal model** is as follows:

Balance Sheet	Income Statement
Assets = Liabilities + Stockholders' equity	← Net Income = Revenues − Expenses

The key to using this model is to keep the balance sheet in balance. The arrow from net income in the income statement to stockholders' equity in the balance sheet indicates that net income affects retained earnings, which is a component of stockholders' equity. For a transaction affecting both the balance sheet and income statement, the balance sheet will balance when the income statement effect on stockholders' equity is considered. In this model, the account name is entered under the appropriate financial statement category, and the dollar effect of the transaction on that account is entered with a plus or minus sign below the account name. For example, the journal entry shown earlier, which records the investment of $30 in the firm by the stockholders, would be shown in this horizontal model as follows:

Balance Sheet		Income Statement
Assets = Liabilities + Stockholders' equity		← Net Income = Revenues − Expenses
Cash	Paid-in Capital	
+ 30	+30	

Accounting Information Systems and Data Protection

A variety of accounting software products have been developed, ranging from off-the-shelf systems that support the basic bookkeeping needs of individuals and small businesses (see quickbooks.intuit.com or sage.com/en-us/products/sage-50-accounting/) to full-scale accounting systems designed for businesses with more complex informational needs (see, generally, sage.com or search for "Microsoft Dynamics SL") to customized, comprehensive enterprisewide resource planning systems used by large multinational corporations (see sap.com or oracle.com).

The methodology for evaluating and selecting a system should focus on matching the decision-making requirements of the business across its functional areas (finance, production, marketing, human resources, and information services) with the functionality and scalability of the software. Important elements to consider include the initial investment and ongoing cost, hardware and human resource requirements, system performance expectations, supplier reliability and service levels, and implementation and training procedures in light of the existing accounting system. Many firms use a structured methodology referred to as the *System Life Cycle (SLC)* to identify their organizational needs and system requirements. The SLC includes phases for planning, analysis, design, implementation, and use of the system.

Reviews of accounting system software products appear regularly in computer and accounting periodicals. Product information is available at supplier websites and normally includes downloadable demos. Online review services such as ctsguides.com are also available to provide insight into the functionality, cost, and service levels of various systems.

In any computerized system, transaction information should be entered only once. For an individual, this may be when a check is written. For a business, this may be when an order is placed with a supplier or when an order is received from a customer. Such processes are often automated, as with the bar code scanners used to record sales and inventory transactions at retail stores. By linking business systems electronically, the initial recording of a transaction can be extended from a seller's system to the systems used by its suppliers and/or customers. For example, after a purchase order is entered into the purchasing system, it may also automatically update the supplier's system for the sales transaction.

To be certain, the majority of e-commerce activity today is represented by these business-to-business transactions, and nobody doubts that the Internet economy has dramatically reduced many of the "data-capturing" costs of doing business. Unfortunately, the data security risks associated with doing business in the electronic age are significant and cannot

Business in
Practice

be ignored. Corporate management must learn to prioritize information assets and to safeguard them against the dangers associated with cyberfraud, viruses, computer crime, and breaches of trust by employees. Disaster prevention and recovery plans should be in place and should include access firewalls, intrusion detection systems within the network architecture, audit logs of system usage, timely virus protection updates, and insurance policies that cover hacker invasions. In today's business environment, the integrity of the accounting information system must be carefully protected to ensure that transaction data can be used to develop relevant and reliable information that supports the management planning, control, and decision-making processes.

To further illustrate the model's use, assume a transaction in which the firm paid $12 for advertising. The effect on the financial statements is as follows:

Balance Sheet	Income Statement
Assets = Liabilities + Stockholders' equity	← Net Income = Revenues − Expenses
Cash −12	Advertising Expense −12

The journal entry would be:

Dr. Advertising Expense	12	
Cr. Cash		12

Notice that in the horizontal model, the amount of advertising expense is shown with a minus sign. This is so because the expense reduces net income, which reduces stockholders' equity. A plus or minus sign is used in the context of each financial statement equation (A = L + SE, and NI = R − E). Thus, a minus sign for expenses means that net income is reduced (expenses are greater), not that expenses are lower.

It is possible that a transaction can affect two accounts in a single balance sheet or income statement category. For example, assume a transaction in which a firm collects $40 that was owed to it by a customer for services performed in a prior period. The effect of this transaction is shown as follows:

Balance Sheet	Income Statement
Assets = Liabilities + Stockholders' equity	← Net Income = Revenues − Expenses
Cash +40	
Accounts Receivable −40	

The journal entry would be:

Dr. Cash	40	
Cr. Accounts Receivable		40

It is also possible for a transaction to affect more than two accounts. For example, assume a transaction in which a firm provided $60 worth of services to a client, $45 of which was collected when the services were provided and $15 of which will be collected later. Here is the effect on the financial statements:

Balance Sheet	Income Statement
Assets = Liabilities + Stockholders' equity	← Net Income = Revenues − Expenses
Cash +45 Accounts Receivable +15	Service Revenues +60

The journal entry would be:

Dr. Cash	45	
Dr. Accounts Receivable	15	
Cr. Service Revenues		60

Recall that revenues and expenses from the income statement are increases and decreases, respectively, to stockholders' equity. Thus, the horizontal model and its two financial statement equations can be combined into this single equation:

$$\text{Assets} = \text{Liabilities} + \text{Stockholders' equity} + \text{Revenues} - \text{Expenses}$$

Notice that as the balance sheet equation (Assets = Liabilities + Stockholders' equity) is expanded to include the results of the income statement (Net income = Revenues − Expenses), the model includes each of the five broad categories of accounts. Remember that dividends reduce retained earnings, which is part of the stockholders' equity term. A separate "Dividends" term has not been included in the model because dividends are not considered a separate account *category*. Note that the operational equal sign in the horizontal model is the one between assets and liabilities. You can check that a transaction recorded in the horizontal model keeps the balance sheet in balance by mentally (or actually) putting an equal sign between assets and liabilities as you use the model to record transaction amounts.

Spend some time now becoming familiar with the horizontal model (e.g., by working Exercise 4.5) so it will be easier for you to understand the effects on the financial statements of transactions that you will encounter later in this book and in the "real world." As a financial statement user (in contrast to a financial statement preparer), you will find that the horizontal model is an easily used tool. With practice, you will become proficient at understanding how an amount shown on either the balance sheet or income statement probably affected other parts of the financial statements when it was recorded.

5. What does it mean to say that "the books are in balance"?

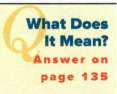

What Does It Mean?
Answer on page 135

Adjustments

After the end of the accounting period, bookkeepers normally have to record an **adjustment** to certain account balances to reflect **accrual** accounting in the financial statements. As discussed in Chapters 1 and 2, accrual accounting recognizes revenues and expenses as they occur, even though the cash receipt from the revenue or the cash disbursement related to the expense may occur before or after the event that causes revenue or expense recognition. Although prepared after the end of the accounting period (when all of the necessary information has been gathered), adjustments are dated and recorded as of the end of the period.

Adjustments result in revenues and expenses being reported in the appropriate fiscal period. For example, revenue may be *earned* in fiscal 2019 from selling a product or providing a service, yet the customer may not pay until fiscal 2020. (Most firms pay for products purchased or services received within a week to a month after receiving the product or service.) It is also likely that some expenses that were *incurred* in fiscal 2019 will not be paid until fiscal 2020. (Utility costs and employee wages are examples.) Remember, however, that revenues are recorded throughout the fiscal period as they are earned and expenses are likewise recorded as they are incurred. The recording of such transactions may take place on a daily, weekly, or monthly basis. As a result, most such transactions will have been recorded in the appropriate fiscal period (2019) but the year-end cutoff for revenue and expense transactions will need to be analyzed to determine whether any adjustments are required for unrecorded transactions as well as over and under-recorded transactions.

It is also possible for a company to receive cash from a customer for a product or service in fiscal 2018, but the product will not be sold or the service provided until fiscal 2019 or beyond. (Subscription fees and insurance premiums are usually received in advance and occasionally for more than one fiscal year in advance.) Likewise, a payment for goods or services may be made in fiscal 2018, but the expense associated with that payment applies instead to fiscal 2019 and possibly later years as well. (Insurance premiums and rent are usually paid in advance.) Note that cash receipt and cash payment transactions are recorded on a daily basis, but the associated revenues and expenses must be matched to the fiscal period(s) in which they were earned or incurred, respectively. Period-end adjustments may be necessary depending on how the initial cash receipt and payment transactions were recorded, relative to how much revenue has been earned (or expense incurred) during the fiscal period in which the cash transaction took place.

These alternative activities are illustrated on the following timeline:

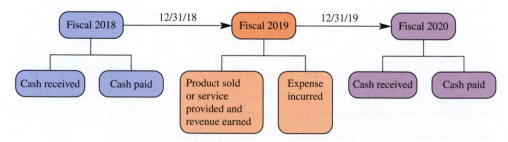

There are two categories of adjustments:

1. *Accruals*—Transactions for which cash has not yet been received or paid, but the effect of which must be recorded in the accounts (at the end of the accounting

period) to accomplish a matching of revenues and expenses and accurate financial statements. In the preceding illustration, if the cash is not expected to be received (or paid) until 2020 but some or all of the associated revenue has been earned (or expense incurred) in 2019, an accrual adjustment would be necessary at the end of 2019 to accurately reflect net income on the accrual basis of accounting. Note that accruals are necessitated by *cash lags* (see Study Suggestion).

2. *Reclassifications*—The initial recording of a transaction, although a true reflection of the transaction at the time, does not result in an appropriate assigning of revenues to the period in which they were earned or expenses to the period in which they were incurred. As a result, an amount must be reclassified from one account to another (at the end of the accounting period) to reflect the appropriate balance in each account. Note that reclassification adjustments are often necessitated by *cash leads* (see Study Suggestion).

The first type of adjustment is illustrated by the accrual of wages expense and wages payable. For example, work performed by employees during March, for which they will be paid in April, results in wages expense to be included in the March income statement and a wages payable liability to be included in the March 31 balance sheet. To illustrate this accrual, assume that employees earned $60 in March that will be paid to them in April. Using the horizontal model, the **accrued** wages adjustment has the following effect on the financial statements:

Balance Sheet	Income Statement
Assets = Liabilities + Stockholders' equity	← Net Income = Revenues − Expenses
Wages Payable +60	Wages Expense −60

Most period-end adjustments are necessitated by the timing differences between when a company receives (or pays) cash versus when the associated revenues are earned (or expenses are incurred).

A *cash lead* occurs when cash is received (or paid) prior to the end of the current fiscal period (2018 in the preceding illustration), but part or all of the associated revenue (or expense) has not yet been earned (or incurred). As such, a reclassification adjustment is required to accurately reflect the revenues earned (or expenses incurred) during the period in which the cash is received (or paid).

A *cash lag* occurs when revenues have been earned (or expenses have been incurred) in a period prior (2019) to when the cash settlement transaction is expected to take place (2020). Cash lags necessitate accrual adjustments at the end of the year in which revenues have been earned but not yet received, or expenses have been incurred but not yet paid.

Understanding when the underlying cash transactions have taken place, or are expected to take place, will help you to know which types of period-end adjustments will be required to reflect the effects of accrual accounting in the financial statements. If the cash transaction has already taken place, then a reclassification will required at period-end; if the cash transaction has not yet taken place, then an accrual will be required at period-end.

Study

Suggestion

The journal entry would be:

Dr. Wages Expense	60	
Cr. Wages Payable		60

Thus, the March 31 balance sheet will reflect the wages payable liability, and the income statement for March will include all of the wages expense incurred during March. Again note that the recognition of the expense of $60 is shown with a minus sign because, as expenses increase, net income and stockholders' equity (retained earnings) decrease. The balance sheet remains in balance after this adjustment because the $60 increase in liabilities is offset by the $60 decrease in stockholders' equity. When the wages are paid in April, both the Cash and Wages Payable accounts will be decreased. (Wages Expense will not be affected by the cash payment entry because it was already affected when the accrual was made.)

Similar adjustments are made to accrue revenues (such as for services performed but not yet billed or for interest earned but not yet received) and to accrue expenses—including various operating expenses, interest expense, and income tax expense—that have been incurred but not yet paid. In each of these examples, there is a cash lag that necessitates the accrual adjustment since revenues/expenses have been earned/incurred in a period prior to the expected receipt/disbursement of cash to settle the transaction.

The effect on the financial statements, using the horizontal model, of accruing $50 of interest revenue that has been earned but not yet received is shown as follows:

Balance Sheet	Income Statement
Assets = Liabilities + Stockholders' equity	← Net Income = Revenues − Expenses
Interest Receivable +50	Interest Revenue +50

The journal entry would be:

Dr. Interest Receivable	50	
Cr. Interest Revenue		50

An example of the second kind of adjustment is the reclassification for supplies. If the purchase of supplies at a cost of $100 during February was initially recorded as an increase in the Supplies (asset) account (and a decrease in Cash), the cost of supplies used during February must be removed from the asset account and recorded as Supplies Expense. Assuming that supplies costing $35 were used during February, the reclassification adjustment would be reflected in the horizontal model as follows:

Balance Sheet	Income Statement
Assets = Liabilities + Stockholders' equity	← Net Income = Revenues − Expenses
Supplies −35	Supplies Expense −35

The journal entry would be:

Dr. Supplies Expense	35	
Cr. Supplies		35

Conversely, if the purchase of supplies during February at a cost of $100 was originally recorded as an increase in Supplies Expense for February, the cost of supplies still on hand at the end of February ($65, if supplies costing $35 were used during February) must be removed from the Supplies Expense account and recorded as an asset. The reclassification adjustment for the $65 of supplies still on hand at the end of February would be reflected in the horizontal model as follows:

Balance Sheet		Income Statement	
Assets = Liabilities + Stockholders' equity		← Net Income = Revenues − Expenses	
Supplies +65			Supplies Expense +65

The journal entry would be:

Dr. Supplies	65	
Cr. Supplies Expense		65

What's going on here? Supplies costing $100 were originally recorded as an expense (a minus 100 in the expense column because more expense means less net income). This was offset by a minus 100 of cash in the asset column, which reflects the cash payment that was made to purchase the supplies. The expense for February should be only $35 because $65 of the supplies are still on hand at the end of February. Thus, the Supplies Expense account balance is adjusted to $35 by showing a plus $65 in the expense column (a reduction in expenses increases net income). The model is kept in balance by increasing Supplies in the asset column by $65.

Adjustments for revenues received in advance (cash received from customers before the service has been performed or the product has been sold) and for prepaid insurance (insurance premiums paid in a fiscal period before the insurance expense has been incurred) are also reclassification types of adjustments. Note that these are examples of cash leads because cash was received or paid in a fiscal period prior to that in which some or all of the associated revenue was earned or expense was incurred.

Generally speaking, every period-end adjustment affects both the income statement and the balance sheet. That is, if one part of the entry—either the debit or the credit—affects the income statement, the other part of the entry affects the balance sheet. The result of adjustments is to make both the income statement for the accounting period and the balance sheet at the end of the accounting period more accurate. After all necessary adjustments are made, all revenues earned during the period are reported, all expenses incurred in generating those revenues are subtracted to arrive at net income, and all asset and liability account balances are appropriately stated. By properly applying the matching concept, the entity's ROI, ROE, and liquidity calculations will likewise be valid measures of the results of operations and financial position.

After the year-end adjustments have been posted to the ledger accounts, final account balances are determined. The financial statements are prepared using the account balance amounts, which usually are summarized to a certain extent. For example, if the company has only one ledger account for cash, the balance in that account is shown on the balance sheet as Cash. If the company has several separate selling expense accounts (e.g., Advertising Expense, Salesforce Travel Expense, and Salesforce Commissions), these account balances are added together to determine the Selling Expense amount shown on the income statement.

This entire process is referred to as **closing the books** and usually takes at least several working days to complete. At the end of the fiscal year for a large, publicly owned company, a period from 4 to 10 weeks may be required to close the books and prepare the financial statements because of the complexities involved, including the annual audit by the firm's public accountants. (See Business in Practice—The Closing Process.)

It should be clear that the bookkeeping process itself is procedural and that the same kinds of activities are repeated each fiscal period in a systematic and consistently followed sequence. These procedures and the sequence are system characteristics that make mechanization and computerization feasible. Mechanical bookkeeping system aids were developed many years ago. Today, many computer programs use transaction data as input and with minimal operator intervention complete the bookkeeping procedures and prepare financial statements. Accounting knowledge and judgment are as necessary as ever, however, to ensure that transactions are initially recorded in an appropriate manner, required adjustments are made, and the output of the computer processing is sensible.

What Does It Mean?

Answer on page 136

6. What does it mean when a revenue or expense must be accrued?
7. What does it mean when an adjustment must be made?

Transaction Analysis Methodology

LO 7

Apply the five questions of transaction analysis.

The key to being able to understand the effect of any transaction on the financial statements is having the ability to analyze the transaction. **Transaction analysis methodology** involves answering five questions:

1. What's going on?
2. What accounts are affected?

3. How are they affected?
4. Does the balance sheet balance? (Do the debits equal the credits?)
5. Does my analysis make sense?

1. *What's going on?* To analyze any transaction, it is necessary to understand the transaction—that is, to understand the activity that is taking place between the entity for which the accounting is being done and the other entity involved in the transaction. This is why most elementary accounting texts, including this one, explain many business practices. It is impossible to understand the effect of a transaction on the financial statements if the basic activity being accounted for is not understood.

2. *What accounts are affected?* This question is frequently answered by the answer to "What's going on?" because the specific account names are often included in that explanation. This question may be answered by a process of elimination. First think about whether one of the accounts is an asset, liability, stockholders' equity, revenue, or expense; then apply that same logic to the other account(s) involved in the transaction. From the broad categories identified, it is usually possible to identify the specific accounts affected.

3. *How are they affected?* Answer this question with the word *increasing* or *decreasing,* and then, if you are using the journal entry or T-account model, translate to *debit* or *credit.* Accountants learn to think directly in debit and credit terms after much more practice than you probably have at this point. Note that you can avoid the debit/credit issue by using the horizontal model.

4. *Does the balance sheet balance?* If the horizontal model is being used, it is possible to determine easily that the balance sheet equation is in balance by observing the arithmetic sign and the amounts involved in the transaction. Remember that the operational equal sign in the model is between assets and liabilities. Alternatively, the journal entry for the transaction can be written, or T-accounts can be sketched, and the equality of the debits and credits can be verified. You know by now that if the balance sheet equation is not in balance, or if the debits do not equal the credits, your analysis of the transaction is wrong!

5. *Does my analysis make sense?* This is the most important question, and it involves standing back from the trees to look at the forest. You must determine whether the horizontal model effects or the journal entry that results from your analysis causes changes in account balances and the financial statements that are consistent with your understanding of what's going on. If the analysis doesn't make sense to you, go back to question number 1 and start again.

The Closing Process

From a business perspective, the closing process allows a firm to complete one accounting year and begin another. After the year-end financial statements have been prepared, managers and financial analysts can evaluate the firm's relative profitability, liquidity, or other measures in relation to key competitors, industry performance measures, or the firm's own financial past.

From a bookkeeping perspective, the closing process simply *transfers* the year-end balances of all income statement accounts (revenues, expenses, gains, and losses that have accumulated during the year) to the retained earnings account, which is part of stockholders' equity on the balance sheet. In addition, if any dividends declared during the year were accumulated in a separate "dividends" account, the balance in that account would also be closed to retained earnings.

Business in
Practice

This is nothing new! The following diagram, with slight modifications from the version presented in Chapter 2, illustrates the *articulation* between the income statement for the year and the balance sheet at the end of the year:

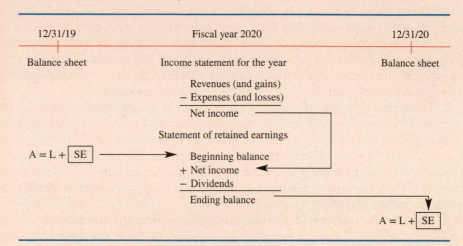

How is the closing process accomplished? Mechanically, the credit balances in all revenue and gain accounts must be reduced to zero by *debiting* each of these accounts for amounts equal to their respective year-end adjusted balances. Conversely, the debit balances in all expense and loss accounts, as well as dividends, are eliminated by *crediting* each of these accounts to close out their year-end adjusted balances. The difference between net income earned and dividends declared during the year goes to retained earnings—it's that simple:

Remember, you are not learning transaction analysis to become an expert in bookkeeping, but to better understand how the amounts reported on financial statements got there, which in turn will improve your ability to make decisions and informed judgments from those statements. Application of this five-question transaction analysis routine is illustrated in Exhibit 4-3.

Transaction analysis methodology and knowledge about the arithmetic operation of a T-account can be used to understand the activity that is recorded in an account.

Exhibit 4-3

Transaction Analysis

Situation:
On September 1, 2019, Cruisers Inc. borrowed $2,500 from its bank; a note was signed providing that the loan principal, plus interest, was to be repaid in 10 months.

Required:
Analyze the transaction and prepare a journal entry, or use the horizontal model, to record the transaction.

Solution:
Analysis of transaction:
What's going on? The firm signed a note at the bank and is receiving cash from the bank.
What accounts are affected? Notes Payable (a liability) and Cash (an asset).
How are they affected? Notes Payable is increasing and Cash is increasing.
Does the balance sheet balance? Using the horizontal model, the effect of the loan transaction on the financial statements is as follows:

Balance Sheet	Income Statement
Assets = Liabilities + Stockholders' equity	← Net Income = Revenues − Expenses
Cash Notes Payable +2,500 +2,500	

Yes, the balance sheet does balance; assets and liabilities each increased by $2,500. The journal entry for this transaction, in which debits equal credits, is as follows:

Sept. 1, 2019	Dr. Cash	2,500	
	Cr. Notes Payable		2,500
	Bank loan received.		

Does my analysis make sense? Yes, because a balance sheet prepared immediately after this transaction will show an increased amount of cash and the liability to the bank. The interest associated with the loan is not reflected in this entry because at this point Cruisers Inc. has not incurred any interest expense, nor does the firm owe any interest; if the loan were to be immediately repaid, there would not be any interest due to the bank. Interest expense and the liability for the interest payable will be recorded as adjustments over the life of the loan.

To get a preview of things to come, let's look at how the interest would be accrued each month (the expense has been incurred, but the liability has not yet been paid) and at how the ultimate repayment of the loan and accrued interest would be recorded. Assume that the interest rate on the note is 12% (remember, an interest rate is an annual rate unless otherwise specified). Interest expense for one month would be calculated as follows:

$$\text{Annual interest} = \text{Principal} \times \text{Annual rate} \times \text{Time (in years)}$$
$$\text{Monthly interest} = \text{Principal} \times \text{Annual rate} \times \text{Time}/12$$
$$= \$2{,}500 \times 0.12 \times 1/12$$
$$= \$25$$

It is appropriate that the monthly financial statements of Cruisers Inc. reflect accurately the firm's interest expense for the month and its interest payable liability at the end of the month. To achieve this accuracy, an adjustment would need to be made at the end of every month of the 10-month life of the note. The effects of each of the monthly adjustments would be as shown here:

(continued)

Exhibit 4-3 *continued*

Balance Sheet	Income Statement
Assets = Liabilities + Stockholders' equity	← Net Income = Revenues − Expenses
Interest Payable +25	Interest Expense −25

Remember, a minus sign for expenses means that net income is reduced as expenses are increased, not that expenses are reduced.

Here is the entry to record this monthly adjustment:

At month-end (each month)	Dr. Interest Expense	25	
	Cr. Interest Payable		25
	To accrue monthly interest on bank loan.		

As explained earlier, if the two financial statement equations are combined into the single equation

$$\text{Assets} = \text{Liabilities} + \text{Stockholders' equity} + \text{Revenues} - \text{Expenses}$$

the equation's balance will be preserved after each transaction or adjustment.

At the end of the 10th month, when the loan and accrued interest are paid, the following effects on the financial statements occur:

Balance Sheet	Income Statement
Assets = Liabilities + Stockholders' equity	← Net Income = Revenues − Expenses
Cash Notes Payable −2,750 −2,500	
Interest Payable −250	

The entry to record this transaction is as follows:

June 30, 2020	Dr. Notes Payable	2,500	
	Dr. Interest Payable	250	
	Cr. Cash		2,750
	Payment of bank loan and accrued interest.		

Apply the five questions of transaction analysis to both the monthly interest expense/interest payable accrual and to the payment. Also think about the effect of each of these entries on the financial statements. What is happening to net income each month? What has happened to net income for the 10 months?

For example, assume that the Interest Receivable account shows the following activity for a month:

Interest Receivable			
Beginning balance	2,400		
		Transactions	1,700
Month-end adjustment	1,300		
Ending balance	2,000		

What transactions caused the credit to this account? Recall that a credit to an asset account represents a reduction in the account balance; thus, the question can be rephrased as "What transaction would cause Interest Receivable to decrease?" The answer: Receipt of cash from entities that owed this firm interest. What is the month-end adjustment that caused the debit to this account? The rephrased question is "What causes Interest Receivable to increase?" The answer: Accrual of interest revenue that was earned this month but not yet received.

Using the horizontal model, the financial statement effects of this transaction and adjustment are as follows:

Balance Sheet	Income Statement
Assets = Liabilities + Stockholders' equity	← Net Income = Revenues – Expenses
Transaction: Cash +1,700 Interest Receivable −1,700 *Adjustment:* Interest Receivable +1,300	 Interest Revenue +1,300

Here are the journal entries to record this transaction and adjustment:

Dr. Cash	1,700	
Cr. Interest Receivable		1,700
Dr. Interest Receivable	1,300	
Cr. Interest Revenue		1,300

The T-account format is a useful way of visualizing the effect of transactions and adjustments on the account balance. In addition, because of the arithmetic operation of the T-account (beginning balance +/− transactions and adjustments = ending balance), if all of the amounts except one are known, the unknown amount can be calculated.

You should invest practice and study time to learn to use transaction analysis procedures and to understand the horizontal model, journal entries, and T-accounts because these tools are used in subsequent chapters to describe the impact of transactions on the financial statements. Although these models are part of the bookkeeper's "tool kit," you are not learning them to become a bookkeeper—you are learning them to become an informed user of financial statements.

---

8. What does it mean to analyze a transaction?

9. What does it mean to use a T-account to determine which activities have affected the account during a period?

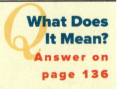

What Does It Mean?

Answer on page 136

Demonstration Problem

The **Demonstration Problem** walkthrough for this chapter is available in *Connect.*

Summary

Financial statements result from the bookkeeping (procedures for sorting, classifying, and presenting the effects of a transaction) and accounting (the selection of alternative methods of reflecting the effects of certain transactions) processes. Bookkeeping procedures for recording transactions are built on the framework of the accounting equation (Assets = Liabilities + Stockholders' equity), which must be kept in balance.

The income statement is linked to the balance sheet through the retained earnings component of stockholders' equity. Revenues and expenses of the income statement are really subparts of retained earnings that are reported separately as net income (or net loss) for a fiscal period. Net income (or net loss) is then added to (or subtracted from) the retained earnings balance at the beginning of the fiscal period in the process of determining retained earnings at the end of the fiscal period. Dividends are a subtraction in the process of determining the ending retained earnings balance. **(LO 3)**

Bookkeeping procedures involve establishing an account for each asset, liability, stockholders' equity element, revenue, and expense. Accounts can be represented by a T; the left side is the debit side and the right side is the credit side. Transactions are recorded in journal entry format:

Dr. Account Name	Amount	
Cr. Account Name		Amount

The journal entry is the source of amounts recorded in an account. The ending balance in an account is the positive difference between the debit and credit amounts recorded in the account, including the beginning balance. Asset and expense accounts normally have a debit balance; liability, stockholders' equity, and revenue accounts normally have a credit balance. **(LO 4)**

The horizontal model is an easy and meaningful way of understanding the effect of a transaction on the balance sheet and/or income statement. The representation of the horizontal model is:

Balance Sheet	Income Statement
Assets = Liabilities + Stockholders' equity	← Net Income = Revenues − Expense

The key to using this model is to keep the balance sheet in balance. The arrow from net income in the income statement to stockholders' equity in the balance sheet indicates that net income affects retained earnings, which is a component of stockholders' equity. For a transaction affecting both the balance sheet and the income statement, the balance sheet will balance when the income statement effect on stockholders' equity is considered. In this model, the account name is entered under the appropriate financial statement category, and the dollar effect of the transaction on that account is entered with a plus or minus sign below the account name. The horizontal model can be shortened to this single equation: **(LO 1, 2, 5)**

Assets = Liabilities + Stockholders' equity + Revenues − Expenses

Adjustments describe accruals or reclassifications rather than transactions. Adjustments usually affect both a balance sheet account and an income statement account. Adjustments are part of accrual accounting, and they are required to achieve a matching of revenue and expense so that the financial statements reflect accurately the financial position and results of operations of the entity. **(LO 6)**

Transaction analysis is the process of determining how a transaction affects the financial statements. Transaction analysis involves asking and answering five questions:

1. What's going on?
2. What accounts are affected?
3. How are they affected?
4. Does the balance sheet balance? (Do the debits equal the credits?)
5. Does my analysis make sense? **(LO 7)**

Transactions can be initially recorded in virtually any way that makes sense at the time. Prior to the preparation of period-end financial statements, a reclassification adjustment can be made to reflect the appropriate asset/liability and expense/revenue recognition with respect to the accounts affected by the transaction (e.g., purchase of supplies) and subsequent activities (e.g., use of supplies).

Key Terms and Concepts

account balance (p. 99)   The arithmetic sum of the additions and subtractions to an account through a given date.

accrual (p. 106)   The process of recognizing revenue that has been earned but not collected, or an expense that has been incurred but not paid.

accrued (p. 107)   Describes revenue that has been earned and a related asset that will be collected, or an expense that has been incurred and a related liability that will be paid.

adjustment (p. 106)   An entry usually made during the process of "closing the books" that results in more accurate financial statements. Adjustments involve accruals and reclassifications. Adjustments are sometimes made at the end of interim periods, such as month-end or quarter-end, as well.

balance (p. 100)   See *account balance*.

charge (p. 99)   In bookkeeping, a synonym for *debit*.

chart of accounts (p. 99)   An index of the accounts contained in a ledger.

closing the books (p. 110)   The process of posting transactions, adjustments, and closing entries to the ledger and preparing the financial statements.

credit (p. 100)   The right side of an account. A decrease in asset and expense accounts; an increase in liability, stockholders' equity, and revenue accounts.

debit (p. 100)   The left side of an account. An increase in asset and expense accounts; a decrease in liability, stockholders' equity, and revenue accounts.

entry (p. 101)   A journal entry or a posting to an account.

horizontal model (p. 102)   A representation of the balance sheet and income statement relationship that is useful for understanding the effects of transactions and adjustments on the financial statements. The model is as follows:

Balance Sheet	Income Statement
Assets = Liabilities + Stockholders' equity	← Net Income = Revenues − Expenses

journal (p. 98)   A chronological record of transactions.

journal entry (p. 101)   A description of a transaction in a format that shows the debit account(s) and amount(s) and credit account(s) and amount(s).

ledger (p. 98)   A book or file of accounts.

on account (p. 97)   Used to describe a purchase or sale transaction for which cash will be paid or received at a later date. A "credit" transaction.

post (p. 98)   The process of recording a transaction in the respective ledger accounts using a journal entry as the source of the information recorded.

source document (p. 102)   Evidence of a transaction that supports the journal entry recording the transaction.

T-account (p. 100)   An account format with a debit (left) side and a credit (right) side.

transaction analysis methodology (p. 110)   The process of answering five questions to ensure that a transaction is understood:

1.   What's going on?
2.   What accounts are affected?
3.   How are they affected?
4.   Does the balance sheet balance? (Do the debits equal the credits?)
5.   Does my analysis make sense?

transactions (p. 95)   Economic interchanges between entities that are accounted for and reflected in financial statements.

---

connect **Mini-Exercises**

All applicable Mini-Exercises are available in *Connect*.

Mini-Exercise
4.1

LO 2, 6, 7

Record transactions and adjustments   The transactions and adjustments related to the first month of operations of Zoe Amelia Corp. were as follows:

a.   Issued common stock to the initial stockholders in exchange for their cash investment.
b.   Signed a lease for office space and paid the first three months of rent in advance.
c.   Purchased office equipment and shelving for cash.
d.   Purchased merchandise inventory; made a partial payment in cash, and agreed to pay the balance within 30 days.
e.   Sold merchandise inventory on account for an amount greater than the cost of the inventory sold.
f.   Paid employees for the first two weeks of the month.
g.   At the end of the month, accrued wages owed to employees for the second two weeks of the month.

h. Recognized rent expense for one month of the payment of rent in advance in transaction **b** (as a reclassification adjusting entry).

Required:
Enter the following column headings across the top of a sheet of paper:

Transaction/ Adjustment	A	=	L	+	SE	Net Income

Enter the transaction/adjustment in the first column, and show the effect, if any, of the transaction entry or adjusting entry on the appropriate balance sheet category or on net income by indicating the account name(s) affected and whether each is an addition (+) or subtraction (−). Items that affect net income should not be shown as affecting stockholders' equity.

Record transactions and adjustments The transactions and adjustments related to the second month of operations of Zoe Amelia Corp. were as follows:

Mini-Exercise 4.2

LO 2, 6, 7

a. Paid wages that had been accrued at the end of the prior month.
b. Collected accounts receivable from sales recorded in the prior month.
c. Paid accounts payable owed for purchases made in the prior month.
d. Borrowed cash from a local bank on a short-term promissory note.
e. Purchased merchandise inventory for cash.
f. Incurred and paid utilities expense for the month.
g. At the end of the month, accrued interest on the short-term promissory note recorded in transaction **d.**
h. Recognized rent expense for one month of the three-month payment of rent in advance made in the prior month (as a reclassification adjusting entry).

Required:
Enter the following column headings across the top of a sheet of paper:

Transaction/ Adjustment	A	=	L	+	SE	Net Income

Enter the transaction/adjustment in the first column, and show the effect, if any, of the transaction entry or adjusting entry on the appropriate balance sheet category or on net income by indicating the account name(s) affected and whether each is an addition (+) or subtraction (−). Items that affect net income should not be shown as affecting stockholders' equity.

Transaction analysis using T-accounts

Mini-Exercise 4.3

LO 6, 7

a. Accounts Payable had a balance of $9,000 at the beginning of the month and $10,200 at the end of the month. During the month, purchases on account amounted to $18,300. Calculate the payments to suppliers during the month.
b. Accounts Receivable had a balance of $10,700 at the beginning of the month and $9,900 at the end of the month. Cash collected from customers totaled $38,000 during the month. Calculate credit sales during the month, assuming that all sales were made on account.

Required:

Solve for the missing amounts using a T-account for the balance sheet accounts in each situation. Assume that there is only one debit entry and one credit entry in the account during the month.

Mini-Exercise
4.4
LO 6, 7

Transaction analysis using T-accounts

a. The Supplies account had a balance of $2,400 at the beginning of the month and $3,200 at the end of the month. The cost of supplies purchased during the month was $7,800. Calculate the cost of supplies used during the month.

b. Wages Payable had a balance of $5,800 at the end of the month. During the month, $28,000 of wages were paid to employees. Wages expense accrued during the month totaled $29,500. Calculate Wages Payable at the beginning of the month.

Required:

Solve for the missing amounts using a T-account for the balance sheet accounts in each situation. Assume that there is only one debit entry and one credit entry in the account during the month.

connect **Exercises**

All applicable Exercises are available in *Connect*.

Exercise 4.5
LO 2, 6, 7

Record transactions and calculate financial statement amounts The transactions relating to the formation of Blue Co. Stores Inc., and its first month of operations follow. Prepare an answer sheet with the columns shown. Record each transaction in the appropriate columns of your answer sheet. Show the amounts involved and indicate how each account is affected (+ or −). After all transactions have been recorded, calculate the total assets, liabilities, and stockholders' equity at the end of the month and calculate the amount of net income for the month.

a. The firm was organized and the stockholders invested cash of $16,000.

b. The firm borrowed $10,000 from the bank; a short-term note was signed.

c. Display cases and other store equipment costing $3,500 were purchased for cash. The original list price of the equipment was $3,800, but a discount was received because the seller was having a sale.

d. A store location was rented, and $2,800 was paid for the first month's rent.

e. Inventory of $30,000 was purchased; $18,000 cash was paid to the suppliers, and the balance will be paid within 30 days.

f. During the first week of operations, merchandise that had cost $8,000 was sold for $13,000 cash.

g. A newspaper ad costing $200 was arranged for; it ran during the second week of the store's operations. The ad will be paid for in the next month.

h. Additional inventory costing $8,400 was purchased; cash of $2,400 was paid, and the balance is due in 30 days.

i. In the last three weeks of the first month, sales totaled $27,000, of which $19,200 was sold on account. The cost of the goods sold totaled $18,000.

j. Employee wages for the month totaled $3,700; these will be paid during the first week of the next month.

k. The firm collected a total of $6,320 from the sales on account recorded in transaction **i.**

l. The firm paid a total of $9,440 of the amount owed to suppliers from transaction **e.**

Answer sheet:

			Assets = Liabilities + Stockholders' equity								
Transaction Cash +	Accounts Receivable +	Merchandise Inventory +	Equipment	= Notes Payable +	Accounts Payable +	Paid-In Capital +	Retained Earnings +	Revenues − Expenses			

Prepare an income statement and balance sheet After you have completed parts **a** through **l** in Exercise 4.5, prepare an income statement for Blue Co. Stores Inc. for the month presented and a balance sheet at the end of the month using the captions shown on the answer sheet.

Optional continuation of Exercise 4.5

Record transactions and calculate financial statement amounts The following are the transactions relating to the formation of Gray Mowing Services Inc. and its first month of operations. Prepare an answer sheet with the columns shown. Record each transaction in the appropriate columns of your answer sheet. Show the amounts involved and indicate how each account is affected (+ or −). After all transactions have been recorded, calculate the total assets, liabilities, and stockholders' equity at the end of the month and calculate the amount of net income for the month.

Exercise 4.6
LO 2, 6, 7

a. The firm was organized and the initial stockholders invested cash of $12,000.

b. The company borrowed $18,000 from a relative of one of the initial stockholders; a short-term note was signed.

c. Two zero-turn lawn mowers costing $7,600 each and a professional trimmer costing $2,600 were purchased for cash. The original list price of each mower was $10,200, but a discount was received because the seller was having a sale.

d. Gasoline, oil, and several packages of trash bags were purchased for cash of $1,800.

e. Advertising flyers announcing the formation of the business and a newspaper ad were purchased. The cost of these items, $3,400, will be paid in 30 days.

f. During the first two weeks of operations, 94 lawns were mowed. The total revenue for this work was $14,100; $9,300 was collected in cash, and the balance will be received within 30 days.

g. Employees were paid $8,400 for their work during the first two weeks.

h. Additional gasoline, oil, and trash bags costing $2,200 were purchased for cash.

i. In the last two weeks of the first month, revenues totaled $18,400, of which $7,500 was collected.

j. Employee wages for the last two weeks totaled $10,200; these will be paid during the first week of the next month.

k. It was determined that at the end of the month the cost of the gasoline, oil, and trash bags still on hand was $600.

l. Customers paid a total of $3,000 due from mowing services provided during the first two weeks. The revenue for these services was recognized in transaction **f.**

Answer sheet:

Assets = Liabilities + Stockholders' equity

| | Accounts | | | Notes | Accounts | Paid-In | Retained | | |
| Transaction Cash + Receivable + Supplies + Equipment | | | | = Payable + | Payable + | Capital + | Earnings + | Revenues − | Expenses |

Optional continuation of Exercise 4.6

Prepare an income statement and balance sheet After you have completed parts **a** through **l** in Exercise 4.6, prepare an income statement for Gray Mowing Services Inc. for the month presented and a balance sheet at the end of the month using the captions shown on the answer sheet.

Exercise 4.7
LO 6

Write journal entries Write the journal entry(ies) for each of the transactions of Exercise 4.5.

Exercise 4.8
LO 6

Write journal entries Write the journal entry(ies) for each of the transactions of Exercise 4.6.

Exercise 4.9
LO 2, 6, 7

Record transactions and adjustments Prepare an answer sheet with the column headings shown after the following list of transactions. Record the effect, if any, of the transaction entry or adjusting entry on the appropriate balance sheet category or on the income statement by entering the account name and amount and indicating whether it is an addition (+) or subtraction (−). Column headings reflect the expanded balance sheet equation; items that affect net income should not be shown as affecting stockholders' equity. The first transaction is provided as an illustration.

(*Note:* As an alternative to using the columns, you may write the journal entry for each transaction or adjustment.)

a. During the month, the Supplies (asset) account was debited $3,600 for supplies purchased. The cost of supplies used during the month was $2,800. Record the adjustment to properly reflect the amount of supplies used and supplies still on hand at the end of the month.

b. An insurance premium of $960 was paid for the coming year. Prepaid Insurance was debited.

c. Wages of $6,400 were paid for the current month.

d. Interest revenue of $500 was received for the current month.

e. Accrued $1,400 of commissions payable to sales staff for the current month.

f. Accrued $260 of interest expense at the end of the month.

g. Received $4,200 on accounts receivable accrued at the end of the prior month.

h. Purchased $1,200 of merchandise inventory from a supplier on account.

i. Paid $320 of interest expense for the month.

j. Accrued $1,600 of wages at the end of the current month.

k. Paid $1,000 of accounts payable.

Transaction/ Adjustment	Assets	Liabilities	Stockholders' Equity	Net Income
a.	Supplies −2,800			Supplies Exp. −2,800
				(Note: An increase to Supplies Expense decreases Net Income.)

Record transactions and adjustments Prepare an answer sheet with the column headings shown after the following list of transactions. Record the effect, if any, of the transaction entry or adjusting entry on the appropriate balance sheet category or on the income statement by entering the account name and amount and indicating whether it is an addition (+) or subtraction (−). Column headings reflect the expanded balance sheet equation; items that affect net income should not be shown as affecting stockholders' equity. The first transaction is provided as an illustration.

Exercise 4.10

LO 2, 6, 7

(*Note:* As an alternative to using the columns, you may write the journal entry for each transaction or adjustment.)

a.   During the month, Supplies Expense was debited $2,600 for supplies purchased. The cost of supplies used during the month was $1,900. Record the adjustment to properly reflect the amount of supplies used and supplies still on hand at the end of the month.

b.   During the month, the board of directors declared a cash dividend of $14,400, payable next month.

c.   Employees were paid $10,500 in wages for their work during the first three weeks of the month.

d.   Employee wages of $3,600 for the last week of the month have not been recorded.

e.   Revenues from services performed during the month totaled $22,200. Of this amount, $9,300 was received in cash, and the balance is expected to be received within 30 days.

f.   A contract was signed with a newspaper for a $1,200 advertisement; the ad ran during this month but will not be paid for until next month.

g.   Merchandise that cost $4,650 was sold for $8,800. Of this amount, $3,300 was received in cash, and the balance is expected to be received within 30 days.

h.   Independent of transaction **a**, assume that during the month, supplies were purchased at a cost of $1,230 and debited to the Supplies (asset) account. A total of $990 of supplies were used during the month. Record the adjustment to properly reflect the amount of supplies used and supplies still on hand at the end of the month.

i.   Interest of $540 has been earned on a note receivable but has not yet been received.

j.   Issued 1,200 shares of $10 par value common stock for $26,400 in cash.

Transaction/ Adjustment	Assets	Liabilities	Stockholders' Equity	Net Income
a.	Supplies +700			Supplies Exp. +700 (Note: A decrease to Supplies Expense increases Net Income.)

Record transactions and adjustments Enter the following column headings across the top of a sheet of paper:

Exercise 4.11

LO 2, 6, 7

Transaction/ Adjustment	Assets	Liabilities	Stockholders' Equity	Net Income

Enter the transaction or adjustment letter in the first column and show the effect, if any, of the transaction entry or adjusting entry on the appropriate balance sheet category or on the income statement by entering the amount and indicating whether it is an addition (+) or a subtraction (−). Column headings reflect the expanded balance sheet equation; items that affect net income should not be shown as affecting stockholders' equity. In some cases, only one column may be affected because all the specific accounts affected by the transaction are included in that category. Transaction **a** has been completed as an illustration.

(*Note:* As an alternative to using the columns, you may write the journal entry for each transaction or adjustment.)

a.   Provided services to a client on account; revenues totaled $1,100.
b.   Paid an insurance premium of $720 for the coming year. An asset, Prepaid Insurance, was debited.
c.   Recognized insurance expense for one month from the premium transaction in **b** via a reclassification adjusting entry.
d.   Paid $1,600 of wages accrued at the end of the prior month.
e.   Paid $5,200 of wages for the current month.
f.   Accrued $1,200 of wages at the end of the current month.
g.   Received cash of $3,000 on accounts receivable accrued at the end of the prior month.

Transaction/ Adjustment	Assets	Liabilities	Stockholders' Equity	Net Income
a.	+1,100			+1,100

Exercise 4.12
LO 2, 6, 7

Record transactions and adjustments Enter the following column headings across the top of a sheet of paper:

Transaction/ Adjustment	Assets	Liabilities	Stockholders' Equity	Net Income

Enter the transaction or adjustment letter in the first column and show the effect, if any, of the transaction entry or adjustment on the appropriate balance sheet category or on the income statement by entering the amount and indicating whether it is an addition (+) or a subtraction (−). Column headings reflect the expanded balance sheet equation; items that affect net income should not be shown as affecting stockholders' equity. In some cases, only one column may be affected because all the specific accounts affected by the transaction are included in that category. Transaction **a** has been completed as an illustration.

(*Note:* As an alternative to using the columns, you may write the journal entry for each transaction or adjustment.)

a.   During the month, Supplies Expense was debited $5,200 for supplies purchased. The cost of supplies used during the month was $3,800. Record the adjustment to properly reflect the amount of supplies used and supplies still on hand at the end of the month.
b.   Independent of transaction **a**, assume that during the month, Supplies (asset) was debited $5,200 for supplies purchased. The total cost of supplies used during the

month was $3,800. Record the adjustment to properly reflect the amount of supplies used and supplies still on hand at the end of the month.

c. Received $3,400 of cash from clients for services provided during the current month.

d. Paid $1,900 of accounts payable.

e. Received $1,500 of cash from clients for revenues accrued at the end of the prior month.

f. Received $800 of interest revenue accrued at the end of the prior month.

g. Received $1,650 of interest revenue for the current month.

h. Accrued $740 of interest revenue earned in the current month.

i. Paid $4,200 of interest expense for the current month.

j. Accrued $1,480 of interest expense at the end of the current month.

k. Accrued $3,200 of commissions payable to sales staff for the current month.

Transaction/ Adjustment	Assets	Liabilities	Stockholders' Equity	Net Income
a.	+1,400			+1,400

Calculate retained earnings On February 1, 2019, the balance of the retained earnings account of Blue Power Corporation was $315,000. Revenues for February totaled $61,000, of which $57,500 was collected in cash. Expenses for February totaled $65,000, of which $54,000 was paid in cash. Dividends declared and paid during February were $6,000.

Exercise 4.13
LO 3

Required:
Calculate the retained earnings balance at February 28, 2019.

Cash receipts versus revenues During the month of April, Riley Co. had cash receipts from customers of $780,000. Expenses totaled $624,000, and accrual basis net income was $218,000. There were no gains or losses during the month.

Exercise 4.14
LO 6, 7

Required:
a. Calculate the revenues for Riley Co. for April.

b. Explain why cash receipts from customers can be different from revenues.

Notes receivable—interest accrual and collection On April 1, 2019, Tabor Co. received an $18,000 note from a customer in settlement of an $18,000 account receivable from that customer. The note bore interest at the rate of 15% per annum, and the note plus interest was payable March 31, 2020.

Exercise 4.15
LO 6, 7

Required:
Use the horizontal model to show the effects of each of these transactions and adjustments:

a. Receipt of the note on April 1, 2019.

b. The accrual of interest at December 31, 2019.

c. The collection of the note and interest on March 31, 2020.

(*Note:* As an alternative to using the horizontal model, write the journal entries to show each of these transactions and adjustments.)

Exercise 4.16
LO 6, 7

Notes payable—interest accrual and payment Proco had an account payable of $63,000 due to Shirmoo Inc., one of its suppliers. The amount was due to be paid on January 31. Proco did not have enough cash on hand then to pay the amount due, so Proco's treasurer called Shirmoo's treasurer and agreed to sign a note payable for the amount due. The note was dated February 1, had an interest rate of 9% per annum, and was payable with interest on May 31.

Required:

Use the horizontal model to show the effects of each of these transactions and adjustments for Proco on the following:

a.   February 1, to show that the account payable had been changed to a note payable.
b.   March 31, to accrue interest expense for February and March.
c.   May 31, to record payment of the note and all of the interest due to Shirmoo.

(*Note:* As an alternative to using the horizontal model, write the journal entries to show each of these transactions and adjustments.)

Exercise 4.17
LO 6, 7

Effect of adjustments on net income Assume that Cater Co.'s accountant neglected to record the payroll expense accrual adjustment at the end of October.

Required:
a.   Explain the effect of this omission on net income reported for October.
b.   Explain the effect of this omission on net income reported for November.
c.   Explain the effect of this omission on total net income for the two months of October and November taken together.
d.   Explain why the accrual adjustment should have been recorded as of October 31.

Exercise 4.18
LO 6, 7

Effects of adjustments A bookkeeper prepared the year-end financial statements of Giftwrap, Inc. The income statement showed net income of $216,000, and the balance sheet showed ending retained earnings of $810,000. The firm's accountant reviewed the bookkeeper's work and determined that adjustments should be made that would increase revenues by $60,000 and increase expenses by $84,000.

Required:
Calculate the amounts of net income and retained earnings after the preceding adjustments are recorded.

Exercise 4.19
LO 6, 7

T-account analysis Answer these questions that are related to the following Interest Payable T-account:

a.   What is the amount of the February 28 adjustment?
b.   What account would most likely have been credited for the amount of the February transactions?
c.   What account would most likely have been debited for the amount of the February 28 adjustment?
d.   Why would this adjusting entry have been made?

Interest Payable			
		February 1 balance	6,000
February transactions	7,500	February 28 adjustment	?
		February 28 balance	10,500

Transaction analysis using T-accounts This exercise provides practice in understanding the operation of T-accounts and transaction analysis. For each situation, you must solve for a missing amount. Use a T-account for the balance sheet account, show in a horizontal model, or prepare journal entries for the information provided. In each case, there is only one debit entry and one credit entry in the account during the month.

Exercise 4.20
LO 6, 7

Example:
Accounts Payable had a balance of $6,000 at the beginning of the month and $5,400 at the end of the month. During the month, payments to suppliers amounted to $16,000. Calculate the purchases on account during the month.

Solution:

Accounts Payable			
	Beginning balance	6,000	
Payment 16,000	Purchase	?=15,400	
	Ending balance	5,400	

Dr. Accounts
     Payable 16,000
   Cr. Cash   16,000
Payments to suppliers.

Dr. Inventory 15,400
   Cr. Accounts
        Payable 15,400
Purchases on account.

a. Accounts Receivable had a balance of $25,200 at the beginning of the month and $10,600 at the end of the month. Credit sales totaled $90,000 during the month. Calculate the cash collected from customers during the month, assuming that all sales were made on account.

b. The Supplies account had a balance of $40,000 at the beginning of the month and $49,600 at the end of the month. The cost of supplies used during the month was $157,200. Calculate the cost of supplies purchased during the month.

c. Wages Payable had a balance of $7,600 at the beginning of the month. During the month, $30,200 of wages were paid to employees. Wages Expense accrued during the month totaled $39,000. Calculate the balance of Wages Payable at the end of the month.

Problems

connect

All applicable Problems are available in *Connect*.
Record transactions and adjustments Use the horizontal model, or write the journal entry, for each of the following transactions and adjustments that occurred during the first year of operations at Kissick Co.

Problem 4.21
LO 2, 6, 7

a. Issued 100,000 shares of $5-par-value common stock for $500,000 in cash.

b. Borrowed $250,000 from Oglesby National Bank and signed a 12% note due in three years.

c. Incurred and paid $190,000 in salaries for the year.

d. Purchased $320,000 of merchandise inventory on account during the year.

e. Sold inventory costing $290,000 for a total of $455,000, all on credit.

f. Paid rent of $55,000 on the sales facilities during the first 11 months of the year.

g. Purchased $75,000 of store equipment, paying $25,000 in cash and agreeing to pay the difference within 90 days.

h. Paid the entire $50,000 owed for store equipment and $310,000 of the amount due to suppliers for credit purchases previously recorded.

i. Incurred and paid utilities expense of $18,000 during the year.

j. Collected $412,000 in cash from customers during the year for credit sales previously recorded.

k. At year-end, accrued $30,000 of interest on the note due to Oglesby National Bank.

l. At year-end, accrued $5,000 of past-due December rent on the sales facilities.

Problem 4.22

LO 1

Prepare an income statement and balance sheet from transaction data

a. Based on your answers to Problem 4.21, prepare an income statement (ignoring income taxes) for Kissick Co.'s first year of operations and a balance sheet as of the end of the year. (*Hint:* You may find it helpful to prepare a T-account for the Cash account since it is affected by most of the transactions.)

b. Provide a brief written evaluation of Kissick Co.'s results from operations for the year and its financial position at the end of the year. In your opinion, what are the likely explanations for the company's net loss?

Problem 4.23

LO 6, 7

Calculate income from operations and net income Selected information taken from the financial statements of Verbeke Co. for the year ended December 31, 2019, follows:

Gross profit	$206,000
General and administrative expenses	41,000
Net cash used by investing activities	53,000
Dividends paid	26,000
Interest expense	31,000
Net sales	372,000
Advertising expense	38,000
Accounts payable	51,000
Income tax expense	19,000
Other selling expenses	21,000

a. Calculate income from operations (operating income) for the year ended December 31, 2019. (*Hint:* You may want to review Exhibit 2-2.)

b. Calculate net income for the year ended December 31, 2019.

Calculate income from operations and net income Selected information taken from the financial statements of Fordstar Co. for the year ended December 31, 2019, follows:

Problem 4.24
LO 6, 7

Net cash provided by operations	$12,000
Cost of goods sold	36,000
Selling, general, and administrative expenses	21,000
Accounts payable	11,000
Dividends paid	17,000
Research and development expenses	5,000
Merchandise inventory	24,000
Provision for income taxes	7,000
Net sales	110,000
Interest expense	9,000

a. Calculate income from operations (operating income) for the year ended December 31, 2019. (*Hint:* You may wish to review Exhibit 2-2.)
b. Calculate net income for the year ended December 31, 2019.

Alternative adjustments—supplies On January 10, 2019, the first day of the spring semester, the cafeteria of The Defiance College purchased for cash enough paper napkins to last the entire 16-week semester. The total cost was $4,800.

Problem 4.25
LO 6, 7

Required:
Use the horizontal model to show the effects of recording the following:
a. The purchase of the paper napkins, assuming that the purchase was initially recorded as an expense.
b. At January 31, it was estimated that the cost of the paper napkins used during the first three weeks of the semester totaled $950. Use the horizontal model to show the adjustments that should be made as of January 31 so that the appropriate amount of expense will be shown in the income statement for the month of January.
c. Use the horizontal model to show the effects of the alternative way of recording the initial purchase of napkins.
d. Use the horizontal model to show the effects of the adjustment that should occur at January 31 if the initial purchase had been recorded as in **c**.
e. Consider the effects that entries **a** and **b** would have on the financial statements of The Defiance College. Compare these effects to those that would be caused by entries **c** and **d**. Are there any differences between these alternative sets of entries on the
  1. Income statement for the month of January?
  2. Balance sheet at January 31?

(*Note:* As an alternative to using the horizontal model, write the journal entries to show each of these transactions and adjustments.)

Alternative adjustments—rent Calco Inc. rents its store location. Rent is $9,000 per month, payable quarterly in advance. On July 1, a check for $27,000 was issued to the landlord for the July–September quarter.

Problem 4.26
LO 6, 7

Required:

Use the horizontal model to show the effects on the financial statements of Calco Inc.:

a. To record the payment on July 1, assuming that all $27,000 is initially recorded as Rent Expense.

b. To record the adjustment that would be appropriate at July 31 if your entry in **a** had been made.

c. To record the payment on July 1, assuming instead that all $27,000 is initially recorded as Prepaid Rent.

d. To record the adjustment that would be appropriate at July 31 if your entry in **c** had been made.

e. To record the adjustment that would be appropriate at August 31 and September 30, regardless of how the payment on July 1 had been initially recorded (and assuming that the July 31 adjustment had been made).

f. If you were supervising the bookkeeper, how would you suggest that the July 1 payment be recorded? Explain your answer.

(*Note:* As an alternative to using the horizontal model, write the journal entries to show each of these transactions and adjustments.)

Problem 4.27
LO 6, 7

Analyze several accounts using Campbell Soup Company annual report data Set up a horizontal model in the following format:

	Assets			**Liabilities**	**Revenues**	**Expenses**	
	Cash and Cash Equivalents	Accounts Receivable, Net	Inventories	Payable to Suppliers and Others	Net Sales	Cost of Products Sold	Marketing, Selling, and Administrative Expenses
Beginning balance							
Net sales							
Cost of products sold							
Marketing, selling, and administrative expenses							
Purchases on account							
Collections of accounts receivable							
Payments to suppliers and others							
Ending balance							

Campbell's

Required:

a. Enter the beginning (July 31, 2016) and ending (July 30, 2017) account balances for Accounts Receivable, Inventories, and Payable to Suppliers and Others. Find these amounts on the balance sheet for Campbell Soup Company in the appendix.

b. From the income statement for Campbell Soup Company for the year ended July 30, 2017, in the appendix, record the following transactions in the model:

1. Net Sales, assuming that all sales were made on account.

2. Cost of Products Sold, assuming that all costs were transferred from inventories.

3. Marketing, Selling, and Administrative Expenses, assuming all of these expenses were accrued in the Payable to Suppliers and Others liability category as they were incurred.

    (*Hint:* Campbell's Marketing, Selling, and Administrative Expenses are contained in two separate captions. Note that Payable to Suppliers and Others is another term for Accounts Payable.)

c. Assuming that the only other transactions affecting these balance sheet accounts were those described next, calculate the amount of each transaction:

    1. Purchases of inventories on account.
    2. Collections of accounts receivable.
    3. Payments to suppliers and others.

Make corrections and adjustments to income statement and balance sheet Big Blue Rental Corp. provides rental agent services to apartment building owners. Big Blue Rental Corp.'s preliminary income statement for August 2019 and its August 31, 2019, preliminary balance sheet did not reflect the following:

Problem 4.28
LO 6, 7

a. Rental commissions of $1,500 had been earned in August but had not yet been received from or billed to building owners.

b. When supplies are purchased, their cost is recorded as an asset. As supplies are used, a record of those used is kept. The record sheet shows that $1,080 of supplies were used in August.

c. Interest on the note payable is to be paid on May 31 and November 30. Interest for August has not been accrued—that is, it has not yet been recorded. (The Interest Payable of $240 on the balance sheet is the amount of the accrued liability at July 31.) The interest rate on this note is 10%.

d. Wages of $780 for the last week of August have not been recorded.

e. The Rent Expense of $3,060 represents rent for August, September, and October, which was paid early in August.

f. Interest of $840 has been earned on notes receivable but has not yet been received.

g. Late in August, the board of directors met and declared a cash dividend of $8,400, payable September 10. Once declared, the dividend is a liability of the corporation until it is paid.

BIG BLUE RENTAL CORP.
Income Statement
August 2019

	Preliminary	Adjustments/Corrections		Final
		Debit	Credit	
Commissions revenue	$27,000	$	$	$
Interest revenue	5,100			
Total revenue	$32,100	$	$	$
Rent expense	$ 3,060	$	$	$
Wages expense	7,140			
Supplies expense	—			
Interest expense	—			
Total expenses	$10,200	$	$	$
Net income	$21,900	$	$	$

(continued)

		Adjustments/Corrections		
	Preliminary	Debit	Credit	Final
BIG BLUE RENTAL CORP. Balance Sheet August 31, 2019				

	Preliminary	Debit	Credit	Final
Assets				
Cash	$ 2,400	$	$	$
Notes receivable	78,000			
Commissions receivable	—			
Interest receivable	—			
Prepaid rent	—			
Supplies	3,900			
Total assets	$84,300	$	$	$
Liabilities and Stockholders' Equity				
Accounts payable	$ 720	$	$	$
Notes payable	14,400			
Interest payable	240			
Wages payable	—			
Dividends payable	—			
Total liabilities	$15,360	$	$	$
Paid-in capital	$14,400	$	$	$
Retained earnings:				
Balance, August 1	$32,640	$	$	$
Net income	21,900			
Dividends	—			
Balance, August 31	$54,540	$	$	$
Total stockholders' equity	$68,920	$	$	$
Total liabilities and stockholders' equity	$84,300	$	$	$

Required:

a. Using the columns provided on the income statement and balance sheet for Big Blue Rental Corp., make the appropriate adjustments/corrections to the statements, and enter the correct amount in the Final column. Key your adjustments/corrections with the letter of the item in the preceding list. Captions/account names that you will have to use are on the statements. (*Hint:* Use the five questions of transaction analysis. What is the relationship between net income and the balance sheet?)

b. Consider the entries that you have recorded in your answer to part **a**. Using these items as examples, explain why adjusting entries normally have an effect on both the balance sheet and the income statement.

c. Explain why the Cash account on the balance sheet is not usually affected by adjustments. In your answer, identify the types of activities and/or events that normally cause the need for adjustments to be recorded. Give at least one example of an adjustment (other than those provided in the problem data).

Cases

All applicable Cases are available in *Connect.*

Capstone analytical review of Chapters 2, 3, and 4. Calculate liquidity and profitability measures and explain various financial statement relationships for a realty firm DeBauge Realtors Inc. is a realty firm owned by Jeff and Kristi DeBauge. The DeBauge family owns 100% of the corporation's stock. The following summarized data (in thousands) are taken from the December 31, 2019, financial statements:

Case 4.29
LO 6, 7

For the Year Ended December 31, 2019:	
Commissions revenue	$426
Cost of services provided	177
Advertising expense	84
Operating income	$165
Interest expense	15
Income tax expense	48
Net income	$102

At December 31, 2019:	
Assets	
Cash and short-term investments	$ 90
Accounts receivable, net	120
Property, plant, and equipment, net	375
Total assets	$585
Liabilities and Stockholders' Equity	
Accounts payable	$270
Income taxes payable	15
Notes payable (long term)	150
Paid-in capital	60
Retained earnings	90
Total liabilities and stockholders' equity	$585

At December 31, 2018, total assets were $615 and total stockholders' equity was $150. There were no changes in notes payable or paid-in capital during 2019.

Required:

a. What particular expense do you suppose accounts for the largest portion of the $177 cost of services provided?

b. The cost of services provided amount includes all operating expenses (i.e., selling, general, and administrative expenses) except advertising expense. What do you suppose the primary reason was for DeBauge Realtors Inc. to separate advertising from other operating expenses?

c. Calculate the effective interest rate on the notes payable for DeBauge Realtors Inc.

d. Calculate the company's average income tax rate. (*Hint:* You must first determine the earnings before taxes.)

e. Calculate the amount of dividends declared and paid to Jeff and Kristi DeBauge during the year ended December 31, 2019. (*Hint:* Do a T-account analysis of retained earnings.) What is the company's dividend policy? (What proportion of the company's earnings are distributed as dividends?)

f. DeBauge Realtors Inc. was organized and operates as a corporation rather than a partnership. What is the primary advantage of the corporate form of business to a realty firm? What is the primary disadvantage of the corporate form?

g. Explain why the amount of income tax expense is different from the amount of income taxes payable.

h. Calculate the amount of working capital and the current ratio at December 31, 2019. Assess the company's overall liquidity.

i. Calculate ROI (including margin and turnover) and ROE for the year ended December 31, 2019. Explain why these single measures may not be very meaningful for this firm.

Case 4.30   **Capstone analytical review of Chapters 2–4. Calculate liquidity and profit-**
LO 6, 7   **ability measures and explain various financial statement relationships for an**
excavation contractor Gerrard Construction Co. is an excavation contractor. The following summarized data (in thousands) are taken from the December 31, 2019, financial statements:

For the Year Ended December 31, 2019:	
Net revenues	$ 96,600
Cost of services provided	34,200
Depreciation expense	19,500
Operating income	$ 42,900
Interest expense	11,400
Income tax expense	9,600
Net income	$ 21,900

At December 31, 2019:	
Assets	
Cash and short-term investments	$ 8,400
Accounts receivable, net	29,400
Property, plant, and equipment, net	232,200
Total assets	$270,000
Liabilities and Stockholders' Equity	
Accounts payable	$ 4,500
Income taxes payable	4,800
Notes payable (long term)	142,500
Paid-in capital	30,000
Retained earnings	88,200
Total liabilities and stockholders' equity	$270,000

At December 31, 2018, total assets were $246,000 and total stockholders' equity was $97,800. There were no changes in notes payable or paid-in capital during 2019.

Required:

a.   The cost of services provided amount includes all operating expenses (selling, general, and administrative expenses) except depreciation expense. What do you suppose the primary reason was for management to separate depreciation from other operating expenses? From a conceptual point of view, should depreciation be considered a "cost" of providing services?

b.   Why do you suppose the amounts of depreciation expense and interest expense are so high for Gerrard Construction Co.? To which specific balance sheet accounts should a financial analyst relate these expenses?

c.   Calculate the company's average income tax rate. (*Hint:* You must first determine the earnings before taxes.)

d.   Explain why the amount of income tax expense is different from the amount of income taxes payable.

e.   Calculate the amount of total current assets. Why do you suppose this amount is so low, relative to total assets?

f.   Why doesn't the company have a Merchandise Inventory account?

g.   Calculate the amount of working capital and the current ratio at December 31, 2019. Assess the company's overall liquidity.

h.   Calculate ROI (including margin and turnover) and ROE for the year ended December 31, 2019. Assess the company's overall profitability. What additional information would you like to have to increase the validity of this assessment?

i.   Calculate the amount of dividends declared and paid during the year ended December 31, 2019. (*Hint:* Do a T-account analysis of retained earnings.)

ANSWERS TO
What Does
It Mean?

1. It means that you are being asked to determine whether the account is for an asset, a liability, stockholders' equity element, revenue, or expense. Frequently, the account classification is included in the account title. In other cases, it is necessary to understand what transactions affect the account.

2. It means that the sum of the debit entries from transactions affecting the account, plus any beginning debit balance in the account, is larger than the sum of any credit entries from transactions affecting the account plus any beginning credit balance in the account.

3. It means that because the balance of these accounts is increased by a debit entry, an asset or expense account will usually have a debit balance.

4. It means that a transaction results in increasing the balance of these kinds of accounts.

5. It means that the sum of all accounts with debit balances in the ledger equals the sum of all accounts with credit balances in the ledger.

6. It means that revenue has been earned by selling a product or providing a service, or that an expense has been incurred, but that cash has not yet been received (from a revenue) or paid (for an expense) so an appropriate receivable or payable account, respectively, must be recognized.

7. It means that a more accurate income statement—matching of revenue and expense—and a more accurate balance sheet will result from the accrual or reclassification accomplished by the adjustment.

8. It means that the effect of the transaction on the affected accounts and financial statement categories is determined.

9. It means that by sketching a T and using arithmetic, if any three of the following are known—balance at the beginning of the period, total debits during the period, total credits during the period, or balance at the end of the period—the fourth can be calculated. The kinds of transactions or adjustments most likely to have affected the account are determined by knowing what the account is used for.

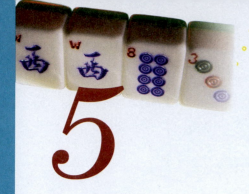

5

Accounting for and Presentation of Current Assets

Current assets include cash and other assets that are expected to be converted to cash or used up within one year, or an **operating cycle**, whichever is longer. An entity's operating cycle is the average time it takes to convert an investment in inventory back to cash. This is illustrated in the following diagram:

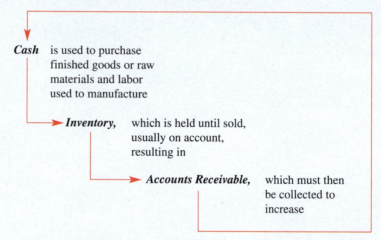

Cash is used to purchase finished goods or raw materials and labor used to manufacture

> *Inventory,* which is held until sold, usually on account, resulting in

> > *Accounts Receivable,* which must then be collected to increase

For most firms, the normal operating cycle is less than one year. As you learn more about each of the current assets discussed in this chapter, keep in mind that a shorter operating cycle permits a lower investment in current assets. This results in an increase in turnover, which in turn increases return on investment (ROI). Many firms attempt to reduce their operating cycle and increase overall profitability by trying to sell inventory and collect accounts receivable as quickly as possible.

Current asset captions usually seen in a balance sheet are the following:

Cash and Cash Equivalents

Short-Term Marketable Securities

Accounts and Notes Receivable

Inventories

Prepaid Expenses or Other Current Assets

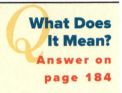

Refer to the Consolidated Balance Sheets of Campbell Soup Company in the appendix. Note that Campbell's reports $1,900 million (exactly $1.9 billion) as total current assets at July 30, 2017, representing 25 percent of the company's total assets. Look at the components of current assets. Notice that Cash and Cash Equivalents, Accounts Receivable, and Inventories are the largest current asset amounts. Now refer to the balance sheets in other annual reports that you may have and examine the composition of current assets. Do they differ significantly from Campbell's balance sheet? The objective of this chapter is to permit you to make sense of the current asset presentation of any balance sheet.

---

1. What does it mean when an asset is referred to as a current asset?

What Does It Mean?

Answer on page 184

LEARNING OBJECTIVES (LO)

After studying this chapter, you should understand and be able to

LO 5-1   Explain what is included in the cash and cash equivalents amount reported on the balance sheet.

LO 5-2   Describe the key features of a system of internal control and explain why internal controls are important.

LO 5-3   Explain the bank reconciliation procedure.

LO 5-4   Explain how short-term marketable securities are reported on the balance sheet.

LO 5-5   Discuss how accounts receivable are reported on the balance sheet, including the valuation allowances for estimated uncollectible accounts and estimated cash discounts.

LO 5-6   Explain how notes receivable and related accrued interest are reported on the balance sheet.

LO 5-7   Explain how inventories are reported on the balance sheet.

LO 5-8   Discuss the alternative inventory cost flow assumptions and generalize about their respective effects on the income statement and balance sheet when price levels are changing.

LO 5-9   Discuss the impact of inventory errors on the balance sheet and income statement.

LO 5-10   Explain what prepaid expenses are and how they are reported on the balance sheet.

Chapters 5, 6, 7, 8 and 9 are organized around the financial statements, starting with the asset side of the balance sheet in Chapters 5 and 6, moving over to the liability and stockholders' equity side in Chapters 7 and 8, and then on to the income statement and statement of cash flows in Chapter 9. Exhibit 5-1 highlights the balance sheet accounts covered in detail in this chapter and shows the income statement and statement of cash flows components affected by these accounts.

Exhibit 5-1

Financial Statements—
The Big Picture

Balance Sheet

Current Assets	Chapter	Current Liabilities	Chapter
Cash and cash equivalents	5, 9	Short-term debt	7
Short-term marketable securities	5	Current maturities of long-term debt	7
Accounts receivable	5, 9	Accounts payable	7
Notes receivable	5	Unearned revenue or deferred credits	7
Inventories	5, 9	Payroll taxes and other withholdings	7
Prepaid expenses	5	Other accrued liabilities	7
Noncurrent Assets		**Noncurrent Liabilities**	
Land	6	Long-term debt	7
Buildings and equipment	6	Deferred tax liabilities	7
Assets acquired by lease	6	Other long-term liabilities	7
Intangible assets	6	**Stockholders' Equity**	
Natural resources	6	Common stock	8
Other noncurrent assets	6	Preferred stock	8
		Additional paid-in capital	8
		Retained earnings	8
		Treasury stock	8
		Accumulated other comprehensive income (loss)	8

Income Statement

	Chapter
Sales	5, 9
Cost of goods sold	5, 9
Gross profit (or gross margin)	5, 9
Selling, general, and administrative expenses	5, 6, 9
Income from operations	9
Gains (losses) on sale of assets	6, 9
Interest income	5, 9
Interest expense	7, 9
Income tax expense	7, 9
Unusual items	9
Net income	5, 6, 7, 8, 9
Earnings per share	9

Statement of Cash Flows

	Chapter
Operating Activities	
Net income	5, 6, 7, 8, 9
Depreciation expense	6, 9
(Gains) losses on sale of assets	6, 9
(Increase) decrease in current assets	5, 9
Increase (decrease) in current liabilities	7, 9
Investing Activities	
Proceeds from sale of property, plant, and equipment	6, 9
Purchase of property, plant, and equipment	6, 9
Financing Activities	
Proceeds from long-term debt*	7, 9
Repayment of long-term debt*	7, 9
Issuance of common stock and/or preferred stock	8, 9
Purchase of treasury stock	8, 9
Payment of dividends	8, 9

Primary topics of this chapter.
Other affected financial statement components.
*May include short-term debt items as well.

Petty Cash Funds

Business in
Practice

Although most of an entity's cash disbursements should be made by check for security and record-keeping purposes, a petty cash fund could be used for small payments for which writing a check would be inconvenient. For example, postage due, **collect on delivery (COD)** charges, or the cost of an urgently needed office supply item often is paid from the petty cash fund to avoid the delay and expense associated with creating a check.

The petty cash fund is an **imprest account**, which means that the sum of the cash on hand in the petty cash box and the receipts in support of disbursements (called *petty cash vouchers*) should equal the amount initially put in the petty cash fund.

Periodically (usually at the end of the accounting period) the petty cash fund is reimbursed to bring the cash in the fund back to the original amount. It is at this time that the expenses paid through the fund are recognized in the accounts.

The amount of the petty cash fund is included in the cash amount reported on the entity's balance sheet.

Cash and Cash Equivalents

The vast majority of publicly traded corporations report their most liquid assets in the *cash* and *cash equivalents* category. **Cash** includes money on hand in change funds, **petty cash** funds (see Business in Practice—Petty Cash Funds), undeposited receipts (including currency, checks, money orders, and bank drafts), and any funds immediately available to the firm in its bank accounts ("demand deposits" such as checking and savings accounts). **Cash equivalents** are short-term investments readily convertible into cash with a minimal risk of price change due to interest rate movements.

LO 1
Explain what is included in the cash and cash equivalents amount reported on the balance sheet.

Because cash on hand or in checking accounts earns little if any interest, management of just about every organization will develop a cash management system to permit investment of cash balances not currently required for the entity's operation. The broad objective of the cash management program is to maximize earnings by having as much cash as feasible invested for the longest possible time. Cash managers are interested in minimizing investment risks, and this is accomplished by investing in U.S. Treasury securities, securities of agencies of the federal government, bank certificates of deposit, money market mutual funds, and commercial paper. (**Commercial paper** is like an IOU issued by a very creditworthy corporation.) Securities selected for investment usually will have a maturity date that is within a few months of the investment date and that corresponds to the time when the cash manager thinks the cash will be needed. Cash equivalents included with cash on the balance sheets of Campbell Soup Company are defined as "all highly liquid debt instruments purchased with a maturity of three months or less" (see the appendix).

Campbell's

LO 2
Describe the key features of a system of internal control and explain why internal controls are important.

In addition to an organization's cash management system, policies to minimize the chances of customer theft and employee embezzlement also will be developed. These are part of the **internal control system** (see Business in Practice—The Internal Control System), which is designed to help safeguard all of an entity's assets, including cash.

2. What does it mean to have an effective system of internal control?

What Does It Mean?
Answer on page 184

Business in
Practice

The Bank Reconciliation as a Control over Cash

Many transactions either directly or indirectly affect the receipt or payment of cash. For instance, a sale of merchandise on account normally leads to a cash receipt when the account receivable is collected. Likewise, a purchase of inventory on account results in a cash payment when the account payable is paid. In fact, cash (in one form or another) is eventually involved in the settlement of virtually all business affairs.

As a result of the high volume of cash transactions and the ease with which money can be exchanged, it is appropriate to design special controls to help safeguard cash. At a minimum, all cash received should be deposited in the company's bank account

at the end of each business day, and all cash payments (other than petty cash disbursements) should be made from the company's bank account using prenumbered checks. Using this simple control system, a duplicate record of each cash transaction is automatically maintained—one by the company and the other by the bank.

To determine the amount of cash available in the bank, it is appropriate that the Cash account balance as shown in the general ledger (or your checkbook) be reconciled with the balance reported by the bank. The **bank reconciliation** process, which you do (or should do) for your own checking account, involves bringing into agreement the account balance reported by the bank on the bank statement with the account balance in the ledger. The balances might differ for two reasons: timing differences and errors.

Timing differences arise because the company knows about some transactions affecting the cash balance about which the bank is not yet aware, or the bank has recorded some transactions about which the company is not yet aware. Following are the most common timing differences:

LO 3

Explain the bank reconciliation procedure.

- **Deposits in transit,** which have been recorded in the company's Cash account but which have not yet been added to the company's balance in the bank's records. From the company's point of view, the deposit in transit represents cash on hand because it has been received. In the bank reconciliation process, deposits in transit are added to the bank's indicated (prereconciled) balance.

- **Outstanding checks,** which have been recorded as credits (reductions) to the company's cash balance, but which have not yet been presented to the bank for payment. From the company's point of view, outstanding checks should not be included in its cash balance because its intent was to disburse cash when it issued the checks. In the reconciliation process, outstanding checks are subtracted from the bank's indicated balance.

- **Bank service charges** against the company's account, and interest income added to the company's balance during the period by the bank. The bank service charge and interest income should be recognized by the company in the period incurred or earned, respectively, because both of these items affect the cash balance at the end of the period. In the reconciliation process, bank service charges are subtracted from the company's indicated balance; interest income is added to the company's indicated balance.

- **NSF (not sufficient funds) checks,** which are checks that have "bounced" from the maker's bank because the account did not have enough funds to cover the check. Because the company that received the check recorded it as a cash receipt and added the check amount to the balance of its Cash account, it is necessary to establish an account receivable for the amount due from the maker of the NSF check. In the reconciliation process, NSF checks are subtracted from the company's indicated balance.

Errors, which can be made by either the company or the bank, are detected in what may be a trial-and-error process if the book balance and bank balance do not reconcile after timing differences have been recognized. Finding errors is a tedious process involving verification of the timing difference amounts (e.g., double-checking the makeup and total of the list of outstanding checks), verifying the debits and credits to the company's ledger account, and verifying the arithmetic and amounts included on the bank statement. If the error is in the recording of cash transactions on the company's books, an appropriate journal entry must be made to correct the error. If the bank has made the error, the bank is notified but no change is made to the Cash account balance. In the reconciliation process, an addition or subtraction is made to correct the error on the side that made the error (either the bank or the company).

There are a number of ways of mechanically setting up the bank reconciliation. The reverse side of the bank statement usually has a reconciliation format printed on it. Many computer-based bookkeeping systems contain a bank reconciliation module that can facilitate the bank reconciliation process. When the bank statement lists returned checks in numerical order, the process is made even easier. A simple and clear technique for setting up the reconciliation is illustrated in Exhibit 5-2.

Even in today's world of electronic banking, the need to reconcile checking accounts on a regular basis retains its importance. Although deposits are now recorded instantaneously in many e-banking systems, checks still take time to clear, banks still charge fees for their services, and NSF checks and errors are every bit as likely to occur as in older systems.

What Does It Mean?
Answer on page 184

3. What does it mean to reconcile a bank account?

Short-Term Marketable Securities

LO 4

Explain how short-term marketable securities are reported on the balance sheet.

As emphasized in the discussion of cash and cash equivalents, a firm's ROI can be improved by developing a cash management program that involves investing cash balances over and above those required for day-to-day operations in **short-term marketable securities.** An integral part of the cash management program is the forecast of cash receipts and disbursements (forecasting, or budgeting, is discussed in Chapter 14). Recall from Chapter 2 that current assets are defined as *cash and other assets that are likely to be converted into cash or used to benefit the entity within one year of the balance sheet date.* Thus, any debt investments that mature beyond one year from the balance sheet date, and any equity securities that management has the ability and intent to hold for more than one year from the balance sheet date, would be reported as "long-term marketable securities."

Balance Sheet Valuation

Short-term marketable debt securities that fall in the *held-to-maturity* category are reported on the balance sheet at the entity's *cost,* which is usually about the same as market value, because of their high quality and the short time until maturity. The majority of investments made by most firms are of this variety because the excess cash

Exhibit 5-2

A Bank Reconciliation Illustrated

Assumptions:

- The balance in the Cash account of Cruisers Inc. at September 30 was $4,614.58.
- The bank statement showed a balance of $5,233.21 as of September 30.
- Included with the bank statement were notices that the bank had deducted a service charge of $42.76 and had credited the account with interest of $28.91 earned on the average daily balance.
- An NSF check for $35.00 from a customer was returned with the bank statement.
- A comparison of deposits recorded in the Cash account with those shown on the bank statement showed that the September 30 deposit of $859.10 was not on the bank statement. This is not surprising because the September 30 deposit was put in the bank's night depository on the evening of September 30.
- A comparison of the record of checks issued with the checks returned in the bank statement showed that the amount of outstanding checks was $1,526.58.

Reconciliation as of September 30:

From Bank Records		**From Company's Books**	
Indicated balance	$5,233.21	Indicated balance	$4,614.58
Add: Deposit in transit	859.10	Add: Interest earned	28.91
		Less: Service charge	(42.76)
Less: Outstanding checks	(1,526.58)	NSF check	(35.00)
Reconciled balance	$4,565.73	Reconciled balance	$4,565.73

   The balance in the company's general ledger account before reconciliation (the "Indicated balance") must be adjusted to the reconciled balance. Using the horizontal model, the effect of this adjustment on the financial statements is as follows:

Balance Sheet	**Income Statement**	
Asset = Liabilities + Stockholders' equity	← Net income = Revenues − Expenses	
Accounts Receivable +35.00 Cash −48.85	Interest Income +28.91	Service Charge Expense −42.76

The journal entry to reflect this adjustment is as follows:

Dr.	Service Charge Expense	42.76	
Dr.	Accounts Receivable	35.00	
	Cr. Interest Income		28.91
	Cr. Cash		48.85

Alternatively, a separate adjustment could be made for each reconciling item. The amount from this particular bank account to be included in the cash amount shown on the balance sheet for September 30 is $4,565.73. There would not be an adjustment for the reconciling items that affect the bank balance because those items have already been recorded on the company's books.

available for investment will soon be needed to meet working capital obligations. If an entity owns marketable debt securities that are not likely to be converted to cash within a few months of the balance sheet date, or marketable equity securities that are subject to significant fluctuation in market value (like common and preferred stock), the balance sheet valuation and related accounting become more complex. Debt and equity securities that fall in the *trading* and *available-for-sale* categories are reported at *market value,* and any unrealized gains or losses are recognized. This is an application of the matching concept because the change in market value is reflected in the fiscal period in which it occurs.

What Does It Mean?

Answer on page 184

4. What does it mean to invest cash in short-term marketable securities?

Interest Accrual

It is appropriate that interest income on short-term marketable debt securities be accrued as earned so that both the balance sheet and income statement more accurately reflect the financial position at the end of the period and results of operations for the period. The asset involved is called *Interest Receivable,* and *Interest Income* is the income statement account. Here is the effect of the interest accrual on the financial statements:

Balance Sheet	Income Statement
Assets = Liabilities + Stockholders' equity	← Net income = Revenues − Expenses

+ Interest
   Receivable
	+ Interest
	   Income

The accrual is made with the following entry:

Dr. Interest Receivable	xx	
Cr. Interest Income		xx

The amount in the Interest Receivable account is combined with other receivables in the current asset section of the balance sheet.

What Does It Mean?

Answer on page 184

5. What does it mean when interest income from marketable securities must be accrued?

Accounts Receivable

Recall from the Campbell Soup Company balance sheet that Accounts Receivable was a significant current asset category at July 30, 2017. Accounts receivable from customers for merchandise and services delivered are reported at **net realizable value**—the amount that is expected to be received from customers in settlement of their obligations. Two factors will cause this amount to differ from the amount of the receivable originally recorded: bad debts and cash discounts.

Bad Debts/Uncollectible Accounts

Whenever a firm permits its customers to purchase merchandise or services on credit, it knows that some of the customers will not pay. Even a thorough check of the potential customer's credit rating and history of payments to other suppliers will not ensure that the customer will pay in the future. Although some bad debt losses are inevitable when a firm makes credit sales, internal control policies and procedures exist in most firms to keep losses at a minimum and to ensure that every reasonable effort is made to collect all amounts that are due to the firm. Some companies, however, willingly accept high credit risk customers and know that they will experience high bad debt losses. These firms maximize their ROI by having a very high margin and requiring a down payment that equals or approaches the cost of the item being sold. Sales volume is higher than it would be if credit standards were tougher; thus, even though bad debts are relatively high, all or most of the product cost is recovered, and bad debt losses are more than offset by the profits from greater sales volume.

LO 5
Discuss how accounts receivable are reported on the balance sheet, including the valuation allowances for estimated uncollectible accounts and estimated cash discounts.

Based on recent collection experience, tempered by the current state of economic affairs of the industry in which a firm is operating, credit managers can estimate with a high degree of accuracy the probable **bad debts expense** (or **uncollectible accounts expense**) of the firm. Many firms estimate bad debts based on a simplified assumption about the collectibility of all credit sales made during a period (percentage of credit sales method). Other firms perform a detailed analysis and aging of their year-end accounts receivable to estimate the net amount most likely to be collected (aging of receivables method). For instance, a firm may choose the following age categories and estimated collection percentages: 0–30 days (98%), 31–60 days (95%), 61–120 days (85%), and 121–180 days (60%). The firm also may have an administrative internal control policy requiring that all accounts more than six months overdue be immediately turned over to a collection agency. Such a policy is likely to increase the probability of collecting these accounts, facilitate the collection efforts for other overdue accounts, and reduce the overall costs of managing accounts receivable. The success of any bad debts estimation technique ultimately depends on the careful application of professional judgment, using the best available information.

When the amount of accounts receivable estimated to be uncollectible has been determined, a **valuation adjustment** can be recorded to reduce the **carrying value** of the asset and recognize the bad debt expense. The effect of this adjustment on the financial statements is as follows:

Balance Sheet	Income Statement
Assets = Liabilities + Stockholders' equity	← Net income = Revenues − Expenses
− Allowance for Bad Debts	− Bad Debts Expense

Here is the adjustment:

Dr. Bad Debts Expense (or Uncollectible Accounts Expense)	xx
Cr. Allowance for Bad Debts (or Allowance for	
Uncollectible Accounts)	xx

In bookkeeping language, the **Allowance for Uncollectible Accounts** (or Allowance for Bad Debts) account is considered a **contra asset** because it is reported as a subtraction from an asset in the balance sheet. The debit and credit mechanics of a contra asset account are the opposite of those of an asset account; that is, a contra asset increases with credit entries and decreases with debit entries, and it normally has a credit balance. The presentation of the Allowance for Bad Debts in the current asset section of the balance sheet (using assumed amounts) is as follows:

Accounts receivable	$10,000
Less: Allowance for bad debts	(500)
Net accounts receivable	$ 9,500

or, as more commonly reported:

Accounts receivable, less allowance	
for bad debts of $500	$9,500

The Allowance for Bad Debts account communicates to financial statement readers that an estimated portion of the total amount of accounts receivable is expected to become uncollectible.

So why not simply reduce the Accounts Receivable account directly for estimated bad debts? The problem with this approach is that the firm hasn't yet determined *which* customers will not pay—only that *some* will not pay. Before accounts receivable can be reduced, the firm must be able to identify which specific accounts need to be written off as uncollectible. Throughout the year, as specific accounts are determined to be uncollectible, they are written off against the allowance account. The effect of this entry on the financial statements follows:

Balance Sheet	Income Statement
Assets = Liabilities + Stockholders' equity	← Net income = Revenues − Expenses

− Accounts
   Receivable
 	
+ Allowance
   for Bad Debts	

The write-off entry is this:

Dr. Allowance for Bad Debts	xx
Cr. Accounts Receivable	xx

Note that the **write-off** of an account receivable has no effect on the income statement, nor should it. The expense was recognized in the year in which the revenue from the transaction with this customer was recognized. The write-off entry removes from Accounts Receivable an amount that is never expected to be collected. Also note that the write-off of an account will not affect the net accounts receivable reported on the balance sheet because the financial statement effects on the asset (Accounts Receivable) and the contra asset (Allowance for Bad Debts) are offsetting. Assume that $100 of the accounts receivable in the previous example was written off. The balance sheet presentation now would be:

Accounts receivable	$9,900
Less: Allowance for bad debts	(400)
Net accounts receivable	$9,500

Providing for bad debts expense in the same year in which the related sales revenue is recognized is an application of the matching concept. The Allowance for Bad Debts (or Allowance for Uncollectible Accounts) account is a **valuation account,** and its credit balance is subtracted from the debit balance of Accounts Receivable to arrive at the amount of net receivables reported in the Current Asset section of the balance sheet. This procedure results in stating Accounts Receivable at the amount expected to be collected (net realizable value). If an appropriate allowance for bad debts is not provided, Accounts Receivable and net income will be overstated, and the ROI, ROE, and liquidity measures will be distorted. The amount of the allowance usually is reported parenthetically in the Accounts Receivable caption on the balance sheet, or possibly in a schedule in the notes to the financial statements, so that financial statement users can evaluate the credit and collection practices of the firm.

---

6. What does it mean that the Allowance for Bad Debts account is a contra asset?

What Does It Mean?
Answer on page 184

Cash Discounts

To encourage prompt payment, many firms permit their customers to deduct up to 2 percent of the amount owed if the bill is paid within a stated period—usually 10 days—of the date of the sale (usually referred to as the *invoice date*). Most firms' **credit terms** provide that if the invoice is not paid within the discount period, it must be paid in full within 30 days of the invoice date. These credit terms are abbreviated as 2/10, n30. The *2/10* refers to the discount terms, and the *n30* means that the full amount of the invoice is due within 30 days. To illustrate, assume that Cruisers Inc. has credit sales terms of 2/10, n30. On April 8, Cruisers Inc. made a $5,000 sale to Mount Marina. Mount Marina has the option of paying $4,900 (5,000 − [2% × $5,000]) by April 18 or paying $5,000 by May 8.

Like most firms, Mount Marina will probably take advantage of the **cash discount** because it represents a high rate of return (see Business in Practice—Cash Discounts). The discount is clearly a cost to the seller because the selling firm will not receive the full amount of the account receivable resulting from the sale. The accounting treatment for estimated cash discounts is similar to that illustrated for estimated bad debts. Cash discounts on sales usually are subtracted from Sales in the income statement to arrive

Business in
Practice

at the net sales amount that is reported because the discount is, in effect, a reduction of the selling price. On the balance sheet, it is appropriate to reduce Accounts Receivable by an allowance for estimated cash discounts that will be taken by customers when they pay within the discount period. Estimated cash discounts are recognized in the fiscal period in which the sales are made, based on past experience with cash discounts taken.

Notes Receivable

LO 6

Explain how notes receivable and related accrued interest are reported on the balance sheet.

If a firm has an account receivable from a customer that developed difficulties paying its balance when due, the firm may convert that account receivable to a **note receivable.** Here is the effect of this transaction on the financial statements:

Balance Sheet	Income Statement
Assets = Liabilities + Stockholders' equity	← Net income = Revenues − Expenses
− Accounts Receivable + Notes Receivable	

The entry to reflect this transaction is as follows:

Dr. Notes Receivable	xx	
Cr. Accounts Receivable		xx

One asset has been exchanged for another. Does the entry make sense?

A note receivable differs from an account receivable in several ways. A note is a formal document that includes specific provisions with respect to its maturity date (when it is to be paid), agreements or *covenants* made by the borrower (such as to supply financial statements to the lender or refrain from paying dividends until the note is repaid), identification of security or **collateral** pledged by the borrower to support the loan, penalties to be assessed if it is not paid on the maturity date, and, most important, the interest rate associated with the loan. Although some firms assess an interest charge or service charge on invoice amounts for accounts receivable that are not paid when due, this practice is unusual for regular transactions between firms. Thus, if an account receivable is not going to be paid promptly, the seller will ask the customer to sign a note so that interest can be earned on the overdue account.

Retail firms often use notes to facilitate sales transactions for which the initial credit period exceeds 60 or 90 days, such as an installment plan for equipment sales. In such cases, Notes Receivable (rather than Accounts Receivable) is increased at the point of sale, even though the seller may provide interest-free financing for a period of time.

Under other circumstances, a firm may lend money to another entity and take a note from that entity; for example, a manufacturer may lend money to a distributor that is also a customer or potential customer in order to help the distributor build its business. Such a transaction is another rearrangement of assets: Cash is decreased and Notes Receivable is increased.

Interest Accrual

If interest is to be paid at the maturity of the note (a common practice), it is appropriate that the holder of the note accrue interest revenue, usually monthly. This is appropriate because interest revenue has been earned, and accruing the revenue and increasing interest receivable result in more accurate monthly financial statements. The financial statement effects of doing this are the same as that for interest accrued on short-term marketable securities:

Balance Sheet	Income Statement
Assets = Liabilities + Stockholders' equity	← Net income = Revenues − Expenses

+ Interest
   Receivable
	+ Interest
	   Revenue

The adjustment is as follows:

Dr.	Interest Receivable	xx
	Cr. Interest Revenue	xx

This accrual entry reflects interest revenue that has been earned in the period and increases current assets by the amount earned but not yet received.

Interest Receivable is frequently combined with Notes Receivable in the balance sheet for reporting purposes. Amounts to be received within a year of the balance sheet date are classified as current assets. If the note has a maturity date beyond a year, it will be classified as a noncurrent asset.

It is appropriate to recognize any probable loss from uncollectible notes and interest receivable just as is done for accounts receivable, and the bookkeeping process is the same. Cash discounts do not apply to notes, so there is no discount valuation allowance.

Inventories

LO 7

Explain how inventories
are reported on the
balance sheet.

For service organizations, inventories consist mainly of office supplies and other items of relatively low value that will be used up within the organization, rather than being offered for sale to customers. As illustrated in Chapter 4, recording the purchase and use of supplies is a straightforward process, although year-end adjustments are usually necessary to improve the accuracy of the accounting records.

Campbell's

For merchandising and manufacturing firms, the sale of inventory in the ordinary course of business provides the major, ongoing source of operating revenue. Cost of Goods Sold (Campbell's uses the equally acceptable synonymous term *Cost of Products Sold*) is usually the largest expense that is subtracted from Sales in determining net income, and, not surprisingly, inventories represent the most significant current asset for many such firms. At Campbell Soup Company, inventories account for 47 percent of current assets and 12 percent of total assets.[1] For Wal-Mart Stores Inc., 75 percent of current assets and 22 percent of total assets are tied up in inventories.[2] For Apple Inc., inventories represent less than 4 percent of current assets and less than 2 percent of total assets.[3] Can you think of some possible explanations for these varying results? Obviously not all firms (and not all industries) have the same inventory needs because of differences in their respective products, markets, customers, and distribution systems. Moreover, some firms do a better job than others of managing their inventory by turning it over quickly to enhance ROI. What other factors might cause the relative size of inventories to vary among firms?

Although inventory management practices are diverse, the accounting treatment for inventory items is essentially the same for all firms. Just as warehouse bins and store shelves hold inventory until the product is sold to the customer, the inventory accounts of a firm hold the *cost* of a product until that cost is released to the income statement to be subtracted from (matched with) the revenue from the sale. The cost of a purchased or manufactured product is recorded as an asset and carried in the asset account until the product is sold (or becomes worthless or is lost or stolen), at which point the cost becomes an expense to be reported in the income statement. The cost of an item purchased for inventory includes not only the invoice price paid to the supplier but also other costs associated with the purchase of the item, such as freight and material handling charges. Cost is reduced by the amount of any cash discount allowed on the purchase. The income statement caption used to report this expense is Cost of Goods Sold. Here are the effects of purchase and sale transactions on the financial statements:

Balance Sheet	Income Statement
Assets = Liabilities + Stockholders' equity	← Net income = Revenues − Expenses
Purchase of inventory: + Inventory + Accounts Payable Recognize cost of goods sold: − Inventory	− Cost of Goods Sold

---

[1] Data based on Campbell Soup Company's Form 10-K filing for the year ended August 3, 2014.
[2] Data based on Wal-Mart Stores, Inc.'s Form 10-K filing for the year ended January 31, 2015.
[3] Data based on Apple, Inc.'s Form 10-K filing for the year ended September 27, 2014.

Exhibit 5-3

Flow of Costs from
Inventory to Cost of
Goods Sold

Balance Sheet		Income Statement	
Inventory (asset)		*Cost of Goods Sold (expense)*	
Purchases of merchandise for resale increase Inventory (credit to Accounts Payable or Cash)	When merchandise is sold, the cost flows from the Inventory asset account to ⟶	⟶ the Cost of Goods Sold expense account	

The entries are as follows:

Dr. Inventory	xx	
Cr. Accounts Payable (or Cash)		xx
Purchase of inventory.		
Dr. Cost of Goods Sold	xx	
Cr. Inventory		xx
To transfer cost of item sold to income statement.		

Recognizing cost of goods sold is a process of accounting for the *flow of costs* from the Inventory (asset) account of the balance sheet to the Cost of Goods Sold (expense) account of the income statement. T-accounts also can be used to illustrate this flow of costs, as shown in Exhibit 5-3. Of course the sale of merchandise also generates revenue, but *recognizing revenue is a separate transaction* involving Accounts Receivable (or Cash) and the Sales Revenue accounts. The following discussion focuses only on the accounting for the cost of the inventory sold.

Inventory Cost Flow Assumptions

Accounting for inventories is one of the areas in which alternative generally accepted practices can result in major differences between the assets and expenses reported by companies that otherwise might be alike in all respects. It is therefore important to study this material carefully to appreciate the impact of inventory methods on a firm's financial statements.

The inventory accounting alternative selected by an entity relates to the assumption about how costs flow from the Inventory account to the Cost of Goods Sold account. There are four principal alternative **cost flow assumptions**:

1. Specific identification.
2. Weighted average.
3. First-in, first-out (FIFO) (pronounced FIE-FOE).
4. Last-in, first-out (LIFO) (pronounced LIE-FOE).

It is important to recognize that these are *cost flow assumptions* and that FIFO and LIFO do not refer to the physical flow of product. Thus, it is possible for a firm to have a FIFO physical flow (a grocery store usually tries to accomplish this) and to use the LIFO cost flow assumption.

LO 8

Discuss the alternative inventory cost flow assumptions and generalize about their respective effects on the income statement and balance sheet when price levels are changing.

The IFRS Approach

The LIFO inventory cost flow assumption is not permitted under international financial reporting standards. The primary reason for the disallowance of LIFO appears to be that international standards have a strong balance sheet measurement focus, and efforts have been made to eliminate accounting methods such as LIFO that do not support this so-called balance sheet approach. As discussed in the following sections, during inflationary times, LIFO assigns to inventory the costs of the oldest items acquired by the company, thus causing balance sheet values to become "outdated" as the company grows. As you study this material, think about what the implications would be for U.S. companies if the LIFO cost flow assumption were no longer available as a reporting alternative under U.S. GAAP.

The **specific identification** alternative links cost and physical flow. When an item is sold, the cost of that specific item is determined from the firm's records, and that amount is transferred from the Inventory account to Cost of Goods Sold. The amount of ending inventory is the cost of the items held in inventory at the end of the year. This alternative is appropriate for a firm dealing with specifically identifiable products, such as automobiles, that have an identifying serial number and are purchased and sold by specific unit. This assumption is not practical for a firm having many inventory items that are not easily identified individually.

The **weighted-average** alternative is applied to individual items of inventory. It involves calculating the average cost of the items in the beginning inventory plus purchases made during the year. The average cost per unit of inventory is then used to determine the cost of goods sold and the carrying value of ending inventory. This method is illustrated in Exhibit 5-4. Notice that the average cost is not a simple average

Exhibit 5-4

Inventory Cost Flow Alternatives Illustrated

Situation:

On September 1, 2019, the inventory of Cruisers Inc. consisted of five Model OB3 boats. Each boat had cost $1,500. During the year ended August 31, 2020, 40 boats were purchased on the dates and at the costs that follow. During the year, 37 boats were sold.

Date of Purchase	Number of Boats	Cost per Boat	Total Cost
September 1, 2019 (beginning inventory)	5	$1,500	$ 7,500
November 7, 2019	8	1,600	12,800
March 12, 2020	12	1,650	19,800
May 22, 2020	10	1,680	16,800
July 28, 2020	6	1,700	10,200
August 30, 2020	4	1,720	6,880
Total of boats available for sale	45		$73,980
Number of boats sold	37		
Number of boats in August 31, 2020, inventory	8		

Required:

Determine the ending inventory amount at August 31, 2020, and the cost of goods sold for the year then ended, using the weighted-average, FIFO, and LIFO cost flow assumptions.

(continued)

Solution:

a. Weighted-average cost flow assumption:

$$\text{Weighted-average cost} = \frac{\text{Total cost of boats available for sale}}{\text{Number of boats available for sale}}$$

$$= \frac{\$73,980}{45}$$

$$= \$1,644 \text{ per boat}$$

Cost of ending inventory = $1,644 × 8 = $13,152
Cost of goods sold = $1,644 × 37 = $60,828

b. FIFO cost flow assumption:

The cost of ending inventory is the cost of the eight boats most recently purchased:

4 boats purchased August 30, 2020, @$1,720 ea	=	$ 6,880
4 boats purchased July 28, 2020, @$1,700 ea	=	6,800
Cost of 8 boats in ending inventory		$13,680

The cost of 37 boats sold is the sum of the costs for the first 37 boats purchased:

Beginning inventory	5 boats @ $1,500 =	$ 7,500
November 7, 2019, purchase	8 boats @ 1,600 =	12,800
March 12, 2020, purchase	12 boats @ 1,650 =	19,800
May 22, 2020, purchase	10 boats @ 1,680 =	16,800
July 28, 2020, purchase*	2 boats @ 1,700 =	3,400
Cost of goods sold		$ 60,300

*Applying the FIFO cost flow assumption, the cost of two of the six boats purchased this date is transferred from Inventory to Cost of Goods Sold.

Note that the cost of goods sold also could have been calculated by subtracting the ending inventory amount from the total cost of the boats available for sale:

Total cost of boats available for sale	$73,980
Less cost of boats in ending inventory	(13,680)
Cost of goods sold	$60,300

c. LIFO cost flow assumption:

The cost of ending inventory is the cost of the first eight boats purchased:

5 boats in beginning inventory @ $1,500 ea	=	$ 7,500
3 boats purchased November 7, 2019, @ $1,600 ea =		4,800
Cost of 8 boats in ending inventory	=	$12,300

The cost of the 37 boats sold is the sum of costs for the last 37 boats purchased:

August 30, 2020, purchase	4 boats @ $1,720 =	$ 6,880
July 28, 2020, purchase	6 boats @ 1,700 =	10,200
May 22, 2020, purchase	10 boats @ 1,680 =	16,800
March 12, 2020, purchase	12 boats @ 1,650 =	19,800
November 7, 2019, purchase†	5 boats @ 1,600 =	8,000
Cost of goods sold		$61,680

†Applying the LIFO cost flow assumption, the cost of five of the eight boats purchased this date is transferred from Inventory to Cost of Goods Sold.

Note that the cost of goods sold also could have been calculated by subtracting the ending inventory amount from the total cost of the boats available for sale:

Total cost of boats available for sale	$73,980
Less cost of boats in ending inventory	(12,300)
Cost of goods sold	$61,680

of the unit costs but is instead an average weighted by the number of units in beginning inventory and each purchase.

First-in, first-out, or **FIFO,** means more than first-in, first-out; it means that the first costs *in to inventory* are the first costs *out to cost of goods sold.* The first cost in is the cost of the inventory on hand at the beginning of the fiscal year. The effect of this inventory cost flow assumption is to transfer to the Cost of Goods Sold account the oldest costs incurred (for the quantity of merchandise sold) and to leave in the Inventory asset account the most recent costs of merchandise purchased or manufactured (for the quantity of merchandise in ending inventory). This cost flow assumption is also illustrated in Exhibit 5-4.

Last-in, first-out, or **LIFO,** is an alternative cost flow assumption opposite to FIFO. Remember, we are thinking about cost flow, not physical flow, and it is possible for a firm to have a FIFO physical flow (like the grocery store) and still use the LIFO cost flow assumption. Under LIFO, the most recent costs incurred for merchandise purchased or manufactured are transferred to the income statement (as Cost of Goods Sold) when items are sold, and the inventory on hand at the balance sheet date is costed at the oldest costs, including those used to value the beginning inventory. This cost flow assumption is also illustrated in Exhibit 5-4.

The way these cost flow assumptions are applied depends on the inventory accounting system in use. The two systems—*periodic* and *perpetual*—are described later in this chapter. Exhibit 5-4 uses the periodic system.

To recap the results of the three alternatives presented in Exhibit 5-4:

Cost Flow Assumption	Cost of Ending Inventory	Costs of Goods Sold
Weighted average	$13,152	$60,828
FIFO	13,680	60,300
LIFO	12,300	61,680

Although the differences between amounts seem small in this illustration, under real-world circumstances with huge amounts of inventory the differences often become large and are thus considered to be material (the materiality concept). Why do the differences occur? Because, as you probably have noticed, the cost of the boats purchased changed over time. If the cost had not changed, there would not have been any difference in the ending inventory and cost of goods sold among the three alternatives. But in practice, costs do change. Notice that the amounts resulting from the weighted-average cost flow assumption are between those for FIFO and LIFO; this is to be expected. Weighted-average results will never be outside the range of amounts resulting from FIFO and LIFO.

The crucial point to understand about the inventory cost flow assumption issue is the impact on cost of goods sold, operating income, and net income of the alternative assumptions. Naturally a company's ROI, ROE, and measures of liquidity are also impacted by its choice of inventory cost flow assumptions (Table 5-1 summarizes the cost flow assumptions most commonly used in practice as of 2011. Unfortunately, the AICPA no longer tracks these data). Because of the importance of the inventory valuation to a firm's measures of profitability and liquidity, the impact of alternative cost flow assumptions must be understood if these measures are to be used effectively in making decisions and informed judgments—especially if comparisons are made between entities.

	Number of Companies
Methods:	
Not disclosed	5
First-in, first-out (FIFO)	311
Last-in, first-out (LIFO)	163
Average cost	133
Other	56
Use of LIFO:	
All inventories	4
50% or more of inventories	66
Less than 50% of inventories	71
Not determinable	22
Companies using LIFO	163

Source: Data from *Accounting Trends and Techniques, U.S. GAAP Financial Statements—Best Practices in Presentation and Disclosure,* Tables 2-3 and 2-4, American Institute of Certified Public Accountants, Inc.

Table 5.1

Inventory Cost Flow Assumptions Used by 500 Publicly Owned Industrial and Merchandising Corporations—2011

---

7. What does it mean to identify the inventory cost flow assumption?

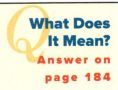

What Does It Mean?

Answer on page 184

The Impact of Changing Costs (Inflation/Deflation)

It is important to understand how the inventory cost flow assumption used by a firm interacts with the direction of cost changes to affect both inventory and cost of goods sold. *In times of rising costs,* LIFO results in lower ending inventory and higher cost of goods sold than FIFO. These changes occur because the LIFO assumption results in most recent, and higher, costs being transferred to cost of goods sold. When purchase costs are falling, the opposite is true. These relationships are illustrated graphically in Exhibit 5-5.

The graphs in Exhibit 5-5 are helpful in understanding the relative impact on cost of goods sold and ending inventory when costs move in one direction. In the real world, costs rise and fall over time, and the impact of a strategy chosen during a period of rising costs will reverse when costs decline. Thus, in the mid-1980s some firms that had switched to LIFO during a prior inflationary period began to experience falling costs. These firms then reported higher profits under LIFO than they would have under FIFO.

Selecting an Inventory Cost Flow Assumption

What factors influence the selection of a cost flow assumption? When rates of inflation were relatively low and the conventional wisdom was that they would always be low, most financial managers selected the FIFO cost flow assumption because that resulted in slightly lower cost of goods sold and hence higher net income. Financial

Exhibit 5-5

Effect of Changing
Costs on Inventory and
Cost of Goods Sold
under FIFO and LIFO

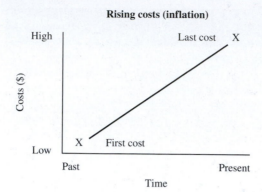

Rising costs (inflation)

FIFO— Lower, older costs transferred
to cost of goods sold.
Higher, more recent costs
stay in inventory.

LIFO— Higher, more recent costs
transferred to cost of goods sold.
Lower, older costs stay
in inventory.

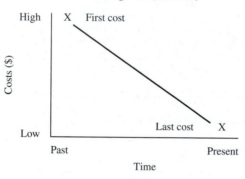

Falling costs (deflation)

FIFO— Higher, older costs transferred
to cost of goods sold.
Lower, more recent costs
stay in inventory.

LIFO— Lower, more recent costs
transferred to cost of goods sold.
Higher, older costs stay
in inventory.

managers have a strong motivation to report higher, rather than lower, net income to the stockholders. However, when double-digit inflation was experienced, the higher net income from the FIFO assumption also resulted in higher income taxes—which, of course, managers prefer not to experience. But why would this occur? When the FIFO cost flow assumption is used during a period of rapidly rising costs, **inventory profits,** or **phantom profits,** result. Under FIFO, the release of older, lower costs to the income statement results in higher profits than if current costs were to be recognized. Taxes must be paid on these profits, and because the current cost of replacing merchandise sold is much higher than the old cost, users of financial statements can be misled about the firm's real economic profitability. See the nearby Study Suggestion, which illustrates this unusual situation with a numerical example.

To avoid inventory profits (and to decrease taxes), many firms changed from FIFO to LIFO for at least part of their inventories during the years of high inflation. (Generally accepted accounting principles do not require that the same cost flow assumption be used for all inventories.) This change to LIFO resulted in higher cost of goods sold than FIFO and lower profits, lower taxes, and (in the opinion of some analysts) more realistic financial reporting of net income. Note, however, that even though net income under LIFO may better reflect a matching of revenues (which also usually rise on a per unit basis during periods of inflation) and costs of merchandise sold, the inventory amount on the balance sheet will be reported at older, lower costs. Thus, under LIFO the balance sheet will not reflect current costs for items in inventory. This is consistent with the original cost concept and underscores the fact that balance sheet amounts do not reflect current values of most assets. It also suggests that, in reality, the

Study

Suggestion

This is a difficult but important concept to grasp, so consider the following example: Assume that Cruisers Inc. sells a boat to a customer for $2,000 and uses the FIFO cost flow assumption. For argument's sake, assume that the cost of goods sold for this boat is $1,500 (taken from the beginning inventory); yet the current cost of replacing the boat has recently increased to $1,900, and the tax rate is 30 percent. The income tax owed by Cruisers Inc. from this sale would be $150, computed as ($2,000 − $1,500) × 30%; when this amount is added to the cost of replacing the boat, the company would experience a negative net cash flow ($2,000 − $1,900 − $150 = −$50) from these transactions! However, on the income statement, net income would be $350 ($2,000 − $1,500 − $150).

use of LIFO only delays the recognition of inventory profits, although this delay can be long-term if prices continue to rise and LIFO inventory layers are not eliminated through liquidations.

But what about consistency—the concept that requires whatever accounting alternative selected for one year to be used for subsequent financial reporting? With respect to the inventory cost flow assumption, the Internal Revenue Service permits a one-time, one-way change from FIFO to LIFO. (Note that if a firm decides to use the LIFO cost flow assumption for tax purposes, federal income tax law requires that LIFO also must be used for financial reporting purposes. This tax requirement, referred to as the *LIFO conformity rule,* is a constraint that does not exist in other areas where alternative accounting methods exist.) When a change in methods is made, the effect of the change on both the balance sheet (inventory) and income statement (cost of goods sold) must be disclosed, so financial statement users can evaluate the impact of the change on the firm's financial position and results of operations.

Look back at Table 5-1, which reports the methods used to determine inventory cost by 500 industrial and merchandising corporations whose annual reports are reviewed and summarized by the AICPA. It is significant that many companies use at least two methods and that only four companies use LIFO for all inventories. The mix of inventory cost flow assumptions used in practice emphasizes the complex ramifications of selecting a cost flow assumption.

---

8. What does it mean to say that net income includes inventory profits?

What Does It Mean?

Answer on page 184

There is obviously a conflict between international financial reporting standards, which do not allow the use of LIFO, and the LIFO conformity rule, which requires that firms using LIFO for tax purposes must also use LIFO for financial reporting purposes. Thus, under current federal income tax law, it seems clear that a U.S. company using LIFO for tax purposes will be in violation of the LIFO conformity rule if it issues financial statements under IFRS. As IFRS and U.S. GAAP standards become more fully integrated in the next few years, this issue will become even more relevant and will require a pragmatic solution.

The IFRS

Approach

Inventory Accounting System Alternatives

The system to account for inventory cost flow is often quite complex in practice because most firms have hundreds or thousands of inventory items. There are two principal **inventory accounting systems:** perpetual and periodic.

In a **perpetual inventory system,** a record is made of every purchase and every sale, and a continuous record of the quantity and cost of each item of inventory is maintained. Computers have made perpetual inventory systems feasible for an increasingly large number of small to medium-sized retail organizations that were forced in previous years to use periodic systems. Advances in the use of product bar coding and scanning devices at cash registers, as well as radio frequency identification tags, have lowered the costs of maintaining perpetual records. The accounting issues involved with a perpetual system are easy to understand (see Business in Practice—The Perpetual Inventory System) after you have learned how the alternative cost flow assumptions are applied in a periodic system (refer to Exhibit 5-4 if you need a review).

In a **periodic inventory system,** a count of the inventory on hand (taking a **physical inventory**) is made periodically—frequently at the end of the fiscal year—and the cost of the inventory on hand, based on the cost flow assumption being used, is determined and subtracted from the sum of the beginning inventory and purchases to determine the cost of goods sold. This calculation is illustrated with the following **cost of goods sold model,** using data from the FIFO cost flow assumption of Exhibit 5-4:

Beginning inventory	$ 7,500
Purchases	66,480
Cost of goods available for sale	$73,980
Less: Ending inventory	(13,680)
Cost of goods sold	$60,300

The examples in Exhibit 5-4 use the periodic inventory system. Although less detailed record keeping is needed for the periodic system than for the perpetual system, the efforts involved in counting and costing the inventory on hand are still significant.

Even when a perpetual inventory system is used, it is appropriate to periodically verify that the quantity of an item shown by the perpetual inventory record to be on hand is the quantity actually on hand. Bookkeeping errors and theft or mysterious disappearance cause differences between the recorded and actual quantities of inventory items. When differences are found, it is appropriate to reflect these as inventory losses, or corrections to cost of goods sold, as appropriate. If the losses are significant, management probably would authorize an investigation to determine the cause of the loss and develop recommendations for strengthening the system of internal control over inventories.

This discussion of accounting for inventories has focused on the products available for sale to the entity's customers. A retail firm would use the term **merchandise inventory** to describe this inventory category; a manufacturing firm would use the term **finished goods inventory.** Besides finished goods inventory, a manufacturing firm will have two other broad inventory categories: raw materials and work in process. In a manufacturing firm, the **Raw Materials Inventory** account is used to hold the costs of raw materials until the materials are released to the factory floor, at which time the costs are transferred to the **Work in Process Inventory** account. Direct labor costs (wages of production workers) and factory overhead costs (e.g., factory utilities, maintenance costs for production equipment, and the depreciation of factory buildings

The Perpetual Inventory System

Under a perpetual inventory system, the cost flow assumption used by the firm is applied on a day-to-day basis as sales are recorded, rather than at the end of the year (or month). This allows the firm to record increases to Cost of Goods Sold and decreases to Inventory on a daily basis. This makes sense from a matching perspective because the sale of inventory is what triggers the cost of goods sold. The following financial statement effects occur at the point of sale:

Balance Sheet	Income Statement
Assets = Liabilities + Stockholders' equity	← Net income = Revenues − Expenses

Record sale of goods:
+ Accounts
   Receivable
   (or Cash)
 	
Recognize cost of goods sold:
− Inventory
	+ Sales
	
	− Cost of
	   Goods
	   Sold

The entries to reflect these transactions are as follows:

Dr.	Accounts Receivable (or Cash)	xx	
	Cr. Sales		xx
Dr.	Cost of Goods Sold	xx	
	Cr. Inventory		xx

Thus, a continuous (or perpetual) record is maintained of the inventory account balance. Under FIFO, the periodic and perpetual systems will always produce the same results for ending inventory and cost of goods sold. Why would this be the case? Even though the FIFO rules are applied at different points in time—at the end of the year (or month) with periodic, and daily with perpetual—the first-in cost will remain in inventory until the next item of inventory is sold. Once first in, always first in, and costs flow from Inventory to Cost of Goods Sold based strictly on the chronological order of purchase transactions. The results are the same under either system because whenever the question "What was the first-in cost?" is asked (daily or annually), the answer is the same.

Under LIFO, when the question "What was the last-in cost?" is asked, the answer will change each time a new item of inventory is purchased. In a perpetual system, the last-in costs must be determined on a daily basis so that cost of goods sold can be recorded as sales transactions occur; the cost of the most recently purchased inventory items is assigned to Cost of Goods Sold each day. But as soon as new items of inventory are purchased, the last-in costs are redefined accordingly. This differs from the periodic approach to applying the LIFO rules. In a periodic system, the last-in costs are assumed to relate only to those inventory items that are purchased toward the end of the year (or month), even though some of the sales transactions occurred earlier in the year (or month).

The weighted-average method becomes a "moving" average under the perpetual system. As with the LIFO method, when the question "What was the average cost of inventory?" is asked, the answer is likely to change each time new inventory items are purchased.

and equipment) are also recorded in the Work in Process Inventory account. These costs, *incurred in making the product,* as opposed to costs of selling the product or administering the company generally, are appropriately related to the inventory items being produced and become part of the product cost to be accounted for as an asset (inventory) until the product is sold. Accounting for production costs is a large part of cost accounting, a topic that will be explored in more detail in Chapter 13.

Study

Suggestion

The effects of inventory errors on cost of goods sold and gross profit can be difficult to reason through. When confronted with having to determine the effects of such errors, two alternative approaches to solving this problem are to use T-accounts for Inventory and Cost of Goods Sold, or to use the cost of goods sold model:

Beginning inventory	$
Cost of goods purchased or manufactured	_____
Cost of goods available for sale	$
Less: Ending inventory	(____)
Cost of goods sold	$ _____

Under either approach, you would do the following:

1. Plug in the "as reported" results for each year.
2. Make the necessary corrections to these amounts to determine the "as corrected" results.
3. Compare your results—before and after the corrections—to determine the effects of the error(s).

LO 9

Discuss the impact of inventory errors on the balance sheet and income statement.

Inventory Errors

Errors in the amount of ending inventory have a direct dollar-for-dollar effect on cost of goods sold and net income. This direct link between inventory amounts and reported profit or loss causes independent auditors, income tax auditors, and financial analysts to look closely at reported inventory amounts. The following T-account diagram illustrates this link:

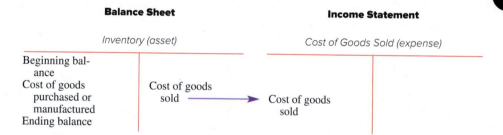

When the periodic inventory system is used, a great deal of effort is made to ensure that the ending inventory count and valuation are as accurate as possible because inventory errors can have a significant impact on both the balance sheet and the income statement for each period affected. As illustrated in Exhibit 5-6, this type of error "washes out" over the two periods taken together (*total* net income is not affected by the error) assuming that the inventory at the end of the second period is counted correctly. Check this out by adding together the total net income for 2019 and 2020 before and after the error is corrected in Exhibit 5-6.

What Does It Mean?

Answer on page 185

9. What does it mean to say that an error in the ending inventory of the current accounting period has an equal but opposite effect on the net income of the subsequent accounting period?

To illustrate the effects of inventory errors, assume that Sample Co. reported the following comparative results:

Exhibit 5-6

Inventory Errors Illustrated

For the year ended December 31:	As Reported	
	2019	2020
Sales	$500,000	$500,000
Cost of goods sold	300,000	300,000
Gross profit	$200,000	$200,000
Operating expenses	100,000	100,000
Net income (ignoring income taxes)	$100,000	$100,000

In early 2021, it was determined that ending inventory on the December 31, 2019, balance sheet was overstated by $10,000 due to the double counting of certain inventory items. All of the inventory items in question were sold during 2020, so the December 31, 2020, inventory count was done correctly and thus the 2020 inventory amount was correct as reported.

As corrected for the effects of the inventory error that occurred at December 31, 2019, Sample Co.'s comparative results would be reported as follows:

For the year ended December 31:	As Corrected	
	2019	2020
Sales	$500,000	$500,000
Cost of goods sold	310,000	290,000
Gross profit	$190,000	$210,000
Operating expenses	100,000	100,000
Net income (ignoring income taxes)	$ 90,000	$110,000

Note that by overstating ending inventory by $10,000 in 2019, cost of goods sold was understated by the same amount ($300,000 as reported rather than $310,000 as corrected). By understating cost of goods sold in 2019, gross profit was overstated ($200,000 rather than $190,000), with a corresponding overstatement of net income in 2019 by the same $10,000 amount.

In 2020, the effects of the 2019 ending inventory error were reversed because the ending inventory on December 31, 2019, became the beginning inventory on January 1, 2020. By overstating beginning inventory, the cost of goods available for sale was overstated, causing cost of goods sold in 2020 to be overstated ($300,000 as reported rather than $290,000 as corrected). By overstating cost of goods sold, gross profit was understated in 2020 ($200,000 rather than $210,000) and net income was understated by the same $10,000 amount.

Balance Sheet Valuation at the Lower of Cost or Market

Inventory carrying values on the balance sheet are reported at the **lower of cost or market.** This reporting is an application of accounting conservatism. The "cost" of lower of cost or market is determined as described in the preceding pages. Inventory is initially recorded for the purchase price (or for the cost of goods manufactured) to the firm. The firm's cost flow assumption (FIFO, LIFO, or weighted average) is then applied to determine the "cost" of ending inventory, which is the amount ordinarily shown as the carrying value of inventory on the balance sheet. However, this "cost" amount must be compared to the market value of the firm's inventory to ensure that

The **IFRS**

Approach

Under international accounting standards, inventories are initially recorded at cost. For financial reporting purposes, inventories are valued at the lower of cost or net realizable value. Net realizable value is the estimated selling price in the ordinary course of business less the estimated costs of completion and estimated selling expenses.

the inventory (an asset) is not overvalued for financial reporting purposes. The "market" of lower of cost or market is generally the replacement cost of the inventory on the balance sheet date. If market value is lower than cost, a loss is reported in the accounting period in which the decline in inventory value occurred. The lower-of-cost-or-market determination can be made with respect to individual items of inventory, broad categories of inventory, or to the inventory as a whole.

LO 10

Explain what prepaid expenses are and how they are reported on the balance sheet.

Prepaid Expenses and Other Current Assets

Other current assets are principally **prepaid expenses**—that is, expenses that have been paid in the current fiscal period but that will not be subtracted from revenue until a subsequent fiscal period. This is the opposite of an accrual and is referred to in accounting and bookkeeping jargon as a *deferral* or *deferred charge* (or *deferred debit* because *charge is a bookkeeping synonym for debit*). An example of a **deferred charge** transaction is a premium payment to an insurance company. It is standard business practice to pay an insurance premium at the beginning of the period of insurance coverage. Assume that a one-year casualty insurance premium of $1,800 is paid on November 1, 2019. At December 31, 2019, insurance coverage for two months has been received, and it is appropriate to recognize the cost of that coverage as an expense. However, the cost of coverage for the next 10 months should be deferred—that is, not shown as an expense but reported as **prepaid insurance,** an asset. Usual bookkeeping practice is to record the premium payment transaction as an increase in the Prepaid Insurance asset account and then to transfer a portion of the premium to the Insurance Expense account as the expense is incurred. Using the horizontal model, this transaction and the adjustment affect the financial statements as follows:

Balance Sheet	Income Statement
Assets = Liabilities + Stockholders' equity	← Net income = Revenues − Expenses
Payment of premium for the year: Cash −1,800 Prepaid Insurance +1,800 Recognition of expense for two months: Prepaid Insurance −300	Insurance Expense −300

The journal entries are as follows:

Nov. 1	Dr. Prepaid Insurance	1,800	
	Cr. Cash		1,800
	Payment of one-year premium.		
Dec. 31	Dr. Insurance Expense	300	
	Cr. Prepaid Insurance		300
	Insurance expense for two months incurred.		

The balance in the Prepaid Insurance asset account at December 31 would be $1,500, which represents the premium for the next 10 months' coverage that has already been paid and will be transferred to Insurance Expense over the next 10 months as the economic benefits associated with the insurance coverage are received and thus the expense of $150 per month is incurred.

Other expenses that could be prepaid and included in this category of current assets include rent, office supplies, postage, and travel expense advances to salespeople and other employees. The key to deferring these expenses is that they can be objectively associated with an economic benefit to be received in a future period. Advertising expenditures are not properly deferred because determining objectively how much of the benefit of advertising was received in the current period and how much of the benefit will be received in future periods is impossible. As with advertising expenditures, research and development costs are not deferred but are instead treated as expenses in the year incurred. The accountant's principal concerns are that the prepaid item be a properly deferred expense and that it will be used up, and become an expense, within the one-year time frame for classification as a current asset.

---

10. What does it mean to defer an expense?

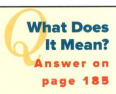

What Does It Mean?

Answer on page 185

Demonstration Problem

The Demonstration Problem walkthrough for this chapter is available in Connect.

Summary

This chapter has discussed the accounting for and the presentation of the following balance sheet current assets and related income statement accounts:

Balance Sheet	Income Statement
Assets = Liabilities + Stockholders' equity	← Net income = Revenues − Expenses
Cash	
Marketable Securities	
Interest Receivable	Interest Revenue
Accounts Receivable	Sales Revenue
(Allowance for Bad Debts)	Bad Debts Expense
Inventory	Cost of Goods Sold
Prepaid Expenses	Operating Expenses

The amount of cash reported on the balance sheet represents the cash available to the company as of the close of business on the balance sheet date. Cash available in bank accounts is determined by reconciling the bank statement balance with the company's book balance. Reconciling items are caused by timing differences (such as deposits in transit or outstanding checks) and errors. **(LO 1, 3)**

Petty cash funds are used as a convenience for making small disbursements of cash. Well-managed companies temporarily invest excess cash in short-term marketable securities to earn interest income. Cash managers invest in short-term, low-risk securities that are not likely to have a widely fluctuating market value. Marketable securities that will be held until maturity are reported in the balance sheet at cost; securities that may be traded or that are available for sale are reported at market value. **(LO 4)**

Accounts receivable are valued in the balance sheet at the amount expected to be collected, referred to as the *net realizable value.* This valuation principle, as well as the matching concept, requires that the estimated losses from uncollectible accounts be recognized in the fiscal period in which the receivable arose. A valuation adjustment recognizing bad debts expense and using the Allowance for Bad Debts account accomplishes this. When a specific account receivable is determined to be uncollectible, it is written off against the allowance account. **(LO 5)**

Many businesses encourage customers to pay their bills promptly by allowing a cash discount if the bill is paid within a specified period, such as 10 days. Cash discounts are classified in the income statement as a deduction from sales revenue. It is appropriate to reduce accounts receivable with an allowance for estimated cash discounts, which accomplishes the same objectives associated with the allowance for bad debts.

Organizations have a system of internal control to promote the effectiveness and efficiency of the organization's operations, the reliability of the organization's financial reporting, and the organization's compliance with applicable laws and regulations. **(LO 2)**

Notes receivable usually have a longer term than accounts receivable, and they bear interest. The accounting for notes receivable is similar to that for accounts receivable. **(LO 6)**

Accounting for inventories involves selecting and applying a cost flow assumption that determines the assumed pattern of cost flow from the Inventory asset account to the Cost of Goods Sold expense account. The alternative cost flow assumptions under U.S. GAAP are specific identification; weighted-average; FIFO; and LIFO. LIFO is not permitted under international financial reporting standards. The assumed cost flow will probably differ from the physical flow of the product. When price levels change, different cost flow assumptions result in different cost of goods sold amounts in the income statement and different Inventory account balances in the balance sheet. Because of the significance of inventories in most balance sheets and the direct relationship between inventory and cost of goods sold, accurate accounting for inventories must be achieved if the financial statements are to be meaningful. **(LO 7, 8, 9)**

Prepaid expenses (or deferred charges) arise in the accrual accounting process. To achieve an appropriate matching of revenue and expense, amounts prepaid for insurance, rent, and other similar items should be recorded as assets (rather than expenses) until the period in which the benefits of such payments are received. **(LO 10)**

Refer to the Campbell Soup Company balance sheet and related notes in the appendix, and to other financial statements you may have, and observe how current assets are presented.

Campbell's

Key Terms and Concepts

administrative controls (p. 142)   Features of the internal control system that emphasize adherence to management's policies and operating efficiency.

Allowance for Uncollectible Accounts (or Allowance for Bad Debts) (p. 148)   The valuation allowance that results in accounts receivable being reduced by the amount not expected to be collected.

bad debts expense (or uncollectible accounts expense) (p. 147)   An estimated expense, recognized in the fiscal period of the sale, representing accounts receivable that are not expected to be collected.

bank reconciliation (p. 143)   The process of bringing into agreement the balance in the Cash account in the company's ledger and the balance reported by the bank on the bank statement.

bank service charge (p. 143)   The fee charged by a bank for maintaining the company's checking account.

carrying value (p. 147)   The balance of the ledger account (net of related contra accounts, if any) of an asset, liability, or stockholders' equity account. Sometimes referred to as *book value*.

cash (p. 141)   A company's most liquid asset; includes money in change funds, petty cash, undeposited receipts such as currency, checks, bank drafts, and money orders, and funds immediately available in bank accounts.

cash discount (p. 149)   A discount offered for prompt payment.

cash equivalents (p. 141)   Short-term, highly liquid investments that can be readily converted into cash with a minimal risk of price change due to interest rate movements; examples include U.S. Treasury securities, bank CDs, money market funds, and commercial paper.

collateral (p. 151)   Assets of a borrower that can be used to satisfy the obligation if payment is not made when due.

collect on delivery (COD) (p. 141)   A requirement that an item be paid for when it is delivered. Sometimes COD is defined as *"cash" on delivery*.

commercial paper (p. 141)   A short-term security usually issued by a large, creditworthy corporation.

contra asset (p. 148)   An account that normally has a credit balance that is subtracted from a related asset on the balance sheet.

cost flow assumption (p. 153)   An assumption made for accounting purposes that identifies how costs flow from the Inventory account to the Cost of Goods Sold account. Alternatives include specific identification; weighted average; first-in, first-out; and last-in, first-out.

cost of goods sold model (p. 160)   The way to calculate cost of goods sold when the periodic inventory system is used. The model is:

$$
\begin{aligned}
&\text{Beginning inventory} \\
+\ &\underline{\text{Purchases}} \\
&\text{Cost of goods available for sale} \\
-\ &\underline{\text{Ending inventory}} \\
=\ &\text{Cost of goods sold}
\end{aligned}
$$

credit terms (p. 149)   A seller's policy with respect to when payment of an invoice is due and what cash discount (if any) is allowed.

deferred charge (p. 164)   An expenditure made in one fiscal period that will be recognized as an expense in a future fiscal period. Another term for a *prepaid expense.*

deposit in transit (p. 143)   A bank deposit that has been recorded in the company's cash account but that does not appear on the bank statement because the bank received the deposit after the date of the statement.

financial controls (p. 142)   Features of the internal control system that emphasize accuracy of bookkeeping and financial statements and protection of assets.

finished goods inventory (p. 160)   The term used primarily by manufacturing firms to describe inventory ready for sale to customers.

first-in, first-out (FIFO) (p. 156)   The inventory cost flow assumption that the first costs in to inventory are the first costs out to cost of goods sold.

imprest account (p. 141)   An asset account that has a constant balance in the ledger; cash on hand and vouchers (as receipts for payments) add up to the account balance. Used especially for petty cash funds.

internal control system (p. 141)   Policies and procedures designed to provide reasonable assurance that objectives are achieved with respect to:

1. The effectiveness and efficiency of the operations of the organization.
2. The reliability of the organization's financial reporting.
3. The organization's compliance with applicable laws and regulations.

inventory accounting system (p. 160)   The method used to account for the movement of items in to inventory and out to cost of goods sold. The alternatives are the periodic system and the perpetual system.

inventory profits (p. 158)   Profits that result from using the FIFO cost flow assumption rather than LIFO during periods of inflation. Sometimes called *phantom profits.*

last-in, first-out (LIFO) (p. 156)   The inventory cost flow assumption that the last costs in to inventory are the first costs out to cost of goods sold.

lower of cost or market (p. 163)   A valuation process that may result in an asset being reported at an amount less than cost.

merchandise inventory (p. 160)   The term used primarily by retail firms to describe inventory ready for sale to customers.

net realizable value (p. 147)   The amount of funds expected to be received upon sale or liquidation of an asset. For accounts receivable, the amount expected to be collected from customers after allowing for bad debts and estimated cash discounts.

note receivable (p. 150)   A formal document (usually interest bearing) that supports the financial claim of one entity against another.

NSF (not sufficient funds) check (p. 143)   A check returned by the maker's bank because there were not enough funds in the account to cover the check.

operating cycle (p. 138) The average time needed for a firm to convert an amount invested in inventory back to cash. For most firms, the operating cycle is measured as the average number of days to produce and sell inventory, plus the average number of days to collect accounts receivable.

outstanding check (p. 143) A check that has been recorded as a cash disbursement by the company but that has not yet been processed by the bank.

periodic inventory system (p. 160) A system of accounting for the movement of items in to inventory and out to cost of goods sold that involves periodically making a physical count of the inventory on hand.

perpetual inventory system (p. 160) A system of accounting for the movement of items in to inventory and out to cost of goods sold that involves keeping a continuous record of items received, items sold, inventory on hand, and cost of goods sold.

petty cash (p. 141) A fund used for small payments for which writing a check is inconvenient.

phantom profits (p. 158) See *inventory profits.*

physical inventory (p. 160) The process of counting the inventory on hand and determining its cost based on the inventory cost flow assumption being used.

prepaid expenses (p. 164) Expenses that have been paid in the current fiscal period but that will not be subtracted from revenues until a subsequent fiscal period when the benefits are received. Usually a current asset. Another term for *deferred charge.*

prepaid insurance (p. 164) An asset account that represents an expenditure made in one fiscal period for insurance that will be recognized as an expense in a subsequent fiscal period to which the coverage applies.

Raw Materials Inventory (p. 160) An asset account that accumulates the costs of materials ready for the production process.

short-term marketable securities (p. 144) Investments made with cash not needed for current operations.

specific identification (p. 154) The inventory cost flow assumption that matches cost flow with physical flow.

uncollectible accounts expense (p. 147) See *bad debts expense.*

valuation account (p. 149) A contra account that reduces the carrying value of an asset to a net realizable value that is less than cost.

valuation adjustment (p. 147) An adjustment that results in an asset being reported at a net realizable value that is less than cost.

weighted average (p. 154) The inventory cost flow assumption that is based on an average of the cost of beginning inventory plus the cost of purchases during the year, weighted by the quantity of items at each cost.

Work in Process Inventory (p. 160) An asset account that accumulates the costs (raw materials, direct labor, and manufacturing overhead) of items that are in the process of being manufactured.

write-off (p. 148) The process of removing a specific account receivable that is not expected to be collected from the Accounts Receivable account. Also used generically to describe the reduction of an asset and the related recognition of an expense or loss.

Mini-Exercises

connect

All applicable Mini-Exercises are available in *Connect*.

Bank reconciliation The balance in Happ Inc.'s general ledger Cash account was $71,580 at September 30, before reconciliation. The September 30 balance shown in the bank statement was $63,780. Reconciling items included deposits in transit, $6,200; bank service charges, $120; NSF check written by a customer and returned with the bank statement, $2,850; outstanding checks, $1,280; and interest credited to the account during September but not recorded on the company's books, $90.

Mini-Exercise 5.1
LO 3

Required:
Prepare a bank reconciliation as of September 30 for Happ Inc.

Bank reconciliation adjustment Refer to Mini-Exercise 5.1.

Required:

a. Show the reconciling items in a horizontal model, or write the adjusting journal entry (or entries) that should be prepared to reflect the reconciling items for Happ Inc. at September 30.

b. What is the amount of cash to be included in the September 30 balance sheet for the company's bank account?

Accounts receivable, bad debts, credit sales, and cash collections analysis At the beginning of the year, accounts receivable were $72,000 and the allowance for bad debts was $5,750. During the year, sales (all on account) were $300,000, cash collections were $290,000, bad debts expense totaled $7,100, and $6,000 of accounts receivable were written off as bad debts.

Required:
Calculate the balances at the end of the year for the Accounts Receivable and Allowance for Bad Debts accounts. (*Hint:* Use T-accounts to analyze each of these accounts, plug in the amounts that you know, and solve for the ending balances.)

Bad debts analysis—Allowance account The Allowance for Bad Debts account had a balance of $19,200 at the beginning of the year and $24,400 at the end of the year. During the year (including the year-end adjustment), bad debts expense of $36,600 was recognized.

Required:
Calculate the total amount of past-due accounts receivable that were written off as uncollectible during the year. (*Hint:* Make a T-account for the Allowance for Bad Debts account, plug in the amounts that you know, and solve for the missing amount.)

Cost flow assumptions—FIFO and LIFO using a periodic system Sales during the year were 700 units. Beginning inventory was 400 units at a cost of $10 per unit. Purchase 1 was 500 units at $12 per unit. Purchase 2 was 300 units at $14 per unit.

Required:
Calculate cost of goods sold and ending inventory under the following cost flow assumptions (using a periodic inventory system):

a. FIFO

b. LIFO

Cost flow assumptions—FIFO and LIFO using a periodic system The beginning inventory was 900 units at a cost of $10 per unit. Goods available for sale during the year were 3,900 units at a total cost of $43,200. In May, 1,800 units were purchased at a total cost of $19,800. The only other purchase transaction occurred during October. Ending inventory was 1,650 units.

Required:

a. Calculate the number of units purchased in October and the cost per unit purchased in October.

b. Calculate cost of goods sold and ending inventory under the following cost flow assumptions (using a periodic inventory system):

  1. FIFO
  2. LIFO

Exercises

All applicable Exercises are available in *Connect*.

Bank reconciliation Prepare a bank reconciliation as of October 31 from the following information:

Exercise 5.7
LO 3

a. The October 31 cash balance in the general ledger is $1,688.

b. The October 31 balance shown on the bank statement is $746.

c. Checks issued but not returned with the bank statement were No. 462 for $26 and No. 483 for $100.

d. A deposit made late on October 31 for $900 is included in the general ledger balance but not in the bank statement balance.

e. Returned with the bank statement was a notice that a customer's check for $150 that was deposited on October 25 had been returned because the customer's account was overdrawn.

f. During a review of the checks that were returned with the bank statement, it was noted that the amount of Check No. 471 was $64 but that in the company's records supporting the general ledger balance, the check had been erroneously recorded as a payment of an account payable in the amount of $46.

Bank reconciliation Prepare a bank reconciliation as of August 31 from the following information:

Exercise 5.8
LO 3

a. The August 31 balance shown on the bank statement is $9,050.

b. There is a deposit in transit of $1,300 at August 31.

c. Outstanding checks at August 31 totaled $1,620.

d. Interest credited to the account during August but not recorded on the company's books amounted to $68.

e. A bank charge of $44 for checks was made to the account during August. Although the company was expecting a charge, the amount was not known until the bank statement arrived.

f. In the process of reviewing the canceled checks, it was determined that a check issued to a supplier in payment of accounts payable of $142 had been recorded as a disbursement of $412.

g. The August 31 balance in the general ledger Cash account, before reconciliation, is $8,436.

Exercise 5.9
LO 3

Bank reconciliation adjustment

a. Show the reconciling items in a horizontal model or write the adjusting journal entry (or entries) that should be prepared to reflect the reconciling items of Exercise 5.7.

b. What is the amount of cash to be included in the October 31 balance sheet for the bank account reconciled in Exercise 5.7?

Exercise 5.10
LO 3

Bank reconciliation adjustment

a. Show the reconciling items in a horizontal model or write the adjusting journal entry (or entries) that should be prepared to reflect the reconciling items of Exercise 5.8.

b. What is the amount of cash to be included in the August 31 balance sheet for the bank account reconciled in Exercise 5.8?

Exercise 5.11
LO 5

Bad debts analysis—Allowance account On January 1, 2019, the balance in Tabor Co.'s Allowance for Bad Debts account was $26,800. During the first 11 months of the year, bad debts expense of $42,924 was recognized. The balance in the Allowance for Bad Debts account at November 30, 2019, was $19,526.

Required:

a. What was the total of accounts written off during the first 11 months? (*Hint:* Make a T-account for the Allowance for Bad Debts account.)

b. As the result of a comprehensive analysis, it is determined that the December 31, 2019, balance of the Allowance for Bad Debts account should be $19,000. Show the adjustment required in the horizontal model or in journal entry format.

c. During a conversation with the credit manager, one of Tabor's sales representatives learns that a $2,460 receivable from a bankrupt customer has not been written off but was considered in the determination of the appropriate year-end balance of the Allowance for Bad Debts account balance. Write a brief explanation to the sales representative explaining the effect that the write-off of this account receivable would have had on 2019 net income.

Exercise 5.12
LO 5

Bad debts analysis—Allowance account On January 1, 2019, the balance in Kubera Co.'s Allowance for Bad Debts account was $25,160. During the year, a total of $65,700 of delinquent accounts receivable was written off as bad debts. The unadjusted balance in the Allowance for Bad Debts account at December 31, 2019, was $30,440.

Required:

a. What was the total amount of bad debts expense recognized during the year? (*Hint:* Make a T-account for the Allowance for Bad Debts account.)

b. As a result of a comprehensive analysis, it is determined that the December 31, 2019, adjusted balance of Allowance for Bad Debts should be $61,600. Show in the horizontal model or in journal entry format the adjustment required.

Exercise 5.13
LO 5

Cash discounts—ROI Annual credit sales of Nadak Co. total $680 million. The firm gives a 2% cash discount for payment within 10 days of the invoice date; 90% of Nadak's accounts receivable are paid within the discount period.

Required:

a. What is the total amount of cash discounts allowed in a year?

b. Calculate the approximate annual rate of return on investment that Nadak Co.'s cash discount terms represent to customers who take the discount.

Cash discounts—ROI

a. Calculate the approximate annual rate of return on investment of the following cash discount terms:

1. 1/15, n30.
2. 2/10, n60.
3. 1/10, n90.

b. Which of these terms, if any, is not likely to be a significant incentive to the customer to pay promptly? Explain your answer.

Exercise 5.14
LO 5

Notes receivable—interest accrual and collection Agrico Inc. accepted a 10-month, 12.8% (annual rate), $9,000 note from one of its customers on May 15, 2019; interest is payable with the principal at maturity.

Exercise 5.15
LO 6

Required:

a. Use the horizontal model or write the journal entry to record the interest earned by Agrico during its year ended December 31, 2019.

b. Use the horizontal model or write the journal entry to record collection of the note and interest at maturity.

Notes receivable—interest accrual and collection Husemann Co.'s assets include notes receivable from customers. During fiscal 2019, the amount of notes receivable averaged $525,000, and the interest rate of the notes averaged 4.2%.

Exercise 5.16
LO 6

Required:

a. Calculate the amount of interest revenue earned by Husemann Co. during fiscal 2019 and show in the horizontal model or write a journal entry that accrues the interest revenue earned from the notes.

b. If the balance in the Interest Receivable account increased by $6,400 from the beginning to the end of the fiscal year, how much interest receivable was collected during the fiscal year? Use the horizontal model, a T-account, or write the journal entry to show the collection of this amount.

LIFO versus FIFO—matching and balance sheet impact Proponents of the LIFO inventory cost flow assumption argue that this costing method is superior to the alternatives because it results in better matching of revenue and expense.

Exercise 5.17
LO 7, 8

Required:

a. Explain why "better matching" occurs with LIFO.

b. What is the impact on the carrying value of inventory in the balance sheet when LIFO rather than FIFO is used during periods of inflation?

Exercise 5.18

LO 7, 8

LIFO versus FIFO—impact on ROI Mannisto Inc. uses the FIFO inventory cost flow assumption. In a year of rising costs and prices, the firm reported net income of $1,500,000 and average assets of $10,000,000. If Mannisto had used the LIFO cost flow assumption in the same year, its cost of goods sold would have been $300,000 more than under FIFO, and its average assets would have been $300,000 less than under FIFO.

Required:

a.   Calculate the firm's ROI under each cost flow assumption (FIFO and LIFO).

b.   Suppose that two years later costs and prices were falling. Under FIFO, net income and average assets were $1,800,000 and $12,000,000, respectively. If LIFO had been used through the years, inventory values would have been $200,000 less than under FIFO, and current year cost of goods sold would have been $100,000 less than under FIFO. Calculate the firm's ROI under each cost flow assumption (FIFO and LIFO).

Exercise 5.19

LO 10

Prepaid expenses—insurance

a.   Use the horizontal model or write the journal entry to record the payment of a one-year insurance premium of $6,000 on March 1, 2019.

b.   Use the horizontal model or write the adjusting entry that will be made at the end of every month to show the amount of insurance premium "used" that month.

c.   Calculate the amount of prepaid insurance that should be reported on the December 31, 2019, balance sheet with respect to this policy.

d.   If the premium had been $12,000 for a two-year period, how should the prepaid amount at December 31, 2019, be reported on the balance sheet?

e.   Why are prepaid expenses reflected as an asset instead of being recorded as an expense in the accounting period in which the item is paid?

Exercise 5.20

LO 10

Prepaid expenses—rent

(*Note:* See Problem 7.25 for the related unearned revenue accounting.)

On November 1, 2019, Wenger Co. paid its landlord $31,800 in cash as an advance rent payment on its store location. The six-month lease period ends on April 30, 2020, at which time the contract may be renewed.

Required:

a.   Use the horizontal model or write the journal entry to record the six-month advance rent payment on November 1, 2019.

b.   Use the horizontal model or write the adjusting entry that will be made at the end of every month to show the amount of rent "used" during the month.

c.   Calculate the amount of prepaid rent that should be reported on the December 31, 2019, balance sheet with respect to this lease.

d.   If the advance payment made on November 1, 2019, had covered an 18-month lease period at the same amount of rent per month, how should Wenger Co. report the prepaid amount on its December 31, 2019, balance sheet?

Exercise 5.21

LO 5, 6, 8

Transaction analysis—various accounts Prepare an answer sheet with the column headings shown here. For each of the following transactions or adjustments, indicate the effect of the transaction or adjustment on the appropriate balance sheet category and on net income by entering for each account affected the account name and amount and indicating whether it is an addition (+) or a subtraction (−). Transaction **a** has been done as an illustration. Net income is *not* affected by every transaction. In some cases only one column may be affected because all of the specific accounts affected by the transaction are included in that category.

	Current Assets	Current Liabilities	Stockholders' Equity	Net Income
a. Accrued interest revenue of $30 on a note receivable.				
	Interest Receivable + 30			Interest Revenue + 30

b. Determined that the Allowance for Bad Debts account balance should be increased by $4,400.

c. Recognized bank service charges of $60 for the month.

d. Received $50 cash for interest accrued in a prior month.

e. Purchased five units of a new item of inventory on account at a cost of $70 each. Perpetual inventory is maintained.

f. Purchased 10 more units of the same item at a cost of $76 each. Perpetual inventory is maintained.

g. Sold eight of the items purchased (in **e** and **f**) and recognized the cost of goods sold using the FIFO cost flow assumption. Perpetual inventory is maintained.

Transaction analysis—various accounts Prepare an answer sheet with the column headings shown here. For each of the following transactions or adjustments, indicate the effect of the transaction or adjustment on the appropriate balance sheet category and on net income by entering for each account affected the account name and amount and indicating whether it is an addition (+) or a subtraction (−). Transaction **a** has been done as an illustration. Net income is *not* affected by every transaction. In some cases only one column may be affected because all of the specific accounts affected by the transaction are included in that category.

Exercise 5.22
LO 5, 8, 10

	Current Assets	Current Liabilities	Stockholders' Equity	Net Income
a. Accrued interest revenue of $30 on a note receivable.				
	Interest Receivable + 30			Interest Revenue + 30

b. Determined that the Allowance for Bad Debts account balance should be decreased by $7,200 because expense during the year had been overestimated.

c. Wrote off an account receivable of $2,600.

d. Received cash from a customer in full payment of an account receivable of $2,500 that was paid within the 2% discount period. A Cash Discount Allowance account is maintained.

e. Purchased six units of a new item of inventory on account at a cost of $130 each. Perpetual inventory is maintained.

f. Purchased 14 more units of the above item at a cost of $140 each. Perpetual inventory is maintained.

g. Sold 16 of the items purchased (in **e** and **f**) and recognized the cost of goods sold using the LIFO cost flow assumption. Perpetual inventory is maintained.

h. Paid a one-year insurance premium of $3,840 that applied to the next fiscal year.

i. Recognized insurance expense related to the preceding policy during the first month of the fiscal year to which it applied.

Exercise 5.23

LO 5, 6, 7

Transaction analysis—various accounts Prepare an answer sheet with the column headings shown here. For each of the following transactions or adjustments, indicate the effect of the transaction or adjustment on the appropriate balance sheet category and on net income by entering for each account affected the account name and amount and indicating whether it is an addition (+) or a subtraction (−). Transaction **a** has been done as an illustration. Net income is *not* affected by every transaction. In some cases only one column may be affected because all of the specific accounts affected by the transaction are included in that category.

		Current Assets	Current Liabilities	Stockholders' Equity	Net Income
a.	Accrued interest revenue of $30 on a note receivable.	Interest Receivable + 30			Interest Revenue + 30

b. Recorded estimated bad debts in the amount of $1,400.

c. Wrote off an overdue account receivable of $1,040.

d. Converted a customer's $2,400 overdue account receivable into a note.

e. Accrued $96 of interest earned on the note (in **d**).

f. Collected the accrued interest (in **e**).

g. Recorded $8,000 of sales, 70% of which were on account.

h. Recognized cost of goods sold in the amount of $6,400.

Exercise 5.24

LO 7, 8, 10

Transaction analysis—various accounts Prepare an answer sheet with the column headings shown here. For each of the following transactions or adjustments, indicate the effect of the transaction or adjustment on the appropriate balance sheet category and on net income by entering for each account affected the account name and amount and indicating whether it is an addition (+) or a subtraction (−). Transaction **a** has been done as an illustration. Net income is *not* affected by every transaction. In some cases only one column may be affected because all of the specific accounts affected by the transaction are included in that category.

	Current Assets	Current Liabilities	Stockholders' Equity	Net Income
a. Accrued interest revenue of $30 on a note receivable.				
	Interest Receivable + 30			Interest Revenue + 30

b. Paid $9,300 in cash as an advance rent payment for a short-term lease that covers the next three months.

c. Recorded an adjustment at the end of the first month (in **b**) to show the amount of rent "used" in the month.

d. Inventory was acquired on account and recorded for $4,810. Perpetual inventory is maintained.

e. It was later determined that the amount of inventory acquired on account (in **d**) was erroneously recorded. The actual amount purchased was only $4,180. No payments have been made. Record the correction of this error.

f. Purchased 12 units of inventory at a cost of $120 each and then four more units of the same inventory item at $140 each. Perpetual inventory is maintained.

g. Sold 13 of the items purchased (in **f**) for $210 each and received the entire amount in cash. Record the sales transaction and the cost of goods sold using the LIFO cost flow assumption. Perpetual inventory is maintained.

h. Assume the same facts (in **g**) except that the company uses the FIFO cost flow assumption. Record only the cost of goods sold.

i. Assume the same facts (in **g**) except that the company uses the weighted-average cost flow assumption. Record only the cost of goods sold.

j. Explain why the sales transaction in **h** and **i** would be recorded in exactly the same way it was in **g**.

Problems

connect

All applicable Problems are available in *Connect*.

Bank reconciliation—compute Cash account balance and bank statement balance before reconciling items Beckett Co. received its bank statement for the month ending June 30, 2019, and reconciled the statement balance to the June

Problem 5.25

LO 3

30, 2019, balance in the Cash account. The reconciled balance was determined to be $9,600. The reconciliation recognized the following items:

1. Deposits in transit were $4,200.
2. Outstanding checks totaled $6,000.
3. Bank service charges shown as a deduction on the bank statement were $100.
4. An NSF check from a customer for $800 was included with the bank statement. Beckett Co. had not been previously notified that the check had been returned NSF.
5. Included in the canceled checks was a check written for $790. However, it had been recorded as a disbursement of $970.

Required:
a. What was the balance in Beckett Co.'s Cash account before recognizing any of the preceding reconciling items?
b. What was the balance shown on the bank statement before recognizing any of the preceding reconciling items?

Problem 5.26
LO 3

Bank reconciliation—compute Cash account balance and bank statement balance before reconciling items Branson Co. received its bank statement for the month ending May 31, 2019, and reconciled the statement balance to the May 31, 2019, balance in the Cash account. The reconciled balance was determined to be $36,400. The reconciliation recognized the following items:

1. A deposit made on May 31 for $22,700 was included in the Cash account balance but not in the bank statement balance.
2. Checks issued but not returned with the bank statement were No. 673 for $4,550 and No. 687 for $9,700.
3. Bank service charges shown as a deduction on the bank statement were $110.
4. Interest credited to Branson Co.'s account but not recorded on the company's books amounted to $88.
5. Returned with the bank statement was a "debit memo" stating that a customer's check for $3,240 that had been deposited on May 23 had been returned because the customer's account was overdrawn.
6. During a review of the checks that were returned with the bank statement, it was noted that the amount of check No. 681 was $680 but that in the company's records supporting the Cash account balance, the check had been erroneously recorded in the amount of $68.

Required:
a. What was the balance in Branson Co.'s Cash account before recognizing any of these reconciling items?
b. What was the balance shown on the bank statement before recognizing any of these reconciling items?

Problem 5.27
LO 5

Bad debts analysis—Allowance account and financial statement effect The following is a portion of the current assets section of the balance sheets of Avanti's, Inc., at December 31, 2020 and 2019:

	12/31/20	12/31/19
Accounts receivable, less allowance for bad debts of $9,100 and $11,600, respectively	$193,400	$226,700

Required:

a. If $10,800 of accounts receivable were written off during 2020, what was the amount of bad debts expense recognized for the year? (*Hint:* Use a T-account model of the Allowance account, plug in the three amounts that you know, and solve for the unknown.)

b. The December 31, 2020, Allowance account balance includes $2,800 for a past due account that is not likely to be collected. This account has *not* been written off. *If it had been written off,* what would have been the effect of the write-off on:
   1. Working capital at December 31, 2020?
   2. Net income and ROI for the year ended December 31, 2020?

c. What do you suppose was the level of Avanti's sales in 2020, compared to 2019? Explain your answer.

Bad debts analysis—Allowance account and financial statement effects The following is a portion of the current asset section of the balance sheets of HiROE Co., at December 31, 2020 and 2019:

Problem 5.28
LO 5

	12/31/20	12/31/19
Accounts receivable, less allowance for uncollectible accounts of $23,000 and $11,000, respectively	$457,000	$359,000

Required:

a. Describe how the allowance amount at December 31, 2020, was most likely determined.

b. If bad debts expense for 2020 totaled $19,000, what was the amount of accounts receivable written off during the year? (*Hint:* Use the T-account model of the Allowance account, plug in the three amounts that you know, and solve for the unknown.)

c. The December 31, 2020, Allowance account balance includes $7,500 for a past due account that is not likely to be collected. This account has *not* been written off. *If it had been written off,* what would have been the effect of the write-off on:
   1. Working capital at December 31, 2020?
   2. Net income and ROI for the year ended December 31, 2020?

d. What do you suppose was the level of HiROE's sales in 2020, compared to 2019? Explain your answer.

e. Calculate the ratio of the Allowance for Uncollectible Accounts balance to the Accounts Receivable balance at December 31, 2020 and 2019. What factors might have caused the change in this ratio?

Problem 5.29

LO 5

Analysis of accounts receivable and allowance for bad debts—determine beginning balances A portion of the current assets section of the December 31, 2020, balance sheet for Carr Co. is presented here:

Accounts receivable	$100,000	
Less: Allowance for bad debts	(14,000)	$86,000

The company's accounting records revealed the following information for the year ended December 31, 2020:

Sales (all on account)	$800,000
Cash collections from customers	820,000
Accounts written off	30,000
Bad debts expense (accrued at 12/31/20)	24,000

Required:

Using the information provided for 2020, calculate the net realizable value of accounts receivable at December 31, 2019, and prepare the appropriate balance sheet presentation for Carr Co., as of that point in time. (*Hint:* Use T-accounts to analyze the Accounts Receivable and Allowance for Bad Debts accounts. Remember that you are solving for the beginning balance of each account.)

Problem 5.30

LO 5

Analysis of accounts receivable and allowance for bad debts—determine ending balances A portion of the current assets section of the December 31, 2019, balance sheet for Gibbs Co. is presented here:

Accounts receivable	$425,000	
Less: Allowance for bad debts	(18,000)	$407,000

The company's accounting records revealed the following information for the year ended December 31, 2020:

Sales (all on account)	$2,600,000
Cash collections from customers	2,375,000
Accounts written off	30,000
Bad debts expense (accrued at 12/31/20)	41,000

Required:

Calculate the net realizable value of accounts receivable at December 31, 2020, and prepare the appropriate balance sheet presentation for Gibbs Co. as of that point in time. (*Hint:* Use T-accounts to analyze the Accounts Receivable and Allowance for Bad Debts accounts.)

Cost flow assumptions—FIFO and LIFO using a periodic system Mower-Blower Sales Co. started business on January 20, 2019. Products sold were snow blowers and lawn mowers. Each product sold for $1,400. Purchases during 2019 were as follows:

	Blowers	Mowers
January 21	20 @ $800	
February 3	40 @ 780	
February 28	30 @ 760	
March 13	20 @ 760	
April 6		20 @ $840
May 22		40 @ 860
June 3		40 @ 880
June 20		60 @ 920
August 15		20 @ 860
September 20		20 @ 840
November 7	20 @ 800	

The December 31, 2019, inventory included 10 blowers and 25 mowers. Assume the company uses a periodic inventory system.

Required:

a. What will be the *difference* between ending inventory valuation at December 31, 2019, under the FIFO and LIFO cost flow assumptions? (*Hint:* Compute ending inventory under each method, and then compare results.)

b. If the cost of mowers had increased to $960 each by December 1, and if management had purchased 30 mowers at that time, which cost flow assumption was probably being used by the firm? Explain your answer.

Cost flow assumptions—FIFO, LIFO, and weighted average using a periodic system The following data are available for Sellco for the fiscal year ended on January 31, 2020:

Sales	1,600 units
Beginning inventory	500 units @ $4
Purchases, in chronological order	600 units @ $5
	800 units @ $6
	500 units @ $8

Required:

a. Calculate cost of goods sold and ending inventory under the following cost flow assumptions (using a periodic inventory system):
   1. FIFO.
   2. LIFO.
   3. Weighted average. Round the unit cost answer to two decimal places and ending inventory to the nearest $10.

b. Assume that net income using the weighted-average cost flow assumption is $80,000. Calculate net income under FIFO and LIFO.

Problem 5.33
LO 7, 8

Cost flow assumptions—FIFO and LIFO using periodic and perpetual systems The inventory records of Kuffel Co. reflected the following information for the year ended December 31, 2019:

Date	Transaction	Number of Units	Unit Cost	Total Cost
1/1	Beginning inventory	150	$60	$ 9,000
1/24	Purchase	70	66	4,620
2/22	Sale	(100)	—	—
3/7	Purchase	90	70	6,300
4/10	Purchase	140	72	10,080
6/11	Sale	(100)	—	—
9/28	Purchase	50	76	3,800
12/4	Sale	(100)	—	—

Required:

a. Assume that Kuffel Co. uses a periodic inventory system. Calculate cost of goods sold and ending inventory under FIFO and LIFO.

b. Assume that Kuffel Co. uses a perpetual inventory system. Calculate cost of goods sold and ending inventory under FIFO and LIFO.

c. Explain why the FIFO results for cost of goods sold and ending inventory are the same in your answers to parts **a** and **b,** but the LIFO results are different.

Problem 5.34
LO 7, 8

Cost flow assumptions—FIFO and LIFO using periodic and perpetual systems The inventory records of Cushing Inc. reflected the following information for the year ended December 31, 2019:

	Number of Units	Unit Cost	Total Cost
Inventory, January 1	400	$13	$ 5,200
Purchases:			
May 30	640	15	9,600
September 28	800	16	12,800
Goods available for sale	1,840		$27,600
Sales:			
April 10	(280)		
June 11	(600)		
November 1	(760)		
Inventory, December 31	200		

Required:

a. Assume that Cushing, Inc., uses a periodic inventory system. Calculate cost of goods sold and ending inventory under FIFO and LIFO.

b. Assume that Cushing, Inc., uses a perpetual inventory system. Calculate cost of goods sold and ending inventory under FIFO and LIFO.

c. Explain why the FIFO results for cost of goods sold and ending inventory are the same in your answers to parts **a** and **b,** but the LIFO results are different.

d. Explain why the results from the LIFO periodic calculations in part **a** cannot possibly represent the actual physical flow of inventory items.

Effects of inventory errors

Problem 5.35
LO 7

a. If the beginning balance of the Inventory account and the cost of items purchased or made during the period are correct, but an error resulted in overstating the firm's ending inventory balance by $15,000, how would the firm's cost of goods sold be affected? Explain your answer by drawing T-accounts for the Inventory and Cost of Goods Sold accounts and entering amounts that illustrate the difference between correctly stating and overstating the ending inventory balance.

b. If management wanted to understate profits, would ending inventory be understated or overstated? Explain your answer.

Effects of inventory errors Following are condensed income statements for Uncle Bill's Home Improvement Center for the years ended December 31, 2020 and 2019:

Problem 5.36
LO 7

	2020	2019
Sales	$760,000	$719,000
Cost of goods sold	(586,000)	(482,000)
Gross profit	$174,000	$237,000
Operating expenses	(117,000)	(143,000)
Net income (ignoring income taxes)	$ 57,000	$ 94,000

Uncle Bill was concerned about the operating results for 2020 and asked his recently hired accountant, "If sales increased in 2020, why was net income so much less than what it was in 2019?" In February of 2021, Uncle Bill got his answer: "The ending inventory reported in 2019 was overstated by $30,000 for merchandise that we were holding on consignment on behalf of Kirk's Servistar. We still keep some of their appliances in stock, but the value of these items was not included in the 2020 inventory count because we don't own them."

a. Recast the 2019 and 2020 income statements to take into account the correction of the 2019 ending inventory error.

b. Calculate the combined net income for 2019 and 2020 before and after the correction of the error. Explain to Uncle Bill why the error was corrected in 2020 before it was actually discovered in 2021.

c. What effect, if any, will the error have on net income and stockholders' equity in 2021?

 **Case**

All applicable Cases are available in *Connect*.

Focus company—accounts receivable and inventory disclosures In Exercise 1.1, you were asked to obtain the most recent annual report of a company that you were interested in reviewing throughout this term.

Required:

Review the note disclosures provided in your focus company's annual report and discuss what you've learned about how your company's accounts receivable and inventory are accounted for and presented.

ANSWERS TO
What Does It Mean?

1. It means that the asset is cash, or it is an asset that is expected to be converted to cash or used up in the operating activities of the entity within one year.

2. It means that from the board of directors down through the organization, the policies and procedures related to effectiveness and efficiency of operations, reliability of financial reporting, and compliance with laws and regulations are understood and followed.

3. It means that the balance in the Cash account in the ledger has been brought into agreement with the balance on the bank statement by recognizing timing differences and errors.

4. It means that cash not immediately required for use by the entity is invested temporarily to earn a return and thus increase the entity's ROI and ROE.

5. It means that interest has not been received by the entity for part of the period for which funds have been invested, even though the interest has been earned, so interest receivable and interest income are recognized by an adjustment.

6. It means that the estimate of accounts receivable that will not be collected is subtracted from the total accounts receivable because it isn't yet known which specific accounts receivable will not be collected.

7. It means to identify the method used to transfer the cost of an item sold from the Inventory asset account in the balance sheet to the Cost of Goods Sold expense account in the income statement. This is different from the physical flow, which describes the physical movement of product from storeroom to customer. The alternative inventory cost flow assumptions are FIFO, LIFO, weighted-average cost, and specific identification.

8. It means that because of applying a particular inventory cost flow assumption (usually FIFO), net income is higher than what it would have been if an alternative cost flow assumption had been used (usually LIFO).

9. It means that an ending inventory error affects cost of goods sold on the income statement for two consecutive periods. Because ending inventory of one period is beginning inventory of the next period, the over/understatement of cost of goods sold in one period will be reversed in the next period.

10. It means to delay the income statement recognition of an expense until a future period to which it is applicable. Even though a cash payment has been made, the expense has not yet been incurred. An asset account is established for the prepaid expense.

Design Elements: Mah-Jongg Tiles: ©Ingram Publishing; Business in Practice: ©Shutterstock/Rawpixel.com; FYI Boxes: ©Stock4B/ Image Source; Study Suggestion Boxes: ©Tetra Images/ Shutterstock; IFRS Boxes: ©Wrangler/ Shutterstock.

6

Accounting for and Presentation of Property, Plant, and Equipment, and Other Noncurrent Assets

Campbell's Noncurrent assets include land, buildings, and equipment (less accumulated depreciation); intangible assets such as leaseholds, patents, trademarks, and goodwill; and natural resources. The presentation of property, plant, and equipment, and other noncurrent assets on the consolidated balance sheets of Campbell Soup Company, in the appendix, appears straightforward. However, several business and accounting matters are involved in understanding this presentation. The objective of this chapter is to show you how to make sense of the noncurrent assets section of any balance sheet.

The primary issues related to the accounting for noncurrent assets are the following:

1. Accounting for the acquisition of assets
2. Accounting for the use (depreciation) of assets
3. Accounting for maintenance and repair costs
4. Accounting for the disposition of assets

LEARNING OBJECTIVES (LO)

After studying this chapter, you should understand and be able to

LO 6-1   Explain how the cost of land, buildings, and equipment is reported on the balance sheet.

LO 6-2   Discuss how the terms *capitalize* and *expense* are used with respect to property, plant, and equipment.

LO 6-3   Describe alternative methods of calculating depreciation for financial accounting purposes and compare the relative effects of each on the income statement and the balance sheet.

LO 6-4   Describe the accounting treatment of repair and maintenance expenditures.

LO 6-5   Explain why depreciation for income tax purposes is an important concern of taxpayers and how tax depreciation differs from financial accounting depreciation.

LO 6-6   Describe the effect on the financial statements of the disposition of noncurrent assets, either by sale or abandonment.

LO 6-7   Describe the difference between an operating lease and a financing lease.

LO 6-8 Explain the similarities in the financial statement effects of buying an asset compared to using a financing lease to acquire the rights to an asset.

LO 6-9 Discuss the meaning of various intangible assets, how their values are measured, and how their costs are reflected in the income statement.

LO 6-10 Explain the role of time value of money concepts in financial reporting and their usefulness in decision making.

Exhibit 6-1 highlights the balance sheet accounts covered in detail in this chapter and shows the income statement and statement of cash flows components affected by these accounts.

Land

Land owned and used in the operations of the firm is shown on the balance sheet at its original cost. All ordinary and necessary costs the firm incurs to get a parcel of land ready for its intended use are considered part of the original cost. These costs include the purchase price of the land, title fees, legal fees, and other costs related to the acquisition. If a firm purchases land with a building on it and razes the building so that a new one can be built to the firm's specifications, the costs of the land, old building, and razing (less any salvage proceeds) all become part of the cost of the land acquired and are *capitalized* (see Business in Practice—Capitalizing versus Expensing) because all these costs were incurred to get the land ready for its intended use.

LO 1
Explain how the cost of land, buildings, and equipment is reported on the balance sheet.

---

1. What does it mean to capitalize an expenditure?

What Does It Mean?
Answer on page 232

Land acquired for investment purposes or for a potential future, but undefined, use is classified as a separate noncurrent and nonoperating asset and reported at its original cost. A land development company treats land under development as inventory, and all development costs are included in the asset carrying value. As lots are sold, the cost of each lot sold is transferred from inventory to cost of goods sold.

Because land is not "used up," no accounting depreciation is associated with land.

When land is sold, the difference between the selling price and cost will be a gain or loss to be reported in the income statement of the period in which the sale occurred. For example, if a parcel of land on which Cruisers Inc. had once operated a plant is sold this year for a price of $140,000 and the land had cost $6,000 when it was acquired 35 years earlier, the effect of this transaction on the financial statements would be as follows:

Balance Sheet	Income Statement
Assets = Liabilities + Stockholders' equity	← Net income = Revenues − Expenses
Cash + 140,000 Land − 6,000	Gain on Sale of Land + 134,000

Balance Sheet

Current Assets	Chapter	Current Liabilities	Chapter
Cash and cash equivalents	5, 9	Short-term debt	7
Short-term marketable securities	5	Current maturities of long-term debt	7
Accounts receivable	5, 9	Accounts payable	7
Notes receivable	5	Unearned revenue or deferred credits	7
Inventories	5, 9	Payroll taxes and other withholdings	7
Prepaid expenses	5	Other accrued liabilities	7
Noncurrent Assets		**Noncurrent Liabilities**	
Land	6	Long-term debt	7
Buildings and equipment	6	Deferred tax liabilities	7
Assets acquired by lease	6	Other long-term liabilities	7
Intangible assets	6	**Stockholders' Equity**	
Natural resources	6	Common stock	8
Other noncurrent assets	6	Preferred stock	8
		Additional paid-in capital	8
		Retained earnings	8
		Treasury stock	8
		Accumulated other comprehensive income (loss)	8
		Noncontrolling interest	8

Income Statement

	Chapter
Sales	5, 9
Cost of goods sold	5, 9
Gross profit (or gross margin)	5, 9
Selling, general, and administrative expenses	5, 6, 9
Income from operations	9
Gains (losses) on sale of assets	6, 9
Interest revenue	5, 9
Interest expense	7, 9
Income tax expense	7, 9
Unusual items	9
Net income	5, 6, 7, 8, 9
Earnings per share	9

Statement of Cash Flows

	Chapter
Operating Activities	
Net income	5, 6, 7, 8, 9
Depreciation expense	6, 9
(Gains) losses on sale of assets	6, 9
(Increase) decrease in current assets	5, 9
Increase (decrease) in current liabilities	7, 9
Investing Activities	
Proceeds from sale of property, plant, and equipment	6, 9
Purchase of property, plant, and equipment	6, 9
Financing Activities	
Proceeds from long-term debt*	7, 9
Repayment of long-term debt*	7, 9
Issuance of common stock and/or preferred stock	8, 9
Purchase of treasury stock	8, 9
Payment of dividends	8, 9

Primary topics of this chapter.

Other affected financial statement components.

* May include short-term debt items as well.

Capitalizing versus Expensing

An expenditure involves using an asset (usually cash) or incurring a liability to acquire goods, services, or other economic benefits. Whenever a firm buys something, it has made an expenditure. All expenditures must be accounted for as either assets (**capitalizing** an expenditure) or expenses (**expensing** an expenditure). Although this jargon applies to any expenditure, it is most prevalent in discussions about property, plant, and equipment.

Expenditures should be capitalized if the item acquired will have an economic benefit to the entity that extends beyond the end of the current fiscal year. However, expenditures for preventive maintenance and normal repairs, even though they are needed to maintain the usefulness of the asset over a number of years, are expensed as incurred. The capitalize versus expense issue is resolved by applying the matching concept, under which costs incurred in generating revenues are subtracted from revenues in the period in which the revenues are earned.

When an expenditure is capitalized, plant assets increase. If the asset is depreciable—and all plant assets except land are depreciable—depreciation expense is recognized over the estimated useful life of the asset. If the expenditure is expensed, the full cost is reflected in the current period's income statement. There is a broad gray area between expenditures that are clearly assets and those that are obviously expenses. This gray area leads to differences of opinion that have a direct impact on the net income reported across fiscal periods.

The materiality concept (see Chapter 2) is often applied to the issue of accounting for capital expenditures. Generally speaking, most accountants will expense items that are not material. Thus, the cost of a $25 wastebasket may be expensed, rather than capitalized and depreciated, even though the wastebasket clearly has a useful life of many years and should theoretically be accounted for as a capital asset.

Another factor that influences the capitalize versus expense decision is the potential income tax reduction in the current year that results from expensing. Although depreciation would be claimed (and income taxes reduced) over the life of a capitalized expenditure, many managers prefer the immediate income tax reduction that results from expensing.

This capitalize versus expense issue is another area in which accountants' judgments can have a significant effect on an entity's financial position and results of operations. Explanations in this text will reflect sound accounting theory. However, recognize that in practice, there may be some deviation from theory.

Business in
Practice

LO 2
Discuss how the terms *capitalize* and *expense* are used with respect to property, plant, and equipment.

The entry for this transaction is as follows:

Dr.	Cash	140,000	
	Cr. Land		6,000
	Cr. Gain on Sale of Land		134,000

Because land is carried on the books at original cost, the unrealized holding gain that had gradually occurred was ignored from an accounting perspective by Cruisers until it sold the land (and realized the gain). Thus, the financial statements for each of the years between purchase and sale would *not* have reflected the increasing value of the land. Instead, the entire $134,000 gain will be reported in this year's income statement. The gain will not be included with operating income; it will be highlighted in the income statement as a nonrecurring, nonoperating item (usually reported as an element of "other income or expense"), so financial statement users will not be led to expect a similar gain in future years.

The original cost valuation of land (and most other categories of noncurrent assets discussed in this chapter) is often criticized for understating asset values on the balance sheet and for failing to provide proper matching on the income statement. Cruisers management would have known that its land was appreciating in value over time, but this appreciation would not have been reflected on the balance sheet. The accounting profession defends the *cost principle* based on its reliability, consistency, and conservatism. To record land at fair value would involve ongoing annual appraisals or other subjective estimates of value that could not be verified until an exchange transaction (sale) occurred. Although approximate fair value would be more relevant than original cost for decision makers, original cost is the basis for accounting for noncurrent assets. You should be aware of this important limitation of the noncurrent asset information shown in balance sheets.

What Does It Mean?
Answer on page 232

2. What does it mean to state that balance sheet values do not represent current fair values of long-lived (noncurrent) assets?

Buildings and Equipment

Cost of Assets Acquired

LO 1

Explain how the cost of land, buildings, and equipment is reported on the balance sheet.

Buildings and equipment are recorded at their original cost, which is the purchase price plus all the ordinary and necessary costs incurred to get the building or equipment ready to use in the operations of the firm. "Construction in Progress," or some similar description, is often used to accumulate the costs of facilities that are being constructed to the firm's specifications until the completed assets are placed in service. Interest costs associated with loans used to finance the construction of a building are capitalized until the building is put into operation. Installation and shakedown costs (costs associated with adjusting and preparing the equipment to be used in production) incurred for a new piece of equipment should be capitalized. If a piece of equipment is made by a firm's own employees, all the material, labor, and overhead costs that would ordinarily be recorded as inventory costs (were the machine being made for an outside customer) should be capitalized as equipment costs. Such costs are capitalized because they are directly related to assets that will be used by the firm over several accounting periods and are not related only to current period earnings.

The IFRS Approach

One of the principal differences between U.S. GAAP and IFRS lies in the balance sheet valuation of noncurrent assets and liabilities. Under U.S. GAAP, most of a firm's noncurrent assets (i.e., property, plant, and equipment) are recorded at original cost. Once recorded, except in rare instances, original cost remains the amount associated with any given noncurrent asset and is likewise the amount used as the base on which depreciation expense is calculated.

International standards focus, instead, on fair value, which may be more than or less than original cost at any point in time. Under IFRS, most noncurrent assets must be revalued on a regular basis, perhaps annually. Revaluation may be applied to an entire class of assets or to individual asset categories. Revaluation increases are recorded as increases in the noncurrent asset's carrying value (on the debit side of the entry) and as increases in "Accumulated other comprehensive income (loss)" within stockholders' equity (on the credit side). Revaluation decreases are recorded in just the opposite manner, as reductions both in "Accumulated other comprehensive income (loss)" and in the relevant noncurrent asset's carrying value. Not surprisingly, significant disclosures are required under IFRS concerning any such revaluations.

Exhibit 6-2

Basket Purchase
Allocation Illustrated

Situation:
Cruisers Inc. acquired a parcel of land, along with a building and some production equipment, from a bankrupt competitor for $200,000 in cash. Current fair values reported by an independent appraiser were land, $20,000; building, $170,000; and equipment, $60,000.

Allocation of Acquisition Cost:

Asset	Appraised Fair Value	Percentage of Total*	Cost Allocation	
Land	$ 20,000	8%	$200,000 × 8% =	$ 16,000
Building	170,000	68%	$200,000 × 68% =	136,000
Equipment	60,000	24%	$200,000 × 24% =	48,000
	$250,000	100%		$200,000

Effect of the Acquisition on the Financial Statements:

Balance Sheet	Income Statement
Assets = Liabilities + Stockholders' equity	← Net income = Revenues − Expenses
Land + 16,000	
Building + 136,000	
Equipment + 48,000	
Cash − 200,000	

Entry to Record the Acquisition:

Dr.	Land	16,000	
Dr.	Building	136,000	
Dr.	Equipment	48,000	
	Cr. Cash		200,000

Original cost is not usually difficult to determine, but when two or more noncurrent assets are acquired in a single transaction for a lump-sum purchase price, the cost of each asset acquired must be measured and recorded separately. In such cases, an allocation of the "basket" purchase price is made to the individual assets acquired based on relative appraisal values on the date of acquisition. Exhibit 6-2 illustrates this allocation process and the related accounting.

Depreciation for Financial Accounting Purposes

In financial accounting, depreciation is an application of the matching concept. The original cost of noncurrent assets represents the *prepaid* cost of economic benefits that will be received in future years. To the extent that an asset is "used up" in the operations of the entity, a portion of the asset's cost should be subtracted from the revenues that were generated through the use of the asset. Thus, the depreciation process involves an allocation of the cost of an asset to the years in which the benefits of the asset are expected to be received. Depreciation is *not* an attempt to recognize a loss in fair value or any difference between the original cost and replacement cost of an asset. In fact, the fair value of noncurrent assets may actually increase as they are used—but appreciation is not presently recorded (as discussed in the land section of this chapter). Depreciation expense is recorded in each fiscal period, and its effect on the financial statements is shown below:

Balance Sheet	Income Statement
Assets = Liabilities + Stockholders' equity	← Net income = Revenues − Expenses
−Accumulated Depreciation	−Depreciation Expense

The adjusting entry to record depreciation is:

Dr. Depreciation Expense	xx	
Cr. Accumulated Depreciation		xx

Accumulated depreciation is another contra asset, and the balance in this account is the cumulative total of all the depreciation expense that has been recorded over the life of the asset up to the balance sheet date. It is classified with the related asset on the balance sheet as a subtraction from the cost of the asset. The difference between the cost of an asset and the accumulated depreciation on that asset is the **net book value** (carrying value) of the asset. The balance sheet presentation of a building asset and its related Accumulated Depreciation account (using assumed amounts) looks like this:

Building	$100,000
Less: Accumulated depreciation	(15,000)
Net book value of building	$ 85,000

or, as more commonly reported, like this:

Building, less accumulated depreciation of $15,000	$85,000

With either presentation, the user can determine how much of the cost has been recognized as expense since the asset was acquired—which would not be possible if the Building account was directly reduced for the amount depreciated each year. This is why a contra asset account is used for accumulated depreciation.

    Note that cash is not involved in the depreciation expense entry. The entity's Cash account was affected when the asset was purchased or as it is being paid for if a liability was incurred when the asset was acquired. The fact that depreciation expense does not affect cash is important in understanding the statement of cash flows, which identifies the sources and uses of a firm's cash during a fiscal period.

    There are several alternative methods of calculating depreciation expense for financial accounting purposes. Each involves spreading the amount to be depreciated, which is the asset's cost minus its estimated salvage value, over the asset's estimated useful life to the entity. The depreciation method selected does not affect the total

Straight-line depreciation

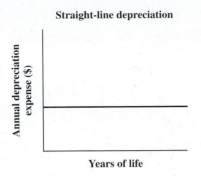

Accelerated depreciation

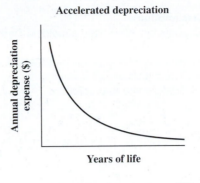

Exhibit 6-3

Depreciation Expense
Patterns

depreciation expense to be recognized over the life of the asset; however, different methods result in different patterns of depreciation expense by fiscal period. There are two broad categories of depreciation calculation methods: straight-line methods and accelerated methods. Depreciation expense patterns resulting from these alternatives are illustrated in Exhibit 6-3.

---

3. What does it mean to say that depreciation expense does not affect cash?

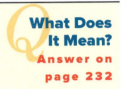

**What Does
It Mean?
Answer on
page 232**

Accelerated depreciation methods result in greater depreciation expense and lower net income than straight-line depreciation during the early years of the asset's life. During the later years of the asset's life, annual depreciation expense using accelerated methods is less than it would be using straight-line depreciation, and net income is higher.

Which method is used, and why? For reporting to stockholders, most firms use the **straight-line depreciation method** because in the early years of an asset's life it results in lower depreciation expense and hence higher reported net income than accelerated depreciation. In later years, when accelerated depreciation is less than straight-line depreciation, *total* depreciation expense using the straight-line method will still be less than under an accelerated method if the amount invested in new assets has grown each year. Such a regular increase in depreciable assets is not unusual for firms that are growing, assuming that prices of new and replacement equipment are rising.

The specific depreciation calculation methods are as follows:

LO 3
Describe alternative
methods of calculat-
ing depreciation for
financial accounting
purposes and compare
the relative effects of
each on the income
statement and the bal-
ance sheet.

Straight-line

Straight-line

Units-of-production

Accelerated

Declining-balance

Sum-of-the-years'-digits

The straight-line, units-of-production, and declining-balance depreciation calculation methods are illustrated in Exhibit 6-4.[1]

---

[1] The sum-of-the-years'-digits method is not illustrated because it is seldom used in practice.

Exhibit 6-4

Depreciation
Calculation Methods

Assumptions:

Cruisers Inc. purchased a molding machine at the beginning of 2019 at a cost of $22,000. The machine is estimated to have a useful life to Cruisers of five years and an estimated salvage value of $2,000. It is estimated that the machine will produce 200 boat hulls before it wears out.

a. Straight-line depreciation:

$$\text{Annual depreciation expense} = \frac{\text{Cost} - \text{Estimated salvage value}}{\text{Estimated useful life}}$$

$$= \frac{\$22,000 - \$2,000}{5 \text{ years}}$$

$$= \$4,000$$

Alternatively, a straight-line depreciation rate could be determined and multiplied by the amount to be depreciated:

$$\text{Straight-line depreciation rate} = \frac{1}{\text{Life in years}} = \frac{1}{5} = 20\%$$

$$\text{Annual depreciation expense} = 20\% \times \$20,000 = \$4,000$$

b. Units-of-production depreciation:

$$\text{Depreciation expense per unit produced} = \frac{\text{Cost} - \text{Estimated salvage value}}{\text{Estimated total units to be produced}}$$

$$= \frac{\$22,000 - \$2,000}{200 \text{ hulls}}$$

$$= \$100$$

Each year's depreciation expense would be $100 multiplied by the number of hulls produced.

c. Declining-balance depreciation:

$$\text{Annual depreciation expense} = \begin{array}{l}\text{Double the straight-line depreciation rate} \\ \times \text{ Asset's net book value at beginning of year}\end{array}$$

$$\text{Straight-line depreciation rate} = \frac{1}{\text{Life in years}} = \frac{1}{5} = 20\%$$

Double the straight-line depreciation rate is 40%.

	Net Book Value at Beginning of Year	Factor			Depreciation Expense for the Year	Accumulated Depreciation	Net Book Value at End of Year
2019	$22,000	×	0.4	=	$8,800	$ 8,800	$13,200
2020	13,200	×	0.4	=	5,280	14,080	7,920
2021	7,920	×	0.4	=	3,168	17,248	4,752
2022	4,752	×	0.4	=	1,901	19,149	2,851
2023	2,851	×	0.4	=	851*	20,000	2,000

Recap of depreciation expense by year and method:

	Straight-Line	Declining-Balance
2019	$ 4,000	$ 8,800
2020	4,000	5,280
2021	4,000	3,168
2022	4,000	1,901
2023	4,000	851
Total	$20,000	$20,000

*Depreciation expense at the end of the asset's life is equal to an amount that will cause the net book value to equal the asset's estimated salvage value.

Note that the total depreciation expense for the five years is the same for both methods; it is the pattern of the expense that differs. Because depreciation is an expense, the effect on operating income of the alternative methods will be opposite; 2019 operating income will be higher if the straight-line method is used and lower if the declining-balance method is used.

Depreciation calculations using the straight-line, units-of-production, and sum-of-the-years'-digits methods involve determining the amount to be depreciated by subtracting the estimated salvage value from the cost of the asset. Salvage value is considered in the declining-balance method only near the end of the asset's life when salvage value becomes the target for net book value.

The declining-balance calculation illustrated in Exhibit 6-4 is known as *double-declining balance* because the depreciation rate used is double the straight-line rate. In some instances the rate used is 1.5 times the straight-line rate; this is referred to as *150% declining-balance depreciation.* Whatever rate is used, a constant percentage is applied each year to the declining balance of the net book value.

Although many firms will use a single depreciation method for all of their depreciable assets, the consistency concept is applied to the depreciation method used for a particular asset acquired in a particular year. Thus, it is possible for a firm to use an accelerated depreciation method for some of its assets and the straight-line method for other assets. Differences can even occur between similar assets purchased in the same or different years. To make sense of the income statement and balance sheet, it is necessary to find out from the notes to the financial statements which depreciation methods are used (see the Campbell's annual report in the appendix).

Table 6-1 summarizes the depreciation methods used for financial reporting purposes by 500 large firms as of the 2011 reporting year. Unfortunately, the AICPA no longer tracks these data.

The estimates made of useful life and salvage value are educated guesses to be sure, but accountants, frequently working with engineers, can estimate these factors with great accuracy. A firm's experience and equipment replacement practices are considered in the estimating process. For income tax purposes (see Business in Practice—Depreciation for Income Tax Purposes), the useful life of various depreciable assets is determined by the Internal Revenue Code, which also specifies that salvage values are to be ignored.

In practice, a number of technical accounting challenges must be considered in calculating depreciation. These include calculating depreciation for assets that were acquired or disposed of during a year (see Business in Practice—Partial-Year Depreciation), changes in the estimated salvage value and/or useful life of an asset that has already been depreciated for several years, asset improvements (or *betterments*), and asset grouping to facilitate the depreciation calculation. Most of these topics are beyond the scope of this text; your task is to understand the alternative calculation methods used in practice and the different effect of each on both depreciation expense in the income statement and accumulated depreciation (and net book value) on the balance sheet.

Methods	Number of Companies
Straight-line	490
Declining-balance	9
Sum-of-the-years'-digits	2
Accelerated method—not specified	9
Units-of-production	12
Group/Composite	17

Table 6.1

Depreciation Calculation Methods Used by 500 Publicly Owned Industrial and Merchandising Corporations—2011

Source: *Accounting Trends and Techniques, U.S. GAAP Financial Statements—Best Practices in Presentation and Disclosure,* Table 3–3, copyright © 2012 by American Institute of Certified Public Accountants, Inc.

Business in
Practice

PARTIAL-YEAR DEPRECIATION

In the illustratration of depreciation calculation methods in Exhibit 6-4, it was assumed that Cruisers Inc. purchased a moulding machine at the beginning of 2019. Assume instead that the machine was purchased on October 1, 2019, and has a five-year useful life, extending to September 30, 2024.

In this case, straight-line depreciation for the year ended December 31, 2019, would be equal the annual depreciation (as calculated in Exhibit 6-4) of $4,000 per year, multiplied by a factor of 3/12, or $1,000. Depreciation expense for each of the next four years (2020–2023) would remain as calculated, or $4,000 per year. In 2024, depreciation expense of $3,000 ($4,000 x 9/12) would be recognized for the final nine months of the asset's useful life. Thus, in practice, it takes one additional calendar year (six years rather than five in this example) to fully depreciate an asset of any given useful life.

Similar partial-year calculations would be made for other depreciation methods, including the double-declining-balance method. For the three-month period ended December 31, 2019, the calculated full-year depreciation expense for the entire 2019 calendar year, of $8,800, would be reduced by a factor of 3/12, to $2,200. This amount would then be subtracted from the asset's cost of $22,000 to arrive at a December 31, 2019, net book value of $19,800. Depreciation expense for 2020 would be $7,920 ($19,800 x 0.4), arriving at an ending net book value of $11,880 ($19,800 − $7,920). Test your understanding of this process by calculating depreciation expense for 2021 and the ending net book value at December 31, 2021, under the double-declining-balance method and with the revised asset purchase date of October 1, 2019. Your answers should be $4,752 and $7,128.

Partial-year (often called year-to-date) depreciation adjustments are also recorded at the time that a depreciable asset is sold or otherwise disposed of during any given year. This ensures that the net book value of the asset sold will be accurately reflected in the company's accounting records at the time the entry to record the asset disposition is recorded.

The IFRS

Approach

International financial reporting standards provide that property, plant, and equipment (PP&E) should be recognized as an asset when it is probable that (1) future economic benefits associated with the asset will flow to the entity and (2) the cost of the asset can be measured reliably. When the cost model is used, each element of PP&E that is significant in relation to the total balance sheet valuation must be depreciated separately. The depreciation method for each element should reflect the pattern in which the asset's economic benefits are likely to be consumed by the entity. When the initial measurement of cost is based on U.S. GAAP, revaluation should be carried out regularly so that asset carrying amounts do not differ materially from fair values at the balance sheet date.

What Does It Mean?

Answer on page 232

4. What does it mean to use an accelerated depreciation method?
5. What does it mean to refer to the tax benefit of depreciation expense?

Repair and Maintenance Expenditures

LO 4
Describe the accounting treatment of repair and maintenance expenditures.

Routine repair costs and preventive maintenance expenditures are clearly expenses of the period in which they are incurred. There is a gray area with respect to some maintenance expenditures, however, and accountants' judgments may differ. If a maintenance expenditure will extend the useful life and/or increase the salvage value of an asset beyond that used in the original depreciation calculation, it is appropriate that the expenditure be capitalized and that the remaining depreciable cost of the asset be depreciated over the asset's remaining useful life.

In practice, most accountants decide in favor of expensing rather than capitalizing for several reasons. Revising the depreciation calculation data is frequently time-consuming with little perceived benefit. Because depreciation involves estimates of useful life and salvage value to begin with, revising those estimates without overwhelming evidence that they are significantly in error is an exercise of questionable value. For income tax purposes, most taxpayers would likewise rather have a deductible expense now (expensing) rather than later (capitalizing and depreciating).

Because of the possibility that net income could be affected either favorably or unfavorably by inconsistent judgments about the accounting for repair and maintenance expenditures, auditors (internal and external) and the Internal Revenue Service usually look closely at these expenditures when they are reviewing a firm's reported results.

---

6. What does it mean to prefer expensing repair and maintenance expenditures rather than capitalizing them?

What Does It Mean?
Answer on page 232

Depreciation for Income Tax Purposes

Depreciation is a deductible expense for income tax purposes. Although depreciation expense does not directly affect cash, it does reduce taxable income. Therefore, most firms would like their deductible depreciation expense to be as large an amount as possible because this means lower taxable income and lower taxes payable. The Internal Revenue Code has permitted taxpayers to use an accelerated depreciation calculation method for many years. Estimated useful life is generally the most significant factor (other than calculation method) affecting the amount of depreciation expense, and for many years this was a contentious issue between taxpayers and the Internal Revenue Service.

In 1981, the Internal Revenue Code was amended to permit use of the **Accelerated Cost Recovery System (ACRS),** frequently pronounced "acres," for depreciable assets placed in service after 1980. The ACRS rules simplified the determination of useful life and allowed rapid write-off patterns similar to the declining-balance methods, so most firms started using ACRS for tax purposes. Unlike the LIFO inventory cost flow assumption (which, if selected for income tax determination purposes, must also be used for financial reporting purposes), there is no requirement that "book" (financial statement) and tax depreciation calculation methods be the same. Most firms continued to use straight-line depreciation for book purposes.

ACRS used relatively short, and arbitrary, useful lives, and ignored salvage value. The intent was more to permit relatively quick "cost recovery" and thus encourage investment than it was

Business in
Practice

LO 5
Explain why depreciation for income tax purposes is an important concern of taxpayers and how tax depreciation differs from financial accounting depreciation.

to recognize traditional depreciation expense. For example, ACRS permitted the write-off of most machinery and equipment over three to five years.

In the Tax Reform Act of 1986 Congress changed the original ACRS provisions. The system has since been referred to as the **Modified Accelerated Cost Recovery System (MACRS).** Recovery periods were lengthened, additional categories for classifying assets were created, and the method of calculating the depreciation deduction was specified. Cost recovery periods are specified based on the type of asset and its class life, as defined in the Internal Revenue Code. Most machinery and equipment is depreciated using the double-declining-balance method, but the 150% declining-balance method is required for some longer-lived assets, and the straight-line method is specified for buildings.

In addition to the MACRS rules, small and medium businesses benefit from a special relief provision that allows certain depreciable assets to be treated as immediate expense deductions as they are purchased. An annual election can be made to expense as much as $1,000,000 (for the 2018 tax year) of the cost of qualifying depreciable property purchased for use in a trade or business, subject to certain limitations and phaseouts. The immediate deduction promotes administrative convenience by eliminating the need for extensive depreciation schedules for qualifying purchases.

Basing depreciation expense for financial accounting purposes on tax law provisions, which are subject to frequent change and influenced by political motivations, is not appropriate. Yet many small to medium-sized business organizations yield to the temptation to do so. Such decisions are based on the inescapable fact that tax depreciation schedules must be maintained to satisfy Internal Revenue Service rules, and therefore the need to keep separate schedules for financial reporting purposes can be avoided.

Disposal of Depreciable Assets

When a depreciable asset is sold or scrapped, both the asset and its related accumulated depreciation account must be removed from the books. For example, scrapping a fully depreciated piece of equipment, for which no salvage value had been estimated, would produce the following financial statement effects:

Balance Sheet	Income Statement
Assets = Liabilities + Stockholders' equity	← Net income = Revenues − Expenses
− Equipment + Accumulated Depreciation	

The entry would be:

LO 6
Describe the effect on the financial statements of the disposition of noncurrent assets, either by sale or abandonment.

Dr.	Accumulated Depreciation	xx	
	Cr. Equipment		xx

Note that this entry does not affect *total* assets or any other parts of the financial statements.

When the asset being disposed of has a positive net book value, either because a salvage value was estimated or because it has not reached the end of its estimated useful life to the firm, a gain or loss on the disposal will result unless the asset is sold for a price that is equal to the net book value. For example, if equipment that cost

$6,000 new has a net book value equal to its estimated salvage value of $900 and is sold for $1,200, the following financial statement effects would occur:

Balance Sheet	Income Statement
Assets = Liabilities + Stockholders' equity	← Net income = Revenues − Expenses
Cash + 1,200 Accumulated Depreciation + 5,100* Equipment − 6,000	Gain on Sale of Equipment + 300

$$*\text{Net book value} = \text{Cost} - \text{Accumulated depreciation}$$
$$900 = 6,000 - \text{Accumulated depreciation}$$
$$\text{Accumulated depreciation} = 5,100$$

Here is the entry to record the sale of equipment:

Dr. Cash	1,200	
Dr. Accumulated Depreciation	5,100	
Cr. Equipment		6,000
Cr. Gain on Sale of Equipment		300
Sold equipment.		

Alternatively, assume that the equipment had to be scrapped without receiving any proceeds. The effect of this entry on the financial statements looks like this:

Balance Sheet	Income Statement
Assets = Liabilities + Stockholders' equity	← Net income = Revenues − Expenses
Accumulated Depreciation + 5,100 Equipment − 6,000	Loss on Disposal of Equipment − 900

The entry would be as follows:

Dr. Accumulated Depreciation	5,100	
Dr. Loss on Disposal of Equipment	900	
Cr. Equipment		6,000
Scrapped equipment.		

The gain or loss on the disposal of a depreciable asset is, in effect, a correction of the total depreciation expense that has been recorded over the life of the asset. If salvage value and useful life estimates had been correct, the net book value of the asset would be equal to the **proceeds** (if any) received from its sale or disposal. Depreciation expense is never adjusted retroactively, so the significance of these gains or losses

You will have no difficulty with the preceding material if you can learn to apply the following formula:

Sales price (of the fixed asset)
− Net book value (original cost − Accumulated depreciation)
= Gain (if the difference is positive) or loss (if negative)

gives the financial statement user a basis for judging the accuracy of the accountant's estimates of salvage value and useful life. Gains or losses on the disposal of depreciable assets are not part of the operating income of the entity. If significant, they will be reported separately as elements of other income or expense. If not material, they will be reported with miscellaneous other income.

Assets Acquired by Lease

LO 7

Describe the difference between an operating lease and a financing lease.

Many firms will lease, or rent, assets rather than purchase them. An **operating lease** is an agreement for the use of an asset that does not involve any substantial attributes of ownership. For example, the renter (lessee) of a car from Hertz or Avis (the lessor) must return the car at the end of the lease term. Therefore, assets rented under a short-term operating lease for periods of 12 months or less are not reflected on the lessee's balance sheet, and the rent expense (or lease expense) involved is reported in the income statement as an operating expense.

Effective for annual periods beginning after December 15, 2018, accounting for assets rented under long-term operating leases (for periods of more than 12 months) by a lessee has become more complex, and is now similar to the treatment of financing leases as described below.

A **financing lease** (sometimes called a *finance lease,* and formerly referred to as a *capital lease*) results in the lessee (renter) assuming virtually all the benefits and risks of ownership of the leased asset. For example, the lessee of a car from an automobile

Focus on the "Big Picture"

A number of technical financial accounting topics are presented in this text at an overview level to provide a basic, user-oriented exposure to the key financial statement accounts and captions that you are likely to encounter at some point in your life as an investor, creditor, or employee of a large, publicly traded company. In this chapter, the accounting for assets acquired by a financing lease and for goodwill represent two such examples. Likewise, brief references were made to the "Accumulated other comprehensive income (loss)" caption, which is reported as an element of stockholders' equity on the balance sheet; this important topic is described in Chapter 8. The authors believe that for students to understand "what the numbers mean," an exposure to these (and similar) types of accounts and captions is not only appropriate but essential, because they represent key components of the modern-day language of accounting and financial reporting. Your attention should be focused on understanding the essential nature of any such "technical" topics as you encounter them, specifically as to how they relate to the "big picture" financial statement model (A = L + SE, and NI = R − E) that you learned in Chapter 2.

dealership may sign a noncancelable lease agreement with a term of five years requiring monthly payments sufficient to cover the cost of the car, plus interest and administrative costs. A lease is a financing lease if it has *any* of the following characteristics:

1. It transfers ownership of the asset to the lessee at the end of the lease term.
2. It permits the lessee to purchase the asset for a nominal sum (a *bargain purchase option* that is reasonably certain to be exercised) at the end of the lease term.
3. The lease term (which does not commence near the end of the economic life of the leased asset) is primarily for the remaining economic life of the leased asset.
4. The **present value** of the lease payments and residual value guarantees is equal, to or more than, substantially all of the fair value of the leased asset. (Please refer to the appendix at the end of this chapter if you are not familiar with the present value concept.)
5. The leased asset has no alternative use to the lessor at the end of its lease term because of its specialized nature.

The economic impact of a financing lease isn't really any different from buying the asset outright and signing a note payable that will be paid off, with interest, over the life of the asset. Therefore, it is appropriate that the asset and related liability be reflected in the lessee's balance sheet. In the lessee's income statement, the cost of the leased asset will be reflected as depreciation expense, rather than rent expense, and the financing cost will be shown as interest expense.

Prior to an FASB standard issued in 1976, many companies did not record assets acquired under a financing lease because they did not want to reflect the related lease liability in their balance sheet. This practice is known as *off-balance-sheet financing* and is deemed inappropriate because the full disclosure concept would be violated were it to be allowed. The new FASB rules requiring the capitalization of long-term operating leases further reduce any incentives management may have once had to use leases as a form of off-balance-sheet financing.

Assets acquired by financing leases (and operating leases for periods of more than 12 months) are referred to as "right-of-use" assets and are now included with purchased assets on the balance sheet. The amount recorded as the cost of the asset involved in a financing lease, and as the related lease liability, is the present value of the lease payments to be made, based on the interest rate used by the lessor to determine the periodic lease payments. Here are the effects of financing lease transactions on the financial statements using the horizontal model:

LO 8
Explain the similarities in the financial statement effects of buying an asset compared to using a financing lease to acquire the rights to an asset.

Balance Sheet	Income Statement
Assets = Liabilities + Stockholders' equity	← Net income = Revenues − Expenses
1. Date of acquisition: + Right-of- + Lease Use Asset Liability	

2. Annual depreciation expense:
− Right-of-
   Use Asset
	− Depreciation
	   Expense

3. Annual lease payments:
− Cash   − Lease
            Liability
	− Interest
	   Expense

The entries to record financing lease transactions are as follows:

1. Date of acquisition.			
Dr. Right-of-Use Asset		xx	
Cr. Lease Liability			xx
2. Annual depreciation expense.			
Dr. Depreciation Expense		xx	
Cr. Right-of-Use Asset			xx
3. Annual lease payments.			
Dr. Interest Expense		xx	
Dr. Lease Liability		xx	
Cr. Cash			xx

The first entry shows the asset acquisition and the related financial obligation that has been incurred. The second shows depreciation expense in the essentially same way it is recorded for purchased assets. (Note that the right-of-use asset is reduced directly rather than crediting an accumulated depreciation account.) The third shows the lease payment effect on cash, reflects the interest expense for the period on the amount that has been borrowed (in substance) from the lessor, and reduces the lease liability by what is effectively a payment on the principal of a loan from the lessor.

To illustrate the equivalence of financing lease payments and a long-term loan, assume that a firm purchased a computer system at a cost of $217,765 and borrowed the money by giving a note payable that had an annual interest rate of 10 percent and that required payments of $50,000 per year for six years. Using the horizontal model, the following is the effect on the financial statements:

Balance Sheet	Income Statement
Assets = Liabilities + Stockholders' equity	← Net income = Revenues − Expenses
Equipment Note + 217,765 Payable + 217,765	

The purchase would be recorded using the following entry:

Dr. Equipment	217,765	
Cr. Note Payable		217,765

Each year the firm will accrue and pay interest expense on the note, and make principal payments, as shown in the following loan amortization table:

Year	Principal Balance at Beginning of Year	Interest at 10%	Payment Applied to Principal ($50,000 − Interest)	Principal Balance at End of Year
1...	$217,765	$21,776	$28,224	$189,541
2...	189,541	18,954	31,046	158,495
3...	158,495	15,849	34,151	124,344
4...	124,344	12,434	37,566	86,778
5...	86,778	8,677	41,323	45,455
6...	45,455	4,545	45,455	−0−

After six years, the note will have been fully paid.

If the firm were to lease the computer system and agree to make annual lease payments of $50,000 for six years instead of borrowing the money and buying the computer system outright, the financial statements should reflect the transaction in essentially the same way. This will happen because the present value of all the lease payments (which include principal and interest) is $217,765. (Referring to Table 6-5 in the appendix to this chapter, in the 10% column and six-period row, the factor is 4.3553. This factor multiplied by the $50,000 annual lease payment is $217,765.) Using the horizontal model, the following is the effect on the financial statements:

Balance Sheet	Income Statement
Assets = Liabilities + Stockholders' equity	← Net income = Revenues – Expenses
Right-of- Lease Use Asset Liability + 217,765 + 217,765	

The entry at the beginning of the lease will be as follows:

Dr. Right-of-Use Asset	217,765	
Cr. Lease Liability		217,765

Each year, the principal portion of the lease payment will reduce the lease liability, and the interest portion will be recognized as an expense. Note that interest expense is reduced each year because the outstanding principal on the loan becomes smaller as payments are made. In addition, the right-of-use asset (representing the equipment) will be depreciated each year on a straight-line basis. Thus, liabilities on the balance sheet and expenses in the income statement will be the same as under the borrow and purchase alternative for each year of the asset's life.

Long-term operating leases are accounted for by lessees in a manner similar to that of financing leases. A right-of-use asset and related lease liability are recognized in equal amounts on the lessee's balance sheet at the inception of the lease. However, the income statement impact of each differs. Financing leases result in greater amounts of total expense (interest plus depreciation) being recognized in the early years of the lease term and smaller amounts in the later years, as demonstrated in the example above. Under long-term operating leases, however, the lease expense recognized by lessees is a straight-line amount equal to the total annual rental payments.

Again, the significance of financing lease accounting is that the economic impact of the lease agreement (as a form of financing the asset) isn't really any different from buying the asset outright; the impact on the financial statements shouldn't differ either. Although long-term operating leases have a different expense recognition pattern, the overall accounting treatment is also similar to that of a purchased asset.

---

7. What does it mean to acquire an asset with a financing lease?

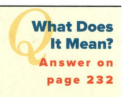

What Does It Mean? Answer on page 232

Intangible Assets

LO 9

Discuss the meaning of various intangible assets, how their values are measured, and how their costs are reflected in the income statement.

Intangible assets are long-lived assets that differ from property, plant, and equipment that have been purchased outright or acquired under a financing lease—either because the asset is represented by a contractual right or because the asset results from a purchase transaction but is not physically identifiable. Examples of the first type of intangible asset are leaseholds, licenses, franchises, brand names, customer lists/relationships, patents, copyrights, and trademarks; the second type of intangible asset is known as *goodwill.*

Just as the cost of plant and equipment is transferred to expense over time through accounting depreciation, the cost of most intangibles is also expensed over time. **Amortization,** which means spreading an amount over time, is the term used to describe the process of allocating the cost of an intangible asset from the balance sheet to the income statement as an expense. The cost of tangible assets is depreciated; the cost of intangible assets is amortized. The terms are different, but the process is the same. Most intangibles are amortized on a straight-line basis based on the useful life to the entity. Although the Accumulated Amortization account is sometimes used, amortization expense is usually recorded as a direct reduction in the carrying value of the related intangible asset. Thus, the effect of periodic amortization on the financial statements would be as follows:

Balance Sheet	Income Statement
Assets = Liabilities + Stockholders' equity	←Net income = Revenues − Expenses

− Intangible
  Asset
	− Amortization
	  Expense

The entry would be:

Dr. Amortization Expense	xx	
Cr. Intangible Asset		xx

Amortization expense is usually included with depreciation expense in the income statement. Note that neither depreciation expense nor amortization expense involves a cash disbursement; cash is disbursed when the asset is acquired or, if a loan is used to finance the acquisition, when the loan payments are made.

Leasehold Improvements

When the tenant of an office building makes modifications to the office space, such as having private offices constructed, the cost of these modifications is a capital expenditure to be amortized over their useful life to the tenant or over the life of the lease, whichever is shorter. The concept is the same as that applying to buildings or equipment, but the terminology is different. Entities that use rented facilities extensively, such as smaller shops or retail store chains that operate in shopping malls, may have a significant amount of **leasehold improvements.**

Patents, Trademarks, and Copyrights

A **patent** is a monopoly license granted by the government giving the owner control of the use or sale of an invention for a period of 20 years. A **trademark** (or trade name), when registered with the Federal Trade Commission, can be used only by the entity that owns it or by another entity that has secured permission from the owner. A trademark has an unlimited life, but it can be terminated by lack of use. A **copyright** is a protection granted to writers and artists that is designed to prevent unauthorized copying of printed or recorded material. A copyright is granted for a period of time equal to the life of the writer or artist, plus 70 years.

To the extent that an entity has incurred some cost in obtaining a patent, trademark, or copyright, that cost should be capitalized and amortized over its estimated remaining useful life to the entity or its statutory life, whichever is shorter. The cost of developing a patent, trademark, or copyright is not usually significant. Most intangible assets in this category arise when one firm purchases a patent, trademark, or copyright from another entity. An intangible that becomes very valuable because of the success of a product (like "Coke") cannot be assigned a value and recorded as an asset while it continues to be owned by the entity that created it. In some cases a firm will include a caption for trademarks, or another intangible asset, on its balance sheet and report a nominal cost of $1 just to communicate to financial statement users that it has this type of asset.

License fees or royalties earned from an intangible asset owned by a firm are reported as operating revenues in the income statement. Likewise, license fees or royalty expenses incurred by a firm using an intangible asset owned by another entity are operating expenses.

Goodwill

Goodwill results from the purchase of one firm by another for a price that is greater than the fair value of the net assets acquired. (Recall from Chapter 2 that *net assets* means total assets minus total liabilities.) Why would one firm be willing to pay more for a business than the fair value of the inventory, plant, and equipment, and other assets being acquired? Because the purchasing firm does not see the transaction as the purchase of assets but instead evaluates the transaction as the purchase of *profits*. The purchaser will be willing to pay such an amount because the profits expected to be earned from the investment will generate an adequate return on the investment. If the firm being purchased has been able to earn a greater than average rate of return on its invested net assets, the owners of that firm will be able to command a price for the firm that is greater than the fair value of its net assets. This greater than average return may result from excellent management, a great location, unusual customer loyalty, a unique product or service, or a combination of these and other factors.

When one firm purchases another, the purchase price is first assigned to the net assets acquired, which includes physical assets and intangible assets. The cost recorded for these net assets is their fair value, usually determined by appraisal. This cost then becomes the basis for depreciating or amortizing the assets, or for determining cost of goods sold if inventory is involved. To the extent that the total price exceeds the fair value of the net assets acquired, the excess is recorded as goodwill. For example, assume that Cruisers Inc. purchased a business by paying $1,000,000 in cash and assuming a note payable liability of $100,000. The fair value of the net assets acquired was $700,000, assigned as follows: Inventory, $250,000; Land, $150,000; Buildings, $400,000; and Notes Payable, $100,000. Here is the effect of this transaction on the financial statements:

Balance Sheet	Income Statement
Assets = Liabilities + Stockholders' equity	←Net income = Revenues − Expenses
Inventory Notes + 250,000 Payable + 100,000 Land + 150,000 Buildings + 400,000 Goodwill + 300,000 Cash − 1,000,000	

The entry would be as follows:

Dr. Inventory	250,000	
Dr. Land	150,000	
Dr. Buildings	400,000	
Dr. Goodwill	300,000	
Cr. Notes Payable		100,000
Cr. Cash		1,000,000

Goodwill is an intangible asset and is *not* amortized. Instead, goodwill must be tested annually for impairment. If the book value of goodwill does not exceed its fair value, goodwill is not considered impaired. However, if the book value of goodwill *does* exceed its fair value, an impairment loss is recorded equal to that excess. Although the details of this test are more appropriate for an advanced accounting course, the financial statement effects of an impairment loss are straightforward. In the preceding Cruisers example, assume that three years after the business was acquired, the fair value of the resulting goodwill of $300,000 was determined to be only $180,000. Here would be the effects on the financial statements of the impairment loss adjustment:

Balance Sheet	Income Statement
Assets = Liabilities + Stockholders' equity	←Net income = Revenues − Expenses
Goodwill − 120,000	Goodwill Impairment Loss − 120,000

The entry for the impairment loss would be as follows:

Dr. Goodwill impairment loss	120,000	
Cr. Goodwill		120,000

Goodwill impairment loss is generally reported as a separate line item within operating income on the income statement. Once goodwill is considered to be impaired and has been written down to its impaired fair value, no subsequent upward adjustments are permitted for recoveries of fair value. In the preceding example, $180,000 would become the new book value for goodwill, and this amount would be compared to the fair value of goodwill in future years to determine if further impairment has occurred.

The prior examples provide a basic illustration of the recording of goodwill and subsequent impairment losses, if any, by an acquiring firm. One way of describing goodwill is to say that—in theory at least—it is the present value of the greater than average earnings on the net assets of the acquired firm, discounted for the period they are expected to last, at the acquiring firm's desired return on investment. In fact, when analysts at the acquiring firm are calculating the price to offer for the firm to be acquired, they use a lot of present value analysis.

Some critics suggest that goodwill is a fictitious asset that should be written off immediately against the firm's retained earnings. Others point out that it is at best a "different" asset that must be evaluated carefully when it is encountered. However, if goodwill is included in the assets used in the return on investment calculation, the ROI measure will reflect management's ability to earn a return on this asset.

---

8.   What does it mean when goodwill results from the acquisition of another firm?

What Does It Mean?

Answer on page 233

Natural Resources

Accounting for natural resource assets, such as coal deposits, crude oil reserves, timber, and mineral deposits, parallels that for depreciable assets. **Depletion,** rather than depreciation, is the term for the using up of natural resources, but the concepts are the same, even though depletion usually involves considerably more complex estimates.

For example, when a firm pays for the right to drill for oil or mine for coal, the cost of that right and the costs of developing the well or mine are capitalized. The cost is then reflected in the income statement as Depletion Expense, which is matched with the revenue resulting from the sale of the natural resource. Depletion usually is recognized on a straight-line basis, based on geological and engineering estimates of the quantity of the natural resource to be recovered. Thus, if $100 million was the cost of a mine that held an estimated 20 million tons of coal, the depletion cost would be $5 per ton. In most cases, the cost of the asset is credited, or reduced directly, in the Depletion Expense entry instead of using an Accumulated Depletion account.

In practice, estimating depletion expense is very complex. Depletion expense allowed for federal income tax purposes frequently differs from that recognized for financial accounting purposes because, from time to time, tax laws have been used to provide special incentives to develop natural resources.

Other Noncurrent Assets

Long-term investments, notes receivable that mature more than a year after the balance sheet date, long-term deferred income tax assets, and other noncurrent assets are included in this category. At such time as they become current (receivable within one year), they will be reclassified to the current asset section of the balance sheet. The notes accompanying the financial statements will include appropriate explanations about these assets if they are significant.

Demonstration Problem

The Demonstration Problem walkthrough for this chapter is available in *Connect.*

Summary

This chapter has discussed the accounting for and presentation of the following balance sheet noncurrent asset and related income statement accounts:

Balance Sheet	Income Statement
Assets = Liabilities + Stockholders' equity	←Net income = Revenues − Expenses
Land	Gain on or Loss on sale* sale*
Purchased Buildings/ Equipment	Repair and Maintenance Expense
Right-of- Lease Use Asset Liability	Interest Expense
(Accumulated Depreciation)	Depreciation Expense
Natural Resources	Depletion Expense
Intangible Assets	Amortization Expense
* For any noncurrent asset.	

Property, plant, and equipment owned by the entity are reported on the balance sheet at their original cost, less (for depreciable assets) accumulated depreciation. **(LO 1)**

Expenditures representing the cost of acquiring an asset that will benefit the entity for more than the current fiscal period are capitalized. Routine repair and maintenance costs are expensed in the fiscal period in which they are incurred. **(LO 2, 4)**

Accounting depreciation is the process of spreading the cost of an asset to the fiscal periods in which the asset is used. Depreciation does not affect cash, nor is it an attempt to recognize a loss in the market value of an asset.

Depreciation expense can be calculated several ways. The calculations result in a depreciation expense pattern that is straight-line or accelerated. Straight-line methods are usually used for book purposes, and accelerated methods (based on the Modified Accelerated Cost Recovery System specified in the Internal Revenue Code) are usually used for income tax purposes. **(LO 3, 5)**

When a depreciable asset is disposed of, both the asset and its related accumulated depreciation are removed from the accounts. A gain or loss normally results, depending on the relationship of any cash (and/or other assets) received in the transaction to the net book value of the asset disposed of. **(LO 6)**

When the use of an asset is acquired in a financing lease transaction, the asset and related lease liability are reported on the balance sheet. The cost of the asset is the present value of the lease payments, calculated using the interest rate used by the lessor to determine the periodic lease payments. The asset is depreciated, and interest expense related to the lease is recorded. **(LO 7, 8, 10)**

Intangible assets are represented by a contractual right or are not physically identifiable. The cost of most intangible assets is spread over the useful life to the entity of the intangible asset and is called *amortization expense.* Intangible assets include leasehold improvements, patents, trademarks, copyrights, and goodwill. Goodwill is not amortized but is tested annually for impairment. The cost of natural resources is recognized as *depletion expense,* which is allocated to the natural resources recovered. **(LO 9)**

Refer to the Campbell Soup Company balance sheet and related notes in the appendix, and to other financial statements you may have, and observe how information about property, plant, and equipment, and other noncurrent assets is presented.

Campbell's

Appendix TO CHAPTER SIX

Time Value of Money

Two financial behaviors learned early in life are that money saved or invested at compound interest can yield large returns and that given the choice of paying a bill sooner or later, it can be financially beneficial to pay later. The first of these situations involves future value, and the second is an application of present value; both are time value of money applications.

LO 10

Explain the role of time value of money concepts in financial reporting and their usefulness in decision making.

Future Value

Future value refers to the amount accumulated when interest on an investment is compounded for a given number of periods. *Compounding* refers to the practice of calculating interest for a period on the sum of the principal and interest accumulated at the beginning of the period (thus, interest is earned on interest). For example, if $1,000 is invested in a savings account earning interest at the rate of 10% compounded annually, and if the account is left alone for four years, the results shown in the following table will occur:

Year	Principal at Beginning of Year	Interest Earned at 10%	Principal at End of Year
1.............	$1,000	$100	$1,100
2.............	1,100	110	1,210
3.............	1,210	121	1,331
4.............	1,331	133	1,464

This is a familiar concept. This process can be illustrated on a timeline as follows:

Today	1 year	2 years	3 years	4 years

$1,000 ⟶ invested at 10% has a future value of ⟶ $1,464

There is a formula for calculating future value, and many computer program packages and business calculators include a future value function. Table 6-2 presents future

Table 6.2   Factors for Calculating the Future Value of $1

No. of Periods	Interest Rate									
	2%	4%	6%	8%	10%	12%	14%	16%	18%	20%
1	1.020	1.040	1.060	1.080	1.100	1.120	1.140	1.160	1.180	1.200
2	1.040	1.082	1.124	1.166	1.210	1.254	1.300	1.346	1.392	1.440
3	1.061	1.125	1.191	1.260	1.331	1.405	1.482	1.561	1.643	1.728
4	1.082	1.170	1.262	1.360	1.464	1.574	1.689	1.811	1.939	2.074
5	1.104	1.217	1.338	1.469	1.611	1.762	1.925	2.100	2.288	2.488
10	1.219	1.480	1.791	2.159	2.594	3.106	3.707	4.411	5.234	6.192
15	1.346	1.801	2.397	3.172	4.177	5.474	7.138	9.266	11.974	15.407
20	1.486	2.191	3.207	4.661	6.727	9.646	13.743	19.461	27.393	38.338
30	1.811	3.243	5.743	10.063	17.449	29.960	50.950	85.850	143.371	237.376
40	2.208	4.801	10.286	21.725	45.259	93.051	188.884	378.721	750.378	1469.772
50	2.692	7.107	18.420	46.902	117.391	289.002	700.233	1670.704	3927.357	9100.438

value factors for a range of interest rates and compounding periods. Note in Table 6-2 that the factor for 10% and four periods is 1.464. This factor is multiplied by the beginning principal to get the future value. The future value of $1,000 at 10% for four periods is $1,464, as shown in the timeline illustration.

Future Value of an Annuity

Sometimes a savings or investment pattern involves adding an amount equal to the initial investment on a regular basis. This is called an **annuity.** When the investment is made at the end of each compounding period, a usual practice, the annuity is in arrears. The future value of an annuity is simply the sum of the future value of each individual investment. Table 6-3 presents the future value factors for a range of interest rates and compounding periods for an annuity in arrears. Note that the factor for an annuity in arrears at 10% for two periods is 2.100. This is the future value of an amount invested at the end of the first period after one more period, plus the amount of

Table 6.3   Factors for Calculating the Future Value of an Annuity of $1 in Arrears

No. of Periods	Interest Rate									
	2%	4%	6%	8%	10%	12%	14%	16%	18%	20%
1	1.000	1.000	1.000	1.000	1.000	1.000	1.000	1.000	1.000	1.000
2	2.020	2.040	2.060	2.080	2.100	2.120	2.140	2.160	2.180	2.200
3	3.060	3.122	3.184	3.246	3.310	3.374	3.440	3.506	3.572	3.640
4	4.112	4.246	4.375	4.506	4.641	4.779	4.921	5.066	5.215	5.368
5	5.204	5.416	5.637	5.867	6.105	6.353	6.610	6.877	7.154	7.442
10	10.950	12.006	13.181	14.487	15.937	17.549	19.337	21.321	23.521	25.959
15	17.293	20.024	23.276	27.152	31.772	37.280	43.842	51.660	60.965	72.035
20	24.297	29.778	36.786	45.762	57.275	72.052	91.025	115.380	146.628	186.688
30	40.568	56.085	79.058	113.283	164.494	241.333	356.787	530.312	790.948	1181.882
40	60.402	95.026	154.762	259.057	442.593	767.091	1342.025	2360.757	4163.213	7343.858
50	84.579	152.667	290.336	573.770	1163.909	2400.018	4994.521	10435.649	21813.094	45497.191

the investment at the end of the second period. What is the future value of an annuity in arrears of $200 invested at 12% (at the end of each year) for 10 years?

Present Value

Whereas future value focuses on the value at some point in the future of an amount invested today, present value focuses on the value today of an amount to be paid or received at some point in the future. Present value is another application of compound interest that is of great significance in accounting and business practice. Organizations and individuals are frequently confronted with the choice of paying for a purchase today or at a later date. Intuition suggests that all other things being equal, it would be better to pay later because in the meantime the cash not spent today could be invested to earn interest. This reflects the fact that money has value over time. Of course, other things aren't always equal, and sometimes the choice is between paying one amount—say, $1,000—today and a larger amount—say, $1,100—a year later. Or in the opposite case, the choice may be between receiving $1,000 today or $1,100 a year from now. Present value analysis is used to determine which of these alternatives is financially preferable.

Present value concepts are well established in financial reporting, having been used traditionally in the valuation of assets and liabilities that characteristically involve far-distant cash flows. In 2000, the Financial Accounting Standards Board extended its Conceptual Framework project to embrace the present value concept more formally as a fundamental accounting measurement technique.[2] Per the FASB:

> The objective of using present value in an accounting measurement is to capture, to the extent possible, the economic difference between sets of estimated future cash flows. Without present value, a $1,000 cash flow due tomorrow and a $1,000 cash flow due in 10 years appear the same. Because present value distinguishes between cash flows that otherwise might appear similar, a measurement based on the present value of estimated future cash flows provides more relevant information than a measurement based on the undiscounted sum of those cash flows.[3]

Present value analysis involves looking at the same compound interest concept from the opposite perspective. Using data in the compound interest table developed earlier, you can say that the present value of $1,464 to be received four years from now, assuming an interest rate of 10% compounded annually, is $1,000. On a timeline representation, the direction of the arrow indicating the time perspective is reversed:

Today	1 year	2 years	3 years	4 years

$1,000 ◄———————— is the present value at 10% of ◄———————— $1,464

If someone owed you $1,464 to be paid four years from now, and if you were to agree with your debtor that 10% was a fair interest rate for that period, you would both be satisfied to settle the debt for $1,000 today. Alternatively, if you owed $1,464 payable

---

[2] See FASB, *Statement of Financial Accounting Concepts No. 7,* "Using Cash Flow Information and Present Value in Accounting Measurements" (Stamford, CT, 2000). Copyright © the Financial Accounting Standards Board, High Ridge Park, Stamford, CT 06905, U.S.A. Excerpted with permission. Copies of the complete document are available from the FASB.

[3] FASB, *Statement of Financial Accounting Concepts No. 7, "Highlights"* (Stamford, CT, 2000). The FASB cautions that highlights are best understood in the context of the full statement.

Business in
Practice

Study
Suggestion

four years from now, both you and your creditor would be satisfied to settle the debt for $1,000 today (still assuming agreement on the 10% interest rate). That is because $1,000 invested at 10% interest compounded annually will grow to $1,464 in four years. Stated differently, the future value of $1,000 at 10% interest in four years is $1,464, and the present value of $1,464 in four years at 10% is $1,000.

Present value analysis involves determining the present amount that is equivalent to an amount to be paid or received in the future, recognizing that money has value over time. The time value of money is represented by the interest that can be earned on money over an investment period. In present value analysis, **discount rate** is a term frequently used for *interest rate*. In our example, the present value of $1,464, discounted at 10% for four years, is $1,000. Thus, the *time value of money* in this example is represented by the $464 in interest that is being charged to the borrower for the use of money over the four-year period.

Present value analysis does not directly recognize the effects of inflation, although inflationary expectations will influence the discount rate used in the present value calculation. Generally, the higher the inflationary expectations, the higher the discount rate used in present value analysis.

Present Value of an Annuity

The preceding example deals with the present value of a *single amount* to be received or paid in the future. Some transactions involve receiving or paying the same amount each period for a number of periods. This sort of receipt or payment pattern is referred to as an *annuity.* The present value of an annuity is the sum of the present value of each of the annuity payment amounts.

There are formulas and computer program functions for calculating the present value of a single amount and the present value of an annuity (see Business in Practice—Using Financial Calculators). In all cases, the amount to be received or paid in the future, the discount rate, and the number of years (or other time periods) are used in the present value calculation. Table 6-4 presents factors for calculating the

Factors for Calculating the Present Value of $1   **Table 6.4**

| No. of Periods | \multicolumn{10}{c}{Discount Rate} |
	2%	4%	6%	8%	10%	12%	14%	16%	18%	20%
1	0.980	0.9615	0.9434	0.9259	0.9091	0.8929	0.8772	0.8621	0.8475	0.8333
2	0.961	0.9246	0.8900	0.8573	0.8264	0.7972	0.7695	0.7432	0.7182	0.6944
3	0.942	0.8890	0.8396	0.7938	0.7513	0.7118	0.6750	0.6407	0.6086	0.5787
4	0.924	0.8548	0.7921	0.7350	0.6830	0.6355	0.5921	0.5523	0.5158	0.4823
5	0.906	0.8219	0.7473	0.6806	0.6209	0.5674	0.5194	0.4761	0.4371	0.4019
6	0.888	0.7903	0.7050	0.6302	0.5645	0.5066	0.4556	0.4104	0.3704	0.3349
7	0.871	0.7599	0.6651	0.5835	0.5132	0.4523	0.3996	0.3538	0.3139	0.2791
8	0.853	0.7307	0.6274	0.5403	0.4665	0.4039	0.3506	0.3050	0.2660	0.2326
9	0.837	0.7026	0.5919	0.5002	0.4241	0.3606	0.3075	0.2630	0.2255	0.1938
10	0.820	0.6756	0.5584	0.4632	0.3855	0.3220	0.2697	0.2267	0.1911	0.1615
11	0.804	0.6496	0.5268	0.4289	0.3505	0.2875	0.2366	0.1954	0.1619	0.1346
12	0.788	0.6246	0.4970	0.3971	0.3186	0.2567	0.2076	0.1685	0.1372	0.1122
13	0.773	0.6006	0.4688	0.3677	0.2897	0.2292	0.1821	0.1452	0.1163	0.0935
14	0.758	0.5775	0.4423	0.3405	0.2633	0.2046	0.1597	0.1252	0.0985	0.0779
15	0.743	0.5553	0.4173	0.3152	0.2394	0.1827	0.1401	0.1079	0.0835	0.0649
16	0.728	0.5339	0.3936	0.2919	0.2176	0.1631	0.1229	0.0930	0.0708	0.0541
17	0.714	0.5134	0.3714	0.2703	0.1978	0.1456	0.1078	0.0802	0.0600	0.0451
18	0.700	0.4936	0.3503	0.2502	0.1799	0.1300	0.0946	0.0691	0.0508	0.0376
19	0.686	0.4746	0.3305	0.2317	0.1635	0.1161	0.0829	0.0596	0.0431	0.0313
20	0.673	0.4564	0.3118	0.2145	0.1486	0.1037	0.0728	0.0514	0.0365	0.0261
21	0.660	0.4388	0.2942	0.1987	0.1351	0.0926	0.0638	0.0443	0.0309	0.0217
22	0.647	0.4220	0.2775	0.1839	0.1228	0.0826	0.0560	0.0382	0.0262	0.0181
23	0.634	0.4057	0.2618	0.1703	0.1117	0.0738	0.0491	0.0329	0.0222	0.0151
24	0.622	0.3901	0.2470	0.1577	0.1015	0.0659	0.0431	0.0284	0.0188	0.0126
25	0.610	0.3751	0.2330	0.1460	0.0923	0.0588	0.0378	0.0245	0.0160	0.0105
30	0.552	0.3083	0.1741	0.0994	0.0573	0.0334	0.0196	0.0116	0.0070	0.0042
35	0.500	0.2534	0.1301	0.0676	0.0356	0.0189	0.0102	0.0055	0.0030	0.0017
40	0.453	0.2083	0.0972	0.0460	0.0221	0.0107	0.0053	0.0026	0.0013	0.0007
45	0.410	0.1712	0.0727	0.0313	0.0137	0.0061	0.0027	0.0013	0.0006	0.0003
50	0.372	0.1407	0.0543	0.0213	0.0085	0.0035	0.0014	0.0006	0.0003	0.0001

Table 6.5   Factors for Calculating the Present Value of an Annuity of $1

No. of Periods	2%	4%	6%	8%	10%	12%	14%	16%	18%	20%
1	0.980	0.9615	0.9434	0.9259	0.9091	0.8929	0.8772	0.8621	0.8475	0.8333
2	1.942	1.8861	1.8334	1.7833	1.7355	1.6901	1.6467	1.6052	1.5656	1.5278
3	2.884	2.7751	2.6730	2.5771	2.4869	2.4018	2.3216	2.2459	2.1743	2.1065
4	3.808	3.6299	3.4651	3.3121	3.1699	3.0373	2.9137	2.7982	2.6901	2.5887
5	4.713	4.4518	4.2124	3.9927	3.7908	3.6048	3.4331	3.2743	3.1272	2.9906
6	5.601	5.2421	4.9173	4.6229	4.3553	4.1114	3.8887	3.6847	3.4976	3.3255
7	6.472	6.0021	5.5824	5.2064	4.8684	4.5638	4.2883	4.0386	3.8115	3.6046
8	7.325	6.7327	6.2098	5.7466	5.3349	4.9676	4.6389	4.3436	4.0776	3.8372
9	8.162	7.4353	6.8017	6.2469	5.7590	5.3282	4.9464	4.6065	4.3030	4.0310
10	8.983	8.1109	7.3601	6.7101	6.1446	5.6502	5.2161	4.8332	4.4941	4.1925
11	9.787	8.7605	7.8869	7.1390	6.4951	5.9377	5.4527	5.0286	4.6560	4.3271
12	10.575	9.3851	8.3838	7.5361	6.8137	6.1944	5.6603	5.1971	4.7932	4.4392
13	11.348	9.9856	8.8527	7.9038	7.1034	6.4235	5.8424	5.3423	4.9095	4.5327
14	12.106	10.5631	9.2950	8.2442	7.3667	6.6282	6.0021	5.4675	5.0081	4.6106
15	12.849	11.1184	9.7122	8.5595	7.6061	6.8109	6.1422	5.5755	5.0916	4.6755
16	13.578	11.6523	10.1059	8.8514	7.8237	6.9740	6.2651	5.6685	5.1624	4.7296
17	14.292	12.1657	10.4773	9.1216	8.0216	7.1196	6.3729	5.7487	5.2223	4.7746
18	14.992	12.6593	10.8276	9.3719	8.2014	7.2497	6.4674	5.8178	5.2732	4.8122
19	15.678	13.1339	11.1581	9.6036	8.3649	7.3658	6.5504	5.8775	5.3162	4.8435
20	16.351	13.5903	11.4699	9.8181	8.5136	7.4694	6.6231	5.9288	5.3527	4.8696
21	17.011	14.0292	11.7641	10.0168	8.6487	7.5620	6.6870	5.9731	5.3837	4.8913
22	17.658	14.4511	12.0416	10.2007	8.7715	7.6446	6.7429	6.0113	5.4099	4.9094
23	18.292	14.8568	12.3034	10.3711	8.8832	7.7184	6.7921	6.0442	5.4321	4.9245
24	18.914	15.2470	12.5504	10.5288	8.9847	7.7843	6.8351	6.0726	5.4509	4.9371
25	19.523	15.6221	12.7834	10.6748	9.0770	7.8431	6.8729	6.0971	5.4669	4.9476
30	22.396	17.2920	13.7648	11.2578	9.4269	8.0552	7.0027	6.1772	5.5168	4.9789
35	24.999	18.6646	14.4982	11.6546	9.6442	8.1755	7.0700	6.2153	5.5386	4.9915
40	27.355	19.7928	15.0463	11.9246	9.7791	8.2438	7.1050	6.2335	5.5482	4.9966
45	29.490	20.7200	15.4558	12.1084	9.8628	8.2825	7.1232	6.2421	5.5523	4.9986
50	31.424	21.4822	15.7619	12.2335	9.9148	8.3045	7.1327	6.2463	5.5541	4.9995

present value of $1 (single amount), and Table 6-5 gives the factors for the present value of an annuity of $1 for several discount rates and number of periods.

To find the present value of any amount, the appropriate factor from the table is multiplied by the amount to be received or paid in the future. Using the data from the initial example just described, we can calculate the present value of $1,464 to be received four years from now, based on a discount rate of 10%:

$1,464 × 0.6830 (from the 10% column, four-period row of
Table 6-4) = $1,000 (rounded)

What is the present value of a lottery prize of $1,000,000, payable in 20 annual installments of $50,000 each, assuming a discount (interest) rate of 12%? Here is the timeline representation of this situation:

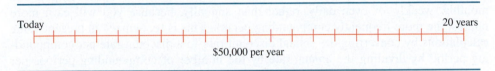

The present value of this annuity is calculated by multiplying the annuity amount ($50,000) by the annuity factor from Table 6-5. The solution is as follows:

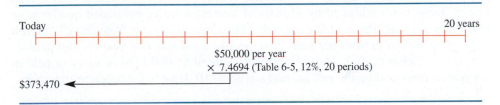

Although the answer of $373,470 shouldn't make the winner feel less fortunate, she certainly has not become an instant millionaire in present value terms. The lottery authority needs to deposit only $373,470 today in an account earning 12% interest to be able to pay the winner $50,000 per year for 20 years beginning a year from now. What is the present value of the same lottery prize assuming that 8% was the appropriate discount rate? What if a 16% interest rate was used? (Take a moment to calculate these amounts.) Imagine how the wife of *The Born Loser* comic strip character must have felt upon learning that he had won a million dollars—payable at $1 per year for a million years! As these examples point out, the present value of future cash flows is directly affected by both the chosen discount rate and the relevant time frame.

Let's look at another example. Assume you have accepted a job from a company willing to pay you a signing bonus, and you must now choose between three alternative payment plans. The plan A bonus is $3,000 payable today. The plan B bonus is $4,000 payable three years from today. The plan C bonus is three annual payments of $1,225 each (an annuity) with the first payment to be made one year from today. Assuming a discount rate of 8%, which bonus should you accept? The solution requires calculation of the present value of each bonus. Here is the timeline approach:

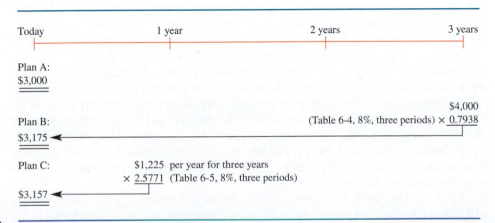

Bonus plan B has the highest present value and for that reason would be the plan selected based on present value analysis.

Impact of Compounding Frequency

The frequency with which interest is compounded affects both future value and present value. You would prefer to have the interest on your savings account compounded monthly, weekly, or even daily, rather than annually, because you will earn more interest the more frequently compounding occurs. This is recognized in present value calculations by converting the annual discount rate to a discount rate per compounding period by dividing the annual rate by the number of compounding periods per year. Likewise, the number of periods is adjusted by multiplying the number of years involved by the number of compounding periods per year. For example, the present value of $1,000 to be received or paid six years from now, at a discount rate of 16% compounded annually, is $410.40 (the factor 0.4104 from the 16% column, six-period row of Table 6-4, multiplied by $1,000). If interest were compounded quarterly, or four times per year, the present value calculation uses the factor from the 4% column (16% per year/four periods per year), and the 24-period row (six years × four periods per year), which is 0.3901. Thus, the present value of $1,000 to be received or paid in six years, compounding interest quarterly, is $390.10. Here is the timeline approach:

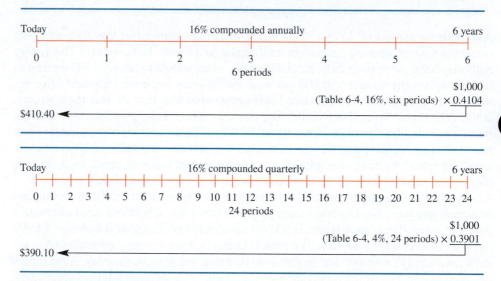

You can make sense of the fact that the present value of a single amount is lower the more frequent the compounding by visualizing what you could do with either $410.40 or $390.10 if you were to receive each of these amounts today rather than receiving $1,000 in six years. Each amount could be invested at 16%, but interest would compound on the $410.40 only once per year, while interest on the $390.10 would compound every three months. Even though you start with different amounts, you'll still have $1,000 after six years in each situation. Test your comprehension of this calculation process by verifying that the present value of an annual annuity of $100 for 10 years, discounted at an annual rate of 16%, is $483.32, and that the present value of $50 paid every six months for 10 years, discounted at the same annual rate (which is an 8% semiannual rate), is $490.91. The present value of an annuity is greater the more frequent the compounding because the annuity amount is paid or received sooner than when the compounding period is longer.

Many of these ideas may seem complicated to you now, but your common sense will affirm the results of present value analysis. Remember that $1 in your hands today is worth more than $1 to be received tomorrow or a year from today. This explains why firms are interested in speeding up the collection of accounts receivable and other cash inflows. The opposite logic applies to cash payments, which explains why firms will defer the payment of accounts payable whenever possible. The prevailing attitude is, "We're better off with the cash in our hands than in the hands of our customers or suppliers." Several applications of present value analysis to business transactions will be illustrated in subsequent chapters. By making the initial investment of time now, you will understand these ideas more quickly later.

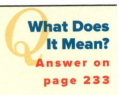

9. What does it mean to say that money has value over time?

10. What does it mean to talk about the present value of an amount of money to be received or spent in the future?

11. What does it mean to receive an annuity?

Key Terms and Concepts

Accelerated Cost Recovery System (ACRS) (p. 197)   The method prescribed in the Internal Revenue Code for calculating the depreciation deduction; applicable to the years 1981–1986.

accelerated depreciation method (p. 193)   A depreciation calculation method that results in greater depreciation expense in the early periods of an asset's life than in the later periods of its life.

amortization (p. 204)   The process of spreading the cost of an intangible asset over its useful life.

annuity (p. 210)   The receipt or payment of a constant amount over fixed periods of time, such as monthly, semiannually, or annually.

capitalizing (p. 189)   To record an expenditure as an asset as opposed to expensing the expenditure.

copyright (p. 205)   An amortizable intangible asset represented by the legally granted protection against unauthorized copying of a creative work.

declining-balance depreciation method (p. 194)   An accelerated depreciation method in which the declining net book value of the asset is multiplied by a constant rate.

depletion (p. 207)   The accounting process recognizing that the cost of a natural resource asset is used up as the natural resource is consumed.

discount rate (p. 212)   The interest rate used in a present value calculation.

expensing (p.189)   To record an expenditure as an expense, as opposed to capitalizing the expenditure.

financing lease (p. 200)   A lease, usually long-term, that has the effect of financing the acquisition of an asset. Sometimes called a *finance lease,* and formerly referred to as a *capital lease.*

future value (p. 209)   The amount that a present investment will be worth at some point in the future, assuming a specified interest rate and the reinvestment of interest in each period that it is earned.

goodwill (p. 205)   A nonamortizable intangible asset arising from the purchase of a business for more than the fair value of the net assets acquired. Goodwill is the present value of the expected earnings of the acquired business in excess of the earnings that would represent an average return on investment, discounted at the investor's required rate of return for the expected duration of the excess earnings.

intangible asset (p. 204)   A long-lived asset represented by a contractual right, or an asset that is not physically identifiable.

leasehold improvement (p. 204)   An amortizable intangible asset represented by the cost of improvements made to a leasehold by the lessee.

Modified Accelerated Cost Recovery System (MACRS) (p. 198)   The method prescribed in the Internal Revenue Code for calculating the depreciation deduction; applicable to years after 1986.

net book value (p. 192)   The difference between the cost of an asset and the accumulated depreciation related to the asset. Sometimes called *carrying value*.

operating lease (p. 200)   A lease that does not involve any substantial attributes of ownership.

patent (p. 205)   An amortizable intangible asset represented by a government-sanctioned monopoly over the use of a product or process.

present value (p. 201)   The value now of an amount to be received or paid at some future date, recognizing an interest (or discount) rate for the period from the present to the future date.

proceeds (p. 199)   The amount of cash (or equivalent value) received in a transaction.

straight-line depreciation method (p. 193)   Calculation of periodic depreciation expense by dividing the amount to be depreciated by the number of periods over which the asset is to be depreciated.

trademark (p. 205)   An amortizable intangible asset represented by a right to the exclusive use of an identifying mark.

units-of-production depreciation method (p. 194)   A depreciation method based on periodic use and life expressed in terms of asset utilization.

■ connect   Mini-Exercises

All applicable Mini-Exercises are available in *Connect*.

Mini-Exercise 6.1

LO 1

Basket purchase allocation Fesco Jewelers Ltd. purchased store fixtures, display cases, and a maximum-security commercial safe for a lump-sum price of $18,000 from a bankrupt competitor. Appraised values were as follows: store fixtures, $9,000; display cases, $13,500; commercial safe, $7,500.

Required:
What cost should be recorded for the commercial safe?

Mini-Exercise 6.2

LO 2

Capitalizing versus expensing Stucki Holdings Corp. incurred the following expenditures: $6,100 cost to replace the transmission in a company-owned vehicle; $21,600 cost of annual property insurance on the company's production facilities; $12,800 cost to develop and register a design patent; $22,700 cost to add a security and monitoring system to the company's distribution center; $600 cost to repair paint damage on a company-owned vehicle caused by normal wear and tear.

Required:
Which, if any, of these expenditures should be capitalized?

Mini-Exercise 6.3

LO 3

Depreciation calculation methods Gandolfi Construction Co. purchased a CAT 336DL earth mover at a cost of $1,000,000 in January 2019. The company's estimated useful life of this heavy equipment is 8 years, and the estimated salvage value is $200,000.

Required:
a. Using straight-line depreciation, calculate the depreciation expense to be recognized for 2019, the first year of the equipment's life, and calculate the equipment's net book value at December 31, 2021, after the third year of the equipment's life.
b. Using declining-balance depreciation at twice the straight-line rate, calculate the depreciation expense to be recognized for 2021, the third year of the equipment's life.

Effect of depreciation on ROI Refer to the information presented in Mini-Exercise 6.3. Assume that Gandolfi Construction Co. calculated depreciation expense for the CAT 336DL earth mover on the straight-line method and reported $960,000 of net income for the year ended December 31, 2019. The company's average total assets for 2019 were $8,000,000.

Mini-Exercise 6.4
LO 3

Required:
a. Calculate Gandolfi's ROI for the year ended December 31, 2019.
b. Calculate what Gandolfi's ROI would have been for the year ended December 31, 2019, had the company used the double-declining-balance depreciation method for the CAT 336DL earth mover. Ignore the effects of income taxes.

Goodwill Backstreets Co. recently acquired all of Jungleland Inc.'s net assets in a business acquisition. The cash purchase price was $12.6 million. Jungleland's assets and liabilities had the following appraised values immediately prior to the acquisition: land, $2.4 million; buildings, $5.8 million; inventory, $3.4 million; long-term notes payable, for which Backstreets Co. assumes payment responsibilities, $2.5 million.

Mini-Exercise 6.5
LO 9

Required:
How much goodwill will result from this transaction?

Present value calculations Congratulations! You have just won $2 billion in the largest Powerball jackpot payoff ever! You will receive payments of $100,000,000 per year for the next 20 years.

Mini-Exercise 6.6
LO 10

Required:
Using a present value table, your calculator, or a computer program present value function, calculate the present value of your lottery winnings, assuming an interest rate of 4%.

Exercises

■ connect

All applicable Exercises are available in *Connect*.

Basket purchase allocation Dorsey Co. has expanded its operations by purchasing a parcel of land with a building on it from Bibb Co. for $255,000. The appraised value of the land is $60,000, and the appraised value of the building is $240,000.

Exercise 6.7
LO 1

Required:
a. Assuming that the building is to be used in Dorsey Co.'s business activities, what cost should be recorded for the land?
b. Explain why, for income tax purposes, management of Dorsey Co. would want as little of the purchase price as possible allocated to land.
c. Explain why Dorsey Co. allocated the cost of assets acquired based on appraised values at the purchase date rather than on the original cost of the land and building to Bibb Co.
d. Assuming that the building is demolished at a cost of $20,000 so that the land can be used for employee parking, what cost should Dorsey Co. record for the land?

Exercise 6.8

LO 1

Basket purchase allocation Crow Co. purchased some of the machinery of Hare Inc., a bankrupt competitor, at a liquidation sale for a total cost of $136,200. Crow's cost of moving and installing the machinery totaled $12,300. The following data are available:

Item	Hare's Net Book Value on the Date of Sale	List Price of Same Item If New	Appraiser's Estimate of Fair Value
Punch press	$85,400	$131,000	$108,000
Lathe	58,200	67,000	45,000
Welder	26,400	42,000	27,000

Required:

a. Calculate the amount that should be recorded by Crow Co. as the cost of each piece of equipment.

b. Which of the following alternatives should be used as the depreciable life for Crow Co.'s depreciation calculation? Explain your answer.

    The remaining useful life to Hare Inc.

    The life of a new machine.

    The useful life of the asset to Crow Co.

Exercise 6.9

LO 2

Capitalizing versus expensing For each of the following expenditures, indicate the type of account (asset or expense) in which the expenditure should be recorded. Explain your answers.

a. $30,000 annual cost of routine repair and maintenance expenditures for a fleet of delivery vehicles.

b. $12,000,000 cost to develop a coal mine, from which an estimated 1 million tons of coal can be extracted.

c. $248,000 cost to replace the roof on a building.

d. $140,000 cost of a radio and television advertising campaign to introduce a new product line.

e. $8,000 cost of grading and leveling land so that a building can be constructed.

Exercise 6.10

LO 2

Capitalizing versus expensing For each of the following expenditures, indicate the type of account (asset or expense) in which the expenditure should be recorded. Explain your answers.

a. $3,700 for repairing damage that resulted from the careless unloading of a new machine.

b. $25,300 cost of designing and registering a trademark.

c. $14,600 in legal fees incurred to perform a title search for the acquisition of land.

d. $5,100 cost of patching a leak in the roof of a building.

e. $325,000 cost of salaries paid to the research and development staff.

Exercise 6.11

LO 3

Effect of depreciation on ROI Alpha Inc. and Beta Co. are sheet metal processors that supply component parts for consumer product manufacturers. Alpha has been in business since 1985 and is operating in its original plant facilities. Much of its equipment was acquired in the 80s and 90s. Beta Co. was started two years ago and acquired its building and equipment then. Each firm has about the same sales revenue, and material and labor costs are about the same for each firm. What would you expect Alpha's ROI to be relative to the ROI of Beta Co.? Explain your answer. What are the implications of this ROI difference for a firm seeking to enter an established industry?

Financial statement effects of depreciation—straight-line versus acceler-ated methods Assume that a company chooses an accelerated method of calculating depreciation expense for financial statement reporting purposes for an asset with a five-year life.

Exercise 6.12
LO 3

Required:
State the effect (higher, lower, no effect) of accelerated depreciation relative to straight-line depreciation on:

a. Depreciation expense in the first year.
b. The asset's net book value after two years.
c. Cash flows from operations (excluding income taxes).

Depreciation calculation methods Millco Inc. acquired a machine that cost $1,200,000 early in 2019. The machine is expected to last for eight years, and its esti-mated salvage value at the end of its life is $180,000.

Exercise 6.13
LO 3

Required:
a. Using straight-line depreciation, calculate the depreciation expense to be recognized in the first year of the machine's life and calculate the accumulated depreciation after the fifth year of the machine's life.
b. Using declining-balance depreciation at twice the straight-line rate, calculate the depreciation expense for the third year of the machine's life.
c. What will be the net book value of the machine at the end of its eighth year of use before it is disposed of, under each depreciation method?

Depreciation calculation methods Barefoot Industrial acquired a new delivery truck at the beginning of its current fiscal year. The truck cost $117,000 and has an estimated useful life of four years and an estimated salvage value of $18,000.

Exercise 6.14
LO 3

Required:
a. Calculate depreciation expense for each year of the truck's life using:
   1. Straight-line depreciation.
   2. Double-declining-balance depreciation.
b. Calculate the truck's net book value at the end of its third year of use under each depreciation method.
c. Assume that Barefoot Industrial had no more use for the truck after the end of the third year and that at the beginning of the fourth year it had an offer from a buyer who was willing to pay $27,900 for the truck. Should the depreciation method used by Barefoot Industrial affect the decision to sell the truck?

Present value calculations Using a present value table, your calculator, or a com-puter program present value function, calculate the present value of:

Exercise 6.15
LO 10

a. A car down payment of $9,000 that will be required in two years, assuming an interest rate of 10%.

b. A lottery prize of $18 million to be paid at the rate of $900,000 per year for 20 years, assuming an interest rate of 10%.

c. The same annual amount as in part **b,** but assuming an interest rate of 14%.

d. A financing lease obligation that calls for the payment of $24,000 per year for 10 years, assuming a discount rate of 8%.

Exercise 6.16

LO 10

Present value calculations—effects of compounding frequency, discount rates, and time periods Using a present value table, your calculator, or a computer program present value function, verify that the present value of $100,000 to be received in five years at an interest rate of 16%, compounded annually, is $47,610. Calculate the present value of $100,000 for each of the following items (parts **a–f**) using these facts, except:

a. Interest is compounded semiannually.

b. Interest is compounded quarterly.

c. A discount rate of 12% is used.

d. A discount rate of 20% is used.

e. The cash will be received in three years.

f. The cash will be received in seven years.

Exercise 6.17

LO 9

Goodwill effect on ROI Assume that fast-food restaurants generally provide an ROI of 12%, but that such a restaurant near a college campus has an ROI of 15% because its relatively large volume of business generates an above-average turnover (sales/assets). The replacement value of the restaurant's plant and equipment is $600,000. If you were to invest that amount in a restaurant elsewhere in town, you could expect a 12% ROI.

Required:

a. Would you be willing to pay more than $600,000 for the restaurant near the campus? Explain your answer.

b. If you purchased the restaurant near the campus for $750,000 and the fair value of the assets you acquired was $600,000, what balance sheet accounts would be used to record the cost of the restaurant?

Exercise 6.18

LO 9

Goodwill—effect on ROI and operating income Goodwill arises when one firm acquires the net assets of another firm and pays more for those net assets than their current fair value. Suppose that Target Co. had operating income of $1,215,000 and net assets with a fair value of $5,400,000. Takeover Co. pays $8,100,000 for Target Co.'s net assets and business activities.

Required:

a. How much goodwill will result from this transaction?

b. Calculate the ROI for Target Co. based on its present operating income and the fair value of its net assets.

c. Calculate the ROI that Takeover Co. will earn if the operating income of the acquired net assets continues to be $1,215,000.

d. What reasons can you think of to explain why Takeover Co. is willing to pay $2,700,000 more than fair value for the net assets acquired from Target Co.?

Transaction analysis—various accounts Prepare an answer sheet with the column headings that follow. For each of the following transactions or adjustments, indicate the effect of the transaction or adjustment on assets, liabilities, and net income by entering for each account affected the account name and amount and indicating whether it is an addition (+) or a subtraction (−). Transaction **a** has been done as an illustration. Net income is *not* affected by every transaction. In some cases, only one column may be affected because all of the specific accounts affected by the transaction are included in that category.

		Assets	Liabilities	Net Income
a.	Recorded $600 of depreciation expense.	Accumulated Depreciation −600		Depreciation Expense −600

b. Sold land that had originally cost $27,000 for $42,000 in cash.

c. Acquired a new machine under a financing lease. The present value of future lease payments, discounted at 10%, was $36,000.

d. Recorded the first annual payment of $6,000 for the leased machine (in part **c**).

e. Recorded a $18,000 payment for the cost of developing and registering a trademark.

f. Recognized periodic amortization for the trademark (in part **e**) using a 40-year useful life.

g. Sold used production equipment for $42,000 in cash. The equipment originally cost $120,000, and the accumulated depreciation account has an unadjusted balance of $66,000. It was determined that a $3,000 year-to-date depreciation entry must be recorded before the sale transaction can be recorded. Record the adjustment and the sale.

Transaction analysis—various accounts Prepare an answer sheet with the following column headings. For each of the following transactions or adjustments, indicate the effect of the transaction or adjustment on assets, liabilities, and net income by entering for each account affected the account name and amount and indicating whether it is an addition (+) or a subtraction (−). Transaction **a** has been done as an illustration. Net income is *not* affected by every transaction. In some cases, only one column may be affected because all of the specific accounts affected by the transaction are included in that category.

		Assets	Liabilities	Net Income
a.	Recorded $600 of depreciation expense.	Accumulated Depreciation −600		Depreciation Expense −600

b. Sold land that had originally cost $55,000 for $42,300 in cash.

c. Recorded a $437,000 payment for the cost of developing and registering a patent.

d. Recognized periodic amortization for the patent (in part **c**) using the maximum statutory useful life.

e. Capitalized $18,400 of cash expenditures made to extend the useful life of production equipment.

f. Expensed $7,100 of cash expenditures incurred for routine maintenance of production equipment.

g. Sold a used machine for $162,000 in cash. The machine originally cost $540,000 and had been depreciated for the first two years of its five-year useful life using the double-declining-balance method. (*Hint:* You must compute the balance of the accumulated depreciation account before you can record the sale.)

h. Purchased a business for $8,000,000 in cash. The fair values of the net assets acquired were as follows: Land, $2,200,000; Buildings, $4,600,000; Equipment, $2,500,000; and Long-Term Debt, $1,800,000.

▪ connect Problems

All applicable Problems are available in *Connect*.

Problem 6.21

LO 2, 4

Capitalizing versus expensing—effect on ROI and operating income During the first month of its current fiscal year, Green Co. incurred repair costs of $40,000 on a machine that had eight years of remaining depreciable life. The repair cost was inappropriately capitalized. Green Co. reported operating income of $225,000 for the current year.

Required:

a. Assuming that Green Co. took a full year's straight-line depreciation expense in the current year, calculate the operating income that should have been reported for the current year.

b. Assume that Green Co.'s total assets at the end of the prior year and at the end of the current year were $1,400,000 and $1,600,000, respectively. Calculate ROI (based on operating income) for the current year using the originally reported data and then using corrected data.

c. Explain the effect on ROI of subsequent years if the error is not corrected.

Problem 6.22

LO 2, 4

Capitalizing versus expensing—effect on ROI Early in January 2019, Tellco Inc. acquired a new machine and incurred $100,000 of interest, installation, and overhead costs that should have been capitalized but were expensed. The company earned net operating income of $750,000 on average total assets of $5,000,000 for 2019. Assume that the total cost of the new machine will be depreciated over 8 years using the straight-line method.

Required:

a. Calculate the ROI for Tellco for 2019.

b. Calculate the ROI for Tellco for 2019, assuming that the $100,000 had been capitalized and depreciated over 8 years using the straight-line method. (*Hint:* There is an effect on net operating income and average assets.)

c. Given your answers to **a** and **b,** why would the company want to account for this expenditure as an expense?

d. Assuming that the $100,000 is capitalized, what will be the effect on ROI for 2020 and subsequent years, compared to expensing the interest, installation, and overhead costs in 2019? Explain your answer.

Depreciation calculation methods—partial year Freedom Co. purchased a new machine on July 2, 2019, at a total installed cost of $132,000. The machine has an estimated life of five years and an estimated salvage value of $18,000.

Problem 6.23

LO 3

Required:

a. Calculate the depreciation expense for each year of the *asset's life* using:
   1. Straight-line depreciation.
   2. Double-declining-balance depreciation.

b. How much depreciation expense should be recorded by Freedom Co. for its fiscal year ended December 31, 2019, under each method? (*Note:* The machine will have been used for one-half of its first year of life.)

c. Calculate the accumulated depreciation and net book value of the machine at December 31, 2020, under each method.

Partial-year depreciation calculations—straight-line and double-declining-balance methods Porter Inc. acquired a machine that cost $720,000 on October 1, 2019. The machine is expected to have a four-year useful life and an estimated salvage value of $80,000 at the end of its life. Porter uses the calendar year for financial reporting. Depreciation expense for one-fourth of a year was recorded in 2019.

Problem 6.24

LO 3

Required:

a. Using the straight-line depreciation method, calculate the depreciation expense to be recognized in the income statement for the year ended December 31, 2021, and the balance of the Accumulated Depreciation account as of December 31, 2021. (*Note:* This is the third calendar year in which the asset has been used.)

b. Using the double-declining-balance depreciation method, calculate the depreciation expense for the year ended December 31, 2021, and the net book value of the machine at that date.

Identify depreciation methods used Grove Co. acquired a production machine on January 1, 2019, at a cost of $480,000. The machine is expected to have a four-year useful life, with a salvage value of $80,000. The machine is capable of producing 50,000 units of product in its lifetime. Actual production was as follows: 11,000 units in 2019; 16,000 units in 2020; 14,000 units in 2021; 9,000 units in 2022.

Problem 6.25

LO 3

Following is the comparative balance sheet presentation of the *net book value* of the production machine at December 31 for each year of the asset's life, using three alternative depreciation methods (items **a–c**):

Production Machine, Net of Accumulated Depreciation

	Depreciation Method?	At December 31			
		2022	**2021**	**2020**	**2019**
a.	_____	80,000	152,000	264,000	392,000
b.	_____	80,000	80,000	120,000	240,000
c.	_____	80,000	180,000	280,000	380,000

Required:

Identify the depreciation method used for each of the preceding comparative balance sheet presentations (items **a–c**). If a declining-balance method is used, be sure to indicate the percentage (150% or 200%). (*Hint:* Read the balance sheet from right to left to determine how much has been depreciated each year. Remember that December 31, 2019, is the end of the first year.)

Problem 6.26

LO 3

Identify depreciation methods used Moyle Co. acquired a machine on January 1, 2019, at a cost of $1,200,000. The machine is expected to have a five-year useful life, with a salvage value of $75,000. The machine is capable of producing 1,500,000 units of product in its lifetime. Actual production was as follows: 300,000 units in 2019; 200,000 units in 2020; 400,000 units in 2021; 250,000 units in 2022; and 350,000 units in 2023.

Items **a** through **d** below are T-account representations of Moyle Co.'s accumulated depreciation account. They reflect the depreciation adjustments that would be made each year for the above described machine using various depreciation calculation methods.

Required:

Identify the depreciation method that would result in each of these annual credit amount patterns to accumulated depreciation. If a declining-balance method is used, indicate the percentage (150% or 200%). (*Hint:* What do the amounts shown for each year represent?)

a.

Accumulated Depreciation	
	480,000 12/31/19
	288,000 12/31/20
	172,800 12/31/21
	103,680 12/31/22
	62,208 12/31/23

c.

Accumulated Depreciation	
	225,000 12/31/19
	225,000 12/31/20
	225,000 12/31/21
	225,000 12/31/22
	225,000 12/31/23

b.

Accumulated Depreciation	
	225,000 12/31/19
	150,000 12/31/20
	300,000 12/31/21
	187,500 12/31/22
	262,500 12/31/23

d.

Accumulated Depreciation	
	360,000 12/31/19
	252,000 12/31/20
	176,400 12/31/21
	123,480 12/31/22
	86,436 12/31/23

Problem 6.27

LO 3, 6

Determine depreciation method used and date of asset acquisition; record disposal of asset The balance sheets of Tully Corp. showed the following at December 31, 2020 and 2019:

	December 31, 2020	December 31, 2019
Equipment, less accumulated depreciation of $240,000 at December 31, 2020, and $150,000 at December 31, 2019.	$180,000	$270,000

Required:

a. If there have not been any purchases, sales, or other transactions affecting this equipment account since the equipment was first acquired, what is the amount of depreciation expense for 2020?

b. Assume the same facts as in part **a**, and assume that the estimated useful life of the equipment is four years and the estimated salvage value is $60,000. Determine:

  1. What the original cost of the equipment was.

  2. What depreciation method is apparently being used. Explain your answer.

  3. When the equipment was acquired.

c. Assume that the equipment is sold on December 31, 2020, for $141,600. Use the horizontal model (or write the journal entry) to show the effect of the sale of the equipment.

Determine depreciation method used and date of asset acquisition; record disposal of asset The balance sheets of HiROE Inc. showed the following at December 31, 2020 and 2019:

Problem 6.28

LO 3, 6

	December 31, 2020	December 31, 2019
Equipment, less accumulated depreciation of $212,625 at December 31, 2020, and $151,875 at December 31, 2019.	$273,375	$334,125

Required:

a. If there have not been any purchases, sales, or other transactions affecting this equipment account since the equipment was first acquired, what is the amount of the depreciation expense for 2020?

b. Assume the same facts as in part **a**, and assume that the estimated useful life of the equipment to HiROE, Inc., is eight years and that there is no estimated salvage value. Determine:

  1. What the original cost of the equipment was.

  2. What depreciation method is apparently being used. Explain your answer.

  3. When the equipment was acquired.

c. Assume that this equipment account represents the cost of five identical machines. Calculate the gain or loss on the sale of one of the machines on January 2, 2021, for $60,000. Use the horizontal model (or write the journal entry) to show the effect of the sale of the machine.

Accounting for financing leases On January 1, 2019, Carey Inc. entered into a noncancelable lease agreement, agreeing to pay $14,000 at the end of each year for four years to acquire a new computer system having a market value of $40,800. The expected useful life of the computer system is also four years, and the computer will be depreciated on a straight-line basis with no salvage value. The interest rate used by the lessor to determine the annual payments was 14%. Under the terms of the lease, Carey has an option to purchase the computer for $1 on January 1, 2023.

Problem 6.29

LO 7, 8, 10

Required:

a. Explain why Carey should account for this lease as a financing lease rather than an operating lease. (*Hint:* Determine which of the five criteria for capitalizing a lease have most likely been met.)

b. Show in a horizontal model or write the entry that Carey should make on January 1, 2019. Round your answer to the nearest $10. (*Hint:* First determine the present value of future lease payments using Table 6-5.)

c. Show in a horizontal model or write the entry that Carey, Inc., should make on December 31, 2019, to record the first annual lease payment of $14,000. Do not round your answers. (*Hint:* Based on your answer to part **b**, determine the appropriate amounts for interest and principal.)

d. What expenses (include amounts) should be recognized for this lease on the income statement for the year ended December 31, 2019?

e. Explain why the accounting for an asset acquired under a financing lease isn't really any different than the accounting for an asset that was purchased with money borrowed on a long-term loan.

Problem 6.30

LO 7, 8, 10

Accounting for financing leases versus purchased assets Ambrose Co. has the option of purchasing a new delivery truck for $63,450 in cash or leasing the truck for $13,725 per year, payable at the end of each year for six years. The truck also has a useful life of six years and will be depreciated on a straight-line basis with no salvage value. The interest rate used by the lessor to determine the annual payments was 8%.

Required:

a. Assume that Ambrose Co. purchased the delivery truck and signed a six-year, 8% note payable for $63,450 in satisfaction of the purchase price. Show in a horizontal model or write the entry that Ambrose should make to record the purchase transaction.

b. Assume instead that Ambrose Co. agreed to the terms of the lease. Show in a horizontal model or write the entry that Ambrose should make to record the financing lease transaction. Round your answer up to the nearest $10. (*Hint:* First determine the present value of future lease payments using Table 6-5.)

c. Show in a horizontal model or write the entry that Ambrose Co. should make at the end of the year to record the first annual lease payment of $13,725. Do not round your answers. (*Hint:* Based on your answer to part **b**, determine the appropriate amounts for interest and principal.)

d. What expenses (include amounts) should Ambrose Co. recognize on the income statement for the first year of the lease?

e. How much would the annual payments be for the note payable signed by Ambrose Co. in part **a**? (*Hint:* Use the present value of an annuity factor from Table 6-5.)

Problem 6.31

LO 8, 10

Present value calculation—financing lease Renter Co. acquired the use of a machine by agreeing to pay the manufacturer of the machine $4,500 per year for 10 years. At the time the lease was signed, the interest rate for a 10-year loan was 12%.

Required:

a. Use the appropriate factor from Table 6-5 to calculate the amount that Renter Co. could have paid at the beginning of the lease to buy the machine outright.

b. What causes the difference between the amount you calculated in part **a** and the total of $45,000 ($4,500 per year for 10 years) that Renter Co. will pay under the terms of the lease?

c. What is the appropriate amount of cost to be reported in Renter Co.'s balance sheet (at the time the lease was signed) with respect to this asset?

Present value calculations Using a present value table, your calculator, or a computer program present value function, answer the following questions:

Required:

a. What is the present value of nine annual cash payments of $58,000, to be paid at the end of each year using an interest rate of 6%?

b. What is the present value of $175,000 to be paid at the end of 20 years, using an interest rate of 18%?

c. How much cash must be deposited in a savings account as a single amount in order to accumulate $1,600,000 at the end of 12 years, assuming that the account will earn 10% interest?

d. How much cash must be deposited in a savings account (as a single amount) in order to accumulate $620,000 at the end of seven years, assuming that the account will earn 12% interest?

e. Assume that a machine was purchased for $210,000. Cash of $40,000 was paid, and a four-year, 8% note payable was signed for the balance.
   1. Use the horizontal model, or write the journal entry, to show the purchase of the machine as described.
   2. How much is the equal annual payment of principal and interest due at the end of each year? Round your answer to the nearest $1.
   3. What is the total amount of interest expense that will be reported over the life of the note? Round your answer to the nearest $1.
   4. Use the horizontal model, or write the journal entries, to show the equal annual payments of principal and interest due at the end of each year.

Cases

connect

All applicable Cases are available in *Connect*.

Focus company—property, plant, and equipment disclosures In Exercise 1.1, you were asked to obtain the most recent annual report of a company that you were interested in reviewing throughout this term.

Required:
Please review the note disclosures provided in your focus company's annual report and discuss what you've learned about how your company's:

a. Property, plant, and equipment is:
   1. Depreciated.
   2. Accounted for and presented.
b. Other noncurrent assets are described and reported.

Case 6.34

LO 3

Financial statement effects of depreciation methods Answer the following questions using data from the Campbell Soup Company annual report in the appendix:

Required:

a. Find the discussion of Property, Plant, and Equipment and depreciation methods used by Campbell's in the appendix. Explain why the particular method is used for the purpose described. What method do you think the company uses for income tax purposes?

b. Calculate the ratio of the depreciation and amortization expense for 2017, which is reported in the appendix, in the Consolidated Statements of Cash Flows to the total cost (*not* net book value) of plant assets reported in the schedule.

c. Based on the ratio calculated in part **b** and the depreciation method being used by Campbell's, what is the average useful life being used for its depreciation calculation?

d. Assume that the use of an accelerated depreciation method would have resulted in 25% more accumulated depreciation than reported at July 30, 2017, and that Campbell's Retained Earnings account would have been affected by the entire difference. By what percentage would this have reduced the retained earnings amount reported at July 30, 2017?

Case 6.35

LO 3, 6

Capstone analytical review of Chapters 5–6. Analyzing accounts receivable, property, plant, and equipment, and other related accounts *(Note: Please refer to Case 4.30 on pages 134–135 for the financial statement data needed for the analysis of this case. You should also review the solution to Case 4.30, provided by your instructor, before attempting to complete this case.)*

You have been approached by Gary Gerrard, president and CEO of Gerrard Construction Co., who would like your advice on a number of business and accounting related matters.

Your conversation with Mr. Gerrard, which took place in February 2020, proceeded as follows:

Mr. Gerrard: "The accounts receivable shown on the balance sheet for 2019 are nearly $30 million and the funny thing is, we just collected a bunch of the big accounts in early December but had to reinvest most of that money in new equipment. At one point last year, more than $60 million of accounts were outstanding! I had to put some pressure on our regular clients who keep falling behind. Normally, I don't bother with collections, but this is our main source of cash flows. My daughter Anna deals with collections and she's just too nice to people. I keep telling her that the money is better off in our hands than in someone else's! Can you have a look at our books? Some of these clients are really getting on my nerves."

Your reply: "That does seem like a big problem. I'll look at your accounts receivable details and get back to you with some of my ideas and maybe some questions you can help me with. What else did you want to ask me about?"

Mr. Gerrard: "The other major problem is with our long-term asset management. We don't have much in the way of buildings, just this office you're sitting in and the service garage where we keep most of the earthmoving equipment. That's where the expense of running this business comes in. I've always said that I'd rather see a dozen guys standing around leaning against shovels than to see one

piece of equipment sit idle for even an hour of daylight! There is nothing complicated about doing 'dirt work,' but we've got one piece of equipment that would
cost over $3 million to replace at today's prices. And that's just it—either you
spend a fortune on maintenance or else you're constantly in the market for the latest and greatest new 'Cat.'"

Your reply: "So how can I help?"

Mr. Gerrard: "Now that you know a little about our business, I'll have my son Nathan
show you the equipment records. He's our business manager. We've got to sell and
replace some of our light-duty trucks. We need to get a handle on the value of some
of the older equipment. What the books say, and what it's really worth, are two different things. I'd like to know what the accounting consequences of selling various
pieces of equipment would be because I don't want to be selling anything at a loss."

Your reply: "Thanks, Gary. I'll have a chat with Anna and Nathan and get back to
you."

After your discussion with Anna, you analyzed the accounts receivable details and
prepared the following aging schedule:

Number of Days Outstanding	Number of Accounts Outstanding	Total Amount Outstanding
0–30	20	$6,720,000
31–60	9	4,800,000
61–120	6	3,960,000
121–180	4	3,240,000
>180	11	10,680,000

You've noted that Gerrard Construction Co. has not written off any accounts receivable
as uncollectible during the past several years. The Allowance for Bad Debts account is
included in the chart of accounts but has never been used. No cash discounts have been
offered to customers, and the company does not employ a collection agency. Reminder
invoices are sent to customers with outstanding balances at the end of every quarter.

After your discussion with Nathan, you analyzed the equipment records related to
the three items that the company wants to sell at this time:

Item Description	Date of Purchase	Cost	Accumulated Depreciation	Book Value	Estimated Market Value
2012 Ford F550	Mar 2012	$ 114,400	$ 77,200	$ 37,200	$ 28,000
2008 Cat D11R dozer	June 2011	1,020,000	544,200	475,800	590,000
2010 Cat 631G scraper	Sept 2013	845,400	453,000	392,400	320,000

Nathan explained that Gerrard Construction Co. uses the units-of-production depreciation method and estimates usage on the basis of hours in service for earthmoving equipment and miles driven for all on-road vehicles. You have recalculated the
annual depreciation adjustments through December 31, 2019, and are satisfied that
the company has made the proper entries. The estimated market values were recently
obtained through the services of a qualified, independent appraiser whom you had
recommended to Nathan.

Required:

a. Explain what Mr. Gerrard meant when he said, "I keep telling her that the money is better off in our hands than in someone else's!"

b. What is your overall reaction concerning Gerrard Construction Co.'s management of accounts receivable? What suggestions would you make to Mr. Gerrard that may prove helpful in the collection process?

c. What accounting advice would you give concerning the accounts receivable balance of $29,400,000 at December 31, 2019?

d. What impact (increase, decrease, or no effect) would any necessary adjustment(s) have on the company's working capital and current ratio? (Note that these items were computed in part **g** of Case 4.30 and do not need to be recomputed now.)

e. Explain what Mr. Gerrard meant when he said, "We need to get a handle on the value of some of the older equipment. What the books say, and what it's really worth, are two different things."

f. Use the horizontal model, or write the journal entries, to show the effect of selling each of the three assets for their respective estimated market values. Partial-year depreciation adjustments for 2020 can be ignored.

g. Explain to Mr. Gerrard why his statement "I don't want to be selling anything at a loss" does not make economic sense.

**ANSWERS TO
What Does
It Mean?**

1. It means that the expenditure is recorded as an asset rather than an expense. If the asset is a depreciable asset, depreciation expense will be recognized over the useful life—to the entity—of the asset.

2. It means that the assets are reported at their original cost, less accumulated depreciation, if applicable. These net book values are likely to be less than fair values.

3. It means that cash is not paid out for depreciation expense. Depreciation expense results from spreading the cost of an asset to expense over the useful life—to the entity—of the asset. Cash is reduced when the asset is purchased or when payments are made on a loan that was obtained when the asset was purchased.

4. It means that relative to straight-line depreciation, more depreciation expense is recognized in the early years of an asset's life and less is recognized in the later years of an asset's life.

5. It means that because depreciation expense is deducted to arrive at taxable income, income taxes are lowered by the tax rate multiplied by the amount of depreciation expense claimed for income tax purposes.

6. It means that, relative to a practice of capitalizing these expenditures, taxable income of the current year will be lower and less time will be spent making depreciation expense calculations than if the expenditures were capitalized.

7. It means that rather than paying cash for the asset when it is acquired, or instead of borrowing funds to pay for the asset, the entity agrees to make payments to the lessor, or a finance company, of specified amounts over a specified period. The agreement is called a lease, but it is really an installment loan agreement.

8. It means that the acquiring firm paid more than the fair value of the net assets acquired because of the potential for earning an above-average return on its investment.

9. It means that money could be invested to earn a return—as interest revenue—if it were invested for a period of time.

10. It means that the future amount has a value today that is equal to the amount that would have to be invested at a given rate of return to grow to the future amount. Present value is less than future value.

11. It means that the same amount will be received each period for a number of periods. For example, large lottery winnings are frequently received as an annuity—that is, equal amounts over 20 years.

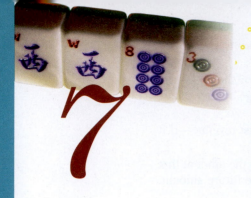

Accounting for and Presentation of Liabilities

Liabilities are obligations of the entity or, as defined by the FASB, "probable future sacrifices of economic benefits arising from present obligations of a particular entity to transfer assets or provide services to other entities in the future as a result of past transactions or events."[1] Note that liabilities are recorded only for *present* obligations that are the result of past transactions or events that will require the probable *future* sacrifice of resources. Thus, the following items would not yet be recorded as liabilities: (1) negotiations for the possible purchase of inventory, (2) increases in the replacement cost of assets due to inflation, and (3) contingent losses on unsettled lawsuits against the entity unless the loss becomes *probable* and can be reasonably estimated.

Most liabilities that meet the preceding definition arise because credit has been obtained in the form of a loan (notes payable) or in the normal course of business—for example, when a supplier ships merchandise before payment is made (accounts payable) or when an employee works one week not expecting to be paid until the next week (wages payable). As has been illustrated in previous chapters, many liabilities are recorded in the accrual process that matches revenues and expenses. The term *accrued expenses* is used on some balance sheets to describe these liabilities, but this is shorthand for *liabilities resulting from the accrual of expenses*. If you keep in mind that revenues and expenses are reported only on the income statement, you will not be confused by this mixing of terms. Current liabilities are those that must be paid or otherwise satisfied within a year of the balance sheet date; noncurrent liabilities are those that will be paid or satisfied more than a year after the balance sheet date. Liability captions usually seen in a balance sheet are the following:

Current Liabilities:
Accounts Payable
Short-Term Debt (Notes Payable)
Current Maturities of Long-Term Debt
Unearned Revenue or Deferred Credits
Other Accrued Liabilities

---

[1] FASB, *Statement of Financial Accounting Concepts No.6,* "Elements of Financial Statements" (Stanford, CT, 1985, para .35.)

Noncurrent Liabilities:
Long-Term Debt (Bonds Payable)
Deferred Tax Liabilities
Other Noncurrent Liabilities

The order in which liabilities are presented within the current and noncurrent categories is a function of liquidity (how soon the debt becomes due) and management preference.

Review the liabilities section of the Campbell Soup Company consolidated balance sheets of the annual report in the appendix. Note that most of these captions have to do with debt, accrued liabilities, and income taxes. The business and accounting practices relating to these items make up a major part of this chapter. Some of the most significant and controversial issues that the FASB has addressed in recent years, including the accounting for income taxes, pensions, and leases, and consolidation of subsidiaries, relate to the liability section of the balance sheet. A principal reason for the interest generated by these topics is that the recognition of a liability usually involves recognizing an expense as well. Expenses reduce net income, and lower net income means lower ROI. Keep these relationships in mind as you study this chapter.

LEARNING OBJECTIVES (LO)

After studying this chapter, you should understand and be able to

LO 7-1   Show the financial statement presentation of short-term debt and current maturities of long-term debt.

LO 7-2   Illustrate the difference between interest calculated on a straight basis and on a discount basis.

LO 7-3   Discuss what unearned revenues are and how they are presented in the balance sheet.

LO 7-4   Describe the accounting for an employer's liability for payroll and payroll taxes.

LO 7-5   Discuss the importance of making estimates for certain accrued liabilities and show how these items are presented in the balance sheet.

LO 7-6   Explain what financial leverage is and how it is provided by long-term debt.

LO 7-7   Describe the different characteristics of a bond, which is the formal document representing most long-term debt.

LO 7-8   Describe why bond discount or premium arises and how it is accounted for.

LO 7-9   Explain what deferred tax liabilities are and why they arise.

Exhibit 7-1 highlights the balance sheet accounts covered in detail in this chapter and shows the income statement and statement of cash flows components affected by these accounts.

Exhibit 7-1

Financial Statements—
The Big Picture

Balance Sheet				
Current Assets	Chapter		**Current Liabilities**	Chapter
Cash and cash equivalents	5, 9		Short-term debt	7
Short-term marketable securities	5		Current maturities of long-term debt	7
Accounts receivable	5, 9		Accounts payable	7
Notes receivable	5		Unearned revenue or deferred credits	7
Inventories	5, 9		Payroll taxes and other withholdings	7
Prepaid expenses	5		Other accrued liabilities	7
Noncurrent Assets			**Noncurrent Liabilities**	
Land	6		Long-term debt	7
Buildings and equipment	6		Deferred tax liabilities	7
Assets acquired by lease	6		Other noncurrent liabilities	7
Intangible assets	6		**Stockholders' Equity**	
Natural resources	6		Common stock	8
Other noncurrent assets	6		Preferred stock	8
			Additional paid-in capital	8
			Retained earnings	8
			Treasury stock	8
			Accumulated other comprehensive income (loss)	8
			Noncontrolling interest	8

Income Statement			Statement of Cash Flows	
Sales	5, 9		**Operating Activities**	
Cost of goods sold	5, 9		Net income	5, 6, 7, 8, 9
Gross profit (or gross margin)	5, 9		Depreciation expense	6, 9
Selling, general, and administrative expenses	5, 6, 9		(Gains) losses on sale of assets	6, 9
Income from operations	9		(Increase) decrease in current assets	5, 9
Gains (losses) on sale of assets	6, 9		Increase (decrease) in current liabilities	7, 9
Interest revenue	5, 9		**Investing Activities**	
Interest expense	7, 9		Proceeds from sale of property, plant, and equipment	6, 9
Income tax expense	7, 9		Purchase of property, plant, and equipment	6, 9
Unusual items	9		**Financing Activities**	
Net income	5, 6, 7, 8, 9		Proceeds from long-term debt*	7, 9
Earnings per share	9		Repayment of long-term debt*	7, 9
			Issuance of common stock and/or preferred stock	8, 9
			Purchase of treasury stock	8, 9
			Payment of dividends	8, 9

Primary topics of this chapter.

Other affected financial statement components.

*May include short-term debt items as well.

Current Liabilities

Short-Term Debt

Most firms experience seasonal fluctuations during the year in the demand for their products or services. For instance, a firm like Cruisers Inc., a manufacturer of small boats, is likely to have greater demand for its product during the spring and early summer than in the winter. To use its production facilities most efficiently, Cruisers Inc. will plan to produce boats on a level basis throughout the year. This means that during the fall and winter seasons, its inventory of boats will be increased in order to have enough product on hand to meet spring and summer demand. To finance this inventory increase and keep its payments to suppliers and employees current, Cruisers Inc. will obtain a **working capital loan** from its bank. This type of short-term loan is made with the expectation that it will be repaid from the collection of accounts receivable that will be generated by the sale of inventory. The short-term loan usually has a **maturity date** specifying when the loan is to be repaid. Sometimes a firm will negotiate a **revolving line of credit** with its bank. The credit line represents a predetermined maximum loan amount, but the firm has flexibility in the timing and amount borrowed. There may be a specified repayment schedule or an agreement that all amounts borrowed will be repaid by a particular date. Whatever the specific loan arrangement may be, a short-term borrowing transaction has the following effect on the financial statements:

LO 1
Show the financial statement presentation of short-term debt and current maturities of long-term debt.

Balance Sheet	Income Statement
Assets = Liabilities + Stockholders' equity	← Net income = Revenues − Expenses
+ Cash + Short-Term Debt	

The entry to record the loan is as follows:

```
Dr.  Cash ................................................      xx
     Cr.  Short-Term Debt ...................................              xx
     Borrowed money from bank.
```

The short-term debt resulting from this type of transaction is sometimes called a **note payable.** The note is a formal promise to pay a stated amount at a stated date, usually with interest at a stated rate and sometimes secured by collateral.

Interest expense is associated with almost any borrowing, and it is appropriate to record interest expense for each fiscal period during which the money is borrowed. The alternative methods of calculating interest are explained in Business in Practice—Interest Calculation Methods.

Prime rate is the term frequently used to express the interest rate on short-term loans. The prime rate is established by the lender, presumably for its most creditworthy borrowers, but is in reality a benchmark rate. The prime rate is raised or lowered by the lender in response to credit market forces. The borrower's rate may be expressed as "prime plus 1," for example, which means that the interest rate for the borrower will be the prime rate plus 1 percent. It is quite possible for the interest rate to change during the term of the loan, in which case a separate calculation of interest is made for each period having a different rate.

Business in
Practice

Interest Calculation Methods

Lenders calculate interest on either a straight (interest-bearing, or simple interest) basis or on a discount (non-interest-bearing) basis. The straight calculation involves charging interest on the money available to the borrower for the length of time it was borrowed. Interest on a **discount loan** is based on the principal amount of the loan, but the interest is subtracted from the principal at the beginning of the loan, and only the difference is made available to the borrower. In effect, the borrower pays the interest in advance. Assume that $1,000 is borrowed for one year at an interest rate of 12 percent.

Straight Interest

The **interest calculation—straight basis** is made as follows:

$$\text{Interest} = \text{Principal} \times \text{Rate} \times \text{Time (in years)}$$
$$= \$1,000 \times 0.12 \times 1$$
$$= \$120$$

At the maturity date of the note, the borrower will repay the principal of $1,000 plus the interest owed of $120. The borrower's *effective interest rate*—the **annual percentage rate (APR)**—is 12 percent:

$$\text{APR} = \text{Interest paid}/[\text{Money available to use} \times \text{Time (in years)}]$$
$$= \$120/\$1,000 \times 1$$
$$= 12\%$$

This is another application of the present value concept described in Chapter 6. The amount of the liability on the date the money is borrowed is the present value of the amount to be repaid in the future, calculated at the effective interest rate—which is the rate of return desired by the lender. To illustrate, the amount to be repaid in one year is $1,120, the sum of the $1,000 principal plus the $120 of interest. From Table 6-4, the factor in the 12% column and one-period row is 0.8929; $1,120 × 0.8929 = $1,000 (rounded). These relationships are illustrated on the following timeline:

1/1/19		12/31/19
├──┤		
$1,000 Principal borrowed	Interest = $1,000 × 0.12 × 1 year = $120	$1,120 Principal and interest repaid

For a loan on which interest is calculated on a straight basis, interest is accrued each period. Here is the effect of this accrual on the financial statements:

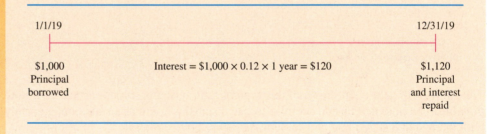

Balance Sheet	Income Statement
Assets = Liabilities + Stockholders' equity	← Net income = Revenues − Expenses
+ Interest Payable	− Interest Expense

Discount

The **interest calculation—discount basis** is made as just illustrated except that the interest amount is subtracted from the loan principal, and the borrower receives the difference. In this case, the loan proceeds would be $880 ($1,000 − $120). At the maturity of the note, the borrower will pay just the principal of $1,000 because the interest of $120 has already been paid—it was subtracted from the principal amount when the loan was obtained. These relationships are illustrated on the following timeline:

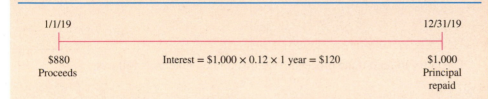

1/1/19 12/31/19

$880 Proceeds   Interest = $1,000 × 0.12 × 1 year = $120 $1,000 Principal repaid

Because the full principal amount is not available to the borrower, the effective interest rate (APR) on a discount basis is much higher than the rate used in the lending agreement to calculate the interest:

$$APR = \text{Interest paid}/[\text{Money available to use} \times \text{Time (in years)}]$$
$$= \$120/\$880 \times 1$$
$$= 13.6\%$$

Applying present value analysis, the carrying value of the liability on the date the money is borrowed represents the amount to be repaid, $1,000, multiplied by the present value factor for 13.6% for one year. The factor is 0.8803 and although it is not explicitly shown in Table 6-4, it can be derived approximately by **interpolating** between the factors for 12% and 14%.

An *installment loan* is repaid periodically over the life of the loan, so only about half of the proceeds (on average) are available for use throughout the life of the loan. Thus, the effective interest rate is about twice that of a *term loan* requiring a lump-sum repayment of principal at the maturity date.

In the final analysis, it isn't important whether interest is calculated using the straight method or the discount method, or whether an installment loan or term loan is arranged; what is important is the APR, or effective interest rate. The borrower's objective is to keep the APR (which must be disclosed in accordance with federal truth in lending laws) to a minimum.

The entry to record accrued interest is as follows:

Dr. Interest Expense	xx	
Cr. Interest Payable		xx
Accrued interest for period.		

Interest Payable is a current liability because it will be paid within a year of the balance sheet date. It may be disclosed in a separate caption or included with other accrued liabilities in the current liability section of the balance sheet.

For a loan on which interest is calculated on a discount basis, the amount of cash **proceeds** represents the initial carrying value of the liability. Using the data from the discount example in the Business in Practice box, the effect on the financial statements of the borrower is as follows:

Balance Sheet	Income Statement
Assets = Liabilities + Stockholders' equity	← Net income = Revenues − Expenses

Cash Short-Term
+ 880 Debt
      + 1,000
 	
      Discount on
      Short-Term Debt
      − 120	

The entry to record the proceeds of a discounted note is as follows:

Dr.	Cash	880	
Dr.	Discount on Short-Term Debt	120	
	Cr. Short-Term Debt		1,000

The Discount on Short-Term Debt account is a **contra liability,** classified as a reduction of Short-Term Debt on the balance sheet. As interest expense is incurred, the Discount on Short-Term Debt is amortized as follows:

Balance Sheet	Income Statement
Assets = Liabilities + Stockholders' equity	←Net income = Revenues − Expenses
+ Discount on Short-Term Debt	− Interest Expense

The entry is as follows:

Dr.	Interest Expense	xx	
	Cr. Discount on Short-Term Debt		xx

The amortization of the discount to interest expense affects neither cash nor interest payable. Net income decreases as interest expense is recorded, and the carrying value of short-term debt increases as the discount is amortized.

What Does It Mean?

Answer on page 273

1. What does it mean to borrow money on a discount basis?

Current Maturities of Long-Term Debt

When funds are borrowed on a long-term basis (a topic to be discussed later in this chapter), it is not unusual for principal repayments to be required on an installment basis; every year a portion of the debt matures and is to be repaid by the borrower. Any portion of a long-term borrowing (e.g., Notes Payable or Bonds Payable) that is to be repaid within a year of the balance sheet date is reclassified from the noncurrent liability section of the balance sheet to the **current maturities of long-term debt** account. These amounts are reported in the current liability section but separately from short-term debt because the liability arose from a long-term borrowing transaction. Interest payable on long-term debt is classified with other interest payable and may be combined with other accrued liabilities for reporting purposes.

Accounts Payable

Amounts owed to suppliers for goods and services that have been provided to the entity on credit are the principal components of **accounts payable.** Unlike accounts receivable, which are reported net of estimated cash discounts expected to be taken, accounts payable to suppliers that permit a cash discount for prompt payment are not usually reduced by the amount of the cash discount expected to be taken. This treatment is supported by the materiality concept because the amount involved is not likely to have a significant effect on the financial position or results of the operations of the firm. However, accounts payable for firms that record purchases net of anticipated cash discounts will be reported at the amount expected to be paid.

Purchase transactions for which a cash discount is allowed are recorded using either the *gross* or the *net* method. The difference between the two is the timing of the recognition of cash discounts. The gross method results in recognizing cash discounts only when invoices are paid within the discount period. The net method recognizes cash discounts when purchases are initially recorded, under the assumption that all discounts will be taken; an expense is then recognized if a discount is not taken.

Unearned Revenue or Deferred Credits

Customers often pay for services or products before the service or product is delivered. An entity collecting cash in advance of earning the related revenue records **unearned revenue,** or a **deferred credit,** which is included in current liabilities. Unearned revenues must then be allocated to the fiscal periods in which the services are performed or the products are delivered, in accordance with the matching concept. The accounting for revenue received in advance was discussed in the context of the adjustments presented in Chapter 4. To illustrate, assume that a magazine publisher requires a subscriber to pay in advance for a subscription. Here are the financial statement effects of this transaction and the subsequent adjustment:

LO 3

Discuss what unearned revenues are and how they are presented in the balance sheet.

Balance Sheet	Income Statement
Assets = Liabilities + Stockholders' equity	← Net income = Revenues − Expenses
Cash received with subscription:	

+ Cash   + Unearned
           Subscription
           Revenue	

Adjustments in fiscal period in which revenue is earned (magazines delivered):	

− Unearned
    Subscription
    Revenue
	+ Subscription
	Revenue

The entry to record this transaction is as follows:

Dr. Cash	xx	
Cr. Unearned Subscription Revenue		xx

The entry to record the adjustment for revenue earned during the fiscal period would be the following:

Dr. Unearned Subscription Revenue	xx	
Cr. Subscription Revenue		xx

As you think about this situation, you should understand that it is the opposite of the prepaid expense/deferred charge transaction described in Chapter 5. In that kind of transaction, cash was *paid* in the current period, and *expense* was recognized in subsequent periods. Unearned revenue/deferred credit transactions involve the *receipt* of cash in the current period and the recognition of *revenue* in subsequent periods.

Deposits received from customers are also accounted for as deferred credits. If the deposit is an advance payment for a product or service, the deposit is transferred from a liability account to a revenue account when the product or service is delivered. Or, for example, if the deposit is received as security for a returnable container, when the container is returned the refund of the customer's deposit reduces (is a credit to) cash and eliminates (is a debit to) the liability.

Unearned revenues/deferred credits are usually classified with other accrued liabilities in the current liability section of the balance sheet.

Payroll Taxes and Other Withholdings

LO 4

Describe the accounting for an employer's liability for payroll and payroll taxes.

The total wages earned by employees for a payroll period, including bonuses and overtime pay, are referred to as their **gross pay,** which represents the employer's Wages Expense for the period. From this amount, several *deductions* are subtracted to arrive at the **net pay** (*take-home pay*) that each employee will receive, which represents the employer's Wages Payable (or Accrued Payroll). The largest deductions are normally for federal and state income tax withholdings and **FICA tax** withholdings, but employees frequently make voluntary contributions for hospitalization insurance, contributory pension plans, union dues, the United Way, and a variety of other items. Employers are responsible for remitting payment to the appropriate entities on behalf of their employees for each amount withheld. Thus, a separate liability account (e.g., Federal Income Taxes Withheld) normally is used for each applicable item. Here is the effect of this transaction on the financial statements:

Balance Sheet	Income Statement
Assets = Liabilities + Stockholders' equity	← Net income = Revenues − Expenses
+ Wages payable + Withholding Liabilities	− Wages Expense

The entry to record a firm's payroll obligation is as follows:

Dr. Wages Expense (for gross pay)	xx	
Cr. Wages Payable (or Accrued Payroll, for net pay)		xx
Cr. Withholding Liabilities (various descriptions)		xx

When the withholdings are paid, both cash and the appropriate withholding liability are reduced.

Most employers are also subject to federal and state *payroll* taxes based on the amount of compensation paid to their employees. These taxes, assessed directly against the employer, include federal and state unemployment taxes and the employer's share of FICA tax. Employer taxes are appropriately recognized when compensation expense is accrued. This involves recognizing payroll tax expense and a related liability. The effect of this transaction on the financial statements is as follows:

Balance Sheet	Income Statement
Assets = Liabilities + Stockholders' equity	← Net income = Revenues − Expenses
+ Payroll Taxes Payable	− Payroll Tax Expense

The entry to record a firm's payroll tax obligation is as follows:

Dr. Payroll Tax Expense	xx	
Cr. Payroll Taxes Payable (or Accrued Payroll Taxes).........		xx

When the taxes are paid, both cash and the liability are reduced.

The liabilities for accrued payroll, payroll withholdings, and accrued payroll taxes are usually classified with other accrued liabilities in the current liability section of the balance sheet.

Other Accrued Liabilities

As just discussed, this caption normally includes the accrued payroll accounts as well as most unearned revenue/deferred credit accounts. Accrued property taxes, accrued interest (if not reported separately), estimated warranty liabilities, and other accrued expenses such as advertising and insurance obligations are often included in this description. This is another application of the matching principle. Each of these items represents an expense that has been incurred but not yet paid. The expense is recognized and the liability is shown so that the financial statements present a more complete summary of the results of operations (income statement) and financial position (balance sheet) than would be presented without the accrual.

To illustrate the accrual of property taxes, assume that Cruisers Inc. operates in a city in which real estate tax bills for one year are not issued until April of the following year and are payable in July. Thus, an adjustment must be made on December 31, 2019, to record the estimated property tax expense for the year then ended. The effect of this adjustment on the financial statements follows:

LO 5
Discuss the importance of making estimates for certain accrued liabilities and show how these items are presented in the balance sheet.

Balance Sheet	Income Statement
Assets = Liabilities + Stockholders' equity	← Net income = Revenues − Expenses
+ Property Taxes Payable	− Property Tax Expense

The entry is as follows:

Dr. Property Taxes Expense	xx	
Cr. Property Taxes Payable		xx

When the tax bill is received at some point in April 2020, the payable account must be adjusted (up or down) to reflect the amount actually owed in July. The adjustment also affects the current year's property tax expense account. The liability and expense amounts reported in the previous year are not retroactively restated because the estimates used were based on the best information available at the time. The resulting estimated amounts were not recorded in "error" because a best efforts, good faith attempt was made to approximate the true, but unknown, settlement amount of the liability.

A firm's estimated liability under product warranty or performance guarantees is another example of an accrued liability. It is appropriate to recognize the estimated warranty expense that will be incurred on a product in the same period in which the revenue from the sale is recorded. Although the expense and liability must be estimated, recent experience and statistical analysis can be used to develop accurate estimates. The following financial statement effects occur in the fiscal periods in which the product is sold and the warranty is honored:

Balance Sheet	Income Statement
Assets = Liabilities + Stockholders' equity	← Net income = Revenues − Expenses

Fiscal period in which product is sold:
 	
    + Estimated
       Warranty
       Liability
 	
Fiscal period in which warranty is honored:
 	
− Cash   − Estimated
   and/or   Warranty
   Repair   Liability
   Parts
   Inventory
	− Warranty
	    Expense

Here is the entry to accrue the estimated warranty liability in the fiscal period in which the product is sold:

Dr. Warranty Expense	xx	
Cr. Estimated Warranty Liability		xx

The entry to record actual warranty cost in the fiscal period in which the warranty is honored is as follows:

Dr. Estimated Warranty Liability	xx	
Cr. Cash (or Repair Parts Inventory)		xx

The accrual for income taxes is usually shown separately because of its significance. The current liability for income taxes is related to the long-term liability for deferred taxes; both are discussed later in this chapter.

What Does It Mean?

Answer on page 273

2. What does it mean to be concerned that an entity's liabilities are not understated?

Noncurrent Liabilities

Long-Term Debt

A corporation's *capital structure* is the mix of debt and stockholders' equity that is used to finance the acquisition of the firm's assets. For many nonfinancial firms, **long-term debt** accounts for up to half of the firm's capital structure. One of the advantages of using debt is that interest expense is deductible in calculating taxable income, whereas dividends (distributions of earnings to stockholders) are not tax deductible. Thus, debt usually has a lower economic cost to the firm than stockholders' equity. For example, assume a firm has an average tax rate of 30 percent and issues long-term debt with an interest rate of 10 percent. The firm's after-tax cost of debt is only 7 percent (calculated as: $10\% \times [1 - 30\%]$), which is probably less than the return sought by stockholders.

Another reason for using debt is to obtain favorable financial leverage. **Financial leverage** refers to the difference between the rate of return earned on assets (ROI) and the rate of return earned on stockholders' equity (ROE). This difference results from the fact that the interest cost of debt is usually a fixed percentage, which is not a function of the return on assets. Thus, if the firm can borrow money at an interest cost of 10 percent and use the money to buy assets on which it earns a return greater than 10 percent, the stockholders will have a greater return on their equity (ROE) than if they had provided all of the funds themselves. In other words, financial leverage relates to the use of borrowed money to enhance the return to stockholders. This is illustrated in Exhibit 7-2.

This simplified illustration shows positive financial leverage. If a firm earns a lower return on investment than the interest rate on borrowed funds, financial leverage will be negative and ROE will be less than ROI. Financial leverage adds risk to the firm because if the firm does not earn enough to pay the interest on its debt, the debt-holders can ultimately force the firm into bankruptcy.

Financial leverage is discussed in greater detail in Chapter 11. For now, you should understand that the use of long-term debt with a fixed interest cost usually results in ROE being different from ROI. Whether financial leverage is good or bad for the stockholders depends on the relationship between ROI and the interest rate on long-term debt.

LO 6

Explain what financial leverage is and how it is provided by long-term debt.

---

3. What does it mean to say that financial leverage has been used effectively?
4. What does it mean that the more financial leverage a firm has, the greater the risk to stockholders and creditors?

What Does It Mean?
Answers on page 273

Recall the discussion and illustration of financing lease liabilities in Chapter 6. Lease payments that are due more than a year from the balance sheet date are included in long-term debt and recorded at the present value of future lease payments.

Most long-term debt, however, is issued in the form of bonds. A **bond** *or* **bond payable** is a formal document, usually issued in denominations of $1,000. Bond prices, both when the bonds are issued and later when they are bought and sold in the market, are expressed as a percentage of the bond's **face amount**—the principal amount printed on the face of the bond. A $1,000 face amount bond that has a market value of $1,000 is priced at 100. (This means 100 percent; usually the term *percent* is neither written nor stated.) A $1,000 bond trading at 102.5 can be purchased for $1,025; such a bond priced at 96 has a market value of $960. When a bond has a market value greater than its face amount, it is trading at a premium; the amount of the **bond premium** is

LO 7

Describe the different characteristics of a bond, which is the formal document representing most long-term debt.

Exhibit 7-2

Financial Leverage

Assumptions:

Two firms have the same assets and operating income. Current liabilities and income taxes are ignored for simplification. The firm without financial leverage has, by definition, no long-term debt. The firm with financial leverage has a capital structure that is 40% long-term debt with an interest rate of 10%, and 60% stockholders' equity. Return on investment and return on equity follow for each firm.

   Note that the return-on-investment calculation has been modified from the model introduced in Chapter 3. ROI is based on income from operations and total assets rather than net income and total assets. Income from operations (which is net income before interest expense) is used because the interest expense reflects a financing decision, not an operating result. Thus, ROI becomes an evaluation of the operating activities of the firm.

Firm without Leverage		**Firm with Leverage**	
Balance Sheet:		**Balance Sheet:**	
Assets	$10,000	Assets	$10,000
Liabilities	$ 0	Liabilities (10% interest) . .	$ 4,000
Stockholders' equity	10,000	Stockholders' equity	6,000
Total liabilities and stockholders' equity	$10,000	Total liabilities and stockholders' equity	$10,000
Income Statement:		**Income Statement:**	
Income from operations . . .	$ 1,200	Income from operations . .	$ 1,200
Interest expense	0	Interest expense	400
Net income	$ 1,200	Net income	$ 800

ROI and ROE Calculations:

Return on investment (ROI = Income from operations/Assets)

$$\text{ROI} = \$1,200/\$10,000 \qquad\qquad \text{ROI} = \$1,200/\$10,000$$
$$= 12\% \qquad\qquad\qquad\qquad = 12\%$$

Return on equity (ROE = Net income/Stockholders' equity)

$$\text{ROE} = \$1,200/\$10,000 \qquad\qquad \text{ROE} = \$800/\$6,000$$
$$= 12\% \qquad\qquad\qquad\qquad = 13.3\%$$

Analysis:

In this case, ROI is the same for both firms because the operating results did not differ—each firm was able to earn 12% on the assets it had available to use. What differed was the way in which the assets were financed (capital structure). The firm with financial leverage has a higher return on stockholders' equity because it was able to borrow money at a cost of 10% and use the money to buy assets on which it earned 12%. Thus, ROE will be higher than ROI for a firm with positive financial leverage. The excess return on borrowed funds is the reward to stockholders for taking the risk of borrowing money at a fixed cost.

Bond Market Basics

Business in
Practice

Bonds are long-term lending agreements between the issuing company (borrower) and the bondholder (lender). Many bonds are traded in highly regulated public securities markets such as the NYSE Bonds. As with most lending arrangements, bonds essentially represent an exchange of cash flows between the parties—bondholders provide a lump sum of cash in exchange for periodic (usually semiannual) fixed-rate interest payments throughout the term of the bond and the return of principal at the bond's maturity. Bond prices vary over time and are influenced by the creditworthiness of the issuing company as well as broad economic factors affecting the overall economy, especially interest rates. What happens to the value of a bond as market interest rates rise? Recall from Chapter 6 that as interest (discount) rates increase, the present value of the future cash flows decreases, which is to say that bond prices fall as market interest rates rise. The opposite is true when market interest rates fall—bond prices rise.

To learn more about bonds, see investopedia.com/university/bonds for a tutorial about bond markets, including how to read a bond table. For a more detailed analysis of the bond market, including commentary from traders, academics, and other bond market experts, visit investinginbonds.com.

Study
Suggestion

You can get a fundamental understanding of the *accounting* for bonds payable, including the amortization of discount or premium, without fighting through the mechanics of present value analysis as it relates to *bond pricing:* Just remember that present value analysis is necessary to determine the *amount* of discount or premium when bonds are issued. When the bond's issue price is determined (the bond may be priced at 96 or 102.5, for example), the difference between the issue price and 100 must be amortized against interest expense over the life of the bond. Present value analysis is included in our examples to illustrate the appropriate conceptual basis for bond pricing, but it can be deemphasized when considering the accounting aspects of bonds.

the excess of its market value over its face amount. A **bond discount** is the excess of the face amount over market value. See the Business in Practice—Bond Market Basics box, including the referenced websites, for a primer on the mechanics of bond pricing.

Accounting and financial reporting considerations for bonds can be classified into three categories: the original issuance of bonds, the recognition of interest expense, and the accounting for bond retirements or conversions.

Original issuance of bonds payable.   If a bond is issued at its face amount, the effect on the financial statements is straightforward:

Balance Sheet	Income Statement
Assets = Liabilities + Stockholders' equity	← Net income = Revenues − Expenses
+ Cash + Bonds Payable	

The journal entry is the following:

Dr. Cash	xx	
Cr. Bonds Payable		xx
Issuance of bonds at face amount.		

As was the case with short-term notes payable, the bonds payable liability is reported at the present value of amounts to be paid in the future with respect to the bonds, discounted at the return on investment desired by the lender (bondholder). For example, assume that a 10 percent bond with a 10-year maturity is issued to investors who desire a 10 percent return on their investment. The issuer of the bonds provides two cash flow components to the investors in the bonds: the annual interest payments and the payment of principal at maturity. Note that the interest cash flow is an annuity because the same amount is paid each period. Using present value factors from Tables 6-4 and 6-5, here are the present values:

Today   10 years

Interest paid annually = Stated rate × Face amount   Maturity value
                       = 10% × $1,000   (face amount)
                       = $100 $1,000

            (Table 6-5,   (Table 6-4,
      10%, 10 periods) × 6.1446   10%, 10 periods) × 0.3855

$614.46 ←
 385.50 ←
$999.96 proceeds

The present value of the liability is the sum of the discounted principal and interest payments. Except for a slight rounding difference in the present value factors, this sum is the same as the face amount of the bonds.

Because of the mechanics involved in a bond issue, there is usually a time lag between the establishment of the interest rate to be printed on the face of the bond and the actual issue date. During this time lag, market interest rates will fluctuate and the market rate on the issue date probably will differ from the **stated rate** (or **coupon rate**) used to calculate interest payments to bondholders. This difference in interest rates causes the proceeds (cash received) from the sale of the bonds to be more or less than the face amount; the bonds will thus be issued at a premium or discount, respectively. This is illustrated in Exhibit 7-3.

LO 8

Describe why bond discount or premium arises and how it is accounted for.

What Does It Mean?

Answer on page 274

5. What does it mean to say that a bond is a fixed-income investment?

Recognition of interest expense on bonds payable.   Because bond premium or discount arises from a difference between the stated interest rate and the market interest rate at the date the bonds are issued, it follows that the premium or discount will affect the amount of interest expense to be recognized by the issuing firm over the life of the bonds. Bond discount represents additional interest expense to be recognized over the life of the bonds. The cash interest that will be paid (based on the stated rate) is less than the interest that would have been paid if it were instead based on the market rate at the date the bonds were issued. Bond discount is a deferred charge that is amortized to interest expense over the life of the bond. The amortization of bond discount increases interest expense over the amount actually paid to bondholders. Bond

As already illustrated, the amount the investor is willing to pay for a bond is the present value of the cash flows to be received from the investment, discounted at the investor's desired rate of return (market interest rate).

Exhibit 7-3

Bond Discount and Premium

Assumptions:
Cruisers Inc. issues a 10%, $1,000 bond when market interest rates are 12%. The bond will mature in eight years. Interest is paid semiannually.

Required:
Calculate the proceeds *(selling price)* of the bond and the premium or discount to be recognized.

Solution:
Note that the interest payments are an annuity because the same amount is paid each period. Because interest is paid semiannually, it is appropriate to recognize semiannual compounding in the present value calculation. This is accomplished by using the number of semiannual periods in the life of the bonds. Because the bonds mature in eight years, there are 16 semiannual periods. However, the interest rate per semiannual period is half of the annual interest rate. To be consistent, the same approach is used to calculate the present value of the principal. Thus, the solution uses factors from the 6% column (one-half the investors' desired ROI of 12%) and the 16-period row (twice the 8-year term of the bonds) of the present value tables. Using present value factors from Tables 6-4 and 6-5, here are the present values:

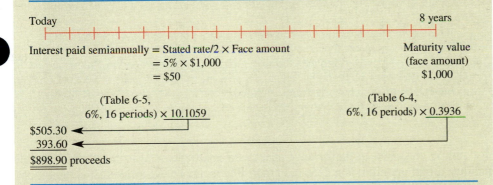

Today   8 years

Interest paid semiannually = Stated rate/2 × Face amount
       = 5% × $1,000
       = $50

Maturity value
(face amount)
$1,000

(Table 6-5, 6%, 16 periods) × 10.1059
(Table 6-4, 6%, 16 periods) × 0.3936

$505.30
 393.60
$898.90 proceeds

The proceeds received by Cruisers Inc., as well as the amount invested by the buyer of the bond, are the sum of the present value of the interest payments and the present value of the principal amount. Because this sum is less than the face amount, the bond is priced at a discount.

This illustration demonstrates two important points about the process of calculating the proceeds from a bond issue:

1. The *stated interest rate* of the bond, adjusted for compounding frequency, is used to calculate the amount of interest paid each payment period; this is the annuity amount ($50 in this case) used in the calculation of the present value of the interest payments.

2. The *market interest rate* (or the investors' desired ROI), adjusted for the compounding frequency, is the discount rate used in the present value calculations.

In this illustration, the market interest rate is higher than the bond's stated interest rate; thus, the investor would pay sufficiently less than the face amount of the bond, such that the $50 of interest to be received each six months and the $1,000 principal to be received at maturity will provide a market rate of return.

(continued)

The issuance of the $1,000 bond by Cruisers Inc. will have the following effects on the financial statements:

Balance Sheet		Income Statement
Assets = Liabilities + Stockholders' equity		←Net income = Revenues − Expenses

Cash   Bonds Payable
+ 898.90 + 1,000
 	
             Discount on
             Bonds Payable
             − 101.10		

The entry to record the issuance of the bond is as follows:

Dr.	Cash	898.90	
Dr.	Discount on Bonds Payable	101.10	
Cr.	Bonds Payable		1,000.00
Issued bond at a discount.			

If the market rate is less than the stated interest rate on the bond, the opposite will be true (the investor will be willing to pay a premium over the face amount of the bond). Use the preceding model to prove to yourself that if the market interest rate is 12%, then a 13% stated rate, $1,000 face amount, 10-year bond on which interest is paid semiannually, would be issued for $1,057.34 (the bond would be issued at a premium of $57.34).

This exhibit illustrates the fundamental reason for bonds being issued for a price (or having a market value) that is different from the face amount. The actual premium or discount is a function of the magnitude of the difference between the stated interest rate of the bond and the market interest rate, and the number of years to maturity. For any given difference between the bond's stated interest rate and the market interest rate, the closer a bond is to maturity, the smaller the premium or discount will be.

discount is classified in the balance sheet as a contra account to the Bonds Payable liability. Bond premium is a deferred credit that is amortized to interest expense, and its effect (which is just the opposite of discount amortization) is to reduce interest expense below the amount actually paid to bondholders. Bond premium is classified in the balance sheet as an addition to the Bonds Payable liability.

Whether a bond is issued at a premium or a discount, the bond's carrying value will converge to its face amount (the principal amount to be repaid at maturity) over the life of the bond as the premium or discount is amortized:

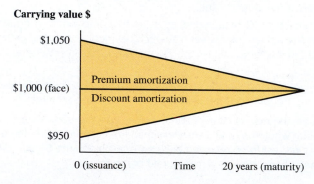

The financial statement effects of recording the interest accrual, interest payment, and discount or premium amortization are as follows:

Balance Sheet	Income Statement
Assets = Liabilities + Stockholders' equity	← Net income = Revenues − Expenses
Interest accrual (each fiscal period, perhaps monthly): 　　　+ Interest 　　　　Payable	− Interest Expense
Interest payment (periodically, perhaps semiannually): − Cash　− Interest 　　　　　Payable	
Amortization (each time interest is accrued): Discount 　　+ Discount 　　on Bonds 　　Payable	− Interest Expense (An increase in interest expense)
Premium 　　− Premium 　　on Bonds 　　Payable	+ Interest Expense (A decrease in interest expense)

These entries record the financial statement effects:

Dr. Interest Expense	xx	
Cr. Interest Payable		xx
Interest accrual (each fiscal period, perhaps monthly).		
Dr. Interest Payable	xx	
Cr. Cash		xx
Interest payment (periodically, perhaps semiannually).		
Dr. Interest Expense	xx	
Cr. Discount on Bonds Payable		xx
Amortization of discount (each time interest is accrued).		
Dr. Premium on Bonds Payable	xx	
Cr. Interest Expense		xx
Amortization of premium (each time interest is accrued).		

Discount or premium usually is amortized on a straight-line basis over the life of the bonds because the amounts involved are often immaterial. However, it is more appropriate to use a compound interest method that results in amortization related to the carrying value (face amount plus unamortized premium or minus unamortized discount) of the bonds. This is referred to as the *effective interest method* and is used when the amount of discount or premium amortization is deemed material. When the effective interest method is used, amortization is smallest in the first year of the bond's life, and it increases in each subsequent year.

Retirements and conversions of bonds payable.   Bonds payable are reported on the balance sheet at their carrying value. Sometimes this amount is referred to as the **book value** of the bonds. As discount is amortized over the life of a bond, the carrying value of the bond increases. At the maturity date, the bond's carrying value is equal to its face amount because the bond discount has been fully amortized. Likewise, as premium is amortized, the carrying value of the bond decreases until it equals the face amount at maturity. Thus, when bonds are paid off (or retired) at maturity, the effect on the financial statements is as follows:

Balance Sheet	Income Statement
Assets = Liabilities + Stockholders' equity	← Net income = Revenues − Expenses
− Cash − Bonds Payable	

The entry is as follows:

Dr.	Bonds Payable	xx	
	Cr. Cash		xx

Most bonds are **callable bonds;** this means the issuer may choose to "call" the bonds and pay off the bondholders before the scheduled maturity date. Bonds will be called if market interest rates have dropped sufficiently below the stated rate being paid on the bonds and the firm can save interest costs by redeeming the existing bonds and refinancing by issuing new bonds at a lower rate. Likewise, if the firm has excess cash that will not be needed in operations in the immediate future, it can redeem the bonds and save more interest expense than could be earned (as interest revenue) by investing the excess cash. The issuer usually is required to pay a **call premium** to bondholders if the bond is called; that is, bondholders receive more than the face amount of the bond because they must reinvest the proceeds, usually at a lower interest rate than was being earned on the called bonds.

If the bonds are called or redeemed prior to maturity, it is appropriate to write off the unamortized balance of premium or discount as part of the transaction. Because a call premium typically is involved in an early retirement of bonds, a loss on the retirement usually will be recognized—although a gain on the retirement is also possible. Here are the financial statement effects of recording an early retirement of $100,000 face amount bonds having a book value of $95,000 by redeeming them for a total payment of $102,000:

Balance Sheet	Income Statement
Assets = Liabilities + Stockholders' equity	← Net income = Revenues − Expenses

Cash   Bonds Payable
− 102,000 − 100,000
 	
               Discount on
               Bonds Payable
               + 5,000
	Loss on
	Retirement
	of Bonds
	− 7,000

The entry is as follows:

Dr.	Bonds Payable	100,000	
Dr.	Loss on Retirement of Bonds	7,000	
	Cr. Cash		102,000
	Cr. Discount on Bonds Payable		5,000

The gain or loss on the retirement of the bonds is reported as other income or expense in the income statement. The gain or loss is not considered part of operating income or interest expense. The firm is willing to retire the bonds and recognize the loss because it will save, in future interest expense, more than the loss incurred.

Additional bond terminology.   A discussion of bonds involves specialized terminology. Although you need not master it all to understand the financial statement impact of bond transactions, it is relevant to understanding bonds.

The contract between the issuer of the bonds and the bondholders is the **bond indenture,** and it is frequently administered by a third party, the **trustee of bonds**— often a bank trust department. Bonds are issued in one of two forms: **registered bonds** and **coupon bonds.**

The name and address of the owner of a registered bond are known to the issuer, and interest payments are mailed to the bondholder on a quarterly, semiannual, or annual basis, as called for in the indenture. The owner of a coupon bond (often called a *bearer bond* or *unregistered bond*) is not known to the issuer; the bondholder receives interest by clipping a coupon on the interest payment date and depositing it in her or his bank account. The coupon is then sent to the trustee and is honored as though it were a check. Coupon bonds are no longer issued because federal income tax regulations have been changed to require interest payers to report the names and Social Security numbers of payees, but coupon bonds issued prior to that regulation are still outstanding.

Bonds are also classified according to the security, or collateral, that is pledged by the issuer. **Debenture bonds (or debentures)** are bonds that are secured only by the general credit of the issuer and, thus, are considered to be unsecured debt securities because they are not secured by specific assets. **Mortgage bonds** are secured by a lien against real estate owned by the issuer. **Collateral trust bonds** are secured by the pledge of securities or other intangible property. Details of bond categories would be found in the notes to the financial statements.

Another classification of bonds relates to when the bonds mature. **Term bonds** require a lump-sum repayment of the face amount of the bond at the maturity date. **Serial bonds** are repaid in installments. The installments may or may not be equal in amount; the first installment is usually scheduled for a date several years after the issuance of the bonds. **Convertible bonds** may be converted into common stock of the issuer corporation at the option of the bondholder. The number of shares of stock into which a bond is convertible is established when the bond is issued, but the conversion feature may not become effective for several years. If the common stock price has risen substantially while the bonds have been outstanding, bondholders may elect to receive shares of stock with the anticipation that the stock investment will be worth more than the face amount of the bonds when the bonds mature.

The specific characteristics, stated interest rate, and maturity date usually are included in a bond's description. For example, you may hear or read about long-term debt described as Cruisers Inc.'s 12 percent convertible debentures due in 2032, callable after 2020 at 102, or its 12.5 percent First Mortgage Serial Bonds with maturities from 2019 to 2030.

---

6. What does it mean when a bond is referred to as a debenture bond?
7. What does it mean to state that bond market values change in the opposite direction from market interest rate changes?
8. What does it mean when a bond is issued at a premium?

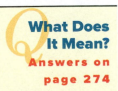

What Does It Mean?
Answers on
page 274

LO 9

Explain what deferred
tax liabilities are and
why they arise.

Deferred Tax Liabilities

Deferred tax liabilities are provided for temporary differences between income tax and financial statement recognition of revenues and expenses. Deferred tax liabilities are normally long term and represent income taxes that are expected to be paid more than a year after the balance sheet date. For many firms, deferred income taxes are one of the most significant liabilities shown on the balance sheet. These amounts arise from the accounting process of matching revenues and expenses; a liability is recognized for the probable future tax consequences of events that have taken place up to the balance sheet date. For example, some revenues that have been earned and recognized for accounting (book) purposes during the current fiscal year may not be taxable until the following year. Likewise, some expenses (such as depreciation) may be deductible for tax purposes before they are recorded in determining book income. These temporary differences between book income and taxable income cause deferred tax liabilities that are postponed until future years.

The most significant temporary difference item resulting in a deferred income tax liability for most firms relates to depreciation expense. As explained in Chapter 6, a firm may use straight-line depreciation for financial reporting and use the Modified Accelerated Cost Recovery System (prescribed by the Internal Revenue Code) for income tax determination. Thus, depreciation deductions for tax purposes are taken earlier than depreciation expense is recognized for book purposes. This temporary difference will eventually reverse; over the life of the asset, the same total amount of book and tax depreciation will be reported. Although the calculations involved are complicated, the effect on the financial statements of accruing income taxes when an increase in the deferred income tax liability is required is straightforward:

Balance Sheet	Income Statement
Assets = Liabilities + Stockholders' equity	← Net income = Revenues − Expenses
+ Income Taxes Payable	− Income Tax Expense
+ Deferred Tax Liabilities	

The entry is as follows:

Dr.	Income Tax Expense	xx	
	Cr. Income Taxes Payable		xx
	Cr. Deferred Tax Liabilities		xx
To accrue current and deferred income taxes.			

If income tax rates do not decrease, the deferred income tax liability of most firms will increase over time. As firms grow, more and more depreciable assets are acquired, and price-level increases cause costs for (new) replacement assets to be higher than the cost of (old) assets being replaced. Thus, the temporary difference between book and tax depreciation grows each year because the excess of book depreciation over income tax depreciation for older assets is more than offset by the excess of tax depreciation over book depreciation for newer assets. Accordingly, some accountants have questioned the appropriateness of showing deferred taxes as a liability because in the aggregate the balance of this account has grown larger and larger for many firms and

Current Assets	Noncurrent Assets	Current Liabilities	Noncurrent Liabilities
360	258	150	350

Source: *Accounting Trends and Techniques, U.S. GAAP Financial Statements—Best Practices in Presentation and Disclosure,* Tables 2-5, 2-9, 2-10, and 2-14, copyright © 2012, by American Institute of Certified Public Accountants, Inc.

Table 7.1

Reporting Frequency of Deferred Income Taxes by Category for 500 Publicly Owned Industrial and Merchandising Corporations—2011

therefore never seems to become payable. They argue that deferred tax liabilities—if recorded at all—should be recorded at the present value of future cash flows discounted at an appropriate interest rate. Otherwise, the amounts shown on the balance sheet will overstate the obligation to pay future taxes.

Most deferred income taxes result from the temporary difference between book and tax depreciation expense, but there are other temporary differences as well. When the temporary difference involves an expense that is recognized for financial accounting purposes before it is deductible for tax purposes, a deferred tax asset can arise. For example, an estimated warranty liability is shown on the balance sheet and warranty expense is reported in the income statement in the year the firm sells a warranted product, but the tax deduction is not allowed until an actual warranty expenditure is made. Because this temporary difference will cause taxable income to be lower in future years, a deferred tax asset is reported. As illustrated in Table 7-1 for the 2011 reporting year (the last available data from the AICPA), the number of companies reporting deferred tax assets actually exceeded the number of companies reporting deferred tax liabilities.

Accounting for deferred tax items is an extremely complex issue that has caused a great deal of debate within the accounting profession. Major changes in accounting for deferred income taxes have occurred in recent years as accounting standards have evolved in response to the needs of financial statement users.

9. What does it mean when a company has a deferred income tax liability?

What Does It Mean?

Answer on page 274

Other Noncurrent Liabilities

Frequently included in this balance sheet category are obligations to pension plans and other employee benefit plans, including deferred compensation and bonus plans. Expenses of these plans are accrued and reflected in the income statement of the fiscal period in which the benefit is earned by the employee. Because benefits are frequently conditional upon continued employment, future salary levels, and other factors, actuaries and other experts estimate the expense to be reported in a given fiscal period. The employer's pension expense will also depend on the ROI earned on funds invested in the pension (or other benefit plan) trust accounts over time. Because of the many significant factors that must be estimated in the expense and liability calculations, accounting for pension plans is a complex topic that has been controversial over the years. In 2006, the FASB issued an accounting standard to increase the uniformity of accounting for pensions. A significant provision of the standard requires the recognition of the over-funded (asset) or underfunded (liability) status of a defined benefit pension plan on the balance sheet. The funded status is measured as the difference between the plan assets at fair value and the projected benefit obligation, which is the present value of all future amounts expected to be paid to current plan participants and retirees.

An issue closely related to pensions is the accounting for postretirement benefit plans other than pensions. These plans provide medical, hospitalization, life insurance, and other benefits to retired employees. The 2006 standard that requires balance sheet recognition of an asset (for overfunded) or liability (for underfunded) pension plans applies to other postretirement benefit plans as well, although for pragmatic reasons the reporting entity's benefit obligation is measured in a different manner. Prior standards for both pension and other postretirement plans had relegated information about the overfunded or underfunded status of such plans to the notes to the financial statements. The present standard provides a better matching of revenues and expenses, a more appropriate balance sheet presentation, and more consistent and understandable note disclosures.

Another item commonly included with other long-term liabilities is the estimated liability under lawsuits in progress and/or product warranty programs. These liabilities are reflected at estimated amounts, and the related expense is reported in the income statement of the period in which the expense was incurred or the liability was identified. Sometimes the term *reserve* is used to describe these items, as in "reserve for product warranty claims." However, the term *reserve* is misleading because this amount refers to an estimated liability, not an amount of money that has been set aside to meet the liability.

The last caption formerly reported as a long-term liability in 2008 and in previous years, was **noncontrolling interest** in subsidiaries (frequently called **minority interest**). Although it was included with noncurrent liabilities in most consolidated balance sheets, some accountants believed that it should have been shown as a separate item between liabilities and stockholders' equity because this amount is not really a liability representing a fixed claim against the consolidated entity. In December 2007, the FASB issued a standard that took this position one step further by requiring that noncontrolling interest be reported within equity, but separate from the parent company's equity, in the consolidated balance sheets of all reporting entities beginning in 2009. The financial reporting and presentation issues concerning noncontrolling interest are discussed further and illustrated in Chapters 8 and 9. For now, understand that this item is no longer reported as a liability, although some financial analysts may continue to treat it as though it were, particularly in their calculations of debt (or financial leverage) measures.

Contingent Liabilities

Contingencies are potential gains or losses, the determination of which depends on one or more future events. **Contingent liabilities** are potential claims on a company's resources arising from such things as pending litigation, environmental hazards, casualty losses to property, and product warranties, to name just a few. But when should a firm recognize a loss and record the related liability on its books due to a mere contingency? The answer is, only in cases where the following two conditions have been met: First, it must be *probable* that the loss will be confirmed by a future transaction or event; and second, the amount of the loss must be *reasonably estimable*. Using product warranties as an example, you learned in this chapter that a firm's annual warranty expense is normally recorded based on estimates made by management. Why are contingent warranty claims recorded as liabilities? Because it is probable that future warranty claims will have to be paid, and the amount of such claims can be estimated with reasonable accuracy at the time the original sales transaction (with the attached product warranty) is made.

Application of these conditions can become difficult in practice, especially with respect to litigation and environmental contingencies, so the note disclosures in annual reports must be carefully analyzed to determine the adequacy of management's estimates. The tobacco and firearms industries, for example, have been battling increasingly complex litigation in recent years, the final outcome of which may not be determinable for years or even decades to come.

Because of accounting conservatism, gain contingencies are not recognized in the financial statements; companies may, however, disclose the nature of a gain contingency in the notes to the financial statements (including estimated amounts), but only where the gain is highly likely to occur.

Demonstration Problem

The Demonstration Problem walkthrough for this chapter is available in _Connect_.

Summary

This chapter discussed the accounting for and presentation of the following liabilities and related income statement accounts. Contra liabilities and reductions of expense accounts are shown in parentheses:

Balance Sheet	Income Statement
Assets = Liabilities + Stockholder's equity	← Net income = Revenues – Expenses
Current Liabilities Short-Term Debt	Interest Expense
(Discount on Short-Term Debt)	Interest Expense
Current Maturities of Long-Term Debt	
Accounts Payable	
Unearned Revenue	Revenue
Other Accrued Liabilities	Various Expenses
Long-Term Liabilities: Bonds Payable	Interest Expense
(Discount on Bonds Payable)	Interest Expense
Premium on Bonds Payable	(Interest Expense)
Deferred Tax Liabilities	Income Tax Expense

Liabilities are obligations of the entity. Most liabilities arise because funds have been borrowed or an obligation is recognized as a result of the accrual accounting process. Current liabilities are those that are expected to be paid within a year of the balance sheet date. Noncurrent, or long-term, liabilities are expected to be paid more than a year after the balance sheet date.

Short-term debt, such as a bank loan, is obtained to provide cash for seasonal buildup of inventory. The loan is expected to be repaid when the inventory is sold and the accounts receivable from the sale are collected. The interest cost of short-term debt sometimes is calculated on a discount basis. **(LO 1, 2)**

Long-term debt principal payments that will be made within a year of the balance sheet date are classified as a current liability. **(LO 1)**

Accounts payable represents amounts owed to suppliers of inventories and other resources. Some accounts payable are subject to a cash discount if paid within a time frame specified by the supplier. The internal control system of most entities will attempt to encourage adherence to the policy of taking all cash discounts offered.

Unearned revenue, other deferred credits, and other accrued liabilities arise primarily because of accrual accounting procedures that result in the recognition of expenses/revenues in the fiscal period in which they are incurred/earned. Many of these liabilities are estimated because the actual liability isn't known when the financial statements are prepared. **(LO 3, 4, 5)**

Long-term debt is a significant part of the capital structure of many firms. Funds are borrowed, rather than invested by the owners, because the firm expects to take advantage of the financial leverage associated with debt. If borrowed money can be invested to earn a higher return (ROI) than the interest cost, the return on the stockholders' investment (ROE) will be greater than ROI. However, the opposite is also true. Leverage adds to the risk associated with an investment in an entity. **(LO 6)**

Long-term debt frequently is issued in the form of bonds payable. Bonds have a stated interest rate (that is almost always a fixed percentage), a face amount or principal, and a maturity date when the principal must be paid. Because the interest rate on a bond is fixed, changes in the market rate of interest result in fluctuations in the market value of the bond. As market interest rates rise, bond prices fall, and vice versa. The market value of a bond is the present value of the interest payments and maturity value, discounted at the market interest rate. When bonds are issued and the market rate at the date of issue is different from the stated rate of the bond, a premium or discount results. Both bond premium and discount are amortized to interest expense over the life of the bond. Premium amortization reduces interest expense below the amount of interest paid. Discount amortization increases interest expense over the amount of interest paid. A bond sometimes is retired before its maturity date because market interest rates have dropped significantly below the stated interest rate of the bond. For the issuer, early retirement of bonds can result in a gain but usually results in a loss. **(LO 7, 8)**

Deferred income taxes result from temporary differences between book and taxable income. The most significant temporary difference is caused by the different depreciation methods used for each purpose. The amount of deferred income tax liability is the amount of income tax expected to be paid in future years, based on tax rates expected to apply in future years multiplied by the total amount of temporary differences. **(LO 9)**

Other long-term liabilities may relate to pension obligations, other postretirement benefit plan obligations, warranty obligations, or estimated liabilities under lawsuits in process. Noncontrolling interest, formerly reported as a long-term liability, is now reported within equity but separate from the parent company's equity, as discussed further in Chapters 8 and 9.

Refer to the Campbell Soup Company balance sheet and related notes in the appendix, and to other financial statements you may have, and observe how information about liabilities is presented.

Campbell's

Key Terms and Concepts

account payable (p. 241)   A liability representing an amount payable to another entity, usually because of the purchase of merchandise or a service on credit.

annual percentage rate (APR) (p. 238)   The effective (true) annual interest rate on a loan.

bond discount (p. 247)   The excess of the face amount of a bond over the market value of a bond (the proceeds of the issue).

bond indenture (p. 253)   The formal agreement between the borrower and investor(s) in bonds.

bond or bond payable (p. 245)   A long-term liability with a stated interest rate and maturity date, usually issued in denominations of $1,000.

bond premium (p. 245)   The excess of the market value of a bond (the proceeds of a bond issue) over the face amount of the bond(s) issued.

book value (p. 251)   The balance of the ledger account (including related contra accounts, if any) for an asset, liability, or stockholders' equity account. Sometimes referred to as *carrying value.*

call premium (p. 252)   An amount paid in excess of the face amount of a bond when the bond is repaid prior to its established maturity date.

callable bonds (p. 252)   Bonds that can be redeemed by the issuer, at its option, prior to the maturity date.

collateral trust bond (p. 253)   A bond secured by the pledge of securities or other intangible property.

contingent liability (p. 256)   A potential claim on a company's resources (i.e., loss) that depends on future events; must be *probable* and *reasonably estimable* to be recorded as a liability on the balance sheet.

contra liability (p. 240)   An account that normally has a debit balance that is subtracted from a related liability on the balance sheet.

convertible bonds (p. 253)   Bonds that can be converted to common stock of the issuer at the bondholder's option.

coupon bond (p. 253)   A bond for which the owner's name and address are not known by the issuer and/or trustee. Interest is received by clipping interest coupons that are attached to the bond and submitting them to the issuer. Coupon bonds, or *bearer bonds* or *unregistered bonds,* are no longer issued, although some are still outstanding.

coupon rate (p. 248)   The rate used to calculate the interest payments on a bond. Sometimes called *stated rate.*

current maturity of long-term debt (p. 241)   Principal payments on long-term debt that are scheduled to be paid within one year of the balance sheet date.

debenture bonds or debentures (p. 253)   Bonds secured by the general credit of the issuer but not secured by specific assets.

deferred credit (p. 241)   An account with a credit balance that will be recognized as a revenue (or as an expense reduction) in a future period. See *unearned revenue.*

deferred tax liability (p. 254)   A long-term liability that arises because of temporary differences between when an item is recognized for book and tax purposes.

discount loan (p. 238)   A loan on which interest is paid at the beginning of the loan period.

face amount (p. 245)   The principal amount of a bond.

FICA tax (p. 242)   Federal Insurance Contribution Act tax used to finance federal programs for old age and disability benefits (Social Security) and health insurance (Medicare).

financial leverage (p. 245)   The use of debt (with a fixed interest rate) that causes a difference between return on investment and return on equity.

gross pay (p. 242)   The total earnings of an employee for a payroll period.

interest calculation—discount basis (p. 239)   Interest calculation in which the interest (called *discount*) is subtracted from the principal to determine the amount of money (the proceeds) made available to the borrower. Only the principal is repaid at the maturity date because the interest is, in effect, prepaid.

interest calculation—straight basis (p. 238)   Interest calculation in which the principal is the amount of money made available to the borrower. Principal and interest are normally repaid by the borrower at the maturity date, although interest may be paid on an interim basis as well.

interpolating (p. 239)   A mathematical term to describe the process of *interpreting* and *relating* two factors from a table to approximate a third factor not shown in the table.

long-term debt (p. 245)   A liability that will be paid more than one year from the balance sheet date.

maturity date (p. 237)   The date when a loan is scheduled to be repaid.

minority interest (p. 256)   Another term for *noncontrolling interest.*

mortgage bond (p. 253)   A bond secured by a lien on real estate.

net pay (p. 242)   Gross pay less payroll deductions; the amount the employer is obligated to pay to the employee.

noncontrolling interest (p. 256)   The portion of equity in a less than 100 percent owned subsidiary not attributable, directly or indirectly, to the parent company; frequently called *minority interest.* Reported within equity, but separate from the parent company's equity, in the consolidated balance sheet; previously reported as a liability by most companies.

note payable (p. 237)   A liability that arises from issuing a note; a formal promise to pay a stated amount at a stated date, usually with interest at a stated rate and sometimes secured by collateral. Can be short-term or long-term.

prime rate (p. 237)   The interest rate charged by banks on loans to large and most creditworthy customers; a benchmark interest rate.

proceeds (p. 240)   The amount of cash received in a transaction.

registered bond (p. 253)   A bond for which the owner's name and address are recorded by the issuer and/or trustee.

revolving line of credit (p. 237)   A loan on which regular payments are to be made but which can be quickly increased up to a predetermined limit as additional funds are borrowed.

serial bond (p. 253)   A bond that is to be repaid in installments.

stated rate (p. 248)   The rate used to calculate the amount of interest payments on a bond. Sometimes called *coupon rate.*

term bond (p. 253)   A bond that is to be repaid in one lump sum at the maturity date.

trustee of bonds (p. 253)   The agent who coordinates activities between the bond issuer and the investors in bonds.

unearned revenue (p. 241)   A liability arising from receipt of cash before the related revenue has been earned. See *deferred credit.*

working capital loan (p. 237)   A short-term loan that is expected to be repaid from collections of accounts receivable.

connect   Mini-Exercises

All applicable Mini-Exercises are available in *Connect*.

Mini-Exercise 7.1
LO 3

Unearned revenues—rent On December 1, 2019, an advance rent payment of $25,800, representing a three-month prepayment for the months of December, January, and February, was received in cash from the company's tenant.

Required:

Use the horizontal model (or write the journal entries) to record the effects of the following items:

a. The three months of rent collected in advance on December 1, 2019.

b. The adjustment that will be made at the end of each month to show the amount of rent "earned" during the month.

Other accrued liabilities—payroll For the payroll period ended on June 25, 2019, gross pay was $143,000, net pay was $102,000, FICA tax withholdings were $10,000, income tax withholdings were $25,000, and medical insurance contributions were $6,000.

Mini-Exercise 7.2
LO 4

Required:

Use the horizontal model (or write the journal entry) to show the effects of the payroll accrual on June 25, 2019.

Other accrued liabilities—warranties The balance of the Estimated Warranty Liability account was $25,000 on January 1, 2019, and $34,400 on December 31, 2019. Based on an analysis of warranty claims during the past several years, this year's warranty provision was established at 1.5% of sales, and sales during the year were $6,500,000.

Mini-Exercise 7.3
LO 5

Required:

a. What amount of warranty expense will appear on the income statement for the year ended December 31, 2019?

b. What were the actual costs of servicing products under warranty during the year?

Bonds payable—various issues On July 1, 2019, $60 million face amount of 7%, 10-year bonds were issued. The bonds pay interest on an annual basis on June 30 each year. The market interest rates were slightly higher than 7% when the bonds were sold.

Mini-Exercise 7.4
LO 8

Required:

a. How much interest will be paid annually on these bonds?

b. Were the bonds issued at a premium or discount? Explain.

c. Will the annual interest expense on these bonds be more than, equal to, or less than the amount of interest paid each year? Explain your answer.

Exercises

connect

All applicable Exercises are available in *Connect*.

Notes payable—discount basis On April 15, 2019, Powell Inc. obtained a six-month working capital loan from its bank. The face amount of the note signed by the treasurer was $1,200,000. The interest rate charged by the bank was 9%. The bank made the loan on a discount basis.

Exercise 7.5
LO 2

Required:

a. Calculate the loan proceeds made available to Powell, and use the horizontal model (or write the journal entry) to show the effect of signing the note and the receipt of the cash proceeds on April 15, 2019.

b. Calculate the amount of interest expense applicable to this loan during the fiscal year ended June 30, 2019.

c. What is the amount of the current liability related to this loan to be shown in the June 30, 2019, balance sheet?

Exercise 7.6

LO 2

Notes payable—discount basis On August 1, 2019, Colombo Co.'s treasurer signed a note promising to pay $2,400,000 on December 31, 2019. The proceeds of the note were $2,340,000.

Required:

a. Calculate the discount rate used by the lender.

b. Calculate the effective interest rate (APR) on the loan.

c. Use the horizontal model (or write the journal entry) to show the effects of
   1. Signing the note and the receipt of the cash proceeds on August 1, 2019.
   2. Recording interest expense for the month of September.
   3. Repaying the note on December 31, 2019.

Exercise 7.7

LO 4

Other accrued liabilities—payroll taxes At March 31, 2019, the end of the first year of operations at Lukancic Inc., the firm's accountant neglected to accrue payroll taxes of $9,600 that were applicable to payrolls for the year then ended.

Required:

a. Use the horizontal model (or write the journal entry) to show the effect of the accrual that should have been made as of March 31, 2019.

b. Determine the income statement and balance sheet effects of not accruing payroll taxes at March 31, 2019.

c. Assume that when the payroll taxes were paid in April 2019, the payroll tax expense account was charged. Assume that at March 31, 2020, the accountant again neglected to accrue the payroll tax liability, which was $10,000 at that date. Determine the income statement and balance sheet effects of not accruing payroll taxes at March 31, 2020.

Exercise 7.8

LO 5

Other accrued liabilities—real estate taxes Glennelle's Boutique Inc. operates in a city in which real estate tax bills for one year are issued in May of the subsequent year. Thus, tax bills for 2019 are issued in May 2020 and are payable in July 2020.

Required:

a. Explain how the amount of tax expense for calendar 2019 and the amount of taxes payable (if any) at December 31, 2019, can be determined.

b. Use the horizontal model (or write the journal entry) to show the effect of accruing 2019 taxes of $44,800 at December 31, 2019.

c. Assume that the actual tax bill, received in May 2020, was for $47,600. Use the horizontal model (or write the journal entry) to show the effects of the appropriate adjustment to the amount previously accrued.

d. Determine the income statement and balance sheet effects of not accruing 2019 taxes at December 31, 2019 (assuming that taxes in **b** are not accrued).

Other accrued liabilities—warranties Kohl Co. provides warranties for many of its products. The January 1, 2019, balance of the Estimated Warranty Liability account was $35,200. Based on an analysis of warranty claims during the past several years, this year's warranty provision was established at 0.4% of sales. During 2019, the actual cost of servicing products under warranty was $15,600, and sales were $3,600,000.

Exercise 7.9
LO 5

Required:

a. What amount of Warranty Expense will appear on Kohl Co.'s income statement for the year ended December 31, 2019?

b. What amount will be reported in the Estimated Warranty Liability account on the December 31, 2019, balance sheet?

Other accrued liabilities—warranties Prist Co. had not provided a warranty on its products, but competitive pressures forced management to add this feature at the beginning of 2019. Based on an analysis of customer complaints made over the past two years, the cost of a warranty program was estimated at 0.7% of sales. During 2019, sales totaled $3,600,000. Actual costs of servicing products under warranty totaled $22,100.

Exercise 7.10
LO 5

Required:

Use the horizontal model (or write the journal entries) to show the effect of having the warranty program during 2019.

Unearned revenues—customer deposits NightWoundsTime Brewing Co. distributes its products in an aluminum keg. Customers are charged a deposit of $60 per keg; deposits are recorded in the Keg Deposits account.

Exercise 7.11
LO 3

Required:

a. Where on the balance sheet will the Keg Deposits account be found? Explain your answer.

b. Use the horizontal model (or write the journal entry) to show the effect of giving a keg deposit refund to a customer for one keg.

c. A keg use analyst who works for NightWoundsTime estimates that 200 kegs for which deposits were received during the year will never be returned. What accounting, if any, would be appropriate for the deposits associated with these kegs?

d. Describe the accounting that would be appropriate for the cost of the kegs that are purchased and used by NightWoundsTime Brewing Co., including how to account for unreturned kegs.

Unearned revenues—ticket sales Kirkland Theater sells season tickets for six events at a price of $378. For the 2019 season, 1,200 season tickets were sold.

Exercise 7.12
LO 3

Required:

a. Use the horizontal model (or write the journal entry) to show the effect of the sale of the season tickets.

b. Use the horizontal model (or write the journal entry) to show the effect of presenting an event.

c. Where on the balance sheet would the account balance representing funds received for performances not yet presented be classified?

Exercise 7.13
LO 8

Bonds payable—record issuance and premium amortization Jessie Co. issued $2 million face amount of 7%, 20-year bonds on April 1, 2019. The bonds pay interest on an annual basis on March 31 each year.

Required:

a. Assume that market interest rates were slightly lower than 7% when the bonds were sold. Would the proceeds from the bond issue have been more than, less than, or equal to the face amount? Explain.

b. Independent of your answer to part **a**, assume that the proceeds were $2,060,000. Use the horizontal model (or write the journal entry) to show the effect of issuing the bonds.

c. Calculate the interest expense that Jessie Co. will show with respect to these bonds in its income statement for the fiscal year ended September 30, 2019, assuming that the premium of $60,000 is amortized on a straight-line basis.

Exercise 7.14
LO 8

Bonds payable—record issuance and discount amortization Alexi Co. issued $75 million face amount of 6%, 10-year bonds on June 1, 2019. The bonds pay interest on an annual basis on May 31 each year.

Required:

a. Assume that the market interest rates were slightly higher than 6% when the bonds were sold. Would the proceeds from the bond issue have been more than, less than, or equal to the face amount? Explain.

b. Independent of your answer to part **a**, assume that the proceeds were $74,580,000. Use the horizontal model (or write the journal entry) to show the effect of issuing the bonds.

c. Calculate the interest expense that Alexi Co. will show with respect to these bonds in its income statement for the fiscal year ended September 30, 2019, assuming that the discount of $420,000 is amortized on a straight-line basis.

Exercise 7.15
LO 8

Bonds payable—calculate market value On August 1, 2011, Bonnie purchased $30,000 of Huber Co.'s 10%, 20-year bonds at face value. Huber Co. has paid the semiannual interest due on the bonds regularly. On August 1, 2019, market rates of interest had fallen to 8%, and Bonnie is considering selling the bonds.

Required:
Using the present value tables in Chapter 6, calculate the market value of Bonnie's bonds on August 1, 2019.

Exercise 7.16
LO 8

Bonds payable—calculate market value On March 1, 2014, Catherine purchased $450,000 of Tyson Co.'s 10%, 20-year bonds at face value. Tyson Co. has regularly paid the annual interest due on the bonds. On March 1, 2019, market interest rates had risen to 12%, and Catherine is considering selling the bonds.

Required:

Using the present value tables in Chapter 6, calculate the market value of Catherine's bonds on March 1, 2019.

Bonds payable—various issues Reynolds Co. issued $85 million face amount of 5% bonds when market interest rates were 4.72% for bonds of similar risk and other characteristics.

Exercise 7.17
LO 8

Required:

a. How much interest will be paid annually on these bonds?

b. Were the bonds issued at a premium or discount? Explain your answer.

c. Will the annual interest expense on these bonds be more than, equal to, or less than the amount of interest paid each year? Explain your answer.

Bonds payable—various issues Atom Endeavour Co. issued $210 million face amount of 8.5% bonds when market interest rates were 8.64% for bonds of similar risk and other characteristics.

Exercise 7.18
LO 8

Required:

a. How much interest will be paid annually on these bonds?

b. Were the bonds issued at a premium or discount? Explain your answer.

c. Will the annual interest expense on these bonds be more than, equal to, or less than the amount of interest paid each year? Explain your answer.

Deferred income tax liability The difference between the amounts of book and tax depreciation expense, as well as the desire to report income tax expense that is related to book income before taxes, causes a long-term deferred income tax liability to be reported on the balance sheet. The amount of this liability reported on the balance sheets of many firms has been increasing over the years, creating the impression that the liability will never be paid. Why has the amount of the deferred income tax liability risen steadily for many firms?

Exercise 7.19
LO 9

Financial leverage A firm issues long-term debt with an effective interest rate of 10%, and the proceeds of this debt issue can be invested to earn an ROI of 12%. What effect will this financial leverage have on the firm's ROE relative to having the same amount of funds invested by the owners/stockholders?

Exercise 7.20
LO 6

Transaction analysis—various accounts Enter the following column headings across the top of a sheet of paper:

Exercise 7.21
LO 4, 5, 8

Transaction/ Adjustment	Current Assets	Current Liabilities	Noncurrent Liabilities	Net Income

Enter the transaction or adjustment letter in the first column and show the effect, if any, of each of the transactions or adjustments on the appropriate balance sheet category or on the income statement by entering the amount and indicating whether it is an addition (+) or a subtraction (−). You may also write the journal entries to record each transaction or adjustment.

a. Wages of $465 for the last three days of the fiscal period have not been accrued.

b. Interest of $340 on a bank loan has not been accrued.

c. Interest on bonds payable has not been accrued for the current month. The company has outstanding $480,000 of 6.5% bonds.

d. The discount related to the bonds in part **c** has not been amortized for the current month. The current month amortization is $150.

e. Product warranties were honored during the month; parts inventory items valued at $1,660 were sent to customers making claims, and cash refunds of $820 were also made.

f. During the fiscal period, advance payments from customers totaling $3,000 were received and recorded as sales revenues. The items will not be delivered to the customers until the next fiscal period. Record the appropriate adjustment.

Exercise 7.22
LO 4, 5, 8

Transaction analysis—various accounts Enter the following column headings across the top of a sheet of paper:

Transaction/ Adjustment	Current Assets	Current Liabilities	Noncurrent Liabilities	Net Income

Enter the transaction or adjustment letter in the first column, and show the effect, if any, of each of the transactions or adjustments on the appropriate balance sheet category or on the income statement by entering the amount and indicating whether it is an addition (+) or a subtraction (−). You may also write the journal entries to record each transaction or adjustment.

a. Wages of $4,100 accrued at the end of the prior fiscal period were paid this fiscal period.

b. Real estate taxes of $5,500 applicable to the current period have not been accrued.

c. Interest on bonds payable has not been accrued for the current month. The company has outstanding $920,000 of 6.3% bonds.

d. The premium related to the bonds in part **c** has not been amortized for the current month. The current-month amortization is $310.

e. Based on past experience with its warranty program, the estimated warranty expense for the current period should be 0.4% of sales of $740,000.

f. Analysis of the company's income taxes indicates that taxes currently payable are $61,000 and that the deferred tax liability should be increased by $22,000.

Exercise 7.23
LO 1, 2, 5, 8, 9

Transaction analysis—various accounts Enter the following column headings across the top of a sheet of paper:

Transaction/ Adjustment	Current Assets	Noncurrent Assets	Current Liabilities	Noncurrent Liabilities	Stockholders' Equity	Net Income

Enter the transaction or adjustment letter in the first column and show the effect, if any, of each transaction or adjustment on the appropriate balance sheet category or on net income by entering for each category affected the account name and amount, and indicating whether it is an addition (+) or a subtraction (−). Items that affect net income should not also be shown as affecting stockholders' equity. You may also write the journal entries to record each transaction or adjustment.

a. Income tax expense of $1,400 for the current period is accrued. Of the accrual, $400 represents deferred tax liabilities.

b. Bonds payable with a face amount of $15,000 are issued at a price of 98.

c. Of the proceeds from the bonds in part **b**, $9,000 is used to purchase land for future expansion.

d. Because of warranty claims, finished goods inventory costing $128 is sent to customers to replace defective products.

e. A three-month, 9% note payable with a face amount of $60,000 was signed. The bank made the loan on a discount basis.

f. The next installment of a long-term serial bond requiring an annual principal repayment of $70,000 will become due within the current year.

Transaction analysis—various accounts Enter the following column headings across the top of a sheet of paper:

Exercise 7.24
LO 5, 8

Transaction/ Adjustment	Current Assets	Noncurrent Assets	Current Liabilities	Noncurrent Liabilities	Stockholders' Equity	Net Income

Enter the transaction or adjustment letter in the first column and show the effect, if any, of each transaction or adjustment on the appropriate balance sheet category or on net income by entering for each category affected the account name and amount, and indicating whether it is an addition (+) or a subtraction (−). Items that affect net income should *not* also be shown as affecting stockholders' equity. You may also write the journal entries to record each transaction or adjustment.

a. Recorded the financing (capital) lease of a truck. The present value of the lease payments is $110,000; the total of the lease payments to be made is $136,000.

b. Recorded the company's payroll for the month. Gross pay was $21,100, net pay was $16,300, and various withholding liability accounts were credited for the difference.

c. Issued $52,000 of bonds payable at a price of 102.

d. Adjusted the estimated liability under a warranty program by reducing previously accrued warranty expense by $7,600.

e. Retired $42,000 face amount of bonds payable with a carrying value of $41,600 by calling them at a redemption value of 104.

f. Accrued estimated annual health care costs for retirees; $62,000 is expected to be paid within a year, and $470,000 is expected to be paid in more than a year.

Problems

McGraw Hill connect

All applicable Problems are available in *Connect*.

Unearned revenues—rent (*Note:* See Exercise 5.20 for the related prepaid expense accounting.) On November 1, 2019, Gordon Co. collected $31,800 in cash from its tenant as an advance rent payment on its store location. The six-month lease period ends on April 30, 2020, at which time the contract may be renewed.

Problem 7.25
LO 3

Required:

a. Use the horizontal model (or write the journal entries) to record the effects of the following items for Gordon Co.:
   1. The six months of rent collected in advance on November 1, 2019.
   2. The adjustment that will be made at the end of each month to show the amount of rent "earned" during the month.

b. Calculate the amount of unearned rent that should be shown on the December 31, 2019, balance sheet with respect to this lease.

c. Suppose the advance collection received on November 1, 2019, covered an 18-month lease period at the same amount of rent per month. How should Gordon Co. report the unearned rent amount on its December 31, 2019, balance sheet?

Problem 7.26

LO 3

Unearned revenues—subscription fees Evans Ltd. publishes a monthly newsletter for retail marketing managers and requires its subscribers to pay $60 in advance for a one-year subscription. During the month of August 2019, Evans Ltd. sold 500 one-year subscriptions and received payments in advance from all new subscribers. Only 350 of the new subscribers paid their fees in time to receive the August newsletter; the other subscriptions began with the September newsletter.

Required:

a. Use the horizontal model (or write the journal entries) to record the effects of the following items:
   1. Subscription fees received in advance during August 2019.
   2. Subscription revenue earned during August 2019.

b. Calculate the amount of subscription revenue earned by Evans Ltd. during the year ended December 31, 2019, for these 500 subscriptions sold in August 2019.

Optional continuation of Problem 7.26—lifetime subscription offer (*Note:* This is an analytical assignment involving the use of present value tables and accounting estimates. Only the first sentence in Problem 7.26 applies to this continuation of the problem.) Evans Ltd. is now considering the possibility of offering a lifetime membership option to its subscribers. Under this proposal, subscribers could receive the monthly newsletter throughout their lives by paying a flat fee of $800. The one-year subscription rate of $60 would continue to apply to new and existing subscribers who choose to subscribe on an annual basis. Assume that the average age of Evans Ltd.'s current subscribers is 38 and their average life expectancy is 78 years. Evans Ltd.'s average interest rate on long-term debt is 10%.

c. Using the information given, determine whether it would be profitable for Evans Ltd. to sell lifetime subscriptions. (*Hint:* Calculate the present value of a lifetime membership for an average subscriber using the appropriate table in Chapter 6.)

d. What additional factors should Evans Ltd. consider in determining whether to offer a lifetime membership option? Explain your answer as specifically as possible.

Problem 7.27

LO 4

Other accrued liabilities—payroll The following summary data for the payroll period ended on April 10, 2018, are available for Brac Construction Ltd.:

Gross pay	$	?
FICA tax withholdings		?
Income tax withholdings		6,880
Medical insurance contributions		560
Union dues		320
Total deductions		10,820
Net pay		29,180

Required:

a. Calculate the missing amounts and then determine the FICA tax withholding percentage.
b. Use the horizontal model (or write the journal entry) to show the effects of the payroll accrual.

Other accrued liabilities—payroll and payroll taxes The following summary data for the payroll period ended December 27, 2018, are available for Cayman Coating Co.:

Problem 7.28
LO 4

Gross pay	$258,000
FICA tax withholdings	?
Income tax withholdings	30,960
Group hospitalization insurance	3,810
Employee contributions to pension plan	?
Total deductions	62,475
Net pay	?

Additional information

- For employees, FICA tax rates for 2018 were 7.65% on the first $128,400 of each employee's annual earnings. However, no employees had accumulated earnings for the year in excess of the $128,400 limit.
- For employers, FICA tax rates for 2018 were also 7.65% on the first $128,400 of each employee's annual earnings.
- The federal and state unemployment compensation tax rates are 0.6% and 5.4%, respectively. These rates are levied against the employer for the first $7,000 of each employee's annual earnings. Only $27,000 of the gross pay amount for the December 27, 2018, pay period was owed to employees who were still under the annual limit.

Required:

Assuming that Cayman Coating Co.'s payroll for the last week of the year is to be paid on January 3, 2019, use the horizontal model (or write the journal entry) to record the effects of the December 27, 2018, entries for:

a. Accrued payroll.
b. Accrued payroll taxes.

Bonds payable—callable Hayden Co. has outstanding $40 million face amount of 7% bonds that were issued on January 1, 2013, for $40,600,000. The 20-year bonds mature on December 31, 2032, and are callable at 103 (that is, they can be paid off at any time by paying the bondholders 103% of the face amount).

Problem 7.29
LO 7

Required:

a. Under what circumstances would Hayden Co. managers consider calling the bonds?

b. Assume that the bonds are called on December 31, 2019. Use the horizontal model (or write the journal entry) to show the effect of the retirement of the bonds. (*Hint:* Calculate the amount paid to bondholders; determine how much of the bond premium would have been amortized prior to calling the bonds; and then calculate the gain or loss on retirement.)

Problem 7.30

LO 7

Bonds payable—callable Hurley Co. has outstanding $420 million face amount of 9% bonds that were issued on January 1, 2007, for $409,500,000. The 20-year bonds mature on December 31, 2026, and are callable at 102 (i.e., they can be paid off at any time by paying the bondholders 102% of the face amount).

Required:

a. Under what circumstances would Hurley Co. managers consider calling the bonds?

b. Assume that the bonds are called on December 31, 2019. Use the horizontal model (or write the journal entry) to show the effect of the retirement of the bonds. (*Hint:* Calculate the amount paid to bondholders; then determine how much of the bond discount would have been amortized prior to calling the bonds; and then calculate the gain or loss on retirement.)

Problem 7.31

LO 8

Bonds payable—calculate issue price and amortize discount On January 1, 2019, Drennen, Inc., issued $5 million face amount of 10-year, 14% stated rate bonds when market interest rates were 12%. The bonds pay semiannual interest each June 30 and December 31 and mature on December 31, 2028.

Required:

a. Using the present value tables in Chapter 6, calculate the proceeds (issue price) of Drennen Inc.'s bonds on January 1, 2019, assuming that the bonds were sold to provide a market rate of return to the investor.

b. Assume instead that the proceeds were $4,820,000. Use the horizontal model (or write the journal entry) to record the payment of semiannual interest and the related discount amortization on June 30, 2019, assuming that the discount of $180,000 is amortized on a straight-line basis.

c. If the discount in part **b** were amortized using the compound interest method, would interest expense for the year ended December 31, 2019, be more than, less than, or equal to the interest expense reported using the straight-line method of discount amortization? Explain.

Problem 7.32

LO 8

Bonds payable—calculate issue price and amortize premium On January 1, 2019, Learned, Inc., issued $105 million face amount of 20-year, 14% stated rate bonds when market interest rates were 16%. The bonds pay interest semiannually each June 30 and December 31 and mature on December 31, 2038.

Required:

a. Using the present value tables in Chapter 6, calculate the proceeds (issue price) of Learned Inc.'s bonds on January 1, 2019, assuming that the bonds were sold to provide a market rate of return to the investor.

b. Assume instead that the proceeds were $108,600,000. Use the horizontal model (or write the journal entry) to record the payment of semiannual interest and the related premium amortization on June 30, 2019, assuming that the premium of $3,600,000 is amortized on a straight-line basis.

c. If the premium in part **b** were amortized using the compound interest method, would interest expense for the year ended December 31, 2019, be more than, less than, or equal to the interest expense reported using the straight-line method of premium amortization? Explain.

d. In reality, the difference between the stated interest rate and the market rate would be substantially less than 2%. The dramatic difference in this problem was designed so that you could use present value tables to answer part **a**. What causes the stated rate to be different from the market rate, and why is the difference likely to be much less than depicted in this problem?

Cases

connect

All applicable Cases are available in *Connect.*

Focus company—noncurrent liability disclosures In Exercise 1.1, you were asked to obtain the most recent annual report of a company that you were interested in reviewing throughout this term.

Case 7.33
LO 7, 9

Required:

Please review the note disclosures provided in your focus company's annual report and identify at least three items being reported as noncurrent (long-term) liabilities. Discuss what you've learned about these items and how they are presented on the balance sheet.

Other accrued liabilities—interest (*Note:* This is an analytical assignment involving the interpretation of financial statement disclosures.) A review of the accounting records at Corless Co. revealed the following information concerning the company's liabilities that were outstanding at December 31, 2020 and 2019, respectively:

Case 7.34
LO 1, 5, 7, 8

Debt (Thousands)	2020	Year-End Interest Rate	2019	Year-End Interest Rate
Short-term debt:				
Working capital loans	$500	8%	$380	7%
Current maturities of long-term debt	160	6%	160	6%
Long-term debt:				
Debenture bonds due in 2037.............	800	9%	800	9%
Serial bonds due in equal annual installments	480	6%	640	6%

Required:

a. Corless Co. has not yet made an adjustment to accrue the interest expense related to its *working capital loans* for the year ended December 31, 2020. Assume that the amount of interest to be accrued can be accurately estimated using an average-for-the-year interest rate applied to the average liability balance. Use the horizontal model (or write the journal entry) to record the effect of the 2020 interest accrual for working capital loans.

b. Note that the dollar amount and interest rate of the *current maturities of long-term debt* have not changed from 2019 to 2020. Does this mean that the $160,000 amount owed at the end of 2019 still has not been paid as of December 31, 2020? (*Hint:* Explain your answer with reference to other information provided in the problem.)

c. Assume that the *debenture bonds* were originally issued at their face amount. However, the market rate of interest for bonds of similar risk has decreased significantly in recent years and is 7% at December 31, 2020. If the debenture bonds were both callable by Corless Co. and convertible by its bondholders, which event is more likely to occur? Explain your answer.

d. Assume the same facts as in part **c.** Would the market value of Corless Co.'s debenture bonds be more than or less than the $800,000 reported amount? Is this good news or bad news to the management of Corless Co.?

e. When the Serial Bonds account decreased during the year, what other account was affected, and how was it affected? Use the horizontal model (or write the journal entry) to record the effect of this transaction.

Case 7.35
LO 5, 7, 8

Analysis of long-term debt Assume that Home and Office City Inc. provided the following comparative data concerning long-term debt in the notes to its 2020 annual report (amounts in millions):

	December 31, 2020	December 31, 2019
3¼% Convertible Subordinated Notes, due October 1, 2021; converted into shares of common stock of the Company at a conversion price of $15.3611 per share in October 2020	$ —	$1,103
6½% Senior Notes, due September 15, 2024; interest payable semiannually on March 15 and September 15 beginning in 2020	500	—
Commercial Paper; weighted average interest rate of 4.8% at January 1, 2019	—	246
Financing Lease Obligations; payable in varying installments through January 31, 2047	216	180
Installment Notes Payable; interest imputed at rates between 5.2% and 10.0%; payable in varying installments through 2038	45	27
Unsecured Bank Loan; floating interest rate averaging 6.05% in fiscal 2020 and 5.90% in fiscal 2019; payable in August 2022	15	15
Variable-Rate Industrial Revenue Bonds; secured by letters of credit or land; interest rates averaging 2.9% during fiscal 2020 and 3.8% during fiscal 2019; payable in varying installments through 2030	3	9
Total long-term debt	$779	$1,580
Less current installments	29	14
Long-term debt, excluding current installments	$750	$1,566

Required:

a. As indicated, Home and Office City's 3¼% Convertible Subordinated Notes were converted into shares of common stock in October 2020. How many shares of stock were issued in conversion of these notes?

b. Regarding the 6½% Senior Notes, Home and Office City Inc. also disclosed that "The Company, at its option, may redeem all or any portion of the Senior Notes by notice to the holder. The Senior Notes are redeemable at a redemption price, plus accrued interest, equal to the greater of (1) 100% of the principal amount of the Senior Notes to be redeemed or (2) the sum of the present values of the remaining scheduled payments of principal and interest on the Senior Notes to maturity."

Redeemable fixed-rate notes, such as those described here, are similar to callable term bonds. Thinking of the 6½% Senior Notes on this basis, would it have been *possible* for Home and Office City Inc. to redeem ("call") these notes for an amount

1. Below face value (at a discount)?
2. Above face value (at a premium)?
3. Equal to face value (at par)?

What circumstances would have been most likely to prompt Home and Office City to redeem these notes?

c. Recall from the discussion of Cash and Cash Equivalents in Chapter 5 that commercial paper is like an IOU issued by a very creditworthy corporation. Home and Office City's note disclosures concerning commercial paper reveal that "The company has a backup credit facility with a consortium of banks for up to $800 million. The credit facility contains various restrictive covenants, none of which is expected to materially impact the company's liquidity or capital resources."

What do you think is meant by this statement?

d. What other information would you have wanted to know about Home and Office City's "Financing Lease Obligations" when making an assessment of the company's overall liquidity and leverage?

e. Regarding the "Installment Notes Payable," what is meant by "interest *imputed* at rates between 5.2% and 10%"?

f. Why do you suppose that Home and Office City's "Unsecured Bank Loan" was immaterial in relation to the company's total long-term debt?

g. Note that the "current installments" due on Home and Office City's long-term debt were immaterial in amount for both years presented. Based on the data presented in this case, explain why this is likely to change over the next five years.

ANSWERS TO
What Does
It Mean?

1. It means that interest on the loan is subtracted from the principal of the loan and the difference is made available for the borrower's use.
2. It means that if liabilities are understated, it is most likely that expenses are also understated and net income is overstated.
3. It means that borrowed funds have been invested to earn a greater rate of return than the interest rate being paid on the borrowed funds.
4. It means that if the firm cannot earn a greater rate of return than the interest rate being paid on borrowed funds, its chances of not being able to repay the debt and of going bankrupt are greater than if it had less financial leverage.

5. It means that the interest rate used to calculate interest payments on the bond is fixed and does not change as market interest rates change.

6. It means that the bond is secured by the general credit of the issuer, not by specific assets.

7. It means that as market interest rates rise, the present value of the fixed interest return on the bond falls, so the market value of the bond falls.

8. It means that the bond has been issued for more than its face amount because the stated interest rate is greater than the market interest rate on the issue date.

9. It means that the firm's deductions for income tax purposes have been greater than expenses subtracted in arriving at net income for book purposes; hence, less income tax will be currently payable than income tax expense based on book net income and the difference represents the company's deferred income tax liability.

8

Accounting for and Presentation of Stockholders' Equity

Stockholders' equity is the claim of the entity's owners/stockholders to the assets shown in the balance sheet. Another term for stockholders' equity is *net assets,* which is assets minus liabilities. Neither the liabilities nor the elements of stockholders' equity are specifically identifiable with particular assets, although certain assets may be pledged as collateral for some liabilities.

The specific terminology used to identify stockholders' equity depends on the form of the entity's legal organization. For an individual proprietorship, the term **proprietor's capital**, or *capital,* perhaps combined with the owner's name, is frequently used. For example, in the balance sheet of a single proprietorship owned by Zoe Petritis, the proprietor's capital account would be labeled Zoe Petritis, Capital. For a partnership, **partners' capital** is the term used, and sometimes the capital account balance of each partner is shown on the balance sheet. In both proprietorships and partnerships, no distinction is made between invested (or paid-in) capital and retained earnings (or earned capital).

Because the corporate form of organization is used for firms that account for most of the business activity in our economy, this text focuses on corporate stockholders' equity. As explained in Chapter 2, there are two principal components of corporate stockholders' equity: paid-in capital and retained earnings. The financial statements of many small businesses that use the corporate form of organization are likely to show in stockholders' equity—only capital stock (which is paid-in capital) and retained earnings. However, as shown by the "shareholders' equity" section of the Consolidated Balance Sheets of Campbell Soup Company in the appendix, the stockholders' equity section can become quite complex. The stockholders' equity section of the balance sheets in other annual reports that you have may appear equally complex. Stockholders' equity captions usually seen in a balance sheet are the following:

Campbell's

1. Paid-in capital:
   a. Preferred stock (sometimes issued)
   b. Common stock (always issued)
   c. Additional paid-in capital
2. Retained earnings (Accumulated deficit if negative)
3. Accumulated other comprehensive income (loss)

	August 31	
	2020	**2019**
Stockholders' equity:		
Paid-in capital:		
Preferred stock, 6%, $100 par value, cumulative, callable at $102, 5,000 shares authorized, issued, and outstanding	$ 500,000	$ 500,000
Common stock, $2 par value, 1,000,000 shares authorized, 244,800 shares issued at August 31, 2020, and 200,000 shares issued at August 31, 2019	489,600	400,000
Additional paid-in capital	3,322,400	2,820,000
Total paid-in capital	$4,312,000	$3,720,000
Retained earnings	2,828,000	2,600,000
Accumulated other comprehensive income (loss)	50,000	(100,000)
Less: Common stock in treasury, at cost; 1,000 shares at August 31, 2020	(12,000)	—
Total stockholders' equity	$7,178,000	$6,220,000

Exhibit 8-1

Stockholders' Equity Section of Racers Inc. Balance Sheets at August 31, 2020 and 2019

4.   Less: Treasury stock

5.   Noncontrolling interest (which is actually the equity interest held by *nonowners* of the reporting entity)

The objective of this chapter is to permit you to make sense of the stockholders' equity presentation of any balance sheet. You will also learn about many characteristics of stockholders' equity that are relevant to personal investment decisions. A brief overview of personal investing is provided as an appendix to this chapter. For the purposes of our discussion, the stockholders' equity section of the balance sheets of Racers Inc. in Exhibit 8-1 is explained.

LEARNING OBJECTIVES (LO)

After studying this chapter, you should understand and be able to

LO 8-1   Describe the characteristics of common stock and show how common stock is presented in the balance sheet.

LO 8-2   Explain what preferred stock is, discuss what its advantages and disadvantages to the corporation are, and show how it is presented in the balance sheet.

LO 8-3   Describe the accounting for a cash dividend and explain the dates involved in dividend transactions.

LO 8-4   Describe what stock dividends and stock splits are and discuss why each is used.

LO 8-5   Recognize what the components of accumulated other comprehensive income (loss) are and explain why these items appear in stockholders' equity.

LO 8-6   Explain what treasury stock is, discuss why it is acquired, and show how treasury stock transactions affect stockholders' equity.

LO 8-7   Show how stockholders' equity transactions for the year are reported in the financial statements.

LO 8-8   Explain what noncontrolling interest is, why it arises, and what it means in the balance sheet.

LO 8-9   Discuss how the presence of a noncontrolling interest affects the presentation of consolidated financial statements.

Exhibit 8-2 highlights the balance sheet accounts covered in detail in this chapter and shows the income statement and statement of cash flows components affected by these accounts.

Paid-In Capital

The captions shown in the paid-in capital category of stockholders' equity (common stock, preferred stock, and additional paid-in capital) represent amounts invested in the corporation by stockholders and are sometimes referred to as *contributed capital.* On the other hand, the retained earnings (or earned capital) category of stockholders' equity represents the entity's cumulative earnings (net income over the life of the entity) less any dividends paid. Naturally, stockholders are interested in the relationship between paid-in capital and retained earnings. The higher the Retained Earnings account balance relative to paid-in capital amounts, the better—because retained earnings reflect, in part, management's ability to earn a return on invested (paid-in) amounts. However, a large retained earnings balance also may lead stockholders to pressure management and the board of directors to pay higher dividends. Remember to keep the distinction between paid-in capital and retained earnings in mind when interpreting the stockholders' equity section of any balance sheet.

Common Stock

LO 1

Describe the characteristics of common stock and show how common stock is presented in the balance sheet.

As already explained, **common stock** (called **capital stock** at times, especially when no other classes of stock are authorized) represents residual ownership. Common stockholders are the ultimate owners of the corporation; they have claim to all assets that remain in the entity after all liabilities and preferred stock claims (described in the next section) have been satisfied. In the case of bankruptcy or forced liquidation, this residual claim may not have any value because the liabilities and preferred stock claims may exceed the amount realized from the assets in liquidation. In this severe case, the liability of the common stockholders is limited to the amount they have invested in the stock; common stockholders cannot be forced by creditors and/or preferred stockholders to invest additional amounts to make up their losses. In the more positive (and usual) case, common stockholders prosper because the profits of the firm exceed the fixed claims of creditors (interest) and preferred stockholders (preferred dividends). All these profits accrue to common stockholders—there is no upper limit to the value of their ownership interest. Of course, it is the market value of common stock that reflects the public perception of profitability (or lack thereof) and ultimate dividend-paying capability of the corporation. However, as residual owners, common stockholders are not entitled to receive any specific dividend amount and may not receive any dividends at all in some years.

Common stockholders have the right and obligation to elect members to the corporation's board of directors. The election process can take one of two forms, as described in Business in Practice—Electing Directors. The board of directors hires

Exhibit 8-2

Financial Statements—
The Big Picture

Balance Sheet

Current Assets	Chapter	Current Liabilities	Chapter
Cash and cash equivalents	5, 9	Short-term debt	7
Short-term marketable securities	5	Current maturities of long-term debt	7
Accounts receivable	5, 9	Accounts payable	7
Notes receivable	5	Unearned revenue or deferred credits	7
Inventories	5, 9	Payroll taxes and other withholdings	7
Prepaid expenses	5	Other accrued liabilities	7
Noncurrent Assets		**Noncurrent Liabilities**	
Land	6	Long-term debt	7
Buildings and equipment	6	Deferred tax liabilities	7
Assets acquired by lease	6	Other long-term liabilities	7
Intangible assets	6	**Stockholders' Equity**	
Natural resources	6	Common stock	8
Other noncurrent assets	6	Preferred stock	8
		Additional paid-in capital	8
		Retained earnings	8
		Treasury stock	8
		Accumulated other comprehensive income (loss)	8
		Noncontrolling interest	8

Income Statement

	Chapter
Sales	5, 9
Cost of goods sold	5, 9
Gross profit (or gross margin)	5, 9
Selling, general, and administrative expenses	5, 6, 9
Income from operations	9
Gains (losses) on sale of assets	6, 9
Interest revenue	5, 9
Interest expense	7, 9
Income tax expense	7, 9
Unusual items	9
Net income	5, 6, 7, 8, 9
Earnings per share	9

Statement of Cash Flows

	Chapter
Operating Activities	
Net income	5, 6, 7, 8, 9
Depreciation expense	6, 9
(Gains) losses on sale of assets	6, 9
(Increase) decrease in current assets	5, 9
Increase (decrease) in current liabilities	7, 9
Investing Activities	
Proceeds from sale of property, plant, and equipment	6, 9
Purchase of property, plant, and equipment	6, 9
Financing Activities	
Proceeds from long-term debt*	7, 9
Repayment of long-term debt*	7, 9
Issuance of common stock and/or preferred stock	8, 9
Purchase of treasury stock	8, 9
Payment of dividends	8, 9

Primary topics of this chapter.
Other affected financial statement components.
* May include short-term debt items as well.

Electing Directors

Directors are elected by a **cumulative voting** procedure or on a slate basis. Under cumulative voting, each stockholder is entitled to cast a number of votes equal to the number of shares owned multiplied by the number of directors to be elected. Thus, if five directors are to be elected, the owner of 100 shares of common stock is entitled to 500 votes; all 500 can be cast for one candidate or 100 can be cast for each of five candidates or they can be cast in any combination between these extremes. In **slate voting**, the common stockholder is entitled to one vote for each share owned, but that vote is applied to an entire slate of candidates.

In most cases, the voting method doesn't affect the outcome. A committee of the board of directors nominates director candidates (equal to the number of directors to be elected), a proxy committee made up of members of the board seeks proxies from the stockholders, and the required number of nominees is duly elected. Occasionally, however, an outside group challenges the existing board; under these circumstances, the election can be exciting. Each group nominates director candidates and solicits stockholder votes. Under slate voting, the successful group will be the one that gets a majority of the vote; that group's entire slate will be elected. Of course, controlling 50.1 percent of the voting shares ensures success. Under cumulative voting, however, it is possible for a minority group of stockholders to concentrate their votes on one or two of their own candidates, thus making it easier to secure representation on the board of directors. For example, if five directors are to be elected, the votes of approximately 17 percent of the outstanding common stock are required to elect one director.

Many people, especially proponents of corporate democracy, favor cumulative voting. Some states require corporations organized under their laws to have cumulative voting for directors. Yet corporations often prefer to maintain a slate voting practice because this method makes getting a seat on the board more difficult for corporate raiders and others. Another tactic designed to reduce an outsider's chance of securing a director position is to provide for rolling terms. For example, for a nine-member board, three directors will be elected each year for a three-year term. Thus, even with cumulative voting, the votes of many more shares are required to elect one director than would be required if all nine directors were elected each year.

corporate officers, and the officers execute strategies for achieving corporate objectives. Some officers may also be directors (**inside directors**), but current practice is that most boards are made up primarily of **independent directors** (individuals not employed by the firm and, thus, also referred to as **outside directors**) who can bring an independent viewpoint to the considerations and deliberations of the board.

Common stockholders also must approve changes to the corporate charter (for example, when the number of shares of stock authorized is changed so that additional shares can be sold to raise more capital) and may have to approve transactions such as mergers or divestitures.

Common stock can have **par value** or it can be of a no-par-value variety. When it is used, par value is usually a nominal amount assigned to each share when the corporation is organized. In today's business world, par value has virtually no economic significance with respect to common stock. In most states, the par value of the issued shares represents the **legal capital** of the corporation. Most state corporation laws provide that stock with par value cannot be issued for a price less than par value, and they provide that total stockholders' equity cannot be reduced to less than legal capital by the distribution of dividends or the purchase from stockholders of previously issued shares of stock. If the stock has par value, the amount reported in the balance sheet in the Common Stock account will be the par value multiplied by the number of shares issued. Any difference between par value and the amount realized from the sale of the stock is recorded as additional paid-in capital. Some firms assign a **stated value** to the common stock, which is essentially par value by another name. If a firm issues true no-par-value stock, then the total amount received from the sale of the shares is recorded as common stock. Campbell Soup Company's capital stock has a par value of $0.0375 per share (see the appendix).

A survey of the 2011 annual reports (the last available data from the AICPA) of 500 publicly owned merchandising and manufacturing companies indicated that only 40 companies had no-par-value common stock. Of those 40 companies, 3 had an assigned or stated value per share.[1]

To illustrate the sale of common stock, assume that during the year ended August 31, 2020, Racers Inc. sold 40,000 additional shares of its $2 par value common stock at a price of $13 per share. The effect of this stock issue on the financial statements of Racers Inc. was as follows:

Balance Sheet		Income Statement	
Assets = Liabilities + Stockholders' equity		← Net income = Revenues − Expenses	
Cash	Common Stock		
+ 520,000	+ 80,000		
(40,000 shares × $13)	(40,000 shares × $2)		
	Additional Paid-In Capital		
	+ 440,000		
	(40,000 shares × $11)		

The entry to record this transaction follows:

```
Dr.  Cash (40,000 shares × $13) .................................   520,000
     Cr.  Common Stock (40,000 shares × $2) ......................            80,000
     Cr.  Additional Paid-In Capital (40,000 shares $11) .............        440,000
```

Refer to Exhibit 8-1 and notice that common stock and additional paid-in capital increased during 2020. (The remaining portion of these increases is explained in the stock dividends section of this chapter.)

On the balance sheet, the number of shares *authorized, issued,* and *outstanding* are disclosed. The number of **authorized shares** is stated in the corporate charter that is filed with the state of incorporation according to its laws regarding corporate organization. This represents the maximum number of shares that the corporation is legally approved to issue; an increase in the number of authorized shares requires shareholder approval. The number of **issued shares** is the number of shares of stock that have actually been transferred from the corporation to shareholders. Issued shares are ordinarily *sold* to stockholders for cash, although it is possible to issue stock in exchange for other assets or for services. The number of **outstanding shares** will be less than the number of issued shares if the firm has **treasury stock.** As explained in more detail later in this chapter, treasury stock is a firm's own stock that has been acquired by the firm from its stockholders. The relationship between these terms and the balance sheet disclosure required for each is summarized in Exhibit 8-3. The difference between the number of shares authorized and the number of shares issued represents the potential for additional shares to be issued.

---

[1] AICPA, *Accounting Trends and Techniques, U.S. GAAP Financial Statements—Best Practices in Presentation and Disclosure* (New York, 2012), Table 5-3.

Exhibit 8-3

Balance Sheet
Disclosure for Shares
of Stock

Terminology	Number of Shares Disclosed	Dollar Amount Disclosed
Shares authorized	Number specified in the corporate charter (maximum approved to be issued)	None
Shares issued	Number of shares that have been issued to stockholders (usually by sale)	Number of shares × par or stated value per share or If no par or stated value, total amount received from sale of shares
Shares outstanding	Number of shares still held by stockholders (shares issued less treasury shares)	None
Treasury stock	Number of issued shares that have been repurchased by the corporation from stockholders and not formally retired	Cost of treasury stock owned by corporation

The common stock of many firms has a **preemptive right,** which gives present shareholders the right to purchase additional shares from any new share issuances in proportion to their present percentage of ownership. The preemptive right is usually most significant in smaller, closely held corporations (those with only a few stockholders) in which existing stockholders want to prevent their ownership interest from being diluted. Even though they are not ordinarily bound by a preemptive right provision, many large corporations offer existing stockholders the right to purchase additional shares when more capital is needed. This maintains stockholder loyalty and can be a relatively inexpensive way to raise capital.

What Does It Mean?
Answers on page 318

1. What does it mean when common stock is referred to as part of paid-in capital?
2. What does it mean when the common stock of a corporation has a par value?
3. What does it mean when a corporation has treasury stock?

Preferred Stock

LO 2
Explain what preferred stock is, discuss what its advantages and disadvantages to the corporation are, and show how it is presented in the balance sheet.

Preferred stock is a class of paid-in capital that is different from common stock in that preferred stock has several debt-like features and a limited claim on assets in the event of liquidation. Also, in most cases, preferred stock does not have a voting privilege. (Common stock represents residual equity—it has claim to all assets remaining after the liabilities and preferred stock claims have been met in the liquidation of the corporation.) Historically, preferred stock has been viewed as having less risk than common stock. In the early years of the Industrial Revolution, when firms sought to raise the large amounts of capital required to finance factories and railroads, investors were more willing to acquire preferred stock in a firm than take the risks associated with common stock ownership. As firms have prospered and many investors have experienced the rewards of common stock ownership, preferred stock has become a less significant factor in the capital structure of many manufacturing, merchandising, and service firms. However, utilities and financial corporations continue to issue preferred stock.

The preferences for preferred stock, relative to common stock, relate to dividends and to the priority of claims on assets in the event of liquidation of the corporation. A **dividend** is a distribution of the earnings of the corporation to its owners/stockholders. The dividend requirement of preferred stock must be satisfied before a dividend can be paid to the common stockholders. Most preferred stock issues call for a quarterly or semiannual dividend, which must be kept current if there is to be a dividend on the common stock. The amount of the dividend is expressed in dollars and cents or as a percentage of the par value of the preferred stock. As shown in Exhibit 8-1, the preferred stock of Racers Inc. is referred to as "6%, $100 par value." This means that each share of preferred stock is entitled to an annual dividend of $6 (6% × $100). The same dividend result could have been accomplished by creating a $6 cumulative preferred stock. The terms of the stock issue will specify whether the dividend is to be paid at the rate of $1.50 per quarter, $3 semiannually, or $6 annually.

Preferred stock issues, including that of Racers Inc., usually provide a **cumulative dividend,** which means that if any dividend payments are not made to preferred stockholders, then the total amount of these missed dividends (or dividends in *arrears* from prior periods) must be paid subsequently before any dividends can be paid to the common stockholders. Occasionally, preferred stock issues have **participating dividends,** which means that after the common stockholders have received a specified dividend, any further dividends are shared by the preferred and common stockholders in a specified ratio. Calculation of preferred stock dividend amounts is illustrated in Exhibit 8-4.

A preferred stock issue's claim on the assets in the event of liquidation (**liquidating value**) or redemption (**redemption value**) is an amount specified when the preferred stock is issued. If the preferred stock has a par value, the liquidating value or redemption value usually is equal to the par value or the par value plus a slight premium. If the

---

Exhibit 8-4

Illustration of Preferred Stock Dividend Calculation

Case 1:
6%, $100 par value cumulative preferred stock, 50,000 shares authorized, issued, and outstanding. Dividend payable semiannually, no dividends in arrears.
Semiannual preferred dividend amount:

$$6\% \times \$100 \times 50{,}000 \text{ shares outstanding} \times 1/2 \text{ year} = \$150{,}000$$

Case 2:
$4.50, $75 par value cumulative preferred stock, 50,000 shares authorized and issued, 40,000 shares outstanding (there are 10,000 shares of treasury stock). Dividend payable quarterly, no dividends in arrears.
Quarterly preferred dividend amount:

$$\$4.50 \times 40{,}000 \text{ shares outstanding} \times 1/4 \text{ year} = \$45{,}000$$

Case 3:
8%, $50 par value cumulative preferred stock, 100,000 shares authorized, 60,000 shares issued, 54,000 shares outstanding (there are 6,000 shares of treasury stock). Dividend payable annually. Dividends were not paid in prior two years. Dividend required in current year to pay dividends in arrears and current year's preferred dividend:

$$8\% \times \$50 \times 54{,}000 \text{ shares outstanding} \times 3 \text{ years} = \$648{,}000$$

preferred stock has no par value, the liquidating value or redemption value is a stated amount. In either case, the claim in liquidation must be fulfilled before the common stockholders receive anything. However, after the liquidating claim is met, the preferred stockholders will not receive any additional amounts.

Callable preferred stock is redeemable (usually at a slight premium over par) at the option of the corporation. **Convertible preferred stock** may be exchanged for common stock of the corporation at the option of the stockholder at a conversion rate (such as six shares of common stock for each share of preferred stock) established when the preferred stock is authorized. For many firms, the call and conversion features of preferred stock cannot be exercised for a number of years after the authorization (or issue) date of the stock; such restrictions are specified in the stock certificate. Note in Exhibit 8-1 that the preferred stock of Racers Inc. is callable at a price of $102.

You probably have noticed that preferred stock has some of the same characteristics as bonds payable. Exhibit 8-5 summarizes the principal similarities and differences of the two. The tax deductibility of interest expense causes many financial managers to prefer debt to preferred stock. After all, they reason, if a fixed amount is going to have to be paid out regularly, it might as well be in the form of deductible interest rather than nondeductible preferred dividends. (As explained in Chapter 7, the after-tax cost of bonds paying 10 percent interest is only 7 percent for a corporation with an average tax rate of 30 percent.) Most investors also prefer bonds because the interest owed to them is a fixed claim that must be paid, but preferred stock dividends may be skipped, even though any arrearage may have to be paid before dividends can be paid on common stock. Of 500 publicly owned industrial and merchandising companies whose annual reports for 2011 were reviewed by the AICPA, only 35 had preferred stock outstanding.[2]

From a creditors' point of view, preferred stock reduces the risk associated with financial leverage (introduced in Chapter 7). Utilities and financial firms (such as banks, insurance companies, and finance companies) frequently have a significant portion of their stockholders' equity represented by preferred stock. This is because a significant proportion of the capital requirements of these firms is provided by investors who prefer the relative security of preferred stock rather than debt and/or common stock.

Exhibit 8-5

Comparison of Preferred Stock and Bonds Payable

Preferred Stock	Bonds Payable
Similarities	
• Dividend is (usually) a fixed claim to income.	• Interest is a fixed claim to income.
• Liquidating or redemption value is a fixed claim to assets.	• Maturity value is a fixed claim to assets.
• Is usually callable and may be convertible.	• Is usually callable and may be convertible.
Differences	
• Dividends may be skipped, even though they usually must be caught up before dividends can be paid on the common stock.	• Interest must be paid or firm faces legal action, possibly leading to bankruptcy.
• No maturity date.	• Principal must be paid at maturity.
• Dividends are not an expense and are not deductible for income tax purposes.	• Interest is an expense and is deductible for income tax purposes.

[2] Ibid., Table 5-4.

The balance sheet disclosures for preferred stock include the following:

- The par value and dividend rate (or the amount of the annual dividend requirement).
- The liquidation or redemption value.
- The number of shares authorized by the corporate charter.
- The number of shares issued.
- The number of shares outstanding.

Any difference between the number of shares issued and the number of shares outstanding is caused by shares held in the firm's treasury, referred to as *treasury stock* (although it is rare in practice to see preferred shares held as treasury stock). In addition, the amount of any preferred dividends that have been missed (that are in arrears) will be disclosed in the notes to the financial statements.

---

4. What does it mean when a corporation has preferred stock?

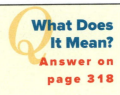

What Does It Mean?

Answer on page 318

Additional Paid-In Capital

As has already been illustrated, **additional paid-in capital** is a stockholders' equity category that reflects the excess of the amount received from the sale of preferred or common stock over par value. (Remember that the amount in the Common Stock and Preferred Stock accounts is equal to the par value per share multiplied by the number of shares issued, or the total amount received from the sale of no-par-value stock.) The Additional Paid-In Capital account is also used for other relatively uncommon capital transactions that cannot be reflected in the Common Stock or Preferred Stock accounts or that should not be reflected in Retained Earnings. **Capital in excess of par value** (or stated value) and *capital surplus* are terms sometimes used to describe additional paid-in capital. The latter term was widely used many years ago before the term *surplus* fell into disfavor because of its connotation as something "extra" and because uninformed financial statement readers might think that this amount was somehow available for dividends.

To summarize and emphasize, the total paid-in capital of a corporation represents the amount invested by the stockholders. If par value stock is involved, paid-in capital includes separate accounts to record the par value and additional paid-in capital components. If no-par-value stock is issued, paid-in capital is represented by the stock accounts alone.

Retained Earnings

Retained earnings reflect the cumulative earnings of the corporation that have been retained for use in the business rather than disbursed to the stockholders as dividends. *Retained earnings are not cash!* Retained earnings are increased by the firm's net income, and the accrual basis of accounting results in a net income amount that is different from the operating cash flows during a fiscal period. To the extent that operating results increase cash, that cash may be used for operating, investing, or financing activities.

Virtually the only factors affecting retained earnings are net income or net loss reported on the income statement, and dividends. (Remember that all revenue, expense, gain, and loss accounts reported on the income statement are indirect changes to the Retained Earnings account on the balance sheet. As these items are recorded throughout the year, retained earnings are, in effect, increased for revenues and gains and decreased for expenses and losses.)

Under certain very restricted circumstances, generally accepted accounting principles permit direct adjustments of retained earnings for the correction of errors (referred to as *prior period adjustments*). For example, if a firm neglected to include a significant amount of inventory in its year-end physical count and this error was not discovered until the following year, a direct adjustment to inventory and retained earnings would be appropriate. Likewise, retained earnings is adjusted for the retrospective application to prior periods' financial statements of most changes in accounting principles. For example, if a company changes from the LIFO to FIFO cost flow assumption, the financial statements of all prior years will be restated as if the FIFO method had always been in use. Such restatements require direct adjustments to retained earnings as well as other affected accounts. However, new information about an estimate made in a prior year (such as for depreciation or bad debts) does not warrant a direct entry to retained earnings because the amounts reported would have reflected the best information available at the time.

Accounting principles emphasize that the income statement is to reflect all transactions affecting stockholders' equity except for the following:

- Dividends to stockholders (which are a reduction in retained earnings).
- Transactions involving the corporation's own stock (which are reflected in the paid-in capital section of the balance sheet).
- Prior period adjustments for the correction of errors (which are direct adjustments to retained earnings).
- Most changes from one generally accepted accounting principle to another generally accepted accounting principle (which are direct adjustments to retained earnings).
- The four main components of accumulated other comprehensive income (which are accounted for within a separate category in stockholders' equity as explained later in this chapter).

If the Retained Earnings account has a negative balance because cumulative net losses and dividends have exceeded cumulative net income, this account is referred to as an **accumulated deficit.**

Cash Dividends

LO 3

Describe the accounting for a cash dividend and explain the dates involved in dividend transactions.

For a corporation to pay a cash dividend, it must meet several requirements: The firm must have retained earnings (although some state corporation laws permit the payment of dividends in excess of retained earnings if certain conditions are met), the board of directors must declare the dividend, and the firm must have enough cash to pay the dividend. If the firm has agreed in a bond indenture or other loan covenant to maintain certain minimum standards of financial health (perhaps a current ratio of at least 1.5:1.0), the dividend must not cause any of these measures to fall below their agreed-upon levels. From both the corporation's and the stockholders' perspectives, several key dates are related to the dividend (see Business in Practice—Dividend Dates). After the board of directors has declared the dividend, it becomes a legally enforceable liability of the corporation. The effects on the financial statements of recording the declaration and subsequent payment of a cash dividend are as follows:

Balance Sheet	Income Statement
Assets = Liabilities + Stockholders' equity	← Net income = Revenues − Expenses

Declaration date
    + Dividends   − Retained
        Payable   Earnings
 	
Payment date
− Cash   − Dividends
            Payable	

The journal entries follow:

On the declaration date:		
Dr. Retained Earnings	XX	
Cr. Dividends Payable		XX
On the payment date:		
Dr. Dividends Payable	XX	
Cr. Cash		XX

Note that *dividends are not an expense* and do not appear on the income statement. Dividends are a distribution of earnings of the corporation to its stockholders and are treated as a direct reduction of retained earnings. If a balance sheet is dated between the date the dividend is declared and the date it is paid, the Dividends Payable account will be included in the current liability section of the balance sheet.

---

5. What does it mean when a corporation's board of directors has declared a cash dividend?

What Does It Mean?

Answer on page 318

Stock Dividends and Stock Splits

In addition to a cash dividend, or sometimes instead of a cash dividend, a corporation may issue a **stock dividend.** A stock dividend is the issuance of additional shares of common stock to the existing stockholders in proportion to the number of shares each currently owns. It is expressed as a percentage; for example, a 5 percent stock dividend would result in the issuance of 5 percent of the previously issued shares. A stockholder who owns 100 shares would receive 5 additional shares of stock, but her proportionate ownership interest in the firm would not change. (Fractional shares are not issued, so an owner of 90 shares would receive 4 shares and cash equal to the market value of half of a share.)

The motivation for a stock dividend is usually to maintain the loyalty of stockholders when the firm does not have enough cash to pay (or increase) the cash dividend.

LO 4

Describe what stock dividends and stock splits are and discuss why each is used.

Business in
Practice

Dividend Dates

Three dates applicable to every dividend are the declaration date, the record date, and the payment date. In addition, there will be an ex-dividend date applicable to companies whose stock is publicly traded. There is no reason that the declaration, record, and payment dates for a closely held company couldn't be the same date.

The **declaration date** is the date on which the board of directors declares the dividend and it becomes a legal liability to be paid. The **record date** is used to determine who receives the dividend; the person listed on the stockholder records of the corporation on the record date is considered the owner of the shares. The stockholder of record is the person to whom the check is made payable and mailed to on the **payment date.** If shares have been sold privately but the ownership change has not yet been noted on the corporation's records, the prior stockholder (the one in the records) receives the dividend (and may have to settle with the new owner, depending on their agreement with respect to the dividend). The **ex-dividend date** relates to this issue of who receives the dividend. When the stock of a publicly traded company is bought or sold, the seller has a settlement period of two business days in which to deliver the stock certificate. The buyer also has two business days to pay for the purchase. Thus, the stock trades "ex-dividend" two business days before the record date to give the corporation a chance to increase the accuracy of its ownership records. On the ex-dividend date, the stock trades without the dividend (the seller retains the right to receive the dividend if the stock is sold on or after the ex-dividend date). If the stock is sold before the ex-dividend date, the buyer is entitled to receive the dividend. All other things being equal, the price of the stock in the market falls by the amount of the dividend on the ex-dividend date.

There is no specific requirement dealing with the number of days that should elapse between the declaration, record, and payment dates for publicly traded stocks. It is not unusual for two to four weeks to elapse between each date.

Although many stockholders like to receive a stock dividend, such a distribution is not income to the stockholders. To understand why there is no income to stockholders, the impact of the stock dividend must be understood from the issuing corporation's point of view. A stock dividend does not cause any change in either assets or liabilities; therefore, it cannot affect *total* stockholders' equity. However, additional shares of stock are issued, and the Common Stock account must be increased by the number of shares issued multiplied by par value per share. Because the issuance of shares is called a *dividend,* it is also appropriate for the Retained Earnings account to be reduced. The amount of the reduction in retained earnings is the number of dividend shares issued multiplied by the market price per share. Any difference between market price and par value is recorded in the Additional Paid-In Capital account. If the shares are without par value, then the Common Stock account is increased by the market value of the dividend shares issued.

To illustrate the effects of a stock dividend transaction, assume that during the year ended August 31, 2020, Racers Inc. issued a 2 percent stock dividend on its $2 par value common stock when the market price was $15 per share. Refer back to Exhibit 8-1 and assume further that the stock dividend occurred at some point after the additional 40,000 shares of common stock had been issued. Thus, a total of

4,800 dividend shares were issued (2% × 240,000 shares previously issued). Using the horizontal model, here is the effect on the financial statements:

Balance Sheet	Income Statement
Assets = Liabilities + Stockholders' equity	← Net income = Revenues − Expenses
Retained Earnings − 72,000 (4,800 shares × $15) Common Stock + 9,600 (4,800 shares × $2) Additional Paid-In Capital + 62,400 (4,800 shares × $13)	

The entry to record this transaction follows:

Dr. Retained Earnings (4,800 shares × $15)	72,000	
Cr. Common Stock (4,800 shares × $2)		9,600
Cr. Additional Paid-In Capital (4,800 shares × $13)		62,400

Note that the stock dividend affects *only* the stockholders' equity of the firm. *Capitalizing retained earnings* is the term sometimes used to refer to the effect of a stock dividend transaction because the dividend permanently transfers some retained earnings to paid-in capital. The income statement is not affected because the transaction is between the corporation and its stockholders (who own the corporation); no gain or loss can result from a capital transaction.

If the stock dividend percentage is more than 20 to 25 percent, only the par value or stated value of the additional common shares issued is transferred from retained earnings to common stock.

What happens to the market value of a share of stock when a firm issues a stock dividend? Is the share owner any wealthier? As already explained, nothing happens to the firm's assets, liabilities, or earning power as a result of the stock dividend; so the *total* market value of the firm should not change. Because more shares of stock are now outstanding and the total market value of all the shares remains the same, the market value of each share will drop. This is why the stock dividend does not represent income to the stockholder. However, under some circumstances the market value per share of the common stock will not settle at its theoretically lower value. This will be true especially if the cash dividend per share is not adjusted to reflect the stock dividend. Thus, if the firm had been paying a cash dividend of $1 per share before the stock dividend, and the same cash dividend rate of $1 per share is continued, there has been an effective increase in the dividend rate simply because each shareholder now owns more shares; the stock price will probably rise to reflect this "good news" to investors.

Sometimes the managers of a firm want to lower the market price of the firm's common stock by a significant amount because they believe that a stock trading in a price range of $20 to $60 per share is a more popular investment than a stock priced at more than $60 per share. A **stock split** will accomplish this objective. A stock split involves issuing additional shares to existing stockholders and, if the stock has a par value, the par value is typically reduced proportionately. For example, if a firm had 60,000 shares of $10 par value stock outstanding, with stock trading in the market at a price of $80 per share, a 4-for-1 stock split would involve issuing three additional shares to each stockholder for each share owned. Then the stockholder who had owned 200 shares would receive an additional 600 shares, bringing the total shares owned to 800. As in the case of a stock dividend, nothing has happened to the assets or liabilities of the firm, so nothing can happen to stockholders' equity. The total market value of the company would not change, but the market price of each share would fall. (Compare the results of 60,000 shares × $80 to 240,000 shares × $20.) No accounting entry is required for a stock split. However, the common stock caption of stockholders' equity indicates the drop in par value per share (if appropriate) and the proportionate increase in the number of shares authorized, issued, and outstanding. If the corporation has used no-par-value stock, only the number of shares changes.

Sometimes a stock split is accomplished in the form of a very large (perhaps 100 percent) stock dividend. As explained earlier, when this happens only the par or stated value of the additional shares issued is transferred from Retained Earnings to the Common Stock account. There is no adjustment to the par value of the stock.

A *reverse stock split* (sometimes called a *share consolidation*) is unusual but may occur when the market price of a firm's common stock has settled at a lower level than management thinks appropriate. Suppose that a stock is trading at $12 per share, and historically it has traded in the $50 to $70 range. A 1-for-5 reverse stock split would reduce the number of shares outstanding to 20 percent of the pre-reverse split quantity, and the market price per share would be expected to increase by a factor of 5, or to approximately $60 in this case. Again, no accounting entries are required for this event, but par value would increase by a factor of 5 and the number of shares authorized, issued, and outstanding would decrease by a factor of 5. The use of reverse splits is extremely uncommon in practice, although this method of price adjustment has been used in the technology, insurance, and banking sectors from time to time. For example, AIG announced a 1-for-20 reverse stock split in 2009 following the market meltdown brought on by the 2008 financial crisis. Likewise, as a result of the lingering effects of the financial crisis, Citigroup Inc.'s shareholders approved a 1-for-10 reverse stock split in 2011. In 2017, Frontier Communications Corp. did 1-for-15 share consolidation, and Xerox Corp. issued a 1-for-4 reverse stock split.

What Does It Mean?

Answers on pages 318–319

6. What does it mean when a corporation's board of directors has declared a stock dividend on the common stock?

7. What does it mean when a corporation has a stock split?

Accumulated Other Comprehensive Income (Loss)

At first glance, it may seem surprising to find the word *income* in the stockholders' equity section of the balance sheet. To put the *comprehensive income* concept into perspective, think back to Chapter 2, where the link between the income statement and balance sheet was first established. Recall that net income is added to retained

Don't be confused by the complicated language used to describe stockholders' equity accounts in annual reports! Just as there are many different types of assets (cash, inventory, land, and so forth), there are also many different forms of ownership (common, preferred, and so on). For most decisions made by financial statement users, having a basic understanding of the broad categories is enough.

Study

Suggestion

earnings within the stockholders' equity section of the balance sheet at the end of each accounting period. This is done through the closing process described in Chapter 4, which emphasizes that income statement accounts are temporary in nature—that is, revenues, gains, expenses, and losses are (in effect) subcategories of stockholders' equity that are "closed" to retained earnings at the end of the accounting period. The balance sheet equation (A = L + SE) and the horizontal model (where net income points back to stockholders' equity) both reinforce this fundamental relationship: *All items of income (or loss) ultimately affect stockholders' equity on the balance sheet.* This is the reason the word *income* appears in this section of the balance sheet.

LO 5
Recognize what the components of accumulated other comprehensive income (loss) are and explain why these items appear in stockholders' equity.

Up until now, stockholders' equity has been described as being composed of two distinct categories: paid-in capital (*contributed* capital such as common and preferred stock) and retained earnings (*earned* capital from cumulative net income in excess of dividends paid). Unfortunately the line between these two is often blurry—and at times, neither category adequately describes certain changes in stockholders' equity. The FASB and its predecessors have debated for years over which items should be included in "net income" for the period (and therefore added to retained earnings) and which items should bypass the income statement and be accounted for directly within the stockholders' equity section of the balance sheet. As a result, several exceptions to the preceding dichotomy were carved out over the years, resulting in a wide array of financial reporting practices among real-world companies.

To improve comparability between firms, the FASB issued an accounting standard in 1997 that defined the term *comprehensive income (loss)* as including all nonshareholder changes in equity. These changes, as amended by subsequent FASB *Accounting Standards Codification Updates* (see ASC 220), include the following classifications:

1. Net income (as reported on the income statement).
2. Cumulative foreign currency translation adjustments.
3. Unrealized gains or losses on available-for-sale investments.
4. Changes during the period in certain pension or other postretirement benefit items.
5. Gains or losses on certain derivative instruments.

A new category of stockholders' equity, referred to as **accumulated other comprehensive income (loss),** was established by this 1997 standard to include items 2 through 5 (as amended) from the preceding list; each of these items is reported net of related income taxes. Note, however, that there is no longer an available-for-sale classification for equity securities if the fair value of these securities can be readily determined; thus, changes in the fair value of such investments will flow through the income statement for fiscal years beginning after December 15. 2017, rather than being included as a component of accumulated other comprehensive income.

Firms are allowed considerable flexibility in *how* other comprehensive income is reported in the financial statements. Alternatives range from extending the income statement to append this information, to reporting line-item details within the stockholders' equity section of the balance sheet (or in a separate statement of stockholders' equity), to reporting only the net accumulated other comprehensive income or loss in the balance sheet and disclosing line-item details in the notes to the financial statements. Campbell's reports the net amount in its balance sheet and provides line-item details in the notes to the financial statements (see Note 4 in the 2017 annual report in the appendix).

Campbell's

Observe that the common characteristic of the four primary items that compose "other comprehensive income" is that each involves *unrealized* changes in stockholders' equity. Because the accounting treatment accorded to each item is essentially the same, only the cumulative foreign currency translation adjustments are explained here.

Cumulative Foreign Currency Translation Adjustment   When the financial statements of a foreign subsidiary are consolidated with those of its U.S. parent company, the financial statements of the subsidiary (originally expressed in the currency of the country in which it operates) must be converted to U.S. dollars. This conversion process is referred to as *foreign currency translation.* Because of the mechanics used in the translation process and because exchange rates fluctuate over time, a debit or credit difference between the translated value of the subsidiary's assets and liabilities and the translated value of the subsidiary's stockholders' equity arises in the translation and consolidation process. Prior to 1981, this debit or credit difference was reported as a loss or gain in the consolidated income statement and, thus, affected net income and retained earnings each year. Because of large gyrations in exchange rates, a firm might have reported a large translation gain in one year and an equally large translation loss in the next year. The translation gain or loss had a material effect on reported results but did not have a significant economic impact because the gain or loss was never actually realized. In fact, the difference between the value of the subsidiaries as measured in U.S. dollars versus foreign currency units will *never* be realized unless the foreign subsidiaries are sold, and there is usually no intention on the part of management to do so. Therefore, the FASB issued an accounting standard that required firms to report the translation gain or loss as a separate account within stockholders' equity rather than as a gain or loss in the income statement. The effect of this accounting standard was to make reported net income more meaningful and to highlight as a separate item in stockholders' equity the cumulative translation adjustment. [This 1981 FASB standard is still in effect, but the cumulative translation gain or loss is now reported as a component of the "accumulated other comprehensive income (loss)" in stockholders' equity.] To the extent that exchange rates of the U.S. dollar rise and fall relative to the foreign currencies involved, the amount of this **cumulative foreign currency translation adjustment** will fluctuate over time. Because the account balance represents a cumulative amount over time, it can and often does swing back and forth from a debit (net cumulative loss) balance, which reduces stockholders' equity, to a credit (net cumulative gain) balance, which increases stockholders' equity. This treatment of the translation adjustment is consistent with the going concern concept because as long as the entity continues to operate with foreign subsidiaries, the translation adjustment will not be realized.

As shown in Exhibits 8-1 and 8-6, the $100,000 accumulated other comprehensive loss for Racers Inc. became a $50,000 accumulated gain as a result of a $150,000 net movement in the cumulative foreign currency translation adjustment during the year ended August 31, 2020.

Exhibit 8-6 Statement of Changes in Stockholders' Equity

RACERS, INC.
Statement of Changes in Stockholders' Equity
For the Year Ended August 31, 2020

	Preferred Stock		Common Stock		Additional Paid-In Capital $	Retained Earnings $	Accumulated Other Comprehensive Income (Loss) $	Common Treasury Stock	
	No. of Shares	$	No. of Shares	$				No. of Shares	$
Balance, August 31, 2019	5,000	$500,000	200,000	$400,000	$2,820,000	$2,600,000	$(100,000)	—	—
Sale of common stock			40,000	80,000	440,000				
Purchase of common treasury stock								1,000	$12,000
Net income						390,000			
Cash dividends:									
Preferred stock						(30,000)			
Common stock						(60,000)			
Stock dividend:									
2% on 240,000 shares when market value was $15 per share			4,800	9,600	62,400	(72,000)			
Net movement in cumulative foreign currency translation adjustment							150,000		
Balance, August 31, 2020	5,000	$500,000	244,800	$489,600	$3,322,400	$2,828,000	$ 50,000	1,000	$12,000

Treasury Stock

LO 6

Explain what treasury stock is, discuss why it is acquired, and show how treasury stock transactions affect stockholders' equity.

Many corporations will, from time to time, purchase shares of their own stock. Any class of stock that is outstanding can be acquired as treasury stock. Rather than being retired, this stock is held for future use for employee stock purchase plans or acquisitions of other companies or is even held to be resold for cash if additional capital is needed. Sometimes treasury stock is acquired as a defensive move to thwart a takeover by another company, and frequently, treasury shares are purchased with excess cash because the market price is low and the company wants to shrink the supply of its own stock in the market. Whatever the motivation, the purchase of treasury stock is in effect a partial liquidation of the firm because the firm's assets are used to reduce the number of shares of stock outstanding. For this reason, treasury stock is not reflected in the balance sheet as an asset; it is instead reported as a contra stockholders' equity account (i.e., treasury stock is deducted from the sum of paid-in capital and retained earnings).

Because treasury stock transactions are capital transactions (between the corporation and its stockholders), the income statement is never affected by the purchase or sale of treasury stock. When treasury stock is acquired, it is recorded at cost. When treasury stock is sold, any difference between its cost and the consideration received is recorded in the Additional Paid-In Capital account. As can be seen in Exhibit 8-1, Racers Inc. purchased 1,000 shares of its own common stock at a total cost of $12,000 during the year ended August 31, 2020. The effect of this transaction on the financial statements was as follows:

Balance Sheet	Income Statement
Assets = Liabilities + Stockholders' equity	← Net income = Revenues − Expenses
Cash − 12,000 Treasury Stock (A contra stockholders' equity account) − 12,000	

The entry to record this purchase looks like this:

Dr. Treasury Stock	12,000	
Cr. Cash		12,000
Purchase of 1,000 shares of treasury stock at a cost of $12 per share.		

If 500 shares of this treasury stock were sold at a price of $15 per share in fiscal 2021, the effect on the financial statements of recording the sale would be as follows:

Balance Sheet	Income Statement
Assets = Liabilities + Stockholders' equity	← Net income = Revenues − Expenses
Cash + 7,500 Treasury Stock + 6,000 Additional Paid-In Capital + 1,500	

Here would be the entry:

Dr. Cash	7,500	
Cr. Treasury Stock.......................................		6,000
Cr. Additional Paid-In Capital		1,500
Sale of 500 shares of treasury stock at a price of $15 per share.		

Cash dividends are not paid on treasury stock. However, stock dividends are issued on treasury stock, and stock splits also affect treasury stock.

For many companies, the dollar amount reported for treasury stock represents a significant reduction in total stockholders' equity. Because treasury stock purchases are recorded at the market price per share, it is not uncommon to find the negative amount reported for treasury stock to exceed the positive stockholders' equity amounts reported for common stock and additional paid-in capital. Why? Suppose that 1,000 shares of no par common stock were issued in 1990 at the prevailing market price of $15 per share. These shares remained outstanding until 2019, when 300 shares were purchased as treasury stock for $80 per share. The $15,000 historical cost of common stock (credit balance) would now be offset by a $24,000 reduction for treasury stock (debit balance). To avoid the confusion that such a situation may cause investors, treasury stock is reported at the bottom of the stockholders' equity section of the balance sheet as an overall negative amount rather than being shown as a direct reduction of total paid in capital. Many successful real-world corporations, such as Coca-Cola, McDonald's, General Electric, and ExxonMobil, reported treasury stock in excess of total paid-in capital in 2017 because of recent share repurchases. Coca-Cola's $50.7 billion of treasury stock was 2.9 times greater than its common stock and additional paid-in capital combined. The primary culprit in this accounting anomaly is, of course, the cost principle.

In recent years many such firms have curtailed their plans to issue new shares while also becoming active market participants in the previously issued shares of their own common stock. This "share buyback" strategy protects existing stockholders from the potential dilution of their ownership interests. Moreover, because treasury stock purchases do not affect net income, ROE is increased due to the reduction in stockholders' equity caused by recording treasury stock purchases.

To summarize and emphasize, you should understand that cash dividends are not paid on treasury stock because the company cannot pay a dividend to itself. However, stock dividends are issued on treasury stock, and stock splits affect treasury stock. What this means, in practical terms, is that cash dividends are based on the number of shares outstanding, whereas stock dividends and stock splits are based on the number of shares previously issued.

Reporting Changes in Stockholders' Equity Accounts

It is appropriate that the reasons for changes to any stockholders' equity account during a fiscal period be presented in the balance sheet, in a separate statement of changes in stockholders' equity, or in the notes to the financial statements. One possible format for a statement of changes in stockholders' equity is presented for Racers Inc. in Exhibit 8-6. (Amounts for net income and dividends on common stock are assumed. You should prove to yourself the amount of the cash dividends on the preferred stock.)

LO 7

Show how stockholders' equity transactions for the year are reported in the financial statements.

Exhibit 8-7

Statement of Changes
in Retained Earnings

RACERS, INC. Statement of Changes in Retained Earnings For the Year Ended August 31, 2020	
Retained earnings balance, beginning of year	$2,600,000
Add: Net income	390,000
Less: Cash dividends:	
Preferred stock	(30,000)
Common stock	(60,000)
2% stock dividend on common stock	(72,000)
Retained earnings balance, end of year	$2,828,000

Alternative formats may be used; this statement is often referred to as the *statement of stockholders' equity,* or *statement of equity.*

Even if there are no changes to the paid-in capital accounts and there is no treasury stock or foreign subsidiary, an analysis of retained earnings is presented. This can be done in a separate statement, as illustrated for Racers Inc. in Exhibit 8-7, or by appending the beginning balance, dividend, and ending balance information to the bottom of the income statement, which then becomes a combined statement of income and retained earnings.

Campbell's

Note that Campbell's presents Consolidated Statements of Equity in its 2017 annual report within the appendix. What approach is used in the other annual reports that you have?

Noncontrolling Interest

LO 8

Explain what non-controlling interest is, why it arises, and what it means in the balance sheet.

As discussed in Chapter 7, a noncontrolling interest, sometimes called a minority interest, is the portion of equity in a subsidiary not attributable, directly or indirectly, to the parent company (reporting entity). It arises in the *consolidation* process, as described below, and signifies to investors and others interested in the financial statements of the reporting entity that a portion of the net assets controlled by the reporting entity are attributable to the ownership interests of outside, non-related parties.

Recall from Chapter 2 (See Business in Practice—Parent and Subsidiary Corporations) that a subsidiary is a corporation that is more than 50 percent owned and controlled by the firm for which the financial statements have been prepared. The financial statements of the parent company and its reported subsidiary(ies) are combined through the consolidation process. The resulting financial statements are referred to as the **consolidated financial statements** of the parent and subsidiary companies. Although separate legal entities, they are treated for financial reporting purposes as though they are one economic entity that is under the common control of the parent company's board and management team. In consolidation, most of the assets and liabilities of the parent and subsidiary companies are added together. Reciprocal amounts (such as a parent's account receivable from a subsidiary and the subsidiary's matching account payable to the parent) are eliminated, or offset. Likewise, the parent's investment in a subsidiary (an asset) is offset against the stockholders' equity of the subsidiary.

Noncontrolling interest arises in the consolidation process when a subsidiary is not 100 percent owned by the parent company. As such, the parent's investment asset will be less than the total stockholders' equity of the subsidiary. Noncontrolling interest is the equity of the other (minority) stockholders in the net assets of the subsidiary.

This amount does not represent what the parent company would have to pay to acquire the rest of the stock of the subsidiary, nor is it a liability in the true sense of the term. Instead, noncontrolling shareholders have an ongoing equity interest in the subsidiary's net assets and thus indirectly can be said to have an equity claim in the consolidated net assets. The noncontrolling interest equity reported on a consolidated balance sheet is included because all of the subsidiary's assets and liabilities (except those eliminated to avoid double counting) have been added to the parent company's assets and liabilities, but only the parent company's share of the subsidiary's stockholders' equity is represented in the consolidated stockholders' equity total. To keep the balance sheet in balance, the noncontrolling stockholders' portion of the stockholders' equity of the subsidiary must be shown.

As per the FASB's reporting requirements (see FASB ASC 810), the ownership interests in subsidiaries held by parties other than the parent must be clearly identified, labeled, and presented in the consolidated balance sheet within equity, but separate from the parent's equity. The effect of this standard is to create, for financial reporting purposes, a new classification scheme allowing the balance sheet model to be *thought of* as being expanded as follows:

LO 9
Discuss how the presence of a noncontrolling interest affects the presentation of consolidated financial statements.

$$\text{Assets} = \text{Liabilities} + (\text{Stockholders' Equity} + \text{Nonowners' Equity})$$

The use of captions such as "Stockholders' Equity" or "Shareholders' Equity" as the lead description for this section of the consolidated balance sheet is no longer appropriate. Instead, the broader term "Equity" is now commonly used, which includes both stockholders' equity and noncontrolling interest, as shown in Exhibit 8-8 for Racers Inc. (using assumed amounts for total assets, total liabilities, and noncontrolling interest).

Exhibit 8-8

Equity Section of Racers Inc. Consolidated Balance Sheet at August 31, 2020

RACERS INC. Consolidated Balance Sheet August 31, 2020	
Assets:	
Total assets	$12,950,000
Liabilities:	
Total liabilities	$ 5,510,000
Equity:	
Racers Inc.'s Stockholders' Equity:	
Preferred stock 6%, $100 par value	$ 500,000
Common stock, $1 par value	489,600
Additional paid-in capital	3,322,400
Retained earnings	2,828,000
Accumulated other comprehensive income (loss)	50,000
Less: Common stock in treasury, at cost	(12,000)
Total Racers Inc. stockholders' equity	$ 7,178,000
Noncontrolling interest	$ 262,000
Total equity	$ 7,440,000
Total liabilities and equity	$12,950,000

In this presentation of the equity section of Racers Inc.'s consolidated balance sheet, no subtotal is shown for Total Paid-In Capital. Many companies will, however, continue to categorize the parent company's stockholders' equity section into the paid-in capital and earned capital components.

The Statement of Changes in Stockholders' Equity for Racers Inc., as depicted in Exhibit 8-6, would be renamed the Consolidated Statement of Changes in Equity, reflecting the fact that both stockholders' and nonowners' equity is represented. Of course, a column for noncontrolling interest would be added as well (normally as the rightmost column), and the parent company's equity accounts would be separately identified and totaled, so that the reader could clearly distinguish the parent company's equity from the noncontrolling interest equity.

What Does It Mean?
Answer on page 319

8. What does it mean when noncontrolling interest is reported in the consolidated balance sheet?

Owners' Equity for Other Types of Entities

Proprietorships and Partnerships

The discussion in this chapter has focused on the owners' equity of corporations, which is referred to as *stockholders' equity.* Neither proprietorships nor partnerships (single and multiple-owner unincorporated businesses, respectively) issue stock, and a distinction between invested capital and retained earnings is not usually made. Owners' equity of these firms is usually referred to as *capital,* as in "Andrew Wiggins, Capital" in the case of a proprietorship, or as "Partners' Capital" in the case of a partnership. For a small partnership, the capital account balance of each partner may be listed separately in the balance sheet. For a partnership with many partners, the capital interest of each may be expressed in "units" or "shares" representing proportional interest, but these shares do not carry the same legal rights as capital stock of a corporation. In fact, partnership shares are frequently used *only* for profit and loss distribution purposes; each partner ordinarily has an equal voice in the management of the firm. The partnership agreement normally specifies how the profits and losses of the partnership are to be allocated to individual partners. Distributions to the owner or owners during the year, including any salaries paid to the proprietor or partners, are treated as reductions of owners' equity rather than expenses. These amounts are frequently accumulated in a "drawing" account, which is similar to the dividends account for a corporation. The statement of changes in owners' equity for the year reports the beginning capital balance, additional capital investments, net income or loss for the year, and capital withdrawals (drawings) to arrive at the ending capital balance.

Not-for-Profit and Governmental Organizations

These types of organizations do not have owners who have *direct* financial interests in the entities. The financial reporting requirements are therefore focused on resource providers (such as taxpayers or donors), rather than investors. Owners' equity in these organizations is referred to as *fund balance.* Because individual resource providers do not have specific claims against the organization's assets, capital accounts are inappropriate, and net income is not reported for most funds. There is usually an operating (or current) fund, and there are frequently several restricted funds for enhancing accountability for certain assets. For example, a university would account for tuition income and operating expenses in its current fund. Money that is donated for student scholarships is accounted for in a restricted fund to help ensure that it is used for its intended purpose. Other funds frequently used are an endowment fund, loan fund, plant fund, and debt retirement fund. The transactions that affect these funds are nonoperating in nature, and specific accountability is required. The statement of owners' equity is called the *statement of changes in fund balances,* which summarizes the activities of each fund. Changes during the year include the excess (or deficiency) of operating revenues over (under) operating expenditures; increases from contributions, grants, or other support; decreases from nonoperating transactions; and transfers to and from other funds. This statement is similar in purpose and content to the statement of stockholders' equity of a corporation and is just as easy to understand.

Demonstration Problem

The Demonstration Problem walkthrough for this chapter is available in *Connect.*

Summary

This chapter described the accounting for and presentation of the following stockholders' equity accounts. (Note that except for the fact that net income is added to retained earnings, transactions affecting stockholders' equity do not affect the income statement.)

Balance Sheet	Income Statement
Assets = Liabilities + Stockholders' equity	← Net income = Revenues − Expenses
Preferred Stock	
Common Stock	
Additional Paid-In Capital	
Retained Earnings	← Net income
Accumulated Other Comprehensive Income (Loss)	
(Treasury Stock)	
Noncontrolling Interest	

Stockholders' equity is also referred to as *net assets.* For single proprietorships and partnerships, the term *capital* is used instead of stockholders' equity. For a corporation, the components of stockholders' equity are paid-in capital, retained earnings, accumulated other comprehensive income (loss), and treasury stock.

Paid-in capital always includes common stock and may include preferred stock and additional paid-in capital. Common stock represents the basic ownership of the corporation. Common stock may have a par value or may have no par value. Additional paid-in capital represents the difference between the par (or stated) value of common stock issued and the total amount paid in to the corporation when the stock was issued. If no-par-value common stock has no stated value, the total amount paid in to the corporation when the stock was issued is reported as the dollar amount of common stock. The principal right and obligation of the common stockholders is to elect the board of directors of the corporation. Voting for directors can be on either a cumulative basis or a slate basis. **(LO 1)**

Preferred stock is different from common stock in that preferred stockholders have a prior claim to dividends and a prior claim on assets when the corporation is liquidated. In most cases, preferred stock does not have a voting privilege. Preferred stock is in some respects similar to bonds payable. However, the most significant difference between the two is that interest on bonds is a tax-deductible expense, whereas dividends on preferred stock are a nondeductible distribution of the corporation's earnings. **(LO 2)**

Retained earnings represent the cumulative earnings reinvested in the business. If earnings are not reinvested, they are distributed to stockholders as dividends. Retained earnings are not cash. The Retained Earnings account is increased by net income and decreased by dividends (and by a net loss).

Dividends are declared by the board of directors and paid to stockholders as of the record date. Although cash dividends can be paid with any frequency, quarterly or semi-annual dividend payments are most common. Stock dividends represent the issuance of additional shares of stock to stockholders in proportion to the number of shares owned on the record date. Stock dividends do not affect the assets, liabilities, or total stockholders' equity of the firm but do transfer an amount of retained earnings to paid-in capital. Stock dividends are expressed as a percentage of the number of pre-dividend shares issued, and that percentage is usually relatively small (less than 20 percent). **(LO 3, 4)**

Stock splits also involve issuing additional shares of stock to stockholders in proportion to the number of shares owned on the record date—but usually result in at least doubling the number of shares held by each stockholder. Stock splits are expressed as a ratio of the number of shares held after the split to the number held before the split (e.g., 2-for-1). The reason for (and effect of) a stock split is to reduce the market value per share of the stock. Reverse stock splits occur on occasion for just the opposite reason—to increase market value per share of the issuer's stock. **(LO 4)**

The cumulative foreign currency translation adjustment is an amount reported in stockholders' equity of corporations having foreign subsidiaries. The adjustment arises in the process of translating the financial statements of subsidiaries (expressed in foreign currency units) to U.S. dollars. Because exchange rates can fluctuate widely, net income could be distorted if this adjustment were reported in the income statement. To avoid this distortion, the adjustment is reported in stockholders' equity as a component of accumulated other comprehensive income (loss). **(LO 5)**

Treasury stock is the corporation's own stock that has been purchased from stockholders and is being held in the treasury for future reissue or other use. Treasury stock is reported as a contra stockholders' equity account. When treasury stock is reissued at a price different from its cost, no gain or loss is recognized, but paid-in capital is affected. **(LO 6)**

Noncontrolling interest, sometimes called minority interest, is the portion of equity in a subsidiary not owned by the parent company (reporting entity). This item must be presented in the consolidated balance sheet within equity, but separate from the parent's equity. **(LO 8, 9)**

Stockholders' equity captions usually seen in a balance sheet include these:

1. Paid-in capital:
   a. Preferred stock (sometimes issued)
   b. Common stock (always issued)
   c. Additional paid-in capital
2. Retained earnings (accumulated deficit if negative)
3. Accumulated other comprehensive income (loss)
4. Less: Treasury stock
5. Noncontrolling interest (which is actually the equity interest held by *nonowners* of the reporting entity) **(LO 7)**

It is possible that a firm may have only common stock (sometimes called *capital stock*) and retained earnings as components of stockholders' equity.

Changes in stockholders' equity (and sometimes nonowners' equity) usually are reported in a comprehensive statement that summarizes the changes of each element of equity. However, if there have not been significant changes in paid-in capital accounts, a statement of changes in retained earnings may be presented by itself. Sometimes the statement of changes in retained earnings is combined with the income statement. **(LO 7)**

Proprietorships, partnerships, and not-for-profit organizations report changes in equity using terminology unique to each type of entity. In the final analysis, the purpose of this statement for these entities is the same as for corporations: to explain the change in net assets of the entity during the reporting period.

Refer to Campbell Soup Company's balance sheets and statements of equity in the appendix, and to other financial statements you may have, and observe how information about stockholders' equity is presented.

Campbell's

Appendix TO CHAPTER EIGHT

Personal Investing

An exciting milestone in any individual's financial life is the beginning of a personal investment program in stocks, bonds, and other securities. A number of questions about one's capability to accept the risks involved must be answered before an investment plan is put into action; it is appropriate for most people to consult a trusted financial adviser to help them understand and answer those questions and to establish a sensible plan.

One investment medium appropriate for many people is an investment company, or mutual fund. Investors purchase shares of the mutual fund, which uses the money received from investors to purchase shares of common stock, preferred stock, and/or bonds. In essence, each investor owns a share of the portfolio of securities owned by the mutual fund. Shares in some mutual funds are purchased through a registered representative employed by a brokerage firm, and in other cases the investor purchases shares directly from the mutual fund. You should understand that not all mutual funds are alike in their operating and investing objectives. Thus, an individual investor should carefully define her own objectives and *then* select a fund that invests in a portfolio of securities consistent with her own views. Whether dealing through a broker or directly with the mutual fund, an investor will receive a prospectus that describes the fund, the costs related to investing in the fund, its operating and investment policies, and the risks to which an investment is exposed.

An alternative method of investing is to make direct purchases of specific corporate securities. This is usually done by opening an account with a brokerage firm, although an employee can invest in the stock of his own employer through a 401(k) plan without having to go through a broker. By taking this approach, the investor has direct ownership of individual stocks and bonds rather than an interest in a portfolio of securities owned by a mutual fund. A prospectus describing the securities purchased and risks involved is *not* furnished when an investor acquires previously issued shares traded on a stock exchange or in the over-the-counter market.

A full discussion of investment characteristics, risks, and alternatives is beyond the scope of this book. It is appropriate to understand the terminology, concepts, and financial reporting practices described here before starting an investment program. Online investing is perhaps the quickest, easiest, and most affordable way to get started. Check out some of the investing sites listed in Exhibit 8-9, especially the Motley Fool site, to learn more about the investing process.

Exhibit 8-9

A Sampling of Investing Websites

1. **Motley Fool** Popular financial forum aims to inform, entertain, and help people make money. Check out portfolios and stock ideas, and get a broker. Offers extensive guides to a host of issues in the realm of personal finance. It's fun and it's free! fool.com

2. **Yahoo Finance** Provides financial news, data, and commentary including stock quotes, press releases, financial reports, and online tools for personal financial management. finance.yahoo.com

3. *Fortune* Online edition of this magazine features an extensive section for investors. Track and analyze up to 150 stocks in a free portfolio. Brief profiles of the 500 leading companies in the United States, including stock quotes, charts, and financial statements. Also access to the Global 500. fortune.com

4. **CNN Money** Get an at-a-glance update on the major U.S. markets, including Dow and Nasdaq indicators, and check on market movers. money.cnn.com/data/us_markets

5. **BigCharts** U.S. investment charting site. Find research on more than 20,000 stocks, mutual funds, and indexes, with intraday historical charts and quotes. bigcharts.com

6. **Dow Jones & Company** Home page of large publisher of business news and information. Details on products and services, including *The Wall Street Journal*. dowjones.com

7. **Bloomberg** Large compendium of global business and financial news. Descriptions of media products and services. bloomberg.com

8. **New York Stock Exchange** Offers stock prices, listing information and links to national and international listed companies, a market summary, and guidelines for investors. nyse.com

9. **Nasdaq** Provides listed company information, investor resources, a tour, a summary of market activity and indexes, and a glossary of market terms. nasdaq.com

10. **Standard & Poor's** Read about the Financial Information Service and Ratings Service. See daily closing values of listed securities. standardandpoors.com

Key Terms and Concepts

accumulated deficit (p. 286)   Retained earnings with a negative (debit) balance.

accumulated other comprehensive income (loss) (p. 291)   A category of stockholders' equity for financial reporting purposes that includes a firm's cumulative foreign currency translation adjustments, unrealized gains or losses on available-for-sale marketable securities, changes during the period in certain pension or other postretirement benefit items, and gains (losses) on certain derivative instruments.

additional paid-in capital (p. 285)   The excess of the amount received from the sale of stock over the par (or stated) value of the shares sold.

authorized shares (p. 281)   The number of shares of a class of stock allowed to be issued per the corporation's charter. The maximum number of shares the corporation can legally issue.

callable preferred stock (p. 284)   Preferred stock that can be redeemed by the corporation at its option.

capital in excess of par value (p. 285)   Another term for *additional paid-in capital.*

capital stock (p. 278)   The generic term for stock issued by a corporation.

common stock (p. 278)   The class of stock that represents residual ownership of the corporation.

consolidated financial statements (p. 296)   Financial statements resulting from the combination of parent and subsidiary company financial statements.

convertible preferred stock (p. 284)   Preferred stock that can be converted to common stock of the corporation at the option of the stockholder.

cumulative dividend (p. 283)   A feature of preferred stock that requires any missed dividends to be paid before dividends are paid on common stock.

cumulative foreign currency translation adjustment (p. 292)   A component of stockholders' equity arising from the translation of foreign subsidiary financial statements.

cumulative voting (p. 280)   A system of voting for the directors of a firm in which the total number of votes that can be cast among one or more candidates is equal to the number of shares of stock owned, multiplied by the number of directors to be elected.

declaration date (p. 288)   The date on which a dividend is approved by the board of directors and becomes a legal liability of the company.

dividend (p. 283)   A distribution of earnings to the owners/stockholders of a corporation.

ex-dividend date (p. 288)   The date on and after which (up to the record date) the buyer of a publicly traded stock will not receive a dividend that has been declared.

independent director (p. 280)   A member of the firm's board of directors who is not an officer or employee of the firm; also referred to as *outside director.*

inside director (p. 280)   A member of the firm's board of directors who is also an officer or employee of the firm.

issued shares (p. 281)   The number of shares of a class of stock that has been issued (usually sold) to stockholders.

legal capital (p. 280)   An amount associated with the capital stock that has been issued by a corporation. Legal capital is generally the par value or stated value of the shares issued.

liquidating value (p. 283)   The stated claim of preferred stock in the event the corporation is liquidated. Sometimes called *redemption value.*

outside director (p. 280)   A member of the firm's board of directors who is not an officer or employee of the firm; another name for *independent director.*

outstanding shares (p. 281)   The number of shares of a class of stock held by stockholders.

par value (p. 280)   An arbitrary value assigned to a share of stock when the corporation is organized. Sometimes used to refer to the stated value or face amount of a security.

participating dividend (p. 283)   A feature of preferred stock that provides a right to preferred stockholders to receive additional dividends at a specified ratio after a base amount of dividends has been paid to common stockholders.

partners' capital (p. 276)   The owners' equity in a partnership.

payment date (p. 288)   The date a dividend is paid.

preemptive right (p. 282)   The right of a stockholder to purchase shares from any additional sales of shares in proportion to the stockholder's present percentage of ownership.

preferred stock (p. 282)   The class of stock representing an ownership interest with certain preferences relative to common stock, usually including a priority claim to dividends.

proprietor's capital (p. 276)   The owners' equity of an individual proprietorship.

record date (p. 288)   The date used to determine the stockholders who will receive a dividend.

redemption value (p. 283)   The stated claim of preferred stock in the event the corporation is liquidated. Sometimes called *liquidating value.*

retained earnings (p. 285)   Cumulative net income that has not been distributed to the owners/stockholders of a corporation as dividends.

slate voting (p. 280)   A system of voting for the directors of a firm in which votes equal to the number of shares owned are cast for a single slate of candidates.

stated value (p. 281)   An arbitrary value assigned to shares of no-par-value stock.

stock dividend (p. 287)   A distribution of additional shares to existing stockholders in proportion to their existing holdings. The additional shares issued usually amount to less than 20 percent of the previously issued shares.

stock split (p. 290)   A distribution of additional shares to existing stockholders in proportion to their existing holdings. The additional shares issued usually amount to 100 percent or more of the previously issued shares.

treasury stock (p. 281)   Shares of a firm's previously issued stock that have been reacquired by the firm.

Mini-Exercises

All applicable Exercises are available in *Connect*.

Mini-Exercise 8.1
LO 1, 3

Common stock—issuance and dividend transactions Altuve Co. was incorporated on January 1, 2019, at which time 250,000 shares of $1 par value common stock were authorized, and 140,000 of these shares were issued for $12 per share. Net income for the year ended December 31, 2019, was $1,200,000. Altuve Co.'s board of directors declared dividends of $2 per share of common stock on December 31, 2019, payable on February 7, 2020.

Required:
Use the horizontal model (or write the entry) to show the effects of

a.   The issuance of common stock on January 1, 2019.

b.   The declaration of dividends on December 31, 2019.

c.   The payment of dividends on February 7, 2020.

Mini-Exercise 8.2
LO 2

Preferred stock—calculate dividend amounts Laura & Marty Ltd. did not pay dividends on its 6.5%, $100 par value cumulative preferred stock during 2018 or 2019. Since 2012, 275,000 shares of this stock have been outstanding. Laura & Marty Ltd.

has been profitable in 2020 and is considering a cash dividend on its common stock that would be payable in December 2020.

Required:
Calculate the amount of dividends that would have to be paid on the preferred stock before a cash dividend could be paid to the common stockholders.

Effects of a stock split Assume that you own 3,600 shares of $10 par value common stock and the company has a 4-for-1 stock split when the market price per share is $68.

Mini-Exercise 8.3

LO 4

Required:
a. How many shares of common stock will you own after the stock split?
b. What will probably happen to the market price per share of the stock?
c. What will probably happen to the par value per share of the stock?

Treasury stock transactions On April 10, 2019, Amelia Inc. purchased 1,800 shares of its own common stock in the market for $23 per share. On September 28, 2019, the company sold 700 of these shares in the open market at a price of $26 per share.

Mini-Exercise 8.4

LO 6

Required:
Use the horizontal model (or write the entry) to show the effects on Amelia Inc.'s financial statements of

a. The purchase of the treasury stock on April 10, 2019.
b. The sale of the treasury stock on September 28, 2019.

Exercises

connect

All applicable Exercises are available in *Connect*.

Review exercise—calculate net income At the beginning of the current fiscal year, the balance sheet of Hughey Inc. showed stockholders' equity of $260,000. During the year, liabilities increased by $11,000 to $116,000, paid-in capital increased by $20,000 to $90,000, and assets increased by $130,000. Dividends declared and paid during the year were $28,000.

Exercise 8.5

Required:
Calculate net income or loss for the year. (*Hint:* Set up the accounting equation for beginning balances, changes during the year, and ending balances; then solve for missing amounts.)

	A	=	L	+	PIC	+	RE
					SE		
Beginning	$	=		+		+	
Changes		=		+		+	
Ending		=		+		+	

Exercise 8.6

Review exercise—calculate net income At the beginning of the current fiscal year, the balance sheet of Cummings Co. showed liabilities of $657,000. During the year, liabilities decreased by $108,000, assets increased by $231,000, and paid-in capital increased by $30,000 to $570,000. Dividends declared and paid during the year were $186,000. At the end of the year, stockholders' equity totaled $1,137,000.

Required:
Calculate net income or loss for the year using the same format as shown in Exercise 8.5.

Exercise 8.7

Review exercise—calculate retained earnings From the following data, calculate the Retained Earnings balance as of December 31, 2020:

Retained earnings, December 31, 2019	$692,800
Cost of buildings purchased during 2020	83,600
Net income for the year ended December 31, 2020	113,800
Dividends declared and paid in 2020	65,000
Increase in cash balance from January 1, 2020, to December 31, 2020	46,000
Increase in long-term debt in 2020	89,200

Exercise 8.8

Review exercise—calculate retained earnings From the following data, calculate the Retained Earnings balance as of December 31, 2019:

Retained earnings, December 31, 2020	$367,800
Net decrease in total assets during 2020	56,100
Net increase in accounts receivable in 2020	12,900
Dividends declared and paid in 2020	50,400
Proceeds from issuance of bonds during 2020	132,600
Net loss for the year ended December 31, 2020	34,500

Exercise 8.9

LO 1

Common stock balance sheet disclosure The balance sheet caption for common stock is the following:

Common stock, $5 par value, 4,000,000 shares authorized, 2,800,000 shares issued, 2,500,000 shares outstanding	$?

Required:
a.   Calculate the dollar amount that will be presented opposite this caption.
b.   Calculate the total amount of a cash dividend of $0.30 per share.
c.   What accounts for the difference between issued shares and outstanding shares?

Exercise 8.10

LO 1

Common stock—calculate issue price and dividend amount The balance sheet caption for common stock is the following:

Common stock without par value, 7,500,000 shares authorized, 3,000,000 shares issued, and 2,700,000 shares outstanding	$38,250,000

Required:

a. Calculate the average price at which the shares were issued.

b. If these shares had been assigned a stated value of $1 each, show how the caption here would be different.

c. If a cash dividend of $1.60 per share were declared, calculate the total amount of cash that would be paid to stockholders.

d. What accounts for the difference between issued shares and outstanding shares?

Preferred stock—calculate dividend amounts Calculate the annual cash dividends required to be paid for each of the following preferred stock issues:

Exercise 8.11

LO 2

Required:

a. $4.75 cumulative preferred, no par value; 400,000 shares authorized, 325,000 shares issued. (The treasury stock caption of the stockholders' equity section of the balance sheet indicates that 40,600 shares of this preferred stock issue are owned by the company.)

b. 5%, $50 par value preferred, 200,000 shares authorized, 172,000 shares issued, and 68,500 shares outstanding.

c. 7.4% cumulative preferred, $100 stated value, $104 liquidating value; 80,000 shares authorized, 63,200 shares issued, 57,600 shares outstanding.

Preferred stock—calculate dividend amounts Calculate the cash dividends required to be paid for each of the following preferred stock issues:

Exercise 8.12

LO 2

Required:

a. The semiannual dividend on 7% cumulative preferred, $60 par value, 40,000 shares authorized, issued, and outstanding.

b. The annual dividend on $5.20 cumulative preferred, 800,000 shares authorized, 240,000 shares issued, 171,600 shares outstanding. Last year's dividend has not been paid.

c. The quarterly dividend on 4.8% cumulative preferred, $100 stated value, $103 liquidating value, 600,000 shares authorized, 445,000 shares issued and outstanding. No dividends are in arrears.

Preferred stock—calculate dividend amounts Rosie Inc. did not pay dividends on its $4.50, $50 par value, cumulative preferred stock during 2018 or 2019, but had met its preferred dividend requirement in all prior years. Since 2014, 42,000 shares of this stock have been outstanding. Rosie Inc. has been profitable in 2020 and is considering a cash dividend on its common stock that would be payable in December 2020.

Exercise 8.13

LO 2

Required:

Calculate the amount of dividends that would have to be paid on the preferred stock before a cash dividend could be paid to the common stockholders.

Preferred stock—calculate dividend amounts Dedrick Inc. did not pay dividends in 2018 or 2019, even though 60,000 shares of its 7.5%, $50 par value cumulative preferred stock were outstanding during those years. The company has 900,000 shares of $2 par value common stock outstanding.

Exercise 8.14

LO 2

Required:

a. Calculate the annual dividend per share obligation on the preferred stock.

b. Calculate the amount that would be received by an investor who has owned 3,100 shares of preferred stock and 29,000 shares of common stock since 2017 if a $0.40 per share dividend on the common stock is paid at the end of 2020.

Exercise 8.15

LO 3

Dividend dates—market price effects O'Garro Inc. has paid a regular quarterly cash dividend of $0.70 per share for several years. The common stock is publicly traded. On February 21 of the current year, O'Garro's board of directors declared the regular first-quarter dividend of $0.70 per share payable on March 30 to stockholders of record on March 15.

Required:

As a result of this dividend action, state what you would expect to happen to the market price of the common stock of O'Garro Inc. on each of the following dates. Explain your answers.

a. February 21.

b. March 13.

c. March 15.

d. March 30.

Exercise 8.16

LO 3

Ex-dividend date—market price effect Find a list of common stock ex-dividend date data. You can go, via Google, to wsj.com. Under the *Markets* tab, select *Market Data;* then click on the arrow next to *U.S. Stocks* to open the pull down menu and select *Dividends* under the Stocks and Trading Statistics category. Scroll down to the Dividend Declarations Table, which includes the relevant ex-dividend dates. Select several stocks, preferably of large and well-known companies. Go to a stock listing on the ex-dividend date and determine what happened to the market price of a share of stock on that date. Does this price action make sense? Explain your answer.

Exercise 8.17

LO 3

Requirements for declaring dividends Anglin Inc. expects to incur a loss for the current year. The chairperson of the board of directors wants to have a cash dividend so that the company's record of having paid a dividend during every year of its existence will continue. What factors will determine whether the board can declare a dividend?

Exercise 8.18

LO 3

Campbell's

Interpret dividend information from an annual report Refer to the Campbell Soup Company annual report in the appendix. From the table of Quarterly Data (unaudited) and the (Selected Financial Data)(sometimes called the Five-Year Review) find the information relating to cash dividends on common stock.

Required:

a. How frequently are cash dividends paid?

b. What has been the pattern of the cash dividend amount per share relative to the pattern of earnings per share?

c. Calculate the rate of change in the annual dividend per share for each of the years from 2014 through 2017.

Exercise 8.19

LO 4

Cash dividends versus stock dividends Under what circumstances would you (as an investor) prefer to receive cash dividends rather than stock dividends? Under what circumstances would you prefer stock dividends to cash dividends?

Calculate stock dividend shares and cash dividend amounts Assume that you own 14,000 shares of Briant Inc.'s common stock and that you currently receive cash dividends of $1.68 per share per year.

Exercise 8.20
LO 4

Required:

a. If Briant Inc. declared a 5% stock dividend, how many shares of common stock would you receive as a dividend?

b. Calculate the cash dividend per share amount to be paid after the stock dividend that would result in the same total cash dividend (as was received before the stock dividend).

c. If the cash dividend remained at $1.68 per share after the stock dividend, what per share cash dividend amount without a stock dividend would have accomplished the same total cash dividend?

d. Why might a company consider having a dividend policy of paying a $0.30 per share cash dividend every year and also issuing a 5% stock dividend every year?

Effects of a stock split Assume that you own 400 shares of $10 par value common stock of a company and the company has a 2-for-1 stock split when the market price per share is $60.

Exercise 8.21
LO 4

Required:

a. How many shares of common stock will you own after the stock split?

b. What will probably happen to the market price per share of the stock?

c. What will probably happen to the par value per share of the stock?

Stock splits versus stock dividends Assume that you own 900 shares of common stock of a company, that you have been receiving cash dividends of $3.15 per share per year, and that the company has a 3-for-2 stock split.

Exercise 8.22
LO 4

Required:

a. How many shares of common stock will you own after the stock split?

b. What new cash dividend per share amount will result in the same total dividend income as you received before the stock split?

c. What stock dividend percentage could have accomplished the same end result as the 3-for-2 stock split?

Problems

🔴 connect

All applicable Problems are available in *Connect*.

Common and preferred stock—issuances and dividends Homestead Oil Corp. was incorporated on January 1, 2019, and issued the following stock for cash:

Problem 8.23
LO 1, 2

800,000 shares of no-par common stock were authorized; 150,000 shares were issued on January 1, 2019, at $38 per share.

200,000 shares of $100 par value, 6.5% cumulative, preferred stock were authorized; 90,000 shares were issued on January 1, 2019, at $122 per share.

Net income for the years ended December 31, 2019 and 2020 was $2,600,000 and $5,600,000, respectively.

No dividends were declared or paid during 2019. However, on December 28, 2020, the board of directors of Homestead declared dividends of $3,600,000, payable on February 12, 2021, to holders of record as of January 19, 2021.

Required:

a. Use the horizontal model (or write the entry) to show the effects of
   1. The issuance of common stock and preferred stock on January 1, 2019.
   2. The declaration of dividends on December 28, 2020.
   3. The payment of dividends on February 12, 2021.

b. Of the total amount of dividends declared during 2020, how much will be received by preferred shareholders?

Problem 8.24
LO 1, 2

Common and preferred stock—issuances and dividends Permabilt Corp. was incorporated on January 1, 2019, and issued the following stock for cash:

2,000,000 shares of no-par common stock were authorized; 750,000 shares were issued on January 1, 2019, at $35 per share.

800,000 shares of $100 par value, 7.5% cumulative, preferred stock were authorized; 540,000 shares were issued on January 1, 2019, at $105 per share.

No dividends were declared or paid during 2019 or 2020. However, on December 22, 2021, the board of directors of Permabilt Corp. declared dividends of $15,000,000, payable on February 12, 2022, to holders of record as of January 8, 2022.

Required:

a. Use the horizontal model (or write the entry) to show the effects of
   1. The issuance of common stock and preferred stock on January 1, 2019.
   2. The declaration of dividends on December 22, 2021.
   3. The payment of dividends on February 12, 2022.

b. Of the total amount of dividends declared during 2021, how much will be received by preferred shareholders?

c. Calculate the common stock dividends per share declared during 2021.

Problem 8.25
LO 6

Treasury stock transactions On May 4, 2019, Docker Inc. purchased 1,200 shares of its own common stock in the market at a price of $19.25 per share. On September 19, 2019, 700 of these shares were sold in the open market at a price of $20.50 per share. There were 48,200 shares of Docker common stock outstanding prior to the May 4 purchase of treasury stock. A $0.40 per share cash dividend on the common stock was declared and paid on June 15, 2019.

Required:

Use the horizontal model (or write the entry) to show the effects on Docker's financial statements of

a. The purchase of the treasury stock on May 4, 2019.

b. The declaration and payment of the cash dividend on June 15, 2019.

c. The sale of the treasury stock on September 19, 2019.

Treasury stock transactions On January 1, 2019, Metco Inc. reported 411,050 shares of $5 par value common stock as being issued and outstanding. On March 24, 2019, Metco Inc. purchased for its treasury 3,600 shares of its common stock at a price of $37 per share. On August 19, 2019, 1,450 of these treasury shares were sold for $43 per share. Metco's directors declared cash dividends of $1.50 per share during the second quarter and again during the fourth quarter, payable on June 30, 2019, and December 31, 2019, respectively. A 4% stock dividend was issued at the end of the year. There were no other transactions affecting common stock during the year.

Problem 8.26
LO 6

Required:

a. Use the horizontal model (or write the entry) to show the effect of the treasury stock purchase on March 24, 2019.

b. Calculate the total amount of the cash dividends paid in the second quarter.

c. Use the horizontal model (or write the entry) to show the effect of the sale of the treasury stock on August 19, 2019.

d. Calculate the total amount of cash dividends paid in the fourth quarter.

e. Calculate the number of shares of stock issued in the stock dividend.

Transaction analysis—various accounts Enter the following column headings across the top of a sheet of paper:

Problem 8.27
LO 1, 2, 4, 6

Transaction	Cash	Other Assets	Liabilities	Paid-In Capital	Retained Earnings	Treasury Stock	Net Income

Enter the transaction letter in the first column and show the effect (if any) of each of the following transactions on each financial statement category by entering a plus (+) or minus (−) sign and the amount in the appropriate column. Do not show items that affect net income in the retained earnings column. You may also write the entries to record each transaction.

a. Sold 8,200 shares of $50 par value 7% preferred stock at par.

b. Declared the annual dividend on the preferred stock.

c. Purchased 1,300 shares of preferred stock for the treasury at $54 per share.

d. Issued 4,000 shares of $1 par value common stock in exchange for land valued at $226,000.

e. Sold 600 shares of the treasury stock purchased in transaction **c** for $58 per share.

f. Split the common stock 2-for-1.

Transaction analysis—various accounts Enter the following column headings across the top of a sheet of paper:

Problem 8.28
LO 1, 2, 4, 6

Transaction	Cash	Other Assets	Liabilities	Paid-In Capital	Retained Earnings	Treasury Stock	Net Income

Enter the transaction letter in the first column and show the effect (if any) of each of the following transactions on each financial statement category by entering a plus (+) or minus (−) sign and the amount in the appropriate column. Do not show items that affect net income in the retained earnings column. You may also write the entries to record these transactions. You should assume that the transactions occurred in the same chronological sequence as listed here:

a.   Sold 4,100 shares of $50 par value preferred stock at $52.50 per share.

b.   Declared the annual cash dividend of $2.20 per share on common stock. There were 5,600 shares of $1 par value common stock issued and outstanding throughout the year.

c.   Issued 8,000 shares of $50 par value preferred stock in exchange for a building when the market price of preferred stock was $54 per share.

d.   Purchased 1,700 shares of preferred stock for the treasury at a price of $57 per share.

e.   Sold 1,100 shares of the preferred stock held in treasury (see **d**) for $58 per share.

f.   Declared and issued a 12% stock dividend on the $1 par value common stock (see **b**) when the market price per share was $44.

Problem 8.29
LO 1, 2, 4, 6

Transaction analysis—various accounts Enter the following column headings across the top of a sheet of paper:

Transaction	Cash	Other Assets	Liabilities	Paid-In Capital	Retained Earnings	Treasury Stock	Net Income

Enter the transaction letter in the first column and show the effect (if any) of each of the following transactions on each financial statement category by entering a plus (+) or minus (−) sign and the amount in the appropriate column. Do not show items that affect net income in the retained earnings column. You may also write the entries to record these transactions. You should assume that the transactions occurred in this chronological sequence and that 80,000 shares of previously issued common stock remain outstanding. (*Hint:* Remember to consider appropriate effects of previous transactions.)

a.   Sold 10,000 previously unissued shares of $1 par value common stock for $18 per share.

b.   Issued 2,000 shares of previously unissued 8% cumulative preferred stock, $40 par value, in exchange for land and a building appraised at $80,000.

c.   Declared and paid the annual cash dividend on the preferred stock issued in transaction **b**.

d.   Purchased 500 shares of common stock for the treasury at a total cost of $9,500.

e.   Declared a cash dividend of $0.15 per share on the common stock outstanding.

f.   Sold 260 shares of the treasury stock purchased in transaction **d** at a price of $20 per share.

g.   Declared and issued a 3% stock dividend on the common stock issued when the market value per share of common stock was $21.

h.   Split the common stock 3-for-1.

Transaction analysis—various accounts Enter the following column headings across the top of a sheet of paper:

Problem 8.30
LO 1, 2, 4, 6

Transaction	Cash	Other Assets	Liabilities	Paid-In Capital	Retained Earnings	Treasury Stock	Net Income

Enter the transaction letter in the first column and show the effect (if any) of each of the following transactions on each financial statement category by entering a plus (+) or minus (−) sign and the amount in the appropriate column. Do not show items that affect net income in the retained earnings column. You may also write the entries to record these transactions. You should assume that the transactions occurred in the listed chronological sequence and that no stock had been previously issued. (*Hint:* Remember to consider appropriate effects of previous transactions.)

a. Issued 7,000 shares of $100 par value preferred stock at par.

b. Issued 4,200 shares of $100 par value preferred stock in exchange for land that had an appraised value of $428,400.

c. Issued 48,000 shares of $5 par value common stock for $16 per share.

d. Purchased 15,000 shares of common stock for the treasury at $18 per share.

e. Sold 9,000 shares of the treasury stock purchased in transaction **d** for $21 per share.

f. Declared a cash dividend of $1.75 per share on the preferred stock outstanding, to be paid early next year.

g. Declared and issued an 8% stock dividend on the common stock when the market price per share of common stock was $25.

Comprehensive problem—calculate missing amounts, dividends, total shares, and per share information Francis Inc. has the following stockholders' equity section in its November 30, 2019, balance sheet:

Problem 8.31
LO 1, 2, 3, 6, 7

Paid-in capital:	
12% preferred stock, $60 par value, 1,000 shares	
authorized, issued, and outstanding	$?
Common stock, $8 par value, 50,000 shares	
authorized, ? shares issued, ? shares outstanding	120,000
Additional paid-in capital on common stock	270,000
Additional paid-in capital from treasury stock	6,500
Retained earnings	48,500
Less: Treasury stock, at cost (1,000 shares of common)	(9,000)
Total stockholders' equity	$?

Required:

a. Calculate the amount of the total annual dividend requirement on preferred stock.

b. Calculate the amount that should be shown on the balance sheet for preferred stock.

c. Calculate the number of shares of common stock that are issued and the number of shares of common stock that are outstanding.

d. On January 1, 2019, the firm's balance sheet showed common stock of $105,000 and additional paid-in capital on common stock of $234,375. The only transaction affecting these accounts during 2019 was the sale of common stock. Calculate the number of shares that were sold and the selling price per share.

e. Describe the transaction that resulted in the additional paid-in capital from treasury stock.

f. The retained earnings balance on January 1, 2019, was $45,150. Net income for the past 11 months was $12,000. Preferred stock dividends for all of 2019 have been declared and paid. Calculate the amount of dividends on common stock during the first 11 months of 2019.

Problem 8.32

LO 1, 2, 3, 4, 6, 7

Comprehensive problem—calculate missing amounts, issue price, net income, and dividends; interpret stock dividend and split Bacon Inc. has the following stockholders' equity section in its May 31, 2019, comparative balance sheets:

	May 31, 2019	April 30, 2019
Paid-in capital:		
Preferred stock, $120 par value, 9%, cumulative, 200,000 shares authorized, 140,000 shares issued and outstanding	$16,800,000	$16,800,000
Common stock, $5 par value, 1,000,000 shares authorized, 600,000 and 540,000 shares issued, respectively	?	2,700,000
Additional paid-in capital	26,100,000	23,220,000
Retained earnings	36,200,000	34,640,000
Less: Treasury common stock, at cost; 72,000 shares and 68,000 shares, respectively	(4,412,000)	(4,148,000)
Total stockholders' equity	$?	$73,212,000

Required:

a. Calculate the amount that should be shown on the balance sheet for common stock at May 31, 2019.

b. The only transaction affecting additional paid-in capital during the month of May was the sale of additional common stock. At what price per share were the additional shares sold?

c. What was the average cost per share of the common stock purchased for the treasury during the month?

d. During May, dividends on preferred stock equal to one-half of the 2019 dividend requirement were declared and paid. There were no common dividends declared or paid in May. Calculate net income for May.

e. Assume that on June 1 the board of directors declared a cash dividend of $0.60 per share on the outstanding shares of common stock. The dividend will be payable on July 15 to stockholders of record on June 15.
1. Calculate the total amount of the dividend.
2. Explain the impact this action will have on the June 30 balance sheet and on the income statement for June.

f. Assume that on June 1 the market value of the common stock was $70 per share and that the board of directors declared a 10% stock dividend on the issued shares of common stock. Use the horizontal model (or write the entry) to show the issuance of the stock dividend.

g. Assume that instead of the stock dividend described in **f**, the board of directors authorized a 2-for-1 stock split on June 1 when the market price of the common stock was $70 per share.
1. What will be the par value, and how many shares of common stock will be authorized after the split?
2. What will be the market price per share of common stock after the split?
3. How many shares of common stock will be in the treasury after the split?

h. By how much will total stockholders' equity change as a result of
1. The stock dividend described in part **f**?
2. The stock split described in part **g**?

Cases

connect

All applicable Cases are available in *Connect*.

Focus company—stockholders' equity disclosures In Exercise 1.1, you were asked to obtain the most recent annual report of a company that you were interested in reviewing throughout this term.

Case 8.33

LO 1, 2, 5, 6, 8, 9

Required:
Please review the note disclosures provided in your focus company's annual report and identify at least three items being reported as stockholders' equity items. Discuss what you've learned about these items and how they are presented on the balance sheet.

Analytical case (part 1)—calculate missing stockholders' equity amounts for 2019 (*Note:* The information presented in this case is also used for Case 8.35. For now you can ignore the 2020 column in the balance sheet; all disclosures presented here relate to the June 30, 2019, balance sheet.) DeZurik Corp. had the following stockholders' equity section in its June 30, 2019, balance sheet (in thousands, except share and per share amounts):

Case 8.34

LO 1, 2, 6, 7

	June 30 (in thousands)	
	2020	**2019**
Paid-in capital:		
$4.50 Preferred stock, $? par value, cumulative, 150,000 shares authorized, 64,000 shares issued and outstanding	_____	$ 5,760
Common stock, $5 par value, 4,000,000 shares authorized, 1,640,000 shares issued, 1,500,000 shares outstanding	_____	_____
Additional paid-in capital on common stock	_____	22,960
Retained earnings	_____	_____
Less: Treasury common stock, at cost, ? shares		
Total stockholders' equity................................	$52,922	$48,000

Required:

a. Calculate the par value per share of preferred stock and determine the preferred stock dividend percentage.

b. Calculate the amount that should be shown on the balance sheet for common stock at June 30, 2019.

c. What was the average issue price of common stock shown on the June 30, 2019, balance sheet?

d. How many shares of treasury stock does DeZurik Corp. own at June 30, 2019?

e. Assume that the treasury shares were purchased for $21 per share. Calculate the amount that should be shown on the balance sheet for treasury stock at June 30, 2019.

f. Calculate the retained earnings balance at June 30, 2019, after you have completed parts **a–e.** (*Hint:* Keep in mind that Treasury Stock is a contra account.)

g. (Optional) Assume that the Retained Earnings balance on July 1, 2018, was $13,400 (in thousands) and that net income for the year ended June 30, 2019, was $908 (in thousands). The 2019 preferred dividends were paid in full, and no other dividend transactions were recorded during the year. Verify that the amount shown in the solution to part **f** is correct. (*Hint:* Prepare a statement of retained earnings or do a T-account analysis to determine the June 30, 2019, balance.)

Case 8.35
LO 1, 2, 3, 4, 6, 7

Analytical case (part 2)—prepare stockholders' equity amounts and disclosures for 2020 using transaction information (*Note:* You should review the solution to Case 8.34, provided by your instructor, before attempting to complete this case.) The transactions affecting the stockholders' equity accounts of DeZurik Corp. for the year ended June 30, 2020, are summarized here:

1. 160,000 shares of common stock were issued at $21.25 per share.
2. 40,000 shares of treasury (common) stock were sold for $21 per share.
3. Net income for the year was $1,480 (in thousands).
4. The fiscal 2020 preferred dividends were paid in full. Assume that all 64,000 shares were outstanding throughout the year ended June 30, 2020.
5. A cash dividend of $0.30 per share was declared and paid to common stockholders. Assume that transactions 1 and 2 occurred before the dividend was declared.
6. The preferred stock was split 2 for 1 on June 30, 2020. (*Note:* This transaction had no effect on transaction 4.)

Required:

a. Calculate the *dollar amounts* that DeZurik Corp. would report for each stockholders' equity caption on its June 30, 2020, balance sheet after recording the effects of transactions 1–6. Note that total stockholders' equity at June 30, 2020 of $52,922 (in thousands), is provided as a check figure. (*Hint:* To determine the Retained Earnings balance, begin with the June 30, 2019, balance of $14,020 (in thousands) as determined in Case 8.34, and then make adjustments for the effects of transactions 3–5.)

b. Indicate how the stockholders' equity caption details for DeZurik Corp. would change for the June 30, 2020, balance sheet, as compared to the disclosures shown in Case 8.34 for the 2019 balance sheet.

c. What was the average issue price of common stock shown on the June 30, 2020, balance sheet?

Capstone analytical review of Chapters 6, 7, and 8. Analyzing financing leases, notes payable, preferred stock, and common stock (*Note:* Please refer to Case 4.30 in Chapter 4 for the financial statement data needed for the analysis of this case. You should also review the solution to Case 4.30, provided by your instructor, before attempting to complete this case.) Your conversation with Mr. Gerrard, which took place in February 2020 (see Case 6.35), continued as follows:

Case 8.36

LO 1, 2, 7

Mr. Gerrard: I've been talking with my accountant about our capital expansion needs, which will be considerable during the next couple of years. To stay in a strong competitive position, we're constantly buying new pieces of earthmoving equipment and replacing machinery that has become obsolete. What it all comes down to is financing, and it's not easy to raise $30 million to $60 million all at once. There are a number of options, including dealer financing, but the interest rates offered by banks are usually lower.

Your reply: From reviewing your balance sheet, I can see that you've got a lot of notes payable already. How is your relationship with your bank?

Mr. Gerrard: Actually, we use several banks and we have an excellent credit history, so getting the money is not a major problem. The problem is that we already owe more than $150 million and I don't want to get overextended.

Your reply: Have you considered long-term leases?

Mr. Gerrard: Yes. This is essentially how dealer financing works. Usually it is arranged as a lease with an option to buy the equipment after a number of years. We've been actively looking into this with our Cat dealer for several scrapers that we need to put on a big job immediately. I can show you one of the contracts involved.

Your reply: OK, I'll have a look at the contracts, but this sounds like a long-term financing lease.

Mr. Gerrard: Yes, I think that's what my accountant called it. What matters most to me is that we get the equipment in place ASAP; but if you could explain what the accounting implications would be of entering into these types of arrangements, that might put me at ease about it.

Your reply: No problem; will do. It would affect both your balance sheet and income statement, but in most respects a long-term financing lease is treated very much like a long-term note payable with a bank. I'll give you a memo about it. But what about looking into other sources of equity financing? Have you considered any of these options?

Mr. Gerrard: We're a family business and want to keep it that way. Our shares are publicly traded, but we're owned mostly by family members and employees. We've got a lot of retained earnings, but that's not the same thing as cash, you know. Should we be issuing bonds?

Your reply: Issuing bonds is possible, but I was thinking more on the lines of preferred stock. Are you familiar with this option?

Mr. Gerrard: Not really. Isn't preferred stock a lot like bonds payable?

Your reply: Maybe this is something else I should include in my memo: an explanation of the differences between common stock, preferred stock, and bonds payable.

Mr. Gerrard: Yes, please do.

Required:

a. When discussing financing leases with Mr. Gerrard, you commented, "It would affect both your balance sheet and income statement, but in most respects a long-term financing lease is treated very much like a long-term note payable with a bank." Explain the accounting treatment of financing leases as compared to the accounting treatment of notes payable in terms that a nonaccountant could easily understand. Include in your answer both the balance sheet and income statement effects of financing leases. (*Note:* You do not need to make reference to the five characteristics that would require a lease to be treated as a financing lease.)

b. Assume you have reviewed the contract Mr. Gerrard provided concerning the dealer financing agreement for the purchase of two new scrapers. You have determined that the lease agreement would qualify as a financing lease. The present value of the lease payments would be $6 million. Use the horizontal model, or write the journal entry, to show Mr. Gerrard how this lease would affect the financial statements of Gerrard Construction Co.

c. Explain what Mr. Gerrard meant by this statement: "We've got a lot of retained earnings, but that's not the same thing as cash, you know." Review the balance sheet at December 31, 2019, provided in Case 4.30. In which assets are most of the company's retained earnings invested?

d. Explain to Mr. Gerrard what the similarities and differences are between bonds payable, preferred stock, and common stock.

e. Why would you recommend to Mr. Gerrard that his company consider issuing $30 million to $60 million of preferred stock rather than bonds payable? (*Hint:* Review the company's balance sheet provided in Case 4.30 in the context of your present conversation with Mr. Gerrard.)

ANSWERS TO What Does It Mean?

1. It means that common stock has been issued to stockholders in exchange for their investment of capital in the corporation. The capital has not been earned; it has been paid in by the stockholders.

2. It means that an arbitrary amount has been assigned as a value for each share of common stock. This arbitrarily assigned value has no effect on the market value of each share of common stock.

3. It means that the corporation has reacquired from stockholders some previously issued shares of stock.

4. It means that the corporation has issued some stock that has many characteristics similar to those of bonds. Relative to common stock, preferred stock has a priority claim to dividends and to assets in the event of liquidation. Unlike bonds, preferred stock does not have to be repaid.

5. It means that the corporation has retained earnings from its operations and cash that the directors want to distribute to the stockholders.

6. It means that the corporation has retained earnings from its operations and that the directors want to transfer some of the retained earnings to paid-in capital rather than distribute cash to the stockholders.

7. It means that the corporation's board of directors wants to lower the market value of each share of common stock. This occurs because the corporation doesn't receive anything for the additional shares issued, so the total market value of the company (which remains unchanged) is split among more shares than were outstanding before the stock split.

8. It means that the ownership interests in subsidiaries held by parties other than the parent must be clearly identified, labeled, and presented in the consolidated balance sheet within equity, but separate from the parent's equity.

9

The Income Statement and the Statement of Cash Flows

The income statement answers some of the most important questions that users of the financial statements have: What were the financial results of the firm's operations for the fiscal period? How much profit (or loss) did the firm have? Are sales increasing relative to cost of goods sold and other operating expenses? Many income statement accounts were introduced in Chapters 5 through 8 when transactions also affecting asset and liability accounts were explained. However, because of the significance of the net income figure to managers, stockholders, potential investors, and others, it is appropriate to focus on the form and content of this financial statement.

The Consolidated Statements of Earnings of Campbell Soup Company can be found in the appendix. This page of the annual report has been reproduced as Exhibit 9-1. Note that comparative statements for the years ended on the Sunday nearest to July 31 of 2017, 2016, and 2015 are presented. This permits the reader of the statement to assess quickly the recent trend of these important data.

Campbell's

As you might expect, Campbell's income statement starts with "net sales." What in popular jargon is referred to as the *bottom line,* or "net income," is reported as "net earnings attributable to Campbell Soup Company." Before arriving at this amount, subtotals are also provided for "earnings before interest and taxes," "earnings before taxes," "earnings from continuing operations," and "net earnings." The significance of the "per share" data will be discussed later in this chapter. The principal objective of the first part of this chapter is to permit you to make sense of any income statement.

The second part of this chapter explores the statement of cash flows in more detail than presented in Chapter 2. Remember that this statement explains the change in the firm's cash from the beginning to the end of the fiscal period by summarizing the cash effects of the firm's operating, investing, and financing activities during the period. The statement of cash flows gives investors a chance to go beyond income statement numbers and determine whether those results are consistent with what is happening in the principal cash flow categories. For example, the first hints of financial difficulties of dot-com highfliers and Enron Corporation were visible in this financial statement.

Income Statement   **Exhibit 9-1**

CAMPBELL SOUP COMPANY
Consolidated Statements of Earnings
(dollars in millions, except per share amounts)

Three Years Ended July 30, 2017	2017 52 weeks	2016 52 weeks	2015 52 weeks
Net sales	$ 7,890	7,961	8,802
Costs and expenses			
Cost of products sold	4,831	5,191	5,300
Marketing and selling expenses	817	893	884
Administrative expenses................................	488	641	601
Research and development expenses	98	124	117
Other expenses / (income)..............................	238	131	24
Restructuring charges	18	31	102
Total costs and expenses..............................	6,490	7,001	7,028
Earnings before interest and taxes......................	1,400	960	1,054
Interest expense	112	115	108
Interest income	5	4	3
Earnings before taxes.................................	1,293	849	949
Taxes on earnings	406	286	283
Net earnings	887	563	666
Less: Net earnings (loss) attributable to noncontrolling interests	—	—	—
Net earnings attributable to Campbell Soup Company......................	$ 887	$ 563	$ 666
Per Share—Basic			
Net earnings attributable to Campbell Soup Company......................	$ 2.91	$1.82	$2.13
Weighted average shares outstanding—basic................................	305	309	312
Per Share—Assuming Dilution			
Net earnings attributable to Campbell Soup Company......................	2.89	1.81	2.13
Weighted average shares outstanding—assuming dilution......................	307	311	313

See accompanying Notes to Consolidated Financial Statements.

Campbell's Consolidated Statements of Cash Flows are presented in the appendix for each
of the past three years. Notice that the subtotal captions describe the activities—operating,
investing, and financing—that caused cash to be provided and used during these years. Pay
more attention to these three "big picture" items than to the detailed captions and amounts
within each category. Notice, however, that Campbell's uses a substantial amount of cash each
year to purchase plant assets (an investing activity) and to pay dividends (a financing activity). As
explained later, these are both signs of a financially healthy firm—especially if the firm can cover
these payments from its cash flows provided by operating activities. Did Campbell's do this for
each year presented?

Campbell's

The income statement and statement of cash flows report what has happened for a *period of time* (usually, but not necessarily, for the fiscal year ended on the balance sheet date). The balance sheet, remember, is focused on a single *point in time*—usually the end of the fiscal year—but one can be prepared as of any date.

What Does It Mean?

Answer on page 366

1. What does it mean when net income is referred to as the "bottom line"?

LEARNING OBJECTIVES (LO)

After studying this chapter, you should understand and be able to

LO 9-1   Explain what revenue is and what the two criteria are that permit revenue recognition.

LO 9-2   Describe how cost of goods sold is determined under both perpetual and periodic inventory accounting systems.

LO 9-3   Discuss the significance of gross profit and describe how the gross profit ratio is calculated and used.

LO 9-4   Identify the principal categories and components of "other operating expenses" and show how these items are reported on the income statement.

LO 9-5   Explain what "income from operations" includes and discuss why this income statement subtotal is significant to managers and financial analysts.

LO 9-6   Describe the components of the earnings per share calculation and discuss the reasons for some of the refinements made in that calculation.

LO 9-7   Compare and contrast the alternative income statement presentation models.

LO 9-8   Discuss the meaning and significance of each of the unusual or infrequently occurring items that may appear on the income statement.

LO 9-9   Describe the purpose and outline the general format of the statement of cash flows.

LO 9-10   Illustrate the difference between the direct and indirect methods of presenting cash flows from operating activities.

LO 9-11   Summarize why the statement of cash flows is significant to financial analysts and investors.

Exhibit 9-2 highlights the income statement and statement of cash flows components that are covered in detail in this chapter. Income statement transactions are often centered on the matching concept and thus have a direct effect on most of the firm's current

Exhibit 9-2

Financial Statements—
The Big Picture

Balance Sheet

Current Assets	Chapter	Current Assets	Chapter
Cash and cash equivalents	5, 9	Short-term debt	7
Short-term marketable securities	5	Current maturities of long-term debt	7
Accounts receivable	5, 9	Accounts payable	7
Notes receivable	5	Unearned revenue or deferred credits	7
Inventories	5, 9	Payroll taxes and other withholdings	7
Prepaid expenses	5	Other accrued liabilities	7
Noncurrent Assets			
Land	6	**Noncurrent Liabilities**	
Buildings and equipment	6	Long-term debt	7
Assets acquired by lease	6	Deferred tax liabilities	7
Intangible assets	6	Other long-term liabilities	7
Natural resources	6		
Other noncurrent assets	6	**Stockholders' Equity**	
		Common stock	8
		Preferred stock	8
		Additional paid-in capital	8
		Retained earnings	8
		Accumulated other comprehensive income (loss)	8
		Treasury stock	8
		Noncontrolling interest	8

Income Statement

	Chapter
Sales	5, 9
Cost of goods sold	5, 9
Gross profit (or gross margin)	5, 9
Selling, general, and administrative expenses	5, 6, 9
Income from operations	9
Gains (losses) on sale of assets	6, 9
Interest revenue	5, 9
Interest expense	7, 9
Income tax expense	7, 9
Unusual items	9
Net income	5, 6, 7, 8, 9
Earnings per share	9

Statement of Cash Flows

	Chapter
Operating Activities	
Net income	5, 6, 7, 8, 9
Depreciation expense	6, 9
(Gains) losses on sale of assets	6, 9
(Increase) decrease in current assets	5, 9
Increase (decrease) in current liabilities	7, 9
Investing Activities	
Proceeds from sale of property, plant, and equipment	6, 9
Purchase of property, plant, and equipment	6, 9
Financing Activities	
Proceeds from long-term debt*	7, 9
Repayment of long-term debt*	7, 9
Issuance of common stock and/or preferred stock	8, 9
Purchase of treasury stock	8, 9
Payment of dividends	8, 9

Primary topics of this chapter.
Other affected financial statement components.
* May include short-term debt items as well.

assets, especially accounts receivable and inventory. The preparation of the statement of cash flows requires analysis of the changes during the year to each and every balance sheet account, with cash as the focal point.

Income Statement

Revenues

LO 1

Explain what revenue is and what the two criteria are that permit revenue recognition.

The FASB defines **revenues** as "inflows or other enhancements of assets of an entity or settlements of its liabilities (or a combination of both) from delivering or producing goods, rendering services, or other activities that constitute the entity's ongoing major or central operations."[1] In its simplest and most straightforward application, this definition means that when a firm sells a product or provides a service to a client or customer and receives cash, creates an account receivable, or satisfies an obligation, the firm has revenue. Most revenue transactions fit this simple and straightforward situation. Revenues generally are measured by the amount of cash received or expected to be received from the transaction. If the cash is not expected to be received within a year, the revenue usually is measured by the present value of the amount expected to be received.

In *Concepts Statement No. 5,* the FASB expands on the preceding definition of revenues to provide guidance in applying the fundamental criteria involved in recognizing revenue. To be recognized, revenues must be realized or realizable and earned. Sometimes one of these criteria is more important than the other.

Realization means that the product or service has been exchanged for cash, claims to cash, or an asset that is readily convertible to a known amount of cash or claims to cash. Thus, the expectation that the product or service provided by the firm will result in a cash receipt has been fulfilled.

Earned means that the entity has completed, or substantially completed, the activities it must perform to be entitled to the revenue benefits (the increase in cash or some other asset, or the satisfaction of a liability).

The realization and earned criteria for recognizing revenue usually are satisfied when the product or merchandise being sold is delivered to the customer or when the service is provided. Thus, revenue from selling and servicing activities is commonly recognized when the sale is made, which means when the product is delivered or when the service is provided to the customer. Here is the effect on the financial statements:

Balance Sheet	Income Statement
Assets = Liabilities + Stockholders' equity	← Net income = Revenues − Expenses
+ Cash, or Accounts Receivable	+ Sales or Service Revenue

The typical entry would be as follows:

Dr.	Cash (or Accounts Receivable)	xx	
	Cr. Sales (or Service Revenue)		xx

---

[1] FASB, *Statement of Financial Accounting Concepts No. 6,* "Elements of Financial Statements" (Stamford, CT, 1985), para. 78. Copyright © by the Financial Accounting Standards Board, High Ridge Park, Stamford, CT 06905, U.S.A. Quoted with permission. Copies of the complete document are available from the FASB.

An example of a situation in which the *earned* criterion is more significant than the realization criterion is a magazine publishing company that receives cash at the beginning of a subscription period. In this case revenue is recognized as earned by delivery of the magazine. On the other hand, if a product is delivered or a service is provided without any expectation of receiving an asset or satisfying a liability (such as when a donation is made), there is no revenue to be recognized because the *realization* criterion has not been fulfilled.

When revenues are related to the use of assets over a period of time—such as the renting of property or the lending of money—they are earned as time passes and are recognized based on the contractual prices that have been established in advance.

Some agricultural products, precious metals, and marketable securities have readily determinable prices and can be sold without significant effort. Where this is the case, revenues (and some gains or losses) may be recognized when production is completed or when prices of the assets change. These are unusual situations, however, and exceptions to the rule that an arm's-length exchange (i.e., sales transaction) must occur to meet the realization and earned criteria.

Due to the increasing complexity of many business activities and other newly developed transactions, a number of revenue recognition problems have arisen over the years. Therefore, the FASB and its predecessors within the American Institute of Certified Public Accountants have issued numerous pronouncements about revenue recognition issues for various industries and transactions. As a result, revenue recognition is straightforward most of the time. However, because they are the key to the entire income statement, revenues that are misstated (usually on the high side) can lead to significantly misleading financial statements. Accordingly, management and internal auditors often design internal control procedures to help promote the accuracy of the revenue recognition process of the firm.

Sales is the term used to describe the revenues of firms that sell purchased or manufactured products. In the normal course of business, some sales transactions will be subsequently voided because the customer returns the merchandise for credit or for a refund. In some cases, rather than have a shipment returned (especially if it is only slightly damaged or defective and is still usable by the customer), the seller will make an allowance on the amount billed and reduce the account receivable from the customer for the allowance amount. If the customer has already paid, a refund is made. These **sales returns and allowances** are accounted for separately for internal control and analysis purposes but are subtracted from the gross sales amount to arrive at **net sales.** In addition, if the firm allows cash discounts for prompt payment, total sales discounts are also subtracted from gross sales for reporting purposes. A fully detailed income statement prepared for use within the company might have the following revenue section captions:

Sales	$
Less: Sales returns and allowances	( )
Less: Sales discounts	( )
Net sales	$

Net sales, or net revenues, is the first caption usually seen in the income statement of a merchandising or manufacturing company (as illustrated in Exhibit 9-1). Many companies provide a detailed calculation of the net sales amount in the accompanying notes of the annual report.

The **IFRS**

Approach

In May 2014, the FASB and IASB issued their long-awaited converged standard on revenue recognition, "Revenue from Contracts with Customers" (IASB 15). For public companies reporting under U.S. GAAP, the new revenue standard became effective for annual reporting periods beginning after January 1, 2018. The model adopted in this standard has affected revenue recognition under both U.S. GAAP and IFRS and has eliminated many of the differences in accounting for revenue between the two frameworks.

The guidance on revenue recognition under U.S. GAAP remains highly detailed and significantly more extensive than that provided under IFRS. Likewise, revenue recognition under U.S. GAAP tends to be industry specific, whereas IFRS takes a broad principles-based approach to be applied across all entities and industries. As a result, the timing of revenue recognition may be different in several instances, with revenue potentially being recognized earlier under IFRS.

Previous U.S. GAAP revenue guidance focused heavily on the "earnings process" as discussed earlier in this chapter with the *realization* and *earned* concepts, but difficulties often arise in determining when revenue is earned. The new model instead employs an asset and liability approach. The FASB and IASB both believe more consistency can be achieved by using a single, contract-based model where revenue recognition is based on changes in contract assets (rights to receive cash or other forms of consideration) and liabilities (obligations to provide a good or perform a service). Under the new model, revenue is now recognized based on the satisfaction of performance obligations.

In applying the new model, entities must follow this five-step process:

1. Identify the contract with a customer.

2. Identify the separate performance obligations in the contract.

3. Determine the transaction price.

4. Allocate the transaction price to the separate performance obligations.

5. Recognize revenue when (or as) each performance obligation is satisfied.

Although this new framework marks a stark change under both U.S. GAAP and IFRS concerning the process of analyzing transactions to determine their revenue effects, the results of such analysis are likely to be the same as dictated under the old (realization and earned) model in most cases. Notice that in step 5, revenue is recognized when each "performance obligation" is satisfied. This normally occurs either when the sale of goods is complete or when the delivery of services has taken place. In other words, although business transactions are now analyzed differently under the new standard, revenue continues to be recognized when it has been realized and earned.

Firms that generate significant amounts of revenue from providing services in addition to (or instead of) selling a product will label the revenue source appropriately in the income statement. Thus, a leasing company might report Rental and Service Revenues as the lead item on its income statement, or a consulting service firm might show Fee Revenues or simply Fees. If a firm has several types of revenue, the amount of each could be shown if each amount is significant and is judged by the accountant to increase the usefulness of the income statement.

From a legal perspective, the sale of a product involves the passing of title (i.e., ownership rights) in the product from the seller to the purchaser. The point at which title passes usually is specified by the shipment terms (see Business in Practice—Shipping Terms). This issue becomes especially significant in two situations. The first involves shipments made near the end of a fiscal period. The shipping terms determine whether revenue is recognized in the period in which the shipment was made or in the subsequent period when the shipment is received by the customer. Achieving an

Shipping Terms

Business in
Practice

Many products are shipped from the seller to the buyer instead of being picked up by the buyer at the time of sale. **Shipping terms** define the owner of products while they are in transit. **FOB destination** and **FOB shipping point** are the terms used. (FOB means *free on board* and is jargon that has carried over from the days when much merchandise was shipped by boat.) When an item is shipped FOB destination, the seller owns the product until it is accepted by the buyer at the buyer's designated location. Thus, title to merchandise shipped FOB destination passes from seller to buyer when the merchandise is received by the buyer. FOB shipping point means that the buyer accepts ownership of the product at the seller's shipping location.

Shipping terms also describe which party to the transaction is to *incur* the shipping cost. The *seller* incurs the freight cost for shipments made FOB destination; the *buyer* incurs the cost of shipments made FOB shipping point. *Payment* of the freight cost is another issue, however. The freight cost for products shipped **freight prepaid** is paid by the seller; when a shipment arrives **freight collect**, the buyer pays the freight cost. Ordinarily, items shipped FOB destination will have freight prepaid, and items shipped FOB shipping point will be shipped freight collect. However, depending on freight company policies or other factors, an item having shipping terms of FOB destination may be shipped freight collect, or vice versa. If this happens, the firm paying the freight subsequently collects the amount paid to the freight company from the other firm, which *incurred* the freight cost under the shipping terms.

accurate "sales cutoff" may be important to the accuracy of the financial statements if the period-end shipments are material in amount. The second situation relates to any loss of or damage to the merchandise while it is in transit from the seller to the buyer. The legal owner of the merchandise, as determined by the shipping terms, is the one who suffers the loss. Of course, this party may seek to recover the amount of the loss from the party responsible for the damage (usually a third-party shipping company).

For certain sales transactions, a firm may take more than a year to construct the item being sold (e.g., a cruise ship builder or a manufacturer of complex custom machinery). In these circumstances, delaying revenue recognition until the product has been delivered may result in the reporting of misleading income statement information for a number of years. Because these items are being manufactured under a contract with the buyer that specifies a price, it is possible to recognize revenue (and costs and profits) under what is known as the **percentage-of-completion method.** If, based on engineers' analyses and other factors, 40 percent of a job has been completed in the current year, 40 percent of the expected revenue (and 40 percent of the expected costs) will be recognized in the current year.

Companies should disclose any unusual revenue recognition methods, such as the percentage-of-completion method, in the notes accompanying the financial statements. Because profits will be directly affected by revenue, the user of the financial statements must be alert to, and understand the effect of, any revenue recognition method that differs from the usual and generally accepted practice of recognizing revenue when the product or service has been delivered to the customer (see Business in Practice—Revenue Recognition Practices of Dot-Com Companies for a glimpse at some of the questionable practices employed in recent years).

Gains, which are increases in an entity's net assets resulting from incidental transactions or nonoperating activities, are usually not included with revenues at the beginning of the income statement. Gains are reported as other income after the firm's operating expenses have been shown and income from operations has been reported.

Revenue Recognition Practices of Dot-Com Companies

Rapidly rising stock values of dot-com companies during the late 1990s seemed to run contrary to traditional value measures such as the price/earnings ratio because many of these companies had no earnings. Financial analysts and investors used revenue growth as a key benchmark. That focus tempted many firms to record revenues in ways that stretched generally accepted revenue recognition practices and bordered on reporting misleading results. Some of these practices were the following:

Recognizing revenue too soon: Revenue was recognized when orders were received but before they were shipped, or revenue was recorded from future software upgrades before the upgrades had been completed, or revenue was recognized from software licenses when a contract was signed rather than over the life of the contract.

Overstating revenue from reselling: When a product or service was resold without ever having been owned by the reseller, revenue was recognized for the full amount charged to the purchaser rather than just for the reseller's markup.

As a result of such questionable practices, the Securities and Exchange Commission (SEC) issued a staff accounting bulletin on revenue recognition in late 1999 that generally delayed the recognition of revenue into future quarters for certain dot-com companies and caused several affected companies to restate prior year earnings. Historically, more than half of all SEC accounting fraud cases have involved revenue hoaxes, so the heightened scrutiny of software company practices did not come as a surprise to many financial analysts.

Interest income is an example of an "other income" item. The reporting of gains will be explained in more detail later in this chapter.

Expenses

The FASB defines **expenses** as "outflows or other using up of assets or incurrences of liabilities (or a combination of both) from delivering or producing goods, rendering services, or carrying out other activities that constitute the entity's ongoing major or central operations."[2] Some expenses (cost of goods sold is an example) are recognized concurrently with the revenues to which they relate. This is another application of the **matching principle,** which has been previously described and emphasized. Some expenses (e.g., administrative salaries) are recognized in the period in which they are incurred because the benefit of the expense is used up simultaneously or soon after incurrence. Other expenses (e.g., depreciation) result from an allocation of the cost of an asset to the periods that are expected to benefit from its use. In each of these categories, expenses are recognized in accordance with the matching principle because they are incurred to support the revenue-generating process. The amount of an expense is measured by the cash or other asset used up to obtain the economic benefit it represents. When the outflow of cash related to the expense will not occur within a year, it is appropriate to recognize the present value of the future cash flow as the amount of the expense.

Most of the time, identifying expenses to be recognized in the current period's income statement is straightforward. Cost of goods sold, compensation of employees,

---

[2] FASB, *Statement of Financial Accounting Concepts No. 6,* "Elements of Financial Statements" (Stamford, CT, 1985), para. 80. Copyright © by the Financial Accounting Standards Board, High Ridge Park, Stamford, CT 06905, U.S.A. Quoted with permission. Copies of the complete document are available from the FASB.

uncollectible accounts receivable, utilities consumed, and depreciation of long-lived assets are all examples. In other cases (e.g., research and development costs and advertising expense), the impact of the expenditure on the revenues of future periods is not readily determinable. For these types of expenditures, there is no sound method of matching the expenditure with the revenues that may be earned over several periods. To avoid the necessity of making arbitrary allocations, all advertising and R&D expenditures are recorded as expenses in the period incurred under U.S. GAAP. This approach is justified by the objectivity and conservatism concepts.

Other types of expense involve complex recognition and measurement issues; income tax expense and pension expense are just two examples. Recall the discussion of these topics in Chapter 7 when the liabilities related to these expenses were discussed.

Losses, which are decreases in an entity's net assets resulting from incidental transactions or nonoperating activities, are not included with expenses. Losses are reported after income from operations, as discussed later in this chapter.

The discussion of expenses in this chapter follows the sequence in which expenses are presented in most income statements.

Cost of Goods Sold

Cost of goods sold (sometimes called "cost of products sold" as is the case for Campbell Soup Company) is the most significant expense for many manufacturing and merchandising companies. Recall from your study of the accounting for inventories in Chapter 5 that the **inventory cost flow assumption** (FIFO, LIFO, weighted-average) being used by the firm affects this expense. **Inventory shrinkage** (the term that describes inventory losses from obsolescence, errors, and theft) usually is included in cost of goods sold unless the amount involved is material. In that case the inventory loss would be reported separately as a loss after operating income has been reported.

Determination of the cost of goods sold amount is a function of the inventory cost flow assumption and the inventory accounting system (periodic or perpetual) used to account for inventories. Recall that under a perpetual system, a record is made of every purchase and every sale, and a continuous record of the quantity and cost of each item is maintained. When an item is sold, its cost (as determined according to the cost flow assumption) is transferred from the inventory asset to the cost of goods sold expense with the following effect on the financial statements:

Campbell's

LO 2

Describe how cost of goods sold is determined under both perpetual and periodic inventory accounting systems.

Balance Sheet	Income Statement
Assets = Liabilities + Stockholders' equity	← Net income = Revenues − Expenses
− Inventory	− Cost of Goods Sold

Here is the entry:

| Dr. | Cost of Goods Sold | xx | |
| | Cr. Inventory | | xx |

The key point about a perpetual inventory system is that cost is determined when the item is sold. As you can imagine, a perpetual inventory system requires much data processing but can give management a great deal of information about which inventory items are selling well and which are not. Advances in point-of-sale technologies (such as standard bar code scanners used by retail stores) have allowed even small merchandising firms to achieve perpetual inventories. Some systems are even tied in with the firms' suppliers so that when inventory falls to a certain level, a reorder is automatically placed. Under any type of perpetual system, regular counts of specific inventory items will be made on a cycle basis during the year, and actual quantities on hand will be compared to the computer record of the quantity on hand. This is an internal control procedure designed to determine whether the perpetual system is operating accurately and to trigger an investigation of significant differences.

Campbell's

In a periodic inventory system, a count of the inventory on hand *(taking a physical inventory)* is made periodically—frequently at the end of a fiscal year—and the cost of inventory on hand (determined according to the cost flow assumption) is determined. This cost is then subtracted from the sum of the cost of the beginning inventory (that is, the ending inventory of the prior period) and the cost of the merchandise purchased during the current period. (A manufacturing firm uses the cost of goods manufactured—discussed in Chapter 13—rather than purchases.) This **cost of goods sold model** is illustrated here using 2017 data from the Campbell Soup Company financial statements in the appendix. Can you find the inventory and cost of goods sold amounts in the appendix? The unknown amounts for net purchases and goods available for sale have been solved for in the model using these known amounts. All amounts are in millions of dollars:

Cost of beginning inventory	$ 940
+ Net purchases (cost of goods manufactured)	4,793
= Cost of goods available for sale	$5,733
− Cost of ending inventory	(902)
= Cost of goods (products) sold	$4,831

The amounts shown for cost of goods sold, inventory, and net purchases include the price paid to the supplier, plus all ordinary and necessary costs related to the purchase transaction (such as freight and material handling charges). Cost is reduced by the amount of any cash discount allowed on the purchase. When the periodic inventory system is used, freight charges, purchase discounts, and **purchase returns and allowances** (the purchaser's side of the sales return and allowance transaction) are usually recorded in separate accounts, and each account balance is classified with purchases. Thus, the net purchases amount is made up of the following:

Purchases	$
Add: Freight charges	
Less: Purchase discounts	( )
Less: Purchase returns and allowances	( )
Net purchases	$

Although the periodic system may require a less complicated recordkeeping system than the perpetual system, the need to take a complete physical inventory to determine accurately the cost of goods sold is a disadvantage. Also, although it can be estimated or developed from special analysis, inventory shrinkage (losses from theft, errors, and so on) is not really known when the periodic system is used because these losses are included in the total cost of goods sold.

Note that selling and administrative expenses (discussed later in the Operating Expenses section of this chapter) are not included as part of cost of goods sold.

Gross Profit or Gross Margin

The difference between sales revenue and cost of goods sold is **gross profit,** or **gross margin.** Using data from Exhibit 9-1, here is the income statement for Campbell Soup Company to this point:

LO 3

Discuss the significance of gross profit and describe how the gross profit ratio is calculated and used.

CAMPBELL SOUP COMPANY			
Consolidated Statements of Earnings			
(dollars in millions)			
Three Years Ended July 30, 2017	**2017**	**2016**	**2015**
Net sales	$7,890	$7,961	$8,082
Cost of products sold	4,831	5,181	5,300
Gross margin	$3,059	$2,780	$2,782

Campbell's

When the amount of gross profit is expressed as a percentage of the sales amount, the resulting **gross profit ratio** (or **gross margin ratio**) is an especially important statistic for managers of manufacturing and merchandising firms. The calculation of the gross profit ratio for Campbell Soup Company for 2017 is illustrated in Exhibit 9-3.

Campbell's

Because the gross profit ratio is a measure of the amount of each sales dollar that is available to cover operating expenses and profit, one of its principal uses by management is to estimate whether the firm is operating at a level of sales that will lead to profitability in the current period. Financial managers know from experience that if the firm is to be profitable, a certain gross profit ratio and level of sales must be achieved. Sales can be determined daily from cash register tapes or sales invoice records, and that amount then can be multiplied by the estimated gross profit ratio to determine the estimated gross profit amount. This amount can be related to estimated operating expenses to estimate the firm's income from operations. In many cases, just knowing the amount of sales is enough to be able to estimate whether the firm has reached profitability. This is especially true for firms that have virtually the same gross profit ratio for every item sold. However, if the gross profit ratio differs by class of merchandise (and it usually

CAMPBELL SOUP COMPANY	
Gross Profit Ratio—2017	
(dollars in millions)	
Net sales (or net revenues)	$7,890
Cost of products sold (or cost of goods sold)	4,831
Gross profit (or gross margin)	$3,059
Gross profit ratio = Gross profit / Net sales	
= $3,059/$7,890	
= 38.8%	

Exhibit 9-3

Gross Profit Ratio

does), then the proportion of the sales of each class to total sales (the **sales mix**) must be considered when estimating total gross profit. For example, assume that Campbell's has average gross profit ratios of 45 percent on simple meals (including sauces, carrot products, refrigerated salad dressings, salsa, hummus, and dips), 35 percent on baked snacks (including cookies, crackers, and biscuits), and 25 percent on beverages. If the sales mix changes frequently, the sales of each product category must be considered to estimate total gross profit anticipated for any given month.

The gross profit ratio can be used to estimate cost of goods sold and ending inventory for periods in which a physical inventory has not been taken, as illustrated in Exhibit 9-4. This is the process used to estimate the amount of inventory lost in a fire, flood, or other natural disaster. Note that the key to the calculation is the estimated gross profit ratio. Many firms prepare quarterly (or monthly) income statements for internal reporting purposes and use this estimation technique to avoid the cost and business interruptions associated with an inventory count.

Another important use of the gross profit ratio is to set selling prices. If the manager knows the gross profit ratio required to achieve profitability at a given level of sales, the cost of the item can be divided by the complement of the gross profit ratio (or the cost of goods sold ratio) to determine the selling price. This is illustrated in Exhibit 9-5. However, competitive pressures, the manufacturer's recommended selling price, and other factors also influence the price finally established, but the desired gross profit ratio and the item's cost are frequently the starting points in the pricing decision.

The gross profit ratio required to achieve profitability will vary among firms as a result of their operating strategies. For example, a discount store seeks a high sales volume and a low level of operating expenses, so a relatively low gross profit ratio is accepted. A boutique, on the other hand, has a relatively low sales volume and higher operating expenses and needs a relatively high gross profit ratio to achieve profitability.

Exhibit 9-4

Using the Gross Profit Ratio to Estimate Ending Inventory and Cost of Goods Sold

Assumptions:

A firm expects to have a gross profit ratio of 30% for the current fiscal year. Beginning inventory is known because it is the amount of the physical inventory taken at the end of the prior fiscal year. Net sales and net purchases are known from the accounting records of the current fiscal year.

Here is the model (with assumed known data entered):

Net sales	$100,000	100%
Cost of goods sold:		
Beginning inventory	$ 19,000	
Net purchases	63,000	
Cost of goods available for sale	$ 82,000	
Less: Ending inventory	?	
Cost of goods sold	$?	
Gross profit	$?	30%

Calculation of estimated ending inventory:

Gross profit = 30% × $100,000 = $30,000
Cost of goods sold = $100,000 − $30,000 = $70,000
Ending inventory = $82,000 − $70,000 = $12,000

Assumptions:

A retail store's cost for a particular carpet is $8 per square yard, and the store owners have a 20% desired gross profit ratio. What selling price per square yard should be established for this product?

$$\text{Selling price} = \text{Cost of product}/(1 - \text{Desired gross profit ratio})$$
$$= \$\,8/(1 - 0.2)$$
$$= \$10$$

Proof:

Calculated selling price	$10 per square yard
Cost of product	8 per square yard
Gross profit	$ 2 per square yard

$$\text{Gross profit ratio} = \text{Gross profit}/\text{Selling price}$$
$$= \$2/\$10$$
$$= 20\%$$

Exhibit 9-5

Using Desired Gross Profit Ratio to Set Selling Price

Even though gross profit and the gross profit ratio are widely used internally by the managers of the firm, many companies (including Campbell's) do not present gross profit as a separate item in their published income statements. However, cost of goods sold usually is shown as a separate item. Thus, the user of the income statement can make the calculation for comparative and other evaluation purposes.

Campbell's

Operating Expenses

The principal categories of other **operating expenses** frequently reported on the income statement are the following:

Selling expenses.
General and administrative expenses.
Research and development expenses.

These categories can be combined in a variety of ways for financial reporting purposes. For instance, Campbell's uses three principal categories: "Marketing and selling expenses," "Administrative expenses," and "Research and development expenses."

The financial statement notes sometimes provide detailed disclosure of the nature and amount of expense items that are combined with others in the income statement. However, management often reports certain operating expenses as separate items to highlight their significance. Common examples include repair and maintenance, research and development, and advertising. Total depreciation and amortization expense is frequently reported as a separate item on the income statement (or disclosed in the notes to the financial statements) because these expenses do not result in the disbursement of cash. The total of depreciation and amortization expense also appears in the statement of cash flows, as will be illustrated later in this chapter. Note that Campbell's includes a separate line item for restructuring charges (discussed in the notes to the consolidated financial statements in Campbell's annual report in the appendix).

LO 4

Identify the principal categories and components of "other operating expenses" and show how these items are reported on the income statement.

Campbell's

Income from Operations

The difference between gross profit and operating expenses represents **income from operations** (or **operating income**), as shown in the following partial income statement from Exhibit 9-1:

LO 5

Explain what "income from operations" includes and discuss why this income statement subtotal is significant to managers and financial analysts.

CAMPBELL SOUP COMPANY Consolidated Statements of Earnings (dollars in millions)			
Three Years Ended July 30, 2017	**2017**	**2016**	**2015**
Net sales	$7,890	$7,961	$8,082
Costs and expenses:			
Cost of products sold	4,831	5,181	5,300
Marketing and selling expenses	817	893	884
Administrative expenses	488	641	601
Research and development expenses	98	124	117
Other expenses (income)	238	131	24
Restructuring charges	18	31	102
Total costs and expenses	6,490	7,001	7,028
Earnings before interest and taxes	1,400	960	1,054

Campbell's

Although only an intermediate subtotal on the income statement, income from operations (reported as "Earnings before interest and taxes" by Campbell's) is frequently interpreted as the most appropriate measure of management's ability to utilize the firm's operating assets. Income from operations normally *excludes* the effects of interest expense, interest revenue, gains and losses, income taxes, and other nonoperating transactions. Thus, many investors prefer to use income from operations data (rather than net income data) to make a "cleaner" assessment of the firm's profitability trend. As discussed in Chapter 3, income from operations is frequently used in the return on investment calculation, which relates operating income to average operating assets.

Although operating income is commonly used as a proxy for net income, investors must pay careful attention to the items that are included in the determination of this important subtotal. In recent years, for example, many firms have reported items such as "restructuring charges" and "asset impairment losses" as operating expenses because the corporate downsizing efforts that lead to such write-offs have been occurring more frequently. Yet other firms report these items in the "other income and expenses" category, which is shown as a *nonoperating* item. Of course, it also is permissible (and quite common) to simply subtract total expenses from total revenues to arrive at net income without indicating a separate amount for income from operations.

Managers of firms that do not report income from operations as a separate item believe that other income and expense items (such as gains and losses) should receive as much attention in the evaluation process as revenues and expenses from the firm's principal operations. After all, nonoperating items do exist and do affect overall profitability. There is no single best presentation for all firms; this is another area in which the accountant's judgment is used to select among equally acceptable financial reporting alternatives.

Other Income and Expenses

Other income and expenses are reported after income from operations. These non-operating items include interest expense, interest revenue, gains, and losses.

Interest expense is the item of other income and expenses most frequently identified separately. Most financial statement users want to know the amount of this expense because it represents a contractual obligation that cannot be avoided. As discussed in Chapter 7, interest expense is associated with financial leverage. The more a firm borrows, the more interest expense it incurs, and the higher its financial leverage. Although this may lead to a greater ROE for stockholders, it also increases the riskiness of their investment.

Interest revenue earned from excess cash that has been temporarily invested is not ordinarily subtracted from interest expense. Interest revenue is reported as a separate item if it is material in amount relative to other nonoperating items. The full disclosure principle is applied to determine the extent of the details reported in this section of the income statement. Significant items that would facilitate the reader's understanding of net income or loss are separately identified, either in the statement itself or in the notes. Items that are not significant are combined in an "other" or "miscellaneous" category. Examples of nonoperating gains or losses are those resulting from litigation, the sale or disposal of depreciable assets (including plant closings), and inventory obsolescence losses; also shown here are items that are unusual or infrequent occurring.

Income before Income Taxes and Income Tax Expense

The income statement usually has a subtotal labeled "**Income before income taxes,**" followed by the caption "Income taxes" or "Provision for income taxes" and the amount of this expense. Some income statements do not use the "Income before income taxes" caption; income taxes are simply listed as another expense in these statements. There will always be a note disclosure of the details of the income tax expense calculation because this is required by generally accepted accounting principles.

---

2. What does it mean to look at the trend of the major subtotals on an income statement?

What Does It Mean?

Answer on page 366

Net Income and Earnings per Share

Net income (or net loss), sometimes called the *bottom line,* is the arithmetic sum of the revenues and gains minus the expenses and losses. Because net income increases retained earnings, which usually is a prerequisite to dividends, stockholders and potential investors are especially interested in net income. Reinforce your understanding of information presented in the income statement by referring again to Exhibit 9-1 and by studying the structure of income statements in other annual reports you may have.

To facilitate interpretation of net income (or loss), it also is reported on a per share of common stock basis. Reported are **basic earnings per share** and, if the firm has issued stock options or convertible securities (long-term debt or preferred stock that is convertible into common stock), **diluted earnings per share.** Basic EPS and diluted EPS (if appropriate) are presented both for income from continuing operations and

LO 6

Describe the components of the earnings per share calculation and discuss the reasons for some of the refinements made in that calculation.

Exhibit 9-6

Weighted-Average
Shares Outstanding
Calculation

Assumptions:

On September 1, 2019, the beginning of its fiscal year, Cruisers Inc. had 200,000 shares of common stock outstanding.

On December 3, 2019, 40,000 additional shares were issued for cash.

On June 28, 2020, 15,000 shares of common stock were acquired as treasury stock (and are no longer outstanding).

Weighted-average calculation:

Period	Number of Months	Number of Shares Outstanding	Months × Shares
9/1–12/3...............................	3	200,000	600,000
12/3–6/28..............................	7	240,000	1,680,000
6/28–8/31...............................	2	225,000	450,000
Totals	12		2,730,000

Weighted-average number of shares outstanding = 2,730,000/12

= 227,500

for net income. Basic earnings per share is calculated by dividing net income by the average number of shares of common stock outstanding during the year. Two principal complications in the calculation should be understood. First, a weighted-average number of shares of common stock is used. This is sensible because if shares are issued early in the year, the proceeds from their sale have been used longer in the income-generating process than the proceeds from shares issued later in the year. For illustration purposes, the weighting basis used is the number of months each block of shares has been outstanding. The weighted-average calculation is illustrated in Exhibit 9-6.

The other complication in the EPS calculation arises when a firm has preferred stock outstanding. Remember that preferred stock is entitled to its dividend before dividends can be paid on common stock. Because of this prior claim to earnings, the amount of the preferred stock dividend requirement is subtracted from net income to arrive at the numerator in the calculation of earnings per share of common stock outstanding. Recall that dividends are not expenses, so the preferred stock dividend requirement is not shown as a deduction in the income statement. To illustrate the basic EPS calculation, assume that Cruisers Inc. had net income of $1,527,000 for the year ended August 31, 2020, and had 80,000 shares of a 7 percent, $50 par value preferred stock outstanding during the year. Using the weighted-average number of shares of common stock outstanding from Exhibit 9-6, the earnings per share of common stock would be calculated as follows:

Net income	$1,527,000
Less preferred stock dividend requirement	
(7% × $50 par value × 80,000 shares outstanding)	280,000
Net income available for common stock	$1,247,000

$$\text{Basic earnings per share of common stock outstanding} = \frac{\text{Net income available for common stock}}{\text{Weighted-average number of shares of common stock outstanding}}$$

$$= \$1,247,000 \,/\, 227,500$$

$$= \$5.48$$

Because of their significance, earnings per share amounts are reported on the income statement just below the amount of net income.

As stated previously, in addition to the basic earnings per share, a firm may be required to report *diluted earnings per share.* If the firm has issued long-term debt or preferred stock that is convertible into common stock, it is possible that the conversion of the debt or preferred stock could reduce basic earnings per share of common stock outstanding. This can happen if the increase in net income available for common stock (if interest expense is reduced, or preferred dividends are not required) is proportionately less than the number of additional common shares issued in the conversion. If a firm has a stock option plan (see Chapter 10), the issuance of additional shares pursuant to the plan likewise has the potential of reducing basic earnings per share. Other incentive and financing arrangements may also require issuance of additional shares, which may similarly decrease basic earnings per share. The reduction in basic earnings per share of common stock is referred to as **dilution.** The effect of the potential dilution is reported on the income statement by showing diluted earnings per share of common stock as well as basic earnings per share. Campbell's diluted earnings per share of $2.89 for 2017 represented a potential dilution of just $0.02 per share due to the potentially dilutive effects of stock options and other share-based payment awards. Refer to the Campbell's annual report in the appendix for details.

The income statement presentation of net income and EPS follows. Data are from the previous Cruisers illustrations, which have no discontinued operations. Note that the diluted earnings per share amount is assumed for illustration:

Net income	$1,527,000
Basic earnings per share of common stock	$ 5.48
Diluted earnings per share of common stock	$ 5.27

If there are any *discontinued operations* reported on the income statement (discussed later in this chapter), the EPS effect(s) of the discontinued operations must be disclosed separately on the face of the income statement. Thus, the reported EPS amounts for both basic and diluted EPS will be the sum of the EPS from income (or loss) from continuing operations and the EPS effect(s) of the discontinued operations.

---

3. What does it mean when earnings per share are subject to dilution?

What Does It Mean?

Answer on page 366

Income Statement Presentation Alternatives

There are two principal alternative presentations of income statement data: the **single-step format** and the **multiple-step format.** These are illustrated in Exhibit 9-7 using hypothetical data for Cruisers for fiscal years 2019 and 2020. (Examples of the unusual or infrequently occurring items that may appear on the income statement are discussed in the next section of this chapter and illustrated in Exhibit 9-8.)

LO 7

Compare and contrast the alternative income statement presentation models.

Exhibit 9-7

Income Statement
Format Alternatives

I. Single-step format:

CRUISERS INC. AND SUBSIDIARIES Consolidated Income Statement For the Years Ended August 31, 2020 and 2019 (000 omitted)		
	2020	**2019**
Net sales	$77,543	$62,531
Cost of goods sold	48,077	39,870
Selling expenses	13,957	10,590
General and administrative expenses	9,739	8,191
Interest expense	3,378	2,679
Other income, net	385	193
Income before taxes	$ 2,777	$ 1,394
Provision for income taxes	1,250	630
Net income	$ 1,527	$ 764
Basic earnings per share of common stock	$ 5.48	$ 2.42

II. Multiple-step format:

CRUISERS INC. AND SUBSIDIARIES Consolidated Income Statement For the Years Ended August 31, 2020 and 2019 (000 omitted)		
	2020	**2019**
Net sales	$77,543	$62,531
Cost of goods sold	48,077	39,870
Gross profit	$29,466	$22,661
Selling, general, and administrative expenses	23,696	18,781
Income from operations	$ 5,770	$ 3,880
Other income (expense):		
Interest expense	(3,378)	(2,679)
Other income, net	385	193
Income before taxes	$ 2,777	$ 1,394
Provision for income taxes	1,250	630
Net income	$ 1,527	$ 764
Basic earnings per share of common stock	$ 5.48	$ 2.42

The principal difference between these two formats is that the multiple-step format provides subtotals for gross profit and income from operations. As previously discussed, each of these amounts is useful in evaluating the performance of the firm, and proponents of the multiple-step format believe that it is appropriate to highlight these amounts.

You may notice an inconsistency in the use of parentheses in the single-step and multiple-step formats in Exhibit 9-7. No parentheses are used in the single-step format; the user is expected to know by reading the captions which items to add and which to subtract in the calculation of net income. In the multiple-step format the caption for "Other income (expense)" indicates that *in this section of the statement,* items without

Exhibit 9-8

Income Statement
Presentation of
Unusual or Infrequently
Occurring Items
*(continued from
Exhibit 9-7)*

Under either the single-step or multiple-step format (see Exhibit 9-7), the "Income before taxes" caption would be shown as "Income from *continuing operations* before taxes," and the rest of the income statement would appear as follows:

	2020	2019
Income from continuing operations before taxes...............	$ 2,777	$1,394
Provision for income taxes	1,250	630
Income from continuing operations...........................	$ 1,527	$ 764
Discontinued operations, net of income taxes:		
Loss from operations	(162)	(122)
Loss on disposal...	(79)	—
Loss from discontinued operations	$ (241)	(122)
Net income...	$ 1,286	$ 642
Basic earnings per share of common stock outstanding:		
Continuing operations......................................	$ 5.48	$ 2.42
Discontinued operations:		
Loss from operations	(0.71)	(0.61)
Loss on disposal..	(0.35)	—
Net income	$ 4.42	$ 1.81

parentheses are added and items in parentheses are subtracted. In other parts of the statement, the caption indicates the arithmetic operation. With either format, the statement reader must be alert to make sense of the information presented in the statement.

The gradual trend during the past several decades has been for more companies to use the multiple-step income statement format. A survey of the year 2011 annual reports (last available data) of 500 publicly owned industrial and merchandising companies indicated that only 87 companies continued to use the single-step format.[3] This trend apparently reflects the increasing complexity of business activities and the demand for more detailed information.

Unusual or Infrequently Occurring Items Sometimes Seen on an Income Statement

One way investors and potential investors use the income statement is to predict probable results of future operations from the results of current operations. Nonrecurring transactions that affect the predictive process are highlighted and reported separately from the results of recurring transactions. The reporting of unusual or infrequently occurring items also facilitates users' comparisons of net income for the current year with that of prior years. Perhaps the most frequently encountered unusual item relates to discontinued operations, which are reported net of their income tax effects. Extraordinary items were previously reported net of income taxes as well, but are no longer reported as a separate income statement category. Another caption sometimes seen on an income statement relates to the noncontrolling (minority) interest in earnings of subsidiaries. Each of these unusual or infrequently occurring items is discussed in the following paragraphs.

LO 8

Discuss the meaning
and significance of each
of the unusual or infre-
quently occurring items
that may appear on the
income statement.

---

[3] AICPA, *Accounting Trends and Techniques* (New York, 2011), Table 3-1.

Discontinued Operations   When a segment, or major portion of a business, is disposed of, it is appropriate to disclose separately the impact that the discontinued operation has had on the current operations of the firm, as well as its impact on any previous year results that are shown for comparative purposes. This separate disclosure is made to help users of the financial statements understand how future income statements may differ because the firm will be operating without the disposed business segment. This is accomplished by reporting the income or loss, after income taxes, of the discontinued operation separately after a subtotal amount labeled **income from continuing operations.** (Income from continuing operations is the income after income taxes of continuing operations.) By reporting discontinued operations as a separate item, net of taxes, all the effects of the discontinued business segment are excluded from the revenues, expenses, gains, and losses of continuing operations. This presentation is illustrated in Exhibit 9-8. Note that earnings per share data are also reported separately for discontinued operations. If Cruisers had issued dilutive securities or stock options, the impact of the discontinued operations on diluted EPS data would also have been reported.

What Does It Mean?

Answer on page 366

4.   What does it mean when income or loss from discontinued operations is shown in the income statement?

Extraordinary Items   Under U.S. GAAP, a transaction that was unusual in nature and occurred infrequently previously qualified for reporting as an **extraordinary item** if the amount involved had a significant after-tax income statement effect. The reason for such separate reporting was to emphasize that the item was extraordinary and that the income statements for subsequent years would not likely include this kind of item. Examples of extraordinary items were pension plan terminations, some litigation settlements, and utilization of tax loss carryforwards. The financial effects of natural disasters such as hurricanes, earthquakes, and major floods or fires were also accounted for as extraordinary items. When an extraordinary item was reported, basic and diluted (if applicable) earnings per share of common stock outstanding were reported for income before the extraordinary item, for the extraordinary item, and for net income (after the extraordinary item).

Although extraordinary items are no longer shown as a separate category for financial reporting purposes under U.S. GAAP, some companies may continue to report the comparative effects of extraordinary items that occurred in years prior to the December 15, 2015, transition date of the new standard.

The current accounting standard now requires that firms report any material events or transactions that are unusual in nature or occur infrequently, or both, as a separate

The IFRS Approach

Under IFRS, there is no distinction between revenues/gains or expenses/losses on the income statement. Extraordinary items are not recognized separately and reported net of tax, but instead are included with other revenues and expenses within operating income. Effective for reporting periods beginning on December 15, 2015, the FASB has adopted this approach for U.S. GAAP as well, thereby eliminating the extraordinary items category for all subsequent years.

component of income from continuing operations. The nature and financial effects of each such material event or transaction are disclosed in the notes to the financial statements. However, the EPS effects of such items are no longer be presented on the face of the income statement, nor are the dollar amounts reported for such items shown net of the related tax effects.

Noncontrolling Interest in Earnings of Subsidiaries   As explained in Chapters 7 and 8, the financial statements of a subsidiary are consolidated with those of the parent even though the parent owns less than 100 percent of the stock of the subsidiary. The consolidated income statement includes all the revenues, expenses, gains, and losses of the subsidiary. However, only the parent company's equity in the subsidiary's earnings should be included in the *bottom line,* **net income attributable to (parent company name)** caption (sometimes referred to as *net income attributable to controlling interest*). The amount of **net income attributable to noncontrolling interest** must also be clearly identified and presented on the face of the consolidated income statement, and is normally subtracted from net income as follows:

>   Revenues
> − Expenses
> = Net income
> − Net income attributable to noncontrolling interest
> = Net income attributable to (parent company name)

Earnings-per-share amounts reported in consolidated financial statements are based on net income attributable to the parent.

Statement of Cash Flows

Content and Format of the Statement

The **statement of cash flows** is a required financial statement that illustrates how accounting evolves to meet the requirements of users of financial statements. The importance of understanding the cash flows of an entity has been increasingly emphasized over the years. The accrual basis income statement is not designed to present cash flows from operations, and except for related revenues and expenses, it shows no information about cash flows from investing and financing activities.

LO 9
Describe the purpose and outline the general format of the statement of cash flows.

    The primary purpose of the statement of cash flows is to provide relevant information about the cash receipts and cash payments of an enterprise during a period. The statement shows why cash (including short-term investments that are essentially equivalent to cash) changed during the period by reporting net cash provided or used by operating activities, investing activities, and financing activities.

Cash Flows from Operating Activities   There are two alternative approaches to presenting the operating activities section of the statement of cash flows: the *direct method presentation* and the *indirect method presentation.* The direct method involves listing each major class of cash receipts transactions and cash disbursements transactions for each of the three activity areas. The operating activity transactions include cash received from customers, cash paid to merchandise or raw material suppliers, cash paid to employees for salaries and wages, cash paid for other operating expenses, cash payments of interest, and cash payments for taxes. A direct method statement of cash flows is illustrated in Section I of Exhibit 9-9. *Notice that under the direct method, each of the captions reported on the statement explains how much cash was received or paid during the year for that item.* For this reason the FASB encourages enterprises to use the direct method.

LO 10
Illustrate the difference between the direct and indirect methods of presenting cash flows from operating activities.

Exhibit 9-9

Statement of Cash
Flows

I. Direct method:

CRUISERS INC. AND SUBSIDIARIES		
Consolidated Statements of Cash Flows		
For the Years Ended August 31, 2020 and 2019		
(000 omitted)		
	2020	**2019**
Cash Flows from Operating Activities:		
Cash received from customers	$ 74,929	$ 63,021
Cash paid to suppliers	(46,784)	(38,218)
Payments for compensation of employees	(17,137)	(16,267)
Other operating expenses paid	(3,873)	(4,002)
Interest paid	(3,675)	(2,703)
Taxes paid	(1,037)	(532)
Net cash provided by operating activities	$ 2,423	$ 1,299
Cash Flows from Investing Activities:		
Proceeds from sale of land	$ —	$ 200
Investment in plant and equipment	(1,622)	(1,437)
Net cash used for investing activities	$ (1,622)	$ (1,237)
Cash Flows from Financing Activities:		
Additional long-term borrowing	$ 7,350	$ 6,680
Payment of long-term debt	(3,268)	(3,053)
Purchase of treasury stock	(1,537)	(1,226)
Payment of dividends on common stock	(2,863)	(2,610)
Net cash used for financing activities	$ (318)	$ (209)
Increase (decrease) in cash	$ 483	$ (147)
Cash balance, August 31, 2019 and 2018	276	423
Cash balance, August 31, 2020 and 2019	$ 759	$ 276
Reconciliation of Net Income and Net Cash Provided by Operating Activities:		
Net income	$ 1,527	$ 764
Add (deduct) items not affecting cash:		
Depreciation expense	926	835
Gain on sale of land	—	(161)
Increase in accounts receivable	(30)	(44)
Increase in inventories	(21)	(168)
Increase in current liabilities	16	66
Other (net)	5	7
Net cash provided by operating activities	$ 2,423	$ 1,299

(continued)

The indirect method explains cash flows from operating activities by explaining the change in each noncash operating account in the balance sheet. A statement of cash flows prepared this way shows net income as the first source of operating cash. However, net income is determined on the accrual basis and must be adjusted for revenues and expenses that do not affect cash. The most significant noncash income statement item is usually total depreciation and amortization expense. Here are the effects of these transactions on the financial statements:

II. Indirect method:

CRUISERS INC. AND SUBSIDIARIES Consolidated Statements of Cash Flows For the Years Ended August 31, 2020 and 2019 (000 omitted)		
	2020	**2019**
Cash Flows from Operating Activities:		
Net income	$ 1,527	$ 764
Add (deduct) items not affecting cash:		
Depreciation expense	926	835
Gain on sale of land	—	(161)
Increase in accounts receivable	(730)	(644)
Increase in inventories	(521)	(368)
Increase in current liabilities	866	716
Other (net)	355	157
Net cash provided by operating activities	$ 2,423	$ 1,299
Cash Flows from Investing Activities:		
Proceeds from sale of land	$ —	$ 200
Investment in plant and equipment	(1,622)	(1,437)
Net cash used for investing activities	$ (1,622)	$ (1,237)
Cash Flows from Financing Activities:		
Additional long-term borrowing	$ 7,350	$ 6,680
Payment of long-term debt	(3,268)	(3,053)
Purchase of treasury stock	(1,537)	(1,226)
Payment of dividends on common stock	(2,863)	(2,610)
Net cash used for financing activities	$ (318)	$ (209)
Increase (decrease) in cash	$ 483	$ (147)
Cash balance, August 31, 2019 and 2018	276	423
Cash balance, August 31, 2020 and 2019	$ 759	$ 276

Balance Sheet	Income Statement
Assets = Liabilities + Stockholders' equity	← Net income = Revenues − Expenses

− Accumulated
  Depreciation
	− Depreciation
	  Expense

− Intangible
  Asset
	− Amortization
	  Expense

The entries to record these items are as follows:

		xx	
Dr.	Depreciation Expense	xx	
	Cr. Accumulated Depreciation		xx

		xx	
Dr.	Amortization Expense	xx	
	Cr. Intangible Asset		xx

Understanding Cash Flow Relationships: Indirect Method

As indicated by the AICPA study, most firms report the statement of cash flows using the indirect method. The primary reason for this preference is that no separate accounting procedures are needed for companies to accumulate cash flow data when the indirect method is used. The statement of cash flows normally is prepared using balance sheet and income statement data and other information readily available from the company's accounting records. However, the operating activities information reported under the direct method is not so readily determinable, and the cost of generating this information can be prohibitive.

The primary objective of the operating activities section of the statement of cash flows (indirect method) is to determine the net cash provided by operating activities. Although net income is determined on an accrual basis, it is ordinarily the most accurate proxy for operating cash flows and thus serves as the starting point in the calculation of this important amount. *Note, however, that none of the adjustments shown in the operating activities section (indirect method) explains how much cash was actually received or paid during the year!* The only operating activity items that convey independent meaning are the amounts shown for net income and net cash provided by operating activities. Review the operating activities section of Exhibit 9-9 for the indirect method. Notice, for example, that accounts receivable increased during both years presented. Does this explain how much cash was received from the collection of accounts receivable during these years? (No, but the direct method shows these amounts.) Once you understand this, the adjustment process for the indirect method can be thought of in a rather mechanical fashion.

Net income is initially assumed to generate operating cash, and this assumption is then adjusted for the effects of noncash (or nonoperating) income statement items. As already explained, the amounts shown for depreciation and amortization expense are added back to net income each year because cash is never paid for these expenses. Similar adjustments are made to remove the effects of noncash revenues or to remove the effects of most nonoperating transactions included in net income (such as gains or losses from the sale of long-term assets). After these income statement adjustments are made, the current (*operating*) accounts on the balance sheet must be analyzed to determine their effects on cash during the year. To simplify the analysis, assume that all changes in account balances from the beginning to the end of the year are attributable to cash transactions. For example, if inventory (a current asset) increased during the year, cash must have decreased (to pay for the increase in inventory). The financial statement effect of this assumed transaction would be as shown in the horizontal model representation as follows:

Because the depreciation and amortization expense amounts do not affect cash, these items are added back to net income to determine more accurately the amount of cash generated from operations. Other income statement items that need to be considered in a similar way include the following:

- Income tax expense not currently payable (that is, deferred income taxes resulting from temporary differences in the recognition of revenues and expenses for book and tax purposes).
- Gains or losses on the sale or abandonment of assets. The *proceeds* from the sale, not the gain or loss, affect cash. Losses are added back to net income, and gains are subtracted from net income. The sale proceeds are reported as an investing activity, as described later.
- Increases (or decreases) to interest expense that result from the amortization of discount (or premium) on bonds payable. Discount amortization is added back to net income, and premium amortization is subtracted from net income.

Changes in the noncash operating accounts must also be shown. Thus, increases in current assets and decreases in current liabilities are reported as operating uses of

Balance Sheet	Income Statement
Assets = Liabilities + Stockholders' equity	← Net income = Revenues − Expenses
+ Inventory − Cash	

The entry is as follows:

Dr. Inventory	xx	
Cr. Cash		xx

Likewise, if accounts payable (a current liability) increased during the year, then cash was not spent and the flow of cash thus increased, as illustrated by the following assumed transaction:

Balance Sheet	Income Statement
Assets = Liabilities + Stockholders' equity	← Net income = Revenues − Expenses
+ Cash + Accounts Payable	

The entry is as follows:

Dr. Cash	xx	
Cr. Accounts Payable		xx

In a similar way, decreases in current asset accounts are assumed to increase cash (for example, the collection of an accounts receivable), and decreases in current liability accounts are assumed to decrease cash (for example, the payment of an account payable). These are only assumptions, but by assuming that cash is involved on the opposite side of every transaction, you will understand the nature of each of the adjustments made within the operating activities section of the statement of cash flows.

cash. Conversely, decreases in current assets and increases in current liabilities are reported as operating sources of cash. An indirect method statement of cash flows is illustrated in Section II of Exhibit 9-9.

Note that the difference between the two methods is only in the presentation of cash flows from operating activities. When the direct method format is used, a separate schedule is required to reconcile net income reported on the income statement with net cash provided by operating activities. This reconciliation is in the form of the indirect method presentation of net cash provided by operating activities. A survey of the annual reports of 500 publicly owned industrial and merchandising companies for the year 2011 (last available data) indicated that 495 firms used the indirect method presentation, whereas only 5 companies used the direct method presentation.[4] Business in Practice—Understanding Cash Flow Relationships: Indirect Method explains the cash flow relationships under the indirect method in more detail.

---

[4] AICPA, *Accounting Trends and Techniques, U.S. GAAP Financial Statements—Best Practices in Presentation and Disclosure* (New York, 2012), Table 6-2.

Cash Flows from Investing and Financing Activities   Investing activities relate primarily to the purchase and sale of noncurrent assets. Cash is often used for the acquisition of assets such as land, buildings, or equipment during the year (these investments are sometimes called *capital additions*). Investments in debt or equity securities of other entities are also shown as investing uses. Likewise, cash received from the sale of noncurrent assets is shown as an investing source of cash. The lending of money and subsequent collection of loans are considered investing activities as well.

Financing activities relate primarily to changes during the year in nonoperating liabilities (such as bonds payable) and in stockholders' equity accounts other than net income (loss), which is treated as an operating activity. Thus, the issuance of bonds or common stock will result in a financing source of cash, and the retirement of bonds will be reported as a financing use. Cash dividends and treasury stock transactions also are reported as financing activities because they affect stockholders' equity.

Interpreting the Statement of Cash Flows

LO 11

Summarize why the statement of cash flows is significant to financial analysts and investors.

The statement of cash flows focuses on cash receipts and cash payments during the period, so the first question to be answered is, "Did the company's cash balance increase or decrease during the period?" The answer is usually found near the bottom of the statement. In the annual report of a publicly owned corporation, comparative statements for the most recent and prior two years will be presented, and the change in each of the years can be noted. If the change in the cash balance during a year has been significant (for example, more than 10 percent of the beginning cash balance), the financial statement user will try to understand the reasons for the change by focusing on the relative totals of each of the three categories of cash flows—operating activities, investing activities, and financing activities. Even if the change in the cash balance during a year is not significant, the relationship between these broad categories will be observed.

A firm should have a positive cash flow provided by operating activities. If operating activities do not generate cash, the firm will have to seek outside funding to finance its day-to-day activities, as well as its investment requirements. Although negative cash flow from operating activities might apply to a firm just starting up, it would be a sign of possible financial weakness for a mature company.

Virtually all financially healthy firms have growth in revenues as a financial objective. This growth usually requires increasing capacity to manufacture or sell products or provide services. Thus, a principal investing activity is the acquisition of plant and equipment. The total cash used for investing activities is compared to the total cash provided by operating activities. If cash provided by operating activities exceeds cash used for investing activities, the indication is that the firm is generating the cash it needs to finance its growth, and that is probably positive. If the cash used for investing activities exceeds the cash provided by operating activities, the difference will have to be provided by financing activities or come from the cash balance carried forward from the prior year. This is not necessarily negative because investment requirements in any one year may be unusually high. If, however, cash used for investing activities exceeds cash provided by operating activities year after year, and the difference is provided from financing activities, a question about the firm's ability to generate additional funds from financing activities must be raised.

Financing activities include the issue and repayment of debt, the sale of stock and purchase of treasury stock, and the payment of dividends on stock. For most companies, it would be desirable to have annual cash dividends covered by the excess of cash provided from operating activities over cash used for investing activities.

After the big picture of the entity's cash flows has been obtained, it may be necessary to look at the details of each category of cash flows for clues that will explain the overall change. For example, if cash flows provided by operating activities are less than cash used for investing activities, or if operating cash flows are decreasing even though profits are increasing, accounts receivable and/or inventories may be increasing at a higher rate than sales. This is a signal that the firm may have liquidity problems that would not necessarily be reflected by the change in working capital, the current ratio, or the acid-test ratio. These liquidity measures include other items besides cash, and the firm's inability to collect its accounts receivable and/or sell its inventory may artificially increase current assets and distort these relationships. Other interpretations of this same trend might also be possible, but the trend itself might not have been observed without a careful analysis of cash flow data.

The details of an entity's investing activities frequently describe its growth strategy. Besides investing in more plant and equipment, some firms acquire capacity by purchasing other companies or by investing in the securities of other companies. Occasionally a firm will sell some of its plant and equipment, in which case cash is provided. The reasons for and consequences of such a sale of assets are of interest to the financial statement user.

To illustrate these interpretation techniques, refer to Campbell's Consolidated Statements of Cash Flows in the annual report in the appendix. Note that a large add-back is made to net income each year for depreciation and amortization because cash is not disbursed for these expense items. Note also that the net cash provided by operating activities exceeded net income by a substantial amount for each of the three years presented. Likewise, net cash provided by operating activities exceeded the net cash used in investing activities for all three years—a relationship generally considered desirable. Purchases of plant assets represented Campbell's primary investment activity each year. Financing activities resulted in a net use of cash for all three years presented, with significant cash outlays being made each year for dividend payments and treasury stock purchases. The overall picture for Campbell's is quite good; net cash provided by operating activities is generally covering all the firm's investing and financing requirements and is creating a surplus of cash for new investment opportunities.

Campbell's

The statement of cash flows provides useful information for owners, managers, employees, suppliers, potential investors, and others interested in the economic activities of the entity. This statement provides information that is difficult, if not impossible, to obtain from the other three financial statements alone.

---

5. What does it mean when the statement of cash flows shows a negative amount of net operating cash flows (i.e., net cash "used by" operating activities)?

6. What does it mean when cash used for investing activities is greater than cash provided by operating activities?

What Does It Mean?

Answers on page 366

Demonstration Problem

The Demonstration Problem walkthrough for this chapter is available in *Connect.*

Summary

This chapter described the income statement and the statement of cash flows. The income statement summarizes the results of the firm's profit-generating or loss-sustaining activities for a fiscal period. The statement of cash flows explains the change in the firm's cash from the beginning to the end of the fiscal period by summarizing the cash effects of the firm's operating, investing, and financing activities during the period.

Revenues are reported at the beginning of the income statement. Revenues result from the sale of a product or the provision of a service, not necessarily from the receipt of cash. The revenues of most manufacturing and merchandising firms are called *sales*. Net sales, which is gross sales minus sales returns and allowances and cash discounts, is usually the first caption of the income statement. Service entities will describe the source of their revenues (such as rental fees or consulting fees) in accordance with the nature of their primary business activities. **(LO 1)**

Expenses are subtracted from revenues in the income statement. A significant expense for many firms is cost of goods sold. The actual calculation of cost of goods sold is determined by the system used to account for inventories. With a perpetual inventory system, cost can be determined and recognized when a product is sold. With a periodic inventory system, cost of goods sold is calculated at the end of the fiscal period using beginning and ending inventory amounts and the purchases (or cost of goods manufactured) amount. Sometimes cost of goods sold is reported separately and subtracted from net sales to arrive at gross profit (sometimes called *gross margin*) in what is called a *multiple-step income statement presentation.* Other firms will include cost of goods sold with operating expenses in a single-step income statement presentation. **(LO 2, 7)**

Gross profit (or gross margin) is frequently expressed as a ratio. The gross profit ratio can be used to monitor profitability, set selling prices, and estimate ending inventory and cost of goods sold. **(LO 3)**

Selling, general, and administrative expenses are the costs of operating the firm. They are deducted from gross profit to arrive at operating income, an important measure of management performance. **(LO 5)**

Interest expense is usually shown as a separate item in the other income and expense category of the income statement. Other significant gains or losses will also be identified. **(LO 4)**

Income before income taxes is frequently reported as a subtotal before income tax expense is shown because taxes are a function of all items reported to this point in the income statement. **(LO 5)**

To facilitate users' comparisons of net income with that of prior years and to provide a basis for future expectations, income or loss from discontinued operations is reported separately in the income statement, net of income taxes, and on a per share basis as well. **(LO 8)**

Net income attributable to noncontrolling interests is reported separately from net income (or net earnings) attributable to the reporting entity; the latter amount is reported in total and on a per share of outstanding common stock basis. If there is potential dilution from convertible debt, convertible preferred stock, or stock options, diluted earnings per share will also be reported. **(LO 6)**

The statement of cash flows shows the change in cash during the year and reports cash provided from or used by operating activities, investing activities, and financing activities. **(LO 9)**

The determination of cash flows from operating activities is essentially a conversion of the accrual accounting income statement to a cash basis income statement. The principal reasons net income doesn't affect cash directly are that not all accounts receivable from sales are collected in the fiscal period of the sale and not all of the expenses reported in the income statement result in the disbursement of cash in the fiscal period in which the expenses are incurred. **(LO 9, 10)**

Investing activities include purchases of plant and equipment, investments in other companies, loans made to other entities, and the sale or collection of these assets (essentially, all significant changes during the year in noncurrent assets are reported as investing activities). **(LO 9)**

Financing activities include the issuance and redemption of bonds and stock, including treasury stock transactions, and cash dividends on stock (essentially, all significant changes during the year in noncurrent liabilities and all stockholders' equity changes, other than net income or net loss, are reported as financing activities). **(LO 9)**

There are two acceptable presentation formats for the statement of cash flows. The difference between the two is in the presentation of cash flows from operating activities. Most entities use the indirect method because no separate accounting procedures are needed to accumulate cash flow data when the indirect method is used. **(LO 10)**

Interpretation of the statement of cash flows involves observing the relationship between the three broad categories of cash flows (operating activities, investing activities, and financing activities) and the change in the cash balance for the year. It is desirable to have cash provided by operating activities that is equal to or greater than cash used for investing activities, although large investment requirements in any one year may cause a reduction in the beginning-of-the-year cash balance. Cash can also be raised from financing activities to offset large investment requirements. The detailed activities of each cash flow category will be reviewed to assess their effect on the overall cash position of the firm. The statement of cash flows provides important information that is not easily obtained from the other financial statements. **(LO 11)**

Refer to the income statement and statement of cash flows for Campbell Soup Company in the appendix, and to these statements in other annual reports you may have, to observe content and presentation alternatives.

Campbell's

Key Terms and Concepts

basic earnings per share (p. 335)   Net income available to common stockholders divided by the weighted-average number of shares of common stock outstanding during the period.

cost of goods sold (p. 329)   Cost of merchandise sold during the period; an expense deducted from net sales to arrive at gross profit.

cost of goods sold model (p. 330)   The formula for calculating cost of goods sold by adding beginning inventory and purchases and subtracting ending inventory.

diluted earnings per share (p. 335)   An amount less than basic earnings per share that assumes that additional shares of common stock have been issued pursuant to convertible debt, convertible preferred stock, and/or stock option plans.

dilution (p. 337)   The reduction in earnings per share of common stock (EPS) that may occur if convertible securities are actually converted to common stock and/or if additional shares of common stock are issued pursuant to a stock option plan.

earned (p. 324)   A revenue recognition criterion that relates to completion of the revenue-generating activity.

expenses (p. 328)   Outflows or other using up of assets or incurrences of liabilities during a period from delivering or producing goods, rendering services, or carrying out other activities that constitute the entity's major operations.

extraordinary item (p. 340)   A gain or loss from a transaction that both was unusual in nature and occurred infrequently; prior to 2015, it was reported separately in the income statement and shown net of taxes. (Some companies may continue to report the comparative effects of extraordinary items that occurred in prior years.)

FOB destination (p. 327)   The shipping term that means that title passes from seller to buyer when the merchandise arrives at its destination.

FOB shipping point (p. 327)   The shipping term that means that title passes from seller to buyer when the merchandise leaves the seller's premises.

freight collect (p. 327)   A freight payment alternative meaning that freight is payable when the merchandise arrives at its destination.

freight prepaid (p. 327)   A freight payment alternative meaning that freight is paid by the shipper.

gains (p. 327)   Increases in net assets from incidental transactions and other events affecting an entity during a period except those that result from revenues or investments by owners.

gross margin (p. 331)   Another term for *gross profit*.

gross margin ratio (p. 331)   Another term for *gross profit ratio*.

gross profit (p. 331)   The difference between net sales and cost of goods sold. Sometimes called *gross margin*.

gross profit ratio (p. 331)   The ratio of gross profit to net sales. Sometimes called *gross margin ratio*.

income before income taxes (p. 335)   An income statement subtotal on which income tax expense is based.

income from continuing operations (p. 340)   An income statement subtotal that is presented before income or loss from discontinued operations.

income from operations (p. 334)   The difference between gross profit and operating expenses. Also called *operating income*.

inventory cost flow assumption (p. 329)   The application of FIFO, LIFO, weighted-average, or specific identification procedures to determine the cost of goods sold.

inventory shrinkage (p. 329)   Inventory losses resulting from theft, deterioration, and record-keeping errors.

losses (p. 329)   Decreases in net assets from incidental transactions and other events affecting an entity during a period except those that result from expenses or distributions to owners.

matching principle (p. 328)   The concept that expenses incurred in generating revenues should be "matched" against revenues earned during some period of time, usually one year, in determining net income or loss for the period.

multiple-step format (p. 337)   An income statement format that includes subtotals for gross profit, operating income, and income before taxes.

net income (p. 335)   The excess of revenues and gains over expenses and losses for a fiscal period.

net income attributable to noncontrolling interest (p. 341)   An income statement item representing the noncontrolling (minority) stockholders' share of the earnings of a subsidiary that have been included in the consolidated income statement.

net income attributable to (parent company name) (p. 341)   Net income, less "net income attributable to noncontrolling interest" in the consolidated income statement: for example, "Net income attributable to Racers Inc." Sometimes referred to as *net income attributable to controlling interest.*

net sales (p. 325)   Gross sales, less sales discounts and sales returns and allowances.

operating expenses (p. 333)   Expenses, other than cost of goods sold, incurred in the day-to-day activities of the entity.

operating income (p. 334)   The difference between gross profit and operating expenses. Also referred to as *income from operations.*

other income and expenses (p. 335)   An income statement category that includes interest expense, interest revenue, and gain or loss items not related to the principal operating activities of the entity.

percentage-of-completion method (p. 327)   A method of recognizing revenue based on the completion percentage of a long-term construction project.

purchase returns and allowances (p. 330)   Reductions in purchases from products returned to the supplier or adjustments in the purchase cost.

realization (p. 324)   A revenue recognition criterion that relates to the receipt of cash or a claim to cash in exchange for the product or service.

revenues (p. 324)   Inflows of cash or increases in other assets, or settlement of liabilities, during a period from delivering or producing goods, rendering services, or performing other activities that constitute the entity's major operations.

sales (p. 325)   Revenues resulting from the sale of product.

sales mix (p. 332)   The proportion of total sales represented by various products or categories of products.

sales returns and allowances (p. 325)   Reductions in sales from product returns or adjustments in selling price.

shipping terms (p. 327)   The description of the point at which title passes from seller to buyer.

single-step format (p. 337)   An income statement format that excludes subtotals, such as gross profit and operating income.

statement of cash flows (p. 341)   The financial statement that explains why cash changed during a fiscal period. Cash flows from operating, investing, and financing activities are shown in the statement.

Mini-Exercises

All applicable Mini-Exercises are available in *Connect*.

Gross profit calculations   Net sales for the year were $450,000 and cost of goods sold was $297,000 for the company's existing products. A new product is presently under development and has an expected selling price of not more than $75 per unit in order to remain competitive with similar products in the marketplace.

Mini-Exercise 9.1
LO 3

Required:
a. Calculate gross profit and the gross profit ratio for the year.

b. What is the maximum cost per unit that can be incurred to manufacture the new product so that the product can be priced competitively and will not result in a reduction to the company's gross profit ratio?

Mini-Exercise 9.2
LO 5

Calculate operating income and net income Selling, general, and administrative expenses were $99,000; net sales were $460,000; interest expense was $10,500; research and development expenses were $47,200; net cash provided by operating activities was $118,800; income tax expense was $11,400; cost of goods sold was $247,500.

Required:
a. Calculate operating income for the period.
b. Calculate net income for the period.

Mini-Exercise 9.3
LO 6

Calculate basic EPS Net income was $659,250 for the year. Throughout the year the company had outstanding 18,000 shares of $2.50, $50 par value preferred stock and 105,000 shares of common stock.

Required:
Calculate basic earnings per share of common stock for the year.

Mini-Exercise 9.4
LO 10

Calculate cash flows from operations—indirect method Net income was $67,100; accounts receivable decreased by $19,500; inventory increased by $10,800; proceeds from the issuance of long-term debt were $22,500; accounts payable decreased by $6,200; equipment purchases were $75,000; depreciation and amortization expense was $36,000.

Required:
Calculate the net cash provided (used) by operating activities for the period.

connect Exercises

All applicable Exercises are available in Connect.

Exercise 9.5
LO 1

Calculate earned revenues Big Blue University has a fiscal year that ends on June 30. The 2019 summer session of the university runs from June 9 through July 28. Total tuition paid by students for the summer session amounted to $168,000.

Required:
a. How much revenue should be reflected in the fiscal year ended June 30, 2019? Explain your answer.
b. Would your answer to part **a** be any different if the university had a tuition refund policy that no tuition would be refunded after the end of the third week of summer session classes? Explain your answer.

Calculate earned revenues Kirkland Theater sells season tickets for six events at a price of $240. In pricing the tickets, the planners assigned the leadoff event a value of $60 because the program was an expensive symphony orchestra. The last five events were priced equally; 1,800 season tickets were sold for the 2019 season.

Exercise 9.6
LO 1

Required:
a. Calculate the theater's earned revenue after the first three events have been presented.
b. About 95% of the season ticket holders attended the first event. Subsequent events were attended by about 80% of the season ticket holders. To what extent, if any, should the attendance data impact revenue recognition? Explain your answer.

Effects of inventory error If the ending inventory of a firm is overstated by $60,000, by how much and in what direction (overstated or understated) will the firm's operating income be misstated? (*Hint:* Use the cost of goods sold model, enter hypothetically "correct" data, and then reflect the effects of the ending inventory error and determine the effect on cost of goods sold.)

Exercise 9.7
LO 2

Effects of inventory error Assume that the ending inventory of a merchandising firm is overstated by $30,000.

Exercise 9.8
LO 2

Required:
a. By how much and in what direction (overstated or understated) will the firm's cost of goods sold be misstated?
b. If this error is not corrected, what effect will it have on the subsequent period's operating income?
c. If this error is not corrected, what effect will it have on the total operating income of the two periods (the period in which there is an error and the subsequent period) combined?

Calculate gross profit ratio and cost of goods sold Refer to the Consolidated Statements of Earnings in the Campbell Soup Company annual report in the appendix.

Exercise 9.9
LO 2, 3

Campbell's

Required:
a. Calculate the gross profit ratio for each of the past three years.
b. Assume that Campbell's net sales for the first four months of 2018 totaled $2.7 billion. Calculate an estimated cost of goods sold and gross profit for the four months.

Calculate gross profit, cost of goods sold, and selling price MBI Inc. had sales of $900 million for fiscal 2019. The company's gross profit ratio for that year was 37.5%.

Exercise 9.10
LO 2, 3

Required:

a. Calculate the gross profit and cost of goods sold for MBI for fiscal 2019.

b. Assume that a new product is developed and that it will cost $1,625 to manufacture. Calculate the selling price that must be set for this new product if its gross profit ratio is to be the same as the average achieved for all products for fiscal 2019.

c. From a management viewpoint, what would you do with this information?

Exercise 9.11

LO 5

Operating income versus net income If you were interested in evaluating the profitability of a company and could have only limited historical data, would you prefer to know operating income or net income for the past five years? Explain your answer.

Exercise 9.12

LO 5

Campbell's

Operating income versus net income Refer to the selected financial data (five-year financial summary) in the Campbell Soup Company annual report in the appendix.

Required:

Compare the trend of the operating income (earnings before interest and taxes) data with the trend of net income (net earnings attributable to Campbell Soup Company) data from 2013 through 2017. Which series of data is more meaningful? Explain your answer.

Exercise 9.13

LO 7

Calculate basic EPS Ringmeup Inc. had net income of $223,925 for the year ended December 31, 2019. At the beginning of the year, 20,000 shares of common stock were outstanding. On May 1, an additional 5,000 shares were issued. On December 1, the company purchased 2,500 shares of its own common stock and held them as treasury stock until the end of the year. No other changes in common shares outstanding occurred during the year. During the year, Ringmeup paid the annual dividend on the 16,000 shares of 7%, $100 par value preferred stock that were outstanding the entire year.

Required:

Calculate basic earnings per share of common stock for the year ended December 31, 2019.

Exercise 9.14

LO 7

Calculate basic EPS, and explain the EPS effect of convertible preferred Thrifty Co. reported net income of $573,650 for its fiscal year ended January 31, 2020. At the beginning of that fiscal year, 100,000 shares of common stock were outstanding. On October 31, 2019, an additional 30,000 shares were issued. No other changes in common shares outstanding occurred during the year. Also during the year, the company paid the annual dividend on the 40,000 shares of 6%, $50 par value preferred stock that were outstanding the entire year.

Required:

a. Calculate basic earnings per share of common stock for the year ended January 31, 2020.

b. If Thrifty Co.'s preferred stock were convertible into common stock, what additional calculation would be required?

Accrual to cash flows For each of the following items, calculate the cash sources or cash uses that should be recognized on the statement of cash flows for Baldin Co. for the year ended December 31, 2019:

Exercise 9.15

LO 10

a. Sales on account (all are collectible) amounted to $560,000, and accounts receivable decreased by $34,000. How much cash was collected from customers?

b. Income tax expense for the year was $118,000, and income taxes payable decreased by $44,000. How much cash was paid for income taxes?

c. Cost of goods sold amounted to $338,000, accounts payable increased by $49,000, and inventories increased by $34,000. How much cash was paid to suppliers?

d. The net book value of buildings increased by $290,000. No buildings were sold, and depreciation expense for the year was $130,000. How much cash was paid to purchase buildings?

Cash flows to accrual For each of the following items, calculate the amount of revenue or expense that should be recognized on the income statement for Pelkey Co. for the year ended December 31, 2019:

Exercise 9.16

LO 10

a. Cash collected from customers during the year amounted to $147,000, and accounts receivable increased by $31,000. How much were sales on account for the year ended December 31, 2019?

b. Cash payments for income taxes during the year were $85,000, and income taxes payable increased by $13,000. How much was income tax expense?

c. Cash paid to suppliers during the year amounted to $168,000, accounts payable decreased by $26,700, and inventories decreased by $14,000. How much was cost of goods sold?

d. The net book value of buildings increased by $275,000. No buildings were sold, and a new building costing $430,000 was purchased during the year. How much was depreciation expense?

Income statement format and EPS disclosures Refer to the Consolidated Statements of Earnings in the Campbell Soup Company annual report in the appendix.

Exercise 9.17

LO 6, 7

Campbell's

Required:
a. Does Campbell's use the single-step format or the multiple-step format? Which format do you prefer? Explain your answer.

b. Refer to the basic and diluted earnings per share data and the related note disclosures in the appendix. Explain why this disclosure is appropriate.

Statement of cash flows analysis Refer to the Consolidated Statements of Cash Flows in the Campbell Soup Company annual report within the appendix.

Exercise 9.18

LO 11

Campbell's

Required:
a. Identify the two most significant sources of cash from operating activities during 2017. How much of a cash source amount do these items represent?

b. What was the firm's most significant investing activity during 2017, and how much cash did this activity use or generate?

c. Identify the three most significant financing activities during 2017. What was the net effect on cash of these items?

▪connect   **Problems**

All applicable Problems are available in *Connect*.

Problem 9.19
LO 5

Calculate operating income and net income The following information is available from the accounting records of Manahan Co. for the year ended December 31, 2019:

Net cash provided by financing activities	$168,000
Dividends paid	27,000
Loss from discontinued operations, net of tax savings of $70,000	155,000
Income tax expense	39,000
Other selling expenses	20,000
Net sales	966,000
Advertising expense	67,000
Accounts receivable	186,000
Cost of goods sold	552,000
General and administrative expenses	214,000

Required:

a. Calculate the operating income for Manahan Co. for the year ended December 31, 2019.

b. Calculate the company's net income for 2019.

Problem 9.20
LO 5

Calculate operating income and net income The following information is available from the accounting records of Spenser Co. for the year ended December 31, 2019:

Selling, general, and administrative expenses	$106,000
Accounts payable	170,000
Research and development expenses	77,000
Loss from discontinued operations, net of tax savings of $8,000	24,000
Provision for income taxes	35,000
Net sales	948,000
Interest expense	97,000
Net cash provided by operations	296,000
Cost of goods sold	521,000

Required:

a. Calculate the operating income for Spenser Co. for the year ended December 31, 2019.

b. Calculate the company's net income for 2019.

Problem 9.21
LO 3

Use gross profit ratio to calculate inventory loss Franklin Co. has experienced gross profit ratios for 2019, 2018, and 2017 of 33%, 30%, and 31%, respectively. On April 3, 2020, the firm's plant and all its inventory were destroyed by a tornado.

Accounting records for 2020, which were available because they were stored in a protected vault, showed the following:

Sales from January 1 through April 2	$71,340
January 1 inventory amount	31,795
Purchases of inventory from	
January 1 through April 2	59,326

Required:
Calculate the amount of the insurance claim to be filed for the inventory destroyed in the tornado. (*Hint:* Use the cost of goods sold model and a gross profit ratio that will result in the largest claim.)

Use gross profit ratio to calculate inventory loss On April 8, 2019, a flood destroyed the warehouse of Stuco Distributing Co. From the waterlogged records of the company, management was able to determine that the firm's gross profit ratio had averaged 45% for the past several years and that the inventory at the beginning of the year was $314,200. It also was determined that during the year until the date of the flood, sales had totaled $638,400 and purchases totaled $355,140.

Problem 9.22
LO 3

Required:
Calculate the amount of inventory loss from the flood.

Cash flows from operations—indirect method The financial statements of Simon Co. include the following items (amounts in thousands):

Problem 9.23
LO 10

Income Statement	For the Year Ended December 31, 2020
Net income	$840
Depreciation and amortization expense	640

	At December 31	
Balance Sheets	2020	2019
Accounts receivable	$250	$340
Inventory	340	300
Accounts payable	160	180
Income taxes payable	100	30

Required:
a. Calculate the net cash flow provided by operations for Simon Co. for the year ended December 31, 2020.
b. Explain why net income is different from the net cash provided by operations.

Problem 9.24

LO 10

Prepare a statement of cash flows—indirect method The financial statements of Pouchie Co. included the following information for the year ended December 31, 2019 (amounts in millions):

Depreciation and amortization expense	$ 130
Cash dividends declared and paid	165
Purchase of equipment	410
Net income	192
Beginning cash balance	60
Proceeds of common stock issued	74
Proceeds from sale of building (at book value)	106
Accounts receivable increase	8
Ending cash balance	20
Inventory decrease	19
Accounts payable increase	22

Required:

Complete the following statement of cash flows, using the indirect method:

POUCHIE CO.
Statement of Cash Flows
For the Year Ended December 31, 2019

Cash Flows from Operating Activities:	
Net income	$ 192
Add (deduct) items not affecting cash:	
_____	
_____	
_____	
_____	
Net cash provided (used) by operating activities	$ ___
Cash Flows from Investing Activities:	
_____	
_____	
Net cash provided (used) by investing activities	$ ___
Cash Flows from Financing Activities:	
_____	
_____	
Net cash provided (used) by financing activities	$ ___
Net increase (decrease) in cash for the year	$ ___
Cash balance, January 1, 2019	60
Cash balance, December 31, 2019	$ 20

Problem 9.25

LO 10

Cash flows from operating, investing, and financing activities—direct method The following information is available from Bromfield Co.'s accounting records for the year ended December 31, 2019 (amounts in millions):

Cash dividends declared and paid	$1,020
Interest and taxes paid	270
Collections from customers	4,050
Payment of long-term debt	660
Purchase of land and buildings	510
Cash paid to suppliers and employees	2,430
Issuance of preferred stock	900
Proceeds from the sale of equipment	120

Required:

a. Calculate the net cash provided (used) by operating activities for Bromfield Co. for the year ended December 31, 2019.

b. Calculate the net cash provided (used) by investing activities.

c. Calculate the net cash provided (used) by financing activities.

d. Calculate the net increase (decrease) in cash for the year.

Cash flows from operating, investing, and financing activities—direct method   **Problem 9.26**

The following information is available from Gray Co.'s accounting records for the year   **LO 10**
ended December 31, 2019 (amounts in millions):

Cash dividends declared and paid	$ 950
Retirement of bonds payable at maturity	600
Interest and taxes paid	440
Proceeds of common stock issued	1,250
Proceeds from the sale of land	500
Collections from customers	8,940
Cash paid to suppliers and employees	?
Purchase of buildings and equipment	?

Required:

a. The net cash provided by operating activities for Gray Co. for the year ended December 31, 2019, is $3,200 million. Calculate the cash paid to suppliers and employees.

b. The increase in cash for the year was $800 million. Calculate the amount of cash used to purchase buildings and equipment. Your answer to part **a** should be considered in your calculation. (*Hint:* Set up a model of the statement of cash flows to determine the net cash provided [used] by operating and investing activities, and then solve for the missing amounts.)

Complete balance sheet and prepare a statement of cash flows—indirect   **Problem 9.27**

method Following is a partially completed balance sheet for Hoeman Inc. at   **LO 10, 11**
December 31, 2020, together with comparative data for the year ended December 31, 2019. From the statement of cash flows for the year ended December 31, 2020, you determine the following:

- Net income for the year ended December 31, 2020, was $47,000.
- Dividends paid during the year ended December 31, 2020, were $33,500.

- Accounts receivable decreased $5,000 during the year ended December 31, 2020.
- The cost of new buildings acquired during 2020 was $62,500.
- No buildings were disposed of during 2020.
- The land account was not affected by any transactions during the year, but the fair value of the land at December 31, 2020, was $89,000.

HOEMAN INC. Comparative Balance Sheets At December 31, 2020 and 2019		
	2020	**2019**
Assets		
Current assets:		
Cash	$ 26,000	$ 23,000
Accounts receivable		67,000
Inventory	78,000	88,000
Total current assets	$	$178,000
Land	$	70,000
Buildings		145,000
Less: Accumulated depreciation	(60,000)	(52,500)
Total land and buildings	$	$162,500
Total assets	$	$340,500
Liabilities		
Current liabilities:		
Accounts payable	$	$ 98,500
Note payable	77,500	62,000
Total current liabilities	$161,000	$160,500
Long-term debt	$	$ 69,500
Stockholders' Equity		
Common stock	$ 25,000	$ 22,500
Retained earnings		88,000
Total stockholders' equity	$	$110,500
Total liabilities and stockholders' equity	$	$340,500

Required:

a. Complete the December 31, 2020, balance sheet. (*Hint:* Long-term debt is the last number to compute to make the balance sheet balance.)

b. Prepare a statement of cash flows for the year ended December 31, 2020, using the indirect method.

Problem 9.28

LO 10, 11

Complete balance sheet and prepare a statement of changes in retained earnings Following is a statement of cash flows (indirect method) for Hartford Inc. for the year ended December 31, 2020. Also shown is a partially completed comparative balance sheet as of December 31, 2020 and 2019:

HARTFORD INC.
Statement of Cash Flows
For the Year Ended December 31, 2020

Cash Flows from Operating Activities:

Net income	$ 54,000
Add (deduct) items not affecting cash:	
Depreciation expense	270,000
Decrease in accounts receivable	138,000
Increase in inventory	(42,000)
Increase in notes payable	72,000
Decrease in accounts payable	(36,000)
Net cash provided by operating activities	$ 456,000
Cash Flows from Investing Activities:	
Purchase of equipment	$(300,000)
Purchase of buildings	(288,000)
Net cash used by investing activities	$(588,000)
Cash Flows from Financing Activities:	
Proceeds from short-term debt	$ 30,000
Cash used for retirement of long-term debt	(150,000)
Proceeds from issuance of common stock	60,000
Payment of cash dividends on common stock	(18,000)
Net cash used by financing activities	$ (78,000)
Net decrease in cash for the year	$ (210,000)

HARTFORD INC.
Comparative Balance Sheets
At December 31, 2020 and 2019

	2020	2019
Assets		
Current assets:		
Cash	$	$ 528,000
Accounts receivable		438,000
Inventory	336,000	
Total current assets	$	$
Land	$	$ 240,000
Buildings and equipment	1,560,000	
Less: Accumulated depreciation		(738,000)
Total land, buildings, and equipment	$	$
Total assets	$	$
Liabilities		
Current liabilities:		
Accounts payable	$	$ 174,000
Short-term debt	192,000	
Notes payable		216,000
Total current liabilities	$	$
Long-term debt	$ 510,000	$
Stockholders' Equity		
Common stock	$ 240,000	$
Retained earnings		
Total stockholders' equity	$	$
Total liabilities and stockholders' equity	$	$

Required:

a. Complete the December 31, 2020 and 2019 balance sheets.
b. Prepare a statement of changes in retained earnings for the year ended December 31, 2020.

Problem 9.29
LO 10, 11

Prepare balance sheet and retained earnings statement using statement of cash flows data Following are a statement of cash flows (indirect method) for Harris Inc. for the year ended December 31, 2020, and the firm's balance sheet at December 31, 2019:

HARRIS INC.
Statement of Cash Flows
For the Year Ended December 31, 2020

Cash Flows from Operating Activities:	
Net income	$ 39,000
Add (deduct) items not affecting cash:	
Depreciation expense	87,000
Increase in accounts receivable	(18,000)
Decrease in merchandise inventory	90,000
Increase in accounts payable	9,000
Net cash provided by operating activities	$ 207,000
Cash Flows from Investing Activities:	
Purchase of buildings	(270,000)
Proceeds from sale of land at its cost	21,000
Net cash used by investing activities	$(249,000)
Cash Flows from Financing Activities:	
Payment of short-term debt	(12,000)
Payment of notes payable	(27,000)
Proceeds from issuance of long-term debt	45,000
Proceeds from issuance of common stock	24,000
Payment of cash dividends on common stock	(15,000)
Net cash provided by financing activities	$ 15,000
Net decrease in cash for the year	$ (27,000)

HARRIS INC.
Balance Sheet
At December 31, 2019

Assets	
Cash	$ 45,000
Accounts receivable	183,000
Merchandise inventory	228,000
Total current assets	$456,000
Land	102,000
Buildings	354,000
Less: Accumulated depreciation	(216,000)
Total land and buildings	$240,000
Total assets	$696,000

Liabilities

Accounts payable	$174,000
Short-term debt	48,000
Notes payable	99,000
Total current liabilities	$321,000
Long-term debt	150,000

Stockholders' Equity

Common stock, no par	$ 60,000
Retained earnings	165,000
Total stockholders' equity	$225,000
Total liabilities and stockholders' equity	$696,000

Required:

a. Using the preceding information, prepare the balance sheet for Harris at December 31, 2020.

b. Prepare a statement of changes in retained earnings for the year ended December 31, 2020.

Prepare statement of cash flows (indirect method) using balance sheet data Following are comparative balance sheets for Millco Inc. at January 31 and February 28, 2020:

Problem 9.30
LO 10, 11

MILLCO INC.
Balance Sheets
February 28 and January 31, 2020

	February 28	January 31
Assets		
Cash	$126,000	$111,000
Accounts receivable	192,000	159,000
Merchandise inventory	243,000	282,000
Total current assets	$561,000	$552,000
Plant and equipment:		
Production equipment	498,000	456,000
Less: Accumulated depreciation	(72,000)	(63,000)
Total assets	$987,000	$945,000
Liabilities		
Accounts payable	$111,000	$123,000
Short-term debt	132,000	132,000
Other accrued liabilities	63,000	72,000
Total current liabilities	$306,000	$327,000
Long-term debt	99,000	138,000
Total liabilities	$405,000	$465,000
Stockholders' Equity		
Common stock, no par value, 80,000 shares authorized, 60,000 and 56,000 shares issued, respectively	$312,000	$288,000
Retained earnings:		
Beginning balance	$192,000	$129,000
Net income for month	108,000	87,000
Dividends	(30,000)	(24,000)
Ending balance	$270,000	$192,000
Total stockholders' equity	$582,000	$480,000
Total liabilities and stockholders' equity	$987,000	$945,000

Required:

Prepare a statement of cash flows that explains the change that occurred in cash during the month. You may assume that the change in each balance sheet amount is due to a single event (e.g., the change in the amount of production equipment is not the result of both a purchase and sale of equipment). (*Hints:* What is the purpose of the statement of cash flows? How is this purpose accomplished?) Use the space to the right of the January 31 data to enter the difference between the February 28 and January 31 amounts of each balance sheet item; these are the amounts that will be in your solution.

connect   Cases

All applicable Cases are available in *Connect*.

Case 9.31
LO 3, 5, 7, 8

Focus company—income statement analysis In Exercise 1.1, you were asked to obtain the most recent annual report of a company that you were interested in reviewing throughout this term.

Required:

a. Which method, single-step or multiple-step, is used in the statement?

b. What are the captions of the intermediate profit amounts reported by this company that are *not* reported by Campbell Soup Company?

c. Calculate the gross profit ratio for each of the years reported. Briefly evaluate the trend of these results.

d. Is operating income increasing or decreasing for the years reported?

e. Does the company report any discontinued operations? If so, what are the effects on net income and earnings per share?

[Campbell's]

Case 9.32
LO 9, 10, 11

Focus company—statement of cash flows analysis In Exercise 1.1, you were asked to obtain the most recent annual report of a company that you were interested in reviewing throughout this term.

Required:

a. Which method, direct or indirect, is used in the statement?

b. List the principal sources and uses of cash for this firm.

c. Evaluate the change in cash. Has the firm generated most of its cash requirements from operations, or has it borrowed extensively? Has the firm's uses of cash been balanced between investments and dividends?

d. Have there been significant treasury stock transactions?

e. Has the cash balance been increasing or decreasing? What seem to be the implications of this pattern for dividends?

Case 9.33
LO 11

Using cash flow information—The Coca-Cola Company Following are comparative statements of cash flows, as reported by The Coca-Cola Company in its 2017 annual report:

THE COCA-COLA COMPANY AND SUBSIDIARIES
Consolidated Statements of Cash Flows
Year Ended December 31 (in millions)

	2017	2016	2015
Operating Activities (details omitted):			
Net cash provided by operating activities	$ 6,995	$ 8,796	$ 10,528
Investing Activities:			
Purchases of investments	(16,520)	(15,499)	(15,831)
Proceeds from disposals of investments	15,911	16,624	14,079
Acquisitions of businesses, equity method investments, and nonmarketable securities	(3,900)	(838)	(2,491)
Proceeds from disposals of businesses, equity method investments, and nonmarketable securities	3,821	1,035	565
Purchases of property, plant, and equipment	(1,675)	(2,262)	(2,553)
Proceeds from disposals of property, plant, and equipment	104	150	85
Other investing activities	(126)	(209)	(40)
Net cash provided by (used in) investing activities	(2,285)	(999)	(6,186)
Financing Activities:			
Issuances of debt	29,857	27,281	40,434
Payments of debt	(28,768)	(25,615)	(37,738)
Issuances of stock	1,595	1,434	1,245
Purchases of stock for treasury	(3,682)	(3,681)	(3,564)
Dividends	(6,320)	(6,043)	(5,741)
Other financing activities	(91)	79	251
Net cash provided by (used in) financing activities	(7,409)	(6,545)	(5,113)
Cash Flows from Discontinued Operations:			
Net cash provided by (used in) operating activities of discontinued operations	111	—	—
Net cash provided by (used in) investing activities of discontinued operations	(65)	—	—
Net cash provided by (used in) financing activities of discontinued operations	(38)	—	—
Net cash provided by (used in) discontinued operations.	8	—	—
Effect of Exchange Rate Changes on Cash and Cash Equivalents:	242	(6)	(878)
Cash and Cash Equivalents:			
Net increase (decrease) during the year	(2,549)	1,246	(1,649)
Balance at beginning of the year	8,555	7,309	8,958
Balance at end of year	$ 6,006	$ 8,555	$ 7,309

Required:

a.   Briefly review the consolidated statements of cash flows, and then provide an overall evaluation of the "big picture" during the three years presented for Coca-Cola. Have operating cash flows been sufficient to meet investing needs and to pay dividends?

b.   Were there significant changes to any of the specific line-item details that you think would require further explanation or analysis?

1. It means that although net income is not the literal bottom line on the income statement, many financial statement users consider it the most important amount on the income statement.

2. It means that to have the "big picture" of the entity's results, one must look at more than the amounts opposite one or two captions. It is especially important to be aware of unusual items that may appear on the income statement.

3. It means that additional shares of common stock may be issued because of the existence of convertible bonds, convertible preferred stock, or stock options. Issuance of shares for these items could reduce earnings per share of common stock and the market value of the common stock.

4. It means that future income statements will not be affected by the results of the discontinued operations and that by highlighting this item it should be possible for a financial statement user to make adjustments when anticipating future results for the firm.

5. It means that the firm has not generated cash from its operations—a situation that should not exist for long. To keep operating, the firm will need to have generated cash from investing or financing activities and/or used some of the cash on hand at the beginning of the reporting period.

6. It means that during the year, the firm may have made some significant investments financed by creditors or stockholders and/or used some of the cash on hand at the beginning of the reporting period.

10

Corporate Governance, Notes to the Financial Statements, and Other Disclosures

The principal objectives of this chapter are to help you understand the issues of **corporate governance** and to enable you to make sense of the notes and other financial information found in most corporate annual reports.

A brief discussion of several recent corporate governance developments is provided to give you a sense of the current regulatory environment and to help establish the background necessary for your study of the notes. The role of the Public Company Accounting Oversight Board (PCAOB) as the watchdog of the accounting and auditing profession is examined in the context of financial reporting. Yet despite the heightened awareness of corporate governance issues in recent years, a variety of financial reporting misstatements continue to escape the attention of independent auditors; some of the reasons for these misstatements will be explored.

Because of the complexities related to financial reporting, and because of the number of alternative generally accepted accounting principles that can be used, **notes to the financial statements** are included as an integral part of the financial statements. As explained in Chapter 2, the full disclosure concept means that companies are required to report all necessary information to prevent a reasonably astute user of the financial statements from being misled. The notes, or **financial review,** are referred to on each page of the individual financial statements and are presented immediately following the financial statements. In the Campbell Soup Company 2017

Campbell's

annual report in the appendix, the notes to the consolidated financial statements can be found here.

At first glance, the notes to the financial statements can appear quite intimidating because they frequently require more pages than the financial statements themselves. They contain a great deal of detailed information and include much financial management terminology. However, the reader cannot fully understand the financial statements without referring to the notes.

Financial statements of companies whose securities are publicly traded must be audited by independent auditors, and the annual report of such a company must include disclosures required by the Securities and Exchange Commission. An understanding of the auditors' report and a review of the note disclosures lead to a more complete picture of a company's financial condition, results of operations, and cash flows.

LEARNING OBJECTIVES (LO)

After studying this chapter, you should understand and be able to

LO 10-1   Discuss the significance of corporate governance.

LO 10-2   Identify the types of financial reporting misstatements that have occurred in recent years.

LO 10-3   Explain why the notes are an integral part of the financial statements.

LO 10-4   Discuss the kinds of significant accounting policies that are explained in the notes.

LO 10-5   Describe the nature and content of various note disclosures.

LO 10-6   Explain the role of the Securities and Exchange Commission and some of its reporting requirements.

LO 10-7   Explain why a statement of management's responsibility is included with the notes.

LO 10-8   Describe the significance of management's discussion and analysis of the firm's financial condition and results of operations.

LO 10-9   Identify what is included in the five-year (or longer) summary of financial data.

LO 10-10   Discuss the meaning and content of the independent auditors' report.

Corporate Governance

LO 1

Discuss the significance of corporate governance.

In addition to the numbers presented in the financial statements, the strategies, behaviors, and actions of the company and its directors, managers, and employees affect the success or lack thereof of the entity. Governance activities and the signals they send to the marketplace form the public's perception of the entity's acknowledgment and performance of its citizenship responsibilities. However, corporate governance is more than a set of structures, control mechanisms, rules, and regulations that directors, officers, and employees must follow. At the core of the governance concept are issues of business ethics, social responsibility, equitable treatment of stakeholders, full and fair disclosure, and the responsibilities of the board of directors and its various committees.

The focus on corporate governance has been heightened since the global stock market meltdown of the late 1980s. The unusual number of high-level corporate failures during the late 1980s and early 1990s initiated significant discussion and movement toward legislative and regulatory reform, including efforts by Congress, the SEC, and the FASB to strengthen financial disclosure requirements and clarify auditor independence issues. Although such efforts contributed to a management focus on ethical behavior, the cycle of business failures was repeated again in the late 1990s and early 2000s with some of the largest corporate bankruptcies in history. The size of failed organizations such as Enron and MCI Inc. (formerly WorldCom Inc.), and the intensity of the fallout of these failures in the United States and overseas resulted in a perceived legitimacy challenge to the accounting profession and a general deterioration in investor confidence.

The failure of corporations to self-control, self-regulate, and fully disclose financial information to the marketplace and to investors in particular was a failure of corporate governance that led to a series of governmental and quasi-governmental reform measures, as well as private sector initiatives to help improve the financial reporting process. The most powerful legislation to date has been the Sarbanes–Oxley Act (SOX) of 2002, which created the Public Company Accounting Oversight Board (PCAOB) as the authoritative watchdog over the accounting and auditing profession. The SOX legislation was aimed primarily to curtail the misbehavior of senior management of corporate entities: Chief executive officers (CEOs) and chief financial officers (CFOs) are required under SOX to attest (in front of a notary) to the correctness of their company's financial statements. (See the appendix for examples of these disclosures.) Companies registered with the SEC must also report in a separate section of their annual 10-K report any "Changes in and Disagreements with Accountants on Accounting and Financial Disclosure" as an added measure of transparency and management accountability. *The simple answer provided by* Campbell Soup Company *for this required disclosure in its 2017 annual report was "None" (see Item 9 in the appendix).*

Campbell's

During the years leading up to the SOX legislation, the question of whether accounting firms should be allowed to provide certain nonaudit services to their audit clients prompted considerable controversy. Many viewed the provision of consulting services by a company's independent auditor as constituting a conflict of interest and thus urged an outright ban on such services. Rather than taking such a severe approach, SOX prohibited specific nonaudit services, including financial information systems design and implementation (information technology work), performance of internal auditing, and "expert" services. Beyond these prohibited services, SOX further required companies retaining their independent auditor to perform nonaudit services to get preapproval from the audit committee of the board of directors and to adequately disclose the details of any nonaudit services performed by the independent auditor.

In 2004, a rather strict interpretation of Section 404 of SOX was implemented. As a result, all public registrants have since been required to thoroughly document, test, and take responsibility for the effectiveness of their accounting and financial reporting safeguards. A separate "Management's Report on Internal Control over Financial Reporting" must be included with all 10-K filings. In making this assessment of internal control effectiveness, the company's management must now use the criteria set forth by the Committee of Sponsoring Organizations of the Treadway Commission (COSO) in *Internal Control—Integrated Framework (2013).* Likewise, in addition to expressing an audit opinion on the company's financial statements and related note disclosures, independent auditors are required to express an opinion on the effectiveness of the company's internal control systems. A separate internal controls report may be presented immediately after the report on the financial statements, or both reports may be combined into a single auditors' report. (See the appendix for an example of the combined report format.)

In response to the financial crisis of 2007–2008, Congress passed the Wall Street Reform and Consumer Protection Act of 2010 (referred to as the *Dodd–Frank Act*). Although most of the act dealt with financial regulation, several Dodd–Frank provisions imposed new corporate governance rules not just on Wall Street banks but also on Main Street public corporations. For instance, the "say on pay" mandate required periodic shareholder advisory votes on executive compensation and golden parachute provisions. Likewise, all board compensation committees must now be composed solely of independent directors. Moreover, companies are now required to have clawback policies in place to recoup executive compensation in the event of financial reporting restatements (even absent misconduct). Another Dodd–Frank provision requires companies to disclose the reasons that they have chosen to have either the same person or separate people serve as the CEO and board chair. The act also authorizes, but does not require, the SEC to implement rules to permit shareholders to use management's proxy materials for the purpose of nominating their own directors.

With the Dodd–Frank Act, the tenor of federal regulation in corporate governance matters shifted from a focus on systems and safeguards (such as the internal controls and auditor independence rules created under SOX) to a focus on eliminating or at least greatly reducing any temptations for wrongdoing on the part of board members and senior management. Yet, while many of the Dodd–Frank provisions were aimed squarely at regulating executive compensation, shareholder empowerment represented another shift in focus, with several provisions aimed at enhancing voting rights and access to information. Considering the magnitude of the LIBOR rate-fixing scandal revealed in 2012 as well as the Toshiba accounting scandal exposed in 2015 (overstating profits by $1.2 billion over a six-year period), it seems likely that the corporate governance provisions enacted under both SOX and Dodd–Frank will get a heavy workout in the federal court system in the years to come.

In addition to adhering to enhanced reporting requirements, many companies have become more active in recent years in communicating their corporate governance policies and related social responsibility matters. Campbell's devotes a section of its website to governance-related issues, clearly demonstrating the company's commitment to a "best-practices" approach to corporate citizenship (see campbellsoup.com; click on *All Campbell Brands* at the top of the home page, then click on *Investors,* and select *Corporate Governance*). Campbell's 2017 annual report also contains useful corporate governance disclosures (see the Campbell's 2017 annual report). Similar examples can be found for nearly every large U.S.-based corporation. Yet, despite the increased attention paid to governance and related matters in recent years, a variety of financial reporting problems continue to exist today.

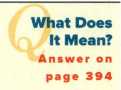

1. What does it mean to state that corporate governance issues have become increasingly important in recent years?

What Does It Mean?
Answer on page 394

Financial Reporting Misstatements

When financial reporting misstatements occur, companies are either required to completely reissue ("Big R" restatements) the full set of financial statements and related note disclosures that were previously filed with the Securities and Exchange Commission, or simply revise ("little r" restatements) the financial statements and notes previously filed. Big R restatements involve material errors, while little r restatements involve immaterial misstatements or adjustments made in the normal course of business. Big R restatements rose significantly between 2004 and 2006, but have since rapidly declined between 2007 and 2016. In 2006, a peak total of 941 Big R restatements were filed due to accounting errors, as compared to only 317 in 2011 and an all-time low of 130 such filings in 2016. Moreover, 59 percent of the total restatements in 2016 (Big R and little r) had no impact on earnings.

What's going on? The full answer to that question is larger than the WorldCom Inc., Enron, and Arthur Andersen scandals dating back to 2001, although researchers will study and report about these and other incidents for years to come. Suffice it to say that the stock market boom of the late 1990s was fueled by the greed and arrogance of certain CEOs and CFOs, auditors, investors, investment bankers, and others; greed and arrogance led them, in some instances, to engage in outright fraud and in other instances to make inappropriate decisions that stretched the financial accounting and reporting processes beyond the limits of general acceptability. Enhanced regulation, in the form of the Sarbanes–Oxley Act of 2002, forced a rising tide of financial restatements from 2004 to 2006; SOX also led to tighter internal controls and an improvement in the reliability of financial reporting. As this enhanced and more effective regulatory environment became the "new normal" in accounting and auditing practice, a dramatic and sustained downward trend in reported misstatements naturally followed. Yet, despite these positive strides witnessed in the post-SOX era, the temptation to "cook the books" will always exist. Thus, it is appropriate to examine several of the common types of financial reporting misstatements to gain some insight on the issues still facing the accounting profession.

Howard Schilit, founder of the Financial Shenanigans Detection Group LLC, and his coauthor, Jeremy Perler, have identified 13 financial shenanigans.[1] Many of their findings have been supported by Arthur Levitt, former chair of the SEC, in an address titled "What the Numbers Mean." Typically these behaviors included inappropriate reporting of revenues and expenses and manipulation of liability numbers, but they also included manipulation of cash flow information and other key metrics. The 13 types of manipulative behaviors ("shenanigans") are listed in Exhibit 10-1.

Exhibit 10-1

Financial Shenanigans

LO 2

Identify the types of financial reporting misstatements that have occurred in recent years.

Earnings Manipulation Shenanigans

1. *Recording revenue too soon.*
   - Recording revenue before completing any obligations under the contract.
   - Recording revenue far in excess of work completed on the contract.
   - Recording revenue before the buyer's final acceptance of the product.
   - Recording revenue when the buyer's payment remains uncertain or unnecessary.

2. *Recording bogus revenue.*
   - Recording revenue from transactions that lack economic substance.
   - Recording revenue from transactions that lack a reasonable arm's-length process.
   - Recording revenue on receipts from non-revenue-producing transactions.
   - Recording revenue from appropriate transactions, but at inflated amounts.

3. *Boosting income using one-time or unsustainable activities.*
   - Boosting income using one-time events.
   - Boosting income through misleading classifications.

4. *Shifting current expenses to a later period.*
   - Improperly capitalizing normal operating expenses.
   - Amortizing costs too slowly.
   - Failing to write down assets with impaired value.
   - Failing to record expenses for uncollectible receivables and devalued investments.

(continued)

---

[1] Howard Schilit and Jeremy Perler, *Financial Shenanigans: How to Detect Accounting Gimmicks and Fraud in Financial Reports,* 3rd ed. (New York: McGraw-Hill, 2010).

Exhibit 10-1

5. *Employing other techniques to hide expenses or losses.*
   - Failing to record an expense from a current transaction.
   - Failing to record an expense for a necessary accrual or reversing a past expense.
   - Failing to record or reducing expenses by using aggressive accounting assumptions.
   - Reducing expenses by releasing bogus reserves from previous charges.
6. *Shifting current income to a later period.*
   - Creating reserves (often in conjunction with an acquisition) and releasing them into income in a later period.
   - Improperly accounting for derivatives in order to smooth income.
   - Recording current-period sales in a later period.
7. *Shifting future expenses to an earlier period.*
   - Improperly writing off assets in the current period to avoid expenses in a future period.
   - Improperly recording charges to establish reserves used to reduce future expenses.

Cash Flow Shenanigans
1. *Shifting financing cash inflows to the operating section.*
   - Recording bogus cash flows from operations from a normal bank borrowing.
   - Boosting cash flows from operations by selling receivables before the collection date.
   - Inflating cash flows from operations by faking the sale of receivables.
2. *Shifting normal operating cash outflows to the investing section.*
   - Inflating cash flows from operations with boomerang transactions.
   - Improperly capitalizing normal operating costs.
   - Recording the purchase of inventory as an investing outflow.
3. *Inflating operating cash flow using acquisitions or disposals.*
   - Inheriting operating inflows in a normal business acquisition.
   - Acquiring contracts or customers rather than developing them internally.
   - Boosting cash flows from operations by creatively structuring the sale of a business.
4. *Boosting operating cash flow using unsustainable activities.*
   - Boosting cash flows from operations by paying vendors more slowly.
   - Boosting cash flows from operations by collecting from customers more quickly.
   - Boosting cash flows from operations by purchasing less inventory.
   - Boosting cash flows from operations with one-time benefits.

Key Metrics Shenanigans
1. *Showcasing misleading metrics that overstate performance.*
   - Highlighting a misleading metric as a surrogate for revenue.
   - Highlighting a misleading metric as a surrogate for earnings.
   - Highlighting a misleading metric as a surrogate for cash flow.
2. *Distorting balance sheet metrics to avoid showing deterioration.*
   - Distorting accounts receivable metrics to hide revenue problems.
   - Distorting inventory metrics to hide profitability problems.
   - Distorting financial asset metrics to hide impairment problems.
   - Distorting debt metrics to hide liquidity problems.

Source: Howard Schilit and Jeremy Perler, *Financial Shenanigans: How to Detect Accounting Gimmicks and Fraud in Financial Reports,* 3rd ed. (New York: McGraw-Hill, 2010).

Most of the shenanigans identified by Schilit and Perler are clearly contrary to the generally accepted accounting principles discussed in preceding chapters. Some of the examples they provide relate to managers' judgments concerning whether to include the effect of a particular transaction as a recurring item or as a nonrecurring item. In some cases, the amounts involved are subject to managers' estimates of future amounts based on various assumptions. In any event, as explained in earlier chapters, a careful review of the statement of cash flows, the notes to the financial statements, and management's discussion and analysis may help to warn financial statement users about financial difficulties being experienced by the company issuing the statements.

The fundamentals of financial accounting that have been explained in Chapters 2–9 will continue to apply to business transactions for years to come, even though some specific changes in accounting and reporting will occur. Efforts by operating and financial executives to have their company's financial statements reflect as favorable a picture as possible of the entity's financial position, results of operations, and cash flows will continue. Therefore, as it has always been, it continues to be the responsibility of financial statement users to dig into the financial statements, notes, and other financial information and to perform financial statement analysis to achieve an understanding of what the numbers mean. The material presented in the balance of this chapter, along with that in Chapter 11, will assist you in this process.

General Organization of Notes to the Financial Statements

LO 3

Explain why the notes are an integral part of the financial statements.

The notes that refer to specific financial statement items generally are presented in the same sequence as the financial statements and in the same sequence that items appear within the individual statements. The financial statement sequence usually is as follows:

1. Income statement.
2. Statement of comprehensive income.
3. Balance sheet.
4. Statement of cash flows.
5. Statement of equity (or statement of stockholders' equity).

Placement of the statement of comprehensive income and statement of equity (or statement of stockholders' equity) depends on the complexity of those statements. If the reporting entity does not have significant elements of "other comprehensive income," a statement of comprehensive income may not be presented as a separate financial statement; details regarding the elements of comprehensive income, in addition to net income, may instead be presented in a schedule in the accompanying notes. If there have been several capital stock transactions during the year, a full statement of equity (or stockholders' equity)—which includes changes in paid-in capital, retained earnings, accumulated other comprehensive income, and noncontrolling interests—would normally be presented separately following the statement of cash flows, although it sometimes follows the balance sheet instead. Some companies present the statement of equity as a note disclosure rather than as a separate financial statement. For a small business, if paid-in capital has not changed during the year, a statement of retained earnings (or statement of changes in retained earnings) may be presented following the income statement and may even be combined with it because net income is the principal item affecting retained earnings.

The notes are an integral part of the financial statements because they contain important disclosures that are not contained in the financial statements themselves. Thus, for the financial statements to be relevant, reliable, and understandable, users must read and interpret the notes to make informed decisions and judgments.

In addition to the notes, sometimes called the *financial review,* annual reports include a narrative section called **management's discussion and analysis (MD&A).** This is a description of the firm's activities for the year, including comments about its financial condition and results of operations. Also included in most annual reports is a comparative summary of key financial data for several years. Both of these components can be quite helpful to users of the annual report.

---

2. What does it mean when a note at the bottom of the financial statements states, "The accompanying notes are an integral part of these statements"?

What Does It Mean?

Answer on page 395

Notes to the Financial Statements

Significant Accounting Policies

As emphasized in earlier chapters, management must make a number of choices among alternative accounting practices that are generally acceptable. Because these choices differ among firms, disclosure of the specific practices being followed by any given firm is necessary for readers to make sense of that firm's financial statements. Users also need information about **significant accounting policies** to make intelligent comparisons of the financial position and results of operations of different firms in the same industry. The following discussion highlights the importance of many of these accounting policy disclosures. The comments in italic refer to the 2017 annual report of Campbell Soup Company in the appendix.

LO 4
Discuss the kinds of significant accounting policies that are explained in the notes.

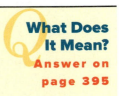
Campbell's

Depreciation Method   The method (straight-line, units-of-production, sum-of-the-years'-digits, or declining-balance) being used for financial reporting purposes and the range of useful lives assumed for broad categories of asset types are usually disclosed. The amount of depreciation expense may also be disclosed in the notes, although it is also reported in the statement of cash flows as an add-back to net income. *Campbell's uses straight-line depreciation for financial reporting purposes (see Note 1 in the appendix). How much depreciation and amortization expense did* Campbell's *report for 2017? (This amount is reported in the statement of cash flows in the appendix.)*

Inventory Valuation Method   The method (weighted-average, FIFO, or LIFO) being used is disclosed. If different methods are being used for different categories of inventory, the method used for each category is disclosed. When LIFO is used, a comparison of the cumulative difference in the balance sheet inventory valuation under LIFO with what it would have been under FIFO (sometimes referred to as the "LIFO Reserve") usually is disclosed. *All of* Campbell's *inventories are "valued at the lower of average cost or net realizable value."*

Basis of Consolidation   A brief statement confirms the fact that the consolidated financial statements include the financial data of all subsidiaries—or if not, why not.

Income Taxes   The Tax Cuts and Jobs Act of 2017 represents the most significant tax changes to both individuals and corporations in more than 30 years; it has reduced the U.S. statutory federal income tax rate for corporations from 35 percent to a flat 21 percent, effective on January 1, 2018. The global average corporate tax rate is about 25 percent, so this move is designed to make the U.S. more globally competitive, which should in turn keep more corporate profits (and jobs) in the United States.

A reconciliation of the statutory income tax rate (35 percent in 2017 and prior years) with the effective tax rate (indicated by the firm's income tax expense as a percentage of pretax income) is provided. Reasons for this difference include the effects of state taxes, non-U.S. income taxed at different rates, export sales benefits, and other special treatment given certain items for income tax purposes. This disclosure is especially pertinent for firms having a substantial business presence in a foreign country. In the United Kingdom, for example, the normal corporate income tax rate is 19 percent (for 2018). Because of the U.S. tax loss carryover rules, the effective tax rate can also differ from the statutory rate for a firm that has reported a net loss in a recent year. Campbell's *reports its effective tax rate for each of the past three years (see Note 11 in the appendix). You can verify these calculations by dividing the "Taxes on earnings" reported on the statements of earnings by the "Earnings before taxes." Try this with the statements of earnings data reported in the appendix. For 2017, this calculation should reconcile with the reported 31.4 percent effective tax rate.*

An explanation is also made of the deferred taxes resulting from differences between the fiscal year in which an expense (or revenue) is reported for book purposes and the fiscal year in which it is reported for tax purposes. As already discussed, the principal factor in deferred taxes for most firms is the use of straight-line depreciation for book purposes and accelerated depreciation for tax purposes. However, many firms also report significant deferred tax amounts for a variety of other items (as discussed in Chapter 7). Campbell's *reports a detailed table of deferred income tax assets and liabilities for the past two years (see Note 11 in the appendix).*

Employee Benefits   The cost of employee benefit plans included as an expense in the income statement will be disclosed. The significant actuarial assumptions made with respect to funding pension plans may be discussed, and certain estimated future pension liabilities may be disclosed. The key to understanding the funded status of a defined benefit pension plan is to compare the *projected benefit obligation* (the present value of expected future payments to retirees) to the *fair value of plan assets* that are currently held in the pension fund.

An additional schedule is provided to show the components of **net pension expense (income)** for each of the past three years if this amount is material. Several elements of pension expense (income) will be reported, including the service cost, interest cost of the projected benefit obligation, and the expected return on plan assets. The latter item is treated as a reduction of pension expense because future funding requirements will decrease as income is earned on invested assets. Service costs represent the actuarially determined cost to provide future pension benefits based on employees' earnings and service in the current and prior years. Although the accounting for pension plans is complex, these key items are easy to identify in the schedules provided by most firms. Campbell's *provides a detailed discussion of its pension and postretirement benefit plans, including schedules that reconcile the changes during 2017 and 2016 in the benefit obligation and the fair value of plan assets. Details concerning the "net periodic benefit expense (income)" are also provided in separate schedules for both pension and postretirement benefits (see Note 10 in the appendix).*

Campbell's

Goodwill and Other Acquisition-Related Intangibles   If the balance sheet contains the intangible asset goodwill, the method of recognizing its initial cost (arising from business acquisitions) will be described. Further details will be provided concerning reductions in the cost of goodwill due to impairment losses and other similar adjustments. The cost of acquisition-related intangibles (other than goodwill) and the amortization methods used for these assets will also be disclosed. As discussed in Chapter 6, the accounting for goodwill is a sticky problem for accountants and is likely to generate further debate for many years to come. Campbell's *discloses its accounting policies concerning goodwilland provides further discussion of goodwill and intangible assets such as customer relationships, technology, and trademarks, in the appendix (see Note 5).*

Earnings per Share of Common stock   An explanation of the calculation will be provided, perhaps including details of the calculation of the weighted-average number of shares outstanding and the adjustments to net income for preferred stock dividends. The potential dilution of the earnings per share (EPS) figure resulting from convertible bonds or convertible preferred stock if conversions had taken place during the year, and the potential dilution from stock option plans, will also be explained. Campbell's *provides a schedule detailing its EPS calculation process in the appendix (see Note 8).*

Stock Option and Stock Purchase Plans   Many firms have a **stock option plan** under which directors, officers, and key employees are given an option to buy a certain number of shares of stock *at some time in the future* but at a price equal to the market value of the stock when the option is granted. The stock option presumably provides an incentive to increase the profitability of the firm so that the stock price will rise.

Stock options are accounted for under the *fair value* method, which requires the use of an option-pricing model (usually the Black–Scholes model) for estimation purposes. The Black–Scholes model calculates the present value of the stock option at the grant date, based upon specific information about the terms of the option and assumptions about future stock price performance. After the fair value of the stock options has been determined, this amount is amortized to expense over the service periods presumed to apply to the group of executives and other employees who received the options.

During 2006, it was determined that some publicly owned corporations had engaged in a practice of backdating stock option grants. For example, options granted on May 20 were dated as of March 10, when the market price of the stock was lower. This resulted in an immediate advantage to the grantee, as long as the market price did not fall before the option was exercised, because the difference between the respective market prices resulted in additional gain to the grantee. In addition, because the market price on the false grant date was lower than the market price on the actual grant date, the compensation expense recognized by the corporation and the amount received from the option holder were both less than they should have been. More than 100 companies were involved in this scandal, and several chief executive officers and chief financial officers lost their jobs. The companies involved were required to restate previously reported earnings to reflect the additional compensation expense related to these backdating practices. In addition, several of the companies involved were fined by the SEC. Although not a scandal on the scope of the Enron Corporation or WorldCom affairs, let alone the LIBOR rate-fixing debacle that came to light in 2012, stock option backdating represents another breakdown in the ethical behavior of some managers.

When stock options are exercised, the owner has an immediate profit that is in effect additional compensation for a job well done. The effect on the issuer's financial statements is the same as that of an ordinary common stock issuance (the cash, common stock, and additional paid-in capital accounts will each be increased) except that the issue price will be less than the prevailing market price of the stock at the date of exercise.

Under a *stock purchase plan,* employees can purchase shares of their company's common stock at a slight discount from market value. The objective is to permit the employees to become part owners of the firm and thus to have more of an owner's attitude about their jobs and the company. Stock purchase plans are also accounted for under the fair value method. *Campbell's has a long-term incentive plan that authorizes the issuance of shares of common stock to satisfy awards of stock options, stock appreciation rights, and total shareholder return (TSR) performance restricted stock units. Details of the company's stock-based compensation are discussed in Note 17 in the appendix.*

Campbell's

From the employees' point of view, stock option and stock purchase plans are usually good fringe benefits. From the investors' point of view, the shares that are issuable under these plans represent potential dilution of equity. Thus, the nature of these plans is described, and the potential dilution is disclosed.

Details of Other Financial Statement Amounts

LO 5

Describe the nature and content of various note disclosures.

Many firms will include in the notes to the financial statements the details of amounts that are reported as a single item in the financial statements. For example, details may be provided for the amount of research and development expenses included in a broader operating expense category on the income statement, the "other income" category of the income statement, or the cost and accumulated depreciation of plant and equipment that are reported in total on the balance sheet. Long-term debt, frequently reported as a single amount on the balance sheet, is usually made up of several obligations. A descriptive listing of the obligations, including a schedule of the principal payments required for each of the next five years, is a mandatory reporting requirement if the amounts involved are material. The extent of such detail to be reported is decided by the financial officers of the firm and is generally based on their judgment of the benefit of such detail to the broad user audience that will receive the financial statements. In some cases, disclosure requirements of the SEC and the desire to conform the stockholders' report with the Form 10-K report required to be filed with the SEC result in these details (see Business in Practice—Reporting to the Securities and Exchange Commission on page 379).

Other Disclosures

Accounting Changes   An **accounting change** is a change in the application of an accounting principle that has a material effect on the comparability of the current period financial statements with those of prior periods. The effects of recently adopted accounting changes must be disclosed. For example, if a firm changes its inventory cost flow assumption from FIFO to LIFO, this fact and the dollar effects of the change on both the income statement and balance sheet must be disclosed. Likewise, a change in depreciation methods, a change in the method of accounting for pension costs, or any other change having a significant effect on the financial statements must be disclosed.

Sometimes accounting changes are the result of recent FASB codification updates. Some of the most common changes reported by U.S. companies in recent years were of this variety and involved the accounting for business combinations, noncontrolling interests, fair value measurements, leases, and revenue recognition issues.

Reporting to the Securities and Exchange Commission

The Securities and Exchange Commission (SEC) was created by the Securities and Exchange Act of 1934 to administer the provisions of that act and the Securities Act of 1933. Subsequently Congress assigned to the SEC the authority and responsibility for administering other securities laws. Securities issued by corporations (principally stocks and bonds) that are offered for sale to more than a very few investors must be registered with the SEC. The basic objective of this registration is to provide to potential investors a full and fair disclosure of the securities being issued, the issuer's business activities and financial position, and an explanation of the use to be made of the proceeds of the security issue. Registration does not result in a "seal of approval" or a guarantee against loss. It is up to investors to decide whether their objectives are likely to be achieved. Registration is required for additional issues of previously unregistered securities (e.g., if the corporation wants to raise capital by selling additional shares of stock) and for issues of newly created securities (e.g., bonds that will be offered to the public). A **prospectus** summarizing the complete registration statement must be provided to investors prior to, or concurrently with, their purchase of the security. A prospectus is provided by the company or the broker through whom the securities are being sold.

Registered securities can be traded publicly on a stock exchange or in the over-the-counter market. Firms that issue these securities are required to file an annual informational report with the SEC. This report is referred to as *Form 10-K*. The requirements of Form 10-K have had a significant impact on the scope of material included in the annual report to stockholders. Nearly all public companies include in their annual report to stockholders all the financial statement information and related note disclosures required in the Form 10-K, and many companies now send to stockholders (or make available electronically) a copy of the entire Form 10-K. This information, along with a separate brochure describing the company and its products/services, forms the basis of the annual report to stockholders.

Form 10-K requires some information not usually found in the financial statements, including data about executive compensation and ownership of voting stock by directors and officers. This information is also included in the *proxy statement* sent to stockholders along with the notice of the *annual general meeting (AGM)* and a description of the items expected to be acted upon by the stockholders at that meeting. Stockholders who do not expect to attend the AGM are invited to return a **proxy**. Although the proxy gives another person (usually a director of the corporation) the right to vote the stockholder's shares, the owner can indicate her or his preference for how the shares are to be voted on the indicated issues.

The registration statement, prospectus, Form 10-K, and proxy statement are public documents, and copies can be obtained from the corporation or from the SEC. Try the website of a corporation in which you are interested, or access the Electronic Data Gathering, Analysis, and Retrieval (EDGAR) system on the SEC's website at sec.gov/edgar.shtml#.VP9s4fnF_0Q/.

Business Combinations   If the firm has been involved in a **business combination** (a merger, acquisition, or disposition), the transaction(s) involved will be described and the effect on the financial statements will be explained. Recall that in the case of the disposition of part of the business, the income statement will segregate the impact of discontinued operations on the current year's results.

Mergers and acquisitions are accounted for using the **acquisition method.** Under the acquisition method, the net assets acquired are recorded by the acquiring company at their *fair value* at the date of acquisition. Any amount paid for the acquired net assets (or company) in excess of the fair value of the net assets is recorded as goodwill—an intangible asset that is evaluated annually for possible impairment losses but is *not* amortized, as discussed in Chapter 6.

Contingencies and Commitments   It is not unusual for a firm to be involved in litigation, the results of which are not known when the financial statements are prepared. If the firm is denying liability in a lawsuit in which it is a defendant, it is appropriate to disclose the fact of the lawsuit to readers of the financial statements. Of course the concept of matching revenue and expense requires the recognition of any anticipated cost of verdicts that the company expects to have to pay. An expense or a loss and a related liability should be reported in the period affected. Even if the lawsuit is one that management and legal counsel believe will not result in any liability to the company, the fact of the potential loss and liability should be disclosed. The nature of the legal action, the potential damages, and a statement to the effect that the claims against the company are not likely to be sustained are included in the notes. *Campbell's brief "Contingencies" note does not describe any particular lawsuits pending against the company, but it does acknowledge that the company is party to legal proceedings and claims arising out of the ordinary course of business. In management's opinion, these proceedings and claims are "not likely to have a material adverse effect" on the company's financial statements (see Note 18 in the appendix).*

In some cases a firm or one of its subsidiaries may act as a guarantor of the indebtedness of another entity. In such cases it is appropriate for the amount of the potential liability and a brief description of the circumstances to be disclosed in the notes. Under certain circumstances a liability may actually need to be recorded for such guarantees. It was the lack of this type of disclosure by Enron Corporation that caused a great deal of criticism of the company's management and auditors after Enron's bankruptcy. *Campbell's guarantees certain bank loans made to Pepperidge Farm independent contractor distributors that could potentially obligate the company for up to $204 million (see Note 18 in the appendix).*

If the firm has made commitments to purchase a significant amount of plant and equipment or has committed to pay significant amounts of rent on leased property for several years into the future, these commitments will be disclosed. This is done because the commitment is like a liability but is not recorded on the balance sheet because the actual purchase transaction has not yet occurred. *Campbell's provides a schedule of rental payments that will be owed over the next several years under operating lease agreements for warehouse and office facilities and retail store space (see Note 18 in the appendix).*

A firm may have quite a few other kinds of **contingencies** and **commitments;** most will have an adverse effect on the financial position of the firm and its results of operations if they materialize. The purpose of disclosing these items is to provide full disclosure to the user of the financial statements.

Events Subsequent to the Balance Sheet Date   If, subsequent to the balance sheet date, a significant event occurs that has a material impact on the balance sheet or income statement, it is appropriate to provide an explanation of the probable impact of the subsequent event on future financial statements. Examples of such significant events include the issuance of a large amount of long-term debt, the restructuring of long-term debt, the issuance of a large amount of capital stock, the sale of a significant part of the company's assets, and the agreement to enter into a business combination.

Impact of Inflation   It has been emphasized that the financial statements do not reflect the impact of inflation. The original cost concept and the objectivity principle result in assets being recorded at their historical cost to the entity, based on current dollars at the time the transactions are initially recorded. The FASB encourages, but does not require, companies to provide supplementary information on the effects of changing prices (inflation) in the notes to the financial statements. In practice, very few companies voluntarily do so. However, the SEC's Regulation S-K requires registrants to "discuss" the effects of inflation and other changes in prices in the Management's Discussion and Analysis (MD&A) section of the 10-K if such effects are considered material; in practice, most companies discuss inflation briefly in their MD&A but do not provide specific financial data. These lax reporting requirements with respect to the effects of inflation are largely due to the fact that inflation has not been an issue of grave importance in the United States for several decades. If the U.S. economy experiences high rates of inflation in the future, the present SEC disclosure requirements are likely to be reexamined and enhanced.

Segment Information Most large corporations operate in several lines of business and in several international geographic areas. In addition, some firms have major customers (frequently other large corporations or the U.S. government) that account for a significant part of the total business. A **business segment** is a group of the firm's business activities that has a common denominator. The components of each business segment are identified and defined by management. Segments may reflect the company's organizational structure, manufacturing processes, product line groups, or industries served. The required disclosure of segment, geographic, and major customer information is designed to permit the financial statement user to make judgments about the impact on the firm of factors that might influence specific lines of business, geographic areas, or specific major customers.

As you have learned, a company presents only one set of financial statements, regardless of how many industries or countries it serves. Segment data disaggregate one company into smaller components so that readers can have more useful information for decision making. Data shown for each segment include sales to unaffiliated customers, operating profit, capital expenditures, depreciation and amortization expense, and identifiable assets. Note that from these data it is possible to make a DuPont model return-on-investment calculation and to prepare for each segment a simple statement of cash flows showing cash flows from operating activities (net income plus depreciation and amortization expense) minus cash used for investing activities (capital expenditures). This simple statement of cash flows omits financing activities (such as long-term debt and dividend transactions), but it does highlight the principal cash flows related to each segment. Although these segment measures cannot be combined to equal the total company's ROI or cash flows (because assets and expenses applicable to the corporation as a whole have not been arbitrarily allocated to segments), segment trends over time can be determined. *Campbell's manages its business in three segments, focused mainly on product categories and likewise reports on three geographic segments as described in the appendix. (See Note 6 in the appendix for the reported business segment amounts.)*

Campbell's

Sales to unaffiliated customers, operating profits, and identifiable assets are also reported by geographic areas in which the firm operates. For example, the areas in the geographic breakdown used by Campbell's include only the United States, Australia, and "Other Countries." Campbell's presence is not strong enough in any other specific country (such as the UK or Canada) to meet any of the minimum reporting thresholds as a separately identifiable segment. Note that ROI calculations can also be made based on geographic areas, but cash flow information cannot be approximated because the required geographic disclosures do not include capital expenditures or depreciation and amortization expense.

If a firm has a major customer that accounts for more than 10 percent of its consolidated sales, it is appropriate to disclose this fact to the financial statement user so that a judgment can be made about the influence of this customer on the firm's continued profitability. However, the name of the major customer is not required to be disclosed. Campbell's reports, *"Our largest customer, Wal-Mart Stores, Inc. and its affiliates, accounted for approximately 20% of consolidated net sales in 2017, 2016 and 2015."*

Management's Statement of Responsibility

LO 7
Explain why a statement of management's responsibility is included with the notes.

Many firms include in the notes **management's statement of responsibility,** which explains that the responsibility for the financial statements lies with the management of the firm, not the external auditor and certified public accountants who express an opinion about the fairness with which the financial statements present the financial condition and results of operations of the company. The statement of responsibility usually refers to the internal audit function, the audit committee of the board of directors, the company's code of conduct, and other policies and procedures designed to ensure that the company operates at a high level of ethical conduct. In addition to these voluntary disclosures, SOX requires management to include in its annual report an assessment of the effectiveness of the company's internal control over financial reporting.

Management's Discussion and Analysis

LO 8
Describe the significance of management's discussion and analysis of the firm's financial condition and results of operations.

For many years, the Securities and Exchange Commission has required companies that must file a Form 10-K annual report with the commission to include in the report a section entitled "Management's Discussion and Analysis of Financial Condition and Results of Operations" (referred to as *MD&A*). MD&A is being included in more and more annual reports to stockholders, and most publicly traded companies now provide links to downloadable versions of their full 10-K reports on their websites. MD&A is designed to enhance public disclosure of information about the corporation and is a part of the annual report that should be read by current and potential investors.

Of particular interest to investors and potential investors are disclosures often provided in MD&A concerning non-GAAP financial measures and key performance indicators that are used to assess the company's financial and operating results. The reporting entity may use several non-GAAP financial measures, not to replace the presentation of financial results in accordance with U.S. generally accepted accounting principles but to supplement other metrics used by management to internally evaluate its businesses and to facilitate the comparison of past and present operations. Any reported non-GAAP measures must be reconciled with the most directly comparable GAAP measures in a table included with the disclosures.

Campbell's

In the Campbell Soup Company report in the appendix, the pages devoted to MD&A have been omitted from those selected for inclusion in this text (see pages 14–32 in the full version of Campbell's 2017 annual report, which can be downloaded from the company's website).

What Does It Mean?
Answer on page 395

3. What does it mean to state that management's discussion and analysis is essential to understanding the firm's activities and financial statements?

Five-Year (or Longer) Summary of Financial Data

Most corporate annual reports present a summary of financial data for at least the five most recent years. Many firms report these data for longer periods, and at least one firm reports these data for every year since it was organized. Included in the summary are key income statement data or even the entire income statement in condensed form. In addition to amounts, significant ratios such as earnings as a percentage of sales, average assets, and average stockholders' equity may also be included. Earnings and dividends per share, the average number of shares outstanding each year, and other operating statistics may be reported. Year-end data from the balance sheet, such as working capital; property, plant, and equipment (net of accumulated depreciation); long-term debt; and stockholders' equity usually are reported. Book value per share of common stock (explained in Chapter 11) and the year-end market price of common stock frequently are reported. When stock dividends or stock splits have occurred, the per share data of prior years are adjusted retroactively so that the per share data are comparable.

As an illustration of the adjustment of per share data for stock dividends or stock splits, assume that Cruisers Inc. reported basic earnings per share and cash dividends per share of $4.50 and $2.00, respectively, for fiscal 2018. Assume also that in 2019 the firm had a 2-for-1 stock split. In the annual report for 2019, earnings and dividends for 2018 should reflect that because of the split, there are now twice as many shares of common stock outstanding as there were when 2018 amounts were first reported. Therefore, in the 2019 annual report, 2018 basic earnings per share and dividends per share will be reported at $2.25 and $1.00, respectively. Assume further that in 2020, Cruisers had a 10 percent stock dividend that resulted in 110 shares outstanding for every 100 shares that were outstanding before the stock dividend. The 2020 annual report will report 2018 basic earnings per share and dividends per share as $2.05 ($2.25 / 1.10) and $0.91 ($1.00 / 1.10), respectively. Diluted earnings per share data (if required to be reported) would also be adjusted.

The **five-year (or longer) summary** is not included in the scope of the independent auditors' work, nor does their opinion relate to the summary. Likewise, the summary is not a part of the notes to the financial statements; it is a supplementary disclosure that may appear before or after the financial statements and notes. Campbell's annual report includes a five-year financial summary in the appendix (see Item 6 "Selected Financial Data").

LO 9
Identify what is included in the five-year (or longer) summary of financial data.

4. What does it mean to review the trends in the five-year (or longer) summary of financial data?

What Does It Mean?
Answer on page 395

Independent Auditors' Report

The independent auditors' report is a brief (usually four paragraphs), often easily overlooked report that relates to the financial statements and the accompanying explanatory notes. The SEC requires an audit of the financial statements of a publicly owned company. Many privately owned firms will likewise have an audit of their financial statements to support their bank loan negotiations.

LO 10
Discuss the meaning and content of the independent auditors' report.

The independent auditors' report (officially referred to as the "Report of Independent Registered Public Accounting Firm") for The Coca-Cola Company for the period ended December 31, 2017, is reproduced in Exhibit 10-2. This report format is a recent variation of that which has been standardized by the Auditing Standards Board of the AICPA (as amended by the Public Company Accounting Oversight Board); it rearranges the order of the introductory, scope and opinion paragraphs (discussed below) to emphasize the audit firm's opinion, followed by the basis for their opinion. Note that Coca-Cola

Exhibit 10-2

Report of Independent Registered Public Accounting Firm

Board of Directors and Shareowners
The Coca-Cola Company

Opinion on the Financial Statements

We have audited the accompanying consolidated balance sheets of The Coca-Cola Company and subsidiaries (the Company) as of December 31, 2017 and 2016, the related consolidated statements of income, comprehensive income, shareowners' equity, and cash flows for each of the three years in the period ended December 31, 2017, and the related notes (collectively referred to as the "financial statements"). In our opinion, the financial statements present fairly, in all material respects, the consolidated financial position of the Company as of December 31, 2017 and 2016, and the consolidated results of its operations and its cash flows for each of the three years in the period ended December 31, 2017, in conformity with U.S. generally accepted accounting principles.

We also have audited, in accordance with the standards of the Public Company Accounting Oversight Board (United States) (PCAOB), the Company's internal control over financial reporting as of December 31, 2017, based on criteria established in Internal Control—Integrated Framework issued by the Committee of Sponsoring Organizations of the Treadway Commission (2013 framework) and our report dated February 23, 2018, expressed an unqualified opinion thereon.

Basis for Opinion

These financial statements are the responsibility of the Company's management. Our responsibility is to express an opinion on the Company's financial statements based on our audits. We are a public accounting firm registered with the PCAOB and are required to be independent with respect to the Company in accordance with the U.S. federal securities laws and the applicable rules and regulations of the Securities and Exchange Commission and the PCAOB.

We conducted our audits in accordance with the standards of the PCAOB. Those standards require that we plan and perform the audit to obtain reasonable assurance about whether the financial statements are free of material misstatement, whether due to error or fraud. Our audits included performing procedures to assess the risks of material misstatement of the financial statements, whether due to error or fraud, and performing procedures that respond to those risks. Such procedures include examining, on a test basis, evidence regarding the amounts and disclosures in the financial statements. Our audits also included evaluating the accounting principles used and significant estimates made by management, as well as evaluating the overall presentation of the financial statements. We believe that our audits provide a reasonable basis for our opinion.

Ernst & Young, LLP

We have served as the Company's auditor since 1921.
Atlanta, Georgia
February 23, 2018

received an *unqualified,* or "clean," audit opinion, meaning that its financial statements were "present[ed] fairly, in all material respects. . . in conformity with U.S. generally accepted accounting principles." This is by far the most commonly presented opinion in annual reports because most firms would prefer to make the necessary "auditor-suggested adjustments" to financial statement amounts and note disclosures than to receive a *qualified* audit opinion.

The report usually is addressed to the board of directors and stockholders of the corporation. The first paragraph, or *introductory paragraph,* identifies the financial statements that were audited and briefly describes the responsibilities of both management and the auditors with respect to the financial statements. It is important to note here that management is responsible for the financial statements; the auditors' task is to express an opinion about them.

The second paragraph is the *scope paragraph,* and it describes the nature and extent of the auditors' work. Note that their concern is with obtaining reasonable assurance about whether the financial statements are free of material misstatements and that their work involves tests. Auditors give no guarantee that the financial statements are free from fraudulent transactions or from the effects of errors. Remember that the accuracy of the financial statements is the responsibility of management, not of the auditors. However, the standards of the PCAOB do require extensive audit procedures as a means of obtaining reasonable assurance that the financial statements are free of material misstatements, whether by error or fraud.

The third paragraph is the *opinion paragraph,* and in that sense it is the most important. The benchmark for fair presentation is U.S. generally accepted accounting principles. Again, note the reference to materiality. If during the audit the auditor determines that the financial statements taken as a whole do not "present fairly," the auditor will require a change in the presentation or withdraw from the audit. The latter action is very rare.

The fourth paragraph, now required by the PCAOB, refers to the audit of the effectiveness of the company's internal control over financial reporting and to the nature of the opinion (unqualified, qualified, or adverse) expressed thereon. An internal control audit is now conducted in conjunction with the audit of financial statements, and an internal control audit opinion is normally presented on a separate page immediately following the financial statements audit opinion.[2] An alternative presentation approach is to combine the financial statements audit opinion and the internal controls audit opinion into a single auditors' report. This was the approach taken by Campbell Soup Company's auditors (see the appendix).

Campbell's

As mentioned earlier, Ernst & Young rearranged the order of the presentation of these four paragraphs in their report on Coca-Cola's 2017 financial statements to emphasize their opinion as well as the basis for their opinion. The first paragraph includes elements of both the traditional introductory paragraph (identifying the financial statements that have been audited) and the opinion paragraph. The second paragraph refers to their audit of the effectiveness of internal controls, a topic traditionally presented in the fourth paragraph. The third paragraph describes the responsibilities of management and the auditors, as traditionally mentioned in the introductory paragraph. The final paragraph details the nature and extent of the auditors' work and the basis for their opinion, which is usually presented in the scope (or second) paragraph.

---

[2] Public Company Accounting Oversight Board (PCAOB), *Auditing Standard No. 2,* "An Audit of Internal Control over Financial Reporting Performed in Conjunction with an Audit of Financial Statements," March 9, 2004. [Effective pursuant to SEC Release No. 34-49884; File No. PCAOB-2004-03, June 17, 2004.]

Although this variation of the standard independent auditors' report audit represents a significant rearrangement of topics, all of the key elements are preserved, and the resulting communication is equally clear.

The name of the auditing firm, sometimes presented as a facsimile signature, and the date of the report are shown at the bottom of the report. The date of the report is the date the audit work was completed, and a required audit procedure is to review transactions subsequent to the balance sheet date up to the date of the report. As discussed earlier in this chapter, unusual transactions that occur during this period must be disclosed in the financial statements or in the notes.

Occasionally the auditors' report includes additional language and/or an explanatory paragraph that describes a situation that does not affect fair presentation but that should be disclosed to keep the financial statements from being misleading. Examples of circumstances requiring departures from the standard auditors' report include the following:

1. Basing the opinion in part on the work of another auditor.
2. Uncertainties about the outcome of a significant event that would have affected the presentation of the financial statements if the outcome could have been estimated.
3. Substantial doubt about the entity's ability to continue as a going concern.
4. A material change from a prior accounting period in the application of an accounting principle.

The auditor can issue a *qualified* opinion if the scope of the audit was restricted and essential audit work could not be performed or if there is a material departure from generally accepted accounting principles that affects only part of the financial statements. The reason for the qualification is explained in the report, and the opinion about fair presentation is restricted to the unaffected parts of the financial statements. Qualified opinions rarely occur in practice.

It is also possible for the auditing firm to issue an *adverse* opinion, indicating that the financial statements are misrepresented, misstated, and do not "present fairly, in all material respects" the financial position and results of operations of the reporting entity. Adverse opinions are extremely rare in practice, particularly among companies that are publicly-traded and must abide by regular SEC reporting requirements. An adverse opinion has severe consequences, normally causing an immediate delisting of a company's stock from an exchange. Tohsiba Corp. narrowly escaped this fate when PricewaterhouseCoopers (PwC) gave the company a qualified opinion instead of an adverse opinion on its 2017 financial statements. PwC did, however, issue an adverse opinion on the company's system of internal controls, a less serious offense, but one that the company must address to earn back trust within the investing community.

It is appropriate for the financial statement reader to review the independent auditors' report and determine the effect of any departure from the standard report.

What Does It Mean?
Answer on page 395

5. What does it mean to say that the auditors have given a clean opinion about the financial statements?

Financial Statement Compilations

Accounting firms also perform services for client organizations whose debt and equity securities are not publicly traded (and whose financial statements are not required to be audited). Many small businesses use an outside accounting firm to prepare the necessary tax returns and to assemble financial information into conventional financial statements. The accounting firm may prepare financial statements to submit to banks and other major suppliers for purposes of obtaining commercial credit. Because the accounting firm is not engaged in an audit or review, it is necessary that a report be issued that clearly communicates to the user that the accounting firm is not providing any form of assurance about the fairness of the financial statements. Such a report, called a *compilation report*, is shown in Exhibit 10-3.

The user of the financial statements should be aware that the compilation means exactly what it says. If a company's need for capital is great and it borrows substantial amounts from its bank, it is not uncommon for the bank to reject a compilation report and insist on financial statements that have been audited by an independent accountant. Having an audit will cause the company's accounting costs to rise significantly.

The Board of Directors and Shareholders,

Cruisers Inc.:

We have compiled the accompanying balance sheet of Cruisers Inc. as of December 31, 2019, and the related statements of income, retained earnings, and cash flows for the year then ended. We have not audited or reviewed the accompanying financial statements and, accordingly, do not express an opinion or provide any assurance about whether the financial statements are in accordance with accounting principles generally accepted in the United States of America.

Management is responsible for the preparation and fair presentation of the financial statements in accordance with accounting principles generally accepted in the United States of America and for designing, implementing, and maintaining internal control relevant to the preparation and fair presentation of the financial statements.

Our responsibility is to conduct the compilation in accordance with Statements on Standards for Accounting and Review Services issued by the American Institute of Certified Public Accountants. The objective of a compilation is to assist management in presenting financial information in the form of financial statements without undertaking to obtain or provide any assurance that there are no material modifications that should be made to the financial statements.

Management has elected to omit substantially all of the disclosures required by accounting principles generally accepted in the United States of America. If the omitted disclosures were included in the financial statements, they might influence the user's conclusions about Cruisers Inc.'s financial position, results of operations, and cash flows. Accordingly, the financial statements are not designed for those who are not informed about such matters.

[Accounting firm's signature, address, and date]

Exhibit 10-3

Compilation Report

Summary

Corporate governance issues continue to command increased attention of legislators, regulators, investors, and the senior management teams of publicly traded companies. The Sarbanes–Oxley Act (SOX) of 2002 and the creation of the Public Company Accounting Oversight Board (PCAOB) have led to significant improvements in the development of a workable corporate financial reporting model. Further refinements to the reporting requirements now in place for U.S.-based companies are expected in the near future. Yet, the temptation to manipulate reported earnings and cash flow disclosures by following questionable or outwardly dishonest financial reporting practices will always exist. Several of the more common financial reporting shenanigans that have been identified in recent years are listed and discussed. **(LO 1, 2)**

Notes to the financial statements are an integral part of the statements and result from the application of the full disclosure concept discussed in Chapter 2. The notes disclose details of amounts summarized for financial statement presentation, explain which permissible alternative accounting practices have been used by the reporting entity, and provide detailed disclosure of information needed for a full understanding of the financial statements. **(LO 3)**

Accounting policies disclosed include the depreciation method, inventory cost flow assumption, and basis of consolidation. Accounting for the entity's income taxes, employee benefits, and amortization of intangible assets is described. Details of the calculation of earnings per share of common stock are sometimes provided. There is a discussion of employee stock option and stock purchase plans. The materiality concept is applied to the extent of each of these disclosures. **(LO 4)**

If there have been changes in the accounting for a material item, the consistency concept requires disclosure of the effect of the change on the financial statements. Sometimes accounting or reporting changes are required as a result of recent FASB codification updates. **(LO 5)**

There is a full discussion of any business combinations in which the entity has been involved. **(LO 5)**

Significant contingencies and commitments, such as litigation or loan guarantees, as well as significant events that have occurred since the balance sheet date, are described. This is a specific application of the full disclosure concept. **(LO 5)**

The impact of inflation on the historical cost amounts used in the financial statements may be reported; although this information is not currently required to be shown in the notes to the financial statements, most companies are required to discuss the impact of inflation in their MD&A. **(LO 5)**

Segment information summarizes some key financial information for the principal activity areas of the firm. The intent of this disclosure is to permit judgment about the significance to the entity's overall results of its activities in certain business segments and geographic areas. **(LO 5)**

The financial statements are the responsibility of management, not the auditors, and management's statement of responsibility acknowledges this. This acknowledgment usually includes a reference to the system of internal control. **(LO 7)**

Management's discussion and analysis (MD&A) of the firm's financial condition and results of operations provides an important and useful summary of the firm's activities. **(LO 8)**

Although not usually a part of the notes to the financial statements, most annual reports include a summary of key financial data for a period of five years or longer. This summary permits financial statement users to make trend evaluations easily. **(LO 9)**

The independent auditors' report includes their opinion about the fair presentation of the financial statements in accordance with U.S. generally accepted accounting principles and calls attention to special situations. Auditors do not guarantee that the company will be profitable, nor do they give assurance that the financial statements are absolutely accurate. **(LO 10)**

The Securities and Exchange Commission is responsible for administering federal securities laws. One of its principal concerns is that investors have full disclosure about publicly-traded securities and the companies that issue them. The reporting requirements of the SEC have led to many of the disclosures contained in corporate annual reports. **(LO 6)**

Refer to the notes to the consolidated financial statements in the Campbell Soup Company annual report in the appendix and to the comparable parts of other annual reports that you may have. Observe the organization of this part of the financial statements and the comprehensive explanation of the material discussed. Read management's discussion and analysis of the firm's financial condition and results of operations. Find the five-year summary of key financial data and evaluate the trends disclosed for sales, net income, total stockholders' equity, and other items reported in the summary. Chapter 11 will describe and illustrate some of the ways of analyzing financial statement data to support the informed judgments and decisions made by users of financial statements.

Campbell's

Key Terms and Concepts

accounting change (p. 378)   A change in the application of an accounting principle.

acquisition method (p. 379)   The method of accounting for the purchase of another company that records as the cost of the investment the fair value of the cash and/or securities paid, less the liabilities assumed in the transaction.

business combination (p. 379)   A merger between two or more firms, or the purchase of one firm by another.

business segment (p. 381)   A group of the firm's similar business activities; most large firms have several segments.

commitment (p. 380)   A transaction that has been contractually agreed to but that has not yet occurred and is not reflected in the financial statements.

contingency (p. 380)   An event that has an uncertain but potentially significant effect on the financial statements.

corporate governance (p. 368)   The strategies, behaviors, and structures that support the fulfillment by the board of directors and management of an entity's citizenship responsibilities and the achievement of its economic performance.

financial review (p. 368)   Another name for the notes to the financial statements.

five-year (or longer) summary (p. 383)   A summary of key financial data included in an organization's annual report; it is not a financial statement included in the scope of the independent auditors' report.

management's discussion and analysis (MD&A) (p. 375)   A narrative description of the firm's activities for the year, including comments about its financial condition and results of operations.

management's statement of responsibility (p. 382)   A discussion included in the notes to the financial statements describing management's responsibility for the financial statements.

net pension expense (income) (p. 376)   The estimated annual cost of (or income earned by) providing pension-related benefits to current and former employees based on certain actuarial assumptions. Normally reported in a detailed schedule in the notes to the financial statements.

notes to the financial statements (p. 368)   An integral part of the financial statements that contains explanations of accounting policies and descriptions of financial statement details.

prospectus (p. 379)   A summary of the characteristics of a security being offered for sale, including a description of the business and financial position of the firm selling the security.

proxy (p. 379)   An authorization given by a stockholder to another person to vote the shares owned by the stockholder.

significant accounting policies (p. 375)   A brief summary or description of the specific accounting practices followed by the entity.

stock option plan (p. 377)   A plan for compensating directors, officers, and key employees by providing an option to purchase a company's stock at a future date at the market price of the stock when the option is issued (granted).

connect Mini-Exercises

All applicable Mini-Exercises are available in *Connect*.

Mini-Exercise 10.1
LO 9

Calculate restated EPS after stock split   For the year ended December 31, 2019, Spike Inc. reported earnings per share of $5.80. During 2020, the company had a 4-for-1 stock split.

Required:

Calculate the 2019 earnings per share that will be reported in Spike's 2020 annual report for comparative purposes.

Mini-Exercise 10.2
LO 9

Calculate originally reported EPS before stock split   During the fiscal year ended June 30, 2020, Jones Co. had a 3-for-1 stock split. In its annual report for 2020, the company reported earnings per share for the year ended June 30, 2019, on a restated basis, of $1.05.

Required:

Calculate the originally reported earnings per share by Jones Co. for the year ended June 30, 2019.

connect Exercises

All applicable Exercises are available in *Connect*.

Exercise 10.3
LO 1, 2
Campbell's

Read and interpret corporate governance statement   Refer to the corporate governance disclosures provided on Campbell Soup Company's website. Visit www.campbellsoup.com; click on "All Campbell Brands" on the home page, then select "Investors" and then "Corporate Governance." Identify the principal topics covered in those disclosures. Are there other topics that you believe would be appropriate to have included? Explain your answer.

Scan the notes to the financial statements and read other annual report disclosures Refer to the Campbell Soup Company annual report for 2017 in the appendix or to the most recent full annual report that you have downloaded from Campbell's website. Find and scan the notes to consolidated financial statements. Read the independent auditors' report and management's discussion and analysis of financial condition and results of operations. What is your general impression regarding the adequacy of the company's financial disclosures?

Exercise 10.4
LO 2, 3

Campbell's

Interpret auditors' opinion It is impossible for an auditor to "guarantee" that a company's financial statements are free of all error because the cost to the company to achieve absolute accuracy (even if that were possible) and the cost of the auditor's verification would be prohibitively expensive. How does the auditors' opinion recognize this absence of absolute accuracy?

Exercise 10.5
LO 10

Interpret auditors' opinion To what extent is the auditors' opinion an indicator of a company's future financial success and future cash dividends to stockholders?

Exercise 10.6
LO 10

Effects of stock split and stock dividend on EPS For the year ended December 31, 2018, Finco Inc. reported earnings per share of $1.56.

Exercise 10.7
LO 9

Required:

a. During 2019, the company had a 3-for-1 stock split. Calculate the 2018 earnings per share that will be reported in Finco's 2019 annual report for comparative purposes.

b. During 2020, Finco had an additional 2-for-1 stock split. Calculate the 2018 earnings per share that will be reported in Finco's 2020 annual report for comparative purposes.

c. Assume that Finco had issued a 10% stock dividend in 2019 and did not have a stock split. Calculate the 2018 earnings per share that will be reported in Finco's 2019 annual report for comparative purposes. Round your answer to two decimal places.

Calculate EPS and effect of stock split on EPS During the year ended December 31, 2020, Gluco Inc. split its stock on a 3-for-1 basis. In its annual report for 2019, the firm reported net income of $442,890 for 2019, with an average 155,400 shares of common stock outstanding for that year. There was no preferred stock.

Exercise 10.8
LO 9

Required:

a. What amount of net income for 2019 will be reported in Gluco's 2020 annual report?

b. Calculate Gluco's earnings per share for 2019 that would have been reported in the 2019 annual report.

c. Calculate Gluco's earnings per share for 2019 that will be reported in the 2020 annual report for comparative purposes.

Exercise 10.9
LO 9

Calculate EPS reported before stock split and stock dividend During the fiscal year ended September 30, 2020, Worrell Inc. had a 2-for-1 stock split and a 5% stock dividend. In its annual report for 2020, the company reported earnings per share for the year ended September 30, 2019, on a restated basis, of $1.20.

Required:
Calculate the originally reported earnings per share for the year ended September 30, 2019.

Exercise 10.10
LO 9

Calculate EPS and dividends per share before stock split For several years Orbon Inc. has followed a policy of paying a cash dividend of $0.45 per share and having a 10% stock dividend. In the 2020 annual report, Orbon reported restated earnings per share for 2018 of $2.70.

Required:
a. Calculate the originally reported earnings per share for 2018. Round your answer to two decimal places.
b. Calculate the restated cash dividend per share for 2018 reported in the 2020 annual report for comparative purposes. Round your answer to two decimal places.

connect **Problems**

All applicable Problems are available in *Connect*.

Problem 10.11
LO 2, 4, 9

Understanding note disclosures and financial summary data This problem is based on the 2017 annual report of Campbell Soup Company in the appendix.

Required:
Find in the Selected Financial Data (also known as the Five-Year Review), or calculate, the following data:
a. Net sales in 2014.
b. Operating income (earnings before interest and taxes) in 2013.
c. Difference between operating income (earnings before interest and taxes) and net income (net earnings) in 2015.
d. Year(s) in which net income (net earnings) decreased compared to the previous year.

Find the following data for 2017 in the Notes to Consolidated Financial Statements:
e. Amount of interest paid in 2017.
f. Number of stock options exercisable at July 30, 2017.
g. Net sales to customers outside the United States in 2017.
h. Cost of products sold for the third quarter of 2017.

Problem 10.12
LO 2, 4, 9

Understanding note disclosures and financial summary data This problem is based on the 2017 annual report of Campbell Soup Company in the appendix.

Required:
Find in the Selected Financial Data (also known as the Five-Year Review), or calculate, the following data:
a. Dividends per share declared in 2017.
b. Capital expenditures in 2016.

c. Year in which total equity grew by the greatest amount over the previous year.

d. Change in total debt from 2013 to 2017.

Find the following data for 2017 in the Notes to Consolidated Financial Statements:

e. Amount of finished products inventory in 2017.

f. The company's effective income tax rate in 2017.

g. Net sales of the Global Biscuits and Snacks segment in 2017.

h. Market price range of common stock for the fourth quarter of 2017.

Cases

connect

All applicable Cases are available in *Connect*.

Focus company—find various accounting policy disclosures In Exercise 1.1, you were asked to obtain the most recent annual report of a company that you were interested in reviewing throughout this term. Please read the "significant accounting policies" and review other note disclosures as necessary to answer the following questions:

Case 10.13
LO 4

Required:

a. What are the principal components included in the firm's receivables (or accounts and notes receivable, or trade receivables)?

b. What inventory valuation method(s) is (are) being used for financial reporting purposes? How much more would ending inventory have been if it were reported on a total FIFO basis? (*Hint:* This disclosure is sometimes referred to as the "LIFO Reserve.")

c. Does the firm report a reconciliation of the statutory income tax rate with the effective tax rate? If so, what are these rates, and what principal temporary differences caused them to differ?

d. Have any significant subsequent events occurred since the balance sheet date? If so, describe the effects that these items will have on future financial statements.

e. What are the principal components included in the firm's cash (or cash and equivalents, or cash and short-term investments)?

f. What depreciation method(s) is (are) being used for financial reporting purposes? How much total depreciation and amortization expense did the firm report?

g. Does the firm have any stock options outstanding? If so, how many option shares are exercisable at the end of the year?

h. Does the firm have any significant contingencies or commitments that have not been reported as liabilities on the balance sheet? If so, describe the potential effects of these items from the perspective of a common stockholder.

Calculate ROI for geographic segments; analyze results—McDonald's Corp. McDonald's conducts operations worldwide and is managed in three primary geographic segments: U.S., International Lead Markets (including Australia, Canada, France, Germany, and the UK), and High Growth Markets (including China, Italy, Korea, Poland, Russia, Spain, Switzerland, and the Netherlands). A hybrid geographic/corporate segment, Foundational Markets & Corporate, reports on the results of all other countries as well as any unallocated amounts. McDonald's allocates resources to, and evaluates the performance of, its segments based on operating income. The

Case 10.14
LO 5

asset totals disclosed by geography are directly managed by those regions and include accounts receivable, inventory, certain fixed assets, and certain other assets. Corporate assets primarily include cash and cash equivalents, investments, deferred tax assets, and other assets. Refer to the following geographic segment data (in millions) from the 2017 annual report of McDonald's Corp.:

		U.S.	International Lead Markets	High Growth Markets	Foundational Markets & Corporate	Total Company
Revenues	2017	$ 8,006.4	$ 7,340.3	$5,533.2	$1,940.5	$22,820.4
	2016	8,252.7	7,223.4	6,160.7	2,985.1	24,621.9
	2015	8,558.9	7,614.9	6,172.8	3,066.4	25,413.0
Operating income	2017	$ 4,022.4	$ 3,166.5	$2,001.4	$ 362.4	$ 9,552.7
	2016	3,768.7	2,838.4	1,048.8	88.6	7,744.5
	2015	3,612.0	2,712.6	841.1	(20.2)	7,145.5
Depreciation and amortization expense	2017	$ 524.1	$ 461.1	$ 231.7	$ 146.5	$ 1,363.4
	2016	510.3	451.6	362.0	192.6	1,516.5
	2015	515.2	460.9	363.9	215.7	1,555.7
Assets	2017	$12,648.6	$11,844.3	$4,480.7	$4,830.1	$33,803.7
	2016	11,960.6	9,112.5	5,208.6	4,742.1	31,023.9
	2015	11,806.1	11,136.3	5,248.6	9,747.7	37,938.7

Required:

a. Based on a cursory review of the data, can you identify any significant trends in the consolidated totals? Are there any notable trends in the data for specific business segments?

b. Using the DuPont model to show margin and turnover, calculate ROI for each of the three primary geographic segments for 2017. Round your percentage answers to one decimal place.

c. Looking only at the data presented here, which business segment appears to offer McDonald's Corp. the greatest potential for high returns in the future?

d. Comment about the difficulties you may encounter when attempting to interpret the Foundational Markets and Corporate segment results.

e. Can you think of any ways in which McDonald's could improve upon its classification of geographic segment data?

1. It means that as a result of the Sarbanes–Oxley Act (SOX) of 2002, the creation of the Public Company Accounting Oversight Board (PCAOB), and the additional requirements imposed by the Dodd–Frank Act of 2010, corporate governance–related issues have become more highly regulated and controlled. These developments have resulted in an improved level of financial disclosure and transparency in annual reports, improved systems of internal control, more effective monitoring of executive compensation arrangements, and enhanced shareholder rights.

2. It means that to understand the financial statements it is necessary to review the related notes to learn about the accounting policies that were followed, details of summary amounts reported in the financial statements, and unusual or significant transactions that affected the financial statements.

3. It means that this part of the annual report contains information that adds substance to the amounts reported in the financial statements.

4. It means that a picture of the firm's recent financial history can be readily obtained by reviewing these data and using them in various calculations (such as ROI and ROE) if those results are not included in the summary.

5. It means that in the opinion of an independent third party, the financial statements (of a public company) present fairly in all material respects, in accordance with the standards of the Public Company Accounting Oversight Board (United States), the financial position, results of operations, and cash flows of the entity for the period. It does not mean that there have not been any fraudulent transactions, that the company has been given an absolute "clean bill of health," or that investors are guaranteed that they will not suffer losses from investing in the company's securities.

11

Financial Statement Analysis

The process of interpreting an entity's financial statements can be facilitated by certain ratio computations, and if one entity's financial condition and results of operations are to be compared to those of another entity, ratio analysis of the financial statements is essential. In Chapter 3, you learned about some of the fundamental interpretations made from financial statement data. The importance of financial statement ratios and the significance of *trends* in the ratio results were explained. The calculation of return on investment (ROI) and the use of the DuPont model, which recognizes margin and turnover in the ROI calculation, were described. In addition, the calculation and significance of return on equity (ROE) and the liquidity measures of working capital, current ratio, and acid-test ratio were explained. It would be appropriate for you to review Chapter 3 if you don't thoroughly understand these analytical tools. In Chapters 5 through 10, you learned about the business, accounting, and financial reporting aspects of most of the transactions that an entity may experience. The effects of these transactions on the financial statements were described and explained. Your understanding of the accounting process and the alternative choices that management must make for financial reporting purposes will permit you to make sense of an entity's financial statements. This chapter builds on the material presented in Chapter 3 and provides a comprehensive discussion of financial statement analysis concepts. The objective of this chapter is to expand your ability to read and interpret financial statements so that you can make decisions and informed judgments about an entity's financial condition and results of operations.

What Does It Mean?

Answer on page 430

1. What does it mean to use the trend of financial statement ratios to compare the financial position and results of operations of one firm with another firm?

LEARNING OBJECTIVES (LO)

After studying this chapter, you should understand and be able to

LO 11-1   Explain how liquidity measures can be influenced by the inventory cost flow assumption used.

LO 11-2   Explain how suppliers and creditors use a customer's payment practices to judge liquidity.

LO 11-3   Discuss the influence of alternative inventory cost flow assumptions and depreciation methods on turnover ratios.

LO 11-4   Discuss how the number of days' sales in both accounts receivable and inventory are used to evaluate the effectiveness of the management of receivables and inventory.

LO 11-5   Discuss the significance of the price/earnings ratio in the evaluation of the market price of a company's common stock.

LO 11-6   Discuss how dividend yield and the dividend payout ratio are used by investors to evaluate a company's common stock.

LO 11-7   Explain what financial leverage is and why it is significant to management, creditors, and owners.

LO 11-8   Explain what book value per share of common stock is, describe how it is calculated, and discuss why it is not a very meaningful amount for most companies.

LO 11-9   Discuss how common size financial statements can be used to evaluate a firm's financial position and results of operations over a number of years.

LO 11-10   Generalize about how operating statistics using physical, or nonfinancial, data can be used to help management evaluate the results of the firm's activities.

Financial Statement Analysis Ratios

The ratios used to facilitate the interpretation of an entity's financial position and results of operations can be grouped into four categories:

1. Liquidity.
2. Activity.
3. Profitability.
4. Debt or financial leverage.

Liquidity Measures

The liquidity measures of working capital, current ratio, and acid-test ratio were discussed in Chapter 3. One point that deserves reemphasis is the **effect of the inventory cost flow assumption on working capital.** The balance sheet carrying value of inventories will depend on whether the weighted-average, FIFO, or LIFO assumption

LO 1
Explain how liquidity measures can be influenced by the inventory cost flow assumption used.

is used. In periods of rising prices, a firm using the FIFO cost flow assumption will report a relatively higher asset value for inventories than a similar firm using the LIFO cost flow assumption. Thus, even though the firms may be similar in all other respects, they will report different amounts of working capital, and they will have different current ratios. Therefore, a direct comparison of the liquidity of the two firms by using these measures is not possible. To ease this reporting difficulty, many firms using the LIFO method disclose a *LIFO reserve* amount in the notes to the financial statements. The LIFO reserve is the difference between the inventory valuation as reported under the LIFO basis and the amount that would have been reported under the FIFO basis.

Even more significant to suppliers or potential suppliers/creditors of the firm than the aggregate working capital or liquidity ratios is the firm's current and recent payment experience. Suppliers/creditors want to know whether the firm is paying its bills promptly. One indication of this is whether all cash discounts for prompt payment (e.g., for payment terms of 2/10, net 30) are being taken. Information about current and recent payment practices can be obtained by contacting other suppliers or credit bureaus and by reviewing Dun & Bradstreet reports (see Business in Practice—Credit Rating and Financial Analysis Services).

LO 2 Explain how suppliers and creditors use a customer's payment practices to judge liquidity.

What Does It Mean?
Answer on page 430

2. What does it mean to assess the liquidity of an entity?

Activity Measures

The impact of efficient use of assets on the firm's return on investment was explained in Chapter 3 in the discussion of the asset turnover component of the DuPont model (ROI = Margin × Turnover). Activity measures focus primarily on the relationship between asset levels and sales (i.e., turnover). Recall that the general model for calculating turnover is the following:

$$\text{Turnover} = \text{Sales} / \text{Average assets}$$

Recall also that average assets are used in the turnover calculation (rather than year-end assets) because the amount invested is compared to sales, which are generated over a period of time. The average assets amount is ordinarily determined by using the balance sheet amounts reported at the beginning and end of the period; however, if appropriate and available, monthly or quarterly balance sheet data can be used in the calculation. Turnover is frequently calculated for the following:

Accounts receivable.
Inventories.
Plant and equipment.
Total operating assets.
Total assets.

LO 3 Discuss the influence of alternative inventory cost flow assumptions and depreciation methods on turnover ratios.

Alternative inventory cost flow assumptions and depreciation methods will affect the comparability of turnover between companies. For example, a company using LIFO and an accelerated depreciation method would report lower amounts for inventory

Business in
Practice

Credit Rating and Financial Analysis Services

To help potential creditors and investors evaluate the financial condition and investment prospects of companies, a credit rating and financial analysis industry has developed. Firms in this industry gather and report data about individual companies, industries, segments of the economy, and the economy as a whole.

Credit-rating firms such as Dun & Bradstreet and credit bureaus collect data from companies and their creditors and sell credit history data to potential suppliers and others. These firms usually have a rating system and assign a credit risk value based on that system. A company being reported on can request to see the data in its file so that erroneous data can be eliminated or corrected.

The financial statements of larger firms whose stock or bonds have been issued to the public are analyzed and reported on by firms such as Standard & Poor's Corporation or Moody's Investors Service Inc. A rating is assigned to bonds to reflect the rating firm's assessment of the risk associated with the security. The ratings range from AAA to C, or no rating at all for a speculative bond. Summary financial statements, ratio calculation results, and bond ratings are published in manuals that are available in many libraries. In addition to rating bonds, these firms and many others (such as Value Line Publishing Inc. and stock brokerage firms) evaluate the common and preferred stock issues of publicly traded companies. They report summary financial data and trends in key ratios, along with their opinions about the investment prospects for the stocks. A potential investor will likely use reports from one or more of these sources as well as the company's annual report to support an investment decision.

and net book value of depreciable assets than would a company using FIFO and the straight-line method. Although the sales volume of the two companies may be identical, the company reporting lower asset values would show a higher asset turnover. Of more significance than intercompany or company–industry comparisons as of a given date is the trend of turnover for the company relative to the trend of turnover for other companies or the industry. Even if the company's turnover data are not directly comparable to industry data because of accounting method choices, the patterns exhibited in the respective trends can be meaningfully compared.

When calculating inventory turnover, most analysts substitute the cost of goods sold amount for the sales amount in the calculation because inventories are reported at cost, not at selling prices. This approach eliminates distortions that could be caused by sales mix changes between product categories with different gross profit ratios or markup percentages. Even if sales are used in the numerator consistently, the inventory turnover trend will not be significantly affected unless there are major relative markup differences and major sales mix changes.

Some analysts use the cost of plant and equipment rather than the net book value (cost minus accumulated depreciation) when calculating plant and equipment turnover. This removes the impact of different depreciation calculation methods and may make intercompany and industry turnover data more comparable. This may be an illusory improvement, however, because the assets of each firm are reported at original cost, not current value or replacement cost. If they were acquired over different periods of time, the cost data are not likely to be comparable.

Exhibit 11-1 illustrates some turnover calculations for Campbell Soup Company with data from the company's 2017 annual report. Note that the calculation results usually are not carried beyond one decimal place because aggregate financial statement data are being used, and the accuracy implied by additional decimal places is not warranted.

Campbell's

Exhibit 11-1

Campbell Soup
Company, Asset
Turnover Calculations
Illustrated

Campbell's

Accounts receivable turnover for 2017 ($ millions):

Sales for 2017	$7,890
Accounts receivable (net) at 7/30/17	605
Accounts receivable (net) at 7/31/16	626

$$\text{Accounts receivable turnover} = \frac{\text{Sales}}{\text{Average accounts receivable}}$$
$$= \frac{\$7,890}{(\$626 + \$605)/2}$$
$$= 12.8 \text{ times}$$

Inventory turnover for 2017 ($ millions):

Cost of goods (products) sold for 2017	$4,831
Inventories at 7/30/17	902
Inventories at 7/31/16	940

$$\text{Inventory turnover} = \frac{\text{Cost of goods sold}}{\text{Average inventories}}$$
$$= \frac{\$4,831}{(\$940 + \$902)/2}$$
$$= 5.2 \text{ times}$$

Plant and equipment turnover for 2017 ($ millions):

Sales for 2017	$7,890
Plant and equipment (net) at 7/30/17	2,454
Plant and equipment (net) at 7/31/16	2,407

$$\text{Plant and equipment turnover} = \frac{\text{Sales}}{\text{Average plant and equipment}}$$
$$= \frac{\$7,890}{(\$2,407 + \$2,454)/2}$$
$$= 3.2 \text{ times}$$

LO 4

Discuss how the number of days' sales in both accounts receivable and inventory are used to evaluate the effectiveness of the management of receivables and inventory.

Two other activity measures that permit assessment of the efficiency of asset management are the **number of days' sales in accounts receivable** and the **number of days' sales in inventory.** The sooner that accounts receivable can be collected, the sooner cash is available to use in the business or to permit temporary investment, and the less cash needs to be borrowed for prompt payment of liabilities. Likewise, the lower that inventories can be maintained relative to sales, the less inventory needs to be financed with debt or stockholders' equity, and the greater the return on investment. However, the risk of having minimum inventories is that an unanticipated increase in demand or a delay in receiving raw materials or finished product can result in an out-of-stock situation that may result in lost sales.

Inventory management is a very important activity for many firms, and several quantitative and operational techniques have been developed to assist in this activity. The just-in-time (JIT) inventory management system was pioneered by some Japanese firms several decades ago and subsequently has been adopted by many firms in the United States and elsewhere throughout the world. The primary objective of a JIT system is to keep the investment in inventories at a minimum by forecasting needs and having suppliers deliver components as they are needed in the production process.

Each of the number of days' sales calculations involves calculating an average day's sales (or cost of sales) and dividing that average into the year-end balance sheet amount. A 365-day year is usually assumed for the average day's sales (or cost of sales) calculation. As in the calculation of inventory turnover, it is more appropriate to use cost of sales data in the days' sales in inventory calculation. Year-end asset values are used instead of average amounts because the focus here is on the number of days' sales (or cost of sales) in the ending balance sheet amounts. The results of these calculations also can be referred to, for receivables, as the *average collection period for accounts receivable* or the *number of days' sales outstanding,* and for inventories, as the *average sales period for inventories.* It must be stressed again that the inventory cost flow assumption will influence the result of the inventory activity calculations. Exhibit 11-2 illustrates these calculations for Campbell Soup Company for 2017.

Number of days' sales in accounts receivable for 2017 ($ millions):

Sales for 2017. . . . . $7,890

Accounts receivable (net) at 7/30/17 605

$$\text{Average day's sales} = \frac{\text{Annual sales}}{365}$$

$$= \frac{\$7,890}{365}$$

$$= \$21.616$$

$$\text{Days' sales in accounts receivable} = \frac{\text{Accounts receivable at year-end}}{\text{Average day's sales}}$$

$$= \frac{\$605}{\$21.616}$$

$$= 28.0 \text{ days}$$

The result of this calculation also can be expressed as the *average age of accounts receivable,* the *number of days' sales outstanding,* or the *average collection period for accounts receivable.*

Number of days' sales in inventory for 2017 ($ millions):

Cost of goods (products) sold for 2017 . . . . $4,831

Inventories at 7/30/17 902

$$\text{Average day's cost of goods sold} = \frac{\text{Annual cost of goods sold}}{365}$$

$$= \frac{\$4,831}{365}$$

$$= \$13.236$$

$$\text{Days' sales in inventory} = \frac{\text{Inventory at year-end}}{\text{Average day's cost of goods sold}}$$

$$= \frac{\$902}{\$13.236}$$

$$= 68.1 \text{ days}$$

The result of this calculation also can be expressed as the *average age of the inventory* or the *average sales period for inventory.*

Again, in evaluating the firm's operating efficiency, it is the trend of these calculation results that is important. A single year's days' sales in receivables or inventory is not very useful. Campbell Soup Company's 28.0 days' sales in accounts receivable would make sense if its credit terms are a combination of 2/10, net 30, and net 30 (without a discount), as is the case for many manufacturing firms. In addition, perhaps certain concessions are granted to major customers (e.g., Walmart) to enhance the market penetration and product placement of Campbell's products. In any event, it is difficult to assess the job performance of Campbell's credit managers without knowing about the firm's credit policies and the details of its accounts receivable balance by customer category. In fact, if the credit manager wanted to know how many days' sales were in receivables at any time, the most accurate result could be determined by doing the following:

1. Obtaining the daily sales amounts for the period ending with the date of the total accounts receivable.
2. Adding the daily sales amounts (working backward by day) until the sum equals the total accounts receivable.
3. Counting the number of days' sales that had to be included to reach this total.

Because of the different operating characteristics of various industries, general rules for activity measures are difficult to develop. In general, the higher the turnover or the fewer the number of days' sales in accounts receivable and inventory, the greater the efficiency. Again, it should be emphasized that the answer from any financial statement analysis calculation is not important by itself; the *trend* of the result over time is most meaningful. An increase in the age of accounts receivable, an increase in inventory relative to sales, or a reduction in plant and equipment turnover are all early warning signs that the liquidity and profitability of a firm may be weakening.

What Does It Mean?
Answers on page 430

3. What does it mean to assess the activity measures of an entity?
4. What does it mean to state that total asset turnover has improved?

Profitability Measures

Two of the most significant measures of profitability, *return on investment* and *return on equity,* were explained and illustrated in Chapter 3. Each of these measures relates net income, or an income statement subtotal (e.g., operating income), to an element of the balance sheet. Operating income, which excludes other income and expense (principally interest expense) and income taxes, is frequently used in the ROI calculation because it is a more direct measure of the results of management's activities than is net income. Interest expense is a function of the board of directors' decisions about capital structure (the relationship between debt and stockholders' equity); income taxes are a function of the tax laws. Thus, ROI based on operating income becomes an evaluation of the operating activities of the firm. The balance sheet elements for these calculations are average total assets (or average operating assets) for ROI, and average common stockholders' equity for ROE. You know enough about accounting principles and

how financial statement data are developed to have some healthy skepticism about the relationship of these rates of return to what a "true" rate of return based on real economic profit related to fair values would be.

The problem is that there is no agreement among managers, accountants, or financial analysts about what constitutes real economic profit or how to objectively determine fair values of the balance sheet data. In addition, the unique characteristics of individual companies and industries make the development of benchmark or target profitability ratios difficult if not impossible. Although many valid exceptions exist, a very broad rule useful for putting ROI in perspective is that average ROI based on net income for most U.S. merchandising and manufacturing companies is normally between 7 and 10 percent. Average ROI based on operating income (earnings before interest and taxes) for the same set of firms is between 10 and 15 percent. Average margin based on net income ranges from about 7 to 10 percent. Using operating income, average margin ranges from 10 to 15 percent. Asset turnover is usually about 1.0 to 1.5. A rule of thumb useful for putting ROE in perspective is that average ROE, for most U.S. merchandising and manufacturing companies, is normally between 12 and 20 percent during times of relative prosperity. However, during recessionary times, these averages decline significantly, making such generalizations even more problematic. Do not draw firm conclusions based on these rules of thumb. Profitability evaluations are likely to be more valid when they are based on the *trend* of one company's ROI and ROE relative to the *trend* of industry and competitors' rates of return.

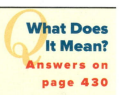

5. What does it mean when ROI has decreased even though net income has increased?

6. What does it mean to use the DuPont model to help explain a decrease in ROI?

What Does It Mean?

Answers on page 430

The **price/earnings ratio,** or simply the P/E ratio, is calculated by dividing the market price of a share of common stock by the earnings per share of common stock (discussed in detail in Chapter 9). The P/E ratio is used extensively by investors to evaluate the market price of a company's common stock relative to that of other companies and relative to the market as a whole. **Earnings multiple** is another term used to describe the price/earnings ratio. This term merely reflects that the market price of stock is equal to the earnings per share multiplied by the P/E ratio. Diluted earnings per share is normally used in the P/E calculation, as illustrated by the following example using data for Campbell Soup Company, as of July 30, 2017.

$$\text{Price/earnings ratio (or earnings multiple)} = \frac{\text{Market price of common stock}[1]}{\text{Diluted earnings per share of common stock}[2]}$$
$$= \$52.85/\$2.89$$
$$= 18.3$$

Campbell's

Campbell's P/E ratio of 18.3 for 2017 is well within a range that would be regarded as normal for a firm supported by strong investor confidence.

LO 5

Discuss the significance of the price/earnings ratio in the evaluation of the market price of a company's common stock.

To understand the significance of the P/E ratio, think about the reason an individual invests in the common stock of a company. The obvious objective is to "make money" (i.e., to achieve the investor's desired return on the investment). It is anticipated that return on investment will be realized in two ways: (1) The firm will pay cash dividends, and (2) the market price of the firm's stock will increase. The change in market value is usually called a *capital gain* or *loss*. A number of factors can cause the market price to change. One of the most significant of these is the prospect for future cash dividends. Both present and future cash dividends are a function of earnings. So, in a very real sense, the market price of a company's common stock reflects investors' expectations about the firm's future earnings. The greater the probability of increased earnings, the more investors are willing to pay for a claim to those earnings. Relating market price and earnings per share in a ratio is a sensible way to express investors' expectations without confusing the issue by focusing on just market price per share. To illustrate, assume the following market price per share of common stock for each of two companies:

	Company A	Company B
Market price per share	$45.00	$63.00

Based on market price alone, the tempting conclusion is that the stock of Company B is more expensive than the stock of Company A. However, when earnings per share are considered, the table looks like this:

	Company A	Company B
Market price per share	$45.00	$63.00
Diluted earnings per share	$1.80	$3.50

The price/earnings ratio can now be calculated by dividing the market price per share by the earnings per share:

	Company A	Company B
Market price per share Diluted earnings per share	$\frac{\$45.00}{\$1.80} = 25$	$\frac{\$63.00}{\$3.50} = 18$

Company A's stock is more expensive because investors are willing to pay 25 times earnings for it, but they will pay only 18 times earnings for the stock of Company B. In essence, investors are showing that they expect greater future earnings growth and dividend payments from Company A than from Company B; therefore, they are willing to pay relatively more for a given amount of current earnings.

---

[1] Campbell's actual year-end closing price of $52.85 can be confirmed by visiting campbellsoup.com and then clicking on *All Campbell Brands; Investors; Stock Information; Historical Price Lookup.* Note that July 28, 2017, was the last trading day before the end of Campbell's fiscal year.

[2] Bottom of consolidated statements of earnings; see the 2017 annual report in the appendix.

The price/earnings ratio, or earnings multiple, is one of the most important measures used by investors to evaluate the market price of a firm's common stock. This is one reason that earnings per share is reported prominently on the face of the income statement. As explained in Chapter 9, the effect of discontinued operations and potential dilution of EPS from any stock options, convertible long-term debt, and/or convertible preferred stock is also disclosed separately on the income statement. It is usually the diluted earnings per share amount that is used to calculate the P/E ratio associated with a company's stock. Because of its significance, the P/E ratio is disclosed in the stock listing tables of *The Wall Street Journal* and other periodicals and electronic data sources.

Although the preceding illustration of the P/E ratio calculation was based on earnings for the past year, analysts sometimes use expected future earnings per share and the current market price in the calculation to evaluate the prospects for changes in the stock's market price. For example, one approach to forecast market price is to use expected future earnings per share multiplied by the current (or expected future) earnings multiple. It should be noted, however, that the P/E ratio applies only to common stock. Because the preferred stock dividend does not fluctuate as earnings change, it would not be meaningful to calculate a preferred stock P/E ratio. A loose rule of thumb for putting the price/earnings ratio in perspective is that for the common stock of most merchandising and manufacturing companies, average P/E ratios have historically ranged from 12 to 18.

The interpretation of P/E ratios for individual firms is fairly straightforward. An above-average P/E ratio indicates that the common stock price is high relative to the firm's current earnings, probably because investors anticipate relatively favorable future developments, such as increased earnings per share or higher dividends per share. Low P/E ratios usually indicate poor earnings expectations. Keep in mind, however, that P/E ratios are significantly influenced by the company's reported earnings. For example, assume that Cruisers Inc. reported diluted earnings per share of $2.42 in 2019 and $5.27 in 2020. Assume also that the year-end market price per share of common stock was $40 in 2019 and $60 in 2020. Thus, the P/E ratio for Cruisers would have fallen from 16.5 ($40/$2.42) to 11.4 ($60/$5.27) even though net income doubled (from $764,000 in 2019 to $1,527,000 in 2020 as illustrated in Exhibit 9-7) and the market price per share of common stock increased by 50 percent, in just one year! In this type of situation, the relatively low P/E ratio at the end of 2020 probably would reflect investors' recognition that 2020 earnings were exceptionally high relative to the company's recent experience. Although the market price per share has increased significantly, it has not adjusted as quickly as earnings have grown. What this demonstrates is that the P/E ratio should not be the sole, or even principal, consideration in an investment decision. Instead, financial analysts might consider a low P/E ratio for a well-established company to be an indicator that the company's stock merits further analysis.

---

7. What does it mean when the price/earnings ratio of a firm's common stock is significantly higher than the P/E ratio for the overall stock market?

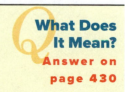

What Does It Mean?

Answer on page 430

Another ratio used by both common stock investors and preferred stock investors is the **dividend yield.** This is calculated by dividing the annual dividend per share

LO 6

Discuss how dividend yield and the dividend payout ratio are used by investors to evaluate a company's common stock.

by the current market price of the stock. This calculation is illustrated here, using assumed amounts for the per share data for Cruisers for the year ended July 30, 2017:

$$\text{Dividend yield} = \frac{\text{Annual dividend per share}}{\text{Market price per share of stock}}$$

Dividend yield on

$$\text{Common stock} = \frac{\$1.60}{\$60.00} = 2.7\%$$

$$\text{Preferred stock} = \frac{\$3.50}{\$56.00} = 6.25\%$$

The dividend yield would be compared to the yield available on alternative investments to help the investor evaluate the extent to which her investment objectives were being met. In many cases, investors will accept a low current dividend yield from a common stock if they believe that the firm is reinvesting the earnings retained for use in the business at a relatively high ROI, because investors anticipate that future earnings will permit higher future dividends. In the case of preferred stock, investors will compare the yield to that available on other fixed-income investments with comparable risk to determine whether to continue holding the preferred stock as an investment. You may have noticed that the dividend yield on Cruisers' preferred stock is lower than the 7 percent stated dividend rate on its $50 par value preferred stock (refer to the EPS illustration on page 336 in Chapter 9). Because preferred dividends are linked to the par value per share, the dividend yield for preferred shareholders decreases as the market price per share increases. The average dividend yield on common stocks has historically been in the range of 3 to 6 percent; for preferred stocks, the yield is usually somewhat greater, in the range of 5 to 8 percent.

What Does It Mean?

Answer on page 430

8. What does it mean when the dividend yield on a firm's common stock is less than the average dividend yield for all common stocks?

Another ratio involving the dividend on common stock is the **dividend payout ratio.** This ratio, computed by dividing the dividend per share of common stock by the earnings per share of common stock (usually diluted earnings per share), reflects the dividend policy of the company. Most firms have a policy of paying dividends that are a relatively constant proportion of earnings (e.g., 40 to 50 percent, or 10 to 15 percent). Knowing the dividend payout ratio permits the investor to project dividends from an assessment of the firm's earnings prospects. Cruisers' dividend payout ratio for fiscal 2020, using assumed amounts, would be the following:

$$\text{Dividend payout ratio} = \frac{\text{Annual dividend per share}}{\text{Earnings per share}}$$

$$= \frac{\$1.60}{\$5.27}$$

$$= 30.4\%$$

Most firms try to avoid having significant fluctuations in the amount of the cash dividend per share because investors prefer to be relatively assured of the dividend amount. Therefore, very few firms use the payout ratio as the sole, or even the principal, determinant of the dividend amount. To help communicate its dividend policy to the stockholders, a firm refers to its dividends in two ways: **Regular dividends** are the stable, or gradually changing, periodic (i.e., quarterly, semiannual, or annual) dividends; **extra dividends** are additional dividends that may be declared and paid after an especially profitable year. The significance of the extra dividend is that it indicates to stockholders that they should not expect to receive the larger amount every year. The most dramatic example of this practice was Microsoft's payment of a one-time dividend of $3 per share toward the end of 2004, which represented a whopping $32.6 billion extra dividend!

As a rule of thumb, the dividend payout ratio for most merchandising and manufacturing companies is usually in the range of 25 to 50 percent. Keep in mind, however, that this range can vary significantly—especially when a firm has a low (or even negative) earnings year but wants to maintain its dividend per share amount. For smaller, growth companies, the average payout ratio can be as low as 10 percent.

From the preferred stockholders' point of view, the ratio of net income to the total preferred stock dividend requirement indicates the margin of safety of the preferred dividend. If net income is less than three or four times the preferred dividend requirement and has been falling over time, the preferred stockholders would become concerned about the firm's ability to generate enough earnings and cash to be able to pay the preferred dividend. This **preferred dividend coverage ratio** for Cruisers for fiscal 2020 (data from Chapter 9) was a somewhat healthy 5.5, calculated as follows:

$$\text{Preferred dividend coverage ratio} = \frac{\text{Net income}}{\text{Preferred dividend requirement}}$$

$$= \frac{\$1,527,000}{\$280,000}$$

$$= 5.5 \text{ times}$$

Financial Leverage Measures

Financial leverage (frequently called just *leverage*) refers to the use of debt (and, in the broadest context of the term, preferred stock) to finance the assets of the entity. Leverage adds risk to the operation of the firm because if the firm does not generate enough cash to pay principal and interest payments, creditors may force the firm into bankruptcy. However, because the cost of debt (i.e., interest) is a fixed charge regardless of the amount of earnings, leverage also magnifies the return to the owners (ROE) relative to the return on assets (ROI). The magnification effect of financial leverage is illustrated in Exhibit 11-3; please study the exhibit before reading the following discussion.

As Exhibit 11-3 illustrates, borrowing money at an interest rate that is less than the rate of return that can be earned on that money increases (or magnifies) the return on stockholders' equity. This makes common financial sense; who wouldn't borrow money at a 9 percent interest cost if the money could be invested to earn substantially more than 9 percent (20 percent in this illustration)? Of course, if the return on investment were less than the cost of borrowing, the result would be a reduction of stockholders' equity (a loss) at best and bankruptcy at worst. This is the risk of leverage—the magnification works both ways! Highly leveraged firms or individuals (i.e., those with substantial debt relative to stockholders' equity) are exposed to the risk of

LO 7

Explain what financial leverage is and why it is significant to management, creditors, and owners.

Exhibit 11-3

Financial Leverage

I. Without financial leverage:

Assume the following balance sheet and income statement:

$$\frac{\text{Return on investment (assets)}}{\text{before interest and taxes}} = \frac{\text{Earnings before interest}}{\text{and taxes}/\text{Total assets}}$$

$$= \$2,000/\$10,000$$
$$= 20\%$$

$$\text{Return on equity, after taxes} = \text{Net income}/\text{Stockholders' equity}$$
$$= \$1,200/\$10,000$$
$$= 12\%$$

Return on investment measures the efficiency with which management has used the operating assets to generate operating income. Note that the return on investment calculation is based on earnings before interest and taxes (operating income) and total assets, rather than net income and total assets. Earnings before interest and taxes (operating income) are used because the amount of interest expense reflects a financing decision, not an operating result, and income taxes are beyond the control of operating management. Thus, ROI becomes an evaluation of the operating activities of the firm. Return on equity measures the rate of return that net income provides to the owners/stockholders. In this illustration, ROI and ROE differ for the firm *without* financial leverage only because income taxes have been excluded from ROI but have been included in ROE.

II. With financial leverage:

Assume the following balance sheet and income statement:

$$\frac{\text{Return on investment (assets)}}{\text{before interest and taxes}} = \frac{\text{Earnings before interest}}{\text{and taxes}/\text{Total assets}}$$

$$= \$2,000/\$10,000$$
$$= 20\%$$

$$\text{Return on equity, after taxes} = \text{Net income}/\text{Stockholders' equity}$$
$$= \$984/\$6,000$$
$$= 16.4\%$$

The use of financial leverage has not affected ROI; financial leverage refers to how the assets are financed, not how efficiently the assets are used to generate operating income.

The use of financial leverage has caused the ROE to increase from 12% to 16.4% because ROI (20%) exceeds the cost of the debt (9%) used to finance a portion of the assets.

losses or bankruptcy if the return on investment falls below the cost of borrowing. This often happens in economic recessions and industry business cycles. Accordingly, most nonfinancial firms try to limit the debt in their capital structure to no more than 50 percent of total capital (debt plus stockholders' equity).

The effect of leverage can be seen in the graphs of Exhibit 3-2, on which are plotted ROI and ROE for Campbell Soup Company, for the period 2013–2017 (see page 80 in Chapter 3). Notice that ROE is several multiples of ROI for each year presented. By looking at the vertical difference between the ROI and ROE graphs in Exhibit 3-2

Campbell's

(keeping the scale in mind), you can see that Campbell's use of leverage has been fairly consistent over the period presented.

Debt and preferred stock provide leverage because the interest cost (or dividend rate) is fixed. When debt is issued, the interest rate is set and remains unchanged for the life of the debt issue. If the interest rate on the debt were to fluctuate as a function of the firm's ROI, or as a result of inflation or deflation in the economy, the magnification of ROE would be diminished or eliminated.

Another feature of debt illustrated in Exhibit 11-3 is the deductibility of interest as an expense in determining income subject to income taxes. The after-tax cost of debt is its interest rate multiplied by the complement of the firm's tax rate. In this example, the assumed tax rate is 40 percent, so the after-tax cost of the debt is $9\% \times (1 - 40\%) = 5.4\%$. Because preferred stock dividends are not deductible as an expense, financial managers strongly prefer to use debt, rather than preferred stock, as the source of fixed-cost capital.

Two **financial leverage measures,** the debt ratio and the debt/equity ratio, are used to indicate the extent to which a firm is using financial leverage. Each ratio expresses the relationship between debt and equity in a slightly different manner. The **debt ratio** is the ratio of total liabilities to the total of liabilities and stockholders' equity. The **debt/equity ratio** is the ratio of total liabilities to total stockholders' equity. Thus, a debt ratio of 50 percent would be the same as a debt/equity ratio of 1 (or 1:1). To illustrate these ratios, assume the following *capital structure* (i.e., right side of the balance sheet) for a firm:

Liabilities.	$ 40,000
Stockholders' equity.	60,000
Total liabilities and stockholders' equity.	$100,000

$$\text{Debt ratio} = \frac{\text{Total liabilities}}{\text{Total liabilities and stockholders' equity}}$$
$$= \frac{\$40,000}{\$100,000}$$
$$= 40\%$$

$$\text{Debt/equity ratio} = \frac{\text{Total liabilities}}{\text{Total stockholders' equity}}$$
$$= \frac{\$40,000}{\$60,000}$$
$$= 66.7\%$$

As already indicated, most nonfinancial firms usually have a debt ratio below 50 percent—which means a debt/equity ratio of less than 1—because of the risk associated with having a greater proportion of debt in the capital structure. However, many firms have been forced into unusually high financial leverage positions in recent years in order to survive competitive pressures (see Business in Practice—The Leveraged Buyout).

The Leveraged Buyout

In 2006 through mid-2008, the activities of hedge funds and private equity firms marked a period of relatively high corporate ownership rearrangement activity that featured friendly and unfriendly mergers and acquisitions, as well as leveraged buyouts. In a merger or acquisition, one firm acquires another, either by issuing stock of the surviving company to the stockholders of the firm being acquired (usually on a merger) or by buying the stock of the company being acquired by paying cash (and sometimes other securities) to the stockholders of the other firm. This is referred to as a *takeover.* Changes in top management and operations of the acquired company frequently result. A leveraged buyout is a transaction in which the present top management of a publicly held firm buys the stock of the nonmanagement stockholders, and the firm becomes "privately owned" (i.e., its shares are no longer traded in the public market). Neither management nor the operations of the firm change significantly. Some firms that have been takeover targets in recent years have "gone private" through a leveraged buyout to avoid being acquired by another firm.

The leveraged buyout transaction gets its label from the fact that the company goes heavily into debt to obtain the funds needed to buy the shares of the public stockholders. In many cases, the debt ratio will be substantially higher than is usually considered prudent, but investors are willing to invest in the firm's bonds because of their confidence in management's proven ability to operate the firm profitably.

The debt issued in a leveraged buyout is usually considered speculative or high risk (the term *junk bond* has been applied to much of it). Investors are often concerned about the impact of a major economic recession on the ability of such firms to meet their interest and principal payment requirements. During the recession of the early 1990s, many firms were forced into bankruptcy or mergers with other firms, and some of the firms that survived were forced to sell off many of their assets. Other financially healthier firms took advantage of rising stock market values to realign their capital structure by selling stock (going public again) and using the proceeds to reduce high-cost, long-term debt.

Because the deferred income tax liability and most of an entity's current liabilities are not interest-bearing, many financial analysts exclude these items from the numerator of the debt ratio and the debt/equity ratio. This allows analysts to get a better sense of what proportion of the entity's capital structure is financed by long-term, interest-bearing debt. Other liabilities that do not add risk to the entity's operations may also be excluded from these calculations.

Holders of a company's long-term debt frequently want to know the **times interest earned ratio** for the firm. This measure is similar to the preferred dividend coverage ratio previously explained; it shows the relationship of earnings before interest and taxes (operating income) to interest expense. The greater the ratio, the more confident the debtholders can be about the firm's prospects for continuing to have enough earnings to cover interest expense, even if the firm experiences a decline in the demand for its products or services. Using data from Cruisers Inc.'s income statement for fiscal 2020, as shown in Exhibit 9-7, the calculation of times interest earned is as follows:

Earnings before income taxes	$2,777 million
Add back interest expense	3,378 million
Earnings before interest and taxes	$6,155 million

$$\text{Times interest earned} = \frac{\text{Earnings before interest and taxes}}{\text{Interest expense}}$$

$$= \frac{\$6,155}{\$3,378}$$

$$= 1.8 \text{ times}$$

The debtholders of Cruisers would be concerned about the company's ability to continue to earn enough to cover its interest expense. As a general rule, a times interest earned ratio of 5 or higher is considered by creditors to indicate a relatively low risk that a firm will experience any difficulty meeting its interest obligations in the future. Campbell's times interest earned for 2017 was a very healthy 12.5. This can be verified by reference to the consolidated statements of earnings in the appendix.

Campbell's

What Does It Mean?

Answers on page 430

9. What does it mean to state that a firm is highly leveraged?
10. What does it mean that the more financial leverage a firm has, the greater the risk to stockholders and creditors?

Other Analytical Techniques

Book Value per Share of Common Stock

The **book value per share of common stock** is a frequently cited ratio in the financial press that can be easily misunderstood by investors who do not carefully interpret its meaning. Book value per share is calculated by dividing the total common stockholders' equity by the number of shares of common stock outstanding. If there is preferred stock in the capital structure of the firm, the liquidating value of the preferred stock is subtracted from total stockholders' equity to get the common stockholders' equity. *Net asset value per share of common stock* is another name for this measure.

The following illustration using data as of July 30, 2017, for Campbell Soup Company, illustrates the calculation (in millions of dollars):

LO 8
Explain what book value per share of common stock is, describe how it is calculated, and discuss why it is not a very meaningful amount for most companies.

Campbell's

$$\text{Book value per share of common stock}^3 = \frac{\text{Common stockholders' equity}}{\text{Number of shares of common stock outstanding}}$$

$$= \frac{\$1,637 \text{ million}}{301 \text{ million}}$$

$$= \$5.44$$

Because total common stockholders' equity reflects the application of generally accepted accounting principles and the specific accounting policies that have been

---

[3] The numerator is reported as "Total Campbell Soup Company shareowners' equity" in the consolidated balance sheets in the appendix; the denominator is reported at the bottom of the consolidated statements of equity in the appendix as 323 million shares of capital stock issued less 22 million shares held as treasury stock.

selected, book value per share is not a number that can be meaningfully compared to the market value per share of stock for most companies, especially if the market value is greater than the book value (which is usually the case). For Campbell's, the 2017 year-end market price per share was $52.85, which was obviously unrelated to its $5.44 book value per share. Although book value per share is not a very useful measure most of the time, you should be aware of how it is calculated and understand its limitations.

What Does It Mean?
Answer on page 430

11. What does it mean to state that a company's book value per share of common stock is less than its market value per share of common stock?

LO 9

Discuss how common size financial statements can be used to evaluate a firm's financial position and results of operations over a number of years.

Common Size Financial Statements

When comparing and evaluating the operating results of a company over a number of years, many analysts like to express the balance sheet and income statement in a percentage format. This type of presentation is referred to as a **common size statement.** To prepare a common size balance sheet, each asset is expressed as a percentage of total assets, and each liability and stockholders' equity amount is expressed as a percentage of that total. For the income statement, the sales amount is set at 100 percent, and each item on the income statement is expressed as a percentage of sales. This type of percentage analysis makes spotting trends in the composition of balance sheet and income statement items much easier than looking at dollar amounts. For example, inventories that represent an increasing percentage of total assets may indicate a weakness in inventory control procedures. An increase in the ratio of cost of goods sold to sales (which would be a decrease in the gross profit ratio) would indicate that management is either unable or unwilling to increase selling prices in response to cost increases, thus causing downward pressure on operating income. However, a well-designed graphical display of key balance sheet and income statement percentage data can also greatly help a reader interpret the data.

Campbell's

Exhibit 11-4 presents common size income statements for Campbell Soup Company for each of the years 2013 through 2017. When analyzing common size financial statement data, you should look first at the "big picture" items and make quick comparisons from year to year. By glancing at the trends for earnings before interest and taxes and net earnings, you will see that Campbell's had a relatively stable earnings pattern from 2013–2017. Check this out by scanning across each of the lines shown in bold in Exhibit 11-4. A line-by-line analysis of a company's common size data often will reveal additional information in support of a reader's basic interpretation of major trends. The actual dollar amounts associated with each of the common size percentage representations should also be considered. A wise investor or financial analyst will make appropriate use of all available information and refrain from drawing quick conclusions.

As mentioned at the beginning of this section, common size balance sheets can also be prepared using total assets as 100 percent. For any given year, each of the individual asset, liability, and stockholders' equity captions would be compared to total assets to determine its relative percentage. This process, illustrated in Exhibit 11-4

Exhibit 11-4

Common Size Income Statements

Campbell's

CAMPBELL SOUP COMPANY Common Size Income Statements For the Five Years Ended July 30, 2017					
	2017	**2016**	**2015**	**2014**	**2013**
Net sales.............................	100.0%	100.0%	100.0%	100.0%	100.0%
Costs and expenses:					
Cost of products sold....................	61.2	65.1	65.6	64.9	63.8
Marketing and selling expenses......................................	10.4	11.2	10.9	11.3	11.8
Administrative expenses..............	6.2	8.1	7.4	6.9	8.4
Research and development expenses......................................	1.2	1.6	1.4	1.5	1.6
Other expenses (income)............	3.0	1.6	0.3	0.3	0.4
Restructuring charges..................	0.2	0.4	1.3	0.7	0.6
Total costs and expenses	82.2%	87.9%	87.0%	85.6%	86.6%
Earnings before interest and taxes.......................................	**17.7**	**12.1**	**13.0**	**14.4**	**13.4**
Interest expense, net........................	1.4	1.4	1.3	1.4	1.6
Earnings before taxes	16.4	10.7	11.7	13.0	11.8
Taxes on earnings.............................	5.1	3.6	3.5	4.2	3.4
Earnings from continued operations..	11.2	7.1	8.2	8.8	8.4
Earnings (loss) from discontinued operations..	0.0	0.0	0.0	1.0	(2.8)
Net earnings..	**11.2%**	**7.1%**	**8.2%**	**9.8%**	**5.6%**

with Campbell's income statement data, is often referred to as *vertical* common size analysis because each financial statement is examined from top to bottom on an annual basis. It is likewise possible, and often useful, to prepare *horizontal* common size financial statements. With horizontal analysis, several years' financial data are stated in terms of a base year. The amount reported for *each* item on the income statement or balance sheet in the base year is equal to 100 percent, and the amounts reported for all other years are stated as a percentage of this base. To illustrate, consider the net sales and net earnings (as restated) results that Campbell's has reported in recent years:

	2017	2016	2015	2014	2013
Net sales (millions).................................	$7,890	$7,961	$8,082	$8,268	$8,052
Net earnings (millions)..........................	887	563	666	855	703

In Campbell's case, the net sales trend shows more stability than the net earnings trend, which is to be expected. Unfortunately, these raw data do not answer all the questions you may have. For example, how rapidly have sales been increasing, and has net earnings kept pace with sales? Horizontal analysis answers these questions directly:

	2017	2016	2015	2014	2013
Net sales..	98%	99%	100%	103%	100%
Net earnings	126%	80%	95%	122%	100%

Note that the selection of the base year influences the presentation of horizontal analysis trend results. With 2013 selected as the base year, the trends from 2015 through 2017 for net sales and net earnings are shown in a more favorable light than would have been the case had 2014 been selected as the base year. Why? Simply because Campbell's reported higher dollar amounts for net sales and net earnings in 2014 than in 2013.

LO 10

Generalize about how operating statistics using physical, or nonfinancial, data can be used to help management evaluate the results of the firm's activities.

Other Operating Statistics

Physical measures of activity, rather than the financial measures included in the financial statements, are frequently useful. For example, reporting sales in units provides a perspective that may be hidden by price changes when only sales dollars are reported. Likewise, reporting the total number of employees (or employees by division or department) may be more useful for some purposes than reporting payroll costs.

Many analysts combine physical and financial measures to develop useful statistics to show trends or make comparisons between firms. For example, both sales dollars per employee and operating income per employee indicate a type of productivity measure. Plant operating expenses per square foot of plant space or gross profit per square foot of selling space might also be useful indicators of efficiency. There are no "cookbooks" of quantitative measures for management to follow; the challenge is to understand the firm's objectives and procedures, and then to develop measurement and reporting techniques to help people accomplish their goals.

What Does It Mean?

Answers on page 430

12. What does it mean to prepare common size financial statements?
13. What does it mean to use more than financial ratios to evaluate a company's financial position and/or performance?

Demonstration Problem

The Demonstration Problem walkthrough for this chapter is available in *Connect*.

Summary

Financial statement analysis using ratio measurements and trend analysis assists the user of financial statements in making informed judgments and decisions about an entity's financial condition and results of operations. Keep in mind, however, that an analysis of an entity's financial data should be tempered by the fact that all of the data reviewed are historical. As a result, the analyst is making decisions about future events based primarily on past events. Without diminishing the value of financial ratio computations, it must be recognized that they do little to foretell the future. Therefore, the analyst must give due consideration to many other factors before making a decision about the entity.

Creditors especially are interested in the entity's liquidity. Working capital and the calculation of the current ratio and acid-test ratio were also discussed in Chapter 3. **(LO 2)**

Because alternative accounting methods affect financial statement data differently, it is important that readers know which alternatives (e.g., FIFO versus LIFO for inventory) have been used in the financial statements being analyzed. **(LO 1, 3)**

Activity measures reflect the efficiency with which assets have been used to generate sales revenue. Most activity ratios focus on turnover. Activity also can be expressed in terms of the number of days of activity (e.g., sales) in the year-end balance (e.g., accounts receivable). **(LO 4)**

Rate of return calculations in general, and the return on investment (ROI) and return on equity (ROE) measures in particular, are essential in evaluating profitability. These measures were discussed in detail in Chapter 3.

The trend of a ratio over time contains much more information than a single ratio at one point in time. Trend comparisons between the entity and broad industry averages are also useful.

In addition to ROI and ROE based on total data, certain per share ratios are also important. The price/earnings ratio, dividend yield, dividend payout ratio, and preferred dividend coverage ratios are examples. **(LO 5, 6)**

Leverage ratios focus on the financial leverage of the firm. Financial leverage magnifies ROE relative to ROI and adds risk to the securities issued by the firm. **(LO 7)**

Book value per share of common stock is frequently reported, but because it is based on the financial statement value of the firm's assets instead of their market value, book value is not very useful in most circumstances. **(LO 8)**

An effective way to compare the financial condition and results of operations of different size firms is to express balance sheet data as percentages of total assets and income statement data as percentages of sales. This process results in *vertical* common size financial statements. It is also useful to prepare *horizontal* common size financial statements that show trends in individual items over several years in comparison to a base year. **(LO 9)**

Investors, managers, employees, and others are frequently interested in other operating statistics that use data not contained in the financial statements. More than financial data are needed to develop a complete picture about a company. **(LO 10)**

Financial statement analysis ratios are summarized here by category of ratio:

I. Liquidity measures
A. Working capital

$$\text{Working capital} = \text{Current assets} - \text{Current liabilities}$$

The arithmetic relationship between current assets and current liabilities is a measure of the firm's ability to meet its obligations as they come due.

B. Current ratio

$$\text{Current ratio} = \frac{\text{Current assets}}{\text{Current liabilities}}$$

This ratio permits an evaluation of liquidity that is more comparable over time and between firms than the amount of working capital.

C. Acid-test ratio

$$\text{Acid-test ratio} = \frac{\text{Cash (including temporary cash investments)} + \text{Accounts receivable}}{\text{Current liabilities}}$$

By excluding inventories and other nonliquid current assets, this ratio gives a conservative assessment of the firm's bill-paying ability.

II. Activity measures
A. Turnover
1. Total asset turnover

$$\text{Total asset turnover} = \frac{\text{Sales}}{\text{Average total assets}}$$

Turnover shows the efficiency with which assets are used to generate sales. Refer also to the DuPont model under profitability measures.

2. Variations include turnover calculations for accounts receivable, plant and equipment, and total operating assets. Each variation uses sales in the numerator and the appropriate average amount in the denominator.
3. Inventory turnover

$$\text{Inventory turnover} = \frac{\text{Cost of goods sold}}{\text{Average inventories}}$$

Inventory turnover focuses on the efficiency of the firm's inventory management practices. Cost of goods sold is used in the numerator because inventories are carried at cost, not selling price.

B. Number of days' sales in
1. Accounts receivable

$$\frac{\text{Number of days' sales in}}{\text{accounts receivable}} = \frac{\text{Accounts receivable at year-end}}{\text{Average day's sales}}$$

$$\text{Average day's sales} = \frac{\text{Annual sales}}{365}$$

This measure shows the average age of the accounts receivable and reflects the efficiency of the firm's collection policies relative to its credit terms.

2. Inventory

$$\frac{\text{Number of days'}}{\text{sales in inventory}} = \frac{\text{Inventory at year-end}}{\text{Average day's cost of goods sold}}$$

$$\frac{\text{Average day's cost}}{\text{of goods sold}} = \frac{\text{Annual cost of goods sold}}{365}$$

This measure shows the number of days' sales that could be made from the inventory on hand. The trend of this measure reflects management's ability to control inventories relative to sales.

III. Profitability measures
A. Return on investment (ROI)
1. General model

$$\text{ROI} = \frac{\text{Return}}{\text{Investment}}$$

Return is frequently net income, and investment is frequently average total assets. This ratio gives the rate of return that has been earned on the assets invested and is the key measure of profitability.

2. DuPont model

$$ROI = Margin \times Turnover$$

$$= \frac{Net\ income}{Sales} \times \frac{Sales}{Average\ total\ assets}$$

Margin expresses the net income resulting from each dollar of sales. Turnover shows the efficiency with which assets are used to generate sales.

3. Variations of the general model use operating income, income before taxes, or some other intermediate income statement amount in the numerator and average operating assets in the denominator to focus on the rate of return from operations before taxes.

B. Return on equity (ROE)

1. General model

$$ROE = \frac{Net\ income}{Average\ total\ stockholders'\ equity}$$

This ratio gives the rate of return on that portion of the assets provided by the owners/stockholders of the entity.

2. A variation of the general model occurs when there is preferred stock. Net income is reduced by the amount of the preferred stock dividend requirement, and only common stockholders' equity is used in the denominator. This distinction is made because the ownership rights of the preferred and common stockholders differ.

C. Price/earnings ratio (P/E ratio)

$$\frac{Price/earnings\ ratio}{(or\ earnings\ multiple)} = \frac{Market\ price\ per\ share}{Earnings\ per\ share}$$

This ratio expresses the relative expensiveness of a share of a firm's common stock because it shows how much investors are willing to pay for the stock relative to earnings. Generally speaking, the greater a firm's ROI and rate of earnings growth, the higher the P/E ratio of its common stock will be. Most of the time the *diluted* earnings per share amount is used in this calculation.

D. Dividend yield

$$Dividend\ yield = \frac{Annual\ dividend\ per\ share}{Market\ price\ per\ share\ of\ stock}$$

The dividend yield expresses part of the stockholder's ROI: the rate of return represented by the annual cash dividend. The other part of the stockholder's total ROI comes from the change in the market value of the stock during the year; this is usually called the *capital gain* or *loss.*

E. Dividend payout ratio

$$Dividend\ payout\ ratio = \frac{Annual\ dividend\ per\ share}{Earnings\ per\ share}$$

The dividend payout ratio expresses the proportion of earnings paid as dividends to common stockholders. It can be used to estimate dividends of future years if earnings can be estimated. The diluted earnings per share amount is usually used in this calculation.

F. Preferred dividend coverage ratio

$$\frac{\text{Preferred dividend}}{\text{coverage ratio}} = \frac{\text{Net income}}{\text{Preferred dividend requirement}}$$

The preferred dividend coverage ratio expresses the ability of the firm to meet its preferred stock dividend requirement. The higher this coverage ratio, the lower the probability that dividends on common stock will be discontinued because of low earnings and failure to pay dividends on preferred stock.

IV. Financial leverage measures

A. Debt ratio

$$\text{Debt ratio} = \frac{\text{Total liabilities}}{\text{Total liabilities and stockholders' equity}}$$

B. Debt/equity ratio

$$\text{Debt/equity ratio} = \frac{\text{Total liabilities}}{\text{Total stockholders' equity}}$$

Each of these measures shows the proportion of debt in the capital structure. Note that a debt ratio of 50 percent is the same as a debt/equity ratio of 100 percent. These ratios reflect the risk caused by the interest and principal requirements of debt. Variations of these models involve the definition of total liabilities. Current liabilities and deferred tax liabilities are excluded by some analysts because they are not interest-bearing and do not add as much risk as does long-term debt.

C. Times interest earned

$$\text{Times interest earned} = \frac{\text{Earnings before interest and taxes}}{\text{Interest expense}}$$

This is a measure of the firm's ability to earn enough to cover its annual interest requirement.

Key Terms and Concepts

book value per share of common stock (p. 411)   The quotient of total common stockholders' equity divided by the number of shares of common stock outstanding. Sometimes called *net asset value per share of common stock*. Not a very useful measure most of the time.

common size statement (p. 412)   A financial statement in which amounts are expressed in percentage terms. In a *vertical* common size balance sheet, total assets are 100 percent, and all other amounts are expressed as a percentage of total assets each year; for an income statement, sales are 100 percent each year. *Horizontal* common size financial statements are side-by-side comparisons of several years' data in relation to the selected base year data.

debt/equity ratio (p. 409)   The ratio of total liabilities to total stockholders' equity. Sometimes, only long-term debt is used for the numerator of the ratio.

debt ratio (p. 409)   The ratio of total liabilities to the sum of total liabilities and total stockholders' equity. Sometimes, long-term debt is the only liability used in the calculation.

dividend payout ratio (p. 406) The ratio of the annual dividend per share of common stock to the earnings per share.

dividend yield (p. 405) The ratio of the annual dividend per share of common stock to the market price per share.

earnings multiple (p. 403) Another term for *price/earnings ratio;* an indicator of the relative expensiveness of a firm's common stock.

effect of the inventory cost flow assumption on working capital (p. 397) When the cost of items being purchased for inventory is changing, the inventory cost flow assumption used (e.g., FIFO or LIFO) influences the inventory account balance, total current assets, and working capital.

extra dividend (p. 407) A dividend that is not likely to be incorporated as part of the regular dividend in the future.

financial leverage measures (p. 409) The debt ratio and debt/equity ratio that indicate the extent to which financial leverage is being used.

number of days' sales in accounts receivable (p. 400) An indicator of the efficiency with which accounts receivable are collected.

number of days' sales in inventory (p. 400) An indicator of the efficiency with which inventories are managed.

preferred dividend coverage ratio (p. 407) The ratio of net income to the annual preferred stock dividend requirement.

price/earnings ratio (p. 403) An indicator of the relative expensiveness of a firm's common stock.

regular dividend (p. 407) A dividend that is likely to be declared on a repetitive, periodic (i.e., quarterly, semiannual, or annual) basis.

times interest earned ratio (p. 410) The ratio of earnings before interest and taxes to interest expense. An indicator of the risk associated with financial leverage.

Mini-Exercises

connect

All applicable Mini-Exercises are available in *Connect*.

(*Note:* Where no specific learning objective is identified, the requirements involve calculating and using several ratios, including those discussed in Chapter 3.)

Calculate liquidity measures The following amounts were reported on the December 31, 2019, balance sheet:

Mini-Exercise 11.1

Cash	$ 16,000
Accounts receivable	44,000
Common stock	80,000
Wages payable	10,000
Retained earnings	160,000
Land	40,000
Accounts payable	30,000
Bonds payable	240,000
Merchandise inventory	60,000
Buildings and equipment, net of accumulated depreciation	360,000

Required:

a. Calculate working capital at December 31, 2019.
b. Calculate the current ratio at December 31, 2019.
c. Calculate the acid-test ratio at December 31, 2019.

Mini-Exercise **Calculate activity measures** The following information was available for the year
11.2 ended December 31, 2019:

Net sales	$292,000
Cost of goods sold	233,600
Average accounts receivable for the year	14,600
Accounts receivable at year-end	16,000
Average inventory for the year	73,000
Inventory at year-end	78,400

Required:

a. Calculate the inventory turnover for 2019.
b. Calculate the number of days' sales in inventory for 2019, using year-end
inventories.
c. Calculate the accounts receivable turnover for 2019.
d. Calculate the number of days' sales in accounts receivable for 2019, using
year-end accounts receivable.

Mini-Exercise **Calculate profitability measures** The following information was available for the
11.3 year ended December 31, 2019:

Sales	$ 400,000
Net income	60,000
Average total assets	1,000,000
Average total stockholders' equity	600,000
Dividends per share	2.40
Earnings per share	6.00
Market price per share at year-end	96.00

Required:

a. Calculate margin, turnover, and ROI for the year ended December 31, 2019.
b. Calculate ROE for the year ended December 31, 2019.
c. Calculate the price/earnings ratio for 2019.
d. Calculate the dividend payout ratio for 2019.
e. Calculate the dividend yield for 2019.

Calculate financial leverage measures The following information was available for the year ended December 31, 2019:

Mini-Exercise 11.4

Earnings before interest and taxes (operating income)	$120,000
Interest expense	24,000
Income tax expense	30,000
Net income	66,000
Total assets at year-end	400,000
Total liabilities at year-end	280,000

Required:

a. Calculate the debt ratio at December 31, 2019.
b. Calculate the debt/equity ratio at December 31, 2019.
c. Calculate the times interest earned for the year ended December 31, 2019.

Exercises

All applicable Exercises are available in *Connect*.

Identify information used in an investment decision Look forward to the day when you will have accumulated $5,000, and assume that you have decided to invest that hard-earned money in the common stock of a publicly owned corporation. What data about that company will you be most interested in, and how will you arrange those data so they are most meaningful to you? What information about the company will you want on a weekly basis, on a quarterly basis, and on an annual basis? How will you decide whether to sell, hold, or buy some more of the firm's stock?

Exercise 11.5

Obtain an annual report and discuss information sources If your library has a common stock investment advisory service such as *Moody's Handbook of Common Stocks* or online access to an investment advisory service such as *Value Line Research Center: Historical Reports,* use one of those sources to locate a report about a company you have heard about or in which you have an interest. Alternatively, visit a brokerage firm office and ask for a report from one of the above sources or a report prepared by the brokerage firm's research division. Review the report and notice the analytical data that it contains. What other data besides those in the report would you like to obtain? Why do you want these other data? How would you get them?

Exercise 11.6

Effect of transactions on various financial ratios Indicate the effect that each transaction/event listed here will have on the financial ratio listed opposite it, and provide an explanation for your answer. Use + for increase, − for decrease, and (NE) for no effect. Assume that current assets exceed current liabilities in all cases, both before and after the transaction/event.

Exercise 11.7

Transaction/Event	Financial Ratio
a. Split the common stock 2 for 1.	Book value per share of common stock
b. Collected accounts receivable.	Number of days' sales in accounts receivable
c. Issued common stock for cash.	Total asset turnover
d. Sold treasury stock.	Return on equity
e. Accrued interest on a note receivable.	Current ratio
f. Sold inventory on account.	Acid-test ratio
g. Wrote off an uncollectible account.	Accounts receivable turnover
h. Declared a cash dividend.	Dividend yield
i. Incurred operating expenses.	Margin
j. Sold equipment at a loss.	Earnings per share

Exercise 11.8   **Effect of transactions on various financial ratios** Indicate the effect that each transaction/event listed here will have on the financial ratio listed opposite it, and provide an explanation for your answer. Use + for increase, − for decrease, and (NE) for no effect. Assume that current assets exceed current liabilities in all cases, both before and after the transaction/event.

Transaction/Event	Financial Ratio
a. Purchased inventory on account.	Number of days' sales in inventory
b. Sold inventory for cash, at a profit.	Inventory turnover
c. Issued a 10% stock dividend.	Earnings per share
d. Issued common stock for cash.	Debt ratio
e. Sold land at a gain.	Return on investment
f. Purchased treasury stock for cash.	Debt/equity ratio
g. Accrued interest on a note payable.	Times interest earned
h. Accrued wages that have been earned by employees.	Current ratio
i. Purchased equipment for cash.	Plant and equipment turnover
j. Issued bonds at an interest rate that is less than the company's ROI.	Return on equity

 connect   **Problems**

All applicable Problems are available in *Connect*.

Problem 11.9

LO 9

Campbell's

Prepare a common size balance sheet, 2016 Refer to the consolidated balance sheets of the Campbell Soup Company annual report in the appendix.

Required:
Prepare a common size balance sheet at July 31, 2016, using the following captions:

     Total current assets

     Plant assets, net of depreciation

     Goodwill

     Total other long-term assets

     Total assets

Total current liabilities
Total long-term liabilities (including deferred taxes)
Total equity
Total liabilities and equity

Campbell's

Prepare a common size balance sheet, 2017 Solve the requirements of Problem 11.9 for the year ended July 30, 2017.

Problem 11.10
LO 9

Review problem—understanding liquidity measures Assume that the current ratio for Arch Company is 2.0, its acid-test ratio is 1.5, and its working capital is $900,000. Answer each of the following questions *independently,* always referring to the original information.

Problem 11.11
LO 1

a.   How much does the firm have in current liabilities?
b.   If the only current assets shown on the balance sheet for Arch Company are Cash, Accounts Receivable, and Merchandise Inventory, how much does the firm have in Merchandise Inventory?
c.   If the firm collects an account receivable of $300,000, what will its new current ratio and working capital be?
d.   If the firm pays an account payable of $300,000, what will its new current ratio and working capital be?
e.   If the firm sells inventory that was purchased for $150,000 at a cash price of $180,000, what will its new acid-test ratio be?

Effect of transactions on liquidity measures Selected balance sheet accounts for Tibbetts Company on September 30, 2019, are as follows:

Problem 11.12
LO 1

Cash	$ 48,000
Marketable securities......................................	87,000
Accounts receivable, net.................................	129,000
Inventory..	135,000
Prepaid expenses..	21,000
Total current assets..	$420,000
Accounts payable..	$147,000
Other accrued liabilities..	33,000
Short-term debt..	60,000
Total current liabilities..	$240,000

Required:
a.   Calculate the working capital, current ratio, and acid-test ratio for Tibbetts Company as of September 30, 2019.
b.   Summarized here are the transactions/events that took place during the fiscal year ended September 30, 2020. Indicate the effect of each item on Tibbetts Company's working capital, current ratio, and acid-test ratio. Use + for increase, − for decrease, and (NE) for no effect. [*Hint:* It may be helpful to use the horizontal model or to record the journal entry(ies) for each item before considering the effects on liquidity measures.]

Transaction/Event	Working Capital	Current Ratio	Acid-Test Ratio
0. Example: Paid accounts payable, $585,000.	NE	+	+
1. Credit sales for the year amounted to $360,000. The cost of goods sold was $234,000.			
2. Collected accounts receivable, $378,000.			
3. Purchased inventory on account, $252,000.			
4. Issued 250 shares of common stock for $54 per share.			
5. Wrote off $10,500 of uncollectible accounts using the allowance for bad debts.			
6. Declared and paid a cash dividend, $30,000.			
7. Sold marketable securities costing $39,000 for $46,500 in cash.			
8. Recorded insurance expense for the year, $18,000. The premium for the policy was paid in June 2019.			
9. Borrowed cash on a short-term bank loan, $15,000.			
10. Repaid principal of $60,000 and interest of $4,500 on a long-term bank loan.			

Problem 11.13

Ratio analysis—comprehensive problem Presented here are summarized data from the balance sheets and income statements of Wiper Inc.:

WIPER, INC.
Condensed Balance Sheets
December 31, 2020, 2019, 2018
(in millions)

	2020	2019	2018
Current assets	$ 650	$ 900	$ 700
Other assets	2,750	2,050	1,750
	$3,400	$2,950	$2,450
Current liabilities	$ 500	$ 800	$ 700
Long-term liabilities	1,500	1,000	800
Stockholders' equity	1,400	1,150	950
Total liabilities and stockholders' equity	$3,400	$2,950	$2,450

WIPER INC.
Selected Income Statement and Other Data
For the Years Ended December 31, 2020 and 2019
(in millions)

	2020	2019
Income statement data:		
Sales	$3,300	$2,900
Operating income	380	300
Interest expense	80	70
Net income	300	230
Other data:		
Average number of common shares outstanding	44	42
Total dividends paid	$ 50	$ 30

Required:

a.   Calculate return on investment, based on net income and average total assets, for 2020 and 2019. Show both margin and turnover in your calculation.

b.   Calculate return on equity for 2020 and 2019.

c.   Calculate working capital and the current ratio for each of the past three years.

d.   Calculate earnings per share for 2020 and 2019.

e.   If Wiper's stock had a price/earnings ratio of 14 at the end of 2020, what was the market price of the stock?

f.   Calculate the cash dividend per share for 2020 and the dividend yield based on the market price calculated in part **e.**

g.   Calculate the dividend payout ratio for 2020.

h.   Assume that accounts receivable at December 31, 2020, totaled $310 million. Calculate the number of days' sales in receivables at that date.

i.   Calculate Wiper's debt ratio and debt/equity ratio at December 31, 2020 and 2019.

j.   Calculate the times interest earned ratio for 2020 and 2019.

k.   Review the results of these calculations, evaluate the profitability and liquidity of this company, and state your opinion about its suitability as an investment for a young, single professional with funds to invest in common stock.

Ratio analysis—comprehensive problem, 2017 data   This problem is based on the 2017 annual report of Campbell Soup Company in the appendix.

Problem 11.14

Required:

Campbell's

a.   Compute the following profitability measures for the year ended July 30, 2017:
   1.   Return on investment, based on net earnings (perform a DuPont analysis).
   2.   Return on equity, based on net earnings and total equity.
   3.   Price/earnings ratio. Use $52.85 as the year-end market price.
   4.   Dividend yield.
   5.   Dividend payout ratio.

b.   Compute the following liquidity measures at July 30, 2017:
   1.   Working capital.
   2.   Current ratio.
   3.   Acid-test ratio.

c.   Compute the following activity measures for the year ended July 30, 2017:
   1.   Number of days' sales in accounts receivable, based on a 365-day year.
   2.   Number of days' sales in inventory, based on a 365-day year.
   3.   Accounts receivable turnover.
   4.   Inventory turnover.
   5.   Turnover of net property, plant, and equipment.

d.   Compute the following financial leverage measures at July 30, 2017:
   1.   Debt ratio.
   2.   Debt/equity ratio.

e.   Compute the following physical measures of Campbell's profitability at July 30, 2017:

1.   Net sales per employee.
2.   Operating income per employee. (*Note:* In a page not reproduced in the appendix, Campbell's 2017 annual report disclosed that on July 30, 2017, the company had approximately 18,000 employees.)

▣ connect   Cases

All applicable Cases are available in *Connect*.

Case 11.15   **Focus company—comprehensive financial statement analysis** In Exercise 1.1, you were asked to obtain the most recent annual report of a company that you were interested in reviewing throughout this term.

Required:
Liquidity:
a.   Calculate working capital, the current ratio, and the acid-test ratio as of the most recent balance sheet date.
b.   Based on your calculations in part **a,** assess the company's overall liquidity position. Explain which ratios indicate particular strengths and/or weaknesses within the company. Assume the following industry averages: current ratio = 2.0; acid-test ratio = 1.6.
c.   Explain how working capital and the current ratio are related. Would you expect a company with a large amount of working capital to always have a high current ratio?

Profitability:
d.   Calculate ROI, showing margin and turnover, for the most recent year.
e.   Calculate ROE for the most recent year.
f.   Calculate the price/earnings ratio for the most recent year, using the company's year-end market price per share of common stock in the numerator and diluted earnings per share in the denominator.
g.   Calculate the dividend payout and dividend yield ratios for the most recent year.
h.   Based on the results of your calculations in parts **d, e,** and **f,** assess the company's overall profitability. Explain which ratios indicate particular strengths and/or weaknesses within the company. Assume the following industry averages: ROI = 15%; margin = 10%; turnover = 1.5; ROE = 20%; price/earnings = 14.0; dividend payout = 40%; dividend yield = 5%.
i.   As an investor in this company's stock, would you be pleased with this year's dividend yield? How would your dividend yield "expectations" change, if at all, if the company's ROI was 5% higher? Explain.

Financial leverage:
j.   Calculate the debt ratio and the debt/equity ratio as of the most recent balance sheet date.
k.   Based on the results of your calculations in part **j,** assess the company's overall leverage position. What would you estimate the industry averages to be for the debt ratio and debt/equity ratio? Explain.
l.   Explain the relationship between ROI and ROE, and the concept of financial leverage. Would you expect the percentage difference between ROI and ROE to be high or low for a firm that makes substantial use of financial leverage?

Activity measures:

m. Calculate the accounts receivable turnover and number of days' sales in accounts receivable (based on a 365-day year) for the most recent year.

n. Based on your analysis in part **m,** do you believe that the company is doing an effective job at managing accounts receivable? What would you estimate the industry averages to be for the accounts receivable turnover and number of days' sales in accounts receivable? Explain.

o. Calculate the inventory turnover and number of days' sales in inventory (based on a 365-day year) for the most recent year.

p. Based on your analysis in part **o,** to what extent does the company need to be concerned about its inventory management policies? In assessing the inventory management policies, would you be more interested in knowing current ratio or acid-test ratio information? Explain.

Overall assessment:

q. Assume that you have $5,000 that you would like to invest in a single company. Evaluate the common stock of your focus company as a potential investment. From the data available in your focus company's financial statements, identify the five most important criteria that you would use to make your investment decision, and explain why each is important.

Analytical case—comparative analysis of profitability and financial leverage **Case 11.16**
measures The annual reports of the Coca-Cola Co. and PepsiCo Inc. indicate the following for the year ended December 31, 2017 (amounts in millions):

	Coca-Cola Co.	PepsiCo Inc.
Net revenues	$35,410	$63,525
Net income	1,283	4,908
Total assets, January 1, 2017	87,270	73,490
Total liabilities, January 1, 2017	64,050	62,291
Total liabilities, December 31, 2017	68,919	68,823
Total stockholders' equity, December 31, 2017	18,977	10,981

Required:

a. Calculate ROI and ROE for each company for 2017. (*Hint:* You will need to calculate some of the numbers used in the denominator of these ratios.)

b. Based on the results of your ROI and ROE analysis in part **a,** do you believe that either firm uses financial leverage more effectively than the other? Explain your answer. (*Hint:* Compare the percentage differences between ROI and ROE for each firm. Is there a significant difference that would suggest that one firm uses leverage more effectively than the other?)

c. Calculate the debt ratio and debt/equity ratio for each firm at the end of 2017.

d. Compare the results of your analysis in part **c** to your expectations concerning the relative use of financial leverage in part **b.** Do the debt and debt/equity ratios calculated in part **c** make sense relative to your expectations? Explain your answer.

Analytical case—complete an income statement and balance sheet using **Case 11.17**
financial ratio data Partially completed financial statements for Whittaker Inc. follow:

WHITTAKER INC.
Income Statement
For the Year Ended December 31, 2020

Sales	$?
Cost of goods sold	?
Gross profit	$?
Operating expenses	?
Income from operations	$?
Interest expense	?
Income before taxes	$?
Income taxes (20%)	?
Net income	$?

WHITTAKER INC.
Balance Sheet
December 31, 2020

Current assets:	
Cash	$?
Accounts receivable, net	?
Inventory	?
Total current assets	$342,000
Property, plant, and equipment, net	?
Total assets	$?
Current liabilities	$?
Bonds payable, 15%	140,000
Total liabilities	$?
Stockholders' equity:	
Common stock, $2 par value	$ 20,000
Additional paid-in capital	30,000
Retained earnings	?
Total stockholders' equity	$?
Total liabilities and stockholders' equity	$?

Additional information:

- Financial ratios computed from these financial statements include the following:

Current ratio	1.9 to 1
Acid-test ratio	1.3 to 1
Debt/equity ratio	2.0 to 1
Inventory turnover	4.0 times
Accounts receivable turnover	6.8 times
Times interest earned	4.45 times
Gross profit ratio	40%
Return on investment	12%
Earnings per share	$5.52

- All sales during the year were made on account. Cash collections during the year exceeded sales by $28,000, and no uncollectible accounts were written off.
- The balance of the accounts receivable account was $114,000 on January 1, 2017.
- No common stock was issued during the year.
- Dividends declared and paid during the year were $15,200.
- The balance of the inventory account was $96,000 on January 1, 2017.
- Interest expense on the income statement relates to the 15% bonds payable; $20,000 of these bonds were issued on May 1, 2017; the remaining amount of bonds payable were outstanding throughout the year. All bonds were issued at face amount.

Required:

a. Complete the income statement and balance sheet for Whittaker Inc. Show how each amount was determined.

b. After completing part **a,** use your answers to recompute each of the financial ratios provided as additional information.

Capstone analytical review of Chapters 9–11. Calculate selected financial ratios and explain financial reporting issues   **Case 11.18**

(*Note:* Please refer to Case 4.30 on pages 134–135 for the financial statement data needed for the analysis of this case. You should also review the solution to Case 4.30, provided by your instructor, before attempting to complete this case.)

Required:

a. Case 4.30 presents the 2019 income statement and balance sheet for Gerrard Construction Co. What other financial statements are required? What information would these statements communicate that could not be determined by reviewing only the income statement and balance sheet?

b. Briefly describe the note disclosures that should be provided by Gerrard Construction Co., and explain why note disclosures are considered an integral part of the financial statements.

c. Assume that the balance of "Accounts Receivable, net" at December 31, 2018, was $24,600. Calculate the following activity measures for Gerrard Construction Co. for the year ended December 31, 2019:

   1. Accounts receivable turnover.

   2. Number of days' sales in accounts receivable.

d. Calculate the following financial leverage measures for Gerrard Construction Co. at December 31, 2019:

   1. Debt ratio.

   2. Debt/equity ratio.

e. Gerrard Construction Co. wishes to lease some new earthmoving equipment from Caterpillar on a long-term basis. What impact (increase, decrease, or no effect) would a financing lease of $12 million have on the company's debt ratio and debt/equity ratio? (*Note:* These items were computed in part **d** and do not need to be recomputed for this requirement.)

f. Review the answer to Case 4.30 part **i** at this time. Assume that Gerrard Construction Co. had 4,800,000 shares of $1 par value common stock outstanding throughout 2019, and that the market price per share of common stock at December 31, 2019, was $57.50. Calculate the following profitability measures for the year ended December 31, 2019:

   1. Earnings per share of common stock.

   2. Price/earnings ratio.

   3. Dividend yield.

   4. Dividend payout ratio.

1. It means that comparing the results of a particular ratio over a period of time permits a more valid comparison of the direction of relative performance than a comparison of that ratio at a single point in time. However, it is necessary to understand how alternative accounting practices have affected the financial statement amounts reported for each firm.

2. It means that working capital, the current ratio, and the acid-test ratio are calculated and interpreted to determine whether the entity is likely to be able to pay its current obligations when they come due.

3. It means that to determine how efficiently the firm's assets are being used and/or managed, various turnover ratios are calculated and evaluated.

4. It means that the ratio of sales for the period to average total assets used during the period has risen, indicating that assets were used more efficiently relative to sales generated. Perhaps this was accomplished by producing more product with the same amount of plant and equipment and/or by reducing inventories.

5. It means that the firm is less profitable in the sense of earnings related to assets used to generate earnings.

6. It means to break ROI into its margin and turnover components to help determine whether the decrease in ROI is due to reduced profitability or less efficient use of assets, or both.

7. It means that investors are willing to pay more, in relative terms, for a share of the firm's common stock than for a share of common stock of most other firms. This may be caused by investor expectations for much higher growth in profitability in the immediate future for the firm relative to expectations for other firms.

8. It means that the firm is retaining and reinvesting proportionately more of its earnings than other companies. This may be because the firm anticipates needing more capital for expansion, and the board of directors prefer to retain earnings for that use rather than raise capital by selling more stock or issuing debt.

9. It means that the firm has a relatively high proportion of debt to equity in its capital structure.

10. It means that if the firm cannot earn a greater rate of return than the interest rate being paid on borrowed funds, its chances of not being able to meet its obligations and of going bankrupt are greater than if it had less financial leverage.

11. It doesn't mean much at all because book value is based on balance sheet values, which are not market values or replacement values.

12. It means that instead of using currency amounts in the statements, elements of the financial statements are expressed as a percentage of total assets (for the balance sheet) or as a percentage of sales (for the income statement). This is an easy and effective way of making comparisons over time for a single company and of comparing one company with another—as long as consideration is given to the effects of different accounting practices that may have been used.

13. It means that other statistics, such as rate of employee turnover, market share, and/or sales per employee, are frequently relevant and useful to the evaluator.

12

Managerial Accounting and Cost–Volume–Profit Relationships

You have learned in Part 1 of *Accounting: What the Numbers Mean* that financial accounting refers to the process that results in the preparation of the financial statements for an entity. These financial statements are oriented to the external user who is not in a position to be aware of the day-to-day financial and operating activities of the entity. In Part 2 of the book, you will learn about accounting for managers of the entity, which will provide yet additional insight to the phrase "what the numbers mean." When asked by the marketing or production manager what a certain item or activity costs, the management accountant who responds "Why do you want to know?" is not being disrespectful. As you will learn, costs used for assigning a value to the inventory produced are different from the costs that should be considered when analyzing a modification to the product or a potential new product.

In **managerial accounting**, sometimes called *management accounting,* economic and financial information is used to plan and control many activities of the entity and to support the management decision-making process. Managerial accounting has an internal orientation, in contrast to the primarily external orientation of financial accounting. The transactions generated by the accounting information system and used for financial reporting also are used in managerial accounting, but the latter are more likely to have a future orientation, such as in the preparation of budgets or decision making. As with financial accounting, managerial accounting has special terminology or, as many would say, *jargon.* Most of these terms relate to different types of costs. An important early lesson about managerial accounting is that *different costs are used for different purposes.*

In this chapter, we will explain the management process, identify several contributions that management accounting makes to that process, and then introduce a model for classifying costs. Subsequent chapters will describe these costs and illustrate how they are used in the planning, control, and decision-making processes.

Cost–volume–profit (CVP) analysis involves using cost behavior patterns to interpret and forecast how changes in operating income result from changes in revenues, costs, or volume of activity. One especially important application of CVP analysis is the determination of the break-even point for a company (or one of its units or products). Because CVP analysis emphasizes the cost behavior pattern of various costs and the impact on costs and profits of changes in the volume of activity, it is useful for planning and for evaluating the results of actual operations.

1. What does it mean to state that there are different costs for different purposes?

What Does It Mean?
Answer on page 474

LEARNING OBJECTIVES (LO)

After studying this chapter, you should understand and be able to

LO 12-1   Explain the management planning and control cycle.

LO 12-2   Identify the major differences between financial accounting and managerial accounting.

LO 12-3   Describe the difference between variable and fixed cost behavior patterns and the simplifying assumptions made in this classification method.

LO 12-4   Demonstrate why expressing fixed costs on a per unit of activity basis is misleading and may result in faulty decisions.

LO 12-5   Explain what types of costs are likely to have variable and fixed cost behavior patterns, respectively.

LO 12-6   Use the high–low method to determine the cost formula for a cost that has a mixed behavior pattern.

LO 12-7   Explain and illustrate the difference between the traditional income statement format and the contribution margin income statement format.

LO 12-8   Use the contribution margin format to analyze the impact of cost and sales volume changes on operating income.

LO 12-9   Calculate the contribution margin ratio and explain how it can be used in CVP analysis.

LO 12-10   Analyze how changes in the sales mix can affect projections using CVP analysis.

LO 12-11   Describe the meaning and significance of the breakeven point and illustrate how the breakeven point is calculated.

LO 12-12   Use operating leverage to evaluate cost structures.

Managerial Accounting Contrasted to Financial Accounting

Managerial accounting supports the internal future-oriented planning decisions made by management. Financial accounting has more of a scorekeeping, historical orientation, although data produced by the financial accounting process form some of the foundation on which plans are based. Planning is a key part of the **management process**; and although there are many descriptions of that process, a generally acceptable

LO 1

Explain the management planning and control cycle.

definition would include reference to the process of planning, organizing, and controlling an entity's activities so that the organization can achieve its desired outcomes. A general model of the process looks like this:

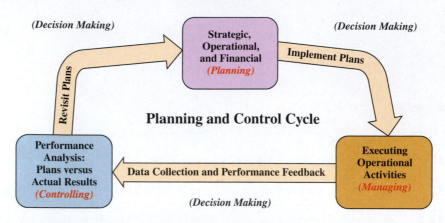

The model suggests that control is achieved through feedback. Actual results are compared to planned results; if a difference exists between the two, then either the plan or the actions, or perhaps both, are changed. Management decision making occurs in each phase of the planning and control cycle using information provided by the accounting information system in an effort to continuously improve organizational performance.

Not all of a firm's objectives are stated in financial terms by any means. For example, market share, employee morale, absence of layoffs, and responsible corporate citizenship are all appropriate objectives that are expressed in nonfinancial terms. However, many of the firm's goals will be financial (ROI, ROE, growth in sales, earnings, and dividends, to name just a few). Managerial accounting plays a major role in identifying these goals, helping to achieve them, and measuring the degree to which they have been accomplished.

LO 2

Identify the major differences between financial accounting and managerial accounting.

Emphasis on the future is a principal characteristic that makes managerial accounting different from financial accounting. Anticipating what revenues will be and forecasting the expenses that will be incurred to achieve those revenues are critical activities of the budgeting process. Another difference between managerial accounting and financial accounting that is emphasized in planning is breadth of focus. Financial accounting deals primarily with the financial statements for the organization as a whole; managerial accounting is more concerned with operating units within the organization. Thus, even though an overall company ROI objective is established, effective planning requires that the planned impact of the activities and results of each unit (division, product line, plant, sales territory, and so on) of the organization be considered.

Measuring results involves using the historical data of financial accounting; because of the time required to perform financial accounting and auditing procedures, there is usually a time lag of weeks or months between the end of an accounting period and the issuance of financial statements. However, for performance feedback to be most effective, it should be provided as quickly as possible after action has been completed. Management accounting is not constrained by generally accepted accounting principles, so approximate results can be quickly generated for use in the control process. In other words, relevant data, even though not absolutely accurate in a financial accounting sense, are useful for evaluating performance soon after an activity has been completed.

Characteristic	Managerial Accounting	Financial Accounting
Service perspective	Internal to managers.	External to investors and creditors.
Time frame	Present and future for planning and control.	Past—financial statements are historical.
Breadth of concern	Micro—individual units of the organization plan and act.	Macro—financial statements are for the organization as a whole.
Reporting frequency and promptness	Control reports issued frequently (e.g., daily) and promptly (e.g., one day after period-end).	Most financial statements issued monthly, a week or more after month-end.
Degree of precision of data used	Reasonable accuracy desired, but "close counts"— relevance is often more important than reliability.	High accuracy desired, with time usually available to achieve it— reliability is of utmost importance.
Reporting standards	None imposed because of internal and pragmatic orientation.	Imposed by generally accepted accounting principles and the FASB.

Exhibit 12-1

Managerial Accounting Compared to Financial Accounting

Exhibit 12-1 summarizes the principal differences between managerial accounting and financial accounting.

If time and effort have been devoted to developing a plan, it is appropriate to attempt to control the activities of the organization so that the desired outcomes of the plan are achieved. Many activities of the management accountant are related to cost control; this control emphasis will be seen in most of the managerial accounting ideas that are explained in these chapters.

Another important management concept relevant to the control process is that if an individual is to be held accountable, or responsible, for the results of an activity, that individual also must have the authority to influence those results. If a manager is to be held responsible for costs incurred by a unit of the organization, then the financial results reported for that unit should never include costs incurred by other units that have been arbitrarily assigned to the manager being evaluated. In other words, performance results should only reflect costs that the manager being held responsible can control.

Management accountants work extensively with people in other functional areas of the organization. For example, industrial engineers and management accountants work together to develop **production standards**, which are the expected or allowed times and costs to make a product or perform an activity. Management accountants help production managers interpret performance reports, which compare actual and planned production and costs. Sales personnel, the marketing staff, and management accountants are involved in estimating a future period's sales. Human resource professionals and management accountants work together to determine the cost impact of compensation changes. And the management accountant plays a significant role in the firm's systems development life cycle process by providing key insights into the planning, analysis, design, and implementation phases of an organization's information systems projects. These few key examples illustrate the need for management accountants to have a breadth of knowledge and interest about the organization and its operating environment. The examples also suggest that it is appropriate for people in other functional areas of the organization to have a general understanding of managerial accounting. Helping you achieve that general understanding is the primary objective of the remaining chapters in this book.

What Does It Mean?

Answers on page 474

2. What does it mean that the time frame for managerial accounting is different from that for financial accounting?

3. What does it mean to have feedback for control purposes?

Cost Classifications

The term *cost* means different things to different people, and in the management planning and decision-making process, it is important to use costs that are appropriate to the situation. Likewise, management accountants should make sure that everyone participating in a given planning or decision-making activity understands the costs involved. Exhibit 12-2 presents a model for the cost classifications most frequently encountered and highlights the cost topics covered in this chapter.

Cost classifications are not mutually exclusive; you will learn that a cost might be identified as a "controllable, variable, direct, product cost," for example. Overall, this basic concept of *different costs for different purposes* is so fundamental to an understanding of the planning, control, and decision-making process that the cost classification model will be presented again in each managerial accounting chapter that follows. From the perspective of this model you will be introduced to these cost concepts as

Exhibit 12-2   Cost Classifications—The Big Picture

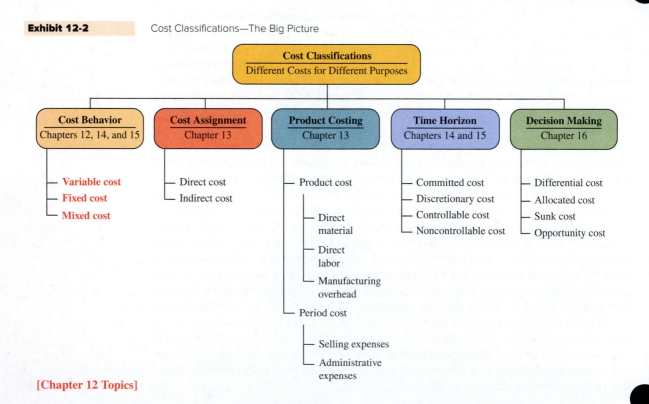

[Chapter 12 Topics]

they relate to the planning, control, or decision-making theme being developed. The cost classification concepts discussed in each chapter will explain the following:

- Relationships between total cost and volume of activity for understanding cost behavior (Chapters 12, 14, and 15).
- Product or activity relationships for cost assignment purposes (Chapter 13).
- Cost accounting to determine the cost of products produced (Chapter 13).
- A time-frame perspective for understanding cost planning and control (Chapters 14 and 15).
- Other analytical purposes to support decision making (Chapter 16).

Relationship of Total Cost to Volume of Activity

The relationship of total cost to volume of activity describes the **cost behavior pattern**, one of the most important cost classification concepts to understand. A **variable cost** is one that changes *in total* as the volume of activity changes. A cost that does not change *in total* as the volume of activity changes is a **fixed cost**. For example, raw material cost incurred to manufacture a product has a variable cost behavior pattern because the more units produced, the higher the total raw material costs incurred. On the other hand, factory building depreciation expense is a fixed cost because total depreciation expense will not change regardless of the level of production (unless, of course, a units-of-production method is used to calculate depreciation, in which case this cost would be variable). The distinction between fixed and variable cost behavior patterns is illustrated graphically in Exhibit 12-3.

Here are several additional examples of variable and fixed costs:

LO 3

Describe the difference between variable and fixed cost behavior patterns and the simplifying assumptions made in this classification method.

Variable Costs	**Fixed Costs**
Manufacturing labor wages	Supervisor's salary
Supplies used in production	Factory rent
Shipping costs	Advertising
Sales commissions	Property taxes
Warranty costs	Sales manager's salary

The fixed or variable label refers to the behavior of *total* cost relative to a change in activity. When referring to the behavior of unit costs, however, the labels may be confusing because variable costs are constant if expressed on a per unit basis, but fixed costs per unit will change as the level of activity changes. Thus, it is necessary to understand the behavior pattern on both a total cost basis and a per unit basis as illustrated in the following chart. Variable costs change in total as activity changes but are

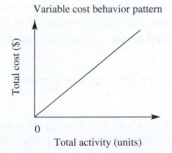

Variable cost behavior pattern

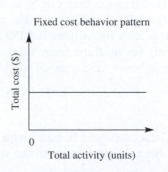

Fixed cost behavior pattern

Exhibit 12-3

Cost Behavior Patterns

constant on a per unit basis. Fixed costs do not change in total as activity changes but will vary if expressed on a per unit of activity basis.

	As Activity Changes	
	Total	**Per Unit**
Fixed Cost	*Remains constant*	Changes inversely
Variable Cost	Changes directly	*Remains constant*

Knowledge of the cost behavior pattern becomes an important analytical tool for the planning process, and several simplifying assumptions are made to facilitate its use. The most fundamental assumption relates to the range of activity over which the identified cost behavior pattern exists. This is the **relevant range** assumption, and it is applicable to fixed costs. Returning to the depreciation expense example, at some point an increase in the volume of production would require more plant capacity, and depreciation expense would increase. On the other hand, if substantially lower production volumes were anticipated in the future, some of the plant would be closed down or converted to another use, and depreciation expense would decrease. To say that depreciation expense is fixed is to say that over some relevant range of production activity, the total cost will not change. Different fixed expenses will have different relevant ranges over which they have a fixed cost behavior pattern. When a cost is identified as fixed and cost projections are made based on that cost behavior pattern classification, the limits of the relevant range assumption must be considered.

The other major simplifying assumption is that the cost behavior pattern is *linear,* not curvilinear. This assumption relates to variable costs. Because of economies of scale, quantity purchase discounts, and other factors, variable costs will change slightly when expressed on a per unit basis. These changes are usually not significant; but if they are, appropriate adjustments in unit costs should be made in the analyses based on cost behavior patterns. These assumptions are illustrated and described in more detail later in this chapter.

Not all costs can be classified as either variable or fixed. Some costs are partly fixed and partly variable. Sometimes costs with this mixed behavior pattern are called **semivariable costs**. Factory utility cost, for example, has a mixed behavior pattern because when the plant isn't operating, some lights must be kept on for safety and security, but as production increases more electricity is required. Analytical techniques can break this type of cost into its fixed and variable components, and a **cost formula** can be developed:

$$\text{Total cost} = \text{Fixed cost} + \text{Variable cost}$$
$$= \text{Fixed cost} + (\text{Variable rate per unit of activity} \times \text{\# units of activity})$$

This cost formula then can be used to forecast the total cost expected to be incurred at various levels of activity. For example, assume that it has been determined that the fixed cost for utilities is $350 per month and that the variable rate for utilities is 30 cents per machine hour. Total estimated utilities cost for a month in which 6,000 machine hours were planned would be as follows:

$$\text{Total cost} = \$350 + (\$0.30/\text{machine hour} \times 6{,}000 \text{ machine hours})$$
$$= \$2{,}150$$

LO 4

Demonstrate why expressing fixed costs on a per unit of activity basis is misleading and may result in faulty decisions.

Great care must be taken with the use of fixed cost when expressed on a per unit basis because any change in the volume of activity will change the per unit cost. As

Assume the following university student service center office costs per month associated with processing and providing student electronic transcript records:

Salaries	$3,500
Allocated space costs (depreciation, utilities, etc.)	1,100
Total per month	$4,600
If 2,000 transcripts are processed in a month, the "cost" per transcript is ($4,600 / 2,000)	$ 2.30
If 5,000 transcripts are processed in a month, the "cost" per transcript is ($4,600 / 5,000)	$ 0.92

How much does it cost to process a transcript?

What action would students take if they learned that a transcript processing fee was being considered based on the "cost" of processing a transcript during the coming month?

Exhibit 12-4

The Error of Unitizing Fixed Costs

a general rule, *do not unitize fixed expenses because they do not behave on a per unit basis!* For example, most costs of a university student service center office to process electronic transcripts—salaries, depreciation, and utilities—are fixed; to calculate the "cost" of processing student transcript requests by dividing a portion of the service center office costs by the number of student transcripts requested in a period of time will give a misleading result, as illustrated in Exhibit 12-4. Sometimes fixed costs must be unitized, as in the development of a predetermined overhead application rate (described in Chapter 13). It is also important to recognize that the relevant range is often quite wide, and significant increases in activity can be achieved without increasing fixed costs (i.e., when significant idle capacity exists). Whenever fixed costs are unitized, be very careful about the conclusions that may be drawn from the data.

---

4. What does it mean to say that determination of a cost behavior pattern involves some implicit assumptions?

5. What does it mean to develop a cost formula?

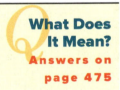

What Does It Mean?

Answers on page 475

Applications of Cost–Volume–Profit Analysis

Cost Behavior Pattern: The Key

Recall the two simplifying assumptions that are made in connection with the determination of cost behavior patterns. First, the behavior pattern is true only within a relevant range of activity; if activity moves out of the relevant range, the cost will change. Second, the cost behavior pattern identified is assumed to be linear within the relevant range, not curvilinear.

The relevant range idea relates to the level of activity over which a particular cost behavior pattern exists. For example, if Cruisers' production capacity of its plant is 90 SeaCruiser sailboats per month, additional equipment would be required to produce 120 boats per month. The investment in additional equipment would increase depreciation expense. On the other hand, if long-term demand for the boat could be satisfied with a capacity of only 50 boats per month, it is likely that management would "mothball" (or dispose of) some of the present capacity, and depreciation expense would fall.

The following graph illustrates a possible relationship between depreciation expense and capacity. The relevant range for depreciation expense of $12,000 per month is production capacity of 60 to 90 boats. As long as capacity remains in this range, the total fixed expense for depreciation will not change; but if capacity changes to another relevant range, the amount of this fixed expense also will change.

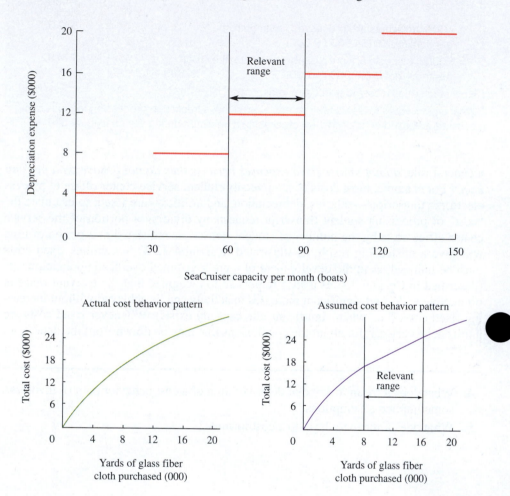

The linearity assumption means that the cost behavior pattern will effectively plot as a straight line within the relevant range. Although applicable to both fixed and variable costs, the significance of this assumption is best illustrated with a variable cost like raw materials such as glass fiber cloth. Because of quantity discounts and shipping efficiencies, the cost per unit of the raw material will decrease as the quantity purchased increases. This is illustrated in the left graph of the second set of graphs. For analytical purposes, however, it may be assumed that the cost is linear within a relevant range, as shown in the right graph. Even though the cost per yard does vary slightly at different activity levels, for purposes of using cost–volume–profit analysis techniques, it will be assumed constant per yard (variable in total) when purchases total between 8,000 and 16,000 yards per month.

It is clear that if these assumptions are overlooked, or if costs are incorrectly classified or described, the results of the analytical process illustrated later in this chapter will be inaccurate. Cost–volume–profit analysis is a valuable and appropriate tool to use in many situations; but the cost behavior assumptions made are crucial to the validity and applicability of its results, and they must be kept in mind when these results are evaluated.

Generally speaking, raw materials and production labor costs of manufacturing units of product are variable costs. In addition, some elements of manufacturing overhead (see the discussion of manufacturing overhead in Chapter 13 for more detail) will have a variable cost behavior pattern. For example, maintenance and housekeeping materials used, as well as the variable portion of factory utilities, will be a function of the quantity of product made. Other manufacturing overhead costs are fixed, including depreciation expense, supervisory salaries, and the fixed portion of utility costs.

Selling, general, administrative, and other operating expenses also fit both patterns. Sales commissions, for example, vary in proportion to sales revenue or the quantity of product sold. The wages associated with employees who process orders from customers, or who handle payments from customers, may be variable if those functions are organized so that the number of workers can be expanded or contracted rapidly in response to changes in sales volume. On the other hand, advertising costs usually are fixed in the short run; once approved, the money is spent, and it is difficult to relate sales volume changes directly to advertising expenditures.

Estimating Cost Behavior Patterns

A particular cost's estimated behavior pattern is determined by analyzing cost and related activity over time. One analytical technique involves using a scattergram to identify high and low cost–to–volume data relationships; then simple arithmetic is used to compute the variable cost per unit and total fixed cost which may then be combined into a cost formula. This "high–low" method is illustrated in Exhibit 12-5. More complex techniques, including simple and multiple regression analysis, also can be used; but at some point, the perceived increase in accuracy is offset by the simplifying assumptions involved in using the cost formula for planning and control purposes.

A Modified Income Statement Format

The traditional income statement format classifies costs according to the reason they were incurred: cost of goods sold, selling expenses, administrative expenses, research and development expenses, and so on. This format is used for financial accounting statements prepared for external use, according to generally accepted accounting principles. For internal purposes, however, managers need an income statement that can serve decision makers' needs. Therefore, the income statement format used in CVP analysis, frequently referred to as the **contribution margin format**, classifies costs according to their cost behavior pattern—variable or fixed. Here are the comparative formats with assumed dollar amounts for illustration:

Traditional Format (Expenses Classified by Function)		Contribution Margin Format (Expenses Classified by Cost Behavior Pattern)	
Revenues	$100,000	Revenues	$100,000
Cost of goods sold	50,000	Variable expenses	60,000
Gross profit	$ 50,000	Contribution margin	$ 40,000
Operating expenses	40,000	Fixed expenses	30,000
Operating income	$ 10,000	Operating income	$ 10,000

Revenues and operating income (income before interest and taxes) are the same under either alternative. The difference is in the classification of expenses: functional in the

LO 5 Explain what types of costs are likely to have variable and fixed cost behavior patterns, respectively.

LO 6 Use the high–low method to determine the cost formula for a cost that has a mixed behavior pattern.

LO 7 Explain and illustrate the difference between the traditional income statement format and the contribution margin income statement format.

Exhibit 12-5

High–Low Method
of Estimating a Cost
Behavior Pattern

Assumption:
During the months of January through June, the following utility costs were incurred at various production volumes:

Month	Total Utility Cost	Total Production Volume
January	$2,500	8,000 units
February	3,500	13,000 units
March	4,000	16,000 units
April	5,500	12,000 units
May	**2,000**	**6,000 units**
June	**5,000**	**18,000 units**

I. The scattergram:

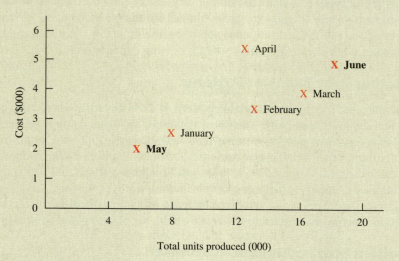

Total units produced (000)

It can be observed in the scattergram that a cost–volume relationship does exist because of the approximate straight-line pattern of most of the observations. However, the April data do not fit the pattern. This condition may be due to an error or some unusual condition that caused utility cost for the month of April to be exceptionally high relative to the level of production activity for April. This observation is an *outlier* and should be investigated for pertinent information about the unusually high cost. However, it will be ignored in the calculation of the cost formula because of its variation from the cost–volume relationship that exists among other data.

II. Calculating the variable cost behavior pattern:
The high–low method of calculating the variable cost behavior pattern, or variable cost rate, relates the change in cost to the change in activity, using the highest and lowest relevant observations:

$$\text{Variable rate} = \frac{\text{High cost} - \text{Low cost}}{\text{High activity} - \text{Low activity}}$$

$$= \frac{\$5,000 - \$2,000}{18,000 \text{ units} - 6,000 \text{ units}}$$

$$= \$3,000/12,000 \text{ units}$$

$$= \$0.25 \text{ per unit}$$

(continued)

Exhibit 12-5

III. Calculating the fixed cost behavior pattern:

With the variable rate known, the fixed cost element can be calculated at either the high or low set of data, and the cost formula can then be developed because total cost is equal to variable cost plus fixed cost.

At 18,000 units of activity, the total variable cost is 18,000 units × $0.25 per unit = $4,500.

Fixed cost calculation:

$$\begin{aligned}
\text{Total cost at 18,000 units} &= \$5,000 \\
\text{Variable cost at 18,000 units} &= \underline{4,500} \\
\text{Fixed cost} &= \$500
\end{aligned}$$

At 6,000 units of activity, the total variable cost is 6,000 units × $0.25 per unit = $1,500.

Fixed cost calculation:

$$\begin{aligned}
\text{Total cost at 6,000 units} &= \$2,000 \\
\text{Variable cost at 6,000 units} &= \underline{1,500} \\
\text{Fixed cost} &= \$500
\end{aligned}$$

IV. The cost formula:

Using the calculated variable and fixed cost behavior patterns, the cost formula for utilities is

$$\begin{aligned}
\text{Total cost} &= \text{Fixed cost} + \text{Variable cost} \\
&= \$500 + \$0.25 \text{ per unit produced}
\end{aligned}$$

V. Using the cost formula:

This cost formula now can be used to estimate total utility costs at any level of activity (within the relevant range). For example, if production volume for the month of July was expected to be 14,000 units, the estimated total utility cost would be as follows:

$$\begin{aligned}
\text{Total cost} &= \text{Fixed cost} + \text{Variable cost} \\
&= \$500 + (\$0.25/\text{unit} \times 14,000 \text{ units}) = \$4,000
\end{aligned}$$

Note that it is considered a coincidence if the cost formula explains total cost accurately at points not used in the high–low calculation. This is so because the calculation assumes a linear relationship between the observations used, and in practice exact linearity will not exist.

---

traditional format and according to cost behavior pattern in the contribution margin format. Although the behavior pattern classification could be carried beyond operating income to other income and expense and income taxes, it usually isn't because the greatest benefits of the contribution margin approach are realized in the planning and control evaluation processes applied to a firm's operations.

The contribution margin format derives its name from the difference between revenues and variable expenses (in managerial accounting, the terms *costs* and *expenses* are often used interchangeably). **Contribution margin** means that this amount is the contribution to fixed expenses and operating income from the sale of products or provision of services. The key to this concept lies in understanding cost behavior patterns. As revenues increase by selling more products or providing more services, variable expenses will increase proportionately, and so will contribution margin. However, *fixed expenses will not increase* because they are not a function of the level of revenue-generating activity.

Use of the traditional income statement model can result in misleading and erroneous conclusions when changes in activity levels are being considered because it is assumed that all expenses change in proportion to changes in activity. This error is made because cost behavior patterns are not disclosed. The error is avoided when

LO 8

Use the contribution margin format to analyze the impact of cost and sales volume changes on operating income.

Business in
Practice

Estimating Cost Behavior Patterns Using Microsoft Excel

Now that you understand the process by which cost behavior patterns are determined using the high–low method, Microsoft Excel can be used to quickly and easily create the cost formula. Several functions in Excel can do this; all of them mathematically calculate the "best fit" of the data to a linear equation that is generated. The data from Exhibit 12-5 are illustrated below. Two functions are highlighted: INTERCEPT, which solves for the fixed cost, and SLOPE, which solves for the variable rate. Recall the discussion from Exhibit 12-5 regarding the April "outlier" and notice how different the solution is when the data are included on the left rather than excluded on the right. Also notice how close the mathematically precise results are when April is excluded from the analysis determined by the high–low method used in Exhibit 12-5.

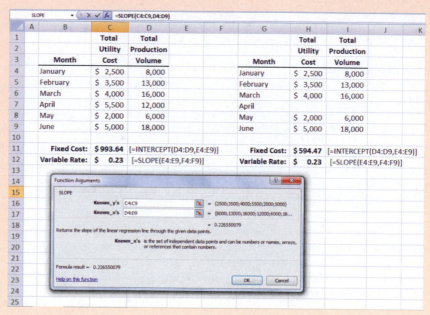

Source: Microsoft Excel 2010

the contribution margin model is used correctly. For example, assume again that the firm illustrated in the income statement presentations earlier currently has revenues of $100,000 and operating income of $10,000. If revenues were to drop by 20 percent to $80,000, a quick conclusion might be that operating income also would decline by 20 percent to $8,000. However, analysis using the contribution margin format results in a much more accurate, and disturbing, result:

	Current Results	Results Assuming a 20% Decline in Revenue
Revenues..............................	$100,000	$80,000
Variable expenses (60%)	60,000	48,000
Contribution margin (40%)	$ 40,000	$32,000
Fixed expenses	30,000	30,000
Operating income	$ 10,000	$ 2,000

Because fixed expenses did not change (the firm did not move into a different relevant range), the $8,000 reduction in contribution margin resulting from the 20 percent

reduction in revenues carried right through to reduce operating income by the same dollar amount. This is an example of why it is misleading to think of fixed costs on a per unit basis. Although fixed costs (and especially the relevant range assumption) should not be overlooked by the manager, it must be recognized that they behave differently from variable costs.

The **contribution margin ratio** is the ratio of contribution margin to revenues. Think of this ratio as the portion of each sales dollar that remains after covering the variable costs and is available to cover fixed costs or provide profits. Continuing with the same data, each sales dollar generated will provide $0.40 ($1.00 × 40%) of contribution margin as follows:

LO 9

Calculate the contribution margin ratio and explain how it can be used in CVP analysis.

	Current Results	%	Relationships
Revenues..............	$100,000	100%	Revenues = 100%
Variable expenses........	60,000	60%	− Variable cost ratio
Contribution margin.......	$ 40,000	40%	= Contribution margin ratio

This contribution margin ratio can then be used to calculate directly the change in contribution margin given a change in revenues. Therefore, a $12,000 increase in revenue would result in a $4,800 (40% × $12,000) increase in contribution margin and a $4,800 increase in operating income because fixed costs will remain unchanged.

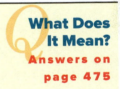

6. What does it mean to rearrange the income statement model from the traditional format to the contribution margin format?

7. What does it mean to state that the contribution margin model is more useful than the traditional model for determining the effect of changes in activity on operating income?

What Does It Mean?

Answers on page 475

An Expanded Contribution Margin Model

The benefits of using the contribution margin model for planning and decision making can be best understood and illustrated by applying the model to a single product. For analytical purposes, an expanded version of the model, using the captions already illustrated but adding some columns, is helpful. Here is the expanded model:

	Per Unit	×	Volume	=	Total	%
Revenue......................	$ Step 1					
Variable expenses	Step 1					
Contribution margin	$ Step 1	×	Step 2	=	$ Step 3	Step 6 %
Fixed expenses.................					Step 4	
Operating income..............					$ Step 5	

The following steps highlight the preferred path through the model:

Step 1   Express revenue, variable expense, and contribution margin on a per unit basis.

Step 2   Enter volume.

Understanding the relationships in the expanded contribution margin model may be the most important concept developed in managerial accounting. The model presented here provides a structure for explaining, in a consistent manner, the effect on operating income of changes in selling price, variable expenses, fixed expenses, or the volume of activity. As you study these examples, you will notice that four relationships are invariably interacting with one another:

1. Revenue − Variable expenses = Contribution margin.

2. Contribution margin / Revenue = Contribution margin ratio.

3. Total contribution margin depends on the volume of activity.

4. Contribution margin must cover fixed expenses before an operating income is earned.

Your goals are to identify these relationships in every cost–volume–profit question and appreciate their interaction as a way of thinking that becomes second nature for you. When you can visualize this interaction of these relationships, you are well on your way to becoming a successful decision maker.

Step 3	Multiply contribution margin per unit by volume to get total contribution.
Step 4	Enter fixed expenses.
Step 5	Subtract fixed expenses for the relevant period from total contribution margin to get operating income. Note that *fixed expenses are never entered on a per unit basis*.
Step 6	Calculate the contribution margin ratio by dividing contribution margin per unit by the per unit selling price. Essentially, you are setting the selling price equal to 100 percent and then expressing the contribution margin as a percentage of the selling price.

Understanding these relationships will allow many what-if questions to be answered when analyzing changes to revenue and will provide support for decision-making.

Contribution Margin in Action—Example 1   To illustrate the use of the model, assume management wants to know the operating income from a product that has the following revenue, cost, and volume characteristics:

Selling price per case.	$ 15
Variable expenses per case	9
Fixed expenses associated with the product for the relevant period	$40,000
Sales volume in cases	8,000 cases

Using these data in the model results in the following analysis:

	Per Unit	×	Volume	=	Total	%
Revenue	$ 15					
Variable expenses	9					
Contribution margin	$ 6	×	8,000	=	$48,000	40%
Fixed expenses					40,000	
Operating income					$ 8,000	

Contribution Margin in Action—Example 2 Now suppose management wants to know what would happen to operating income if a $3 per unit price cut were to result in a volume increase of 5,000 units, to a total of 13,000 units. The solution:

	Per Unit	×	Volume	=	Total	%
Revenue	$ 12					
Variable expenses	9					
Contribution margin	$ 3	×	13,000	=	$39,000	25%
Fixed expenses.					40,000	
Operating income.					$ (1,000)	

Based on the analysis, the price reduction would not be made.

Contribution Margin in Action—Example 3 Next, suppose management proposes the same $3 per unit price cut in conjunction with a $3,000 increase in advertising, with the expectation that volume will increase to 18,000 units. Here is the analysis of the effect on operating income:

	Per Unit	×	Volume	=	Total	%
Revenue	$ 12					
Variable expenses	9					
Contribution margin	$ 3	×	18,000	=	$54,000	25%
Fixed expenses.					43,000	
Operating income.					$11,000	

Note that the advertising expense increase is reflected in fixed expenses. The analysis suggests that if the volume increase can be achieved with the price cut and increased advertising combination, operating income will increase from its present level. But watch out for the relevant range assumption: The impact on fixed expenses of such a large increase in sales volume should be assessed.

Contribution Margin in Action—Example 4 The expanded contribution margin model can also be used to calculate the volume of activity required to achieve a target level of operating income. For example, using the original data for selling price and variable expenses, suppose management wanted to know the sales volume required to have operating income of $23,000. The solution involves entering the known data in the model and working to the middle to obtain the required volume:

	Per Unit	×	Volume	=	Total	%
Revenue	$ 15					
Variable expenses	9					
Contribution margin	$ 6	×	?	=	$63,000	40%
Fixed expenses.					40,000	
Operating income.					$23,000	

The required sales volume is $63,000/$6 = 10,500 units.

Contribution Margin Ratio in Action—Example 5 The contribution margin *ratio* is used to directly calculate the effect on contribution margin and operating income when the change in operations is expressed in terms of total revenues. For example, if the

contribution margin ratio is 40 percent, and total revenues are expected to increase by $12,000, a $4,800 ($12,000 × 40%) increase in contribution margin and operating income would result, assuming that fixed expenses didn't change.

Contribution Margin Ratio in Action—Example 6   Another use of the contribution margin ratio is to determine the increase in revenues and sales volume that would be necessary to cover an increase in fixed expenses. For example, if fixed expenses were to increase by $9,000, contribution margin would have to increase by the same amount to keep operating income constant. If the contribution margin ratio is 40 percent, revenues would have to increase by $22,500 ($9,000/40%) to generate a $9,000 increase in contribution margin. The sales volume increase needed to generate the additional revenue is determined by dividing $22,500 by the $15 selling price per unit. (We could also calculate the volume increase of 1,500 units by dividing the increased contribution margin required, $9,000, by the contribution margin of $6 per unit.)

Contribution Margin Ratio in Action—Example 7   The contribution margin ratio also is used to determine revenue and contribution margin changes when per unit data are not available or not applicable. For example, the contribution margin model is frequently used to analyze the impact on the operating income of an entire product line (perhaps a candy bar brand) that is sold in a variety of package or size configurations, assuming that each configuration has the same, or very nearly the same, contribution margin ratio. Thus, if a product line had a contribution margin ratio of 30 percent, would an advertising program costing $21,000 be cost-effective if it generated an additional $80,000 of revenue?

Increase in contribution margin ($80,000 × 30%)	$24,000
Increase in advertising	21,000
Increase in operating income	$ 3,000

So yes, the program would be cost-effective. Alternatively, dividing the increased fixed expenses by the contribution margin ratio ($21,000/30%) shows that an additional $70,000 of revenue would be needed to cover the increased fixed expense. Because the revenue increase is estimated to be $80,000, which is $10,000 more than required, an operating income increase of $3,000 (30% × $10,000) can be expected.

Contribution Margin Ratio in Action—Example 8   Although all the examples used so far have expressed volume as units of product, the contribution margin model is also useful for organizations that provide services rather than sell products. For example, a day care center could identify variable expenses by type of activity and then set charges to achieve a target contribution margin to cover fixed expenses and operating income. Using the expanded contribution margin model, expected variable expenses of $18 per week per child, and a target contribution margin ratio of 40 percent, the revenue needed per week per child is calculated as follows:

	Per Child	×	Volume	=	Total	%
Revenue	$?					100%
Variable expenses	18					?
Contribution margin	$?	×	?	=	$?	40%

If the contribution margin ratio is 40 percent, the variable expense ratio is 60 percent (revenues = 100%); 60 percent of revenue per child = $18; revenue per child = $18 / 0.60 = $30. This process is virtually the same as that described in Chapter 9 to calculate a required selling price when the cost of the item and the desired gross profit ratio are known.

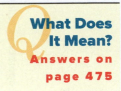

8. What does it mean to expand the contribution margin model?
9. What does it mean to state that the contribution model provides better support for decision making?

What Does It Mean?
Answers on page 475

Multiple Products or Services and Sales Mix Considerations

When the contribution margin model is applied using data for more than one product or service, the *sales* mix issue must be considered. **Sales mix** refers to the relative proportion of total sales accounted for by different products or services. Because different products or services are likely to have different contribution margin ratios, the average contribution margin ratio for a given mix of products or services will change if the sales mix of the products or services changes.

Sales mix is an important concept to understand because almost all firms have multiple products or services. When there is a range of quality to a firm's products (good, better, best), the higher-quality products generally have higher contribution margin ratios, so marketing efforts frequently focus on those products. On the other hand, a strategy that some firms try to follow is to price their products to achieve a contribution margin ratio that is about the same for all products. A company that can achieve this approximate parity in contribution margin ratios among its products doesn't have to be concerned, from a product profitability standpoint, about sales mix changes. Thus, marketing efforts can be more broadly based than if sales mix were a consideration. The effect of a sales mix change is illustrated in Exhibit 12-6.

LO 10
Analyze how changes in the sales mix can affect projections using CVP analysis.

10. What does it mean that fixed expenses should not be unitized because they don't behave that way?
11. What does it mean to state that contribution margin ratio is frequently a more useful measurement than contribution margin per unit?

What Does It Mean?
Answers on page 475

Breakeven Point Analysis

The **breakeven point** is usually expressed as the amount of revenue that must be realized for the firm (or product or activity or group of products or activities) to have neither profit nor loss (i.e., operating income equal to zero). The breakeven point is useful to managers because it expresses a minimum revenue target, and managers frequently find it easier to think in terms of revenues rather than variable and fixed expenses. In addition, the amount of sales (or revenues) generated by the firm is easily determined daily from the accounting information system.

The contribution margin model is used to determine the breakeven point by setting operating income equal to zero and solving the model for the revenue or physical sales

LO 11
Describe the meaning and significance of the breakeven point and illustrate how the breakeven point is calculated.

Exhibit 12-6   Multiple Products and Sales Mix

I. Assume that a company has two products. Per unit revenue, variable expenses, and product volumes for present operations follow:

| | Product A | | | | | | Product B | | | | | | Total Company | |
	Per Unit	×	Volume	=	Total	%	Per Unit	×	Volume	=	Total	%	Total	%
Revenue	$ 40	×	2,000	=	$80,000		$ 30	×	2,000	=	$60,000		$140,000	100%
Variable expenses	30						18							
Contribution margin	$ 10	×	2,000	=	$20,000	25%	$ 12	×	2,000	=	$24,000	40%	$ 44,000	31.4%
Fixed expenses													30,000	
Operating income													$ 14,000	

Note that fixed expenses are shown only in the Total Company column because they apply to the company as a whole, not to individual products.

II. Now assume that the sales mix changes and that, instead of sales volume of 2,000 units of each product, sales volume becomes 2,500 units of product A and 1,500 units of product B. The company's contribution margin format income statement becomes this:

| | Product A | | | | | | Product B | | | | | | Total Company | |
	Per Unit	×	Volume	=	Total	%	Per Unit	×	Volume	=	Total	%	Total	%
Revenue	$ 40	×	2,500	=	$100,000		$ 30	×	1,500	=	$45,000		$145,000	100%
Variable expenses	30						18							
Contribution margin	$ 10	×	2,500	=	$ 25,000	25%	$ 12	×	1,500	=	$18,000	40%	$ 43,000	29.7%
Fixed expenses													30,000	
Operating income													$ 13,000	

Note that even though total sales volume remained 4,000 units in both examples, total revenues increased, but total contribution margin and operating income decreased. This is due to the fact that proportionately more units of product A, with its relatively lower contribution margin ratio, were sold than product B, which has a relatively higher contribution margin ratio. As a result, the company's average contribution margin ratio also decreased.

volume that will cause that result. The calculation of the breakeven point in terms of units and total revenues is illustrated here:

Selling price per unit..	$ 12
Variable expenses per unit..	8
Total fixed expenses..	$45,000

	Per Unit	×	**Volume**	=	**Total**	**%**
Revenue	$ 12					
Variable expenses	8					
Contribution margin	$ 4	×	?	=	?	33.3%
Fixed expenses..........					45,000	
Operating income........					$ 0	

According to the model, contribution margin must be equal to fixed expenses of $45,000.

$$\text{Volume in units at breakeven} = \frac{\text{Fixed expenses}}{\text{Contribution margin per unit}}$$

$$= \$45,000/\$4$$

$$= 11,250 \text{ units}$$

$$\text{Total revenues at breakeven} = \frac{\text{Fixed expenses}}{\text{Contribution margin ratio}}$$

$$= \$45,000/33.3\%$$

$$= \$135,000$$

or

$$\text{Volume in units at breakeven} = \frac{\text{Total revenues required}}{\text{Revenue per unit}}$$

$$= \$135,000/\$12$$

$$= 11,250 \text{ units}$$

Most firms plan for certain desired levels of operating income and would not be satisfied to simply break even. As illustrated earlier, we can use the contribution margin model to determine total revenues and sales volume in units for any amount of desired operating income. The breakeven formula also can be easily modified to determine these amounts by adding the desired operating income to the numerator. To illustrate, assume the same information and a desired operating income of $10,000:

$$\frac{\text{Volume in units for desired}}{\text{level of operating income}} = \frac{\text{Fixed expenses} + \text{Desired operating income}}{\text{Contribution margin per unit}}$$

$$= (\$45,000 + \$10,000)/\$4$$

$$= 13,750 \text{ units}$$

$$\frac{\text{Total revenues for desired}}{\text{level of operating income}} = \frac{\text{Fixed expenses} + \text{Desired operating income}}{\text{Contribution margin ratio}}$$

$$= (\$45,000 + \$10,000)/33.3\%$$

$$= \$165,000$$

Recall the discussion of multiple products and sales mix. Exhibit 12-6 illustrated the negative effect on operating income when the sales mix shifted by selling more units of product A, with its lower contribution margin, relative to product B, with its higher contribution margin. Breakeven analysis can be performed when multiple products exist by using the average contribution margin ratio generated from the current sales mix.

$$\text{Total revenues at breakeven} = \frac{\text{Fixed expenses}}{\text{Average contribution margin ratio}}$$

To illustrate using the sales mix information from Exhibit 12-6, Part I:

$$\text{Total revenues at breakeven} = \$30,000/31.4\%$$
$$= \$95,541$$

To compare using the sales mix information from Exhibit 12-6, Part II:

$$\text{Total revenues at breakeven} = \$30,000/29.7\%$$
$$= \$101,010$$

Just as the shifting of unit sales away from product B to product A produced a negative effect on operating margin, the same negative result is observed with breakeven revenues.

Breakeven analysis is frequently presented in graphical format, as illustrated in Exhibits 12-7 and 12-8 with data from the preceding example. Following are the important relationships to understand for interpreting or preparing a breakeven chart as illustrated in Exhibit 12-7.

Exhibit 12-7

Breakeven Graph

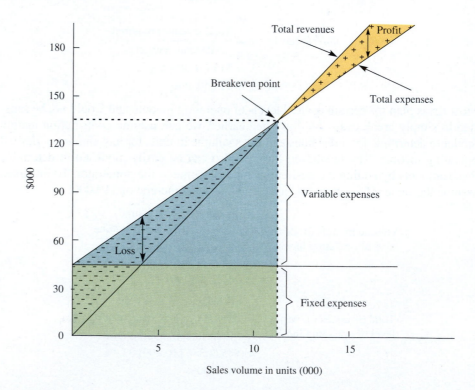

1. The horizontal axis is sales volume in units, and the vertical axis is total dollars.

2. The horizontal line represents fixed expenses of $45,000.

3. Variable expenses of $8 per unit are added to fixed expenses to produce the total expense line.

4. Revenues start at the origin and rise at the rate of $12 per unit in proportion to the sales volume in units.

5. The intersection of the total expense line and the total revenue line is the break-even point.

6. The sales volume required to break even (11,250 units) is on the horizontal axis directly below this point, and total revenues required to break even ($135,000) can be read on the vertical axis opposite the intersection.

7. The amount of operating income or loss can be read as the dollar amount of the vertical distance between the total revenue line and total expense line for the sales volume actually achieved.

8. Sometimes the area between the two lines is marked as "profit area" or "loss area."

Note that the loss area begins with an amount equal to total fixed expenses of $45,000 (at a sales volume of 0 units). As unit sales increase, the loss decreases by the contribution margin per unit of $4 for each unit sold until the breakeven point is achieved; then the profit increases by the $4 contribution margin per unit on sales volume beyond the breakeven point.

Exhibit 12-8 is another version of the breakeven graph. The variable expense line begins at the origin, with fixed expenses added to total variable expenses. Although expenses are rearranged compared to Exhibit 12-7, the total expense line stays the same, and the breakeven point and the profit and loss areas are the same. This version

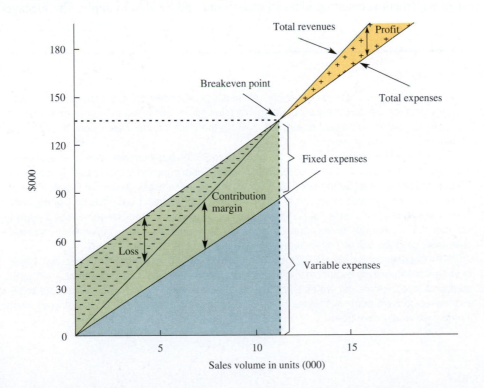

Exhibit 12-8

Breakeven Graph
Featuring Contribution
Margin

permits identification of contribution margin and shows how contribution margin grows as volume increases.

The **margin of safety** is a relative measure of risk that describes a company's current sales performance in relation to its break-even sales. This measure informs the manager about the amount of sales decline that a company can withstand before a loss would be incurred. Assuming sales revenue is currently $150,000 and break-even sales have been calculated to be $135,000, the margin of safety is calculated as

$$\text{Margin of safety} = \text{Total sales} - \text{Breakeven sales}$$
$$= \$150,000 - \$135,000$$
$$= \$15,000$$

Sales can drop by no more than $15,000 before the company would begin to experience a loss. Perhaps expressing the margin of safety as a ratio rather than an absolute dollar amount would be even more meaningful. The margin of safety ratio is calculated as

$$\text{Margin of safety ratio} = \frac{\text{Margin of safety}}{\text{Total sales}}$$
$$= \$15,000/\$150,000$$
$$= 10\%$$

This margin of safety ratio informs the manager that if sales drop by 10 percent, the company will be operating at its breakeven point.

The key to the breakeven point calculation (and graphic presentation) is that fixed expenses remain fixed in total regardless of the level of activity, subject to the relevant range assumption. In addition to that assumption, the linearity and constant sales mix assumptions also must be considered. In spite of these simplifications, the contribution margin model and cost behavior pattern concepts are among the most important management accounting ideas to understand and be able to apply. The manager

Business in
Practice

The 1-Cent Sale

An understanding of cost–volume–profit relationships is shown by the manager of a fast-food and soft ice cream business operating in a midwestern city when a 1-cent sale is held in February. Ice cream sundaes are featured—two for the price of one, plus 1 cent. None of the other menu items are on sale.

Those sundaes usually sell for a price of $2.79 to $3.39, but even with generous estimates, it is hard to come up with variable costs (ice cream, topping, cup, and spoon) much greater than 30 percent of the usual selling price. So even when the price is effectively cut in half, there is still a positive contribution margin. And what happens to the store's fixed costs during the sale? They are probably not affected at all. The fixed costs (including workers' wages) will be incurred whether or not extra customers come in for the sundae special. And, of course, many of those customers probably will buy other items at the regular price.

The net result of the special promotion is that the store builds traffic and business at a time of otherwise low activity (assuming that normal demand for sundaes is low in February). All of the additional sales volume generates a positive contribution margin, fixed expenses are the same as they would have been without the promotion, and operating income is increased over what it otherwise would have been.

encounters many situations in which cost–volume–profit analysis supports decisions that help the organization achieve its objective. One of these applications is described in link Business in Practice—The 1-Cent Sale.

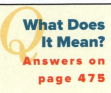

12. What does it mean to break even?

13. What does it mean to be aware of the effect of sales mix changes on a firm's operating income?

What Does It Mean?
Answers on page 475

Operating Leverage

When an entity's revenues change because the volume of activity changes, variable expenses and contribution margin will change proportionately. But the presence of fixed expenses, which do not change as the volume of activity changes, means that operating income will change proportionately more than the change in revenues. This magnifying effect on operating income resulting from a change in revenue is called **operating leverage**. This concept was illustrated in the discussion of the contribution margin format income statement example earlier in this chapter. It showed a 20 percent decline in volume, with revenues, variable expenses, and contribution margin also declining by 20 percent; but operating income declined 80 percent (from $10,000 to $2,000). Note the similarity of operating leverage to the discussion of financial leverage, explained in Chapter 11, in which fixed interest expense causes a proportionately larger change in ROE than the percentage change in ROI resulting from any given change in operating income.

Just as high financial leverage increases the risk that a firm may not be able to meet its required interest payments, high operating leverage increases the risk that a small percentage decline in revenues will cause a relatively larger percentage decline in operating income. *The higher a firm's contribution margin ratio, the greater its operating leverage.* Management can influence the operating leverage of a firm by its decisions about incurring variable versus fixed costs. For example, if a firm substitutes automated production equipment for employee labor, it has changed a variable cost (assuming the employees could be laid off if demand for the firm's products declined) to a fixed cost (the machine will depreciate, be insured, and be included in the property tax base whether or not it is being used); and it has increased its contribution margin ratio and operating leverage. If the management of a firm anticipates a decline in demand for the firm's products or services, it may be reluctant to change its cost structure by shifting variable costs to fixed costs, even though productivity increases could be attained, because the equipment has to be operating to realize the benefits of productivity gains.

The effect of different cost structures on operating leverage is illustrated in Exhibit 12-9. Observe in Part I that with alternative cost structures and a volume of 10,000 units, Company A and Company B achieved an identical amount of operating income of $100,000. This exhibit illustrates an important element of the decision-making process involving the trade-off between fixed cost (capital-intensive) and

LO 12
Use operating leverage to evaluate cost structures.

variable cost (labor-intensive) alternatives and is referred to as the **indifference point**. The indifference point is found by setting the cost structure (total cost) of each alternative (Company A and Company B in this example) equal to one another and solving for the volume of activity that equates total cost:

Company A	Company B
Fixed costs +	Fixed costs +
(Variable cost per unit × Volume) =	(Variable cost per unit × Volume)
$50,000 + ($35 × Volume)	= $200,000 + ($20 × Volume)
$15 × Volume	= $150,000
Volume	= 10,000 units

Parts II and III of Exhibit 12-9 illustrate that as a change in volume moves each company away from the indifference point, the effect on operating income is more dramatic with Company B's higher proportion of fixed cost to variable cost relative to Company A. The relatively higher operating leverage provides faster accumulation of operating income for increases in volume but also indicates that operating income will decrease faster when volume decreases. The effect of operating leverage on operating income is a key information component in the selection of a cost structure. The importance of understanding a company's cost structure and operating leverage, from an investor's perspective, is provided by The Motley Fool (www.fool.com) with excerpts and company examples described in Business in Practice—A Look at Operating Leverage.

Exhibit 12-9   Operating Leverage

I. Assume that two companies make similar products but that the companies have adopted different cost structures. Company A's product is made in a labor-intensive operation with relatively high variable costs but relatively low fixed costs, and Company B's product is made in a capital-intensive operation with relatively low variable costs but relatively high fixed costs. Each firm presently sells 10,000 units of product. A contribution margin model for each firm is presented here:

	Company A— Lower Operating Leverage				Company B— Higher Operating Leverage			
	Per Unit × Volume	**= Total**	**%**		**Per Unit × Volume**	**= Total**	**%**	
Revenue	$ 50				$ 50			
Variable expenses	35				20			
Contribution margin	$ 15 × 10,000	= $150,000	30%		$ 30 × 10,000	= $300,000	60%	
Fixed expenses		50,000				200,000		
Operating income.......		$100,000				$100,000		

(continued)

II. Effect on operating income of an increase in volume from 10,000 to 11,000 units:

	Company A—Lower Operating Leverage				Company B—Higher Operating Leverage			
	Per Unit × Volume	=	Total	%	Per Unit × Volume	=	Total	%
Contribution margin	$ 15 × 11,000	=	$165,000	30%	$ 30 × 11,000	=	$330,000	60%
Fixed expenses . . .			50,000				200,000	
Operating income			$115,000				$130,000	
Percentage change in volume	+10%				+10%			
Percentage change in operating income			+15%				+30%	

Note that Company B's operating income increased at a much higher rate, and to a considerably higher amount, than Company A's operating income. Operating leverage resulted in the operating income of each firm increasing proportionately more than the change in volume of activity. With an increase in volume, the greater contribution margin per unit and contribution margin ratio of Company B's product resulted in a greater increase in its operating income than experienced by Company A.

III. Effect on operating income of a decrease in volume from 10,000 units to 9,000 units:

	Company A—Lower Operating Leverage				Company B—Higher Operating Leverage			
	Per Unit × Volume	=	Total	%	Per Unit × Volume	=	Total	%
Contribution margin	$ 15 × 9,000	=	$135,000	30%	$ 30 × 9,000	=	$270,000	60%
Fixed expenses			50,000				200,000	
Operating income			$ 85,000				$ 70,000	
Percentage change in volume	−10%				−10%			
Percentage change in operating income			−15%				−30%	

Note that Company B's operating income decreased at a much higher rate, and to a considerably lower amount, than Company A's operating income. Operating leverage resulted in the operating income of each firm decreasing proportionately more than the change in volume of activity. With a decrease in volume, the greater contribution margin per unit and contribution margin ratio of Company B's product resulted in a greater reduction of its operating income than experienced by Company A.

A LOOK AT OPERATING LEVERAGE

How Operating Leverage Moves a Business

Do you know what the cost structure of your favorite company looks like—or why it matters? Understanding the relationship between fixed and variable costs is an important part of determining a company's operating leverage: how changes in sales, relative to a company's cost structure, can power (or deflate) the business.

Retailers and labor-intensive industries such as restaurants and accounting companies have low operating leverage, while tech companies, utilities, and airlines have high operating leverage. Let's look at two examples to illustrate how operating leverage can affect a business.

High Operating Leverage: IPG Photonics

If a company has high operating leverage, that means it can squeeze more money out of each additional sale. When a company's cost structure is largely based on fixed costs, it doesn't need to spend additional dollars when a new business prospect comes along or a current customer increases its order. The company already has the necessary assets in place—such as manufacturing facilities, equipment, and those well-paid executives—so it doesn't need to spend tons of money to meet the increased demand. Those savings help raise the profit margin, and earnings grow at a faster rate than sales. But there are risks. Fixed costs must be paid whether or not business is booming, so when sales struggle, margins and profit deteriorate quickly.

A perfect example of a company with high fixed costs and operating leverage is IPG Photonics. As David Meier wrote on the company's standout second quarter, "The dramatic increases were a function of the turnaround in sales and the nature of IPGP's business model. A vertically integrated business can generate incredible returns if it is sized correctly. But if sales are too light, the high fixed costs eat away the margins, which is what happened during the downturn in 2008–2009." Happily, IPG is benefiting from increasing sales, and because of its fixed cost structure, this is leading to a significant rise in margins and cash flow.

Low Operating Leverage: Costco

On the flip side, companies with low operating leverage have variable cost structures, which better positions them to do well when times are tough. Variable costs fall when the economy is struggling, and companies without the burden of high fixed costs can be nimble and adapt more quickly. This can allow a company to turn a profit even when it brings in less revenue.

A great example is Costco. Inventory and part-time labor make up a large part of its cost structure. When times are good, Costco will spend more on inventory, stocking its shelves with a ton of merchandise. It will also bring on more part-time workers. But if things turn south for a bit, Costco can lighten up on inventory and cut most of its workforce's hours, helping the company continue to wring out a profit.

Foolish bottom line

To sum up, there are three things to keep in mind when looking at the operating leverage of a potential investment:

- Companies with fixed cost structures enjoy a rapid rise in margins and profit when there is an increase in sales.

- Companies with variable cost structures can make money with lower sales, but they have less upside to their margins.

- In an economic downturn, variable cost structures help companies cut costs quickly.

Source: "A Look at Operating Leverage," From the Motley Fool: https://www.fool.com/investing/general/2010/08/19/a-look-at-operating-leverage.aspx.

14. What does it mean to state that a firm has a relatively high degree of operating leverage?

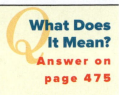

What Does It Mean?
Answer on page 475

Demonstration Problem

The Demonstration Problem walkthrough for this chapter is available in *Connect*.

Summary

Management is the process of planning, organizing, and controlling an organization's activities to accomplish its goals. Managerial accounting (sometimes called *management accounting*) supports the management process. **(LO 1)**

Managerial accounting differs from financial accounting in several ways. Managerial accounting has an internal orientation and a future perspective, and it often focuses on individual units within the firm rather than on the organization as a whole. Reasonably accurate data are acceptable for internal analysis, and performance reports tend to be issued frequently for managerial control and decision making. **(LO 2)**

Costs are classified differently for different purposes, and cost terminology is important to understand if cost data are to be used appropriately. The behavior pattern of a cost relates to the change in total cost given a change in activity. Variable costs change, in total, as activity changes, such as sales commissions or supplies used in production. Fixed costs remain constant in total as activity changes, such as sales salaries or rent. Assumptions about linearity and relevant range are implicit when a cost is described as variable or fixed. Many costs have a mixed behavior pattern (they are partly variable and partly fixed). A cost formula expresses the total amount of a cost for a given level of activity by combining the fixed and variable elements of the total cost. It is inappropriate, and may be misleading, to express a fixed cost on a per unit basis because by definition a fixed cost is constant over a range of activity. **(LO 3, 4, 5)**

Cost–volume–profit (CVP) analysis uses knowledge about cost behavior patterns to interpret and forecast changes in operating income resulting from changes in revenue, cost, or the volume of activity.

When a particular cost is partly fixed and partly variable, the high–low method can be used to develop a cost formula that recognizes both the variable and fixed elements of the cost. **(LO 6)**

The contribution margin format income statement reclassifies the functional cost categories of the traditional income statement to cost behavior pattern categories. Contribution margin is the difference between revenues and variable expenses. Unless there are changes in the composition of variable expenses, contribution margin changes in proportion to the change in revenues. **(LO 7)**

The expanded contribution margin format model provides a framework for analyzing the effect of revenue, cost, and volume changes on operating income. A key to using this model is that fixed costs are recognized only in total; they are never expressed on a per unit basis. **(LO 8)**

The contribution margin ratio (contribution margin / sales revenue) sometimes can be used to determine the effect of a volume change on operating income more quickly and more easily than using unit revenue, variable expense, and volume. **(LO 9)**

Sales mix describes the relative proportion of total sales accounted for by specific products. When different products or product lines have significantly different contribution margin ratios, changes in the sales mix will cause the percentage change in total contribution margin to differ from the percentage change in revenues. **(LO 10)**

The breakeven point is the total sales volume (in units or dollars) at which operating income is zero. With the contribution margin model, the breakeven point is achieved when total contribution margin is equal to fixed expenses. Breakeven analysis also can be illustrated graphically to provide a visual representation of profit and loss areas and to demonstrate the impact of the contribution margin per unit on operating income (or loss). **(LO 11)**

Operating leverage describes the percentage change in operating income for a given percentage change in revenues. The higher a firm's fixed expenses relative to its variable expenses, the greater the operating leverage and the greater the risk that a change in the level of activity will cause a relatively larger change in operating income than with less leverage. Operating leverage should inform management's decisions about whether to incur variable costs or fixed costs. **(LO 12)**

Key Terms and Concepts

breakeven point (p. 449)   The amount of revenue required to have neither operating profit nor operating loss.

contribution margin (p. 443)   The difference between revenues and variable costs.

contribution margin format (p. 441)   An income statement format in which variable costs are subtracted from revenues to show contribution margin, from which fixed costs are subtracted to determine operating income.

contribution margin ratio (p. 445)   The ratio of contribution margin to revenues.

cost behavior pattern (p. 437)   Identification of whether a cost is fixed or variable.

cost formula (p. 438)   An algebraic expression that reflects the fixed and variable elements of a cost.

cost–volume–profit (CVP) analysis (p. 432)   Analysis of the impact on profit of volume and cost changes using knowledge about the behavior pattern of the costs involved.

fixed cost (p. 437)   A cost that does not change in total as the level of activity changes within the relevant range.

indifference point (p. 456)   The activity level that produces the same total cost when two different cost formulas or cost structures are compared.

management process (p. 433)   Planning, organizing, and controlling the activities of an organization so it can accomplish its purpose.

managerial accounting (p. 432)   Accounting that uses economic and financial information to plan and control many activities of the entity and to support the management decision-making process. Sometimes called *management accounting*.

margin of safety (p. 454)   The amount by which current sales exceed breakeven sales, providing a relative measure of risk before an operating loss would be incurred.

operating leverage (p. 455)   The concept that operating income changes proportionately more than revenues for any change in the level of activity given the relative trade-off of variable versus fixed costs in a firm's cost structure.

production standards (p. 435)   Expected or allowed times and costs to make a product or perform an activity.

relevant range (p. 438)   The range of activity over which the fixed or variable cost behavior pattern exists.

sales mix (p. 449)   The proportion of total sales represented by various products or categories of products.

semivariable cost (p. 438)   A cost that has both fixed and variable elements—a mixed cost.

variable cost (p. 437)   A cost that changes in total as the volume of activity changes.

Mini-Exercises

All applicable Mini-Exercises are available in *Connect*.

Using cost behavior patterns MFG Company experiences the following cost behavior patterns each week:

Mini-Exercise 12.1
LO 3, 5

> Fixed costs: supervisor's salary $1,000; factory rent $2,500
> Mixed costs: utilities $1,500 + $5.25 per unit
> Variable costs per unit: manufacturing labor wages $20; supplies used in production $8.50; packaging cost $2.25; warranty cost $4

Required:
Compute total costs to be incurred for a week with 2,750 units of activity.

High–low method During a year, Mark's monthly sales compensation ranged between $18,000 and $24,000 per month and units sold ranged between 2,000 and 3,000 units for those same months.

Mini-Exercise 12.2
LO 6

Required:
Use the high–low method to determine Mark's monthly salary and commission rate per unit sold and then calculate the total number of units sold in a year when Mark's total compensation amounted to $168,000.

Prepare a contribution margin format income statement China Imports Inc. sold 18,000 units in May. Per unit selling price and variable expense were $25 and $17, respectively. Fixed expense incurred for May totaled $120,000.

Mini-Exercise 12.3
LO 7

Required:
Prepare the May income statement for China Imports in the contribution margin format.

CVP analysis Current operating income for Bay Area Cycles Co. is $74,000. Selling price per unit is $120, the contribution margin ratio is 30%, and fixed expense is $250,000.

Mini-Exercise 12.4
LO 8

Required:

Calculate Bay Area Cycle's per unit variable expense and contribution margin. How many units are currently being sold? How many additional unit sales would be necessary to achieve operating income of $110,000?

Mini-Exercise
12.5
LO 9, 11

Break-even analysis Refer to the current information for Bay Area Cycle Co. in Mini-Exercise 12.4.

Required:

Calculate Bay Area Cycle's breakeven point in units and total sales dollars. Calculate Bay Area Cycle's margin of safety and margin of safety ratio.

Mini-Exercise
12.6
LO 9, 10, 11

Multiple Products and CVP Analysis Assume MIX Inc. has sales volume of $1,000,000 for two products with May sales and contribution margin ratios as follows:

Product A: Sales $400,000; Contribution Margin Ratio 30%
Product B: Sales $600,000; Contribution Margin Ratio 60%

Required:

Assume MIX's fixed expenses are $300,000. Calculate the May total contribution margin, operating income, average contribution margin ratio, and breakeven sales volume.

Mini-Exercise
12.7
LO 9, 10, 11

Sales Mix Shift and CVP Analysis Assume MIX Inc. has sales volume of $1,000,000 for two products with June sales and contribution margin ratios as follows:

Product A: Sales $500,000; Contribution Margin Ratio 30%
Product B: Sales $500,000; Contribution Margin Ratio 60%

Required:

Assume MIX's fixed expenses are $300,000. Calculate the June total contribution margin, operating income, average contribution margin ratio, and breakeven sales volume. Refer to your answers for Mini-Exercise 12.6 and explain why MIX is expiring such different operating results from May to June when total sales volume is $1,000,000 in both months.

Mini-Exercise
12.8
LO 12

Operating leverage The cost structure of two firms competing in the same industry is represented by the following cost formulas:

Company X = $1,350,000 + $37/unit;
Company Z = $825,000 + $72/unit.

The selling price is $140 per unit for both companies.

Required:

Calculate the indifference point between the two cost structures; that is, the amount of unit sales that produce the same operating income for Company X and Company Z. If sales volume were expected to increase by 20% over the next two years, which cost structure would you prefer? Why?

Exercises

All applicable Exercises are available in *Connect*.

Cost classifications For each of the following costs, check the column(s) that most likely applies (apply):

Exercise 12.9
LO 3

Cost	Variable	Fixed
Wages of assembly-line workers	_____	_____
Depreciation—plant equipment	_____	_____
Glue and thread	_____	_____
Shipping costs	_____	_____
Raw materials handling costs	_____	_____
Salary of public relations manager	_____	_____
Production run setup costs	_____	_____
Plant utilities	_____	_____
Electricity cost of retail stores	_____	_____
Research and development expense	_____	_____

Cost classifications For each of the following costs, check the column(s) that most likely applies (apply):

Exercise 12.10
LO 3

Cost	Variable	Fixed
Raw materials	_____	_____
Tape used to secure packed boxes of product	_____	_____
Plant janitors' wages	_____	_____
Inventory clerks' wages	_____	_____
Advertising expenses	_____	_____
Production workers' wages	_____	_____
Production supervisors' salaries	_____	_____
Sales force commissions	_____	_____
Office supplies used	_____	_____
Controller's salary	_____	_____
Electricity cost	_____	_____
Real estate taxes for:	_____	_____
Plant	_____	_____
Office building	_____	_____

Estimating costs based on behavior patterns Larry estimates that the costs of insurance, license, and depreciation to operate his car total $320 per month and that the gas, oil, and maintenance costs are 14 cents per mile. Larry also estimates that, on average, he drives his car 1,400 miles per month.

Exercise 12.11
LO 3

Required:

a. How much cost would Larry expect to incur during April if he drove the car 1,529 miles?

b. Would it be meaningful for Larry to calculate an estimated average cost per mile for a typical 1,400-mile month? Explain your answer.

Exercise 12.12
LO 3

Estimating costs based on behavior patterns The following information provides the amount of cost incurred in March for the cost items indicated. During March, 4,000 units of the firm's single product were manufactured.

Raw materials.	$20,800
Factory depreciation expense	40,500
Direct labor.	49,600
Production supervisor's salary	5,000
Computer rental expense	3,100
Maintenance supplies used	600

Required:

a. How much cost would you expect to be incurred for each of these items during April when 5,600 units of the product are planned for production?

b. Calculate the average total cost per unit for the 4,000 units manufactured in March. Explain why this figure would not be useful to a manager interested in predicting the cost of producing 5,600 units in April.

Exercise 12.13
LO 7, 9

Understanding CVP relationships Calculate the missing amounts for each of the following firms:

	Sales	Variable Costs	Contribution Margin Ratio	Fixed Costs	Operating Income (Loss)
Firm A	$320,000	?	32%	?	$38,300
Firm B	?	$465,050	?	$118,000	71,950
Firm C	134,000	?	26%	36,700	?
Firm D	?	59,000	20%	?	(4,920)

Exercise 12.14
LO 7, 9

Understanding CVP relationships Calculate the missing amounts for each of the following firms:

	Units Sold	Selling Price	Variable Costs per Unit	Contribution Margin	Fixed Costs	Operating Income (Loss)
Firm A	10,000	$25.00	?	$100,000	$40,000	?
Firm B	9,000	?	$19.00	?	66,000	$33,000
Firm C	?	7.00	4.00	12,000	?	(6,000)
Firm D	4,000	?	50.00	40,000	48,000	?

Calculate selling price of new product with a target CM ratio Backus Inc. makes and sells many consumer products. The firm's average contribution margin ratio is 35%. Management is considering adding a new product that will require an additional $15,000 per month of fixed expenses and will have variable expenses of $7.80 per unit.

Exercise 12.15
LO 8, 9

Required:
a. Calculate the selling price that will be required for the new product if it is to have a contribution margin ratio equal to 35%.
b. Calculate the number of units of the new product that would have to be sold if the new product is to increase the firm's monthly operating income by $6,000.

Calculate selling price of new product; what-if questions; breakeven D&R Corp. has annual revenues of $375,000, an average contribution margin ratio of 32%, and fixed expenses of $150,000.

Exercise 12.16
LO 8, 9, 10, 11

Required:
a. Management is considering adding a new product to the company's product line. The new item will have $9.52 of variable costs per unit. Calculate the selling price that will be required if this product is not to affect the average contribution margin ratio.
b. If the new product adds an additional $26,880 to D&R's fixed expenses, how many units of the new product must be sold at the price calculated in part **a** to break even on the new product?
c. If 16,000 units of the new product could be sold at a price of $15.50 per unit, and the company's other business did not change, calculate D&R's total operating income and average contribution margin ratio.
d. Describe how the analysis of adding the new product would be complicated if it were to "steal" some volume from existing products.

Special promotion—effects of a two-for-one sale Pam and Lenny's ice cream shop charges $1.25 for a cone. Variable expenses are $0.35 per cone, and fixed costs total $1,800 per month. A "sweetheart" promotion is being planned for the second week of February. During this week, a person buying a cone at the regular price would receive a free cone for a friend. It is estimated that 400 additional cones would be sold and that 600 cones would be given away. Advertising costs for the promotion would be $120.

Exercise 12.17
LO 8, 9

Required:
a. Calculate the effect of the promotion on operating income for the second week of February.
b. Do you think the promotion should occur? Explain your answer.

Special promotion—effects of a 1-cent sale The management of Rocko's Pizzeria is considering a special promotion for the last two weeks of May, which is normally a relatively low-demand period. The special promotion would involve selling two medium pizzas for the price of one, plus 1 cent. The medium pizza normally sells for $11.99 and has variable expenses of $4. Expected sales volume without the special promotion is 400 medium pizzas per week.

Exercise 12.18
LO 8, 9

Required:

a. Calculate the total contribution margin generated by the normal volume of medium pizzas in a week.

b. Calculate the total number of medium pizzas that would have to be sold during the 1-cent sale to generate the same amount of contribution margin that results from the normal volume.

c. What other factors should management consider in evaluating the pros and cons of the special promotion?

▓connect **Problems**

All applicable Problems are available in *Connect*.

Problem 12.19

LO 6

High–low method A department of Alpha Co. incurred the following costs for the month of September. Variable costs, and the variable portion of mixed costs, are a function of the number of units of activity:

Activity level in units.	5,000
Variable costs	$10,000
Fixed costs.	30,000
Mixed costs	20,000
Total costs.	$60,000

During October, the activity level was 8,000 units, and the total costs incurred were $70,500.

Required:

a. Calculate the variable costs, fixed costs, and mixed costs incurred during October.

b. Use the high–low method to calculate the cost formula for mixed cost.

Problem 12.20

LO 6

High–low method—missing amounts The following data have been extracted from the records of Puzzle Inc.:

	February	August
Production level, in units.	10,000	20,000
Variable costs	$24,000	$?
Fixed costs.	?	36,000
Mixed costs.	20,000	?
Total costs.	$80,000	$118,000

Required:

a. Calculate the missing costs.

b. Calculate the cost formula for mixed cost using the high–low method.

c. Calculate the total cost that would be incurred for the production of 16,000 units.

d. Identify the two key cost behavior assumptions made in the calculation of your answer to part **c.**

Prepare a contribution margin format income statement; answer what-if questions Shown here is an income statement in the traditional format for a firm with a sales volume of 8,000 units. Cost formulas also are shown:

Problem 12.21
LO 7, 8, 9

Revenues	$32,000
Cost of goods sold ($6,000 + $2.10/unit).	22,800
Gross profit	$ 9,200
Operating expenses:	
Selling ($1,200 + $0.10/unit).	2,000
Administration ($4,000 + $0.20/unit).	5,600
Operating income	$ 1,600

Required:

a. Prepare an income statement in the contribution margin format.

b. Calculate the contribution margin per unit and the contribution margin ratio.

c. Calculate the firm's operating income (or loss) if the volume changed from 8,000 units to
1. 12,000 units.
2. 4,000 units.

d. Refer to your answer to part **a** for total revenues of $32,000. Calculate the firm's operating income (or loss) if unit selling price and variable expenses per unit do not change and total revenues
1. Increase $12,000.
2. Decrease $7,000.

Prepare a contribution margin format income statement; answer what-if questions Shown here is an income statement in the traditional format for a firm with a sales volume of 18,000 units:

Problem 12.22
LO 7, 8, 9, 12

Revenues	$108,000
Cost of goods sold ($10,000 + $2.80/unit)	60,400
Gross profit.	$ 47,600
Operating expenses:	
Selling ($2,200 + $1.00/unit)	20,200
Administration ($5,000 + $0.40/unit)	12,200
Operating income.	$ 15,200

Required:

a. Prepare an income statement in the contribution margin format.

b. Calculate the contribution margin per unit and the contribution margin ratio.

c. Calculate the firm's operating income (or loss) if the volume changed from 15,000 units to
1. 20,000 units.
2. 10,000 units.

d. Refer to your answer to part **a** when total revenues were $108,000. Calculate the firm's operating income (or loss) if unit selling price and variable expense per unit do not change and total revenues
1. Increase by $15,000.
2. Decrease by $10,000.

Problem 12.23
LO 7, 8, 9, 11

Prepare a contribution margin format income statement; calculate break-even point Presented here is the income statement for Big Shot Inc. for the month of May:

Sales	$65,000
Cost of goods sold	56,000
Gross profit.	$ 9,000
Operating expenses.	14,000
Operating loss	$ (5,000)

Based on an analysis of cost behavior patterns, it has been determined that the company's contribution margin ratio is 20%.

Required:
a. Rearrange the preceding income statement to the contribution margin format.
b. If sales increase by 30%, what will be the firm's operating income?
c. Calculate the amount of revenue required for Big Shot to break even.

Problem 12.24
LO 7, 8, 9, 11

Prepare a contribution margin format income statement; calculate breakeven point Presented here is the income statement for Fairchild Co. for March:

Sales	$100,000
Cost of goods sold	54,000
Gross profit.	$ 46,000
Operating expenses.	37,000
Operating income.	$ 9,000

Based on an analysis of cost behavior patterns, it has been determined that the company's contribution margin ratio is 30%.

Required:
a. Rearrange the preceding income statement to the contribution margin format.
b. Calculate operating income if sales volume increases by 10%. (*Note:* Do not construct an income statement to get your answer.)
c. Calculate the amount of revenue required for Fairchild to break even.

Problem 12.25
LO 7, 8, 9, 10

CVP analysis—what-if questions; breakeven Monterey Co. makes and sells a single product. The current selling price is $15 per unit. Variable expenses are $9 per unit, and fixed expenses total $27,000 per month.

Required:
(Unless otherwise stated, consider each requirement separately.)

a. Calculate the breakeven point expressed in terms of total sales dollars and sales volume.

b. Calculate the margin of safety and the margin of safety ratio. Assume current sales are $75,000.

c. Calculate the monthly operating income (or loss) at a sales volume of 5,400 units per month.

d. Calculate monthly operating income (or loss) if a $2 per unit reduction in selling price results in a volume increase to 8,400 units per month.

e. What questions would have to be answered about the cost–volume–profit analysis simplifying assumptions before adopting the price cut strategy of part **d**?

f. Calculate the monthly operating income (or loss) that would result from a $1 per unit price increase and a $6,000 per month increase in advertising expenses, both relative to the original data. Assume a sales volume of 5,400 units per month. Is the increase in advertising expense justified by the price increase?

g. Management is considering a change in the sales force compensation plan. Currently each of the firm's two salespeople is paid a salary of $2,500 per month. Calculate the monthly operating income (or loss) that would result from changing the compensation plan to a salary of $400 per month, plus a commission of $0.80 per unit, assuming a sales volume of
   1. 5,400 units per month.
   2. 6,000 units per month.

h. Assuming that the sales volume of 6,000 units per month achieved in part **g** could also be achieved by increasing advertising by $1,000 per month instead of changing the sales force compensation plan, which strategy would you recommend? Explain your answer.

CVP analysis—what-if questions; sales mix issue Ozark Metal Co. makes a single product that sells for $42 per unit. Variable costs are $27.30 per unit, and fixed costs total $65,415 per month.

Problem 12.26
LO 7, 8, 9, 10, 11

Required:

a. Calculate the number of units that must be sold each month for the firm to break even.

b. Assume current sales are $220,000. Calculate the margin of safety and the margin of safety ratio.

c. Calculate operating income if 5,000 units are sold in a month.

d. Calculate operating income if the selling price is raised to $45 per unit, advertising expenditures are increased by $8,000 per month, and monthly unit sales volume becomes 5,400 units.

e. Assume that the firm adds another product to its product line and that the new product sells for $20 per unit, has variable costs of $14 per unit, and causes fixed expenses in total to increase to $83,000 per month. Calculate the firm's operating income if 5,000 units of the original product and 4,000 units of the new product are sold each month. For the original product, use the selling price and variable cost data given in the problem statement.

f. Calculate the firm's operating income if 4,000 units of the original product and 5,000 units of the new product are sold each month.

g. Explain why operating income is different in parts **e** and **f**, even though sales totaled 9,000 units in each case.

Problem 12.27
LO 7, 8, 9, 10, 11

CVP application—expand existing product line? Collegiate Canvas Co. currently makes and sells two models of a backpack. Data applicable to the current operation are summarized in the following columns labeled Current Operation. Management is considering adding a Value model to its current Luxury and Economy models. Expected data if the new model is added are shown in the following columns labeled Proposed Expansion:

	Current Operation		Proposed Expansion		
	Luxury	**Economy**	**Luxury**	**Economy**	**Value**
Selling price per unit	$ 20	$ 12	$ 20	$ 12	$ 15
Variable expenses per unit	8	7	8	7	8
Annual sales volume—units	10,000	20,000	6,000	17,000	8,000
Fixed expenses for year	Total of $70,000		Total of $84,000		

Required:

a. Calculate the company's current total contribution margin and the current average contribution margin ratio.

b. Calculate the company's current amount of operating income.

c. Calculate the company's current breakeven point in dollar sales.

d. Explain why the company might incur a loss, even if the sales amount calculated in part **c** was achieved and selling prices and costs didn't change.

e. Calculate the company's total operating income under the proposed expansion.

f. Based on the proposed expansion data, would you recommend adding the Value model? Why or why not?

g. Would your answer to part **f** change if the Value model sales volume were to increase to 10,000 units annually and all other data remained the same? Why or why not?

Problem 12.28
LO 8, 9, 10, 11

CVP application—eliminate product from operations? Muscle Beach Inc. makes three models of high-performance weight-training benches. Current operating data are summarized here:

	MegaMuscle	**PowerGym**	**ProForce**
Selling price per unit	$ 140	$ 220	$ 290
Contribution margin per unit	42	77	58
Monthly sales volume—units	3,000	2,000	1,000
Fixed expenses per month		Total of $320,000	

Required:

a. Calculate the contribution margin ratio of each product.

b. Calculate the firm's overall contribution margin ratio.

c. Calculate the firm's monthly breakeven point in sales dollars.

d. Calculate the firm's monthly operating income.

e. Management is considering the elimination of the ProForce model due to its low sales volume and low contribution margin ratio. As a result, total fixed expenses can be reduced to $270,000 per month. Assuming that this change would not affect the other models, would you recommend the elimination of the ProForce model? Explain your answer.

f. Assume the same facts as in part **e.** Assume also that the sales volume for the PowerGym model will increase by 500 units per month if the ProForce model is eliminated. Would you recommend eliminating the ProForce model? Explain your answer.

CVP analysis—effects of changes in cost structure; breakeven Riveria Co. makes and sells a single product. The current selling price is $32 per unit. Variable expenses are $20 per unit, and fixed expenses total $43,200 per month. Sales volume for May totaled 4,100 units.

Problem 12.29
LO 8, 9, 11

Required:

a. Calculate operating income for May.

b. Calculate the breakeven point in terms of units sold and total revenues.

c. Management is considering installing automated equipment to reduce direct labor cost. If this were done, variable expenses would drop to $14 per unit, but fixed expenses would increase to $67,800 per month.

1. Calculate operating income at a volume of 4,100 units per month with the new cost structure.

2. Calculate the breakeven point in units with the new cost structure. (Round your answer.)

3. Why would you suggest that management seriously consider investing in the automated equipment and accept the new cost structure?

4. Why might management not accept your recommendation but decide instead to maintain the old cost structure?

CVP analysis—effects of change in cost structure; breakeven Austin Inc. produces small-scale replicas of vintage automobiles for collectors and museums. Finished products are built on a 1/20 scale of originals. The firm's income statement showed the following:

Problem 12.30
LO 8, 9, 11, 12

Revenues (1,200 units)	$792,000
Variable expenses	435,600
Contribution margin	$356,400
Fixed expenses	260,000
Operating income	$ 96,400

An automated stamping machine has been developed that can efficiently produce body frames, hoods, and doors to the desired scale. If the machine is leased, fixed expenses will increase by $29,000 per year. The firm's production capacity will increase, which is expected to result in a 25% increase in sales volume. It is also estimated that labor costs of $33 per unit could be saved because less polishing and finishing time will be required.

Required:

a. Calculate the firm's current contribution margin ratio and breakeven point in terms of revenues. (Round your answer.)

b. Calculate the firm's contribution margin ratio and breakeven point in terms of revenues if the new machine is leased.

c. Calculate the firm's operating income assuming that the new machine is leased.

d. Do you believe that management of Austin should lease the new machine? Explain your answer.

---

connect   **Cases**

All applicable Cases are available in *Connect*.

Case 12.31
LO 8, 9, 11

CVP application—allow special discount? Assume you are a sales representative for Sweet Tooth Candy Company. One of your customers is interested in buying some candy that will be given to the members of a high school Substance Abuse Awareness Club. The club members will be marching in a community parade and will give the candy to children who are watching the parade. Your customer has asked that you discount the normal selling price of the candy to be given to the club by 30%. You know that the contribution margin ratio of the candy, based on the regular selling price, is 40%.

Required:
Identify the pros and cons of complying with the customer's request, and state the recommendation you would make to your sales manager.

Case 12.32
LO 5, 8, 9

CVP application—determine offering price Tommy Appleton is in charge of arranging the "attitude adjustment" period and dinner for the monthly meetings of the local chapter of the Management Accountants Association. Tommy is negotiating with a new restaurant that would like to have the group's business, and Tommy wants to apply some of the cost–volume–profit analysis concepts he has learned. The restaurant is proposing its regular menu prices of $4 for a before-dinner drink and $22 for dinner. Tommy has determined that, on average, the people attending the meeting have 1.5 drinks before dinner. He also believes that the contribution margin ratios for the drinks and dinner are 50% and 40%, respectively.

Required:
Prepare a memo to Tommy outlining the possible offers he might make to the restaurant owner, and recommend which offer he should make.

Case 12.33
LO 12

Comparison of operating leverage and financial leverage The concept of financial leverage was introduced in Chapter 7 and expanded on in Chapter 11. In Exercise 7.20 you were asked to describe the risks associated with financial leverage.

Required:

a. Describe the risks associated with operating leverage.

b. Outline the similarities and differences between operating leverage and financial leverage. (*Hint:* Compare Exhibit 12-9 to the discussion and analysis in Exhibits 7-2 and 11-3.)

Understanding the effects of operating leverage HighTech Inc. and OldTime Co. compete within the same industry and had the following operating results in 2019:

Case 12.34
LO 12

	HighTech, Inc.	OldTime Co.
Sales	$420,000	$420,000
Variable expenses	84,000	252,000
Contribution margin	$336,000	$168,000
Fixed expenses	294,000	126,000
Operating income	$ 42,000	$ 42,000

Required:

a. Calculate the breakeven point for each firm in terms of revenue.

b. What observations can you draw by examining the breakeven point of each firm given that they earned an equal amount of operating income on identical sales volumes in 2019?

c. Calculate the amount of operating income (or loss) that you would expect each firm to report in 2020 if sales were to

1. Increase by 20%.
2. Decrease by 20%.

d. Using the amounts computed in requirement **c,** calculate the increase or decrease in the amount of operating income expected in 2020 from the amount reported in 2019.

e. Explain why an equal percentage increase (or decrease) in sales for each firm would have such differing effects on operating income.

f. Calculate the ratio of contribution margin to operating income for each firm in 2019. (*Hint:* Divide contribution margin by operating income.)

g. Multiply the expected increase in sales of 20% for 2020 by the ratio of contribution margin to operating income for 2019 computed in requirement **f** for each firm. (*Hint:* Multiply your answer in requirement **f** by 0.2.)

h. Multiply your answer in requirement **g** by the operating income of $42,000 reported in 2019 for each firm.

i. Compare your answer in requirement **h** with your answer in requirement **d.** What conclusions can you draw about the effects of operating leverage from the steps you performed in requirements **f, g,** and **h**?

Breakeven analysis; CVP application using Internet tools You have recently been engaged by Dominic's Italian Cafe to evaluate the financial impact of adding gourmet pizza items to the menu. A survey of the clientele indicates that demand for

Case 12.35
LO 11

the product exists at an average selling price of $18 per pizza. Fixed costs related to new equipment would be $12,000 per month. Variable costs for ingredients, labor, and electricity for the oven would average $6 per pizza. You decide that a good starting point is to conduct an initial breakeven analysis on the new project.

Knowing that many commercial Internet companies provide free downloads or online demos of their products for your evaluation and testing pleasure, you decide to conduct the breakeven analysis using breakeven calculators that have been located at several websites.

Required:

a. Calculate the breakeven point in pizzas per month and print your results using the online break-even analysis tools at each of the following websites:

1.   entrepreneur.com/calculators/breakeven.html

2.   calcxml.com/calculators/breakeven-analysis

3.   anz.com/aus/Small-Business/Tools-Forms-And-Guides/Benchmark-Your-Business/Breakeven-Analyser/default.asp

4.   dinkytown.net/java/BreakEven.html

b. Write a comparative analysis of each of the four tools that you used to calculate the breakeven point. You might discuss strengths, weaknesses, usefulness, and user interaction for each tool.

c. Dominic's now is interested in the amount of operating income available from the gourmet pizza operation if sales are initially expected to be 2,000 pizzas each month. Calculate the operating income and print your results using the "PDF Report" button available with the calcxml.com breakeven analysis tool.

d. Dominic's now would like to understand the effect on operating income if certain changes in costs or volume occur. Use the calcxml.com "PDF Report" results to present and evaluate each of the following independent cases assuming sales are initially expected to be 2,000 pizzas each month:

1.   Selling price is decreased by 10%, and pizza sales are expected to increase by 5%.

2.   Selling price is increased to $20, and pizza sales are expected to decrease by 20%.

3.   Higher-quality ingredients are used at a cost increase of $2 to $8 per pizza, and pizza sales are expected to increase to 2,200 pizzas per month.

4.   A more efficient pizza oven is available that would reduce the electricity used in baking each pizza. Variable costs would be reduced to $5 per pizza. The more efficient oven would increase the fixed costs to $15,000 per month.

e. Write a memo to Dominic's explaining the results of your analysis.

ANSWERS TO
What Does
It Mean?

1. It means that *cost* is a very broad term that must be qualified so communication about cost is clear. It is important to understand cost terminology.

2. It means that managerial accounting is more future-oriented, whereas financial accounting is concerned primarily with reporting events that have already occurred.

3. It means that planned results are compared to actual results, and either actions or plans are changed so future results come closer to planned results.

4. It means that classification of a cost as fixed or variable is based on the simplifying assumptions of linearity and relevant range.

5. It means that a formula for predicting the total cost at some level of activity has been developed and that it recognizes both the fixed and variable elements of the cost's behavior pattern.

6. It means that instead of using cost of goods sold and operating expense functional categories, expenses are classified according to their cost behavior pattern as variable or fixed; then variable expenses are subtracted from sales to arrive at contribution margin, from which fixed expenses are subtracted to arrive at operating income.

7. It means that because costs are classified based on behavior patterns (contribution margin format), the effect of changes in activity on expenses and operating income can be more easily and accurately determined.

8. It means that contribution per unit (revenue less variable expenses) is multiplied by volume to obtain total contribution margin, and fixed costs are subtracted to arrive at operating income.

9. It means that by organizing the relationships between revenues, variable expenses, fixed expenses, and volume into a model that provides a consistent way to better understand the interaction of these items, improved decision making should occur.

10. It means that because total fixed expenses don't change as the volume of activity changes, to express fixed expenses on a per unit basis doesn't make sense.

11. It means that because many firms have multiple products, overall planning and control are more easily accomplished by focusing on contribution margin ratio rather than the contribution margin of individual products.

12. It means that revenues equal expenses, so operating income is zero.

13. It means that because different products have different contribution margin ratios, changes in the proportion of sales of one product to total sales compared to the proportion of sales of another product to total sales—that is, a change in the sales mix—will affect operating income based on the products' relative contribution margin ratios.

14. It means that the firm has a relatively high proportion of fixed to variable costs, so the effect of changes in sales volume on contribution margin and operating income will be magnified relative to a firm with a lower operating leverage.

13

Cost Accounting and Reporting

"What does it cost?" may be the most important question addressed by an organization's accounting information system. As you will come to realize, accurate cost information is necessary to guide managers in making pricing decisions, evaluating productivity and efficiency, developing operating budgets, determining whether component product parts/services will be manufactured/performed internally or outsourced, analyzing whether production technology will replace human efforts, and appraising performance—in addition to helping address many other questions that will be explored throughout the remaining chapters of this text. **Cost accounting** is a subset of both financial and managerial accounting that relates primarily to the accumulation and determination of product, process, or services costs. The costing system used to accumulate, assign, and report these costs for financial reporting purposes must also be flexible enough to provide answers to support the broad array of managerial questions for planning, control, and decision making purposes.

The economic recession of 2008–2009, and then the road to eventual recovery and a more robust economy a decade later, led many managers to seek more effective and less costly ways of performing their activities. These include seeking more efficient methods of processing and manufacturing, an activity frequently labeled "continuous improvement," or making the organization "leaner." This trend has led to the development of "lean accounting," a system that focuses on product or process cost accumulation by element of the value chain. The development of lean accounting reflects the requirement for managers to have increasingly relevant cost data and illustrates the need for cost information to continuously evolve in order to meet decision-making needs more effectively.

LO 1
Explain the role of cost accounting as it relates to financial and managerial accounting.

Cost accounting plays a very important role in the income measurement and inventory valuation aspects of financial accounting. You will recall that the fundamental focus of financial accounting is external to the organization: providing information to stockholders, creditors, the government, and others about the financial position and results of operations of the organization in accordance with generally accepted principles of accounting. To that end, the cost accounting system reports the cost of goods manufactured and sold, as well as the cost of goods manufactured and not sold—inventory valuation—along with other costs that are carried in the accounts of a manufacturing company. Exhibit 13-1 presents these relationships.

In this chapter, we explore the cost accounting and reporting systems that serve the needs of both financial and managerial accounting.

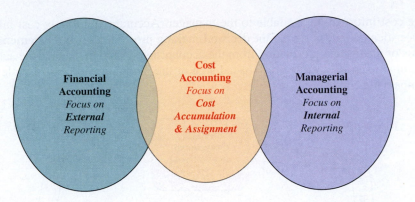

Relationship of Cost
Accounting to Financial
Accounting and
Managerial Accounting

1. What does it mean to state that cost accounting serves both financial and managerial accounting?

**What Does
It Mean?**
Answer on
page 518

LEARNING OBJECTIVES (LO)

After studying this chapter, you should understand and be able to

LO 13-1   Explain the role of cost accounting as it relates to financial and managerial accounting.

LO 13-2   Describe how cost management plays a strategic role in the organization's value chain.

LO 13-3   Contrast direct and indirect costs and illustrate how they relate to a product or activity.

LO 13-4   Distinguish between product costs and period costs and identify the three components of product cost.

LO 13-5   Explain the general operation of a product costing system and illustrate how costs flow through the inventory accounts to cost of goods sold.

LO 13-6   Calculate predetermined overhead application rates and demonstrate how they are used.

LO 13-7   Prepare and interpret a statement of cost of goods manufactured.

LO 13-8   Explain and illustrate the difference between absorption and direct (or variable) costing.

LO 13-9   Perform activity-based costing and describe activity-based management.

Cost Management

Recall from the planning and control cycle that management attention is given to planning, executing, and controlling the entity's activities so that the organization can achieve its strategic goals. Along each step of that process, decisions are made based on the cost information available to the manager. Accurate and timely cost information is critical to the success of the decision-making process. **Cost management** is the process of using cost information from the accounting system to manage the activities of the organization (see the gray shaded area of the planning and control cycle in the accompanying figure).

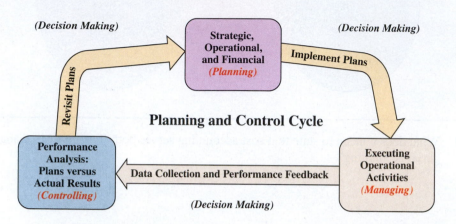

LO 2

Describe how cost management plays a strategic role in the organization's value chain.

Considering the broad scope and function of an organization's activities helps one to appreciate how important quality cost information is to the manager. Too often, cost accounting is viewed in its traditional role of determining the cost of producing products or providing services and the related accounting for those activities—a results-oriented, short-term view of cost. A more contemporary view is that costs must be understood and managed at each stage of an organization's value chain to provide an awareness of cost over the entire life cycle of a product or service—a prescriptive, long-term view of cost where cost management clearly becomes a strategic initiative. A **value chain** is the sequence of functions and related activities that, over the life of a product or service, can ultimately create a "value" difference for the customer. The significance of viewing each function as a link in a chain is that each is critical to managing the firm's activities for each product or service at each stage of the value chain, and a weakness in any element of the value chain could impair management's desired outcome. The sequence of functions that compose the value chain and examples of cost management initiatives at each stage of the value chain are shown in Exhibit 13-2.

Viewing the organization's value chain highlights many questions that can be answered about activities by analyzing their cost. For example, focusing cost control questions independently on the production activity may be too late, from an ability to control cost perspective, because the current product design will provide only marginal opportunities to improve cost performance. Costs that will be incurred during production are effectively "locked in" during the product design process. Therefore, the objective is to improve or sustain any competitive advantage the firm may have in the marketplace while maintaining an appropriate level of product or service quality and to provide for an appropriate return on investment. Later in this chapter, activity-based costing is introduced as a technique for analyzing activities within the value chain to improve the relevance and accuracy of the costing process.

As can be seen in the example of value chain functions in Exhibit 13-2, there exists an emphasis on "different costs for different purposes," as was explained in Chapter 12.

Exhibit 13-2

Value Chain Functions

Product/Service Idea

Cost Management Initiatives

- Is the cost of generating new ideas and experimentation justified?
- What portion of the operating budget should be used for R&D?
- How much is the competition spending?

- Can a product or process flow be designed with a resulting cost that allows effective competition in the market and that generates appropriate ROI?

- What is the cost of acquiring raw materials and converting them into a finished product?
- How much should it cost to produce each unit?
- Should the production of certain product component parts be outsourced?

- What is the cost to promote and sell the firm's products?
- Is the use of a digital marketing strategy cost effective?

- How much is delivery costing per mile? Per pound?
- Are more effective carriers available for certain deliveries?

- What is the after-sale cost of product support activities?
- What is the cost of an unsatisfied customer?

An entire course could be devoted to developing cost management initiatives across the entire value chain. Thus, our focus throughout the remaining chapters of this text is primarily on the production stage and explaining the process for cost accumulation and assignment. Cost accumulation is the easy part; accounting systems always have focused on the collection and recording of transactions, and automated data collection systems are available for manufacturing environments today. Cost assignment, on the other hand, is much more complex because to answer the question "What does it cost?" *it* must be carefully defined and cost relationships must be understood.

What Does It Mean?

Answer on page 518

2. What does it mean to say that cost assignment is more complex than cost accumulation?

Cost Accumulation and Assignment

A cost is incurred to acquire the resources that are used in carrying out the activities in each function of the value chain. Managers are interested in planning and controlling these costs. After costs are accumulated, they are assigned to a point of reference for which the manager is interested in observing a separate cost measurement. This point of reference is referred to as a **cost object,** and it may represent a job, a machine, a product line, a service activity, a department, a plant, a customer, a sales territory, a division of the corporation, or any other organizational reference point where a need to understand cost exists.

   Cost accumulation is the process of collecting and recording transaction data through the accounting information system. These systems can be highly automated and provide a real-time view of cost information to allow timely decisions as the activity is occurring. The total amount of cost accumulated by the system is then logically categorized in different ways, such as by the production department. This classification of cost emphasizes the managerial point of reference and is referred to as a **cost pool**. **Cost assignment** is the process of attributing an appropriate amount of cost in the cost pool to each cost object. The process of cost pooling and assignment is illustrated here:

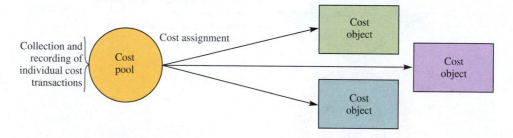

The following diagram illustrates this concept for a production department where management is interested in knowing the amount of cost assigned to each job the department produces:

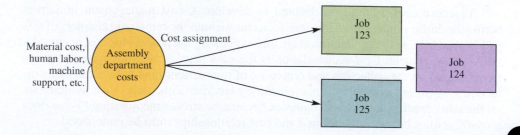

Cost Classifications—The Big Picture   **Exhibit 13-3**

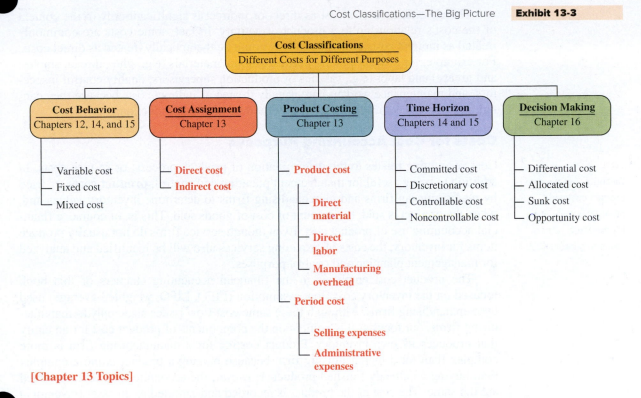

[Chapter 13 Topics]

Does the illustrated sequence seem simple enough? The answer is yes for some costs; but *let's think about this more carefully* is the more logical response. Certain costs in the cost pool, such as a raw material, are clearly traceable to the cost object, but common costs such as machine depreciation will need to be allocated to the cost object. The term *cost* means different things to different people depending upon one's point of reference. This chapter develops cost terminology further as two additional paths of the cost classification model introduced in Chapter 12 are explored. These are highlighted in Exhibit 13-3.

Cost Relationship to Products or Activity

Direct cost and **indirect cost** are terms used to relate a cost to a product or activity (i.e., a cost object). Whether a cost is direct or indirect depends on the context within which the term is being used. When we describe the cost of a specific product, such as a book, the amount of paper used is clearly traceable to each book and is a direct cost, but the amount of electricity used by the printing press is not as obviously traceable to each book and therefore is an indirect cost. However, when we evaluate the profitability of the printing press, the amount of electricity used by the press would now be a direct cost, as would other costs traceable to the operation of the printing press. The cost of a training program designed to make all press operators more efficient would be an indirect cost of printing a book. One way of distinguishing between a direct and an indirect cost is to think of a direct cost as a cost that would *not* be incurred if the product or activity did not exist. An indirect cost is one that would continue to be incurred even if the product or activity were discontinued.

LO 3

Contrast direct and indirect costs and illustrate how they relate to a product or activity.

The classification of a cost as direct or indirect is significant only in the context of the cost's relationship to a product or activity. In fact, some costs are commonly treated as indirect costs even though they could be theoretically treated as direct costs. For example, for product costing purposes, some materials (e.g., glue, thread, staples, and grease) and labor (e.g., salaries of production supervisors, quality control inspectors, and maintenance workers) are usually treated as indirect costs because they cannot be easily traced or identified with individual units of production.

Costs for Cost Accounting Purposes

LO 4

Distinguish between product costs and period costs and identify the three components of product cost.

Cost accounting relates to the determination of product, process, or service costs. In addition to being useful for management planning and control, **product costs** are used by manufacturing firms and merchandising firms to determine inventory values and, when the product is sold, the amount of cost of goods sold. This is, of course, a financial accounting use of product cost. Even though service firms do not usually produce items for inventory, the costs of providing services also will be identified and analyzed for management planning and control purposes.

The product cost emphasis in the financial accounting chapters of this book focused on the inventory cost flow assumption (FIFO, LIFO, weighted-average) used by merchandising firms. Although these same cost flow issues also apply to manufacturing firms, our focus at this point is on the components of product cost for an entity that produces its own inventory. Product costing for a manufacturing firm is more complex than for a merchandising firm because making a product is more complex than buying an already finished product. However, the accounting concepts involved are the same. The cost of the product is recorded and reported as an asset (inventory) until the product is sold, at which point the cost is transferred to the income statement (cost of goods sold) as an expense to be matched with the revenue that resulted from the sale. The difference between a manufacturer and a merchandiser is illustrated in the following diagram:

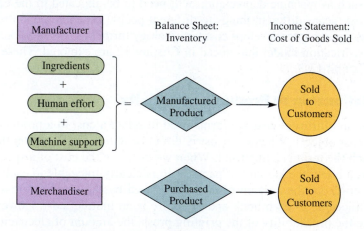

The cost associated with each of the manufacturing inputs is classified as raw materials, direct labor, or manufacturing overhead.

Raw materials are the ingredients of the product—the materials that are put into the production process and from which the finished product is made. The cost of raw materials includes the same items as the product cost of a merchandiser. The finished product of one process or company may be the raw material of another process or company. For example, corn is the raw material of a corn processor, and one of the processor's finished products may be corn syrup. The candy manufacturer uses the corn syrup as a raw material of its products.

Direct labor is the effort provided by workers who are directly involved with the manufacture of the product. For example, workers who perform machine operations on raw materials, workers who operate or control raw material conversion equipment (e.g., melters, mixers, heat treaters, coolers, and evaporators), and workers who assemble or package the product are directly involved in manufacturing activities. Their compensation costs would be considered direct labor costs.

Manufacturing overhead, or **overhead,** includes all manufacturing costs except those for raw materials and direct labor. Overhead is an indirect cost because it is not feasible to trace, or specifically relate, overhead items to individual products. Examples of overhead costs include factory utilities, indirect materials (e.g., nails, thread, glue) for the product, maintenance and housekeeping costs (both materials and labor), depreciation expense for the factory building and production equipment, and compensation of production managers and supervisors.

As the manufacturing process becomes more complex and technology-driven, overhead costs generally become more significant. For example, the development of robotic production methods has resulted in increased overhead costs. Thus, planning and controlling overhead has become a significantly important activity in many manufacturing firms.

Costs not included in inventory as product costs are reported in the income statement as incurred. These are the selling, general, and administrative costs (or operating expenses) of the firm that are not related to production activities. These items are called **period costs** because they are recorded as expenses in the accounting period in which they are incurred. Accounting for product and period costs is illustrated in Exhibit 13-4. Section I of the exhibit illustrates the effect of product and period costs on the financial statements when viewed as transactions in the horizontal model. Section II provides a cost flow view of the differences in accounting for product and period costs and their impact on the financial statements.

---

3. What does it mean that a cost is a direct, product, and variable cost?

4. What does it mean that product costs flow through inventory on their way to the income statement?

What Does It Mean?

Answers on pages 518

Cost Accounting Systems

Cost Accounting Systems—General Characteristics

Every manufacturing firm uses a cost accounting system to accumulate the cost of products made. Although some firms manufacture a single, unique product, one unit at a time, most firms produce large quantities of identical products in a more or less continuous process (i.e., production runs). As you can imagine, cost accounting systems vary considerably in terms of complexity because they are designed for the specific needs of individual companies, but virtually all systems have the general characteristics described here.

LO 5
Explain the general operation of a product costing system and illustrate how costs flow through the inventory accounts to cost of goods sold.

Exhibit 13-4	Accounting for Product and Period Costs

I. Viewed as transactions in the horizontal model:

	Balance Sheet			Income Statement
	Assets = Liabilities + Stockholders' equity			←Net income = Revenues − Expenses
Product costs: Become an asset until the product is sold				
Raw Materials	+ Inventory (when incurred)	+ Accounts Payable		
Direct Labor	+ Inventory (when incurred)	+ Accrued Wages Payable		
Manufacturing Overhead	+ Inventory (when incurred)	+ Other Accrued Liabilities		
	− Inventory (when sold)			− Cost of Goods Sold
Period costs: Nonproduct costs such as selling expense, advertising expense, and interest expense are recognized as expenses when incurred	+ Accounts Payable + Other Accrued Liabilities + Interest Payable			− Selling Expense − Advertising Expense − Interest Expense

II. Viewed as a flow of costs:

Cost	Balance Sheet	Income Statement
Product costs: Raw materials Direct labor Manufacturing overhead ⟶	Become an asset until the product is sold When the cost is transferred to the income statement as ⟶	Cost of goods sold (an expense)
Period costs: Nonproduct costs such as selling expenses advertising interest expense ⟶		Are recognized as expense when incurred

A manufacturing cost accounting system involves three inventory accounts: *Raw Materials, Work in Process,* and *Finished Goods.*

- **Raw Materials Inventory** holds the cost of parts, assemblies, and materials (e.g., for a sailboat manufacturer—glass fiber cloth, manufacturer—glass fiber cloth, sailcloth, deck fittings, and rope) that will be used in the manufacturing process.
- **Work in Process Inventory** is used to accumulate all of the manufacturing costs, including raw materials, direct labor, and manufacturing overhead while the product is being manufactured. When the manufacturing process is complete, the cost of the items made is transferred.
- **Finished Goods Inventory** holds the total cost of items manufactured that are now complete and available for sale.

At the end of the accounting period, each of these inventory accounts may have a balance. For Raw Materials and Finished Goods, the balance represents the cost of the items on hand at the end of the period. For Work in Process, the balance represents the sum of the costs incurred for products that were started in production but have not been completed at the end of the period. The Work in Process Inventory account balance will be relatively small (or zero) for production processes that are of short duration or that are cleared out at the end of the period (e.g., candy manufacturing or food processing). Work in Process Inventory is likely to exist for firms that have relatively long-duration manufacturing processes, but the account balance will usually be low relative to Raw Materials and Finished Goods. For Campbell Soup Company, Work in Process Inventory does not exist in the 2016 and 2017 balance sheets, which illustrates their relatively short manufacturing process (see the appendix).

When a manufactured item is sold, its cost is transferred from the balance sheet Finished Goods Inventory account to cost of goods sold in the income statement. Exhibit 13-5 illustrates and compares the flow of product costs for a manufacturing firm and a merchandising firm. Section I of the exhibit illustrates the transaction effect of the cost flows on the financial statements when viewed in the horizontal model. Section II provides a cost flow view and presents a logical way to think about the sequence of activities involved in the conversion of raw materials into a finished product that is ultimately sold.

Product Costing

The cost of a single unit of a manufactured product is determined by averaging the total material, labor, and overhead costs incurred in the manufacture of some quantity of the product (for example, the average cost per unit in a production run). Determining the raw material and direct labor costs is usually fairly easy, as direct costs they are clearly traceable to the product; raw material inventory usage records and time records for direct labor workers provide these data. It is the assignment of overhead costs, as indirect costs, that presents the challenge. Most cost systems apply overhead to production by using a single surrogate measure of overhead behavior—or at most very few. One commonly used measure of activity has been direct labor hours. Other measures include direct labor cost, machine hours, raw material usage, and the number of units made. The simplifying assumption is that overhead is incurred because products are being made, and the number of direct labor hours (or other base) used on a particular production run is a fair indicator of the overhead incurred for that production run.

LO 6
Calculate predetermined overhead application rates and demonstrate how they are used.

Exhibit 13-5   Flow of Cost Comparison—Manufacturer and Merchandiser

I. Viewed as transactions in the horizontal model:

A. Manufacturer:

Balance Sheet						Income Statement		
Assets	=	Liabilities	+	Stockholders' equity		←Net income	= Revenues −	Expenses

Raw Materials Inventory
+ The cost of raw materials *purchased* is recorded as an asset
− The cost of raw materials *used* in production is transferred to ⌐

Work in Process Inventory
+ Raw materials *used*
+ Direct labor *incurred*
+ Manufacturing overhead costs *applied*
− The cost of products *manufactured* and transferred to the warehouse is added to ⌐

Finished Goods Inventory
+ Cost of goods manufactured
− Cost of products sold

Liabilities:
+ Accounts Payable
+ Accrued Wages Payable
+ Other Accrued Liabilities

Income Statement:
− Cost of Goods Sold

B. Merchandiser:

Balance Sheet						Income Statement		

Merchandise Inventory
+ The cost of products *purchased*
− Cost of products sold

Liabilities:
+ Accounts Payable

Income Statement:
− Cost of Goods Sold

(continued)

II. Viewed as a flow of costs:
A. Manufacturer:

Balance Sheet

Raw Materials Inventory

The cost of raw materials *purchased* is recorded as an asset in raw materials inventory

The cost of raw materials *used* in production is moved from raw materials inventory to work in process inventory

Work in Process Inventory

Raw materials *used,* direct labor *incurred,* and manufacturing overhead costs *applied* are recorded as an asset in work in process inventory

The cost of products *manufactured* and transferred to the warehouse is removed from work in process inventory and added to finished goods inventory as

Finished Goods Inventory

Cost of goods manufactured

The cost of manufactured products *sold* is removed from finished goods inventory to become

Income Statement

Cost of Goods Sold

Cost of goods sold—an expense in the income statement

B. Merchandiser:

Balance Sheet

Merchandise Inventory

The cost of products *purchased* is recorded as an asset in merchandise inventory

The cost of products sold is *removed* from merchandise inventory to become

Income Statement

Cost of Goods Sold

Cost of goods sold—an expense in the income statement

Given this relationship, at the beginning of the year an estimate is made of both the total overhead expected to be incurred during the year and the total direct labor hours (or other base) expected to be used. Estimated total overhead cost is divided by the estimated total direct labor hours (or other base) to get a **predetermined overhead application rate** per direct labor hour (or other base).

To illustrate product costing and other cost and managerial accounting concepts, the hypothetical firm Cruisers Inc., a manufacturer of fiberglass sailboats, will be used. Exhibit 13-6 illustrates how the cost of a boat (the cost object) made during the month of April is calculated. Note the following product costing process steps:

1. The first step is the determination of the predetermined overhead application rate. This is shown in Section I of Exhibit 13-6.
2. Then overhead is assigned to specific production runs based on this predetermined overhead application rate. This cost assignment is illustrated in Section II of Exhibit 13-6. Note that if multiple overhead application bases are used, the estimated overhead cost associated with each base must be divided by the

Exhibit 13-6

Product Costing
Illustration

I. Calculation of predetermined overhead application rate:

Assumptions:

Cruisers Inc. incurs overhead costs in proportion to the number of direct labor hours worked; therefore, the predetermined overhead application rate is based on direct labor hours.

The estimated annual production level is 1,250 sailboats, and each sailboat should require 240 direct labor hours to complete.

Estimated total overhead cost to be incurred for the year: $4,200,000.

Estimated total direct labor hours to be worked in the year: 300,000.

$$\text{Overhead application rate} = \frac{\text{Estimated total overhead cost}}{\text{Estimated total direct labor hours}}$$
$$= \$4,200,000/300,000 \text{ hours}$$
$$= \$14/\text{direct labor hour}$$

II. Calculation of product cost:

Assumptions:

Cruisers Inc. produced 86 SeaCruiser sailboats during April; a total of 20,640 labor hours were worked, and the following costs were incurred:

Raw materials	$368,510
Direct labor	330,240

The cost of each boat is determined by dividing the total manufacturing costs incurred by the number of boats produced:

Raw materials	$368,510
Direct labor	330,240
Overhead (20,640 direct labor hours × the overhead application rate of $14/hour)	288,960
Total manufacturing cost incurred	$987,710
Cost per boat ($987,710/86 boats)	$ 11,485

Working with manufacturing overhead for product costing can be confusing. Thinking of this process as one of cost pooling and assignment, as illustrated earlier in the chapter, will help you. The purpose is to assign an appropriate amount of overhead cost (otherwise indirect and therefore not traceable) to each sailboat (a cost object) that Cruisers Inc. manufactures. Direct labor hours (the cost driver) incurred to produce each sailboat style will determine the amount of overhead (from the cost pool) that will be assigned to each sailboat.

Study

Suggestion

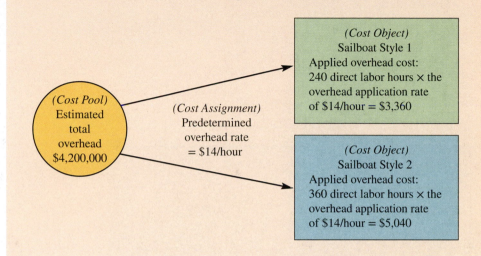

(Cost Pool) Estimated total overhead $4,200,000

(Cost Assignment) Predetermined overhead rate = $14/hour

(Cost Object) Sailboat Style 1 Applied overhead cost: 240 direct labor hours × the overhead application rate of $14/hour = $3,360

(Cost Object) Sailboat Style 2 Applied overhead cost: 360 direct labor hours × the overhead application rate of $14/hour = $5,040

estimated usage of each base to develop the separate **overhead application rates.** For example, overhead may be applied based on 140 percent of direct labor cost, plus $3.10 per pound of a certain raw material used in the production process.

3. Next, total manufacturing costs incurred is determined by accumulating the raw materials, direct labor, and overhead cost applied to the units produced.

4. Finally, the total manufacturing costs incurred are then averaged over the number of units produced to get the cost of a single unit.

Study Exhibit 13-6 to see how cost components are accumulated and then averaged to get the cost of a single unit.

Although the costing process involves estimates and provides an overall average, many firms do an excellent job of estimating both total overhead costs and total activity, resulting in quite accurate overhead application and product costing. Because the predetermined overhead application rate calculation is based on estimates, at the end of the year there will be a difference between the total overhead costs actually incurred and the costs applied to production during the year. This difference is called **overapplied overhead** or **underapplied overhead.** At the end of the year, if the overapplied or underapplied overhead is small relative to total overhead costs incurred, it is transferred to cost of goods sold. If it is material in amount, it is allocated between inventories and cost of goods sold in proportion to the total overhead included in each. On a monthly basis, the overapplied or underapplied overhead is carried forward in the Manufacturing Overhead account. The reason for this is that estimates for the whole year were used to calculate the predetermined overhead application rate, and variations in cost and activity that occur in one month may be offset in a subsequent month. Thus, a better matching of revenue

Exhibit 13-7   Cruisers Inc. Flow of Costs for April

I. Viewed as transactions in the horizontal model:

	Assets	=	Liabilities	+	Stockholders' equity	← Net income	=	Revenues	−	Expenses
Raw Materials Inventory										
(1) Beginning balance	126,900									
Cost of raw materials *purchased* in April	+347,860		+ Accounts Payable 347,860							
(2) Cost of raw materials *used*	−368,510									
Ending balance	106,250									
Manufacturing Overhead										
Beginning balance (overapplied balance at March 31)	(1,873)									
(4) Actual manufacturing costs *incurred* during April	+292,518		+ Various Liabilities 292,518˙							
(5) Manufacturing overhead costs *applied* at a predetermined overhead application rate	−288,960									
Ending balance (underapplied)	1,685									
Work in Process Inventory										
(2) Beginning balance	0									
Raw materials *used*	+368,510									
(3) Direct labor *incurred*	+330,240		+ Accrued Wages Payable 330,240*							
(5) Manufacturing overhead costs *applied*	+288,960									

(continued)

Balance Sheet				Income Statement			
Assets	=	Liabilities	+	Stockholders' equity	←Net income	= Revenues	− Expenses
(6) Cost of goods *manufactured* and transferred to finished goods	−987,710						
Ending balance	0						
Finished Goods Inventory							
Beginning balance	243,820						
(6) Cost of goods *manufactured*	+987,710						
(7) Cost of products *sold*	−1,103,930						− Cost of Goods Sold 1,103,930
Ending balance	127,600						

Explanation of transactions:

(1) Purchase of raw materials on account.

(2) Cost of raw materials used is transferred to Work in Process.

(3) Direct labor costs for the month increase Work in Process and increase Wages Payable.*

(4) Actual manufacturing overhead costs incurred for the month increase Manufacturing Overhead and increase Accounts Payable, Accrued Wages Payable, or Other Accrued Liabilities.*

(5) Manufacturing Overhead is applied to Work in Process using the predetermined overhead application rate and the actual activity base (direct labor hours, for example).

(6) Cost of goods manufactured is transferred from Work in Process to Finished Goods.

(7) Cost of goods sold is transferred from Finished Goods inventory to Cost of Goods Sold.

*Some transactions may result in a decrease of Cash if cash payment occurs at the time of the transaction.

(continued)

Exhibit 13-7

II. Viewed as a flow of costs:

Raw Materials

Beginning balance	126,900
Raw materials purchased (1) 347,860	(2) 368,510
Ending balance	106,250

Work in Process

Beginning balance	0
Raw materials used (2) 368,510	Cost of goods manufactured (6) 987,710
Direct labor (3) 330,240	
Manufacturing overhead applied (5) 288,960	
Ending balance	0

Finished Goods

Beginning balance	243,820
Cost of goods manufactured (6) 987,710	Cost of goods sold (7) 1,103,930
Ending balance	127,600

Cost of Goods Sold

(7) 1,103,930	

Accounts Payable, Accrued Wages Payable, Other Accrued Liabilities, or Cash

	(1) 347,860
	(3) 330,240
	(4) 292,518

Manufacturing Overhead

Beginning balance	1,873
Actual manufacturing overhead costs incurred (4) 292,518	Manufacturing overhead applied (5) 288,960
	Ending balance (underapplied) 1,685

Note: Transaction numbers (1), etc. refer to explanations at the end of Part I of the exhibit, which are printed on the preceding page.

and expense occurs if the overapplied or underapplied overhead adjustment is made only at the end of the year.

Exhibit 13-7 illustrates the flow of these product costs through the accounts of Cruisers Inc. for April. Note the use of the Manufacturing Overhead account—this is an account that functions as an asset-type clearing account. *Actual* manufacturing overhead costs incurred are recorded as increases (debits) in this account, and the manufacturing overhead *applied* to Work in Process is a reduction (credit) to the account. The Manufacturing Overhead account will not have any balance at the beginning or end of the year because, as already stated, overapplied or underapplied overhead is transferred to Cost of Goods Sold or allocated between Work in Process, Finished Goods, and Cost of Goods Sold. However, at month-ends during the year, the account is likely to have a relatively small overapplied or underapplied balance. This case is illustrated in Exhibit 13-7.

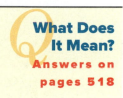

5. What does it mean that manufacturing overhead is applied to inventory?
6. What does it mean when there is underapplied overhead at the end of the year?

What Does It Mean?
Answers on pages 518

Statement of Cost of Goods Manufactured

Manufacturing costs can be summarized and reported in a **statement of cost of goods manufactured.** Such a statement using amounts for Cruisers for April is illustrated in Exhibit 13-8. Although it was assumed that there were no beginning or ending inventories for work in process, Exhibit 13-8 illustrates how work in process balances would be reported in this statement.

LO 7
Prepare and interpret a statement of cost of goods manufactured.

To calculate cost of goods sold for April, the cost of goods manufactured is added to the beginning inventory of finished goods to get the cost of goods available for

CRUISERS INC. Statement of Cost of Goods Manufactured For the Month of April		
Raw materials:		
Inventory, March 31	$ 126,900	
Purchases during April	347,860	
Raw materials available for use	$ 474,760	
Less: Inventory, April 30	(106,250)	
Cost of raw materials used		$368,510
Direct labor cost incurred during April		330,240
Manufacturing overhead applied during April		288,960
Total manufacturing costs incurred during April		$987,710
Add: Work in process inventory, March 31		-0-
Less: Work in process inventory, April 30		-0-
Cost of goods manufactured during April		$987,710

Exhibit 13-8

Statement of Cost of Goods Manufactured

sale. The cost of the ending inventory of finished goods is then subtracted from goods available for sale to arrive at cost of goods sold as illustrated in the cost of goods sold model:

Beginning inventory	$ 243,820
Cost of goods manufactured	987,710
Cost of goods available for sale	$1,231,530
Less: Ending inventory	(127,600)
Cost of goods sold	$1,103,930

To summarize, product costs are attached to the product being manufactured and are treated as an expense when the product is sold (or is lost, becomes worthless from obsolescence, or is otherwise no longer an asset to the firm). Period costs—selling, general, and administrative expenses—are reported in the income statement of the period in which such costs are incurred. *Another way to distinguish between product and period costs is to think of product costs as manufacturing costs and period costs as nonmanufacturing costs.*

In the Exhibit 13-7 illustration of the flow of product costs for Cruisers, the end result was that cost of goods sold was $1,103,930 for the month of April. Revenues and nonmanufacturing (i.e., period) costs were omitted from the transaction data in Exhibit 13-7 for the sake of clarity. An income statement for Cruisers, using assumed amounts, is presented in Exhibit 13-9. Notice that selling, general, and administrative expenses represent a significant portion of the total expenses. Nonoperating expenses reported for interest and income taxes also are significant. You should keep these relationships in mind as you study the next two sections of this chapter. Each of the alternative cost accounting systems (job order costing and process costing) described in these sections emphasizes the flow of product costs and determination of cost of goods sold.

Cost of goods sold represents the largest expense for most manufacturing firms and overall profitability especially depends on the firm's ability to control these costs. This point is illustrated in Campbell Soup Company's consolidated statements of earnings, which appear in the appendix. In 2015, net sales were reported at $8.082 billion

Exhibit 13-9

Income Statement

CRUISERS INC. Income Statement For the Month of April	
Sales	$2,012,400
Cost of goods sold	(1,103,930)
Gross profit	$ 908,470
Selling, general, and administrative expenses	(562,110)
Income from operations	$ 346,360
Interest expense	(78,420)
Income before taxes	$ 267,940
Income tax expense	(93,779)
Net income	$ 174,161

and by 2017 had declined $172 million to $7.890 billion. Over the same three years, however, the cost of product sold, as a percent of net sales, improved from 65.6 percent of net sales to 61.2 percent, indicating that the cost of product sold expense was better controlled, improving 4.4 percent of net sales. This product cost savings means that for every sales dollar generated, an extra 4.4 cents remained as gross profit in 2017 and while at first glance a 4.4 cent improvement may not seem all that impressive, but on $7.890 billion in net sales it contributed to an increase of $277 million in gross profit in 2017 over 2015, and remember that increase in gross profit was realized over a three-year period when net sales declined by $172 million.

Cost Accounting Systems—Job Order Costing, Process Costing, and Hybrid Costing

The general cost accounting system illustrated in the prior section must be adapted to fit the manufacturing environment of the entity. A **job order costing system** is used when discrete products, such as sailboats, are manufactured. Each production run is treated as a separate "job." Costs are accumulated for each job, as illustrated in Exhibit 13-6 for Cruisers' production of 86 SeaCruiser sailboats, and the cost per unit is determined by dividing the total costs incurred by the number of units produced. During any accounting period, a number of jobs, or production runs of different products, may be worked on. For any job or production run, costs are accumulated, and the cost per unit of product made is calculated as illustrated for the SeaCruiser sailboat.

When the manufacturing environment involves essentially homogeneous products that are made in a more or less continuous process, frequently involving several departments, it is not feasible to accumulate product cost by job, so a **process costing system** is used. The processing of corn into meal, starch, and syrup is an example of an activity for which process costing would be applicable. The objectives of process costing and job order costing are the same: to assign raw material, direct labor, and manufacturing overhead costs to products and to provide a means to compute the unit cost of each item produced. In process costing, costs are accumulated by department (rather than by job) and are assigned to the products that are processed through the department.

The accumulation of costs by department is relatively straightforward, but the existence of partially completed work in process inventories adds a complexity to the determination of the number of units of product over which departmental costs are to be spread. For example, assume the following:

- During October, 100,000 completed units were transferred from the assembly department to the finishing department
- At the end of October an additional 15,000 units were still in process, which were only 50 percent completed.

Because of the likelihood of a certain number of units remaining in process at the end of any given period, for process costing, production during the month is stated in **equivalent units of production**—the number of units that would have been produced if all production efforts during the month had resulted in completed products, calculated for October as follows:

$$\text{Assembly department equivalent units of production} = \text{Units completed and transferred} + (\text{units in process} \times \text{percent complete})$$
$$= 100,000 + (15,000 \times 50\%)$$
$$= 107,500 \text{ units}$$

In this example, the costs incurred by the assembly department during the period (including costs in the beginning inventory) would then be spread over 107,500 units to get the weighted-average cost per equivalent unit for this department. This is the cost per unit for items transferred to the finishing department (100,000 units) and the cost used to value the assembly department's ending inventory (7,500 equivalent units). Costs of subsequent departments include costs transferred in from prior departments. Ultimately, all production costs are transferred to Finished Goods Inventory after the final department completes the production cycle.

As manufacturing firms have sought to increase efficiency and to lower costs in recent years, production processes have been developed that mix elements of job order and continuous process manufacturing environments. Whether labeled flexible manufacturing, batch manufacturing, just-in-time manufacturing, or something else, most of these processes involve streamlined work flow, tighter inventory controls, and extensive use of automated equipment. Hybrid costing systems have evolved for these processes. Hybrid cost accounting systems mix elements of job order and process costing systems to accomplish the objective of assigning manufacturing costs to units produced. It is important to recognize that cost accounting systems will change, as illustrated with the evolution of lean accounting described in the Chapter 13 introduction, in response to technology advances in the manufacturing process.

Cost Accounting Methods—Absorption Costing and Direct Costing

LO 8

Explain and illustrate the difference between absorption and direct (or variable) costing.

The cost accounting method described thus far is that of **absorption costing** because all manufacturing costs incurred are absorbed into the cost of the product. An alternative method, called **direct costing** or **variable costing**, assigns only variable costs to products; fixed manufacturing costs are treated as operating expenses of the period in which they are incurred. (Variable and fixed costs were described in Chapter 12.) Absorption costing must be used for financial reporting and income tax purposes because fixed manufacturing overhead is considered part of the cost of a product. However, some managers are willing to incur the additional expense of using direct (or variable) costing for internal planning and control purposes because it results in product and inventory values that reflect the more direct relationship between total cost and volume of activity, which is important in CVP analysis and decision making.

The distinction between absorption costing and direct costing focuses on *manufacturing overhead* costs only. Raw material and direct labor are always product costs, and selling, general, and administrative expenses are always treated as operating expenses of the period in which they are incurred. Under absorption costing, *both* variable and fixed manufacturing overhead are considered product costs and are applied to work in process. Under direct costing, however, only variable manufacturing overhead is a product cost applied to work in process; fixed manufacturing overhead is treated as a period cost and recorded as an operating expense when incurred. The reasoning behind this treatment is that fixed manufacturing cost is really the cost of having manufacturing capacity available for any given period. Underutilized capacity in a period cannot be recovered in subsequent periods. Therefore these fixed capacity costs should be treated as period costs. Exhibit 13-10 provides a cost flow illustration of these alternative methods.

The significance of the distinction between absorption costing and direct costing is a function of any change in ending inventory. If inventories have increased, under

Exhibit 13-10   Cost Flows—Absorption Costing and Direct (Variable) Costing

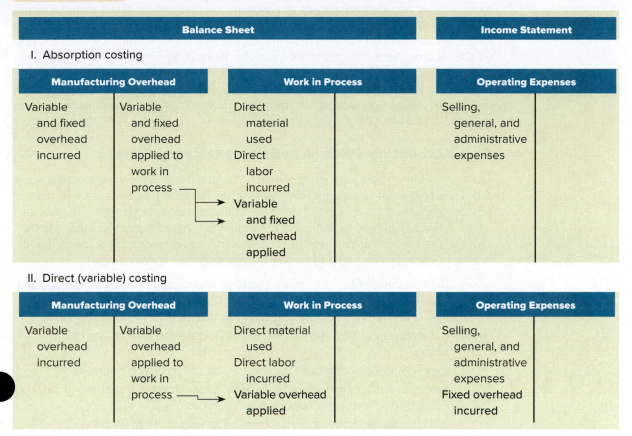

absorption costing the fixed manufacturing overhead related to the inventory increase is an asset in the balance sheet, but under direct costing it is an expense in the income statement. Thus, when inventories increase, expenses are lower and profits are higher under absorption costing than under direct costing. The opposite is true when inventories decrease. These characteristics are summarized:

	Reporting Differences when Using Absorption Costing vs. Direct Costing	
Production to Sales Results	Units in Ending Inventory	Operating Income
Units produced = Units sold	No change	No change
Units produced > Units sold	Increase	Higher
Units produced < Units sold	Decrease	Lower

Direct costing advocates point out that absorption costing gives an erroneous profit signal to managers and question whether higher profits should result in periods when the firm's production has exceeded sales and inventories increase. Can you now appreciate how important it is when evaluating profit performance of a manufacturing organization to consider the impact of any related inventory change?

For financial reporting and income tax purposes, firms that use direct costing must make a year-end adjustment to reclassify that part of the fixed manufacturing overhead incurred during the year that relates to the ending inventory. The effect of this reclassification is to decrease the balance of the Operating Expense account on the income statement and to increase the Work in Process and Finished Goods Inventory account balances on the balance sheet. The amount of fixed manufacturing overhead to be reclassified can be calculated fairly easily based on the proportion of the variable cost of ending inventory to the total variable manufacturing costs incurred during the year.

Cost Accounting Systems in Service Organizations

The discussion of cost accounting systems has emphasized the need to collect and assign costs in manufacturing environments. But the reality of competing in today's service- and information-oriented economy is that nonmanufacturing businesses also have a fundamental need to accurately determine the cost of the services they provide. Think about the unique sequence of service activities represented by each of the following examples when trying to answer the question "What does it cost?"

- The accounting firm of Ernst & Young provides audit services for clients, and many professionals from the firm participate in these engagements.
- FedEx delivers your priority package to a client by 10 a.m. tomorrow morning.
- The emergency room at County General Hospital treats an auto accident victim.
- Tony's Auto Repair replaces the transmission of a Buick Rendevous.
- American Airlines operates a St. Louis–Chicago route that carries passengers multiple times every day between the two cities.
- ADP processes a small business's payroll checks every two weeks.

Regardless of the type of services a company provides, the basic cost accounting principles are identical to those of manufacturing firms—certain costs will be direct to a particular service activity being measured and other costs will be common to all services provided by the organization. For Tony's Auto Repair, a system similar to job order costing described earlier in the chapter would be utilized to capture the cost of parts (direct materials) and the mechanic's time (direct labor), as well as to apply a share of the shop's indirect costs (overhead) to each repair order. Many software companies specialize in providing cost accounting solutions for specific service industries that not only efficiently collect direct time and materials costs and provide a basis for applying overhead but also automate many other important activities, such as estimating job costs and job scheduling.

Activity-Based Costing

LO 9

Perform activity-based costing and describe activity-based management.

Overhead costs (i.e. those costs that can't be easily and directly traced to a particular cost object) have become an increasingly significant part of product cost, and managers have needed higher-quality cost information to permit greater control and better responses to the pressures of increased competition. R&D, design, marketing, distribution, and customer service costs in each stage of the value chain have become as important as product costs in this environment. As a result, the application of overhead on the basis of a few broad rates based on direct labor hours and/or machine hours has been replaced in many firms by an **activity-based costing (ABC)** system.

An ABC system involves identifying the activity that causes the incurrence of a cost; this activity is known as a **cost driver.** Examples of cost drivers are machine setup, quality inspection, production order preparation, and materials handling activities. The number of times each activity is performed and the total cost of the activity are estimated, and a predetermined cost per activity is calculated. These activity-based costs are applied to products, manufacturing processes, and even administrative and marketing efforts. There are likely to be significantly more cost drivers than direct labor hours or machine hours. The development of an ABC system is a complex process involving considerable analysis and a significant investment. Comprehensive computerized databases are a necessary prerequisite to effective activity-based costing.

ABC systems have led to more accurate costing than traditional overhead application methods and have supported more effective management of the production, administrative, and marketing functions. Exhibit 13-11 presents an example of activity-based costing for the manufacturing overhead related to the SeaCruiser sailboats previously costed in Exhibit 13-6. Notice that the $316,640 of manufacturing overhead applied to the production of the 86 SeaCruiser sailboats in April using activity-based costing is different from the $288,960 applied (using a rate based on direct labor hours) in Exhibit 13-6.

Activity-based costing should be especially emphasized in organizations where multiple products require differing amounts of manufacturing and other value chain activities. Given a basic difference in the complexity of each product, the more diverse an organization's product mix is, the more inaccurate it will be to utilize an

Exhibit 13-11

Activity-Based Costing Illustration

I. Manufacturing overhead cost drivers, and estimated annual costs and activity levels, for Cruisers Inc.:

Activity (Cost Driver)	Estimated Annual Cost	Estimated Total Activity	Predetermined Rate per Unit of Activity
Production order preparation	$ 135,000	180 orders	$ 750/order
Hull and deck mold setup	2,140,000	1,000 setups	2,140/setup
Raw material acquisition	650,000	2,600 receipts	250/receipt
Material handling	450,000	9,000 moves	50/move
Quality inspection	750,000	6,000 inspections	125/inspection
Cleanup and waste disposal	75,000	250 loads	300/load
Total manufacturing overhead	$4,200,000		

II. Actual activity levels required to produce 86 SeaCruiser sailboats in April and manufacturing overhead applied:

Activity (Cost Driver)	Activity Required	Rate per Unit of Activity	Overhead Applied
Production order preparation	11 orders	$750/order	$ 8,250
Hull and deck mold setup	86 setups	2,140/setup	184,040
Raw material acquisition	185 receipts	250/receipt	46,250
Material handling	610 moves	50/move	30,500
Quality inspection	340 inspections	125/inspection	42,500
Cleanup and waste disposal	17 loads	300/load	5,100
Total manufacturing overhead applied			$316,640

overhead application rate based on a single cost driver, such as direct labor hours. Cost distortions will likely occur because a single cost driver too narrowly defines the overhead application process. Products that are less complex to manufacture will likely be assigned a larger share of overhead as compared to products that are more complex, which in turn will likely be assigned a smaller share of overhead.

FYI

The Activity Based Costing Association (ABCA) is an association of companies and organizations with activity-based costing interests. The association conducts benchmarking studies to identify practices that improve the overall operations of the members. ABCA's mission is to identify "best in class" activity-based costing processes, which lead member companies to exceptional performance when implemented. See abcbenchmarking.com for additional information about the objectives, services, and activities of the association.

To illustrate the risk of **cost distortion** when applying overhead by using a single cost driver, information from Cruisers, Inc., will be revisited and the cost for a second product, canoes, will be analyzed. Exhibit 13-12 extends the examples presented earlier in Exhibit 13-6, which calculated an overhead application rate of $14/direct labor hour, and Exhibit 13-11, which developed activity-based rates for applying manufacturing overhead. Notice in Exhibit 13-12 that a considerable shift takes place in the amount of manufacturing overhead applied to sailboats when Cruisers moves from a single cost driver (direct labor hours) to activity-based costing rates. Using direct labor hours, sailboats are assigned $336,000 of the manufacturing overhead and canoes receive $182,000, which represent 65 percent and 35 percent of the total $518,000. Exhibit 13-12 illustrates how activity-based costing reflects the difference in activity required for the production of the more complex sailboats and correspondingly assigns $43,270 more, or a total of 73 percent, of the manufacturing overhead cost pool to the sailboats produced. This difference is significant for both product lines and has important implications when considering how this cost information will ultimately be used by the management team at Cruisers to set selling prices, calculate ROI, evaluate the performance of the production managers, and more.

The advantage of ABC is that it more clearly focuses on the activities causing cost, and it directs management attention to those activities. For example, in analyzing the makeup of what appears to be a very high setup cost, management of Cruisers,

Exhibit 13-12

Cost Distortion
Illustration

I. Manufacturing overhead applied on the basis of direct labor hours:

Assumptions (as modified from Exhibit 13-6):

Cruisers Inc. estimates its production level at 1,250 sailboats and 5,000 canoes. The canoes are produced five times during the year in production runs of 1,000 canoes.

Each sailboat requires 240 direct labor hours and each canoe requires 13 direct labor hours to complete.

Overhead is applied at the rate of $14/direct labor hour. (Assumes total overhead is now estimated to be $5,110,000.)

During May, 100 sailboats were produced, requiring 24,000 labor hours, and 1,000 canoes were produced, requiring 13,000 labor hours.

Calculation of applied overhead:

Sailboats (24,000 direct labor hours × $14/hour)	....	$336,000
Canoes (13,000 direct labor hours × $14/hour)	....	182,000
Total overhead applied	....	$518,000

II. Manufacturing overhead applied using activity-based costing:

(Activity rates calculated in Exhibit 13-11 are used):

Calculation of applied overhead for 100 sailboats:

Activity (Cost Driver)	Activity Required	Rate per Unit of Activity	Overhead Applied
Production order preparation	13 orders	$ 750/order	$ 9,750
Hull deck and mold setup	103 setups	2,140/setup	220,420
Raw material acquisition	222 receipts	250/receipt	55,500
Material handling	732 moves	50/move	36,600
Quality inspection	408 inspections	125/inspection	51,000
Cleanup and waste disposal	20 loads	300/load	6,000
Overhead applied to sailboats			$379,270

Calculation of applied overhead for 1,000 canoes:

Activity (Cost Driver)	Activity Required	Rate per Unit of Activity	Overhead Applied
Production order preparation	1 order	$ 750/order	$ 750
Production run setup	1 setup	2,140/setup	2,140
Raw material acquisition	10 receipts	250/receipt	2,500
Material handling	50 moves	50/move	2,500
Quality inspection	1,000 inspections	125/inspection	125,000
Cleanup and waste disposal	20 loads	300/load	6,000
Overhead applied to canoes			$138,890
Total overhead applied			$518,160

Inc., might develop alternative setup methods that would be less costly. It also might be fruitful to study the material acquisition system to try to make that system more efficient or reduce the number of times raw materials need to be received. To the extent that management can determine cost drivers and understand why and how costs are incurred, the effectiveness of cost controls and the efficiency with which the organization operates can be improved.

Activity-based management (ABM) is the use of activity-based costing information to support the decision-making process. Managers seeking to achieve the broad range of organizational objectives encompassed in the value chain use ABM. The application of this tool is limited only by the collective imagination of the management team and can be relevant to efforts focusing on customer satisfaction, operational productivity and efficiency, product or process design, product mix, and profit and performance measurement, to name just a few. The extension of ABC to these value chain efforts has led to better decisions, and many nonmanufacturing organizations such as banks, professional organizations, technology firms, health care providers, and the government have realized the benefits of ABC as described in Business in Practice—ABC/M and the Municipal Transport Company of Madrid (EMT).

Business in
Practice

ABC/M and the Municipal Transport Company of Madrid (EMT)

Numerous software providers dot the technology landscape offering activity-based costing/management (ABC/M) solutions. SAS is one of the world's leaders in business analytics software, with a goal of providing breakthrough technology to help organizations transform the way they do business. A centerpiece of the SAS Performance Management solution, which includes ABC/M as part of Cost and Profitability Management, is a focus on understanding what drives costs and value in an organization, and the fundamental necessity to control costs. SAS positions its Cost and Profitability Management product to enhance business decision making by providing more accurate cost modeling. The SAS website (sas.com) presents many descriptions of how SAS activity-based management has helped organizations maximize profits, contain costs, and improve operational efficiencies. Following are excerpts from the Success Story titled "How to Know the Real Cost, Efficiency and Profitability of Each Activity," which explains how the Municipal Transport Company of Madrid (EMT) benefits from activity-based cost management:

The Municipal Transport Company of Madrid (EMT) needed to get a clearer view of its costs—which of its operations were profitable, and which weren't? It needed to develop a more precise cost system so it could accurately assess the direct and indirect costs of its activities and transfer those costs to each of the individual lines and buses.

To strengthen its cost control systems, EMT launched an activity-based costing project using SAS Cost and Profitability Management. As a result, it can now obtain accurate information on costs and profitability of each line and bus.

Before this project, EMT—which is responsible for Madrid's public bus transportation—didn't have sufficient cost information to make informed decisions. Its financial control system provided only aggregate information, without much detail. With SAS Cost and Profitability Management, EMT can identify which processes are consuming the most resources, or if any of the activities have costs that outweigh their benefits.

This comprehensive analysis of costs helps EMT make better operational decisions, such as expanding the number of buses on a particular route or improving the customer services and optimizing scarce resources. SAS Activity-Based Management has great flexibility and analytics, which allows EMT to compare costs by different variables such as bus model, operations center, lines and shifts, the profitability of these lines in each time slot, or cost per kilometer of passenger transported.

EMT now understands the costs of its services and activities. This information allows it to improve efficiency by optimizing resources and, therefore, to meet its commitment to provide a quality urban transportation service.

What Does It Mean?

Answer on page 518

7. What does it mean when an activity-based costing system is used?

Demonstration Problem

The Demonstration Problem walkthrough for this chapter is available in *Connect*.

Summary

Cost management is the process of using cost information from the accounting system to manage the activities of the organization. Accurate and timely cost information is critical to the success of the decision-making process. The value chain of the organization is the sequence of functions and related activities that adds value for the customer over the life of a product or service. Viewing the organization in terms of its value chain highlights many questions that must be answered about activities through the analysis and management of the activity cost. **(LO 1, 2)**

Cost accumulation is the process of collecting and recording transaction data through the accounting system. The total amount of cost accumulated by the system is then logically categorized in different ways, such as by production department, which is referred to as a cost pool. Cost assignment is the process of attributing an appropriate amount of cost in the cost pool to each cost object. Costs can be classified as direct or indirect, relative to a particular product or activity (a cost object). **(LO 3)**

Cost accounting systems distinguish between product costs and period costs. Product costs for a merchandising firm are the costs associated with products held for sale. Product costs for a manufacturing firm include raw materials, direct labor, and manufacturing overhead. Period costs, such as selling, general, and administrative expenses, are reported as expenses in the fiscal period in which they are incurred. **(LO 4)**

Cost accounting systems account for the flow of product costs into Work in Process Inventory, the transfer of cost of goods manufactured out of Work in Process Inventory into Finished Goods Inventory, and finally to Cost of Goods Sold when the product is sold. One of the especially challenging objectives of the cost accounting system is to assign manufacturing overhead to products produced. The cost of a single unit of product is the sum of the costs incurred to produce a quantity of units divided by the number of units produced. **(LO 5)**

Overhead is applied to production by using a predetermined overhead application rate, such as direct labor hours. Other bases include direct labor cost, machine hours, raw material usage, and the number of units made. At the beginning of the year an estimate is made of the total overhead expected to be incurred during the year and the total direct labor hours (or other base) expected to be used. Estimated total overhead cost is divided by the estimated total direct labor hours (or other base) to get the predetermined overhead rate. **(LO 6)**

Manufacturing costs are summarized in a statement of cost of goods manufactured. To calculate cost of goods manufactured, the raw material used, direct labor incurred, and manufacturing overhead applied during the period are added to the beginning inventory of work in process to calculate total manufacturing costs. The ending work in process inventory is then subtracted from total manufacturing costs to arrive at cost of goods manufactured. **(LO 7)**

The difference between absorption costing and direct (or variable) costing is in the accounting for fixed manufacturing overhead. In absorption costing, fixed manufacturing overhead is a product cost. In direct (or variable) costing, fixed manufacturing overhead is a period cost. **(LO 8)**

The increased significance of overhead costs has led to the development of activity-based costing as a means of more accurately assigning overhead to production by relating costs to the activities that drive them. **(LO 9)**

Key Terms and Concepts

absorption costing (p. 496)   A product costing method by which both variable and fixed manufacturing costs are included in product costs.

activity-based costing (ABC) (p. 498)   The process of accumulating manufacturing overhead costs by production support activity (e.g., machine setup) and then applying manufacturing overhead to production based on the activity required for each job or product.

activity-based management (ABM) (p. 501)   Use of activity-based costing information by managers to support the decision-making process.

cost accounting (p. 476)   A subset of both financial and managerial accounting that relates to the accumulation and determination of product, process, or service costs.

cost accumulation (p. 480)   The process of collecting and recording transaction data through the accounting system.

cost assignment (p. 480)   The process of allocating an amount of cost to a cost object.

cost distortion (p. 500)   A shift in the relative amount of manufacturing overhead costs applied to the mix of products produced that occurs because a single cost driver application rate is used instead of activity-based costing rates.

cost driver (p. 499)   An activity that causes the incurrence of a cost.

cost management (p. 478)   The process of using cost information to assess and manage the activities of the organization.

cost object (p. 480)   Any reference point for which cost is measured.

cost pool (p. 480)   Costs that have been accumulated for assignment to a cost object.

direct cost (p. 481)   A cost directly related to a product or activity; the cost would not be incurred if the product or activity were discontinued.

direct costing (p. 496)   A product costing method in which only variable manufacturing costs are included in product cost. Sometimes called *variable costing*.

direct labor (p. 483)   Effort provided by workers who are directly involved in the manufacture of a product.

equivalent units of production (p. 495)   In a process costing system, the number of units that would have been produced if all production efforts during the period had resulted in completed products.

Finished Goods Inventory (p. 485)   Inventory account applicable to goods available for sale to customers.

indirect cost (p. 481)   A cost that is indirectly related to the product or activity under consideration; the cost would continue to be incurred if the product or activity were discontinued.

job order costing system (p. 495)   A product costing system used when discrete products, or "jobs," are manufactured.

manufacturing overhead (p. 483)   All manufacturing costs except those classified as raw materials or direct labor.

overapplied overhead (p. 489)   A credit balance in the Manufacturing Overhead account that results from applied overhead in excess of actual overhead costs.

overhead (p. 483)   Another term for *manufacturing overhead*.

overhead application rate (p. 489)   The rate used to allocate overhead to specific production runs. See *predetermined overhead application rate*.

period costs (p. 483)   Noninventoriable costs, including *selling, general, and administrative expenses,* that relate to an accounting period.

predetermined overhead application rate (p. 488)   The rate per unit of activity (e.g., direct labor hour) used to apply manufacturing overhead to work in process.

process costing system (p. 495)   A costing system used to accumulate costs for a production process that is more or less continuous, frequently involving several departments.

product costs (p. 482) Inventoriable costs including raw materials, direct labor, and manufacturing overhead.

raw materials (p. 482) The ingredients of a product.

Raw Materials Inventory (p. 485) Inventory account applicable to materials ready for the production process.

statement of cost of goods manufactured (p. 493) A supplementary financial statement that supports cost of goods sold, which is an element of the income statement. This statement summarizes raw material, direct labor, and manufacturing overhead costs during the period.

underapplied overhead (p. 489) A debit balance in the Manufacturing Overhead account that results from actual overhead costs in excess of applied overhead.

value chain (p. 478) The sequence of functions (R&D, design, production, marketing, distribution, and customer service) and related activities that, over the life of a product or service, adds value for the customer.

variable costing (p. 496) A product costing method in which only variable manufacturing costs are included in product cost. Sometimes called *direct costing*.

Work in Process Inventory (p. 485) Inventory account for the costs (raw material, direct labor, and manufacturing overhead) of items that are in the process of being manufactured.

Mini-Exercises

connect

All applicable Mini-Exercises are available in *Connect*.

Total manufacturing costs Acme Inc. incurs the following costs during May:

Sales expense	$11,500	Administrative expense	$21,500
Direct labor	26,000	Plant depreciation	6,200
Factory supplies	2,500	Indirect labor	8,000
Advertising	2,800	Utilities	10,000*
Raw material used	18,000		

*75% of this amount relates to the factory.

Mini-Exercise 13.1

LO 3, 4

Required:
Calculate Acme's total manufacturing costs for May.

Calculate predetermined overhead rate and unit cost Bentley estimates manufacturing overhead of $1,200,000 for 2019 and will apply overhead to units produced based on 400,000 machine hours. During 2019, Bentley used $1,280,000 of raw materials, paid $1,620,000 of direct labor, generated 420,000 machine hours, and produced 1,000,000 units.

Mini-Exercise 13.2

LO 5, 6

Required:
Calculate Bentley's predetermined overhead rate and cost per unit of production for 2019.

Underapplied overhead analysis Tyler Company applies manufacturing overhead to production at the rate of $4 per direct labor hour and ended August with $12,000 underapplied overhead. Actual manufacturing overhead incurred for August amounted to $88,000.

Mini-Exercise 13.3

LO 6

Required:
How many direct labor hours did Tyler Company incur during August?

**Mini-Exercise
13.4
LO 7**

Statement of cost of goods manufactured The following information is from ABC Company's general ledger: Beginning and ending inventories, respectively, for raw materials were $12,000 and $15,000 and for work in process were $30,000 and $33,000. Raw material purchases and direct labor costs incurred were $54,000 each, and manufacturing overhead applied amounted to $30,000.

Required:

Prepare a statement of cost of goods manufactured for ABC Company.

**Mini-Exercise
13.5
LO 7**

Cost of goods manufactured and sold The following information is from ABC Company's general ledger for the month of February: Beginning and ending finished goods inventory, respectively, were 56,000 and 52,000. Cost of goods sold for February was $136,000.

Required:

How much was ABC Company's cost of goods manufactured in February?

**Mini-Exercise
13.6
LO 8**

Variable versus absorption costing The following cost behavior patterns describe anticipated manufacturing costs for 2019: raw material, $7/unit; direct labor, $10/unit; and manufacturing overhead, $240,000 + $8/unit.

Required:

If anticipated production for 2019 is 30,000 units, calculate the unit cost using variable costing and absorption costing. Explain the difference.

**Mini-Exercise
13.7
LO 8**

Variable versus absorption costing The following cost behavior pattern describes anticipated manufacturing overhead costs for 2019: $240,000 + $8/unit. During the year, 30,000 units were produced and 28,000 units were sold.

Required:

Calculate the manufacturing overhead unit cost for 2019 using variable costing and absorption costing, and then calculate the difference in operating income for 2019 using variable costing versus absorption costing. Explain the difference.

**Mini-Exercise
13.8
LO 9**

Activity-based costing Brooklyn Cycles produces custom bicycles and has used a traditional manufacturing overhead application rate based on direct labor hours. Currently, overhead is applied at the rate of $42/DLH. Brooklyn is now considering using activity-based driver rates to improve manufacturing overhead costing accuracy. Budgeted manufacturing overhead costs for expected driver activity are as follows:

	Budgeted Cost	Budgeted Activity
Machining time	$280,000	8,000 hours
Direct labor time	$300,000	15,000 hours
Inspection time	$ 50,000	5,000 hours

Required:

Calculate manufacturing overhead rates that would be applied to bicycles produced using activity-based costing, and explain how Brooklyn Cycles could achieve improved costing accuracy.

Exercises

All applicable Exercises are available in *Connect*.

Value chain classifications Match each of the following cost items with the value chain business function where you would expect the cost to be incurred:

Exercise 13.9
LO 2

Business Function	Cost Item	Answer
a. Research and development	1. Purchase of raw materials	_____
b. Design	2. Advertising	_____
c. Production	3. Salary of research scientists	_____
d. Marketing	4. Shipping expenses	_____
e. Distribution	5. Reengineering of product assembly process	_____
f. Customer service	6. Replacement parts for warranty repairs	_____
	7. Manufacturing supplies	_____
	8. Sales commissions	_____
	9. Purchase of CAD (computer-aided design) software	_____
	10. Salary of website designer	_____

Value chain classifications Match each of the following cost items with the value chain business function where you would expect the cost to be incurred:

Exercise 13.10
LO 2

Business Function	Cost Item	Answer
a. Research and development	1. Labor time to repair products under warranty	_____
b. Design	2. Radio commercials	_____
c. Production	3. Labor costs of delivering customer orders	_____
d. Marketing	4. Testing of competitor's product	_____
e. Distribution	5. Direct manufacturing labor costs	_____
f. Customer service	6. Development of order tracking system for online sales	_____
	7. Design cost of new product brochures	_____
	8. Hours spent designing childproof bottles	_____
	9. Training costs for representatives to staff the customer call center	_____
	10. Installation of robotics equipment in manufacturing plant	_____

Cost classifications For each of the following costs, check the columns that most likely apply (both variable and fixed might apply for some costs).

Exercise 13.11
LO 3, 4

	Product				
Costs	Direct	Indirect	Period	Variable	Fixed
Wages of assembly-line workers	_____	_____	_____	_____	_____
Depreciation of plant equipment	_____	_____	_____	_____	_____
Glue and thread	_____	_____	_____	_____	_____
Outbound shipping costs	_____	_____	_____	_____	_____

	Product				
Costs	**Direct**	**Indirect**	**Period**	**Variable**	**Fixed**
Raw materials handling costs	___	___	___	___	___
Salary of public relations manager	___	___	___	___	___
Production run setup costs	___	___	___	___	___
Plant utilities	___	___	___	___	___
Electricity cost of retail stores	___	___	___	___	___
Research and development expense	___	___	___	___	___

Exercise 13.12
LO 3, 4

Cost classifications For each of the following costs, check the columns that most likely apply (both variable and fixed might apply for some costs).

	Product				
Costs	**Direct**	**Indirect**	**Period**	**Variable**	**Fixed**
Raw materials	___	___	___	___	___
Tape used to secure packed boxes of product	___	___	___	___	___
Plant janitors' wages	___	___	___	___	___
Inventory clerks' wages	___	___	___	___	___
Promotional expenses	___	___	___	___	___
Production workers' wages	___	___	___	___	___
Production supervisors' salaries	___	___	___	___	___
Sales force commissions	___	___	___	___	___
Maintenance supplies used	___	___	___	___	___
Controller's salary	___	___	___	___	___
Electricity cost for office building	___	___	___	___	___
Real estate taxes for					
Factory	___	___	___	___	___
Office building	___	___	___	___	___

Exercise 13.13
LO 4

Cost classifications Aussie Corp. manufactures rugby jerseys for collegiate sports teams and sells its merchandise through university bookstores.

Required:

Identify a specific item in the company's manufacturing, selling, or administrative processes for which the cost would be classified as

a. Raw material.
b. Direct labor.
c. Variable manufacturing overhead.
d. Fixed manufacturing overhead.
e. Fixed administrative expense.
f. Fixed indirect selling expense.
g. Variable direct selling expense.

Cost classifications   College Carriers manufactures backpacks that are sold to students for use as book bags.

Exercise 13.14
LO 4

Required:

Identify a specific item in this company's manufacturing, selling, or administrative processes for which the cost would be classified as

a.   Raw material.
b.   Direct labor.
c.   Variable manufacturing overhead.
d.   Fixed manufacturing overhead.
e.   Fixed administrative expense.
f.   Fixed indirect selling expense.
g.   Variable direct selling expense.

Product costing—various issues   Clay Co. produces ceramic coffee mugs and pencil holders. Manufacturing overhead is assigned to production using an application rate based on direct labor hours.

Exercise 13.15
LO 5

Required:

a.   For 2019, the company's cost accountant estimated that total overhead costs incurred would be $408,750 and that a total of 54,500 direct labor hours would be worked. Calculate the amount of overhead to be applied for each direct labor hour worked on a production run.

b.   A production run of 750 coffee mugs used raw materials that cost $810 and used 90 direct labor hours at a cost of $9.50 per hour. Calculate the cost of each coffee mug produced.

c.   At the end of October 2019, 530 coffee mugs made in the production run in part **b** had been sold and the rest were in ending inventory. Calculate (1) the cost of the coffee mugs sold that would have been reported in the income statement and (2) the cost included in the October 31, 2019, finished goods inventory.

Product costing—manufacturing overhead   Nautical Footware Inc. manufactures women's boating shoes. Manufacturing overhead is assigned to production on a machine-hour basis. For 2019, it was estimated that manufacturing overhead would total $487,200 and that 33,600 machine hours would be used.

Exercise 13.16
LO 5

Required:

a.   Calculate the predetermined overhead application rate that will be used for absorption costing purposes during 2019.

b.   During May, 5,860 pairs of shoes were made. Raw materials costing $28,468 were used, and direct labor costs totaled $28,800. A total of 2,840 machine hours were worked during the month of May. Calculate the cost per pair of shoes made during May.

c.   At the end of May, 1,578 pairs of shoes were in ending inventory. Calculate the cost of the ending inventory and the cost of the shoes sold during May.

Exercise 13.17

LO 5, 6

Manufacturing overhead—over/underapplied Checker Inc. produces automobile bumpers. Overhead is applied on the basis of machine hours required for cutting and fabricating. A predetermined overhead application rate of $12.70 per machine hour was established for 2019.

Required:

a. If 9,000 machine hours were expected to be used during 2019, how much overhead was expected to be incurred?

b. Actual overhead incurred during 2019 totaled $121,650, and 9,100 machine hours were used during 2019. Calculate the amount of over- or underapplied overhead for 2019.

c. Explain the accounting necessary for the over- or underapplied overhead for the year.

Exercise 13.18

LO 5, 6

Manufacturing overhead—over/underapplied Creative Lighting Inc. makes specialty table lamps. Manufacturing overhead is applied to production on a direct labor hours basis. During June, the first month of the company's fiscal year, $110,880 of manufacturing overhead was applied to Work in Process Inventory using the predetermined overhead application rate of $12 per direct labor hour.

Required:

a. Calculate the number of hours of direct labor used during June.

b. Actual manufacturing overhead costs incurred during June totaled $106,680. Calculate the amount of over- or underapplied overhead for June.

c. Identify two possible explanations for the over- or underapplied overhead.

d. Explain the accounting appropriate for the over- or underapplied overhead at the end of June.

Exercise 13.19

LO 5, 6

Manufacturing overhead—multiple application bases Fredrick Paulson Tie Co. manufactures neckties and scarves. Two overhead application bases are used; some overhead is applied on the basis of raw material cost at a rate of 140% of material cost, and the balance of the overhead is applied at the rate of $7.20 per direct labor hour.

Required:

Calculate the cost per unit of a production run of 530 neckties that required raw materials costing $1,950 and 75 direct labor hours at a total cost of $840.

Exercise 13.20

LO 5, 6

Manufacturing overhead—multiple application bases Staley Toy Co. makes toy flutes. Two manufacturing overhead application bases are used; some overhead is applied on the basis of machine hours at a rate of $7.20 per machine hour, and the balance of the overhead is applied at the rate of 250% of direct labor cost.

Required:

a. Calculate the cost per unit of October production of 1,420 toy flutes that required

   1. Raw materials costing $960.

   2. 36 direct labor hours costing $612.

   3. 60 machine hours.

b.   At the end of October, 1,310 of these toy flutes had been sold. Calculate the end-
     ing inventory value of the toy flutes still in inventory at October 31.

Variable versus absorption costing Wool Creations Inc. manufactures wool   **Exercise 13.21**
sweaters. Costs incurred in making 9,000 sweaters in October included $22,500 of   **LO 8**
fixed manufacturing overhead. The total absorption cost per sweater was $11.60.

Required:

a.   Calculate the variable cost per sweater.
b.   The ending inventory of sweaters was 1,600 units lower at the end of the month
     than at the beginning of the month. By how much and in what direction (higher
     or lower) would cost of goods sold for the month of October be different under
     variable costing than under absorption costing?
c.   Express the sweater cost in a cost formula.

Variable versus absorption costing Colorado Business Tools manufactures   **Exercise 13.22**
calculators. Costs incurred in making 12,500 calculators in February included   **LO 8**
$42,500 of fixed manufacturing overhead. The total absorption cost per calculator
was $11.75.

Required:

a.   Calculate the variable cost per calculator.
b.   The ending inventory of calculators was 925 units higher at the end of the month
     than at the beginning of the month. By how much and in what direction (higher
     or lower) would operating income for the month of February be different under
     variable costing than under absorption costing?
c.   Express the calculator cost in a cost formula.

Problems   ![Connect] **connect**

All applicable Problems are available in *Connect*.

Activity-based costing MedTech Inc. manufactures and sells diagnostic equipment   **Problem 13.23**
used in the medical profession. Its job costing system was designed using an activity-   **LO 9**
based costing approach. Direct materials and direct labor costs are accumulated separately, along with information concerning four manufacturing overhead cost drivers
(activities). Assume that the direct labor rate is $20 per hour and that there were no
beginning inventories. The following information was available for 2019, based on an
expected production level of 400,000 units for the year:

Activity Cost Driver	Budgeted Costs for 2016	Cost Driver Used as Allocation Base	Cost Allocation Rate
Materials handling	$3,600,000	Number of parts used	$ 1.50 per part
Milling and grinding	8,800,000	Number of machine hours	11.00 per hour
Assembly and inspection	6,000,000	Direct labor hours worked	5.00 per hour
Testing	1,200,000	Number of units tested	3.00 per unit

The following production, costs, and activities occurred during the month of August:

Units Produced/Tested	Direct Materials Costs	Number of Parts Used	Machine Hours	Direct Labor Hours
50,000	$3,500,000	275,000	95,000	160,000

Required:

a. Calculate the total manufacturing costs and the cost per unit produced and tested during the month of August for MedTech.

b. Explain the advantages of the ABC approach relative to using a single predetermined overhead application rate based on direct labor hours. (*Note:* You do not have to calculate the overhead that would be applied for the month of August using this alternative method.)

Problem 13.24
LO 9

Activity-based costing versus traditional overhead allocation methods
Woodland Industries manufactures and sells custom-made windows. Its job costing system was designed using an activity-based costing approach. Direct materials and direct labor costs are accumulated separately, along with information concerning three manufacturing overhead cost drivers (activities). Assume that the direct labor rate is $18 per hour and that there were no beginning inventories. The following information was available for 2019, based on an expected production level of 50,000 units for the year, which will require 200,000 direct labor hours:

Activity Cost Driver	Budgeted Costs for 2019	Cost Driver Used as Allocation Base	Cost Allocation Rate
Materials handling	$ 225,000	Number of parts used	$ 0.18 per part
Cutting and lathe work	1,875,000	Number of parts used	1.50 per part
Assembly and inspection	4,400,000	Direct labor hours	22.00 per hour

The following production, costs, and activities occurred during the month of July:

Units Produced	Direct Materials Costs	Number of Parts Used	Direct Labor Hours
3,400	$126,240	74,800	14,320

Required:

a. Calculate the total manufacturing costs and the cost per unit of the windows produced during the month of July (using the activity-based costing approach).

b. Assume instead that Woodland Industries applies manufacturing overhead on a direct labor hours basis (rather than using the activity-based costing system previously described). Calculate the total manufacturing cost and the cost per unit of the windows produced during the month of July. (*Hint:* You will need to calculate the predetermined overhead application rate using the total budgeted overhead costs for 2019.)

c. Compare the per unit cost figures calculated in parts **a** and **b.** Which approach do you think provides better information for manufacturing managers? Explain your answer.

Variable versus absorption costing   TroutPro Co. manufactures fishing equipment. During 2019, total costs associated with manufacturing 15,000 fly-cast fishing rods (a new product introduced this year) were as follows:

Problem 13.25

LO 8

Raw materials	$62,100
Direct labor	16,500
Variable manufacturing overhead	11,250
Fixed manufacturing overhead	18,000

Required:

a. Calculate the cost per fishing rod under both variable costing and absorption costing.
b. If 300 of these fishing rods were in finished goods inventory at the end of 2019, by how much and in what direction (higher or lower) would 2019 operating income be different under variable costing than under absorption costing?
c. Express the fishing rod cost in a cost formula. What does this formula suggest the total cost of making an additional 200 fishing rods would be?

Variable versus absorption costing   Williamson Inc. manufactures digital voice recorders. During 2019, total costs associated with manufacturing 52,000 of the new EZ 9900 model (introduced this year) were as follows:

Problem 13.26

LO 8

Raw materials	$447,200
Direct labor	$738,400
Variable manufacturing overhead	187,200
Fixed manufacturing overhead	176,800

Required:

a. Calculate the cost per recorder under both variable costing and absorption costing.
b. If 6,800 of these recorders were in finished goods inventory at the end of 2019, by how much and in what direction (higher or lower) would 2019 cost of goods sold and operating income be different under variable costing than under absorption costing?
c. Express the digital voice recorder cost in a cost formula. What does this formula suggest the total cost of making an additional 825 recorders would be?

Cost of goods manufactured, cost of goods sold, and income statement   Maryville Inc. incurred the following costs during August:

Problem 13.27

LO 4, 5, 7

Raw materials used	$33,100
Direct labor	65,200
Manufacturing overhead, actual	44,800
Selling expenses	26,700
Administrative expenses	19,400
Interest expense	9,100

Required:

During the month, 5,300 units of product were manufactured and 4,800 units of product were sold. On August 1, Maryville carried no inventories. On August 31, there were no inventories other than finished goods.

a. Calculate the cost of goods manufactured during August and the average cost per unit of product manufactured.

b. Calculate the cost of goods sold during August.

c. Calculate the difference between cost of goods manufactured and cost of goods sold. How will this amount be reported in the financial statements?

d. *(Optional)* Prepare a traditional (absorption) income statement for Maryville for the month of August. Assume that sales for the month were $244,800 and the company's effective income tax rate was 30%.

Problem 13.28

LO 4, 5, 7

Cost of goods manufactured, cost of goods sold, and income statement GrandSlam Inc. incurred the following costs during March:

Selling expenses	$31,675
Direct labor	56,628
Interest expense	8,213
Manufacturing overhead, actual	40,950
Raw materials used	92,196
Administrative expenses	24,600

Required:

During the month, 3,900 units of product were manufactured and 2,200 units of product were sold. On March 1, GrandSlam carried no inventories. On March 31, there were no inventories for raw materials or work in process.

a. Calculate the cost of goods manufactured during March and the average cost per unit of product manufactured.

b. Calculate the cost of goods sold during March.

c. Calculate the difference between cost of goods manufactured and cost of goods sold. How will this amount be reported in the financial statements?

d. *(Optional)* Prepare a traditional (absorption) income statement for GrandSlam for the month of March. Assume that sales for the month were $207,060 and the company's effective income tax rate was 35%.

Problem 13.29

LO 5, 7

Cost of goods manufactured and cost of goods sold The following table summarizes the beginning and ending inventories of Decatur Manufacturing Inc. for the month of October:

	Sept. 30	Oct. 31
Raw materials	$ 33,500	$27,600
Work in process	71,300	64,800
Finished goods	47,200	41,900

Raw materials purchased during the month of October totaled $123,900. Direct labor costs incurred totaled $312,200 for the month. Actual and applied manufacturing overhead costs for October totaled $188,400 and $192,300, respectively. Over/under-applied overhead is written off to cost of goods sold at the end of the year in December.

Required:

a. Calculate the cost of goods manufactured for October.
b. Calculate the cost of goods sold for October.

Cost of goods manufactured, cost of goods sold, and income statement   **Problem 13.30**
Morrison & Company incurred the following costs during August: **LO 4, 5, 7**

Raw materials purchased	$66,150
Direct labor ($15 per hour)	82,500
Manufacturing overhead (actual)	135,450
Selling expenses	44,700
Administrative expenses	22,050
Interest expense	7,660

Manufacturing overhead is applied on the basis of $25 per direct labor hour. Assume that overapplied or underapplied overhead is transferred to cost of goods sold only at the end of the year. During the month, 5,000 units of product were manufactured and 5,300 units of product were sold. On August 1 and August 31, Morrison & Company carried the following inventory balances:

	August 1	August 31
Raw materials	$27,440	$25,060
Work in process	74,480	79,760
Finished goods	58,520	41,525

Required:

a. Prepare a statement of cost of goods manufactured for the month of August and calculate the average cost per unit of product manufactured.
b. Calculate the cost of goods sold during August.
c. Calculate the difference between cost of goods manufactured and cost of goods sold. How will this amount be reported in the financial statements?
d. *(Optional)* Prepare a traditional (absorption) income statement for Morrison & Company for the month of August. Assume that sales for the month were $413,400 and the company's effective income tax rate was 40%.

Cases   ■ connect

All applicable Cases are available in *Connect*.

Cost of goods manufactured, cost of goods sold, and income statement   **Case 13.31**
Determine each of the following missing amounts: **LO 4, 5, 7**

	Firm A	Firm B	Firm C
Beginning raw materials inventory	$ 17,000	$?	$ 42,000
Purchases of raw materials during the year	?	96,000	226,000
Raw materials available for use	?	119,000	?
Ending raw materials inventory	12,000	?	51,000
Cost of raw materials used	90,000	101,000	?
Direct labor costs incurred	130,000	?	318,000
Variable manufacturing overhead applied	?	34,000	72,000
Fixed manufacturing overhead applied	100,000	60,000	?
Total manufacturing costs incurred	370,000	?	?
Beginning work in process	15,000	7,000	19,000
Ending work in process	25,000	11,000	16,000
Cost of goods manufactured	$?	$266,000	$?
Sales	$?	$410,000	$?
Beginning finished goods inventory	30,000	?	61,000
Cost of goods manufactured	?	266,000	?
Cost of goods available for sale	?	303,000	761,000
Ending finished goods inventory	50,000	?	48,000
Cost of goods sold	?	273,000	?
Gross profit	140,000	?	198,000
Selling, general, and administrative expenses	68,000	?	?
Income from operations	$?	$ 32,000	$ 89,000

Case 13.32

LO 4, 5, 7

Product costing—various issues Custom Granite Inc. uses an absorption cost system for accumulating product cost. The following data are available for the past year:

- Raw materials purchases totaled $240,000.
- Direct labor costs incurred for the year totaled $480,000.
- Variable manufacturing overhead is applied on the basis of $6 per direct labor hour.
- Fixed manufacturing overhead is applied on the basis of machine hours used.
- When plans for the year were being made, it was estimated that total fixed overhead costs would be $312,000 and that 96,000 machine hours would be used during the year.
- The direct labor rate is $16 per hour.
- Actual machine hours used during the year totaled 88,000 hours.
- Actual general and administrative expenses for the year totaled $320,000.

Inventory balances at the beginning and end of the year were as follows:

	Beginning of Year	End of Year
Raw materials	$39,000	$ 27,000
Work in process	33,000	51,500
Finished goods	104,000	122,000

Required:

a.   Calculate the predetermined fixed manufacturing overhead rate and explain how it will be used during the year.

b.   Draw a graph for fixed manufacturing overhead showing two lines. The first line should illustrate cost behavior and how Custom Granite's management expects total fixed costs to be incurred for the year. The second line should illustrate product costing and how fixed costs are to be assigned to Custom Granite's production. Comment on your graph.

c.   Repeat requirement **b** for variable manufacturing overhead.

d.   Prepare a T-account for Raw Materials to calculate the cost of raw materials used. Explain the relationship between raw material purchased and raw material used.

e.   Calculate the variable manufacturing overhead applied to work in process. Could the applied amount of variable overhead differ from the actual amount of variable overhead incurred by Custom Granite for the year? If so, why might this occur?

f.   Calculate the fixed manufacturing overhead applied to work in process. Could the applied amount of fixed overhead differ from the actual amount of fixed overhead incurred by Custom Granite for the year? Why or why not?

g.   Prepare a T-account for Work in Process to calculate the cost of goods manufactured.

h.   Prepare a T-account for Finished Goods to calculate the cost of goods sold. Identify the cost of goods manufactured and *not sold.*

i.   Custom Granite estimated that it would use 96,000 machine hours during the year, but actual machine hours used totaled 88,000. Refer to the graph you prepared in requirement **b** and explain the implications for the product costing system of the 8,000 machine hours that Custom Granite failed to generate during the year. What are the implications for Custom Granite's balance sheet and income statement?

Financial reporting, manufacturing firm—Internet assignment Campbell Soup Company provides access to its annual reports online at campbellsoup.com. The annual reports are found in the "All Campbell Brands/Investors/Financial Information/ Annual Reports" area of its website. Locate the following information in the annual reports provided for 2017 and 2015:

Case 13.33

LO 5, 7

1.   From the supplementary financial statement data, find the composition of the beginning and ending inventory for each of the following balance sheet accounts: Raw Material, Work in Process, and Finished Goods.

2.   From the consolidated statements of income, find the amount for Cost of Sales.

3.   From the consolidated balance sheets, find the amount for Inventories.

4.   From the management's discussion and analysis, find the overview section that explains Gross Profit.

Required:

a.   Calculate the cost of goods manufactured for 2017, 2016, and 2015.

b.   Calculate the total amount of combined cost incurred in 2017, 2016, and 2015 for raw material, direct labor, and manufacturing overhead.

c. From the 2017 "Management's Discussion and Analysis of Financial Condition and Results of Operations," identify the ratio of cost of sales to net sales for 2017, 2016, and 2015. Comment on the overall trend.

d. Review Chapter 11 if necessary and calculate the inventory turnover and day's sales in inventory for 2017, 2016, and 2015. Comment on the overall trend.

Case 13.34

LO 9

Activity-based management—Internet assignment SAS is a world leader in business analytics software, delivering breakthrough technology to transform the way organizations do business. At sas.com, many activity-based management (Cost and Profitability Management Solution) success stories are presented from a variety of firms in different industries.

Required:

a. Locate the product fact sheet about SAS's activity-based management solution. Read the product overview and information and write a summary report detailing your findings.

b. Locate the Success Stories for activity-based management (Cost and Profitability Management Solution). Choose an organization and read its testimonial. Write a summary report describing how that organization is using activity-based management.

ANSWERS TO
What Does It Mean?

1. It means that cost accounting provides product cost and inventory value information for financial reporting purposes and provides planning, control, and decision-making information for managerial purposes.

2. It means that after costs are collected and recorded (cost accumulation), an understanding of cost relationships is necessary to complete the costing process (cost assignment), in which an appropriate portion of cost is assigned to a product or activity to determine its costs.

3. It means that the cost is either direct material or direct labor incurred in making a product; as such, total cost will vary with the quantity of product made.

4. It means that these costs are initially recorded as an inventory asset and that when the related product is eventually sold, the cost of the product is recognized as cost of goods sold.

5. It means that a way of assigning these indirect costs to inventory has been developed and used as a means of including manufacturing overhead in product cost.

6. It means that actual overhead incurred during the year is more than overhead applied to work in process by using the predetermined overhead application rate, because actual overhead and/or actual production activity was different from the estimates used at the beginning of the year to develop the overhead application rate.

7. It means that there has been an extensive effort to refine the method of assigning overhead costs to products and processes so cost data are more accurate than was the case with earlier cost systems.

Cost Planning

Have you ever defined a personal goal that you considered so important that you prepared a roadmap to guide you toward your goal? Perhaps your goal was to purchase a new car and the roadmap identified the portion of your paycheck that, given your other current responsibilities, needed to be set aside for the initial down payment and subsequent monthly payments. Or perhaps your goal involved more than a financial component, such as law school, where an academic roadmap was necessary in addition to a financial roadmap. And at the various stages defined in your roadmap, did you reflect and ask yourself the important question: "How well am I doing?" These questions about goals, roadmaps, and performance, from a business perspective, are presented in here in Chapter 14 and in Chapter 15 as we continue to explore the management planning and control cycle.

Planning is an essential part of the management process, and it represents the initial activity in the planning and control cycle (see gray-shaded area in the planning and control cycle model). A **budget** quantifies an organization's plane financial terms; *budgeting* is the process of financial planning. It involves the use of financial accounting concepts because ultimately the results of the organization's activities will be reported in terms of income, cash flows, and financial position—the financial statements. Budgeting also involves the use of managerial accounting concepts, especially cost behavior patterns because the aggregate financial plan of an organization is the sum of

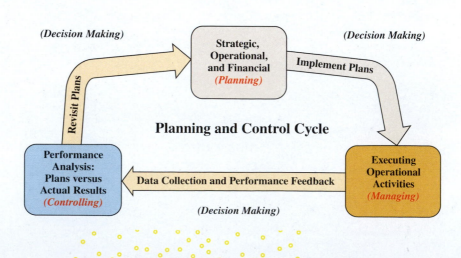

all plans for individual products and units. Budgets are useful because the preparation of a budget forces management to plan. In addition, the budget provides a benchmark against which to compare actual results.

The budget preparation process requires communication and coordination of activities among the different functional areas of the firm—finance, production, marketing, and human resources—if organizational goals are to be aligned. Although it may seem that these benefits should be achieved even without a budget, often they are not realized without a budgeting process because each functional area gets so wrapped up in its own activities that its impact on other functions is overlooked or given secondary significance. When budgets are properly developed and administered, they also serve as motivational tools. Operating managers can focus on the specific goals that will help them achieve their budget objectives, knowing that their success will contribute to the overall success of the firm.

A **standard cost** is a unit budget allowance for a single component—material, labor, or overhead—of a product or service. Standard costs are used in the planning and control processes of manufacturing and service firms that perform repetitive operations in the production of goods or performance of services. Although usually associated with manufacturing, standard costs are also developed in financial and consumer service organizations.

LEARNING OBJECTIVES (LO)

After studying this chapter, you should understand and be able to

LO 14-1   Describe cost terminology that relates to the budgeting process.

LO 14-2   Explain why budgets are useful and how management philosophy can influence the budgeting process.

LO 14-3   Compare how alternative budget time frames can be used.

LO 14-4   Demonstrate the impact of the sales forecast (or revenue budget) on the overall operating budget.

LO 14-5   Prepare a purchases/production budget.

LO 14-6   Illustrate the importance of cost behavior patterns in developing the operating expense budget.

LO 14-7   Explain why and how a budgeted income statement and balance sheet are prepared, and prepare a cash budget.

LO 14-8   Explain why and how standards are useful in the planning and control process.

LO 14-9   Determine how the standard cost of a product is developed.

LO 14-10   Describe how standard costs are used in the cost accounting system.

Cost Classifications

Relationship of Total Cost to Volume of Activity

LO 1

Describe cost terminology that relates to the budgeting process.

For planning purposes, it is necessary to review and understand how costs are expected to change as the level of planned activity changes. For example, the raw material or direct labor requirements will depend on the planned level of production. Similarly, the planned level of production will depend on the planned level of sales. Raw material and direct labor, as discussed in Chapter 12, are **variable costs** that increase or decrease in total with the volume of activity but remain constant when expressed on a per unit basis. Many individual items classified within manufacturing overhead or selling and administrative costs are variable, and the amount of total cost expected will be a function of the amount of cost driver activity. Exhibit 14-1 highlights cost classification topics covered in this chapter.

Costs such as property taxes, executive salaries, and plant depreciation will not change (within the relevant range of activity) with plans for sales and related production requirements because these items represent **fixed costs**. The idea that a cost is classified as a fixed cost does not necessarily suggest that the amount to plan for in the budget will not change from year to year. The important point is that fixed costs will not change as the volume of activity changes (within the relevant range) but could change as a result of the managerial decision-making process, as explained in the next section of this chapter.

Other costs, such as utilities, maintenance, and compensation of salespeople who receive a salary plus commission, suggest that a certain fixed amount of cost can be

Exhibit 14-1   Cost Classifications—The Big Picture

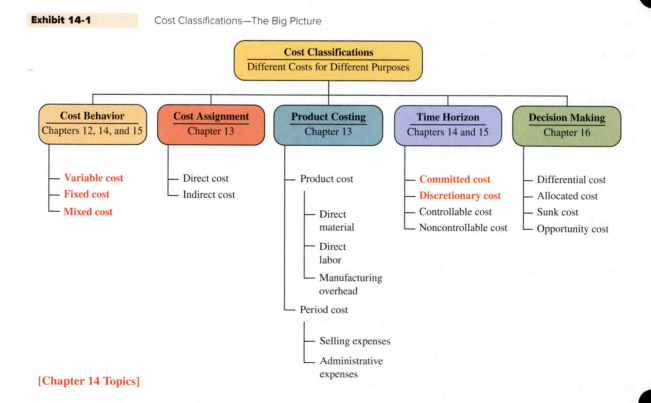

[Chapter 14 Topics]

expected regardless of the level of activity, but another part of these costs also will change as activity changes. These behavior patterns were referred to as **mixed costs** in Chapter 12, and the high–low method was illustrated as a simple technique for separating the variable and fixed components of the mixed cost. Knowing the cost behavior pattern for each line item of the operating budget is an essential prerequisite for effective planning.

Cost Classification According to a Time-Frame Perspective

Planning for exclusively variable cost items is strictly a function of the amount of cost driver activity expected each period, whereas planning for many fixed cost items becomes more a function of the time horizon. Fixed costs classified according to a time-frame perspective are known as *committed costs* and *discretionary costs.* A committed cost is one that will be incurred to execute long-range policy decisions to which the firm has "committed." Collectively, these **committed cost** investments provide the organization with the capacity resources necessary to carry out the basic activities along its value chain—R&D, design, production, marketing, distribution, and customer service. A **discretionary cost** is one that can be adjusted in the short run (usually on an annual basis) as management evaluates the organization's available resources and prioritizes the annual budget requests. Examples of each type of cost include the following:

Committed Costs	Discretionary Costs
Salaries of top management	Company softball team
Real estate taxes	Advertising expenditures
Technology infrastructure	Charitable contributions
Quality control	Management development programs
Depreciation	Internships for college students
Insurance	Employee tuition reimbursement program
	Copy machine upgrades

With respect to committed costs, the control issue for managers is whether the cost is appropriate for the value received from the expenditure. On the other hand, when adding or curtailing discretionary costs, managers do have short-term discretion about the level of cost to be incurred. As suggested by the preceding examples, significant nonfinancial considerations also must be evaluated with respect to discretionary costs for establishing priorities.

Budgeting

The Budgeting Process in General

Many organizations commit substantial time and resources to the budgeting process. A useful budget is not prepared in a few hours or a few days; usually, several months and the efforts of many people are devoted to the process. After development, a budget is not put on the shelf; it should become a resource to guide and help managers accomplish the goals that have been established.

How the budget is used in an organization will depend on the management philosophy of the organization's top executives. In a highly structured, autocratically managed firm, the budget may be seen as being "carved in stone," and managers may develop dysfunctional practices to avoid being criticized for failing to meet budgeted results. For example, the sales force may defer entering customer orders in a month in

LO 2

Explain why budgets are useful and how management philosophy can influence the budgeting process.

which the sales target has already been achieved, sacrificing customer service levels and sales to get a head start on the next month's quota. Or a manager may commit funds for supplies that aren't really needed in order to use the full budget allowance, on the premise that doing so will facilitate justifying a budget allowance of at least an equal amount for the next period. These and other budget "games" waste valuable time and resources.

The budget should be seen as a guide that reflects management's best thinking at the time it is prepared. However, the plan may need to change if circumstances evolve differerently from those envisioned when the budget was prepared. Otherwise, large differences between budgeted amounts and actual amounts may have to be anticipated and accepted. The objective of the organization should not be to have actual results equal budgeted results; the objective should be to operate profitably, as expressed and measured by rate of return, growth in profits, market share, levels of service, and other metrics that reflect the mission and strategy of the organization.

Organizations will generally differ in its management philosophy and approach to budget preparation and these differences are reflected in the following process characteristics:

- **Top-down budgeting** is an authoritarian approach that implies that little or no input during the budget process will originate with lower levels of management.
- **Participative budgeting** is an interactive, collaborative approach in which lower-level managers provide significant input to the budgeting process.

These differences are extreme and one approach is not necessarily better than the other in all situations. A participative approach would result in lower-level managers identifying more closely with and likely "owning" the budget objectives; but there may be times, such as when a firm is under heavy pressure to survive, that dictated objectives are appropriate.

Another important differentiation to consider in the budgeting process is where to begin:

- **Incremental budgeting** starts with actual performance for the current period. The manager first determines what the revenues and/or costs have been recently and then adjusts these amounts for changes that are expected to occur in the next period.
- **Zero-based budgeting** starts with a clean slate and involves identifying, justifying and prioritizing the activities carried out by a department, determining the costs associated with each, and then authorizing for the future only those activities that satisfy certain priority constraints.

Again, these differences are extreme. A disadvantage of the incremental approach is that inefficiencies in the present way of doing things tend to be carried into the future, and those organizations that embarked on a purely zero-based budgeting program all but discontinued it because of the heavy administrative and recordkeeping burdens it requires. The answer for where to begin lies somewhere in the middle. Available resources to support ongoing operations should be analyzed with respect to current performance and any increments are prioritized according to expected activity changes in the next period. Alternatively, budget requests for new operating activities or initiatives are more likely to compete for any available resources through the justification and prioritization characteristics of a zero-based approach.

---

1. What does it mean to have a participative budgeting process?

What Does It Mean?

Answer on
page 561

The Budget Time Frame

Budgets can be prepared for a single period or for several periods. A **single-period budget** for a fiscal year would be prepared in the months preceding the beginning of the year and used for the entire year. The disadvantage of this approach is that some budget estimates must be made more than a year in advance. For example, a firm operating on a calendar year basis will prepare its 2019 budget during the last few months of 2018; November and December 2019 activities are being planned before actual results for those months of 2018 are known.

LO 3

Compare how alternative budget time frames can be used.

A multiperiod or **rolling budget** involves planning for segments of a year on a repetitive basis. For example, in a three-month/one-year rolling budget, a budget for each quarter of 2019 will be prepared late in 2018. During the first quarter of 2019, a budget for the next four quarters will be prepared. This will be the second budget prepared for each of the last three quarters of 2019 and the first budget for the first quarter of 2020. This process will continue each quarter, as illustrated in Exhibit 14-2.

The advantage of such a **continuous budget** is that the final budget for any quarter should be much more accurate because it has been prepared more recently. The obvious disadvantage to this process is the time, effort, and cost required. However, in a rapidly changing environment, the benefit of a budget that requires frequent assessment of the organization's plans may be worth the cost. The multiperiod budget can be prepared with any reporting frequency that makes sense for the organization and for the activity being budgeted. Thus, full financial statements may be budgeted on a

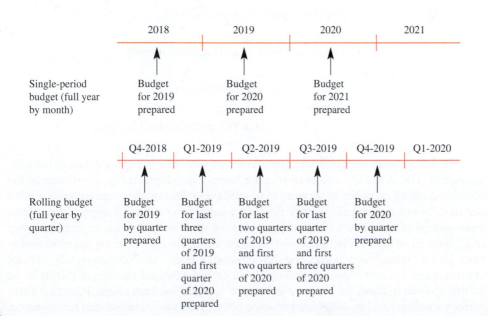

Exhibit 14-2

Budget Time Frames

six-month/one-year cycle, but cash receipt and disbursement details may be budgeted on a one-week/four-week cycle or even a daily/one-week/four-week cycle (i.e., every day a budget by day for the next several days is prepared, and every week a budget by week for the next four weeks is prepared).

What Does It Mean?

Answer on page 561

2. What does it mean to have a rolling or continuous budget?

The Budgeting Process

The first step in the budgeting process is to develop and communicate a set of broad assumptions about the economy, the industry, and the organization's strategy for the budget period. This is frequently done by planners and economists and is approved by top management. These assumptions represent the foundation on which the action plans for the budget period are built.

The **operating budget,** sometimes called the **master budget,** is the operating plan expressed in financial terms; it is made up of a number of detailed budgets with commonsense dependencies that must be appreciated, such as:

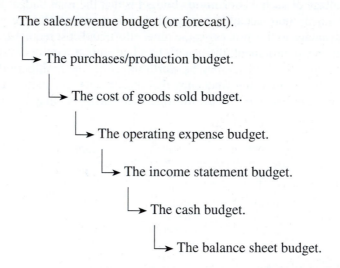

The sales/revenue budget (or forecast).

↳→ The purchases/production budget.

↳→ The cost of goods sold budget.

↳→ The operating expense budget.

↳→ The income statement budget.

↳→ The cash budget.

↳→ The balance sheet budget.

LO 4

Demonstrate the impact of the sales forecast (or revenue budget) on the overall operating budget.

The key to every budget is the forecast of "activity" that is expected during the budget period. This is usually a sales or revenue forecast developed using an estimate of the physical quantity of goods or services to be sold multiplied by the expected selling price per unit. Merchandising firms may develop a **sales forecast** using expected revenues from groups of products. Commodity processing firms may forecast expected activity (e.g., bushels of corn to be processed) because revenues are based on the commodity price plus a "spread" or markup, and the commodity price can fluctuate widely. Service organizations forecast expected activity based on the expected number of clients to be served and the quantity of service likely to be required by each client. Based on these activity measures and an anticipated revenue per service, total revenues can be estimated.

The sales forecast is the most challenging part of the budget to develop accurately because the organization has little or no control over a number of factors that influence revenue-producing activities. These include the state of the economy, regulatory restrictions, seasonal demand variations, and competitors' actions. A variety of computerized modeling tools, including regression analysis and forecasting models, are available to assist in developing the sales forecast. The past experience of managers provides valuable input to the forecast. Information provided by the sales force and market research studies is also important. The firm's pricing policies, advertising effectiveness, and production capacity also may be considered. But in the final analysis, the sales forecast is only an educated guess resulting from a great deal of effort. Although the rest of the budgeting process flows from it, managers must remember that variations from the sales forecast will occur, and good managers will be prepared to respond quickly to those variations.

After the sales forecast has been developed, the other budgets can be prepared because the items being budgeted are a function of sales (or a similar measure of activity). For example, the quantity of product to purchase or manufacture depends on planned sales and desired inventory levels. Selling expenses will be a function of sales, and other operating expenses depend on quantities purchased (or manufactured) and sold. After revenues and expenses have been forecast, an income statement can be completed. Next, the cash budget (or projected statement of cash flows) can be prepared, given the budgeted operating results and plans for investing and financing activities. Finally, by considering all these expectations, a balance sheet as of the end of the period can be prepared. This hierarchy of budgets is illustrated in Exhibits 14-3 and 14-4. An overview of the overall operating budget is presented in Exhibit 14-3 to illustrate the sequencing dependencies in the budget development process. Exhibit 14-4 illustrates the way each budget relates to the income statement and balance sheet and illustrates their effect on the horizontal model. Keep in mind that the key assumption in the entire budgeting process is the sales forecast.

---

3. What does it mean to say that the key to the entire budget (e.g., the sales budget) is the forecast of operating activity?

What Does It Mean?

Answer on page 561

The Purchases/Production Budget

Recall that the following model was used to determine cost of goods sold under a periodic inventory system:

LO 5
Prepare a purchases/production budget.

Beginning inventory	$
Add: Purchases	
Goods available for sale	$
Less: Ending inventory	( )
Cost of goods sold	$

Exhibit 14-3

Overview of the
Operating Budget
Development Sequence

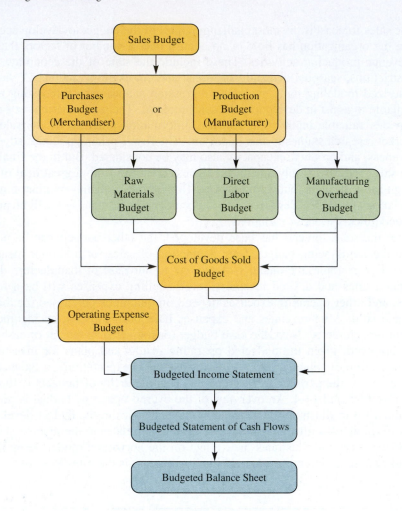

By changing dollars to physical quantities, the same model can be used to determine the quantity of merchandise to be purchased or manufactured. The captions change slightly, and the model would be revised as follows:

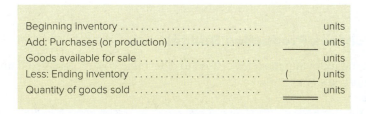

Beginning inventory		units
Add: Purchases (or production)	_____	units
Goods available for sale		units
Less: Ending inventory	(_____)	units
Quantity of goods sold	======	units

To use the model:

1. First enter the beginning and ending inventory quantities based on the firm's inventory management policies.
2. Next enter the quantity of goods sold from the sales forecast.

Exhibit 14-4 Hierarchy of Budgets and Financial Statement Relationships

Budgets (in Order of Preparation)	Balance Sheet			Income Statement			Explanation
	Assets = Liabilities + Stockholders' equity			Net income = Revenues − Expenses			
1. Sales forecast	+ Cash + Accounts Receivable − Inventories				+ Revenues (i.e., sales)	− Cost of Goods Sold	Assets are increased by the difference between sales and cost of goods sold.
2. Purchases/production	+ Inventories − Cash	+ Accounts Payable					Purchase/production of inventory requires the use of cash and/or incurrence of a liability.
3. Operating expenses	− Cash	+ Other Accrued Liabilities				− Operating Expenses	Examples include wages, utilities, rent, insurance, advertising, and research and development.
4. Budgeted income statement	− Accumulated Depreciation		+ Retained Earnings	Net income = Revenues		− Depreciation Expense −−−−−−− − Expenses	Summarizes the income statement effects caused by the above budgets.
5. Cash: (Operating) (Investing) (Financing)	+/− Cash +/− Accounts Receivable +/− Inventories +/− Cash +/− Plant and Equipment +/− Cash	+/− Accounts Payable +/− Other Accrued Liabilities +/− Long-term Debt	+ Capital Stock − Dividends − Treasury Stock				Includes effects caused by the above budgets (i.e., cash sales and payments for operating expenses) and all other anticipated effects on cash. Broken down by categories to facilitate the preparation of a budgeted statement of cash flows, if desired.
6. Budgeted balance sheet	Assets =	Liabilities	+ Stockholders' equity				A detailed balance sheet is prepared based on the results of all other budgets.

3. The goods available for sale amount in units is then calculated by working from the bottom up—the ending inventory is added to quantity of goods sold.

4. Finally, the beginning inventory is subtracted from goods available for sale to get the purchase or production quantity.

The model could be rearranged to permit calculation of the purchase or production quantity in a traditional equation format:

$$\text{Purchases or production} = \text{Ending inventory} + \text{Quantity sold} - \text{Beginning inventory}$$

A firm's inventory management policies should recognize the average lead time to receive or make finished goods and/or raw materials. Likewise, these policies will ordinarily provide an allowance for forecast errors. For example, a finished goods inventory policy might be to have a desired ending inventory equal to 1.4 times the quantity expected to be sold in the subsequent month (or period). Remember that one period's ending inventory is the next period's beginning inventory. The beginning inventory for the first budget period could be estimated using the firm's inventory policy or the estimated ending inventory of the current period.

The results of the production and purchases budget model will frequently be adjusted to reflect production efficiencies or appropriate order quantities. For example, if the production budget calls for significantly different quantities of production each month for several months, management may elect to plan a constant production level and ignore the ending inventory policy because the benefits of production efficiencies are greater than the costs of carrying any excess inventory. Likewise, if the purchases budget indicates that 38,400 units of raw material should be purchased, but standard shipping containers include 2,000 units each, the actual quantity ordered will be either 38,000 or 40,000 units. Inventories will absorb the difference between the budget calculation and the practical order quantity. Remember that in most cases, the budget calculations result in a guide to action; they do not produce absolute amounts to be followed at all costs.

When the number of units to be produced is known, the quantity of each raw material input to be purchased would be forecast using the same model. The quantity of each raw material used per unit of production must be substituted into the model, as follows:

Beginning inventory	units
Add: Purchases of raw materials	units
Raw materials available for use	units
Less: Ending inventory	( ) units
Quantity of materials used in production	units

Exhibit 14-5 illustrates the development of a manufacturing firm's production budget to support the sales forecast, and the raw materials purchases budget to support the budgeted level of production. A merchandising firm's purchases budget would be similar to a manufacturer's production budget. To complete a budgeted income statement, physical quantities developed in the production budget and raw materials purchases budget must be converted to dollars. This conversion is done by multiplying

I. Assumptions:

A. Sales forecast in units per month:

January	10,000 units
February	12,000 units
March	15,000 units
April	11,000 units

B. Inventory policy:

Finished goods ending inventory should equal 1.4 times the subsequent month's forecasted sales. Raw materials ending inventory should equal 50% of the subsequent month's budgeted raw material usage.

C. Three pounds of raw materials are required for each unit of finished product.

II. Production budget calculations:

A. Ending inventory of finished goods required:

	December	January	February	March
Ending inventory units required (1.4 × sales forecast for subsequent month)...........	14,000	16,800	21,000	15,400

B. Production budget using the cost of goods sold model (assuming that December 31 inventory is equal to that required by the finished goods inventory policy):

	January	February	March
Beginning inventory (units)	14,000	16,800	21,000
Add: Production (units)	?	?	?
Goods available for sale (units)	?	?	?
Less: Ending inventory (units)	(16,800)	(21,000)	(15,400)
Quantity of goods sold (units)	10,000	12,000	15,000
By working from the bottom up, the quantity of goods available for sale is calculated first, and then beginning inventory is subtracted from goods available for sale to get production in units	12,800	16,200	9,400

III. Raw materials purchases budget calculations:

	January	February	March
A. Quantity of raw material used each month to produce the number of units called for by the production budget (3 pounds of raw materials per unit of finished product)	38,400	48,600	28,200
B. Ending inventory required (equal to 50% of next month's usage in pounds)	24,300	14,100	_____ *

C. Purchases budget using cost of goods sold model with known data (assuming that December 31 inventory is equal to that required by the raw materials inventory policy):

	January	February
Beginning inventory (pounds)	19,200	24,300
Add: Purchases	?	?
Raw materials available for use (pounds)	?	?
Less: Ending inventory (pounds)	(24,300)	(14,100)
Quantity of materials used (pounds)	38,400	48,600
By working from the bottom up, the quantity of raw materials available for use is calculated first, and then beginning inventory is subtracted from raw materials available for use to get purchases in pounds.	43,500	38,400

Note that the purchases budget for March cannot be established until the sales budget for May is available, because the inventory of finished goods at the end of March is a function of April production requirements.

*Won't be known until the April production budget is established.

the cost of a unit by the budgeted quantity for each element of the model. The computations involved are not complex, but they are numerous, and automated applications are widely used in the process.

If quantity forecast data are not desired because the cost of using the preceding approach is greater than its benefit, the approach can be easily modified to provide a dollar amount forecast for purchases or production. This is accomplished by using the complement of the budgeted gross profit ratio to calculate budgeted cost of goods sold. Beginning and ending inventories can be expressed as a function of budgeted cost of goods sold, and the dollar amount of budgeted purchases can then be determined. This process is illustrated in Exhibit 14-6.

The cost of goods manufactured budget will include budgeted amounts for direct labor and manufacturing overhead. Determining these budget amounts frequently involves the use of a standard cost system (discussed later in this chapter), which is based on an analysis of the labor and overhead inputs required per unit of product.

Many manufacturing firms increase the accuracy of their cost of production and cost of goods sold forecasts by using the contribution margin model for manufacturing costs. (Note that in a merchandising firm, the cost of goods sold is a variable expense.) Variable costs of manufacturing (raw materials, direct labor, and variable overhead) are determined, and the variable cost ratio (variable manufacturing costs as a percentage of selling price) is calculated. This ratio is then used instead of the cost of goods sold ratio, as illustrated in Exhibit 14-6. Fixed manufacturing expenses are budgeted separately because they are not a function of the quantity produced or sold.

Exhibit 14-6   Budgeted Purchases Using the Gross Profit Ratio

I. Assumptions:
Sales forecast as shown below.
Gross profit ratio budgeted at 30%.
Ending inventory planned to be 80% of next month's cost of goods sold.

II. Required:
Calculate the budgeted purchases for April, May, and June.

III. Budget calculations:

	March	April	May	June	July
Sales forecast	$75,000	$ 55,000	$ 70,000	$ 80,000	$90,000
Cost of goods sold (Sales × [1 − 0.3])	52,500	38,500	49,000	56,000	63,000
Ending inventory (equal to 80% of next month's cost of goods sold)	30,800	39,200	44,800	50,400	
Beginning inventory		$ 30,800	$ 39,200	$ 44,800	
Add: Purchases		?	?	?	
Goods available for sale		$?	$?	$?	
Less: Ending inventory		(39,200)	(44,800)	(50,400)	
Cost of goods sold		$ 38,500	$ 49,000	$ 56,000	
By working from the bottom up, the amount of goods available for sale is calculated first, and then beginning inventory is subtracted from goods available for sale to get purchases		$ 46,900	$ 54,600	$ 61,600	

Calculations involving inventory accounts are sometimes easier to understand when viewed graphically. The key to understanding inventory is to think of "goods available" by looking at where those goods available come from and where they end up. Goods available come from two sources: beginning inventory and goods purchased (or produced) during the period. Goods available end up being sold or left unsold as ending inventory. Knowing any three of these components allows you to solve for the remaining item. This concept is illustrated here:

Study

Suggestion

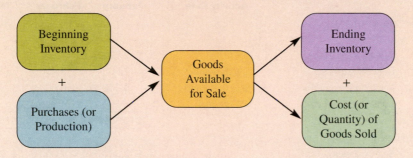

The Cost of Goods Sold Budget

The cost of goods sold budget summarizes changes in the Merchandise Inventory account for the merchandising firm and changes in the Finished Goods Inventory account for the manufacturing firm as indicated by the results of the sales budget, the purchases/production budget, and the required ending inventory levels determined by management. For the merchandising firm, the cost of goods available for sale is determined by adding the beginning merchandise inventory and the purchases planned in the purchases budget. Ending inventory requirements are then subtracted from goods available for sale to calculate the budgeted cost of goods sold. This process is identical for the manufacturing firm except that the merchandising firm has purchases and the manufacturing firm has the cost of goods manufactured as determined by the budgeted costs of each component of the production budget—the raw materials budget, the direct labor budget, and the manufacturing overhead budget.

The Operating Expense Budget

The cost behavior patterns of selling, general, administrative, and other operating expenses are determined, and these expenses are budgeted accordingly. For example, sales commissions will be a function of the forecast of either sales dollars or units. The historical pattern of some expenses will be affected by changes in strategy that management may plan for the budget period. In a participative budgeting system, the manager of each department or cost responsibility center will submit the anticipated cost of the department's planned activities, along with descriptions of the activities and explanations of significant differences from past experience. After review by higher levels of management, and perhaps negotiation, a final budget will be established. Exhibit 14-7 illustrates the significance of cost behavior patterns on the operating expense budget.

Operating managers have a natural tendency to submit budget estimates that are slightly higher than what the costs are really expected to be. This practice gives the manager some **budget slack** for contingencies or cost increases that may not have been

LO 6

Illustrate the importance of cost behavior patterns in developing the operating expense budget.

Exhibit 14-7

Operating Expense
Budget

I. Assumptions:

	January	February	March
Sales units	10,000	12,000	15,000
Sales revenue	$50,000	$60,000	$75,000

II. Budget calculations:

	Variable Activity Rate	January	February	March
Selling expenses:				
Variable selling expenses:				
Sales commissions	5% of sales	$ 2,500	$ 3,000	$ 3,750
Delivery expense	$0.25 per unit	2,500	3,000	3,750
Marketing promotions	$0.50 per unit	5,000	6,000	7,500
Bad debt expense	1% of sales	500	600	750
Total variable expense		$10,500	$12,600	$15,750
Fixed selling expenses:				
Sales salaries		$ 2,000	$ 2,000	$ 2,000
Advertising		3,000	3,000	3,000
Depreciation		960	960	960
Other fixed expenses		520	520	520
Total fixed expense		$ 6,480	$ 6,480	$ 6,480
Total selling expense		$16,980	$19,080	$22,230
Administrative expenses:				
Administrative salaries		$ 5,000	$ 5,000	$ 5,000
Facility expense		8,000	8,000	8,000
Depreciation		1,680	1,680	1,680
Property taxes		300	300	300
Other fixed expenses		480	480	480
Total administrative expense		$15,460	$15,460	$15,460
Budgeted operating expense		$32,440	$34,540	$37,690

anticipated. Adding budget slack or "padding the budget" can result in a significantly misleading budget for the organization as a whole. In spite of budget managers' pleas and/or threats that padding be eliminated, the practice probably continues in virtually all organizations. Some budget managers deal with the problem by judgmentally reducing the grand total of all departmental expense budgets when the company budget is prepared.

The Budgeted Income Statement

LO 7

Explain why and how a budgeted income statement and balance sheet are prepared, and prepare a cash budget.

The sales forecast, cost of goods sold budget, and operating expense budget data are used by management accountants to prepare a budgeted income statement. This process can be complex but necessary if the anticipated overall results of the budget period are to be evaluated in a meaningful way.

In many cases, if the budgeted income statement shows unacceptable results, top management will request that operating departments review their budget proposals and make appropriate adjustments so that profitability goals can be achieved.

The Cash Budget

The cash budget is very much like a budgeted statement of cash flows but with a relatively short time frame. The financial manager must be able to anticipate short-term borrowing requirements because arrangements for borrowing must be made in advance of the date when additional cash might be needed. When considering a loan proposal, the bank lending officer will want to know how much cash will be needed, how soon it will be needed, and when the borrower expects to repay the loan. A potential borrower who cannot answer these questions because a cash budget has not been prepared may be denied an otherwise reasonable loan request or may be charged a higher interest rate because of the perceived risk caused by these uncertainties. The financial manager also must know when temporarily excess cash is available for investment opportunities so that cash can be invested to earn interest income.

A number of assumptions about the timing of cash receipts and disbursements must be made when the cash budget is prepared. For example, how long after the sale will an account receivable be collected? The days' sales in receivables analysis will help answer this question. Again, the sales forecast comes into play. For example, assume that, based on past experience, the entity expects that 25 percent of a month's sales will be collected in the month of sale, 60 percent will be collected in the month following the month of sale, and 12 percent will be collected in the second month following the month of sale. (The last 3 percent will be collected over several months but is ignored in the budgeting process because of its relatively small amount and uncertain collection pattern. Some of these accounts may eventually be written off as uncollectible.) A cash receipts analysis for March and April might look like this:

	January	February	March	April
Sales forecast	$50,000	$60,000	$75,000	$55,000
Collections:				
25% of current month's sales			$18,750	$13,750
60% of prior month's sales			36,000	45,000
12% of second prior month's sales			6,000	7,200
Total collections			$60,750	$65,950

If this cash receipts forecast were being made in late December for the next four months, collections of sales made prior to January probably would be based on an estimate of when the accounts receivable at the end of December would be collected. This approach, and an alternative format for the cash receipts forecast analysis, would look like this:

	January	February	March	April
Sales forecast	$50,000	$60,000	$75,000	$55,000
Collections:				
From December 31 accounts receivable of $68,423 (amounts assumed)	$38,000	$25,000	$ 3,000	$ 1,000
From January sales	12,500	30,000	6,000	
From February sales		15,000	36,000	7,200
From March sales			18,750	45,000
From April sales				13,750
Total collections	$50,500	$70,000	$63,750	$66,950

Note that the difference between the budgeted cash receipts for March and April in the two formats is the estimated collections of December 31 accounts receivable. Even though the estimated collections from sales occur over three months, the estimated collections of December 31 accounts receivable are more realistically spread over a longer period, and it has been recognized that not all of the receivables are likely to be collected. It should be apparent that the keys to an accurate cash receipts forecast are the accuracy of the sales forecast and the accuracy of the collection percentage estimates.

On the cash disbursement side, the payment pattern for purchases must be determined. If suppliers' terms are 2/10, net 30, the financial manager will assume that two-thirds of a month's purchases will be paid for in the same month as the purchase, and one-third will be paid for in the subsequent month. The format of the analysis of payments of accounts payable will be similar to that illustrated for cash receipts. As was the case for the cash receipts forecast, the accuracy of the cash payments forecast is a function of the accuracy of the sales forecast and the payment pattern estimates. (Remember that the sales forecast impacts the finished goods budget and the raw materials purchases budget. Therefore, cash disbursements also will be impacted by the sales forecast.) A cash disbursements forecast for purchases budgeted for the months of April through June as calculated in Exhibit 14-6 would look like this:

	April	May	June
Purchases forecast	$46,900	$54,600	$61,600
Payments:			
From March purchases	$13,766		
From April purchases	31,267	$15,633	
From May purchases		36,400	$18,200
From June purchases			41,067
Total payments	$45,033	$52,033	$59,267

In addition to the payments for purchases, a number of other cash disbursements must be estimated. For example, the frequency with which the company pays its employees will be related to projected payroll expense to determine this significant disbursement. All other operating expense outlays need to be included in cash disbursements. Capital expenditure plans and anticipated dividend payments will also need to be considered. Projected depreciation and amortization expenses are ignored in cash budgeting because these are not expenses requiring the use of cash.

After the assumptions about the timing of cash receipts and disbursements have been made, the preparation of the cash budget is a straightforward process. Budgeted cash receipts are added to the beginning cash balance, budgeted disbursements are subtracted, and a preliminary ending balance is determined. The organization will have an established minimum cash balance to be maintained. This "inventory" of cash serves the same purpose as an inventory of product; it is a cushion that can absorb forecast errors. If the cash forecast indicates a preliminary balance that is less than the desired minimum, temporary investments must be liquidated or a loan must be planned to bring the forecast balance up to the desired level. If the preliminary balance is greater than the minimum desired working balance, the excess is available for repayment of loans or for investment. The cash budget will be prepared for monthly periods at least; many organizations forecast cash flows on a daily basis for a week or two, and then weekly for a month or two, so optimum cash management results can be achieved. Exhibit 14-8 illustrates a cash budget format and shows sources of the budget amounts.

Cash Budget Illustration and Assumptions | **Exhibit 14-8**

| CRUISERS, INC. |
| Cash Budget |
| For the Months of March and April |

Date Budget Prepared: February 25

Activity	March	April	Source/Comments
Beginning cash balance	$19,425	$ 8,842	March: Forecast balance for March 1. April: Indicated cash balance at end of March.
Cash Receipts:			
From sales made in prior periods	45,000	53,200	Analysis of accounts receivable detail when budget prepared, and sales forecast for subsequent periods with collection estimates based on past experience.
From sales made in current period	18,750	13,750	Sales forecast and estimates based on past experience.
From investing activities	1,000	—	Plans for sale of assets.
From financing activities	5,000	—	Plans for new borrowings or sale of stock.
Total cash available	$89,175	$ 75,792	
Cash Disbursements:			
To suppliers for inventory purchases	$44,333	$ 45,033	Analysis of accounts payable detail for purchases that have been made and of purchases budget for subsequent periods with estimates based on supplier terms and past payment practices.
To other creditors and employees for operating expenses and wages	20,000	24,000	Analysis of accrued liability detail for transactions that have occurred and of production budget and operating expense budget for subsequent periods, and knowledge of past payment practices.
For investing activities	8,000	17,000	Plans for purchase of plant and equipment, and other investments.
For financing activities	3,000	—	Plans for dividend payments, debt repayments, or purchases of treasury stock.
Total disbursements	$75,333	$ 86,033	
Indicated cash balance	$13,842	$(10,241)	
Desired cash balance	5,000	5,000	Based on financial operating needs and amount of "cushion" for error that is desired.
Excess (deficiency)	$ 8,842	$(15,241)	Excess available for temporary investment or repayment of loans. Deficiency indicates a need to liquidate temporary investments or arrange financing.

The Budgeted Balance Sheet

The impact of all of the other budgets on the balance sheet is determined, and a budgeted balance sheet is prepared. This hierarchy is illustrated in Exhibits 14-3 and 14-4. For example, the production and purchases budgets include inventory budget estimates. The operating expense budget is the source of the depreciation and amortization impact on the balance sheet. The budgeted income statement indicates the

effect of net income or loss on retained earnings. The cash budget, with its assumptions about collections of accounts receivable and payments of accounts payable and other liabilities, purchases of equipment, and payment of dividends and other financing activities, is the source of many budgeted balance sheet amounts. All of the current assets (except inventories) are derived from the cash budget, as are the budgeted amounts for plant assets, liabilities, paid-in capital, treasury stock, and the dividend impact on retained earnings. In effect, the financial accounting process is applied using planned transaction amounts to generate an anticipated balance sheet. This balance sheet will be analyzed to determine that all the appropriate financial ratios are within the limits established by top management. The reasons for any discrepancies will be determined, and appropriate changes in plans will be considered. This process may very well require modifications to some of the other budgets, and if so, the entire budgeting process may need to be adjusted or repeated. Although this may seem like a tedious and frustrating thing to do, it is better done in the planning process than after the company has already acted. Recovery at that stage may be very difficult to accomplish, and the firm's financial condition may have been adversely affected.

If desired, a budgeted statement of cash flows can be prepared from the budgeted income statement and balance sheet data. The process for doing this is the same as illustrated in Chapter 9. Many organizations prepare cash budgets on a monthly basis, along with an overall annual cash budget, which serves the same purpose as a statement of cash flows.

The most challenging parts of the budgeting process are developing the sales forecast, coming up with the assumptions related to the timing of cash receipts and disbursements, and establishing policies for ending inventory quantities, the minimum desired cash balance, and other targets. The budget calculations are easily made for most organizations using computer spreadsheet models or software solutions designed to provide comprehensive budgeting support. These tools make it feasible for planners to change various assumptions and to quickly and easily see the effect on budgeted results.

What Does It Mean?

Answer on page 561

4. What does it mean when the cash budget forecasts a cash deficiency?

Standard Costs

Using Standard Costs

Standard costs are are best understood when thinking of them as budgets for a single unit of product. Standards are used in the planning and control phases of the management process and in financial accounting to value the inventory of a manufacturing firm. A standard cost has two elements: the quantity of input and the cost per unit of input. The quantity of input could be weight or volume of raw materials, hours of labor, kilowatt hours of electricity, number of welding rods, or any other measure of physical input use. Standard cost systems are traditionally and most extensively used in the manufacturing environment, but their use in the service sector economy has grown significantly as well.

Because the standard represents a unit budget (i.e., the expected quantity and cost of the resources required to produce a unit of product or provide a unit of service), standards are used extensively in the budget preparation process. After the sales forecast has been developed and expressed in units, standards are used to plan for the inputs that will need to be provided to make the product or provide the service.

As the budget period proceeds, actual inputs used can be compared to the standard inputs that should have been used to make or service the actual output achieved. This comparison, which helps managers focus their efforts on achieving goals, is made in a performance report that will be discussed in detail in Chapter 15.

Frequently, control focuses on the quantity dimensions of the standard cost rather than the dollar amount of the standard cost (the product of quantity multiplied by unit cost) because the supervisor responsible can relate more easily to the physical quantity than to the dollar cost. For example, the supervisor responsible for raw material use and the supervisor responsible for order-processing activity probably relate more easily to pounds used and number of orders processed per employee, respectively, than they would to the costs of those inputs used during a reporting period.

Standard costs that have been appropriately developed (see the following discussion) can be used in the cost accounting system described in Chapter 13. This approach results in a cost system that is easier to use than one involving actual costs because when it comes to valuing inventory, standard costs have been developed prior to the accounting period, whereas actual costs aren't known until after the accounting period has been completed.

LO 8

Explain why and how standards are useful in the planning and control process.

Developing Standards

Because standards are budgets for individual units of product, all the management philosophy and individual behavior considerations identified in the discussion of the budgeting process in general also apply to standards. There are three strategic approaches to developing standards:

LO 9

Determine how the standard cost of a product is developed.

- Ideal, or engineered, standards.
- Attainable standards.
- Past experience standards.

An **ideal standard** assumes that operating conditions will be ideal and that material and labor inputs will be provided at maximum levels of efficiency at all times. One of the work measurement techniques used by industrial engineers is called *motion and time study*. This technique involves a very detailed analysis of the activities involved in performing a task, with the objective of designing work-station layout and operator movements so that the task can be performed most efficiently. Industrial engineers recognize that individual fatigue and other factors will result in actual performance over a period of time that will be less than 100 percent efficient, as defined by motion and time study analysis. However, these factors are ignored when an ideal standard is established. The principal disadvantage of ideal standards is that the standard will almost never be achieved, and as a result, supervisors and employees will not employ the standard as a realistic performance target.

An **attainable standard** recognizes that there will be some operating inefficiencies relative to ideal conditions. Actual performance will not always meet the standard, but employees are more likely to strive to achieve this type of standard than an ideal standard because of the sense of accomplishment that comes from meeting a legitimate goal. An attainable standard may present varying degrees of "tightness" or "looseness," depending on management philosophy and operating circumstances. For example, some firms create a highly competitive work environment and establish tight standards that require considerable effort to achieve. When an attainable standard is established, it is not set forever. Changes in worker efficiency and/or changes in the work environment may call for changes in the standard.

A **past experience standard** has the disadvantage of including all the inefficiencies that have crept into the operation over time. Such a standard is typically not challenging, and performance is not likely to improve over time. Such a standard reflects current performance but is not likely to provide much incentive for improvement.

The following table summarizes the performance expectations and related behavioral responses from employees that would likely be experienced with each standard setting strategy:

Standard-Setting Approach	Performance Expectation	Behavioral Implications
Ideal (engineered) standard	Operate at 100% efficiency 100% of the time	Attainment can realistically never be achieved
Attainable (practical) standard	Allow for practical adjustments relative to ideal operating conditions	Challenging but realistically perceived to be attainable as a genuine goal
Past experience standard	Current performance is acceptable and should continue	Currently attainable and not likely to motivate for improvement

Establishing performance standards for an organization that has not used them before is a significant management challenge. It is only natural for workers to be uncomfortable with the idea that someone will now be measuring and watching their efficiency. The usefulness of standards for planning and control purposes will increase over time as those affected by them learn and become accustomed to how supervisors and managers use the resulting performance reports. Many organizations have experienced productivity and profitability increases, and workers have experienced increases in job satisfaction and compensation as a result of well-designed and carefully implemented standard cost systems.

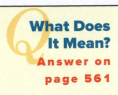

What Does It Mean?

Answer on page 561

5. What does it mean to develop a standard cost?
6. What does it mean to have an attainable standard?

Costing Products with Standard Costs

The process of establishing a standard cost for a product involves aggregating the individual standard costs for each of the inputs to the product: raw materials, direct labor, and manufacturing overhead. After the standard quantities allowed have been developed, as explained in the prior section, a standard cost for each unit of input is developed, and finally the standard cost for a unit of product is determined.

Developing the standard cost for each unit of input involves estimating costs for the budget period. The purchasing agent will provide input for raw material costs; the human resources department will be involved in establishing standard labor rates; and the production, purchasing, and human resources departments will provide data for estimating the various overhead costs. Because of the necessity to recognize cost behavior patterns for planning and control purposes, overhead costs will be classified as variable or fixed. Variable overhead usually will be expressed in terms of direct labor hours, machine hours, or some other physical measure that reflects the causes of overhead expenditures. Fixed overhead is expressed as a total cost per accounting period for planning and control purposes, and it is allocated to individual products for product costing purposes. Recall from Chapter 13 that this allocation is made by developing a fixed overhead application rate that is established by dividing the total fixed overhead budget amount by an estimated total volume of activity (such as direct labor hours, machine hours, or some other measure of activity). But remember, because fixed overhead does not behave on a per unit basis, this approach is not valid for planning and controlling fixed overhead: It is used only to allocate fixed overhead to individual products for product costing purposes.

The result of this process is a standard cost calculation that might look like this for a SeaCruiser sailboat hull manufactured by Cruisers Inc.:

LO 10

Describe how standard costs are used in the cost accounting system.

Variable costs:	
Raw materials:	
218 yd of fiberglass cloth @ $2.10/yd	$ 457.80
55 gal of epoxy resin @ $0.92/gal	50.60
1 purchased keel plate @ $132.16	132.16
Total raw materials	$ 640.56
Direct labor:	
26 hours of "build-up" labor @ $12.80/hr	$ 332.80
8 hours of finishing labor @ $19.30/hr	154.40
Total direct labor	$ 487.20
Variable overhead (based on total direct labor hours):	
34 hours @ $3.20/hr	$ 108.80
Total standard variable cost per unit	$1,236.56
	(continued)

Fixed costs:

Fixed overhead (the $10.80 rate is based on total budgeted fixed overhead for the year divided by total estimated direct labor hours to be worked during the year):

34 hours @ $10.80/hr	$ 367.20
Total standard cost per unit	$1,603.76

Note: For consistency purposes, the total variable and fixed manufacturing overhead cost equals $14 per direct labor hour, as shown in Exhibit 13-6. This is the predetermined overhead application rate used for cost accounting. The fixed overhead component of that rate is determined as explained in Exhibit 13-6; the variable component is developed by building a standard based on the relationship between the elements of variable overhead (e.g., utilities and maintenance) and the chosen activity base. In this example, that activity base is direct labor hours, but it can be any other physical measure that has a causal relationship with the cost.

In a similar fashion, the standard cost of every component of the boat would be developed. The standard cost of the SeaCruiser is the sum of the standard costs for all its components. The standard cost of all other models would be compiled in the same way. A great deal of effort and organizational resources are involved in implementing a standard cost system; but the benefit should be positive because of the planning, control, and product costing uses of the system. Many firms revise standard quantities allowed when necessary because of performance and operating changes, and they revise standard costs per unit of input on an annual basis. However, some large firms with many products involving hundreds of raw material and direct labor inputs have adopted a different strategy. Standards may be reviewed and revised on a cyclical basis over a two- or three-year period, or they may be retained for several years, anticipating and accepting differences between standard and actual cost that result from quantity or price changes. Managers of any firm using standards must weigh the trade-offs involved in keeping the standards current compared to revising them periodically.

Other Uses of Standards

In addition to being used for product costing in a manufacturing environment, standards can be developed and used for planning and control of period costs and for qualitative goals in both manufacturing and service organizations. For example, a day care center could develop a standard cost for the food provided to its clients and/or a standard for the number of staff required for a given number of clients of a given age.

Both manufacturing firms and service organizations are seeking to respond to increased competitive pressures by becoming more efficient. One outcome of this effort has been the development of goals, which can be expressed as standards, for such activities as these:

- Quality control, including total quality management programs and statistical quality control measures.
- Inventory control, including just-in-time inventory management systems and flexible manufacturing environments.
- Machine usage, including downtime for setup, preventive maintenance, and unscheduled repairs.
- Service levels, including customer/client response times, out-of-stock frequencies, and delivery times.

Few of these standards are expressed in terms of dollars per unit of product; they need not be expressed in dollars to be useful for management planning and control.

For manufacturing firms, standards often are developed to express organizational goals based on the notion of *continuous improvement* (e.g., "zero defects" or "100 percent on-time deliveries"). Even though absolute perfection cannot be realistically achieved, many firms use this type of standard to emphasize the importance of making progress and showing improvement rather than simply meeting standards. To monitor progress toward such goals, performance must be measured in *real time*—as production occurs—so that feedback can be provided continually. Machine adjustments and/or changes in the work flow can be made as the need arises, and many problems can be solved on the factory floor. Management's feedback loop is shortened significantly under this approach, which has the effect of increasing *throughput* (i.e., the output rate or cycle time) in the manufacturing process and reducing machine *downtime*.

A similar approach can be taken to monitor the "quality" of production and/or customer service. For production quality, an important measure is the first-time pass rate for each process, as indicated by the number (or percentage) of defective units per batch inspected. The higher the first-time pass rate, the less rework and scrap, which in turn reduces labor and material costs, respectively. Perhaps more important, poor production quality leads to unhappy customers and lost sales opportunities. To monitor customer service quality, procedures must be established to ensure that immediate and appropriate actions will be taken to resolve all customer complaints that management deems it feasible to resolve. The true "cost" of losing a valued customer may be unknown, but it is likely to exceed many of the readily measurable costs for which standards traditionally have been developed.

Budgeting for Other Analytical Purposes

Although this chapter emphasizes the budgeting of dollars and units of production for manufacturing firms, organizations in the service sector of the economy also use budgeting techniques for other important resources, such as personnel time, or for nonfinancial measures, such as the utilization of productive capacity. Consider the following examples:

- Law firms and public accounting firms often are concerned with "time" budgets and the ability of professional staff to generate "billable hours."
- Merchandising firms, especially large retail organizations, may be concerned with budgeted "sales dollars per square foot" of floor space.
- State and municipal governments must determine the best use of tax and other revenues and budget these resources to provide services or operate certain social programs, which are measured on a "per capita" basis.
- NFL teams must budget player contracts to operate within the "salary cap" requirement.
- Universities may make resources available to academic units based on budgeted "credit hours" for which they expect students to enroll.
- Not-for-profit agencies funded by the United Way may attempt to demonstrate the outreach achieved by their programs when seeking a share of annual campaign contributions.

Within a manufacturing firm, budgets also can be developed to meet the needs of other functional areas, such as the research and development, marketing, or customer service departments. Likewise, activity-based costing principles (discussed in Chapter 13) can be extended to the budgeting process. *Activity-based budgeting* is an

Business in
Practice

Do Companies Get Budgets All Wrong?

As we've learned throughout this chapter in significant detail, budgeting is the process of financial planning—a process that should be obviously critical to you by now which establishes a financial roadmap to guide the success of any organization. The budget should be a living document and become a practical tool to help managers accomplish the organization's goals. But while the framework we've studied is straightforward and the necessary mechanics to produce the operating budget are relatively modest, it's the behavioral side of budgeting that presents some interesting dynamics.

A 2013 *Wall Street Journal (WSJ) Leadership Report* suggests that while almost all companies prepare a budget, almost all companies do it wrong. Leaders are reported to be critical of both the typical process for creating the budget as well as the way budgets are eventually used by the organization. Related concerns and shortcomings are identified in the report as follows:

- The budget process distracts managers from doing their jobs and discourages risk-taking.
- The process also undermines integrity, distorts information, and leads to bad decisions.
- Meetings are endless and numbers are crunched that have long gone out of date.
- Budget targets are defined in backward-looking financial terms and don't reflect current organizational successes or challenges.
- The budget process provides underserving and unscrupulous managers the opportunity for self-aggrandizement and enrichment:
  - Those managers most skilled in negotiating easy budget targets will often earn the best performance ratings.
  - Some managers will manipulate numbers in their budget reports to inflate results in order to achieve budget targets.
  - Other managers will spend money wastefully in order to avoid future budget reductions.

The *WSJ* report stresses that if the annual budget process is to accomplish all of the positive results it is expected to, organizations will need to blow apart traditional budgeting by adopting the following blueprint to refocus the process:

1. Start dynamic planning—Since traditional annual budgets become quickly obsolete, update plans whenever new, more relevant information is identified that has a material impact on the business.
2. Allocate money where it is needed, when it is needed—No business unit should have to wait until next year for additional resources when new circumstances present opportunities or new needs arise.
3. Don't use budgets to evaluate performance—Budgets are notoriously poor evaluation tools and a manager's performance should be judged on how the business unit actually faired when compared to peer organizations or other defined performance standards.
4. Devise a richer set of performance metrics—Financial results alone are too narrow to accurately evaluate the performance. Multiple criteria that clearly articulate success factors and serve as leading indicators of coming financial performance are necessary.
5. Make bonuses incremental—Aligning compensation opportunity with minimum performance levels must consider the temptation by managers to manipulate results. Bonuses aligned with varying degrees of measured performance would minimize this temptation.

In conclusion, the strategic design of the budgeting process and related performance evaluation is to align the goals of individual managers and business units with the goals of the organization as a whole. A more adaptive and innovative organization that can respond quickly to new opportunities and threats should also enjoy a team of motivated managers making better business decisions with more timely, relevant, and unbiased information.

Source: wsj.com/articles/SB10001424127887323873904578571810482331202.

attempt to relate the cost of performing each unit of activity (cost driver) to the demand for that activity. The budgeted cost per unit of activity (e.g., cost per part handled or cost per unit inspected) can be compared to the actual cost incurred for the level of activity performed during the period, and corrective action can be taken if necessary.

Standard costs for raw materials, direct labor, and manufacturing overhead, as budgets for a single unit of product, provide benchmarks for evaluating actual performance. This control process, which is referred to as *variance analysis,* will be developed in Chapter 15. Capital budgeting (discussed in Chapter 16) involves long-term strategic planning and the commitment of a significant amount of the firm's resources for extended periods of time. Whereas the operating budget reflects the firm's strategic plans to achieve current-period profitability, the capital budget provides an overall blueprint to help the firm meet its long-term growth objectives.

Demonstration Problem

The Demonstration Problem walkthrough for this chapter is available in
Connect.

Summary

A budget is a financial plan. Many organizations have a policy to require budgets because budgets force planning, provide a benchmark against which performance can be compared, and require coordination between the functional areas of the organization. To budget effectively a clear understanding of cost behavior, *variable and fixed costs,* it is necessary to appreciate how costs are expected to change as budgeted levels of activity change. Fixed costs classified according to a time-frame perspective are known as *committed costs* and *discretionary costs.* A committed cost is one that will be incurred to execute long-range policy decisions to which the firm has committed. A discretionary cost is one that can be adjusted in the short run at management's discretion. **(LO 1)**

To a large extent, the budgeting process is influenced by behavioral considerations. How the budget is used by management will influence the validity of the budget as a planning and control tool. In most instances, an interactive, participative approach to budget preparation, together with an attitude that the budget is an operating plan, results in a most useful budget document. **(LO 2)**

Budgets can be prepared for a single period or on a multiperiod, rolling basis. Which is most appropriate for any activity depends on the degree of control over the activity and the speed with which the environment of the activity changes. Different activities may have different budget time frames. **(LO 3)**

An operating budget is made up of several component budgets. The sales forecast (or revenue budget) is the starting point for all the other budgets that become part of the operating budget. The operating budget consists of a hierarchy of budgets, and the results of one budget provides input for the preparation of another budget. **(LO 4)**

The purchases/production budget is prepared after the sales forecast has been determined and an inventory policy has been established. Ending inventory is expressed as a function of the expected sales or usage of the subsequent period. One period's ending inventory is the next period's beginning inventory. **(LO 5)**

Operating managers have a natural tendency to build slack into their budget estimates. When budget managers combine departmental budgets into an overall organizational budget, the cumulative slack can cause the overall budget to lose significance. Budget managers must be aware of the slack issue and deal with it in ways that promote organizational goals. The operating expense budget is a function of the sales forecast, cost behavior patterns, and planned changes from past levels of advertising, administrative, and other activities. **(LO 6)**

A budgeted income statement shows planned operating results for the entity as a whole. If top management is not satisfied with budgeted net income, changes in operations may be planned and/or various elements of the operating budget may be returned to operating managers for revision. **(LO 7)**

After the income statement budget has been settled, a cash budget can be prepared. Cash flows from operating activities are forecast by adjusting net income for noncash items included in the income statement, as well as expectations about cash receipts and disbursements related to revenues and expenses. Cash flows from investing and financing activities are estimated, and the estimated cash balance at the end of the fiscal period is determined. Cash in excess of a minimum operating balance is available for investment. A deficiency in cash means that plans should be made to liquidate temporary investments or borrow money, or that cash payment assumptions must be revised. **(LO 7)**

The budgeted balance sheet uses data from all the other budgets. Management uses this budget to evaluate the entity's projected financial position. If the result is not satisfactory, appropriate operating, investing, and financing plans will be revised. **(LO 7)**

A standard cost is a unit budget for a single component of a product or service. As such, standards are used like any budget in planning and controlling. Standards can also facilitate the calculation of product costs for inventory valuation purposes. Because a standard is a unit budget, it can be used in the process of building the various component budgets of the operating budget. Standards also provide a benchmark for evaluating performance. Standards are typically expressed in monetary terms ($/unit) but can also be useful when expressed in physical quantities (lb/unit). **(LO 8)**

Standards are usually established on the basis of engineering studies and should be attainable. Ideal standards and past experience standards are less useful because they are not likely to serve as positive motivators. **(LO 9)**

The standard cost for a product is the sum of the standard costs for raw materials, direct labor, and manufacturing overhead used in making the product. A fixed manufacturing overhead standard is a unitized fixed expense and therefore must be used carefully because fixed expenses do not behave on a per unit basis. **(LO 10)**

Standards are useful for the entire range of planning and control activities; they are not restricted to use in product costing. Thus, many service organizations and manufacturing firms have developed standards for period costs. Standards can also be developed for qualitative goals that may not be expressed in financial terms. **(LO 10)**

Key Terms and Concepts

attainable standard (p. 540)   A standard cost or production standard that is achievable under actual operating conditions.

budget (p. 520)   A financial plan.

budget slack (p. 533)   Allowances for contingencies built into a budget. Sometimes called *padding* or *cushion.*

committed cost (p. 523)   A cost that is incurred because of a long-range policy decision.

continuous budget (p. 525)   A budget that is prepared for several periods in the future and then revised several times prior to the budget period. Sometimes called a *rolling budget.*

discretionary cost (p. 523)   A cost that can be raised or lowered in the short run.

fixed cost (p. 522)   A cost that does not change in total as the level of activity changes within the relevant range.

ideal standard (p. 539)   A standard cost or a production standard that assumes ideal operating conditions and maximum efficiency at all times.

incremental budgeting (p. 524)   A budgeting process that starts with actual performance for the current budget period and then adjusts these amounts for changes that are expected to occur in the next budget period.

master budget (p. 526)   An operating plan comprising the sales forecast (or revenue budget), the purchases/production budget, the operating expense budget, the income statement budget, the cash budget, and the budgeted balance sheet. Sometimes called an *operating budget.*

mixed cost (p. 523)   A cost that has both fixed and variable elements.

operating budget (p. 526)   An operating plan comprising the sales forecast (or revenue budget), the purchases/production budget, the operating expense budget, the income statement budget, the cash budget, and the budgeted balance sheet. Sometimes called a *master budget.*

participative budgeting (p. 524)   A budgeting process that involves the input and negotiation of several layers of management.

past experience standard (p. 540)   A standard cost or production standard that is based on historical data.

planning (p. 520)   The management process of identifying and quantifying the goals of the organization.

rolling budget (p. 525)   A budget that is prepared for several periods in the future and then revised several times prior to the budget period. Sometimes called a *continuous budget.*

sales forecast (p. 526)   Expected sales for future periods; a key to the budgeting process.

single-period budget (p. 525)   A budget that has been prepared only once prior to the budget period. This contrasts with a *continuous budget.*

standard cost (p. 521)   A unit budget allowance for a cost component of a product or activity.

top-down budgeting (p. 524)   A budgeting approach that implies little or no input from lower levels of management.

variable cost (p. 522)   A cost that changes in total as the volume of activity changes.

zero-based budgeting (p. 524)   A budgeting process that involves justifying resource requirements based on an analysis and prioritization of unit objectives without reference to prior period budget allowances.

Mini-Exercises

All applicable Mini-Exercises are available in *Connect.*

Sales forecast and budget   ABC Company's actual unit sales in the current year for January, February, and March was 15,000, 12,000, and 18,000 units, respectively. Current year selling price is $20. An analysis of general economic trends and specific initiatives at ABC forecasts increases for the coming budget year: sales volume by 10% and sales price by 5%.

Mini-Exercise 14.1

LO 4

Required:

Prepare ABC Company's budgeted unit sales and total sales volume for the first quarter of the coming year.

**Mini-Exercise
14.2
LO 4, LO 5**

Production budget ABC Company's budgeted sales for June, July, and August are 12,000, 16,000, and 14,000 units, respectively. ABC requires 30% of the next month's budgeted unit sales as finished goods inventory each month. Budgeted ending finished goods inventory for May is 3,600 units.

Required:

Calculate the number of units to be produced in June and July.

**Mini-Exercise
14.3
LO 4, LO 5**

Purchases budget In addition to the information presented in Mini-Exercise 14.2, each unit that ABC Company produces uses four pounds of raw material. ABC requires 20% of the next month's budgeted production as raw material inventory each month.

Required:

Calculate the number of pounds of raw material to be purchased in June.

**Mini-Exercise
14.4
LO 6**

Operating expense budget In addition to the information presented in Mini-Exercise 14.2, the following cost behavior patterns are budgeted for ABC Company's operating expenses each month:

Fixed costs: salaries, $2,000; rent, $5,000; depreciation, $2,400; advertising, $3,200

Mixed costs: utilities, $3,000 + $0.50 per unit

Variable costs per unit sold: sales commissions, $2.00; marketing promotions, $1.00; supplies, $0.75; bad debt expense, $0.25

Required:

Prepare ABC Company's operating expense budget for June, July, and August.

**Mini-Exercise
14.5
LO 7**

Cash receipts analysis In addition to the information presented in Mini-Exercise 14.2, the selling price for each unit is $20. Based on past experience, ABC expects that 35% of a month's sales will be collected in the month of sale, 53% in the following month, and 10% in the second month following the sale.

Required:

Prepare an analysis of cash receipts from sales for ABC Company for August.

**Mini-Exercise
14.6
LO 7**

Cash disbursements analysis ABC Company's raw materials purchases for June, July, and August are budgeted at $35,000, $25,000, and $50,000, respectively. Based on past experience, ABC expects that 60% of a month's raw material purchases will be paid in the month of purchase and 40% in the month following the purchase.

Required:

Prepare an analysis of cash disbursements from raw materials purchases for ABC Company for August.

**Mini-Exercise
14.7
LO 7**

Cash budget ABC Company has a cash balance of $25,000 on August 1 and requires a minimum ending cash balance of $20,000. Cash receipts from sales budgeted for August are $291,600. Cash disbursements budgeted for August include inventory purchases, $40,000; other manufacturing expenses, $98,000; operating expenses, $76,200; bond retirements, $50,000; and dividend payments, $15,000.

Required:
Prepare a cash budget for ABC Company for August.

Standard product cost In addition to the information presented in Mini-Exercises 14.2 and 14.3, ABC Company currently pays a standard rate of $2 per pound for raw materials. Each unit should be produced in 15 minutes of direct labor time at a standard direct labor rate of $16 per hour. Manufacturing overhead is applied at the standard rate of $20 per direct labor hour.

Mini-Exercise 14.8

LO 9

Required:
Calculate the standard cost per unit for ABC Company.

Exercises

connect

All applicable Exercises are available in *Connect*.

Production and purchases budgets Olympia Productions Inc. makes award medallions that are attached to ribbons. Each medallion requires 18 inches of ribbon. The sales forecast for February is 2,000 medallions. Estimated beginning inventories and desired ending inventories for February are as follows:

Exercise 14.9

LO 4, 5

	Estimated Beginning Inventory	Desired Ending Inventory
Medallions	1,000	800
Ribbon (yards)	50	20

Required:
a. Calculate the number of medallions to be produced in February.
b. Calculate the number of yards of ribbon to be purchased in February.

Production and purchases budgets Gillman Co. is forecasting sales of 80,600 units of product for August. To make one unit of finished product, five pounds of raw materials are required. Actual beginning and desired ending inventories of raw materials and finished goods are as follows:

Exercise 14.10

LO 4, 5

	August 1 (Actual)	August 31 (Desired)
Raw materials (pounds)	97,100	88,600
Finished goods (units)	7,700	10,800

Required:
a. Calculate the number of units of product to be produced during August.
b. Calculate the number of pounds of raw materials to be purchased during August.

Exercise 14.11
LO 5

Purchases budget Each gallon of Old Guard, a popular aftershave lotion, requires two ounces of ocean scent. Budgeted *production* of Old Guard for the first three quarters of 2019 is as follows:

Quarter I	10,000 gallons
Quarter II	18,000 gallons
Quarter III	11,000 gallons

Management's policy is to have on hand at the end of every quarter enough ocean scent inventory to meet 25% of the next quarter's production needs. At the beginning of Quarter I, 5,000 ounces of ocean scent were on hand.

Required:
a.   Calculate the number of ounces of ocean scent to be purchased in each of the first two quarters of 2019.
b.   Explain why management plans for an ending inventory instead of planning to purchase each quarter the amount of raw materials needed for that quarter's production.

Exercise 14.12
LO 4, 5

Production and purchases budgets Osage Inc. has actual sales for May and June and forecast sales for July, August, September, and October as follows:

Actual:	
May	8,300 units
June	8,700 units
Forecast:	
July	8,400 units
August	9,500 units
September	7,800 units
October	7,400 units

Required:
a.   The firm's policy is to have finished goods inventory on hand at the end of the month that is equal to 80% of the next month's sales. It is currently estimated that there will be 6,600 units on hand at the end of June. Calculate the number of units to be produced in each of the months of July, August, and September.
b.   Each unit of finished product requires four pounds of raw materials. The firm's policy is to have raw material inventory on hand at the end of each month that is equal to 70% of the next month's estimated usage. It is currently estimated that 26,000 pounds of raw materials will be on hand at the end of June. Calculate the number of pounds of raw materials to be purchased in each of the months of July and August.

Exercise 14.13
LO 4, 7

Cash receipts budget Fox Trail Center's sales are all made on account. The firm's collection experience has been that 30% of a month's sales are collected in the month the sale is made, 50% are collected in the month following the sale, and 18% are collected in the second month following the sale. The sales forecast for the months of May through August is as follows:

May	$240,000
June	280,000
July	300,000
August	350,000

Required:
Calculate the cash collections that would be included in the cash budgets for July and August.

Cash receipts budget Scottsdale Co. has actual sales for July and August and forecast sales for September, October, November, and December as follows:

Exercise 14.14
LO 4, 7

Actual:	
July	$294,000
August	315,000
Forecast:	
September	342,000
October	282,000
November	366,000
December	321,000

Based on past experience, it is estimated that 40% of a month's sales are collected in the month of sale, 50% are collected in the month following the sale, and 9% are collected in the second month following the sale.

Required:
Calculate the estimated cash receipts for September, October, and November.

Developing direct labor cost standards Brass Creations Co. makes decorative candle pedestals. An industrial engineer consultant developed ideal time standards for one unit of the Cambridge model pedestal. The standards follow, along with the cost accountant's determination of current labor pay rates:

Exercise 14.15
LO 8, 9

Worktype 1	0.15 hour @ $12.30 per hour
Worktype 2	0.30 hour @ $10.90 per hour
Worktype 3	0.60 hour @ $19.50 per hour

Required:
a. Using the preceding data, calculate the direct labor cost for a Cambridge model pedestal.
b. Would it be appropriate to use the cost calculated in part **a** as a standard cost for evaluating direct labor performance and valuing inventory? Explain your answer.

Exercise 14.16

LO 8, 9

Developing raw material cost standards Lakeway Manufacturing Co. manufactures and sells household cleaning products. The company's research department has developed a new cleaner for which a standard cost must be determined. The new cleaner is made by mixing 15 quarts of triphate solution and 6 pounds of sobase granules and boiling the mixture for several minutes. After the solution has cooled, 3 ounces of methage are added. This "recipe" produces 12 quarts of the cleaner, which is then packaged in 1-quart plastic dispenser bottles. Raw material costs are as follows:

Triphate solution	$0.40 per quart
Sobase granules	0.86 per pound
Methage	1.30 per ounce
Bottle	0.18 each

Required:

a. Using the preceding data, calculate the raw material cost for one bottle of the new cleaner.

b. Assume that the preceding costs are the current best estimates of the costs at which required quantities of the raw material can be purchased. Would you recommend that any other factors be considered in establishing the raw material cost standard for the new cleaner?

c. Explain the process that would be used to develop the direct labor cost standard for the new product.

Exercise 14.17

LO 9, 10

Standard absorption cost per unit DMA Inc. processes corn into corn starch and corn syrup. The company's productivity and cost standards follow:

From every bushel of corn processed, 12 pounds of starch and three pounds of syrup should be produced.

Standard direct labor and variable overhead total $0.42 per bushel of corn processed.

Standard fixed overhead (the predetermined fixed overhead application rate) is $0.35 per bushel processed.

Required:

a. Calculate the standard absorption cost per pound for the starch and syrup produced from the processing of 15,000 bushels of corn if the average cost per bushel is $2.83.

b. Comment about the usefulness of this standard cost for management planning and control purposes.

Exercise 14.18

LO 9, 10

Standard absorption cost per unit A cost analyst for Stamper Manufacturing Co. has assembled the following data about the Model 24 stamp pad:

The piece of sheet metal from which eight pad cases can be made costs $0.18.

This amount is based on the number of sheets in a 4,000-pound bundle of sheet metal, which is the usual purchase quantity.

The foam pad that is put in the case costs $0.05, based on the number of pads that can be cut from a large roll of foam.

Production standards, based on engineering analysis recognizing attainable performance, provide for the manufacture of 2,000 pads by two workers in an eight-hour shift. The standard direct labor pay rate is $14 per hour.

Manufacturing overhead is applied to units produced using a predetermined overhead application rate of $18 per direct labor hour, of which $8 per hour is fixed manufacturing overhead.

Required:

a. Calculate the standard absorption cost of a package of 12 stamp pads.

b. Stamper Manufacturing Co.'s management is considering a special promotion that would result in increased sales of 1,000 packages of 12 pads per package. Calculate the cost per package that is relevant for this analysis.

Problems

All applicable Problems are available in *Connect*.

Purchases budget Brooklyn Furniture, a retail store, has an average gross profit ratio of 46%. The sales forecast for the next four months follows:

Problem 14.19
LO 4, 5

July	$250,000
August	220,000
September	310,000
October	400,000

Management's inventory policy is to have ending inventory equal to 300% of the cost of sales for the subsequent month, although it is estimated that the cost of inventory at June 30 will be $410,000.

Required:

Calculate the purchases budget, in dollars, for the months of July and August.

Purchases budget—analytical Precious Stones Ltd. is a retail jeweler. Most of the firm's business is in jewelry and watches. The firm's average gross profit ratio for jewelry and watches is 70% and 40%, respectively. The sales forecast for the next two months for each product category is as follows:

Problem 14.20
LO 4, 5

	Jewelry	Watches
May	$186,000	$90,000
June	144,000	76,500

The company's policy, which is expected to be achieved at the end of April, is to have ending inventory equal to 150% of the next month's cost of goods sold.

Required:

a. Calculate the cost of goods sold for jewelry and watches for May and June.

b. Calculate a purchases budget, in dollars, for each product for the month of May.

Problem 14.21

LO 4, 7

Cash budget—part 1 PrimeTime Sportswear is a custom imprinter that began operations six months ago. Sales have exceeded management's most optimistic projections. Sales are made on account and collected as follows: 50% in the month after the sale is made and 45% in the second month after sale. Merchandise purchases and operating expenses are paid as follows:

In the month during which the merchandise is purchased or the cost is incurred	75%
In the subsequent month	25%

PrimeTime Sportswear's income statement budget for each of the next four months, newly revised to reflect the success of the firm, follows:

	September	October	November	December
Sales	$42,000	$54,000	$68,000	$59,000
Cost of goods sold:				
Beginning inventory	$ 6,000	$14,400	$20,600	$21,900
Purchases	37,800	44,000	48,900	33,100
Cost of goods available for sale	$43,800	$58,400	$69,500	$55,000
Less: Ending inventory	(14,400)	(20,600)	(21,900)	(20,000)
Cost of goods sold	$29,400	$37,800	$47,600	$35,000
Gross profit	$12,600	$16,200	$20,400	$24,000
Operating expenses	10,500	12,800	14,300	16,100
Operating income	$ 2,100	$ 3,400	$ 6,100	$ 7,900

Cash on hand August 31 is estimated to be $40,000. Collections of August 31 accounts receivable were estimated to be $20,000 in September and $15,000 in October. Payments of August 31 accounts payable and accrued expenses in September were estimated to be $24,000.

Required:

a. Prepare a cash budget for September.

b. What is your advice to management of PrimeTime Sportswear?

Problem 14.22

LO 4, 7

Cash budget—part 2 Refer to the PrimeTime Sportswear data presented in Problem 14.21.

Required:

a. Prepare a cash budget for October and November. What are the prospects for this company if its sales growth continues at a similar rate?

b. Assume now that PrimeTime Sportswear is a mature firm, and that the September–November data represent a seasonal peak in business. Prepare a cash budget for December, January, and February, assuming that the income statements for January and February are the same as December's. Explain how the cash budget would be used to support a request to a bank for a seasonal loan.

Problem 14.23

LO 7

Cash budget The monthly cash budgets for the second quarter of 2019 follow ($000 omitted) for Forest Hills Mfg. Co. A minimum cash balance of $30,000 is required to start each month, and a $100,000 line of credit has been arranged with a local bank at a 8% interest rate.

	April	May	June	Total
Cash balance, beginning	$ 26	$?	$?	$ 26
Add collections from customers	?	108	?	?
Total cash available	$ 94	$?	$166	$338
Less disbursements:				
Purchase of inventory	$?	$ 60	$ 48	$?
Operating expenses	30	?	?	?
Capital additions	34	8	?	44
Payment of dividends	–	–	?	8
Total disbursements	$?	$108	$ 82	$304
Excess (deficiency) of cash available over disbursements	$(20)	$?	$ 84	$?
Borrowings	?	–	–	?
Repayments (including interest)	–	–	?	?
Cash balance, ending	$?	$ 30	$?	$ 33

Required:
Calculate the missing amounts. (*Hint:* The total cash available includes collections from customers for all three months, plus the beginning cash balance from April 1, 2019.)

Cash budget—comprehensive Following are the budgeted income statements for the second quarter of 2019 for SeaTech Inc.:

Problem 14.24
LO 7

	April	May	June
Sales	$112,000	$136,000	$152,000
Cost of goods sold*	76,800	91,200	100,800
Gross profit	$ 35,200	$ 44,800	$ 51,200
Operating expenses†	17,600	20,000	21,600
Operating income	$ 17,600	$ 24,800	$ 29,600

*Includes all *product costs* (i.e., direct materials, direct labor, and manufacturing overhead).
†Includes all *period costs* (i.e., selling, general, and administrative expenses).

The company expects about 40% of sales to be cash transactions. Of sales on account, 65% are expected to be collected in the first month after the sale is made, and 35% are expected to be collected in the second month after sale. Depreciation, insurance, and property taxes represent $9,600 of the estimated monthly cost of goods sold and $6,400 of the estimated monthly operating expenses. The annual insurance premium is paid in January, and the annual property taxes are paid in August. Of the remainder of the cost of goods sold and operating expenses, 90% are expected to be paid in the month in which they are incurred, and the balance is expected to be paid in the following month.

Current assets as of April 1, 2019, consist of cash of $11,200 and accounts receivable of $119,840 ($84,000 from March credit sales and $35,840 from February credit sales). Current liabilities as of April 1 consist of $14,400 of accounts payable for product costs incurred in March; $3,680 of accrued liabilities for operating expenses incurred in March; and a $38,000, 12%, 120-day note payable that is due on April 17, 2019.

An estimated income tax payment of $36,000 will be made in May. The regular quarterly dividend of $12,800 is expected to be declared in May and paid in June. Capital expenditures amounting to $13,760 will be made in April.

Required:

a. Complete the monthly cash budgets for the second quarter of 2019 using the following format. Note that the ending cash balance for June is provided as a check figure.

SEATECH INC. Cash Budget For the Months of April, May, and June 2019	April	May	June
Beginning cash balance	$11,200	$	$
Cash Receipts:			
From cash sales made in current month			
From credit sales made in:			
February			
March			
April			
May			
Total cash available	$	$	$
Cash Disbursements:			
For cost of goods sold and operating expenses incurred in:			
March	$	$	$
April			
May			
June			
For payment of note payable and interest			
For capital expenditures			
For payment of income taxes			
For payment of dividends			
Total disbursements	$	$	$
Ending cash balance	$	$	$21,760

b. Assume that management of SeaTech Inc. desires to maintain a minimum cash balance of $10,000 at the beginning of each month and has arranged a $50,000 line of credit with a local bank at an interest rate of 10% to ensure the availability of funds. Borrowing transactions are to occur only at the end of months in which the budgeted cash balance would otherwise fall short of the $10,000 minimum balance. Repayments of principal and interest are to occur at the end of the earliest month in which sufficient funds are expected to be available for repayment. Explain how this minimum cash balance requirement would affect the monthly cash budgets prepared in part **a**.

Sales, production, purchases, and cash budgets Soprano Co. is in the process of preparing the second quarter budget for 2019, and the following data have been assembled:

Problem 14.25
LO 4, 5, 7

- The company sells a single product at a selling price of $40 per unit. The estimated sales volume for the next six months is as follows:

March	6,000 units	June	8,000 units
April	7,000 units	July	9,000 units
May	10,000 units	August	6,000 units

- All sales are on account. The company's collection experience has been that 40% of a month's sales are collected in the month of sale, 55% are collected in the month following the sale, and 5% are uncollectible. It is expected that the net realizable value of accounts receivable (i.e., accounts receivable less allowance for uncollectible accounts) will be $132,000 on March 31, 2019.

- Management's policy is to maintain ending finished goods inventory each month at a level equal to 50% of the next month's budgeted sales. The finished goods inventory on March 31, 2019, is expected to be 3,500 units.

- To make one unit of finished product, three pounds of materials are required. Management's policy is to have enough materials on hand at the end of each month to equal 40% of the next month's estimated usage. The raw materials inventory is expected to be 10,200 pounds on March 31, 2019.

- The cost per pound of raw material is $6, and 80% of all purchases are paid for in the month of purchase; the remainder is paid in the following month. The accounts payable balance for raw material purchases is expected to be $26,280 on March 31, 2019.

Required:

a. Prepare a sales budget in units and dollars, by month and in total, for the second quarter (April, May, and June) of 2019.

b. Prepare a schedule of cash collections from sales, by month and in total, for the second quarter of 2019.

c. Prepare a production budget in units, by month and in total, for the second quarter of 2019.

d. Prepare a materials purchases budget in pounds, by month and in total, for the second quarter of 2019.

e. Prepare a schedule of cash payments for materials, by month and in total, for the second quarter of 2019.

Sales, production, purchases, and cash budgets Freese Inc. is in the process of preparing the fourth quarter budget for 2019, and the following data have been assembled:

Problem 14.26
LO 4, 5, 7

- The company sells a single product at a price of $50 per unit. The estimated sales volume for the next six months is as follows:

September	26,000 units
October	24,000 units
November	28,000 units
December	40,000 units
January	18,000 units
February	20,000 units

- All sales are on account. The company's collection experience has been that 33% of a month's sales are collected in the month of sale, 65% are collected in the month following the sale, and 2% are uncollectible. It is expected that the net realizable value of accounts receivable (i.e., accounts receivable less allowance for uncollectible accounts) will be $845,000 on September 30, 2019.
- Management's policy is to maintain ending finished goods inventory each month at a level equal to 40% of the next month's budgeted sales. The finished goods inventory on September 30, 2019, is expected to be 9,600 units.
- To make one unit of finished product, five pounds of materials are required. Management's policy is to have enough materials on hand at the end of each month to equal 30% of the next month's estimated usage. The raw materials inventory is expected to be 38,400 pounds on September 30, 2019.
- The cost per pound of raw material is $4, and 75% of all purchases are paid for in the month of purchase; the remainder is paid in the following month. The accounts payable for raw material purchases is expected to be $126,600 on September 30, 2019.

Required:

a. Prepare a sales budget in units and dollars, by month and in total, for the fourth quarter (October, November, and December) of 2019.

b. Prepare a schedule of cash collections from sales, by month and in total, for the fourth quarter of 2019.

c. Prepare a production budget in units, by month and in total, for the fourth quarter of 2019.

d. Prepare a materials purchases budget in pounds, by month and in total, for the fourth quarter of 2019.

e. Prepare a schedule of cash payments for materials, by month and in total, for the fourth quarter of 2019.

---

connect Cases

All applicable Cases are available in *Connect*.

Case 14.27
LO 9

Standard-setting process Canada Printing Group Inc. (CPGI) has recently begun the process of acquiring small to medium-size local and regional printing firms across the country to facilitate its corporate strategy of becoming the low-cost provider of graphic arts and printing services in Canada. To emphasize the importance of cost control, CPGI uses a standard cost system in all its printing plants. Most of the smaller firms that CPGI has acquired have never used a standard cost system before. Therefore, when CPGI acquires a new printing plant, its first task is to evaluate the operation and set standards for the printing presses.

One such recent acquisition was Pierre's Lithographing of Montreal. Pierre has a five-year-old, 40-inch, four-color press that is in very good condition. Specifications provided by the manufacturer of the press indicate that under ideal conditions, the press should be able to produce 10,000 impressions per hour. CPGI has many similar presses throughout its organization, and in most locations, the standard has been set at 9,000 impressions per hour. Many of Pierre's jobs have been for smaller run quantities, which means that the presses are stopped many times during the day as the press operator sets up the press for each new job. Additionally, the jobs that Pierre attracts are very complex and require high-quality results. Pierre suggests that even if everything ran perfectly throughout a day, the most he could expect the press to run would be 8,000 impressions per hour.

As usual with new acquisitions, CPGI has prepared a time study of the press for the past six months to determine how productive each of the operators has been. The results of the time study are as follows:

Press Operator	Average Impressions per Hour
M. Lemieux	6,800
G. LeFleur	5,700
M. Richard	7,400
P. Roy	6,100
P. Turgeon	6,500
Overall average	6,500

Required:

a. CPGI is considering five possibilities for setting the press standard for impressions per hour: 10,000, 9,000, 8,000, 7,400, or 6,500. Discuss the appropriateness, including a list of pros and cons, of setting the press standard at each level identified.

b. What qualitative factors should CPGI consider when setting a standard for the same model press at other sites across Canada?

c. Which level would you choose for the press standard at Pierre's Lithographing of Montreal? Explain your answer.

Budget of the U.S. government: Internet assignment The Office of Management and Budget (OMB) provides access to the budget of the United States government through the U.S. Government Printing Office's Federal Digital System (FDsys) at gpo.gov/fdsys. At this site, you will find a link to the specific collection, the "Budget of the United States Government," or it may be found at www.gpo.gov/fdsys/browse/collectionGPO.action?collectionCode=BUDGET. As the featured collection description states, "The Budget of the United States Government is a collection of documents that contains the budget message of the President, information about the President's budget proposals for a given fiscal year, and other budgetary publications that have been issued throughout the fiscal year. Other related and supporting budget publications are included, which may vary from year to year."

Case 14.28

One particularly useful supporting publication that appeared from 1996 through 2002 was "A Citizen's Guide to the Federal Budget," which provided information about the budget and the budget process for the general public. This guide was designed to give the reader a walking tour of the budget of the United States. Access the guide for fiscal year 2002, and complete the following requirements:

Required:

a.   Why was the guide designed, and what information is presented at this site?

b.   What is the federal budget?

c.   What percentage of the gross domestic product does spending for federal programs represent? What percentage does state and local government spending represent?

d.   What was the amount of total receipts? Where did they come from?

e.   What was the amount of total outlays? Where did they go?

f.   Explain the process used by the government to create a budget.

g.   How is the federal budget monitored?

h.   What is meant by a *budget surplus*? A *budget deficit*?

i.   Why is a budget deficit important? A budget surplus?

j.   How does the government's budget process compare to the operating budgeting process described in the chapter? What are the similarities and differences?

Case 14.29   **Budgeting software review, collaborative project: Internet assignment**   Form a group of three or four students to research, evaluate, and report on software solutions available to support the budgeting needs of an organization. Choose three planning/budgeting products from the following list of company websites, and review the information about the software solutions available on each company's website. The list provided is meant to serve only as a starting point for this case; it is not a comprehensive listing of all budgeting software tools on the market. In fact, you are encouraged to search for other products and include them in your analysis.

Your information gathering should focus on things such as company history, product features and functionality, for what size organization the product is designed, product scalability, technology requirements, budgeting process employed by the system, customer references and/or testimonials, product demos, training, and/or other services available for implementation. After you have compiled information about each product, write a summary report that provides a comparative assessment of the three products.

Software Company	Website Address
A3 Solutions Inc.	a3solutions.com
Adaptive Insights	adaptiveinsights.com
Centage Corporation	centage.com
GoHagit Inc.	upyourcashflow.com
Kepion Incorporated	kepion.com
Host Analytics Inc.	hostanalytics.com
PlanGuru LLC	planguru.com
Prophix Software Inc.	prophix.com
Questica Inc.	questica.com
XLerant Inc.	xlerant.com

1. It means that the final budget results from the joint efforts of people at every level of management.

2. It means that the budget is prepared for several periods in the future, so continuous budgeting involves refining the budgets previously prepared for subsequent periods, plus preparing the first budget for a new period added at the end of the budget horizon.

3. It means that the level of planned operating activity determines the quantity of product or the capacity for services needed to fulfill the plan, and that this in turn influences the level of operating expenses and other costs that will be incurred as well as the level of cash and other resources that will be needed to support fulfillment of the plan.

4. It means that the amount of cash available for the period (beginning cash balance + cash receipts) is exceeded by the cash requirements (cash disbursements + desired ending cash balance) for the period. Having an understanding of this situation allows management to take the steps necessary to secure borrowings from its bank to ensure that all cash requirements will be fulfilled.

5. It means that a budgeted unit cost for material, labor, and overhead is developed to facilitate the determination of a product or process cost and for use in the planning and control activities of the firm.

6. It means that barring unusual circumstances, workers should be able to acquire and use materials, perform direct labor, and support the manufacturing process at the standard.

Cost Control

15

Answering the question "How well am I doing?" is a fundamental extension of the planning process and an important dimension of managerial accounting. Every strategic plan is, or should be, accompanied by an appropriate set of metrics that identify success. Every operational budget has a related analysis activity that compares actual performance to the budget. And every daily to-do list either receives a check mark indicating completion or grows longer when tasks fail to be completed on time.

Performance reporting is a controlling activity that involves comparing actual results with planned results, with the objective of highlighting those activities for which actual and planned results differ, favorably or unfavorably, so appropriate action can be taken by either changing the way activities are carried out or adjusting goals (see the gray shaded area of the planning and control cycle). Ideally, a well-designed control system will provide leading indicators that identify when performance begins to drift from expectations so that corrective actions can be initiated as soon as possible.

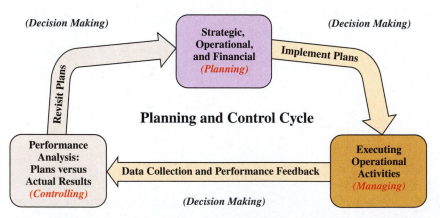

Performance reporting tools, such as effectively designed measurement systems and the technology to deliver timely performance information to managers, are necessary for a successful control environment. This chapter reviews the process of performance analysis as an extension of the planning and managing activities described in Chapters 13 and 14. It then explains how

variances (the differences between planned and actual results) are analyzed so that managers can identify why they occurred and plan appropriate response actions.

As you study the material presented in this chapter, remember that budgets and standards should be used in conjunction with a performance reporting system that is designed to meet the information needs of management but also serves to motivate those whose performance is being evaluated and aligned to the goals defined in the plan. When appropriately designed and implemented, a control system establishes performance targets and provides benchmarks against which actual results can be compared to answer the fundamental question, "How well am I doing?"

LEARNING OBJECTIVES (LO)

After studying this chapter, you should understand and be able to

LO 15-1 Explain why all costs are controllable by someone at some time, but in the short run, some costs may be classified as noncontrollable.

LO 15-2 Discuss how performance reporting facilitates the management by exception process.

LO 15-3 Construct a flexible budget and describe how it is used.

LO 15-4 Calculate and explain the two components of a standard cost variance.

LO 15-5 Name and compare the specific variances assigned to different product inputs.

LO 15-6 Analyze and explain how the control of fixed overhead variances and that of variable cost variances differ.

LO 15-7 Illustrate the alternative methods of accounting for variances.

LO 15-8 Demonstrate how the operating results of segments of an organization can be reported most meaningfully.

LO 15-9 Explain and compare how return on investment and residual income are used to evaluate investment center performance.

LO 15-10 Explain the benefits of a balanced scorecard.

Cost Classifications

Relationship of Total Cost to Volume of Activity

Exhibit 15-1 highlights cost classification topics covered in this chapter. Chapter 14 emphasized that for planning purposes, it is necessary to understand how costs are expected to change as the level of planned activity changes. For control purposes, understanding the behavior patterns of fixed and variable cost items is equally important. Rarely, if ever, does an organization perform *exactly* as planned. In the process of analyzing performance, any differences between planned and actual costs should be evaluated. Actual cost is compared to expected cost *for the level of activity achieved*

Exhibit 15-1   Cost Classifications—The Big Picture

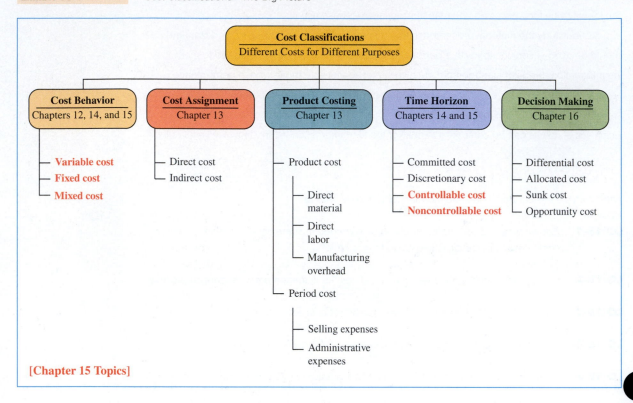

[Chapter 15 Topics]

based on the fixed and/or variable cost behavior pattern of each cost item. As activity changes from that originally planned, the expected total amount of variable cost would also be expected to change to an amount determined by multiplying the variable rate for that activity by the amount of activity achieved—just as the total variable amount would have been determined in the original budget. The total amount of fixed cost expected would not change if the actual and expected level of activity were different. Later in this chapter, a flexible budget is introduced to implement this concept.

Cost Classification According to a Time-Frame Perspective

LO 1

Explain why all costs are controllable by someone at some time, but in the short run, some costs may be classified as noncontrollable.

Frequently, reference is made to a "noncontrollable" cost, which implies that there is really nothing the manager can do to influence the amount of the cost. This may be true in the short run (e.g., for the coming quarter or year), but in the long run, every cost incurred by the organization is controllable by someone at some time. For example, real estate taxes on a firm's plant and office facilities usually cannot be influenced by management in the short run because the assessed valuation and tax rates are established by taxing authorities. However, when the decision was made to build or buy the facilities, the relative level of property taxes was established. Land in a prime location and a fancy building with plenty of space for possible expansion could be expected to result in higher property taxes over the years than more modest facilities. The point is not whether appropriate facilities were obtained, but that the decision makers (top management or the board of directors) had control over the general level of property taxes when the decision was being made. It is not appropriate to think of any cost as being noncontrollable over all time frames.

Performance Reporting

Characteristics of the Performance Report

The performance report compares actual results to budgeted amounts. The performance reporting system is an integral part of the control process because those activities that are accomplished differently from expectations are highlighted, and the managers responsible for achieving goals are provided with information about activities that need attention.

The general format of a performance report is as follows:

(1)	(2)	(3)	(4)	(5)
	Budget	Actual	Variance	
Activity	Amount	Amount	(2) – (3)	Explanation

The variance usually is described as *favorable* or *unfavorable,* depending on the nature of the activity and the relationship between the budget and actual amounts. For revenues, a **favorable variance** is the excess of actual revenues over the budget amount. An actual expense that is greater than a budgeted expense causes an **unfavorable variance**. Similarly, actual revenues that fall short of the budgeted amount cause an unfavorable variance, and when actual expenses are less than budgeted expenses, a favorable variance exists. These relationships are summarized as follows:

	Variance	
	Actual > Budget	**Actual < Budget**
Revenue item	*Favorable (F)*	*Unfavorable (U)*
Expense item	*Unfavorable (U)*	*Favorable (F)*

Sometimes, the favorable or unfavorable nature of the variance must be determined based on the relationship of one variance to another. For example, if a favorable variance in advertising expense resulted from not placing as many ads as planned, and this caused lower sales than were forecast, the variance is not really favorable because it ultimately resulted in an undesirable outcome for the company.

The explanation column of the performance report is used to communicate to upper-level managers concise explanations of significant variances. Because top management probably doesn't want to be inundated with details, a system of responsibility reporting is used by many organizations. **Responsibility reporting** involves successive degrees of summarization, so that each layer of management receives detailed performance reports for the activities directly associated with that layer but summaries of the results of activities of lower layers in the chain of command.

The principal concern of a manager should be with the actions that are going to be taken to eliminate unfavorable variances and to capture favorable variances that result in desirable outcomes. Performance reports should not be used to find fault or place blame; such uses are likely to result in dysfunctional behavior when developing budget amounts and/or reporting actual results.

Management by exception is frequently used in connection with performance reporting to permit managers to concentrate their attention on only those activities that are not performing according to plan. The presumption is that management time is scarce and that if a thorough job of planning is completed, a manager's attention need be devoted only to those areas not performing according to plan. To facilitate the use of management by exception, the variance is frequently expressed as a percentage of the budget, and only those variances in excess of a predetermined percentage

LO 2
Discuss how performance reporting facilitates the management by exception process.

(e.g., 10 percent) are investigated. The objective of this analysis is to understand why an unusual variance occurred and, if appropriate, to take action to eliminate unfavorable variances and capture favorable variances that result in desirable outcomes.

Performance reports must be issued soon after the period in which the activity takes place if they are to be useful for influencing future activity. Otherwise, it would be difficult to link results to the actions that caused those results. If the time lag is too long between the activity and the analysis, the actions are forgotten or confused with later activities. Not all performance reports need to be issued with the same frequency. Thus, production supervisors might receive weekly cost and volume reports, a supervisor responsible for the use of a high-cost raw material might receive a daily usage report, and the advertising manager might receive only a monthly expenditure report.

An issue that arises in the design of a performance report is the extent of the cost-generating activities listed for a particular responsibility area relative to the degree of short-term control that the manager has over those activities. For example, should the performance report for a production line show the depreciation expense, property taxes, insurance cost, and other "noncontrollable" expenses associated with that production line? Or should the performance report be limited to those expenses over which the supervisor has real short-term control?

- Advocates of the all-inclusive report format suggest that it is appropriate for the supervisor to be aware of all costs, even though she or he may not be able to influence them in the short run.
- Advocates of the limited format believe that the report should focus only on those costs that the supervisor can control. They argue that the inclusion of other costs causes confusion and may focus attention on the wrong costs (i.e., those that can't be controlled in the short run).

There is no "right" answer to this issue. One middle-ground solution is to periodically provide the supervisor with all cost data but to focus the performance report on those costs that can be controlled in the short run on a timelier basis. Notice that at the heart of the issue is the allocation of fixed costs, and recall the previously discussed warning not to allocate fixed costs arbitrarily because "they don't behave that way."

A performance report for the April 2019 production of SeaCruiser sailboats made by Cruisers Inc. is presented in Exhibit 15-2. (Actual costs in this exhibit have been brought forward from Exhibit 13-6.) Note that the manufacturing overhead has been classified according to cost behavior. This classification is appropriate because the efforts made to control these costs will be a function of their cost behavior pattern. The performance report in Exhibit 15-2, although interesting and perhaps helpful to top management's determination of why budgeted results were not achieved, is not very useful for operating managers and supervisors. Here are some questions raised by this report:

1. Were there significant but offsetting variances within raw materials?
2. Which workers were not efficient?
3. Were any new workers being paid a lower-than-budget wage rate until they became proficient?
4. Is the training program for new workers effective?
5. How does the manufacturing overhead variance affect the validity of the predetermined overhead application rate used to apply overhead to production?

A method for answering these questions, and others, and for preparing a performance report that is useful for the cost-controlling efforts of operating managers and supervisors is discussed later in this chapter.

Exhibit 15-2   Performance Report Illustration

CRUISERS INC.				
Performance Report—SeaCruiser Sailboats				
April 2019				
Activity	**Budget**	**Actual**	**Variance***	**Explanation**
Raw materials	$370,300	$368,510	$ 1,790 F	Variance not significant in total.
Direct labor	302,680	330,240	27,560 U	New workers not as efficient as planned.
Manufacturing overhead:				
Variable	89,400	103,160	13,760 U	Related to additional hours caused by labor inefficiency.
Fixed	193,200	185,800	7,400 F	Plant fire insurance premium credit received.
Totals	$955,580	$987,710	$32,130 U	

* F is favorable, U is unfavorable.

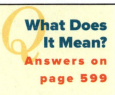

1. What does it mean to use a performance report to evaluate the results achieved during a period?
2. What does it mean to have a favorable variance?
3. What does it mean to capture favorable variances that result in desirable outcomes and eliminate unfavorable variances?

What Does It Mean?
Answers on page 599

The Flexible Budget

Consider the following partial performance report for the hull manufacturing department of Cruisers Inc. for the month of March:

Activity	**Budget Amount**	**Actual Cost**	**Variance**	**Explanation**
Raw materials	$ 54,936	$ 46,125	$ 8,811 F	Produced fewer boats than planned.
Direct labor	39,936	32,893	7,043 F	Same as above.
Variable overhead	9,984	8,128	1,856 F	Same as above.
Fixed overhead	36,720	37,320	600 U	Immaterial.
Total	$141,576	$124,466	$17,110 F	

Now suppose you find out that the budget amount was based on the expectation that 120 hulls would be built during March but that 100 hulls were actually built. Because we know that some of these product costs are variable and would change in total as more or less activity occurs, does it make sense to compare costs that were budgeted for 120 hulls to actual costs incurred to produce 100 hulls? What could be done to make this performance report more useful for managers?

The purpose of a flexible budget is to highlight the significance of cost behavior for planning and control purposes and to avoid the pitfall associated with comparing actual performance for the period with a budget that was constructed for a different

LO 3
Construct a flexible budget and describe how it is used.

level of activity. A flexible budget can be prepared for any level of activity, as illustrated here:

Activity	Variable Rate/Hull	Flexible Budget Allowance		
		100 Hulls	120 Hulls	140 Hulls
Raw materials	$ 457.80	$ 45,780	$ 54,936	$ 64,092
Direct labor	332.80	33,280	39,936	46,592
Variable overhead	83.20	8,320	9,984	11,648
	$873.80	$ 87,380	$104,856	$122,332
Fixed overhead		36,720	36,720	36,720
Total		$124,100	$141,576	$159,052

Notice that the variable rates for direct materials, direct labor, and variable overhead are used to calculate a budget allowance for any level of activity—but in particular for the level of activity achieved this period—so that a valid comparison can be made against actual costs incurred for that level of activity. (Why isn't the fixed overhead budget amount also adjusted?) Adjusting the original budget so it reflects budgeted amounts for actual activity is called *flexing the budget.*

The performance report using the **flexible budget** approach would look like this:

Activity	Budget Allowance	Actual Cost	Variance	Explanation
Raw materials	$ 45,780	$ 46,125	$345 U	Immaterial.
Direct labor	33,280	32,893	387 F	Immaterial.
Variable overhead	8,320	8,128	192 F	Immaterial.
Fixed overhead	36,720	37,320	600 U	Immaterial.
Total	$124,100	$124,466	$366 U	

The variances now are relatively insignificant, and the initial conclusion made from this report is the correct one: The production manager is performing according to plan for the number of hulls that were actually produced.

Of course, there is a question about why 100 hulls were produced when the original budget called for production of 120 hulls. The answer to that question, while significantly important, is not relevant to controlling costs for the number of hulls that were actually produced.

Using a flexible budget approach does not affect the predetermined overhead application rate used to apply overhead to production. To the extent that the actual level of production differs from the activity estimate used in developing the predetermined overhead application rate, fixed manufacturing overhead will be overapplied or underapplied. However, this is not a cost control issue. It is an accounting issue, usually resolved by closing the amount of overapplied or underapplied overhead to Cost of Goods Sold at year end.

Flexible budgeting means that *the budget allowance for variable costs should be flexed to show the costs that should have been incurred for the level of activity actually experienced.* As illustrated with the Cruisers example, this is done by multiplying the variable cost per unit of *each* variable cost item (i.e., direct materials, direct labor, and variable manufacturing overhead) by the actual activity level (e.g., number of units produced in a month) to determine the *budget allowance* against which actual costs can be meaningfully compared. The variance in the level of activity should be investigated and explained so that improvements in activity forecasting can be achieved, but this is a separate and distinct issue from the analysis of cost performance.

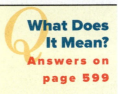
Standard Cost Variance Analysis

Analysis of Variable Cost Variances

To achieve the control advantages associated with the standard cost system discussed in Chapter 14, performance reports must be provided to individuals responsible for incurring costs. Remember, the term *standard cost* was described as a budget for a single unit of product for its related components—raw materials, direct labor, and manufacturing overhead. The total variance for any particular cost component is referred to as the **budget variance** because it represents the difference between actual cost and standard cost. The budget variance is caused by two factors: the difference between actual and standard *unit costs* of the input, and the difference between actual and standard *quantities* of the input. Even if the same individual were responsible for both price and quantity, it would be desirable to break the budget variance into the **cost per unit of input variance** and the **quantity variance**. However, because different managers are usually responsible for each component of the total variance, it is essential to separate the two components so that each manager can take the appropriate action to eliminate unfavorable variances or capture those that are favorable. A summary overview of the budget variance is illustrated here:

LO 4

Calculate and explain the two components of a standard cost variance.

```
Actual          ┐
cost            │
                ├──►  Budget   ──┬──►  Cost per unit of
Standard        │     variance   │     input variance
cost            ┘                └──►  Quantity
                                        variance
```

As is the case with much of managerial and financial accounting, different organizations use different terms for these variances. In the discussion that follows, the cost per unit of input variance will be referred to as a *price, rate,* or *spending variance,* and the quantity variance will be referred to as a *usage* or *efficiency* variance. These terms are generally, but not exclusively, used in practice. In addition, variances will be referred to here as *favorable* or *unfavorable*. In some organizations, a favorable variance is shown as a positive but otherwise unlabeled amount, and an unfavorable variance is shown as a negative amount. Whether a variance is favorable or unfavorable, and therefore good or bad, respectively, must be determined in the context of the item being evaluated and the goals of the organization. Spending less for raw materials because lower-than-specified-quality materials were purchased may give rise to an arithmetically favorable variance (actual cost was less than standard cost) that is not desirable because of the negative impact on product quality. Thus, a "favorable" variance might lead to an unfavorable outcome, so the labeling of a variance as F or U should not be understood as automatically leading to a favorable or unfavorable outcome.

To illustrate the two components of the budget variance, we will focus on the "build-up" labor of the SeaCruiser hull for which the standard cost was summarized in Chapter 14. Assume that 100 hulls were made last month. The following table summarizes the actual and standard labor hours and the hourly rates for build-up labor inputs. Note that variances are also indicated (F is favorable, U is unfavorable).

Actual	2,540 hours @ $12.95/hr	$32,893
Standard	2,600 hours @ $12.80/hr	33,280
Budget variance	60 F $ 0.15 U	$ 387 F

The analysis of the budget variance into the cost per unit of input variance and the quantity variance is as follows:

Variance due to rate difference:	
$0.15/hr × 2,540 hours (actual hours)	$381 U
Variance due to hours difference:	
60 hours × $12.80 (standard rate)	$768 F
Budget variance	$387 F

The cost per unit of input variance (due to the difference between the actual and standard hourly pay rates) is called the **direct labor rate variance**. In this case, the rate variance is unfavorable because workers were paid a higher rate than allowed at standard. The quantity variance (due to the difference between the actual hours worked and the standard hours allowed) is called the **direct labor efficiency variance** because it relates to the efficiency with which labor was used. In this case, the efficiency variance is favorable because the 100 hulls were produced in fewer build-up labor hours than were allowed at standard. Note that standard quantities for variable cost inputs are based on the flexible budget concept described earlier in this chapter; the standard quantity allowed is adjusted in response to the number of units produced.

The rate variance would be reported to the human resources manager or other individual responsible for pay rates. The efficiency variance would be reported to the supervisor responsible for direct labor inputs to the product. Management by exception procedures are appropriate, and, if a variance is significant, the reasons for it will be determined so that appropriate action can be taken to eliminate unfavorable variances and capture favorable ones.

The variances are labeled favorable or unfavorable based on the arithmetic difference between actual and standard, but these labels are not necessarily synonymous with "good" and "bad," respectively. This example illustrates a trade-off that can frequently be made. Even though the workers were paid more than the standard rate, the work was performed efficiently enough to more than make up for the unfavorable rate variance. If this occurred because of a conscious decision by the production supervisor, it may be appropriate to make a permanent change in the way the work is done and to change the standards accordingly. Alternatively, achieving a favorable rate variance by using less-skilled employees may result in a more-than-offsetting unfavorable efficiency variance.

The budget variance for raw materials and variable overhead can also be analyzed and separated into the two components, as illustrated for direct labor. The label assigned to each of the components varies from input to input, but the calculations are the same. The labels generally used are **raw materials price variance**, **raw materials** usage variance, **variable overhead spending variance**, and **variable overhead effi-ciency variance**. These variable manufacturing cost variances are summarized here:

LO 5

Name and compare the specific variances assigned to different product inputs.

	Variance due to Difference between Standard and Actual	
Input	**Cost per Unit of Input**	**Quantity**
Raw materials	Price	Usage
Direct labor	Rate	Efficiency
Variable overhead	Spending	Efficiency

The terms used for cost per unit of input variances are consistent with the way costs are usually referred to: *price* for raw materials and *rate* for employee wages. *Spending* is used for variable overhead because of the number of different cost items that compose overhead; although an overall spending rate is calculated, the variance reflects the fact that actual over-head costs differ from the spending that was anticipated when the rate was established. The terms *usage* and *efficiency* refer to quantity of input; from the perspective of direct labor, efficiency relates to the quantity of labor hours actually used relative to the quantity called for by the standard. The variable overhead quantity variance is called the *efficiency variance* because variable overhead is, in most cases, assumed to be related to direct labor hours.

The general model for calculating each variance is:

$$\begin{array}{c} \text{Cost per unit} \\ \text{of input} \\ \text{variance} \end{array} = \left(\begin{array}{c} \text{Standard} \\ \text{cost per} \\ \text{unit} \end{array} - \begin{array}{c} \text{Actual} \\ \text{cost per} \\ \text{unit} \end{array} \right) \times \begin{array}{c} \text{Actual} \\ \text{quantity} \\ \text{used} \end{array}$$

$$\text{Quantity variance} = \left(\begin{array}{c} \text{Standard} \\ \text{quantity} \\ \text{allowed} \end{array} - \begin{array}{c} \text{Actual} \\ \text{quantity} \\ \text{used} \end{array} \right) \times \begin{array}{c} \text{Standard} \\ \text{cost per} \\ \text{unit} \end{array}$$

This model can also be expressed in the following way:

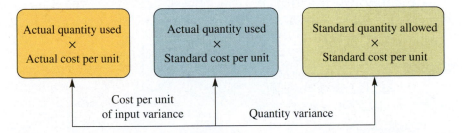

The arithmetic sign of the variance calculated using either of the preceding versions of the model indicates whether the variance is favorable (+) or unfavorable (−). Variance calculation examples for some of the SeaCruiser hull costs are illustrated in Exhibit 15-3.

Although the total budget variance of $234 F calculated in Exhibit 15-3 is easily considered immaterial, some of the individual variances are much more significant. It just happens that they are largely offsetting. This emphasizes the need to analyze the variances for each standard. Thus, although not illustrated in Exhibit 15-3, vari-ances for the other raw material, direct labor, and variable overhead components of the SeaCruiser hulls would also be computed.

What use will be made of the information in Exhibit 15-3? Remember that the objectives of variance analysis are to highlight deviations from planned results. With respect to raw materials, it is possible that the favorable price variance of $1,125 was caused by buying lower-quality fiberglass that resulted in the unfavorable usage

Study
Suggestion

Integrate your knowledge! When studying the analysis of standard cost variances, realizing that the model is an application of the flexible budget concept presented earlier in the chapter is useful. Actual costs are at one end of the model. To evaluate actual results (cost × quantity), the question is, "*How much cost should have been incurred* (standard cost × standard quantity) *given the actual units produced?*" Calculating total standard cost as the standard quantity allowed × standard cost per unit is simply "flexing the budget" *for the actual units produced* during the period.

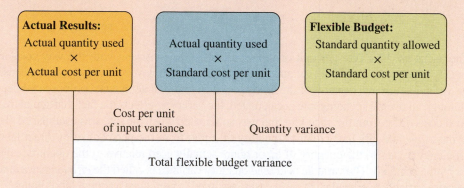

Exhibit 15-3

Calculation of Standard Cost Variances

I. Assumptions:

The following performance report summarizes budget and actual usage and costs for the items shown for a month in which 100 SeaCruiser hulls were produced:

	Budget	Actual	Variance
Raw materials:			
Glass fiber cloth:	$45,780	$46,125	$345 U
Budget: Standard/hull of 218 yd			
@ $2.10/yd × 100 hulls			
Actual: 22,500 yd @ $2.05/yd			
Direct labor:			
Build-up labor:	33,280	32,893	387 F
Budget: Standard/hull of 26 hr			
@ $12.80/hr × 100 hulls			
Actual: 2,540 hr @ $12.95/hr			
Variable overhead:			
Related to build-up labor:	8,320	8,128	192 F
Budget: Standard/hull of 26 hr			
@ $3.20/hr × 100 hulls			
Actual: 2,540 hr @ $3.20/hr			
Totals	$87,380	$87,146	$234 F

II. Required:

Analyze the budget variance for each item by calculating the cost per unit of input and quantity variances.

III. Solution:

$$\text{Cost per unit of input variance} = \left(\begin{array}{c}\text{Standard} \\ \text{cost per} \\ \text{unit}\end{array} - \begin{array}{c}\text{Actual} \\ \text{cost per} \\ \text{unit}\end{array}\right) \times \begin{array}{c}\text{Actual} \\ \text{quantity} \\ \text{used}\end{array}$$

(continued)

Exhibit 15-3

Raw materials
    price variance   = ($2.10/yd − $2.05/yd) × 22,500 yd
                        = $1,125 F

Direct labor
    rate variance   = ($12.80/hr − $12.95/hr) × 2,540 hr
                        = $381 U

Variable overhead
    spending variance   = ($3.20/hr − $3.20/hr) × 2,540 hr
                        = 0

$$\text{Quantity variance} = \left(\begin{matrix} \text{Standard} \\ \text{quantity} \\ \text{allowed} \end{matrix} - \begin{matrix} \text{Actual} \\ \text{quantity} \\ \text{used} \end{matrix} \right) \times \begin{matrix} \text{Standard} \\ \text{cost per} \\ \text{unit} \end{matrix}$$

Raw materials
    usage variance   = [(218 yd × 100 hulls) − 22,500 yd] × $2.10
                        = $1,470 U

Direct labor
    efficiency variance = [(26 hr × 100 hulls) − 2,540 hr] × $12.80
                        = $768 F

Variable overhead
    efficiency variance = [(26 hr × 100 hulls) − 2,540 hr] × $3.20
                        = $192 F

IV. Recap of variances:

	Price/Rate/Spending	**Usage/Efficiency**	**Total**
Raw materials	$1,125 F	$1,470 U	$345 U
Direct labor	381 U	768 F	387 F
Variable overhead	0	192 F	192 F
Totals	$ 744 F	$ 510 U	$234 F

variance of $1,470. As a result of the performance report, there should be communication between the purchasing agent and the raw materials supervisor to resolve the issue. Without this analysis and communication, the purchasing agent, being unaware that the price savings were more than offset by higher usage, might continue to buy lower-quality material. Likewise, the favorable labor efficiency variance of $768 might be the result of using more experienced and higher-paid employees this month, which in turn caused a $381 unfavorable rate variance. After analysis and discussion, the direct labor supervisor, production superintendent, and human resources manager might decide to continue this trade-off. Variance analysis information should result in actions to maintain or increase the profitability of the company. If the benefit of calculating variances is not greater than the cost of doing so, there isn't much sense in making the calculations.

As is the case with any performance reporting system, variances should be communicated to the individuals responsible as promptly as possible after the activity has occurred. This way, the causes of the variances can be easily remembered and appropriate action can be taken. All variances need not be reported with the same frequency. In most organizations, the usage of raw materials and the efficiency of direct labor are most subject to short-term control, so these variances will be reported more frequently than the cost per unit of input variances. In many situations, it is appropriate to report raw materials usage variances and direct labor efficiency variances in physical terms because supervisors are more accustomed to thinking in terms of pounds, square feet, and direct labor hours as opposed to dollars. For example, using the data in Exhibit 15-3, and eliminating standard cost per unit from the model, the quantity variances would be calculated and expressed as follows:

$$\text{Quantity variance} = \left(\begin{array}{cc}\text{Standard} & \text{Actual}\\ \text{quantity} - \text{quantity}\\ \text{allowed} & \text{used}\end{array}\right)$$

$$\begin{array}{l}\text{Raw materials}\\ \quad\text{usage variance}\end{array} = (218 \text{ yd} \times 100 \text{ hulls}) - 22{,}500 \text{ yd}$$
$$= 700 \text{ yd U}$$

$$\begin{array}{l}\text{Direct labor}\\ \quad\text{efficiency variance}\end{array} = (26 \text{ hr} \times 100 \text{ hulls}) - 2{,}540 \text{ hr}$$
$$= 60 \text{ hr F}$$

Some organizations calculate and report the raw materials price variance at the time materials are purchased rather than when they are used. This variance is called the **raw materials purchase price variance**. This is especially appropriate if raw materials inventories are maintained, in contrast to having material purchases put directly into production, because it shows the purchasing manager any price variance soon after the purchase is made rather than later when the material is used. For example, if 25,000 yards of glass fiber cloth were purchased at a cost of $2.05 per yard, and the standard cost was $2.10 per yard, the purchase price variance would be calculated as follows:

General Model

$$\begin{array}{l}\text{Cost per unit}\\ \quad\text{of input}\\ \quad\text{variance}\end{array} = \left(\begin{array}{cc}\text{Standard} & \text{Actual}\\ \text{cost per} - \text{cost per}\\ \text{unit} & \text{unit}\end{array}\right) \times \begin{array}{c}\text{Actual}\\ \text{quantity}\\ \text{used}\end{array}$$

Modification for Purchase Price Variance

$$\begin{array}{l}\text{Cost per unit}\\ \quad\text{of input}\\ \quad\text{variance}\end{array} = \left(\begin{array}{cc}\text{Standard} & \text{Actual}\\ \text{cost per} - \text{cost per}\\ \text{unit} & \text{unit}\end{array}\right) \times \begin{array}{c}\text{Actual}\\ \text{quantity}\\ \textit{purchased}\end{array}$$

$$= (\$2.10 - \$2.05) \times 25{,}000 \text{ yd}$$
$$= \$1{,}250 \text{ F}$$

What Does It Mean?

Answers on page 599

6. What does it mean to have an unfavorable raw materials usage variance?

7. What does it mean to analyze the direct labor budget variance to determine the efficiency variance and rate variance components?

8. What does it mean to state that a favorable usage variance may not really be favorable?

9. What does it mean to state that for variance analysis to be effective, it should result in better communication between managers?

Analysis of Fixed Overhead Variance

LO 6

Analyze and explain how the control of fixed overhead variances and that of variable cost variances differ.

The fixed manufacturing overhead variance is analyzed differently from the variable cost variances because the cost behavior pattern is different. For control purposes, the focus is on the difference between the actual fixed overhead expenditures and the fixed overhead that was budgeted for the period. This difference is labeled a *budget variance* (the same term used to identify the difference between actual and budgeted variable costs). A variance also arises if the number of units of product made during the period differs from planned production. The reason for this is that fixed overhead is applied to production using a predetermined application rate (see Exhibit 13-6) based on planned activity. If actual activity is different from planned activity, the amount of fixed overhead applied to production will be different from that planned to be applied. This variance is called a **volume variance**. *Remember that because fixed costs do not behave on a per unit basis, it is not appropriate to make any per unit fixed overhead variance calculations.*

To illustrate the calculation of fixed overhead variances, we return to the production of SeaCruiser sailboats by Cruisers, Inc. The predetermined fixed overhead application rate shown in the standard cost calculation in Chapter 14 is $10.80 per direct labor hour. To recap from Chapter 13, this rate would have been determined as follows:

Total estimated (budgeted) fixed manufacturing overhead for the year	$3,240,000
Total estimated (budgeted) direct labor hours for the year (1,250 sailboats @ 240 hours each)	300,000 hours
Predetermined fixed overhead application rate ($3,240,000/300,000 hours)	$10.80/direct labor hour

Now assume that the actual fixed manufacturing overhead for the year totaled $3,327,500, and that the actual level of production was 1,288 sailboats. The standard direct labor hours allowed for actual production during the year would be 309,120 hours (1,288 actual sailboats × 240 standard hours allowed per sailboat). The Fixed Manufacturing Overhead account would appear as follows:

Fixed Manufacturing Overhead			
Actual costs incurred	3,327,500	Fixed manufacturing overhead *applied* to production (309,120 direct labor hours × $10.80/direct labor hr)	3,338,496
		Balance (overapplied overhead)	$10,996

The overapplied overhead is made up of a budget variance and a volume variance, as follows:

Budget variance:		
Actual fixed manufacturing overhead		$3,327,500
Budgeted fixed manufacturing overhead		3,240,000
Budget variance		$ 87,500 U
Volume variance:		
Budgeted direct labor hours for year	300,000 hr	
Standard direct labor hours allowed for actual production during year	309,120 hr	
Excess of standard hours allowed for volume of production actually achieved over estimated hours . . .	9,120 hr	
Predetermined fixed overhead application rate	× $10.80/hr	
Volume variance		98,496 F
Net variance (overapplied overhead)		$ 10,996 F

This is another situation in which the net variance is small, but it results from significantly larger offsetting variances that may deserve investigation. The amount of fixed overhead actually incurred versus the amount applied to production during the year could be different for a variety of reasons. The cost category of fixed overhead comprises many individual cost items (e.g., supervisor salaries, depreciation, property taxes, and maintenance), and each line item should be evaluated to understand its individual effect on the budget variance. One possibility is that responsible managers could have paid more or less to acquire a particular fixed overhead item during the year. Conversely, property taxes, which are beyond management's control, may have increased. And just because a variance is favorable does not necessarily mean it is good for the company. For example, a favorable maintenance variance could indicate a manager's attempt to improve his or her performance by delaying or completely ignoring scheduled maintenance of equipment—a savings today that will likely require much higher costs in the long term.

The volume variance explains the effect of treating fixed overhead costs differently for planning and control purposes as opposed to product costing purposes. For planning purposes, fixed costs are expected to total $3,240,000, but for product costing purposes, fixed costs are unitized over 300,000 estimated direct labor hours of activity (at the rate of $10.80/direct labor hour) in order to allow each unit produced to absorb a share of the total budgeted fixed overhead costs. Note that only when Cruisers generates exactly 300,000 direct labor hours will the units produced exactly absorb budgeted fixed overhead costs of $3,240,000. If the company generates more or less than 300,000 direct labor hours, too much or too little fixed overhead will be applied to production. The following graph demonstrates this concept:

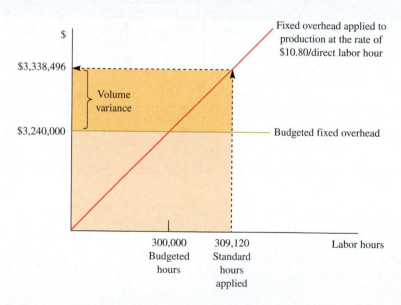

The graph illustrates that when Cruisers generates more than 300,000 direct labor hours, it will apply more than the $3,240,000 amount of expected fixed overhead for the year. Likewise, if Cruisers fails to generate the 300,000 direct labor hours, it will apply less than the $3,240,000 expected fixed overhead. By generating 9,120 more direct labor hours than planned, Cruisers overapplied fixed overhead costs to the units produced in the amount of $98,496 (9,120 direct labor hours × $10.80 per direct labor hour).

This volume variance means that work in process and finished goods inventories as well as cost of goods sold would have been overstated as a result of achieving a larger number of direct labor hours than estimated.

The preceding illustration uses annual data; in practice, the analysis is likely to be made monthly or with a frequency that leads to the most effective control of fixed overhead. As stated earlier, by its very nature, fixed overhead is difficult to control on a short-term basis. Yet, for many firms, it has become a significant cost that may be greater than all of the variable costs combined, so it does receive much management attention.

10. What does it mean to state that the analysis of fixed manufacturing overhead variance is not likely to be done with the same frequency as the analysis of variable cost variances?

What Does It Mean?

Answers on page 599

How Well Am I Doing?

Business in
Practice

Performance reporting is a critical component of the planning and control cycle; it helps managers identify those activities for which actual and planned results differ so appropriate action can be taken. This process ranges from the evaluation of a single raw material used in the production cycle to an analysis of the entire operating budget and provides a yardstick against which further comparisons may be made. To fully appreciate how well a company is performing, however, the dimensions of time and industry should be examined.

The time dimension suggests that the current performance evaluation results be compared with results of prior periods to establish performance trends within the company. This perspective gives managers a longer-run internal view of the effectiveness of their planning strategy to support an objective of continuous improvement. The industry dimension suggests that the current performance evaluation results should be compared with those of similar organizations to establish performance benchmarks within the industry. This perspective gives managers a bigger-picture external view of their performance in the marketplace.

To facilitate evaluation, industry organizations and trade associations provide many sources of specific information. For example, Printing Industries of America Inc. (PIA), at printing.org, is a portal to the industry's largest knowledge resource. For more than 90 years, PIA *Ratios* reports have been the printing industry's premier tool for measuring individual company performance and benchmarking it against industry averages and the performance of industry profit leaders—printers in the top 25 percent of profitability. Under Programs / Print Economics & Management, see the Dynamic Ratios section for related content and information about best practices, benchmarks, PIA ratios, and industry statistics and surveys.

Agile Manufacturing Benchmarking Consortium, at ambcbenchmarking.org, is a group of manufacturing process improvement professionals who identify best practices surrounding manufacturing issues for the overall operations of the members. The organization's mission is to identify "Best in Class" business processes, which, when implemented, lead member companies to exceptional performance.

The American Productivity & Quality Center (APQC), at apqc.org, is a resource for process and performance improvement for organizations of all sizes across all industries. APQC works with organizations to improve productivity and quality. This center provides the tools, information, and support needed to discover and implement best practices.

Accounting for Variances

LO 7
Illustrate the alternative
methods of accounting
for variances.

Some interesting issues arise in connection with accounting for variances. Usually, if the net total of all of the favorable and unfavorable variances is not significant relative to the total of all production costs incurred during the period, the net variance will simply be included with cost of goods sold in the income statement. Because standard costs were used in valuing inventories during the period, standard costs were also released to cost of goods sold; classifying the net variance with this amount has the effect of reporting cost of goods sold at the actual cost of making those items. However, if the net variance is significant relative to total production costs, it may be allocated between inventories and cost of goods sold in proportion to the standard costs included in these accounts. On the other hand, if the standards represent currently attainable targets, a net unfavorable variance can be interpreted as the cost of production inefficiencies that should be recognized as an expense of the current period. If this is the case, none of the net variance should be assigned to inventory because doing so results in postponing the income statement recognition of the inefficiencies until the product is sold. A net variance that is favorable would indicate that the standards were too loose, and so it would be appropriate to allocate the variance between inventory and cost of goods sold. In any event, the financial statements and explanatory notes are not likely to contain any reference to the standard cost system or accounting for variances, because disclosures about these details of the accounting system do not increase the usefulness of the statements as a whole.

Analysis of Organizational Units

Reporting for Segments of an Organization

LO 8
Demonstrate how the
operating results of
segments of an organi-
zation can be reported
most meaningfully.

A **segment** of an organization is a division, product line, sales territory, or other organizational unit. Management frequently reports company results by segment in such a way that the total income for each segment equals the total company net income. For example, assume that Cruisers Inc. has three divisions: sailboats, motorboats, and repair parts. The following income statement might be prepared:

	Total Company	Sailboat Division	Motorboat Division	Repair Parts Division
CRUISERS INC. Segmented Income Statement Quarter Ended July 31, 2019				
Sales	$560,000	$320,000	$160,000	$80,000
Variable expenses ...	240,000	128,000	72,000	40,000
Contribution margin ..	$320,000	$ 192,000	$ 88,000	$40,000
Fixed expenses	282,000	164,000	72,000	46,000
Operating income ...	$ 38,000	$ 28,000	$ 16,000	$ (6,000)

From an analysis of this segmented income statement, management might consider eliminating the repair parts division because it is operating at a loss. In fact, one might think that operating income would increase by $6,000 if this division were eliminated.

Now suppose that a detailed analysis of the fixed expenses identifies that the fixed expenses assigned to each division represents the sum of the fixed expenses incurred in each division (**direct fixed expenses**) plus an allocated share of the corporate fixed expenses (**common fixed expenses**) that would continue to be incurred even if one of the divisions were to be closed. (Would the president's salary—a common fixed expense—be reduced if one of the divisions were closed?) This analysis of fixed expenses might reveal the following:

	Total Company	Sailboat Division	Motorboat Division	Repair Parts Division
Direct fixed expenses	$170,000	$100,000	$40,000	$30,000
Common fixed expenses allocated in proportion to sales	112,000	64,000	32,000	16,000
Total fixed expenses	$282,000	$164,000	$72,000	$46,000

Because the common fixed expenses will continue to be incurred even if the repair parts division is closed, Cruisers would be worse off by $10,000 if the division were eliminated. Why? Because that division's contribution to common fixed expenses and profits (referred to as **segment margin**) would also be eliminated. This is illustrated clearly in a more appropriately designed segmented income statement:

CRUISERS INC. Segmented Income Statement Quarter Ended July 31, 2019				
	Total Company	Sailboat Division	Motorboat Division	Repair Parts Division
Sales	$560,000	$320,000	$160,000	$80,000
Variable expenses	240,000	128,000	72,000	40,000
Contribution margin	$320,000	$ 192,000	$ 88,000	$40,000
Direct fixed expenses	170,000	100,000	40,000	30,000
Segment margin	$ 150,000	$ 92,000	$ 48,000	$ 10,000
Common fixed expenses ...	112,000			
Operating income	$ 38,000			

The key feature of a segmented income statement is that common fixed expenses have not been *arbitrarily allocated* to the segments. The preferred segmented statement reflects the contribution of each segment to the common fixed expenses and company profit. Using this approach should avoid analytical errors like the one that would have resulted in closing the repair parts division.

The segmented statement format separating direct and common fixed expenses should be used whenever both classifications of fixed expenses exist. For example, if the sailboat division's segment margin of $92,000 were to be broken down by sales territory, that division's $100,000 of direct fixed expenses would be analyzed, and the portion that is direct *to each territory* would be subtracted from the territory contribution margin to arrive at the territory's segment margin. The division's fixed expenses

Exhibit 15-4

Methods of Evaluating
Responsibility Centers
(Segments)

Segment	How Performance Is Evaluated
Cost center	Actual costs incurred compared to budgeted costs.
Profit center	Actual segment margin compared to budgeted segment margin.
Investment center	Comparison of actual and budgeted return on investment (ROI) based on segment margin and assets controlled by the segment.

that are common from a territory perspective *would not* be allocated to the territories; they would be subtracted as a single amount from the total territory segment margin to arrive at the division's segment margin of $92,000.

Sometimes the segments of an organization are referred to as *responsibility centers, cost centers, profit centers,* or *investment centers*. A **responsibility center** is an element of the organization over which a manager has been assigned responsibility and authority, and for which performance is evaluated. A **cost center** does not directly generate any revenue for the organization. For example, the industrial engineering department would be a cost center. An organizational segment that is responsible for selling a product, like the sailboat division of Cruisers, could be either a **profit center** or an **investment center**. The methods used to evaluate the performance of each type of center (or segment) are summarized in Exhibit 15-4.

An interesting dynamic in some organizations is when production or service efforts flow sequentially from one segment to another and when management would like to think of these segments in terms of profits rather than costs. Efforts are made to convert what are essentially cost centers into profit centers by treating these internal transactions as "sales" from the providing segment and "purchases" by the receiving segment, which is accomplished by establishing a **transfer price**. Because products, components, or services are now "sold" from one segment of the organization to another, where the revenue of one segment becomes the cost of another segment, it is difficult to establish a transfer price that is considered fair by all concerned.

The "fairness" concerns between segment managers, plus the increased bookkeeping costs, means that significant behavioral and other qualitative benefits must be expected to warrant transfer pricing at the cost center level of an organization. Transfer pricing is more commonly applied to intersegment transactions between major divisions of a company and to affiliates organized as separate legal entities, and especially when markets external to the organization also exist. These transfer prices can influence bonuses, source of supply decisions, and state and national income tax obligations. The determination of an appropriate transfer price in these situations is often quite complex.

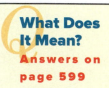

What Does It Mean?

Answers on page 599

11. What does it mean to have a responsibility reporting system?
12. What does it mean to state that common fixed expenses should never be arbitrarily allocated to segments (for example, products or organizational units)?

The Analysis of Investment Centers

The manager of an investment center has a much higher level of responsibility for decision making in the organization than does the manager of a cost center or profit center.

Not only is the investment center manager responsible for the incurrence of cost and the generation of revenue, but she also has autonomy for investing in the assets that will be used in conducting the operating activities of the organizational unit. Because of this additional dimension of responsibility, appropriate measures of performance are important for evaluating investment center managers across the organization. Many times, the performance evaluation system is directly related to a manager's compensation or other bonus opportunities, and logically so; the evaluation system should motivate managers to maximize their individual performance, which, in turn, should contribute to maximizing the performance of the organization as a whole.

LO 9
Explain and compare how return on investment and residual income are used to evaluate investment center performance.

Exhibit 15-4 identified the comparison of actual and budgeted return on investment (ROI) based on income (segment margin) and assets controlled by the investment center manager as the primary method of evaluating performance. The DuPont model for separating ROI into margin and turnover presented in Chapter 3 is a particularly useful tool for this analysis because it gives a manager insight into the various factors within the numerator and denominator of the ROI calculation that can affect the overall ratio. Selected relevant information from the segmented income statement for the year ended July 31, 2019, for Cruisers and information on the amount of operating assets in each division are presented here to illustrate this performance analysis technique:

	Total Company	Sailboat Division	Motorboat Division	Repair Parts Division
Sales	$ 560,000	$320,000	$160,000	$ 80,000
Segment margin	$ 150,000	$ 92,000	$ 48,000	$ 10,000
Divisional operating assets	$1,200,000	$600,000	$500,000	$100,000
DuPont Performance Analysis:				
Margin (Segment margin/Sales)	26.8%	28.8%	30.0%	12.5%
Turnover (Sales/Operating assets)	0.47 turns	0.53 turns	0.32 turns	0.80 turns
ROI (Segment margin/Operating assets) or (Margin × Turnover)	12.5%	15.3%	9.6%	10.0%

With the information from a DuPont analysis, division managers can focus their attention on those activities that would increase profit margin without sacrificing sales, such as increasing revenues and/or reducing expenses, or that would increase turnover by increasing sales while holding operating assets constant and/or while holding sales constant and decreasing operating assets. Also notice how a performance ranking of each division manager changes with the details provided by the DuPont analysis. This information provides each division manager with an understanding of his or her relative performance within the organization:

	Sailboat Division	Motorboat Division	Repair Parts Division
DuPont Performance Analysis:			
Margin	28.8%	30.0%	12.5%
Performance ranked by margin	2	1	3
Turnover	0.53 turns	0.32 turns	0.80 turns
Performance ranked by turnover	2	3	1
ROI	15.3%	9.6%	10.0%
Performance ranked by ROI	1	3	2

If the performance evaluation system is not carefully designed, it will lead to dysfunctional behavior on the part of the investment center manager. *Dysfunctional behavior* means that a manager will act in his or her own best interest without regard to the effect of his or her decision on the organization as a whole. For example, what would happen if the sailboat division manager were faced with an opportunity for a new sailboat line that would generate an ROI of 13.5 percent? If the only measure of performance used by Cruisers to evaluate the manager's performance is ROI, and especially if his performance is tied to compensation, you can be assured that the manager of the sailboat division will reject the opportunity because his current ROI would be lowered if he invested in this sailboat line. But is this decision good for Cruisers? The answer is no because its overall ROI is 12.5 percent, and a new sailboat line earning a return of 13.5 percent would enhance Cruiser's overall ROI. For this reason, known as **suboptimization**, ROI should not be the sole measure of investment center performance.

Another approach used to evaluate the performance of an investment center, which eliminates this risk of suboptimization, is known as **residual income**. This technique evaluates the manager's ability to generate a minimum required ROI. Therefore, the investment center manager's goal is to maximize the dollar amount of earnings above this minimum requirement rather than to maximize a percentage amount of ROI. Residual income is calculated as follows:

Residual income = Operating income − Required ROI $ (Operating assets × Required ROI %)

To illustrate, we will continue with the information from the segmented income statement at July 31, 2019, for Cruisers and assume that the required ROI has been set at 10 percent:

	Total Company	Sailboat Division	Motorboat Division	Repair Parts Division
Divisional operating assets	$1,200,000	$600,000	$500,000	$100,000
Residual Income Analysis:				
Segment margin	$ 150,000	$ 92,000	$ 48,000	$ 10,000
ROI required (Operating assets × 10%)	120,000	60,000	50,000	10,000
Residual income	$ 30,000	$ 32,000	$ (2,000)	$ 0
Performance ranked by residual income		1	3	2

Residual income is positive when the investment center is earning an ROI greater than the required ROI, 10 percent in this example. A negative residual income means that a division is losing organization value by not earning the minimum required ROI, and viewing this underachievement brings greater emphasis to its significance. Notice in the preceding illustration that a performance ranking based on residual income produces the same order as using ROI, but using residual income would now allow the manager of the sailboat division to invest in the new sailboat line with an expected return of 13.5 percent because any opportunity that provides at least a 10 percent ROI would increase the division's residual income. It is clear that no single measure of performance will satisfy all information analysis needs of an organization at the same time while providing the behavioral incentive for managers to act in the best interest of the company as a whole.

What Does It Mean?

Answers on page 600

13. What does it mean when an investment center manager suboptimizes company performance?
14. What does it mean when residual income is zero?

The Balanced Scorecard

A high-level approach to measuring and reporting organizational performance is accomplished by using a balanced scorecard. The **balanced scorecard** is a set of integrated financial and operating performance measures that highlight and communicate an organization's strategic goals and priorities. Developed by Harvard Professor Robert S. Kaplan and David P. Norton, this concept promotes the use of a few key financial and nonfinancial measures of performance. Too often, performance analysis is so intensely focused on financial measures, such as operating income, segment margin, or ROI, that managers lose sight of other key indicators that can provide additional insight to understanding performance. The balanced scorecard approach takes a "big picture" outlook and provides an analytical framework to support an organizationally integrated planning and performance measurement system.

The balanced scorecard framework is integrated through four key perspectives: the financial perspective, which is concerned with financial performance and improvements; the customer perspective, which is concerned with customer satisfaction and the organization's ability to serve the customer in a timely manner; the internal business process perspective, which is concerned with improvements in key operating areas to achieve greater efficiency and productivity; and the learning and growth perspective, which is concerned with empowering employees with new knowledge resources. Within each perspective, the organization will define several key objectives and related performance measurement targets, as illustrated in Exhibit 15-5.

The organizational investment flow and return on investment flow in Exhibit 15-5 illustrate the integrative nature of this measurement and reporting concept. As Cruisers invests in programs and activities that focus on improving customer satisfaction, business

LO 10

Explain the benefits of a balanced scorecard.

The Balanced Scorecard Institute provides training and consulting services to assist companies, nonprofit organizations, and government agencies in applying best practices in balanced scorecard (BSC) and performance measurement for strategic management and organizational transformation. At balancedscorecard.org, you will find a vast resource designed for managers and analysts to obtain information, ideas, tools, and lessons learned in building strategic management and performance measurement systems as they use balanced scorecard concepts. As the institute focuses on the needs of managers involved in deploying strategic plans and improving their organizations' strategic performance, many areas of the website are particularly interesting and provide useful information such as frequently asked questions, the steps to success, performance measurement, and examples of company success stories.

FYI

Exhibit 15-5

Balanced Scorecard for
Cruisers Inc.

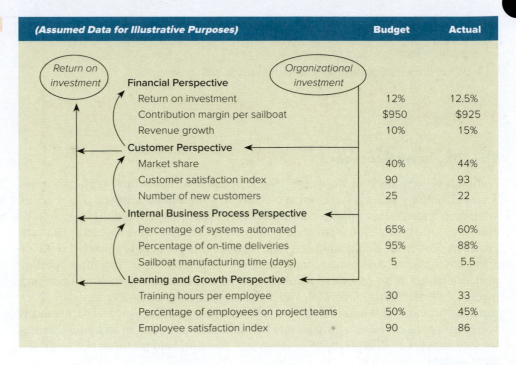

(Assumed Data for Illustrative Purposes)	Budget	Actual
Financial Perspective		
Return on investment	12%	12.5%
Contribution margin per sailboat	$950	$925
Revenue growth	10%	15%
Customer Perspective		
Market share	40%	44%
Customer satisfaction index	90	93
Number of new customers	25	22
Internal Business Process Perspective		
Percentage of systems automated	65%	60%
Percentage of on-time deliveries	95%	88%
Sailboat manufacturing time (days)	5	5.5
Learning and Growth Perspective		
Training hours per employee	30	33
Percentage of employees on project teams	50%	45%
Employee satisfaction index	90	86

processes, and organizational learning, the rewards will be upward flowing and will result in improved financial strength. Talented and happy employees will work toward improvements in business activities and operations, which should add value for the customer and ultimately provide for a greater return on investment for the organization.

Demonstration Problem

The Demonstration Problem walkthrough for this chapter is available in *Connect*.

Summary

All costs are controllable by someone at some time; but in the short run, some costs may be classified as noncontrollable because there is really nothing a manager can do to influence the amount of cost in the short run. **(LO 1)**

Part of the payoff of the budgeting process involves comparing actual results with planned results. This is accomplished in a performance report. The variance shown in the performance report is the difference between the actual and budgeted amounts. Management by exception involves focusing attention on those activities that have a significant variance, with the objective of understanding why the variance occurred and, if appropriate, taking action to eliminate unfavorable variances and capture favorable variances. **(LO 2)**

Flexible budgeting recognizes cost behavior patterns. The original budget amount for variable items based on planned activity is adjusted by calculating a budget allowance based on actual activity for the period. This results in a variable cost variance that is meaningful because the effect of a difference between actual and budgeted volumes of activity is removed from the variance. Only variable cost budgets are flexed. **(LO 3)**

Variances from standard can be caused by a difference between actual and standard costs per unit of input and by a difference between actual and standard quantities. Variance analysis breaks the total budget variance into the amounts caused by each difference. This is necessary because different managers are responsible for each component of the total variance. The objective of reporting variances is to have the appropriate manager take action to eliminate unfavorable variances and to capture favorable variances. Communication between managers is essential to achieve this objective. **(LO 4)**

Variances can be labeled in many ways, but a generally used classification is the following: **(LO 5)**

	Variance due to Difference between Standard and Actual	
Input	**Cost per Unit of Input**	**Quantity**
Raw materials	Price	Usage
Direct labor	Rate	Efficiency
Variable overhead	Spending	Efficiency

Quantity variances for raw materials and direct labor are frequently expressed by unit of measure as well as the dollar amount because the manager responsible for controlling the variance usually thinks in quantity (pounds, gallons, feet, etc.) terms. **(LO 5)**

Fixed manufacturing overhead variances are analyzed differently from variable cost variances because the cost behavior pattern is different. The fixed overhead budget variance is the difference between total actual and total budgeted fixed overhead. The fixed overhead volume variance arises because the actual level of activity differed from that used in calculating the fixed overhead application rate. **(LO 6)**

In most standard cost systems, standard costs are recorded in Work in Process Inventory and Finished Goods Inventory. Variances are usually taken directly to the income statement in the fiscal period in which they arise as an adjustment of Cost of Goods Sold. **(LO 7)**

Segment reporting for an organization involves assigning revenues and expenses to divisions, product lines, geographic areas, or other responsibility centers. In this process, costs that are common to a group of segments should not be arbitrarily allocated to individual segments in that group. **(LO 8)**

Investment center performance is measured by return on investment and is separated into margin and turnover as defined by the DuPont model. Managers are then able to focus on each component of the DuPont formula in order to understand where performance improvements may be achieved. Residual income is an ROI alternative that measures the amount of income an investment center generates above a minimum required return on investment. This method seeks to maximize dollar amounts and eliminates the risk of suboptimization—decisions that result when an investment center manager rejects an opportunity to invest in a project that would increase the ROI of the company as a whole but would lower the ROI of the investment center. **(LO 9)**

A balanced scorecard communicates the set of integrated financial and operating performance measures that highlight an organization's priorities in achieving its strategic goals. **(LO 10)**

Key Terms and Concepts

balanced scorecard (p. 583) A set of integrated financial and operating performance measures that communicates an organization's priorities associated with achieving strategic goals.

budget variance (p. 569) The difference between actual and budgeted amounts.

common fixed expense (p. 579) An expense that is not assigned to an organizational segment in a segmented income statement because the expense would be incurred even if the segment were eliminated.

cost center (p. 580) A responsibility center for which performance is evaluated by comparing actual cost with budgeted cost.

cost per unit of input variance (p. 569) That part of a variable cost budget variance due to a difference between the actual and standard costs per unit of input. See also *raw materials price variance, direct labor rate variance,* and *variable overhead spending variance.*

direct fixed expense (p. 579) An expense assigned to an organizational segment in a segmented income statement that would not be incurred if the segment were eliminated.

direct labor efficiency variance (p. 570) That part of the direct labor budget variance due to the difference between actual hours required and standard hours allowed for the work done.

direct labor rate variance (p. 570) That part of the direct labor budget variance due to the difference between the actual hourly wage rate paid and the standard rate.

favorable variance (p. 565) The excess of actual revenue over budgeted revenue, or budgeted cost over actual cost.

flexible budget (p. 568) A budget adjusted to reflect a budget allowance based on the actual level of activity, rather than the planned level of activity used to establish the original budget.

investment center (p. 580) A responsibility center for which performance is evaluated by comparing actual return on investment with budgeted return on investment.

management by exception (p. 565) A management concept that involves thorough planning and then corrective effort only in those areas that do not show results consistent with the plan.

performance reporting (p. 562) Comparing actual and planned activities or costs.

profit center (p. 580) A responsibility center for which performance is evaluated by comparing actual profit with budgeted profit.

quantity variance (p. 569) The part of a variable cost budget variance due to a difference between the actual and standard quantities of inputs. See also *raw material usage variance, direct labor efficiency variance,* and *variable overhead efficiency variance.*

raw materials price variance (p. 570) That part of the raw materials budget variance due to the difference between actual cost and standard cost of raw materials *used.*

raw materials purchase price variance (p. 574) A variance recognized soon after the purchase of raw materials that is caused by the difference between actual cost and standard cost of raw materials *purchased.*

raw materials usage variance (p. 571) That part of the raw materials budget variance due to the difference between actual usage and standard usage of raw material.

residual income (p. 582) The amount of income an investment center generates above a minimum required return on investment.

responsibility center (p. 580) An element of the organization over which a manager has been assigned responsibility and authority.

responsibility reporting (p. 565) A system of performance reporting that involves successive degrees of summarization as the number of management responsibility levels being reported about increases.

segment (p. 578) A unit of the organization, such as a product line, sales territory, or group of related activities.

segment margin (p. 579)   The contribution of a segment of an organization to the common fixed expenses and operating income of the organization.

suboptimization (p. 582)   The result of an investment center manager rejecting an opportunity to invest in a project that would increase the ROI of the company as a whole but would lower the ROI of the investment center.

transfer price (p. 580)   A price established for the "sale" of goods or services from one segment of the organization to another segment of the organization.

unfavorable variance (p. 565)   The excess of budgeted revenue over actual revenue, or actual cost over budgeted cost.

variable overhead efficiency variance (p. 571)   That part of the variable overhead budget variance due to the difference between actual hours required and standard hours allowed for the work done.

variable overhead spending variance (p. 571)   That part of the variable overhead budget variance due to the difference between actual variable overhead cost and the standard cost allowed for the actual inputs used (based on direct labor hours, for example).

variance (p. 563)   The difference between actual and budget; variances are labeled as "favorable" or "unfavorable," usually on the basis of the arithmetic difference between actual and budget.

volume variance (p. 575)   A fixed manufacturing overhead variance caused by actual activity being different from the estimated activity used in calculating the predetermined overhead application rate.

Mini-Exercises

Mc Graw Hill **connect**

All applicable Mini-Exercises are available in *Connect*.

Flexible budget Acme Company's production budget for August is 17,500 units and includes the following component unit costs: direct materials, $8; direct labor, $10; variable overhead, $6. Budgeted fixed overhead is $35,000. Actual production in August was 17,000 units.

**Mini-Exercise
15.1
LO 3**

Required:
Prepare a flexible budget that would be used to compare against actual production costs for August.

Flexible budget and performance reporting In addition to the information for Acme Company in Mini-Exercise 15.1, actual unit component costs incurred during August include direct materials, $8.25; direct labor, $9.45; variable overhead, $6.82. Actual fixed overhead was $33,500.

**Mini-Exercise
15.2
LO 3, 4**

Required:
Prepare a performance report, including each cost component, using the following headings:

Cost Component	Original Budget	Flexed Budget	Actual Cost	Budget Variance

Direct material variances In addition to the information for Acme Company in Mini-Exercises 15.1 and 15.2, the standard direct material cost per unit consists of

**Mini-Exercise
15.3
LO 4, 5**

10 pounds of raw material at $0.80 per pound. During August, 187,000 pounds of raw material were used that were purchased at $0.75 per pound.

Required:
Calculate the materials price variance and materials usage variance for August.

Mini-Exercise
15.4
LO 4, 5

Direct labor variances In addition to the information for Acme Company in Mini-Exercises 15.1 and 15.2, the standard direct labor cost per unit consists of 0.5 hour of labor time at $20 per hour. During August, $160,650 of actual labor cost was incurred for 7,650 direct labor hours.

Required:
Calculate the labor rate variance and labor efficiency variance for August.

Mini-Exercise
15.5
LO 4, 5, 6

Variable overhead variances In addition to the information for Acme Company in Mini-Exercises 15.1 and 15.2, the standard variable overhead rate per unit consists of $6 per machine hour and each unit is allowed a standard of 1 hour of machine time. During August, $115,940 of actual variable overhead cost was incurred for 18,700 machine hours.

Required:
Calculate the variable overhead spending variance and the variable overhead efficiency variance.

Mini-Exercise
15.6
LO 4, 5, 6

Fixed overhead variances In addition to the information for Acme Company in Mini-Exercises 15.1 and 15.2, the standard fixed overhead application rate per unit consists of $2 per machine hour and each unit is allowed a standard of 1 hour of machine time.

Required:
Calculate the fixed overhead budget variance and the fixed overhead volume variance.

Mini-Exercise
15.7
LO 8

Segmented income statement ABC Company operates two divisions with the following sales and expense information for the month of August:

Division 1: sales, $120,000; contribution margin ratio, 50%; direct fixed expenses, $24,000.

Division 2: sales, $80,000; contribution margin ratio, 70%; direct fixed expenses, $16,000.

ABC Company's total fixed expenses during August was $100,000.

Required:
Prepare a segmented income statement for ABC Company to determine the segment margin for Divisions 1 and 2 and the operating income for ABC Company.

Mini-Exercise
15.8
LO 9

Investment center performance ABC Company operates two divisions with the following operating information for the month of May:

Division 1: sales, $120,000; operating income, $36,000; operating assets, $300,000.

Division 2: sales, $80,000; operating income, $40,000; operating assets, $400,000.

ABC Company expects a minimum return of 10% should be earned from all investments.

Required:
Prepare ABC Company's ROI analysis using the DuPont model for each division, and calculate each division's residual income.

Exercises

All applicable Exercises are available in *Connect*.

Flexible budgeting The cost formula for the maintenance department of Rainbow Ltd. is $19,400 per month plus $7.70 per machine hour used by the production department.

Exercise 15.9
LO 3

Required:

a. Calculate the maintenance cost that would be budgeted for a month in which 6,700 machine hours are planned to be used.

b. Prepare an appropriate performance report for the maintenance department assuming that 7,060 machine hours were actually used in the month of May and that the total maintenance cost incurred was $68,940.

Flexible budgeting Western Manufacturing produces a single product. The original budget for April was based on expected production of 17,500 units; actual production for April was 16,600 units. The original budget and actual costs incurred for the manufacturing department follow:

Exercise 15.10
LO 3

	Original Budget	Actual Costs
Direct materials	$275,625	$270,750
Direct labor	213,500	206,750
Variable overhead	107,625	97,625
Fixed overhead	85,000	86,250
Total	$681,750	$661,375

Required:
Prepare an appropriate performance report for the manufacturing department.

Performance reporting and flexible budgeting Following is a partially completed performance report for a recent week for direct labor in the binding department of a book publisher:

Exercise 15.11
LO 4, 5

	Original Budget	Flexed Budget	Actual	Budget Variance
Direct labor	$1,800		$1,888	

The original budget is based on the expectation that 3,000 books would be bound; the standard is 20 books per hour at a pay rate of $12 per hour. During the week, 2,860 books were actually bound. Employees worked 160 hours at an actual total cost of $1,888.

Required:

a. Calculate the flexed budget amount against which actual performance should be evaluated and then calculate the budget variance.

b. Calculate the direct labor efficiency variance in terms of hours.

c. Calculate the direct labor rate variance.

Exercise 15.12

LO 4, 5

Performance reporting and flexible budgeting For the stamping department of a manufacturing firm, the standard cost for direct labor is $15 per hour, and the production standard calls for 1,000 stampings per hour. During February, 198 hours were required for actual production of 186,000 stampings. Actual direct labor cost for the stamping department for June was $3,168.

Required:

a. Complete the following performance report for February:

	Flexed Budget	Actual	Budget Variance
Direct labor			

b. Analyze the budget variance by calculating the direct labor efficiency and rate variances for February.

c. What alternatives to the preceding monthly report could improve control over the stamping department's direct labor?

Exercise 15.13

LO 4, 5

Direct labor variances—solving for unknowns Ackerman's Garage uses standards to plan and control labor time and expense. The standard time for an engine tune-up is 3.5 hours, and the standard labor rate is $15 per hour. Last week, 24 tune-ups were completed. The labor efficiency variance was 6 hours unfavorable, and the labor rate variance totaled $81 favorable.

Required:

a. Calculate the actual direct labor hourly rate paid for tune-up work last week.

b. Calculate the dollar amount of the labor efficiency variance.

c. What is the most likely explanation for these two variances? Is this a good trade-off for the management of the garage to make? Explain your answer.

Exercise 15.14

LO 4, 5

Direct labor variances—solving for unknowns Four Seasons Industries has established direct labor performance standards for its maintenance and repair shop. However, some of the labor records were destroyed during a recent fire. The actual hours worked during August were 3,000, and the total direct labor budget variance was $900 unfavorable. The standard labor rate was $15 per hour, but recent resignations allowed the firm to hire lower-paid replacement workers for some jobs, and this produced a favorable rate variance of $3,600 for August.

Required:

a. Calculate the actual direct labor rate paid per hour during August.

b. Calculate the dollar amount of the direct labor efficiency variance for August.

c. Calculate the standard direct labor hours allowed for the actual level of activity during August. (*Hint:* Use the formula for the quantity variance and solve for the missing information.)

Direct material variances—solving for unknowns Oakwood Inc. manufactures end tables, armchairs, and other wood furniture products from high-quality materials. The company uses a standard costing system and isolates variances as soon as possible. The purchasing manager is responsible for controlling direct material price variances, and production managers are responsible for controlling usage variances. During November, the following results were reported for the production of American Oak armchairs:

Exercise 15.15
LO 4, 5

Units produced	1,500 armchairs
Direct materials purchased	19,000 board feet
Direct materials issued into production	17,200 board feet
Standard cost per unit (12 board feet × $8)	$96 per unit produced
Purchase price variance	$2,850 unfavorable

Required:

a. Calculate the actual price paid per board foot purchased.
b. Calculate the standard quantity of materials allowed (in board feet) for the number of units produced.
c. Calculate the direct materials usage variance.
d. What is the most likely explanation for the price and usage variances? Is this a good trade-off for management of Oakwood to make? Explain your answer.

Direct material variances—solving for price and usage variances Fiberworks Company is a manufacturer of fiberglass toy boats. The company has recently implemented a standard cost system and has designed the system to isolate variances as soon as possible. During the month of May, the following results were reported for the production of 25,000 toy boats:

Exercise 15.16
LO 4, 5

Direct materials (fiberglass) purchased	50,000 pounds
Direct materials issued into production	40,000 pounds
Standard pounds allowed per boat	1.5 pounds
Standard price per pound	$6.50
Cost of fiberglass purchased	$312,500

Required:

a. Calculate the actual cost per pound of fiberglass purchased during May.
b. Calculate the direct materials purchase price variance for May.
c. Calculate the direct materials usage variance for May.
d. Comment on calculating the material price variance based on pounds purchased rather than pounds issued into production.

Segmented income statement The president of Ravens Inc. attended a seminar about the contribution margin model and returned to her company full of enthusiasm

Exercise 15.17
LO 8

about it. She requested that last year's traditional model income statement be revised, and she received the following report:

	Total Company	Division A	Division B	Division C
Sales	$100,000	$40,000	$25,000	$35,000
Variable expenses	60,000	26,000	15,000	19,000
Contribution margin	$ 40,000	$14,000	$10,000	$16,000
Fixed expenses	30,000	10,000	11,000	9,000
Net income (loss)	$ 10,000	$ 4,000	$ (1,000)	$ 7,000

The president was told that the fixed expenses of $30,000 included $21,000 that had been split evenly between divisions because they were general corporate expenses. After looking at the statement, the president exclaimed, "I knew it! Division B is a drag on the whole company. Close it down!"

Required:

a. Evaluate the president's remark.

b. Calculate what the company's net income would be if Division B were closed down.

c. Write a policy statement related to the allocation of fixed expenses.

Exercise 15.18
LO 8

Segmented income statement Vogel Co. produces three models of heating and air conditioning thermostat components. The following table summarizes data about each model:

	BV19	HV41	MV12
Selling price per unit	$ 24	$ 40	$ 20
Contribution margin per unit	8	12	4
Units sold per month	2,000	1,000	3,000
Total contribution margin	$16,000	$12,000	$12,000
Direct fixed expenses	7,200	5,700	8,100
Segment margin	$ 8,800	$ 6,300	$ 3,900
Allocated company fixed expenses	3,333	1,667	5,000
Operating income (loss)	$ 5,467	$ 4,633	$ (1,100)

Required:

a. Criticize the preceding presentation. On what basis does the $10,000 of company fixed expenses appear to be allocated?

b. Calculate the effect on total company net income if the MV12 model were discontinued.

c. Calculate the contribution margin ratio for each model.

d. If an advertising campaign focusing on a single model were to result in an increase of 5,000 units in the quantity of units sold, which model should be advertised? Explain your answer.

e.   If an advertising campaign focusing on a single model were to result in an increase
     of $15,000 in revenues, which model should be advertised? Explain your answer.

Investment center analysis; ROI and residual income The Central Division
of National Inc. has operating income of $16,000 on sales revenue of $160,000.
Divisional operating assets are $80,000, and management of National has determined
that a minimum return of 12% should be expected from all investments.

Exercise 15.19
LO 9

Required:
a.   Using the DuPont model, calculate the Central Division's margin, turnover,
     and ROI.
b.   Calculate the Central Division's residual income.

Investment center analysis; ROI and residual income Romano Corporation has
three operating divisions and requires a 12% return on all investments. Selected
information is presented here:

Exercise 15.20
LO 9

	Division X	Division Y	Division Z
Revenues	$ 750,000	?	?
Operating income...........	$ 90,000	?	$75,000
Operating assets............	$ 375,000	$225,000	?
Margin.....................	?	12%	?
Turnover	?	1 turn	2 turns
ROI.......................	?	?	?
Residual income	?	?	$18,750

Required:
a.   Calculate the missing amounts for each division.
b.   Comment on the relative performance of each division.
c.   Provide an example to show how residual income improves decision making at
     the divisional level.

Problems

All applicable Problems are available in *Connect*.

Calculate variable cost variances—explain results The standards for one case of
Springfever Tonic are as follows:

Problem 15.21
LO 4, 5

Direct materials	4 lb @ $5.00/lb	= $20
Direct labor	3 hr @ $13.00/hr	= $39
Variable overhead (based		
on direct labor hours)	3 hr @ $6.00/hr	= $18

During the week ended August 28, the following activity took place:

    7,400 lb of raw materials were purchased for inventory at a cost of $4.95 per pound.
    2,000 cases of finished product were produced.
    8,300 lb of raw materials were used.

5,800 direct labor hours were worked at a total cost of $78,300.

$35,670 of actual variable overhead costs were incurred.

Required:

Calculate each of the following variances and provide plausible explanations for the results:

a. Price variance for raw materials purchased.

b. Raw materials usage variance.

c. Direct labor rate variance.

d. Direct labor efficiency variance.

e. Variable overhead spending variance.

f. Variable overhead efficiency variance.

Problem 15.22

LO 4, 5

Calculate variable cost variances—explain results The standards for one case of liquid weed killer are as follows:

Direct materials	6 lb @ $ 7.50/lb
Direct labor.	3.6 hr @ $16.00/hr
Variable overhead (based on machine hours).	1.2 hr @ $ 5.50/hr

During the week ended May 6, the following activity took place:

4,360 machine hours were worked.

22,800 lb of raw material were purchased for inventory at a total cost of $174,420.

3,800 cases of finished product were produced.

22,580 lb of raw material were used.

13,440 labor hours were worked at an average rate of $16.25 per hour.

$23,108 actual variable overhead costs were incurred.

Required:

Calculate each of the following variances and provide plausible explanations for the results:

a. Price variance for raw materials purchased.

b. Raw materials usage variance.

c. Direct labor rate variance.

d. Direct labor efficiency variance.

e. Variable overhead spending variance.

f. Variable overhead efficiency variance.

Problem 15.23

LO 4, 5

Direct labor variances—insurance company application The Foster Insurance Company developed standard times for processing claims. When a claim was received at the processing center, it was first reviewed and classified as simple or complex. The standard time for processing was:

Simple claim.	45 minutes
Complex claim.	2.5 hours

Employees were expected to be productive 7.5 hours per day. Compensation costs were $90 per day per employee. During April, which had 20 working days, the following number of claims were processed:

Simple claims.	3,000 processed
Complex claims.	600 processed

Required:

a. Calculate the number of workers that should have been available to process April claims.

b. Assume that 27 workers were actually available throughout the month of April. Calculate a labor efficiency variance expressed as both a number of workers and a dollar amount for the month.

Direct labor variances—banking application Founders State Bank developed a standard for teller staffing that provided for one teller to handle 15 customers per hour. During June, the bank averaged 50 customers per hour and had five tellers on duty at all times. (Relief tellers filled in during lunch and rest breaks.) The teller compensation cost is $12 per hour. The bank is open eight hours a day, and there were 21 working days during June.

Problem 15.24
LO 4, 5

Required:

a. Calculate the teller efficiency variance during June expressed in terms of number of tellers and cost per hour.

b. Now assume that in June, during the 11 A.M. to 1 P.M. period every day, the bank served an average of 80 customers per hour. During the other six hours of the day, an average of 40 customers per hour were served.

  1. Calculate a teller efficiency variance for the 11 to 1 period expressed in terms of number of tellers per hour and total cost for the month.

  2. Calculate a teller efficiency variance for the other six hours of the day expressed in terms of number of tellers per hour and total cost for the month.

  3. As teller supervisor, explain the significance of the variances calculated in 1 and 2, and explain how you might respond to the uneven work flow during each day.

Fixed overhead variances—various issues Silverstone's production budget for July called for making 40,000 units of a single product. The firm's production standards allow one-half of a machine hour per unit produced. The fixed overhead budget for July was $36,000. Silverstone uses an absorption costing system. Actual activity and costs for July were:

Problem 15.25
LO 5, 6

Units produced	39,000
Fixed overhead costs incurred	$37,000

Required:

a. Calculate the predetermined fixed overhead application rate per machine hour that would be used in July.

b. Calculate the number of machine hours that would be allowed for actual July production.

   c.   Calculate the fixed overhead applied to work in process during July.
   d.   Calculate the over- or underapplied fixed overhead for July.
   e.   Calculate the fixed overhead budget and volume variances for July.

Problem 15.26

LO 5, 6

Variable and fixed overhead variances—various issues Presented here are the original overhead budget and the actual costs incurred during April for Piccolo Inc. Piccolo's managers relate overhead to direct labor hours for planning, control, and product costing purposes. The original budget is based on budgeted production of 20,000 units in 4,000 standard direct labor hours. Actual production of 21,600 units required 4,500 actual direct labor hours.

	Original Budget	Actual Costs
Variable overhead	$30,000	$33,800
Fixed overhead	36,000	37,600

Required:
a.   Calculate the flexed budget allowances for variable and fixed overhead for April.
b.   Calculate the direct labor efficiency variance for April expressed in terms of direct labor hours.
c.   Calculate the predetermined overhead application rate for both variable and fixed overhead for April.
d.   Calculate the fixed and variable overhead applied to production during April if overhead is applied on the basis of standard hours allowed for actual production achieved.
e.   Calculate the fixed overhead budget and volume variances for April.
f.   Calculate the over- or underapplied fixed overhead for April.

---

connect **Cases**

All applicable Cases are available in *Connect.*

Case 15.27

LO 3

Performance reporting The chair of the Science Department of State University has a budget for laboratory supplies. Supplies have a variable cost behavior pattern that is a function of the number of students enrolled in laboratory courses. For planning purposes, when the budget was prepared in March 2019, it was estimated that 300 students would be enrolled in laboratory courses during the fall 2019 semester. Actual enrollment for the fall semester was 318 students.

Required:
a.   Explain what action should be taken with respect to the supplies budget when the actual enrollment is known.
b.   Would your answer to part **a** be any different if the actual enrollment turned out to be 273 students? Explain your answer.
c.   Suppose the budget item in question was the salary for the lab assistant. How would your answer to part **a** and part **b** change, if at all? Explain your answer.

Flexible budgeting One of the significant costs for a nonpublic college or university is student aid in the form of gifts and grants awarded to students because of academic potential or performance, and/or financial need. Gifts and grants are only a part of a financial aid package, usually accounting for no more than 20% of the total package. Federal and state grants, other scholarships, loans, and income from work constitute the rest of financial aid, but these funds are not provided by the institution. Assume that for the 2019–2020 academic year, Wonder College had a gift and grant budget of $900,000 and that all of these funds had been committed to students by May 15, 2019. The college had capacity to enroll up to 200 additional students.

Case 15.28
LO 3

Required:

Explain why and how flexible budgeting should be applied by the management of Wonder College in administering its gift and grant awards budget.

Frequency of performance reporting If a company uses a standard cost system, should all variances be calculated with the same frequency (e.g., monthly), and should they always be expressed in dollar amounts? Explain your answer and include in it the reason for calculating variances.

Case 15.29
LO 4

Rank the importance of eight variances Assume that you are the production manager of a small branch plant of a large manufacturing firm. The central accounting control department sends you monthly performance reports showing the flexed budget amount, actual cost and variances for raw materials, direct labor, variable overhead (which is expressed on a direct labor hour basis), and fixed overhead. The variable cost budget variances are separated into quantity and cost per unit of input variances, and the fixed overhead budget and volume variances are shown. All variances are expressed in dollars.

Case 15.30
LO 5

Required:

a. Rank the eight variances in descending order of their usefulness to you for planning and controlling purposes. Explain your ranking.
b. Given the usefulness ranking in part **a,** explain how the frequency of reporting and the units in which each variance is reported might make the performance reports more useful.

Direct material variances—the price versus usage trade-off Williamson Inc. manufactures quality replacement parts for the auto industry. The company uses a standard costing system and isolates variances as soon as possible. The purchasing manager is responsible for controlling the direct material price variances for hundreds of raw material items that are used in the company's various production processes. Recent experience indicates that, in the aggregate, direct material price variances have been favorable. However, several problems have occurred. Direct material usage variances have become consistently unfavorable for many items, and the company's total budget variance for direct materials has been unfavorable during each of the past six months. Direct laborers have complained about the quality of certain raw material items, and major customers have canceled purchase orders. In the meantime, the company's raw materials inventory has increased by nearly 240%.

Case 15.31
LO 4, 5

Required:

a. Give a probable explanation of why these results have occurred. (*Hint:* What might the purchasing manager be doing that is dysfunctional for the company as a whole?)

b. How could the performance reporting system be improved to encourage more appropriate behavior on the part of the purchasing manager?

Case 15.32
LO 5

Evaluate the effects of erroneous standards During the year ended May 31, 2018, Teller Register Co. reported favorable raw material usage and direct labor and variable overhead efficiency variances that totaled $285,800. Price and rate variances were negligible. Total standard cost of goods manufactured during the year was $1,905,340.

Required:

a. Comment about the effectiveness of the company's standards for controlling material and labor usage.

b. If standard costs are used for valuing finished goods inventory, will the ending inventory valuation be higher or lower than if actual costs are used? Explain your answer.

c. Assume that the ending inventory of finished goods valued at standard cost is $158,780. Calculate the adjustment to finished goods inventory that would be appropriate because of the erroneous standards.

Case 15.33
LO 7

Using standard costs to record inventory transactions York Co. uses a standard cost system. When raw materials are purchased, the standard cost of the raw materials purchased is recorded as an increase in the Raw Materials Inventory account. When raw materials are used, the standard cost of the materials allowed for the units produced is recorded as an increase in the Work in Process Inventory account. Likewise, the standard cost of direct labor and variable manufacturing overhead is recorded as an increase in Work in Process Inventory.

Required:

a. Explain where in the financial statements the difference between the actual and standard cost of raw materials purchased will be recorded.

b. In this system, under what circumstances will the increases and decreases in the Finished Goods Inventory account (due to production and sales, respectively) represent the actual cost of products made and sold?

c. How does the accounting for overapplied or underapplied overhead, originally discussed in Chapter 13, differ from York Co.'s cost accounting system?

Case 15.34

The planning and control environment: Internet assignment The Consortium for Advanced Manufacturing—International (CAM-I) is an international consortium of companies, consultancies, and academics that have elected to work cooperatively in a precompetitive environment to solve problems common to the group. Its sole purpose is to support member companies in their quest for excellence in today's highly competitive global marketplace. This case requires you to use the CAM-I website at cam-i. org to complete the following requirements.

Assume that a start-up manufacturing company has recently hired you, and your first task is to develop a cost planning and control environment for the firm.

Required:

a. Review CAM-I's "Home" page and the "About CAM-I" page. Summarize the history and mission of the organization, and describe how CAM-I's participative model produces value for its members.

b. Read CAM-I's most recent "Deliverables" report to members. Prepare a one-page summary emphasizing important initiatives in progress from your perspective.

c. Read CAM-I's value proposition, and review its membership options (large corporate, medium size, and small organization). Choose a membership option that you expect will be beneficial, and write a memo to your new supervisor describing your rationale to justify the cost of joining this organization.

d. Review CAM-I's body of knowledge publications. Identify two items from the list of publications that would help you with your new responsibility. Explain your choices.

e. Review CAM-I's wiki. Read the main-page overview of CAM-I's Cost Management Systems (CMS) interest group, explore the 10 planning and budgeting "we share your pain" issues presented in the survey results list, and write a brief summary of your findings.

ANSWERS TO
What Does It Mean?

1. It means that actual results are compared to planned or budgeted results, and explanations for variances are determined.

2. It means that actual results are better than planned results; for example, actual sales are greater than forecasted sales, or actual expenses are less than budgeted expenses.

3. It means that managers usually should work to repeat activities that have resulted in favorable variances that result in desirable outcomes and to eliminate activities that have caused unfavorable variances.

4. It means that when the performance report is prepared, the budgeted amounts reflect expected costs at the actual level of activity achieved, rather than originally budgeted costs for the expected level of activity.

5. It means that because fixed expenses are not expected to change if the level of activity changes within the relevant range, it is not appropriate to change the budget for fixed expenses even though actual activity differs from planned activity.

6. It means that more than the standard amount of raw material allowed was used for the production achieved.

7. It means that the variance associated with each cost element—rate paid and hours used—is determined separately and reported to the individuals who are responsible for the rate paid and hours used.

8. It means that the variance may have resulted from an undesirable activity, such as purposely not putting enough ingredients into a batch, that could adversely affect the quality of the product.

9. It means that responsible managers don't operate in a vacuum and that their control activities have to be coordinated to achieve optimum results.

10. It means that because costs are fixed, this type of overhead is difficult to control on a short-term basis by shift or by week. But because fixed costs are becoming increasingly significant for many firms, they are likely to receive a lot of attention.

11. It means that a performance report for a particular area of responsibility reflects those items over which the managers of that area have control.

12. It means that because these expenses would not decrease in total even if the segment disappeared, erroneous conclusions can result from an analysis that includes arbitrarily allocated common fixed expenses.

13. It means that the manager has rejected an opportunity to invest in a project that would increase the ROI of the company as a whole because it would lower the ROI of the investment center.

14. It means that the investment center is earning an ROI exactly equal to the minimum required ROI used to calculate residual income.

16

Costs for Decision Making

American cartoonist Scott Adams, creator of the *Dilbert* comic strip, once declared that "informed decision making comes from a long tradition of guessing and then blaming others for inadequate results." Dilbert's satirical view of planning and control perhaps holds more truth about the art of decision making than one would care to admit as he typically portrays the corporate office culture as an inefficient political environment where mismanagement spawns ridiculous decisions. In this chapter, however, a more systematic approach to the decision-making process is examined for both short- and long-term decisions.

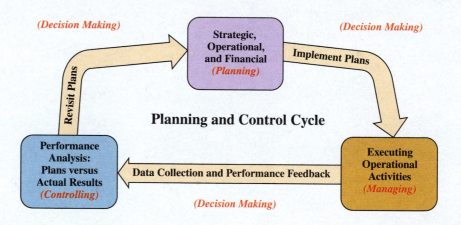

Decision making encompasses the entire planning and control cycle and involves members from all functional areas of the organization. Some decisions required in the planning process are short-term in nature and include the allocation of company resources for those discretionary cost items discussed in Chapter 14, such as advertising, charitable contributions, and employee development programs. Implementing the operational and financial budgets discussed in Chapter 14 requires decisions from those managers responsible for executing the activities defined by those budgets. After feedback information is available from the performance reporting system discussed in Chapter 15, decisions will be required to enhance or correct operational plans and/or activities.

Decisions regarding the long-run competitive strategy for product markets and prices are made in conjunction with the investment in physical capacity resources necessary to meet the objectives of the firm's strategy. **Capital budgeting** is the process of analyzing proposed capital expenditures—investments in plant, equipment, new products, and so on—to determine whether the investment will generate a large enough return on investment (ROI) over time to contribute to the organization's overall ROI objective.

This chapter examines several examples of short- and long-run decisions—and establishes a way of thinking about the costs involved in the decision-making process. The analysis necessary for those unique opportunities that present themselves on a random basis, such as special discounted price offers a firm receives for a one-time sale of its product, is significantly different from the analysis required for the investment in additional plant capacity.

LEARNING OBJECTIVES (LO)

After studying this chapter, you should understand and be able to

LO 16-1   Explain and illustrate the following cost terms: *differential, allocated, sunk,* and *opportunity.*

LO 16-2   Explain how costs are determined to be relevant for short-run decisions.

LO 16-3   Analyze relevant costs for the following decisions: sell or process further, special pricing, target costing, make or buy, continue or discontinue a segment, and product mix.

LO 16-4   Describe the attributes of capital budgeting that make it a significantly different activity from operational budgeting.

LO 16-5   Explain why present value analysis is appropriate and use it in capital budgeting.

LO 16-6   Define the cost of capital and demonstrate its use in capital budgeting.

LO 16-7   Illustrate the use of and differences between various capital budgeting techniques: net present value, present value ratio, and internal rate of return.

LO 16-8   Describe how issues concerning estimates, income taxes, and the timing of cash flows and investments are treated in the capital budgeting process.

LO 16-9   Calculate the payback period of a capital expenditure project.

LO 16-10 Calculate the accounting rate of return of a project and explain how it can be used most appropriately.

LO 16-11 Explain why not all management decisions are made strictly on the basis of quantitative analysis techniques.

Cost Classifications

Cost Classifications for Other Analytical Purposes

LO 1

Explain and illustrate the following cost terms: *differential, allocated, sunk,* and *opportunity.*

Exhibit 16-1 highlights the final branch of the cost classification model and presents the cost terminology and concepts used in the decision-making process.

Differential costs are brought into focus when possible future activities are analyzed. A **differential cost** is one that will differ according to the alternative activity being considered. For example, if a modification of an existing product is being considered, only the changes in cost resulting from the modification need to be considered relative to the additional revenues expected to result from the modification. Those costs that will continue to be incurred whether or not the modification is made are not germane to the decision. Identifying differential costs will be key to successful decision making.

Allocated costs are those that have been assigned to a product or activity (a "cost object") using some sort of systematic process. For example, overhead costs are allocated to production runs using the overhead application rate, for which the process was described in Chapter 13. At this point, a reminder about cost allocations is appropriate. Many cost allocation methods are arbitrary and do not result in assigning costs in a way that reflects the reason why the costs were incurred. (Recall the discussion about common fixed expenses in Chapter 15.) Therefore, managers must be very careful about the conclusions made from any analysis that includes allocated costs. A general rule, similar to the warning against expressing fixed cost on a per unit basis, is appropriate to learn: *Do not arbitrarily allocate costs to a responsibility center because the allocated costs may not behave the way assumed in the allocation method.*

A **sunk cost** is a cost that has been incurred and cannot be unincurred, or reversed, by some future action. For example, if a firm has acquired a special-purpose asset that

Exhibit 16-1   Cost Classifications—The Big Picture

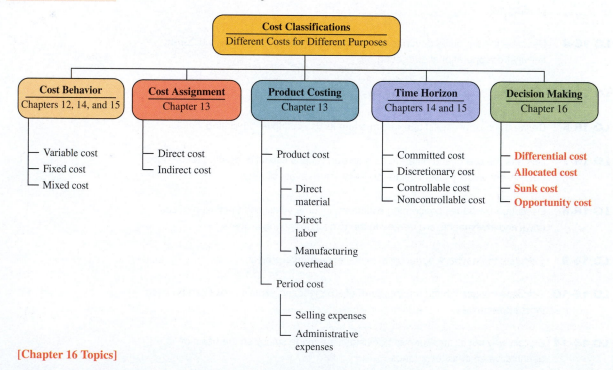

[Chapter 16 Topics]

would not be useful to any other organization, the cost of the asset represents a sunk cost. If the asset is put in use, its cost will be shown as depreciation expense over its life; if scrapped, its net book value will be recorded as a loss. Either way, the cost of the asset will be reflected in the income statement. When a new car is driven out of the dealer's lot, a sunk cost has been incurred that is equal to the loss in value because the car is now "used." *Sunk costs are never relevant to the analysis of alternative future actions (i.e., they are never differential costs) because they have been incurred and will not change.*

Opportunity cost is an economic concept that is too frequently overlooked in accounting analyses. Opportunity cost is the income forgone because an asset was not invested at a rate of return that could have been earned. For example, assume that you keep a $200 minimum balance in a non-interest-bearing checking account for which no service charge is assessed regardless of balance. If your next best alternative is to invest the $200 in a 6 percent savings account, the opportunity cost of your decision is $12 per year (6% × $200). Because opportunity cost relates to a transaction that did not occur, no record of it is made in the financial accounting process; thus, it is often overlooked. Awareness of opportunity cost raises the question, what other alternatives are there for earning a return on a particular asset?

---

1. What does it mean to state that a cost is a sunk cost?

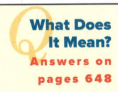

What Does It Mean?

Answers on pages 648

Short-Run Decision Analysis

Relevant Costs

While executing daily responsibilities of managing the operations of an organization, managers are faced with decisions that may affect only the next few days, weeks, or months. These short-run decisions could involve the utilization of resources not otherwise active or the opportunity to reduce costs by outsourcing the production of certain components that will be used in production. Or a manager might have the ability to improve profits by choosing to sell a product at a special price or at a certain point in the production process or by choosing to refine the product further and in doing so attract a higher selling price. **Relevant costs** are those *future* costs that represent differences between these decision alternatives, and they are the key to effective decision making. *Past* transaction costs that are appropriately recorded in the accounting system as a result of the financial accounting process, represent costs that are never

LO 2

Explain how costs are determined to be relevant for short-run decisions.

relevant for decision making and will only confuse the manager presented with the challenge of correctly analyzing costs for a particular decision.

Discussion of the many cost classification concepts presented in Chapters 12 through 15 has emphasized the theme of *different costs for different purposes* by describing how costs are viewed from different perspectives for planning and control purposes. Those same costs are now analyzed as being relevant or irrelevant for decision making and that depends on the question being addressed by the decision alternatives. Variable or fixed costs may or may not be relevant to a decision; it depends on whether they represent a difference between the alternatives.

Relevant Costs in Action—The Sell or Process Further Decision

LO 3

Analyze relevant costs for the following decisions: sell or process further, special pricing, target costing, make or buy, continue or discontinue a segment, and product mix.

The sell or process further decision will be used to introduce relevant cost analysis. Suppose that Air Comfort Inc. produces a heating and cooling system that sells for $7,200 and requires the following production costs:

Direct materials	$2,400
Direct labor	1,600
Variable overhead	800
Fixed overhead	1,200

Next, assume that Air Comfort's design engineers have developed a more efficient air filtration system that would increase the efficiency of the current model. The only changes to the cost structure to produce the more efficient model would be direct materials that would now cost $3,400. Air Comfort's marketing vice president suggests that the more efficient version of the system could sell for $8,000 in the current marketplace for similar systems. What are the relevant costs to consider in deciding whether to sell the current system as is or to produce the more efficient system?

The relevant costs are those costs that are different between the current system and the more efficient system: direct materials in the amount of $1,000 ($3,400 new material cost versus $2,400 current material cost). Note that the analysis requires the decision maker to think independently about each cost item presented; one cannot rely on the general cost classifications presented earlier for planning and control purposes. Costs in this example can be classified as direct (materials and labor) and indirect (overhead), or costs can be classified as variable (materials, labor, and variable overhead) and fixed (fixed overhead). But simply because a cost is direct rather than indirect or variable instead of fixed does not necessarily mean it will be relevant or irrelevant in a decision. Costs for decision-making purposes presented in this chapter are viewed as a *way of thinking* to determine their relevance for any decision by asking the fundamental question "Does it make a difference?"

Should Air Comfort sell the system as is or produce the more efficient system? The relevant cost of producing the more efficient system has been identified as $1,000, but before the final decision can be made, the $1,000 must be compared to the difference in selling price that would be available from the more efficient system. The following relevant cost analysis indicates that it would not be wise to produce and sell the more efficient system given the current marketplace.

Difference in selling price ($8,000 − $7,200)	$ 800
Difference in materials cost ($3,400 − $2,400)	1,000
Difference in profit	$ (200)

In the Air Comfort example, the direct material cost is a differential cost, and the selling price of the more efficient model is an opportunity cost; both items are considered relevant. The fixed overhead in the product cost is an allocated cost, and the design engineering cost is a sunk cost; both costs are considered irrelevant. Understanding these cost classification concepts presented earlier in this chapter is necessary for effective decision analysis:

Relevant	**Irrelevant**
Differential cost—will differ according to alternative activities being considered.	Allocated cost—a common cost that has been arbitrarily assigned to a product or activity.
Opportunity cost—income forgone by choosing one alternative over another.	Sunk cost—has already been incurred and will not change.

2. What does it mean to state that a cost is a relevant cost?

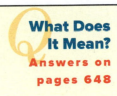

What Does It Mean? Answers on pages 648

Relevant Costs in Action—The Special Pricing Decision

Although many examples illustrate relevant cost analysis for short-run decision making, the special pricing decision offers several compelling issues. The product or service pricing decision, in general, is a long-run decision. In the long run, the product or service price must be adequate to recover all costs identified in the organization's value chain (R&D, design, production, marketing, distribution, and customer service), as well as provide for the necessary ROI. In many situations the marketplace and those firms competing in the marketplace determine the product or service price. If an organization wants to compete, the key issue is whether the firm can strategically manage costs within the value chain over the life of the product or service to produce the desired ROI. This cost management concept is referred to as **target costing**. The target cost is the maximum cost that can be incurred, which—when added to the desired amount of ROI—results in an amount equal to the marketplace selling price.

On certain occasions, the firm may be presented with a special offer for its product or service at a price that is below the normal selling price. In addition to an assessment of relevant costs, the special pricing decision requires an understanding of where the firm is currently operating relative to its capacity. Assume MicroTech Inc. (MTI) produces a high-end laptop computer that normally sells in the marketplace for $2,400. Also assume that World University wants to provide each of its MBA students with a laptop computer so they may participate in online courses with faculty and other students from around the world. World University estimates that in July, it will need to acquire 500 laptops for its MBA students and, therefore, makes an offer to MTI for 500 laptops at the price of $1,800 each.

MTI has the capacity to produce 5,000 laptop computers each month and uses this capacity as the denominator activity for computing predetermined fixed overhead rates. For the month of July, the operating budget calls for the sale and production of 4,400 laptops. In addition to a standard sales commission of 5 percent paid on the sale of each laptop, which would not be paid on the WU special order, standard manufacturing costs are as follows:

Manufacturing costs:	
Direct materials	$ 800
Direct labor	450
Variable overhead	250
Fixed overhead	500
Total unit cost	$2,000

At first glance, it appears that MTI should reject an offer of $1,800 when the cost to produce and sell each laptop is $2,120 ($2,000 manufacturing cost plus $120 commission [$2,400 × 5%]). But the important question is this: "What are the relevant costs for MTI in the decision to accept or reject this special pricing offer?" Exhibit 16-2 presents a relevant cost analysis for this special pricing decision. Notice in Section I that in the month of July, MTI has **idle capacity** of 600 units (5,000 units total capacity less 4,400 units in the current production budget). This unscheduled capacity allows MTI to consider adding 500 units of production without adding production capacity. Note that the analysis is presented in the contribution margin format that highlights cost behavior as activity changes. The current selling price of $2,400 generates $780 of contribution margin per unit toward covering total fixed costs of $2,500,000 and toward providing a profit.

An examination of the relevant costs for the special order of 500 laptops at a price of $1,800 each reveals that the variable cost items of direct material, direct labor, and variable overhead are relevant costs because they represent the additional productive resources necessary to produce 500 additional laptop computers. Variable sales commission, however, is not relevant to the special order because commissions will not be paid on the 500 laptops. Variable costs that can be avoided in the special pricing decision are never relevant costs. The special offer price of $1,800 generates a contribution margin of $300 per unit, and this positive contribution margin flows directly to the bottom line as $150,000 additional operating income since no additional fixed costs were incurred, given the idle capacity. Fixed overhead, assigned for accounting purposes at the predetermined overhead rate of $500 per unit, is not relevant to the special pricing offer but is often incorrectly included in an analysis that does not focus on relevant costs. It should be apparent from Exhibit 16-2 that any price offered above the relevant variable costs of $1,500 will generate a positive contribution margin and should be accepted as long as no other more profitable opportunity for the 600 units of idle capacity can be identified. MicroTech, by accepting the offer of $1,800 per laptop from World University, improved operating income by 16 percent for the month of July.

How would the analysis of relevant costs change if the firm were operating at **full capacity**? Sections II and III of Exhibit 16-2 assume that MTI is currently producing and selling at full capacity of 5,000 laptops in July. Illustrating the option of rejecting the special offer, Section II determines the maximum operating income that MTI can expect to earn with a selling price of $2,400 per laptop. When operating at full capacity, there is no reasonable explanation for considering any price less than the normal selling price unless an opportunity is provided to avoid more cost than the related decrease in price. At full capacity, any combination of price minus variable cost that produces less than $780 of contribution margin will lower total operating income.

Section III of Exhibit 16-2 illustrates the effect on operating income of accepting the special offer when operating at full capacity. Note that operating income has

Relevant Cost Analysis for Special Pricing Decisions | **Exhibit 16-2**

I. Idle capacity = 600 laptops, special offer accepted:

	Current Sales 4,400 Laptops		Special Offer 500 Laptops		July Total 4,900 Laptops
	Unit	Total	Unit	Total	Total
Sales	$2,400	$10,560,000	$1,800	$900,000	$11,460,000
Less: Variable costs:					
Direct material	800	3,520,000	800	400,000	3,920,000
Direct labor	450	1,980,000	450	225,000	2,205,000
Variable overhead	250	1,100,000	250	125,000	1,225,000
Sales commission	120	528,000	—	—	528,000
Contribution margin	$ 780	$ 3,432,000	$ 300	$150,000	$ 3,582,000
Less: Fixed costs*		2,500,000		—	2,500,000
Operating income		$ 932,000		$150,000	$ 1,082,000
Percentage change in operating income				+ 16 %	

II. Full capacity, special offer rejected:

	Current Sales 5,000 Laptops		July Total 5,000 Laptops
	Unit	Total	Total
Sales	$2,400	$12,000,000	$12,000,000
Less: Variable costs:			
Direct material	800	4,000,000	4,000,000
Direct labor	450	2,250,000	2,250,000
Variable overhead	250	1,250,000	1,250,000
Sales commission	120	600,000	600,000
Contribution margin	$ 780	$ 3,900,000	$ 3,900,000
Less: Fixed costs*		2,500,000	2,500,000
Operating income		$ 1,400,000	$ 1,400,000

III. Full capacity, special offer accepted:

	Current Sales 4,500 Laptops		Special Offer 500 Laptops		July Total 5,000 Laptops
	Unit	Total	Unit	Total	Total
Sales	$2,400	$10,800,000	$1,800	$900,000	$11,700,000
Less: Variable costs:					
Direct material	800	3,600,000	800	400,000	4,000,000
Direct labor	450	2,025,000	450	225,000	2,250,000
Variable overhead	250	1,125,000	250	125,000	1,250,000
Sales commission	120	540,000	—	—	540,000
Contribution margin	$ 780	$ 3,510,000	$ 300	$150,000	$ 3,660,000
Less: Fixed costs*		2,500,000		—	2,500,000
Operating income		$ 1,010,000		$150,000	$ 1,160,000
Percentage change in operating income					−17 %

*Total fixed costs for month (5,000 units × $500).

FYI

The Federal Trade Commission was created in 1914 and enforces a variety of federal antitrust and consumer protection laws. The commission seeks to ensure that the nation's markets function competitively and are vigorous, efficient, and free of undue restrictions.

Use the search engine at ftc.gov to locate specific information about the Robinson–Patman Act.

decreased by $240,000 ($1,400,000 − $1,160,000) as a result of generating $480 ($780 − $300) less contribution margin on the 500 special offer laptops ($480 × 500 = $240,000) than earned on sales at full capacity. The difference in contribution margin of $480 per laptop is a relevant opportunity cost—the operating profit forgone by choosing to accept rather than reject the special offer. As discussed in Chapter 12, contribution margin analysis is a powerful tool for managers to use to determine the effects on profits of decisions involving changes in selling prices, variable or fixed costs, or the volume of operating activity.

To summarize, MTI has an opportunity to maximize operating income regardless of whether it is operating at full or idle capacity, and the decision to accept or reject the special offer from World University hinges on the proper interpretation of relevant costs. By accepting the $1,800 offer when operating with idle capacity, MTI will improve its bottom line by 16 percent and put inactive resources to work. On the other hand, by rejecting the $1,800 offer when operating at full capacity, MTI will avoid an unnecessary 17 percent decline in profits.

Relevant cost analysis provides a quantitative framework for the special pricing decision. However, every quantitatively indicated decision should also be evaluated against a qualitative framework that could result in not executing the decision outcome. For example, the special order may not be accepted when operating with idle capacity even though the special price more than covers incremental costs because regular customers might learn of the special price and demand it for their "regular" business. Another example could be related to unanticipated increased volume in the near future; sales at a special price less than the regular price would absorb capacity that could be used for new regular sales. Additionally, management must be certain the special price is not in violation of the Robinson–Patman Act, which does not allow products to be priced differently unless those prices reflect related cost differences. To learn more about this law, see the FYI box.

What Does It Mean?
Answers on pages 648

3. What does it mean when a firm has an offer to sell its product or service at a special price and is operating with idle capacity?

Relevant Costs in Action—The Target Costing Question

Earlier in this chapter, *target costing* was described generally as a long-term concept. Given that the market price for a particular product or service may be a function of the firms competing in that market, the question becomes whether a potential entrant into the market can compete at the established market price and earn a desired amount of profit, thereby requiring the entrant to provide the product or service at the target cost.

This target cost is the minimum cost that can be incurred, which when subtracted from the selling price earns a desired profit:

$$\text{Target cost} = \text{Market price} - \text{Desired profit}$$

Target costing analysis is primarily used to identify cost reduction initiatives in an organization's value chain when it becomes apparent that the firm is no longer competitive and is unable to achieve a desired level of profit at the current marketplace selling price for its products or services. The firm must find a way to reduce cost, or it will eventually be driven out of the market. However, in the short term, the target costing model can be used in a relevant cost analysis to effectively evaluate opportunities that may present themselves. Suppose that MTI is operating under conditions of idle capacity, as described earlier in the chapter, and is looking for opportunities to use that capacity. One of its customers is interested in acquiring 200 tablet-style laptops over the next year, a style that MTI has not produced to date. The marketplace selling price, given a standard configuration and basic features, is already well established at $2,600 per unit. The decision for MTI centers on the question of a target cost: Can MTI produce the 200 tablet laptops at a target cost that will allow it to earn a desired profit, given the selling price of $2,600?

The basic difference in producing the tablet-style laptop compared to MTI's standard laptop is the versatile screen architecture and the notepad user interface, which allows the user to transcribe handwritten notes directly on the tablet screen. What costs are relevant to this decision for MTI? The analysis is in many ways similar to the special pricing decision—the difference being that in the special pricing decision, costs were known up front and in this example some costs that will be new to MTI are not presently known. Obviously these new costs will be differential costs and certainly relevant to the analysis. New costs would likely include design and engineering time, raw material components for the versatile screen user interface, and software enhancements. Another potentially relevant cost could be a labor cost differential if the tablet laptop required more assembly or testing time than the standard laptop. How about equipment? Would new manufacturing equipment, equipment retooling, or other capacity-related costs be necessary?

Assume that MTI requires a 30 percent profit margin to be earned on all laptop products. What is the target cost for the new tablet laptop model?

$$\text{Target cost} = \$2,600 - (\$2,600 \times 30\%)$$
$$\text{Target cost} = \$2,600 - \$780$$
$$\text{Target cost} = \$1,820$$

MTI must be able to produce the tablet laptop at the target cost of $1,820, or less, if it wants to earn its required profit margin of 30 percent. At this point, MTI might consider this opportunity as an opening to compete in the tablet laptop market on a permanent basis; if so, a more long-term life cycle cost analysis would be appropriate. Or MTI's decision may focus on its currently available idle capacity and the 200 tablet-style laptops the customer has asked it to consider. In either case, the importance of understanding costs relevant to the decision is significant.

Relevant Costs in Action—The Make or Buy Decision

Another decision-making situation that illustrates the use of relevant costs is the make or buy decision. For example, how does a manager evaluate the alternatives of producing a component part of a product internally versus buying that component from an outside source? Any number of reasons could exist that might create an advantage for buying from outside the company. This question of **outsourcing** is prevalent in organizations looking to add value to the products and services they provide. The goal is to reduce costs while simultaneously improving the quality and/or functionality of the product or service. Producing a component part internally may be more costly if other organizations specialize in producing that component and it is considered within their core competencies. As such, these outside sources may provide an advantage in terms of newer, more specialized equipment and technologies or certain skilled labor. Alternatively, being presented with a more profitable use of the capacity needed to produce a component part internally might make it desirable to outsource that part's production. Organizational services such as payroll, tax return preparation, information technology resources, or the operation of the employee cafeteria also could be candidates for the outsourcing decision.

What are the relevant costs in a make or buy decision? Suppose that MicroTech Inc. currently produces the motherboards used in the laptop computers that were described in the special pricing decision. As such, MTI incurs the following production costs:

Manufacturing costs:	
Direct materials	$120
Direct labor	80
Variable overhead	50
Fixed overhead	100
Total unit cost	$350

The laptop product manager has determined that a motherboard of comparable quality is now available and could be acquired from Integrated Technologies Inc. at a purchase cost of $300 plus a $5 shipping charge per motherboard. At first glance, this appears to be a simple decision, but until the analysis of relevant costs is performed, the risk of an incorrect decision is considerable.

In a make or buy decision, the relevant cost of making a component or providing a service internally is the cost that can be avoided by acquiring the resource or service from a source outside the company. Therefore, avoidable costs are the relevant costs for this decision. In evaluating each item of cost, the important question to ask is, "Will this cost continue if the resource is purchased from the outside?" If the cost will continue regardless of whether the resource is produced internally or purchased from outside, then it is not relevant to the decision. Using the MTI information to illustrate this concept, assume that 20 percent of the fixed overhead amount that has been allocated to each unit represents the cost (in terms of salary) of the motherboard production manager who would not be retained if the motherboards were not produced by MTI. Also assume that at the present time there is no other use for the production resources being used to produce the motherboards. An analysis of avoidable costs for this decision follows:

	Avoidable Cost to Make	Cost to Buy
Purchase costs:		
Motherboard cost		$300
Shipping cost		5
Manufacturing costs:		
Direct material	$120	
Direct labor	80	
Variable overhead	50	
Fixed overhead ($100 × 20%)	20	
Total unit cost	$270	$305
Advantage to make	$ 35	

It should be clear that the variable production costs will not be necessary if the motherboards are purchased, but notice that only 20 percent of the fixed overhead is included in the relevant cost analysis because the remainder of these fixed costs are sunk, unavoidable, and provide no alternative use.

How would the analysis change if there were alternative uses for the capacity resources currently being used to produce the motherboards? Suppose that MTI could apply the resource capacity being used to produce the motherboards to expand production of wide screen monitors, which provide a contribution margin of $50 per unit. In this scenario, an opportunity cost has been introduced into the scenario, and we must remember that opportunity costs are always relevant for decision making. A revised relevant cost analysis follows:

	Avoidable Cost to Make	Cost to Buy
Purchase costs:		
Motherboard cost		$300
Shipping cost		5
Manufacturing costs:		
Direct material	$120	
Direct labor	80	
Variable overhead	50	
Fixed overhead ($100 × 20%)	20	
Total unit cost	$270	
Opportunity cost of not using available capacity to produce monitors	$ 50	
Total relevant costs	$320	$305
Advantage to buy		$ 15

A final decision to outsource a product component or other service should not be made merely on the basis of the quantitative analysis without considering important qualitative factors. Important dependencies will exist with suppliers, and the need to manage the supplier relationship will be imperative. Concerns about the quality of parts or services received should be addressed, and testing and measurement systems should be defined to ensure the necessary quality. Delivery times and having products or services when they are needed could also be a risk. On the other hand, it is possible that even higher quality and service could be achieved through outsourcing because of the unique expertise or technology that the outside resource or service provider can bring to the organization.

---

4. What does it mean when a cost is avoidable in the make or buy decision?

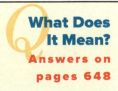

What Does It Mean?

Answers on pages 648

Relevant Costs in Action—The Continue or Discontinue a Segment Decision

Consider next the question of whether to continue or discontinue a particular segment of the organization. You might recall from Chapter 15 that a *segment* is a division, a product or service line, a sales territory, or any other organizational unit.

Because management frequently disaggregates total company operating results into segment results, it is possible that a segment will appear to be operating at a loss. When this occurs, the inevitable question arises as to whether to continue or discontinue the segment. The following illustration of a segmented income statement was presented in Chapter 15 for Cruisers Inc., which showed three divisions: sailboats, motorboats, and repair parts. However, this example assumes annual revenue and expense amounts:

CRUISERS INC.
Segmented Income Statement
For the Year Ended December 31, 2019

	Total Company	Sailboat Division	Motorboat Division	Repair Parts Division
Sales	$2,240,000	$1,280,000	$640,000	$320,000
Variable expenses	960,000	512,000	288,000	160,000
Contribution margin	$1,280,000	$ 768,000	$352,000	$160,000
Fixed expenses	1,128,000	656,000	288,000	184,000
Operating income	$ 152,000	$ 112,000	$ 64,000	$ (24,000)

It appears that if the repair parts division were discontinued, operating income for Cruisers would increase by $24,000. How does an analysis of relevant cost guide the decision maker to the correct outcome? In this type of decision, the relevant cost focus is on those costs that can be eliminated if the segment is eliminated. Otherwise, if a cost will continue even if a segment is discontinued, the cost is not a differential cost and, therefore, not relevant to the decision.

If the repair parts division is discontinued, it should be obvious that sales of $320,000, variable expenses of $160,000, and contribution margin of $160,000 would all be eliminated—these items would be relevant to this decision. What's not so obvious is what happens to the fixed expenses. Cruisers would be willing to discontinue the repair parts division if the company could eliminate more fixed expenses than the amount of contribution margin it would be losing, in this example $160,000.

Now suppose that, as a result of a detailed analysis of fixed expenses, it is learned that the fixed expenses assigned to each division represent the sum of the fixed expenses incurred in each division plus an allocated share of the corporate fixed expenses. The corporate fixed expenses would continue to be incurred even if one of the divisions were to be closed. This analysis of fixed expenses reveals the following:

	Total Company	Sailboat Division	Motorboat Division	Repair Parts Division
Direct fixed expenses	$ 680,000	$400,000	$160,000	$120,000
Common fixed expenses allocated in proportion to sales	448,000	256,000	128,000	64,000
Total fixed expenses	$1,128,000	$656,000	$288,000	$184,000

If Cruisers were to discontinue the repair parts division, $120,000 of direct fixed expenses could be eliminated. Direct fixed expenses would, therefore, be relevant to this decision. However, the $64,000 of corporate fixed expenses allocated to the repair parts division would continue regardless of whether the repair parts division were continued or discontinued. Remember, allocated costs are never relevant. The relevant cost analysis would look like this:

Relevant Cost Analysis of
Discontinuing the Repair Parts Division

Decrease in contribution margin	$(160,000)
Decrease in direct fixed expenses	120,000
Net decrease in segment margin	$ (40,000)

The relevant cost analysis indicates that if the repair parts division is discontinued, Cruisers will experience a $40,000 decrease in company segment margin and, therefore, operating income. It is not logical to give up the $160,000 of contribution margin being generated by the repair parts division if the only benefit is the ability to avoid $120,000 of direct fixed expenses attributable to that division. The following illustration presents a revised segmented income statement for Cruisers Inc., assuming the repair parts division is discontinued with the remaining $64,000 of corporate fixed expenses reallocated to the sailboat and motorboat divisions:

CRUISERS INC.
Segmented Income Statement
For the Year Ended December 31, 2019

	Total Company	Sailboat Division	Motorboat Division
Sales	$1,920,000	$1,280,000	$640,000
Variable expenses	$ 800,000	512,000	288,000
Contribution margin	$1,120,000	$ 768,000	$352,000
Fixed expenses	1,008,000	698,667	309,333
Operating income	$ 112,000	$ 69,333	$ 42,667

The revised segmented income statement for Cruisers shows the decrease in operating income of $40,000 ($152,000 − $112,000) by discontinuing the repair parts division that was suggested by the relevant cost analysis. A careful review and understanding of fixed expenses, as illustrated in this example, emphasizes an important point made earlier in the discussion of relevant costs—just because a cost is classified as fixed (or variable) does not mean that it is always relevant or irrelevant to the decision.

One final note here: Had the original segmented income statement been organized in the preferred format illustrated in Chapter 15, the decision would have been obvious from the beginning. The repair parts division is generating $40,000 of segment margin (sales less variable and direct fixed expenses); by eliminating the segment, the company as a whole would experience a decrease in operating income equal to the $40,000 segment margin. The preferred organization of the segmented income statement is again illustrated here as developed in Chapter 15:

	CRUISERS INC. Segmented Income Statement For the Year Ended December 31, 2019			
	Total Company	Sailboat Division	Motorboat Division	Repair Parts Division
Sales	$2,240,000	$1,280,000	$640,000	$320,000
Variable expenses	960,000	512,000	288,000	160,000
Contribution margin	$1,280,000	$ 768,000	$352,000	$160,000
Direct fixed expenses	680,000	400,000	160,000	120,000
Segment margin	$ 600,000	$ 368,000	$192,000	$ 40,000
Common fixed expenses . . .	448,000			
Operating income	$ 152,000			

What Does It Mean?

Answers on pages 648

5. What does it mean when fixed expenses allocated to a segment are considered to be common corporate expenses?

Relevant Costs in Action—The Short-Term Allocation of Scarce Resources

As a final example of how relevant costs are used in decision making, consider how production resources might be allocated to a mix of products when product demand exceeds the currently available production capacity. The next part of the chapter explains the decision-making tools used to analyze long-term investments in additional production capacity; but in the short term, capacity constraints may force a decision about which product(s) should be produced next when that capacity is completely consumed. The objective is to maximize contribution margin given the demand and capacity constraints. To illustrate, assume that Integrated Technologies Inc. (ITI) produces the following items, which use the same circuitry production line. Demand is such that ITI can produce and sell as much of either product as it can process through the circuitry production line. Selling prices, variable costs, and contribution margins per unit follow:

	Motherboards	Video Circuit Boards
Selling price	$300	$200
Variable costs	150	100
Contribution margin per unit	$150	$100

It would appear that the motherboards are the more profitable product and should be a production priority. However, when capacity constraints exist, it is important to view the contribution margin of each product in terms of the capacity constraint.

Assume that one hour is required to produce a video circuit board and two hours are required to produce a motherboard on the circuitry production line, which has only 120 hours available each week. Does this information about the production time requirements of each product relative to the constrained resource change your view of profitability? Expressing the contribution margin of each product in terms of circuitry production line hours would generate the following results:

	Motherboards	Video Circuit Boards
Selling price	$300	$200
Variable costs	150	100
Contribution margin per unit	$150	$100
Circuitry line hours required	2	1
Contribution margin per hour	$ 75	$100

The contribution margin per circuitry line hour, the scarce resource, indicates that profit will be maximized with the production of video circuit boards. If all 120 available hours were used to produce video circuit boards, the contribution margin generated would be $12,000 ($100 × 120 hours). Only to the extent that any hours were unused for video circuit boards should any motherboards be produced. Of course, an appropriate question to pose at this point, given the current high demand for both products produced on the circuitry production line, is whether additional production capacity should be added. This question presents interesting new considerations that depend on a longer-run view of decision making. These considerations are discussed in the remainder of this chapter.

Long-Run Investment Analysis

Capital Budgeting

Capital budgeting is the process of analyzing proposed capital expenditures—investments in plant, equipment, new products, and so on—to determine whether the investment will generate a large enough return on investment (ROI) over time to contribute to the organization's overall ROI objectives.

Capital budgeting differs from operational budgeting in the time frame being considered. Whereas operational budgeting involves planning for a period that is usually not longer than one year, capital budgeting concerns investments and returns that are spread over a number of years. Thus, the operating budget explained in Chapter 14 reflects the firm's strategic plans to achieve current period profitability, and the capital budget provides an overall blueprint to help the firm meet its long-term growth and profitability objectives.

LO 4
Describe the attributes of capital budgeting that make it a significantly different activity from operational budgeting.

Investment Decision Special Considerations

Investment decisions involve committing financial resources now in anticipation of a return that will be realized over an extended period of time. This extended time frame, which can be many years, adds complexity to the analysis of whether or not to make the investment because of compound interest/present value considerations. The time value of money can be ignored for most operating expenditure decisions because the benefit of an expenditure will be received soon after the expenditure is made, and a simple cost/benefit relationship can be determined. This is not so for capital expenditures because the benefits of the expenditure will be received over several years, and $100 of benefit to be received five years from now is not the same as $100 of benefit to be received one year from now.

LO 5
Explain why present value analysis is appropriate and use it in capital budgeting.

Most business firms and other organizations have more investment opportunities than resources available for investment. Capital budgeting procedures, especially those applying present value analysis techniques, are useful in helping management identify the alternatives that will contribute most to the future profitability of the firm. However, as is the case with most quantitative techniques, the quantitative "answer" will not necessarily dictate management's decision. The quantitative result will be considered along with qualitative factors in the decision-making process. Examples of qualitative factors include top management's willingness to assume competitive risks associated with expanding (or not expanding) into a new market area, the implications for a board of directors retaining control if more stock must be sold to raise funds for the expansion, and, of course, top management's personal goals for the organization. Because capital budgeting involves projections into the future, top management attitudes about the risk of forecasting errors have a major impact on investment decisions.

Most firms involve the board of directors in capital budgeting by having the board approve all capital expenditures above a certain minimum amount. Depending on the company and its financial circumstances, this amount may range from $5,000 to $1 million or more. High-level approval is required because the capital expenditure represents a major commitment of company resources over a multiyear period of time.

What Does It Mean?

Answers on pages 648

6. What does it mean to have a capital budget?

Cost of Capital

LO 6

Define the cost of capital and demonstrate its use in capital budgeting.

The principal financial objective of a firm organized for profit is to earn a return on the assets invested that will permit payment of all borrowing costs (interest) and provide the owners a return on their investment (ROE—return on equity) that compensates them fairly for the financial risks being taken. To meet the requirements of these resource providers, whose claims are shown on the right side of the balance sheet, attention must be focused on the assets that are reported on the left side of the balance sheet. Thus, return on assets (ROI—return on investment) becomes a primary concern of financial managers who evaluate proposed capital expenditures.

The **cost of capital** is the rate of return on assets that must be earned to permit the firm to meet its interest obligations and provide the expected return to owners. Determining the cost of capital of a company is a complex process that is beyond the scope of this text. Suffice it to say here that the cost of capital is a composite of borrowing costs and stockholder dividend and earnings' growth rate expectations. The cost of capital is most useful as a "worry point" guide to management (i.e., an indication of an approximate *minimum* ROI that creditors and owners are expecting). Most firms set a cost of capital rate for investment analysis purposes that is somewhat greater than the "true" economic cost of acquiring funds. This allows for estimation errors in the calculation and provides some cushion for estimation errors in the data used in the investment analysis itself. The cost of capital used for analyzing proposed capital expenditures is also influenced by the perceived riskiness of the proposal being evaluated. Riskier proposals (e.g., new product development or expansion into a new activity) will be required to earn a higher rate of return than less risky proposals (e.g., equipment replacement or expansion of an existing activity). This risk difference is related to the uncertainties associated with operating in a somewhat different environment than that in which the firm is experienced.

The cost of capital is the *discount rate* (i.e., the interest rate at which future period **cash flows** are discounted) used to determine the present value of the investment proposal being analyzed. For most firms, the cost of capital is probably in the range of 10 to 20 percent. In the capital budgeting illustrations presented in this chapter, the cost of capital will be a given. However, you should recognize that in practice the development of the cost of capital rate is a complex but important process.

Capital Budgeting Techniques

Of the four generally recognized capital budgeting techniques, two use present value analysis and two do not. Because money does have value over time, the two methods that recognize this fact are clearly superior, at least conceptually, to those that ignore the time value of money.

Methods That Use Present Value Analysis

Net present value (NPV) method.

Internal rate of return (IRR) method.

Methods That Do Not Use Present Value Analysis

Payback method.

Accounting rate of return method.

Each of these methods uses the amount to be invested in the capital project. The net present value, internal rate of return, and payback methods use the amount of *cash* generated by the investment each year. The accounting rate of return method uses accrual accounting net income resulting from the investment. For most investment projects, the difference between the cash generated each year and accrual accounting net income is depreciation expense—a noncash item that reduces accrual accounting net income. Again, because they recognize the time value of money and focus on cash flows, the NPV and IRR methods are considered more appropriate than either payback or accounting rate of return.

Net Present Value   The **net present value (NPV) method** involves calculating the present value of the expected cash flows from a project using the cost of capital as the discount rate, and then comparing the total present value of the cash flows to the amount of investment required.

Based on this analysis, the following conclusions can be drawn:

LO 7
Illustrate the use of and differences between various capital budgeting techniques: net present value, present value ratio, and internal rate of return.

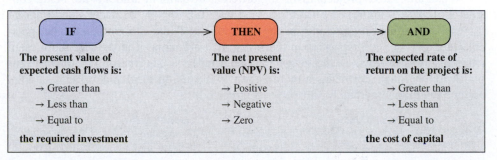

IF	THEN	AND
The present value of expected cash flows is:	The net present value (NPV) is:	The expected rate of return on the project is:
→ Greater than	→ Positive	→ Greater than
→ Less than	→ Negative	→ Less than
→ Equal to	→ Zero	→ Equal to
the required investment		the cost of capital

The discount rate used in net present value analysis is sometimes referred to as the *hurdle rate* because it represents the minimum rate of return required for an investment to yield a positive NPV. The net present value method is illustrated in Exhibit 16-3.

Exhibit 16-3   Net Present Value (NPV) Analysis of a Proposed Investment

I. **Assumptions:**
   A. A new packaging machine costing $100,000, including installation, has an estimated useful life of five years and an estimated salvage value of $6,000 after five years. The new machine will be purchased at the end of 2019.
   B. Installation and use of the machine in the firm's operations will result in labor savings during each of the next five years as follows:

2020	$26,000
2021	27,000
2022	31,000
2023	35,000
2024	38,000

   C. The firm's cost of capital is 16%.

II. **Timeline presentation of cash flows from the investment:**

	12/31/19	2020	2021	2022	2023	2024
Cash flows from investment:						
Savings		$26,000	$27,000	$31,000	$35,000	$38,000
Salvage						6,000
Total		$26,000	$27,000	$31,000	$35,000	$44,000

III. **Net present value calculation at 16%:**

		2020	2021	2022	2023	2024
Present value factors (Table 6-4, 16%)		0.8621	0.7432	0.6407	0.5523	0.4761
Present value of cash flows from investment		$ 22,415	$20,066	$19,862	$19,331	$20,948

Total present value of cash flows
   from investment .... $102,622 ←
Investment .... (100,000)

Net present value at 16% .... $ 2,622

IV. **Conclusion from analysis:**
   The net present value is positive; therefore the projected rate of return on this investment is greater than the 16% cost of capital. Based on this quantitative analysis, the investment should be made.

When alternative projects involving different investment amounts are being considered, the NPV approach must be carried one step further. Projects should not be assigned a profitability ranking on the basis of the dollar amount of the net present value because of disparities in the investment amounts. The ratio of the present value of the cash flows to the investment, referred to as the **present value ratio** (or **profitability index**), provides a more appropriate ranking mechanism. For example, assume the following data for the projects indicated:

Project	Present Value of Cash Flows	Investment	Net Present Value	Present Value Ratio
A	$22,800	$20,000	$2,800	1.14
B	34,000	30,000	4,000	1.13

Even though project B has a greater net present value, it is clear from looking at the present value ratios that project A has a higher present value for every dollar invested

It's time to refresh your learning! A solid understanding of present value concepts and calculations is necessary when using the net present value and internal rate of return methods as capital budgeting techniques. Take a minute to review the discussion and examples presented in the Chapter 6 appendix. Working through Exercises 16.19 and 16.20 will also provide a good review of present value calculations.

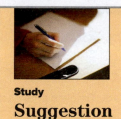

Study

Suggestion

and is thus a more desirable investment. When the NPV approach to investment analysis is used, it is appropriate to take this second step and calculate the present value ratio, especially when a selection must be made from several positive NPV projects.

---

7. What does it mean to state that present value analysis is appropriate for capital budgeting?
8. What does it mean to calculate the net present value of a proposed capital investment?
9. What does it mean if the net present value of a proposed capital expenditure is positive?

What Does It Mean?

Answers on pages 648

Internal Rate of Return   The **internal rate of return (IRR) method** and the NPV method differ in that the discount (interest) rate—the cost of capital—is a given in the NPV approach, whereas the IRR approach solves for the actual rate of return that will be earned by the proposed investment. This is the discount rate at which the present value of cash flows from the project will equal the investment (i.e., the discount rate at which the NPV equals zero). Thus, the IRR method may require several calculations using different discount rates. After the project's internal rate of return is known, a conclusion about the suitability of the investment is made by comparing the IRR to the cost of capital. If the IRR is greater than the cost of capital, the investment will be recommended. If the IRR is less than the cost of capital, the investment will not be recommended.

With respect to the investment proposal illustrated in Exhibit 16-3, the IRR must be greater than 16 percent because the NPV is positive. Determination of the actual IRR requires another set of present value calculations using a higher discount rate (18 percent is the next higher rate in the Chapter 6 tables) and then **interpolating** to determine the actual discount rate at which the present value of cash flows would equal the investment. The IRR method is illustrated in Exhibit 16-4.

There are some theoretical advantages to the NPV approach to evaluate proposed capital expenditures, but many managers use both approaches because they are more comfortable knowing the actual rate of return. Computer applications make the calculations easy; estimating the amount and timing of future cash flows associated with a proposal is the more challenging part of the process.

---

10. What does it mean to state that the net present value calculation technique is easier to use than the internal rate of return calculation method?

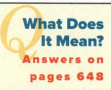

What Does It Mean?

Answers on pages 648

Exhibit 16-4 Internal Rate of Return (IRR) Analysis of a Proposed Investment

I. Assumptions:
Same as in Exhibit 16-3.
The NPV of the proposed investment at a discount rate of 16% is $2,622 (from Exhibit 16-3).

II. Timeline presentation of cash flows from the investment:

	12/31/19	2020	2021	2022	2023	2024
Cash flows from investment:						
Savings		$26,000	$27,000	$31,000	$35,000	$38,000
Salvage						6,000
Total		$26,000	$27,000	$31,000	$35,000	$44,000

III. Net present value calculation at 18%:

	12/31/19	2020	2021	2022	2023	2024
Present value factors (Table 6-4, 18%)		0.8475	0.7182	0.6086	0.5158	0.4371
Present value of cash flows from investment		$22,035	$19,391	$18,867	$18,053	$19,232
Total present value of cash flows from investment	$ 97,578					
Investment	(100,000)					
Net present value at 18%	$ (2,422)					

IV. Interpolation:

Discount rate	16%	17%	18%
Net present value	$2,622	$0	$(2,422)

The discount rate at an NPV of $0 is approximately 17%.

V. Conclusion from analysis:
The internal rate of return of the project is the discount rate at which the NPV = $0, so the IRR is 17%. The expected IRR is more than the firm's 16% cost of capital. Based on this quantitative analysis, the investment should be made.

LO 8

Describe how issues concerning estimates, income taxes, and the timing of cash flows and investments are treated in the capital budgeting process.

Some Analytical Considerations Net present value and internal rate of return are powerful analytical tools that enhance decision making for capital expenditures. The present value concept and related mechanical calculations are relatively straightforward; however, careful attention must be given to the variety of situations that frame the environment surrounding an investment decision spanning many years into the future, and that ultimately impacts the quality of the decision model.

Estimates. The validity of present value calculations will be a function of the accuracy with which future cash flows can be estimated. A great deal of effort will be expended in making estimates. When the project involves a replacement machine, the estimates of future cash flows (inflows from expense savings, and outflows for preventive and periodic maintenance) can be made relatively easily. When the project involves an investment in a new product or a major capacity expansion, the most important (and hardest) data to estimate are revenues. Most firms will require a **postaudit** of the project to determine whether the anticipated benefits are actually being realized. Although it may be too late to affect a project already completed, knowledge about past estimating errors should permit analysts to improve future estimates.

Cash flows far into the future.   Given the challenges of estimating, many capital budgeting analysts will not consider probable cash flows that are expected to occur more than 10 years in the future. In essence, their position is that if the project will not have a satisfactory return considering the cash flows in the first 10 years, then the project is too risky to accept, even if later cash flows will give it a satisfactory rate of return. For example, the present value of $100 to be received in 11 years, at a discount rate of 20 percent, is $13.46, so far-distant cash flows will not add significantly to the total present value of cash flows.

Timing of cash flows within the year.   The present value factors in Tables 6-4 and 6-5 assume that all the cash flows each year are received at the end of the year. It is more likely that the cash flows will be received fairly evenly throughout the year; and although present value can be calculated using that assumption, it is not uncommon for the end-of-the-year assumption to be used because it results in a slightly lower, more conservative present value amount.

Investment made over a period of time.   Capital expenditure projects involving new products, new plants, and capacity expansion usually require expenditures to be made over a period of time. For example, payments are usually made to a building contractor every month during construction, and for a major project, construction may extend over several years. When this is going to occur, the investment amount used in the present value analysis should be determined as of the point at which the project is expected to be put into service. This means that interest on cash disbursements made during the construction or preoperating period should be considered, so the investment amount will include the time value of money invested during that period.

Income tax effect of cash flows from the project.   The cash flows identified with a proposed capital expenditure should include all the associated inflows and outflows, including income taxes. The model for making this calculation is essentially the same as that used in the statement of cash flows to determine cash generated from operating activities. For example, assume that a capital expenditure proposal for a new product reflects the following makeup of operating income, income taxes, and net income for the first year the product is sold:

Revenues	$240,000
Variable expenses	100,000
Contribution margin	$140,000
Direct fixed expenses:	
Requiring cash disbursements	85,000
Depreciation of equipment	20,000
Operating income	$ 35,000
Income taxes @ 40%	14,000
Net income	$ 21,000

To calculate the amount of cash flow from this product, it is necessary to add back the depreciation expense to net income. Remember that depreciation is a deduction for income tax purposes but is not a cash expenditure. Therefore, the cash flow during the first year for this new product would be:

Net income	$21,000
Add: Depreciation expense	20,000
Cash flow from the product	$41,000

In addition, any other differences between accrual basis earnings and cash flows would be recognized when using the NPV and IRR methods.

Working capital investment.   Capital expenditure proposals that involve new products or capacity expansion usually require a working capital increase because accounts receivable and inventories will increase. The working capital increase required is treated as additional investment (i.e., it is a cash outflow at the beginning of the project or later). If the new product or capacity expansion has a definite life, the investment in working capital will be recovered after the product is discontinued or the expansion is reversed. The expected recovery of the working capital investment should be treated as a cash inflow.

Least cost projects.   Not all capital expenditures are made to reduce costs or increase revenues. Some expenditures required by law—environmental controls, for example—will increase operating costs. (The benefit may include the avoidance of a fine.) Alternative expenditures in this category should also be evaluated using present value analysis; however, instead of seeking a positive NPV or IRR, the objective is to have the least negative result. Even though the present value ratio will be less than 1.0, the most desirable alternative is still the one with the highest present value ratio.

LO 9

Calculate the payback period of a capital expenditure project.

Payback.   The **payback method** to evaluate proposed capital expenditures answers this question: How many years will it take to recover the amount of the investment? The answer to this question is determined by adding up the cash flows (beginning with the first year) until the total cash flows equal the investment and then counting the number of years of cash flow required. For example, using the data from Exhibit 16-3, for a machine costing $100,000, the projected annual and cumulative cash flows are determined and illustrated as follows:

Year	Cash Flow	Cumulative Cash Flow	Investment	Unrecovered Investment	Payback Periods
2020	$ 26,000	$ 26,000	$ 100,000	$ 74,000	1
2021	27,000	53,000		47,000	2
2022	31,000	84,000		16,000	3
2023	35,000	119,000			4
2024	44,000	163,000			5

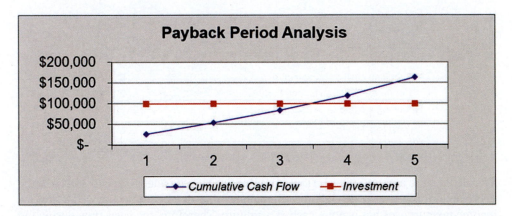

The investment will be recovered during the fourth year after $16,000 of that year's $35,000 has been realized. Expressed as a decimal, 16/35 is 0.46, so the project's payback period would be expressed as 3.46 years.

The obvious advantage of the payback method is its simplicity. Present value analysis is confusing to some people, but anyone can understand payback period. There are two major disadvantages to the payback method. First, it does not consider the time value of money, and this is a serious flaw. Second, as traditionally used, the payback method does not consider cash flows that continue after the investment has been recovered. Thus, a project having a payback period of three years and no subsequent cash flows would appear to be more desirable than a project that has a payback period of four years and cash flows that continue for five more years.

In spite of its flaws, the payback method is used by many firms, especially in connection with equipment replacement decisions. The widespread use of the payback method is due to the clarity of its meaning and the fact that in a rapidly changing technology environment, the speed with which an investment is recovered is critical. Many firms require early and significant cash flows from an investment in new plant and equipment because they don't have the capacity to finance their activities while waiting for the payoff from an investment to begin. Some analysts report the payback period along with NPV (or present value ratio) and IRR just to answer the question "How long until the investment is recovered?"

Accounting Rate of Return   The **accounting rate of return method** focuses on the impact of the investment project on the financial statements. Accounting operating income (or net income) is related to the effect of the investment on the balance sheet. This is done on a year-by-year basis. The calculation for 2020, using data from Exhibit 16-3, is illustrated in Exhibit 16-5.

As explained with the payback method, a serious flaw of the accounting rate of return approach is that the time value of money is not considered. Some financial managers will make the accounting rate of return calculation not for investment evaluation purposes but to anticipate the effect that the investment will have on the financial

LO 10
Calculate the accounting rate of return of a project and explain how it can be used most appropriately.

I. Assumption:

Same as in Exhibit 16-3.

II. Calculation:

$$\text{Accounting rate of return} = \frac{\text{Operating income}}{\text{Average investment}}$$

$$= \frac{\text{Savings } - \text{ Depreciation expense}}{\text{Average investment}}$$

For 2020:

$$= \frac{26,000 - 18,800*}{(100,000 + 81,200^\dagger)/2}$$

$$= \frac{7,200}{90,600}$$

$$= 7.9\%$$

*Straight-line depreciation expense:

(Cost − Salvage value)/Estimated life
(100,000 − 6,000)/5 years = 18,800

†Net book value at end of 2020:

Cost − Accumulated depreciation
100,000 − 18,800 = 81,200

Exhibit 16-5

Accounting Rate of Return Analysis of a Proposed Investment

statements. Large start-up costs for a new product line or new production facility may adversely affect reported results for a year or two. Management should be aware of this and should put stockholders on notice in advance to minimize the impact of the start-up costs on the market price of the firm's common stock.

What Does It Mean?

Answers on pages 648

11. What does it mean to state that both the payback method and the accounting rate of return method are flawed because they do not recognize the time value of money?

LO 11

Explain why not all management decisions are made strictly on the basis of quantitative analysis techniques.

The Investment Decision

As is the case with virtually every management decision, both quantitative and qualitative factors are considered. After the results of the quantitative models just illustrated have been obtained, the project with the highest NPV or IRR may not be selected. Overriding qualitative factors could include the following:

- Commitment to a segment of the business that requires capital investment to achieve or regain competitiveness even though that segment does not have as great an ROI as others.
- Regulations that mandate investment to meet safety, environmental, or access requirements. Fines and other enforcement incentives aside, management's citizenship goals for the organization may result in a high priority for these investments.
- Technology developments within the industry may require new facilities to maintain customers or market share at the cost of lower ROI for a period of time.
- The organization may have limited resources to invest in capital projects, and as a result of the capital rationing process, less ambitious, lower-ROI projects may be approved instead of large-scale, higher-ROI projects for which resources cannot be obtained.

In addition to considering issues such as these, management's judgments about the accuracy of the estimates used in the capital budgeting model may result in the selection of projects for which the estimates are believed to be more accurate.

The important point to be remembered here is that although the use of appropriate quantitative models can significantly improve the management decision-making process, most decisions are significantly influenced by top management's values and experiences—qualitative factors. Whether the decision involves the use of time value of money calculations, cost behavior pattern information, analysis of variances, or other applications you have learned, all important managerial decisions involve uncertainty and require the use of judgment. This is one reason top managers receive top salaries—their jobs are at risk if they make the wrong decisions.

Integration of the Capital Budget with Operating Budgets

Several aspects of the capital budget interact with the development of the operating budget. Contribution margin increases and cost savings from anticipated capital expenditure projects must be built into the expenditure and income statement budgets. Cash disbursements for capital projects must be included in the cash budget. The impact of capital expenditures on the balance sheet forecast must also be considered. Most important, you should understand that capital budgeting expenditures impact the level at which the firm will be able to operate in future years. Investments in equipment, new plant facilities, and other long-term operational assets are necessary to support the firm's growth objectives. Thus, the development of the capital budget is an integral part of the overall budgeting and strategic planning process. To learn how Microsoft Excel provides financial functions for capital budgeting techniques, see Business in Practice—Internal Rate of Return Using Microsoft Excel.

12. What does it mean to integrate the capital budget into the operating budget?

What Does It Mean?

Answers on pages 648

Business in Practice

©Credit/ Credit to come

Internal Rate of Return Using Microsoft Excel

Now that you understand the nature of NPV and IRR as capital budgeting techniques, Microsoft Excel can be used to quickly and easily calculate the IRR (or NPV) of a proposed investment as illustrated here using data from Exhibit 16-4 (or as shown in the Excel Help Index at IRR or NPV).

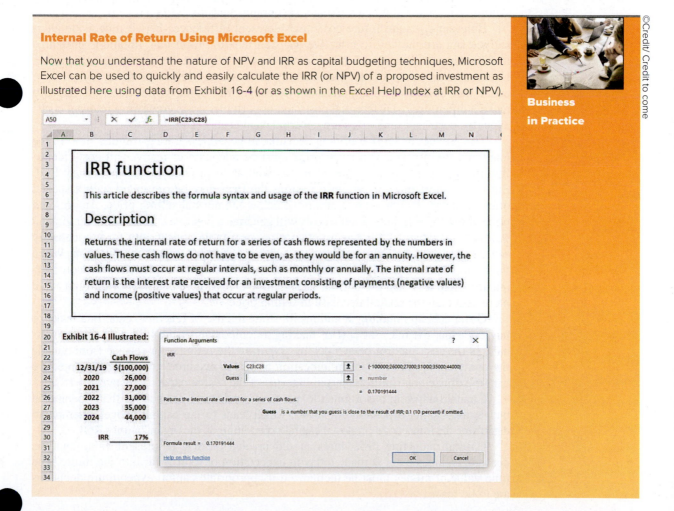

Demonstration Problem

The **Demonstration Problem walkthrough for this chapter is available in** *Connect.*

Summary

Important cost classifications for analyzing decision alternatives include differential costs, allocated costs, sunk costs, and opportunity costs. Differential costs are those costs that differ between alternatives and must be considered in the analysis. Sometimes costs are allocated for accounting purposes; but if the allocation is made on an arbitrary basis rather than by recognizing causal factors, users of the data must be very careful about the conclusions they reach when considering allocated costs in decision making. Sunk costs have been incurred and cannot be reversed, so they should not be included in the analysis. Opportunity costs arise from choosing one alternative over another, and while these costs are not reflected in the accounting records, they should be recognized when making an economic analysis. **(LO 1)**

Relevant costs are future costs that represent differences between decision alternatives and are the key to effective decision making. Cost classifications presented in Chapters 12 through 15 may or may not be relevant for a particular decision. Understanding costs for decision-making purposes is viewed as a *way of thinking* about their relevance to any decision by asking the fundamental question "Does it make a difference?" Differential costs and opportunity costs are always relevant costs; allocated costs and sunk costs are never relevant costs. **(LO 2)**

The product or service pricing decision, in general, is a long-run decision. In the long run, the product or service price must be adequate to recover all costs identified in the organization's value chain, as well as to provide for the necessary ROI. But in the short run, on certain occasions the firm may be presented with a special offer for its product or service at a price below the normal selling price. Any offered price above the relevant variable costs will generate a positive contribution margin and should be accepted as long as no other more profitable opportunity for idle capacity can be identified, or unless overriding qualitative factors impact the decision. When the firm is operating at full capacity, there is no reasonable explanation for considering any price less than the normal selling price unless there is an opportunity to avoid more cost than the related decrease in selling price. **(LO 3)**

Other decision-making situations illustrate the use of relevant costs. In a make or buy decision, the relevant cost of making a component or providing a service internally is the cost that can be avoided by acquiring the resource or service from outside the company. In the short-term allocation of scarce resources decision, the objective is to maximize contribution margin in terms of the scarce capacity resource. **(LO 3)**

Capital budgeting has a much longer-term time-frame perspective than operational budgeting. Capital expenditure analysis, which leads to the capital budget, attempts to determine the impact of a proposed capital expenditure on the organization's ROI. **(LO 4)**

Capital budgeting procedures should involve the use of present value analysis because an investment is made today in expectation of returns far into the future. The time value of money must be recognized if appropriate capital expenditure decisions are to be made. **(LO 5)**

Cost of capital is the minimum ROI that should be earned on the proposed investment. The risk associated with the proposal will affect the cost of capital, or desired ROI, used to evaluate the investment. **(LO 6)**

Net present value and internal rate of return are two investment analysis methods that recognize the time value of money. The net present value approach uses the cost of capital as the discount rate to calculate a difference between the present value of future cash flows from the investment and the amount invested. If the net present value is zero or positive, the proposed investment's ROI is equal to or greater than the cost of capital, and the investment is an appropriate one to make. The present value ratio, or profitability index, provides a means of ranking alternative proposals. The internal rate of return approach solves for the proposal's ROI, which is then compared to the cost of capital. The investment is an appropriate one to make if the ROI of the proposed investment equals or exceeds the cost of capital. **(LO 7)**

Some analytical considerations related to capital budgeting include estimating accuracy, the timing of cash flows within a year, and investments made over a period of time. Many firms require a postaudit of a capital project to evaluate the estimates made in the initial analysis. Some projects will require an increase in working capital, which is considered part of the investment. **(LO 8)**

Payback and accounting rate of return are two investment analysis methods that do not recognize the time value of money and are thus inappropriate analytical techniques. Nevertheless, many analysts and managers use the results of these methods along with the results of the NPV and IRR methods. **(LO 9, 10)**

In addition to considering the results of the various quantitative models used to evaluate investment proposals, management also identifies and considers qualitative factors when deciding whether to proceed with an investment. These qualitative factors could potentially be more significant than the quantitative model results. **(LO 11)**

Key Terms and Concepts

accounting rate of return method (p. 625) A capital budgeting technique that calculates the rate of return on the investment based on the impact of the investment on the financial statements.

allocated cost (p. 604) A cost that has been assigned to a product or activity using some sort of systematic process.

capital budgeting (p. 603) The process of analyzing proposed investments in plant and equipment and other long-lived assets.

cash flows (p. 619) In capital budgeting, the cash receipts and disbursements associated with a capital expenditure over its life.

cost of capital (p. 618) The ROI that must be earned to permit the firm to meet its interest obligations and provide the owners their expected return; the discount rate used in the present value calculations of capital budgeting.

differential cost (p. 604) A cost that will differ based on the selection of an alternative activity.

full capacity (p. 608) The operating condition when all available production resources are being utilized.

idle capacity (p. 608) The operating condition when some available production resources are not being utilized.

internal rate of return (IRR) method (p. 621) A capital budgeting technique that solves for the time-adjusted rate of return on an investment over its life.

interpolating (p. 621)   A mathematical term that describes the process of interpreting and relating two factors from a (present value) table to approximate a third factor not shown in the table.

net present value (NPV) method (p. 619)   A capital budgeting technique that uses a given cost of capital to relate the present value of the returns from an investment to the present value of the investment.

opportunity cost (p. 605)   An economic concept relating to income forgone because an opportunity to earn income was not pursued.

outsourcing (p. 611)   The acquisition of resources or services from outside the organization as opposed to producing those resources or services internally.

payback method (p. 624)   A capital budgeting technique that calculates the length of time for the cash flows from an investment to equal the investment.

postaudit (p. 622)   The process of comparing the assumptions used in a capital project analysis with the actual results of the investment.

present value ratio (p. 620)   The ratio of the present value of the cash flows from an investment to the investment. See *profitability index.*

profitability index (p. 620)   The ratio of the present value of the cash flows from an investment to the investment; used for ranking proposed capital expenditures by profitability.

relevant cost (p. 605)   A cost classification used in analyzing costs of decision alternatives; costs are relevant when they represent future differences between the alternatives.

sunk cost (p. 604)   A cost that has been incurred and that cannot be unincurred, or reversed, by some future action.

target costing (p. 607)   A cost management technique in which the firm determines the required cost for a product or service to earn a desired profit when the selling price is determined by the marketplace.

▨ connect   Mini-Exercises

All applicable Mini-Exercises are available in *Connect.*

Mini-Exercise
16.1
LO 2, 3

Sell or process further? Lakeside Inc. produces a product that currently sells for $36 per unit. Current production costs per unit include direct materials, $10; direct labor, $12; variable overhead, $5; and fixed overhead, $5. Product engineering has determined that certain production changes could refine the product quality and functionality. These new production changes would increase material and labor costs by 20% per unit.

Required:

If Lakeside could sell the refined version of its product for $40 per unit, should it be processed further?

Mini-Exercise
16.2
LO 2, 3

Accept special sales order? In addition to the product cost information for Lakeside Inc. in Mini-Exercise 16.1, Lakeside has received an offer from a nonprofit organization to buy 8,000 units at $28 per unit. Lakeside currently has unused production capacity.

Required:

Should Lakeside accept this special sales order?

Mini-Exercise
16.3
LO 2, 3

The make or buy decision In addition to the product cost information for Lakeside Inc. in Mini-Exercise 16.1, product engineering has determined that a certain part of the product conversion process could be outsourced. Raw material costs would not be affected, but direct labor and variable overhead costs would be reduced by 30%. No other opportunity is currently feasible for unused production capacity.

Required:

Should Lakeside outsource part of the conversion process at a cost of $4 per unit?

Target Costing Lakeside Inc. is considering whether to enter the market to produce and sell Product X. The market selling price for Product X is well established at $300 per unit, and Lakeside requires a profit margin of 25% on product lines.

Mini-Exercise
16.4
LO 2, 3

Required:

Calculate the target cost per unit Lakeside must achieve to produce Product X.

The Product Mix Decision Lakeside Inc. produces Product A and Product B that require special machining time. Machine time capacity is 10,000 machine hours per month. Lakeside estimates April demand for each product and provides additional information as follows:

Mini-Exercise
16.5
LO 2, 3

	Product A	Product B
April demand	3,000 units	2,000 units
Contribution margin	$600 per unit	$500 per unit
Required machine hours	3 per unit	2 per unit

Required:

Determine how many units of each product Lakeside should produce to maximize contribution margin in April.

Net present value Lakeside Inc. is considering replacing old production equipment with state-of-the-art technology that will allow production cost savings of $7,500 per month. The new equipment will have a five-year life and cost $320,000, with an estimated salvage value of $20,000. Lakeside's cost of capital is 12%.

Mini-Exercise
16.6
LO 7

Required:

Calculate the net present value of the new production equipment.

Net present ratio and IRR Use the information presented for Lakeside Inc., in Mini-Exercise 16.6 and your calculation of the net present value of the new production equipment.

Mini-Exercise
16.7
LO 7

Required:

Calculate the present value ratio of the new production equipment, and comment on the internal rate of return of this investment relative to the cost of capital.

Payback period and accounting rate of return Use the information presented for Lakeside Inc. in Mini-Exercise 16.6.

Mini-Exercise
16.8
LO 9, 10

Required:

Calculate the payback period and the accounting rate of return for the new production equipment.

connect   **Exercises**

All applicable Exercises are available in *Connect*.

Exercise 16.9
LO 1

Application of cost terminology Assume that you have decided to drive your car to Florida for the spring break. A classmate learns about your plans and asks about riding along with you. Explain how you would apply each of the following cost concepts to the task of determining how much, if any, cost you would take into consideration for the purposes of setting a price to be charged for taking the classmate with you.

   a. Differential cost.
   b. Allocated cost.
   c. Sunk cost.
   d. Opportunity cost.

Exercise 16.10
LO 1

Give examples of various costs Attending college involves incurring many costs. Give an example of a college cost that could be assigned to each of the following classifications. Explain your reason for assigning each cost to the classification.

   a. Sunk cost.
   b. Discretionary cost.
   c. Committed cost.
   d. Opportunity cost.
   e. Differential cost.
   f. Allocated cost.

Exercise 16.11
LO 2, 3

Sell or process further? American Chemical Company manufactures a chemical compound that is sold for $29 per gallon. A new variant of the chemical has been discovered, and if the basic compound were processed into the new variant, the selling price would be $36 per gallon. American expects the market for the new compound variant to be 5,000 gallons initially and determines that processing costs to refine the basic compound into the new variant would be $40,000.

Required:
Should American produce the new compound variant? Explain your answer.

Exercise 16.12
LO 2, 3

Sell or process further? ADP Mining Company mines an iron ore called Alpha. During the month of August, 350,000 tons of Alpha were mined and processed at a cost of $675,000. As the Alpha ore is mined, it is processed into Delta and Pi, where 60% of the Alpha output becomes Delta and 40% becomes Pi. Each product can be sold as is or processed into the refined products Super Delta and Precision Pi. Selling prices for these products are as follows:

	Delta	Super Delta	Pi	Precision Pi
Selling price	$6/ton	$12/ton	$15/ton	$25/ton

Processing costs to refine Delta into Super Delta are $1,680,000; processing costs to refine Pi into Precision Pi are $1,120,000.

Required:

a. Should Delta and Pi be sold as is or refined into Super Delta and Precision Pi?

b. Identify any costs in the problem that are not relevant to this decision.

c. What is the maximum profit that ADP Mining Company can expect to earn from the production of the 350,000 tons of Alpha?

Accept special sales order? Integrated Masters Inc. (IMI) is presently operating at 50% of capacity and manufacturing 50,000 units of a patented electronic component. The cost structure of the component is as follows:

Exercise 16.13
LO 2, 3

Raw materials	$ 1.50 per unit
Direct labor	1.50 per unit
Variable overhead	2.00 per unit
Fixed overhead	$100,000 per year

An Italian firm has offered to purchase 30,000 of the components at a price of $6 per unit, FOB IMI's plant. The normal selling price is $8 per component. This special order will not affect any of IMI's "normal" business. Management calculated that the cost per component is $7, so it is reluctant to accept this special order.

Required:

a. Show how management came up with a cost of $7 per unit for this component.

b. Evaluate this cost calculation. Explain why it is or is not appropriate.

c. Should the offer from the Italian firm be accepted? Why or why not?

Accept special sales order? SureLock Manufacturing Co. makes and sells several models of locks. The cost records for the ZForce lock show that manufacturing costs total $23.25 per lock. An analysis of this amount indicates that $13.40 of the total cost has a variable cost behavior pattern, and the remainder is an allocation of fixed manufacturing overhead. The normal selling price of this model is $31.00 per lock. A chain store has offered to buy 12,000 ZForce locks from SureLock at a price of $16.25 each to sell in a market that would not compete with SureLock's regular business. SureLock has manufacturing capacity available and could make these locks without incurring additional fixed manufacturing overhead.

Exercise 16.14
LO 2, 3

Required:

a. Calculate the effect on SureLock's operating income of accepting the order from the chain store.

b. If SureLock's costs had not been classified by cost behavior pattern, is it likely that a correct special order analysis would have been made? Explain your answer.

c. Identify the key qualitative factors that SureLock managers should consider with respect to this special order decision.

Target costing EagleEye Company, a manufacturer of digital cameras, is considering entry into the digital binocular market. EagleEye Company currently does not produce binoculars of any style, so this venture would require a careful analysis of relevant

Exercise 16.15
LO 2, 3

manufacturing costs to correctly assess its ability to compete. The market price for this binocular style is well established at $98 per unit. EagleEye has enough square footage in its plant to accommodate the new production line, although several pieces of new equipment would be required; their estimated cost is $3,750,000. EagleEye requires a minimum ROI of 12% on any product line investment and estimates that if it enters this market with its digital binocular product at the prevailing market price, it is confident of its ability to sell 15,000 units each year.

Required:

a.   Describe, in general terms, any costs that EagleEye Company would consider relevant to the decision of entering the digital binocular market.

b.   Calculate the target cost per unit for entry into the digital binocular market.

Exercise 16.16
LO 2, 3

Target costing Rainbow Cruises operates a weeklong cruise tour through the Hawaiian Islands. Passengers currently pay $1,500 for a two-person cabin, which is an all-inclusive price that includes food, beverages, and entertainment. The current cost to Rainbow per two-person cabin is $1,200 for the weeklong cruise, and at this cost, Rainbow is able to earn the minimum profit margin needed to operate the business. Rainbow competes with two other cruise lines and, to date, $1,500 has been the prevailing market price for the weeklong cruises. Each cruise line provides exactly the same services to their passengers, but recently one of Rainbow's competitors found a way to permanently lower its price to $1,250 per two-person cabin.

Required:

a.   At a new market price of $1,250 per two-person cabin, calculate the target cost that will allow Rainbow to earn the same profit margin percentage it currently earns.

b.   Calculate the target cost reduction that Rainbow must achieve if it expects to remain competitive.

c.   Describe several cost reduction initiatives that Rainbow might explore to achieve its target cost reduction requirements.

Exercise 16.17
LO 2, 3

The make or buy decision Lakeview Engine Inc. produces engines for the watercraft industry. An outside manufacturer has offered to supply several component parts used in the engine assemblies, which are currently being produced by Lakeview. The supplier will charge Lakeview $270 per engine for the set of parts. Lakeview's current costs for those part sets are direct materials, $160; direct labor, $80; and manufacturing overhead applied at 100% of direct labor. Variable manufacturing overhead is considered to be 20% of the total, and fixed overhead will not change if the part sets are acquired from the outside supplier.

Required:
Should Lakeview Engine continue to make the part sets or accept the offer to purchase them for $270?

Exercise 16.18
LO 2, 3

The make or buy decision Redbud Company uses a certain part in its manufacturing process that it buys from an outside supplier for $36 per part plus another $5 for shipping and other purchasing-related costs. The company will need 18,000 of these parts in the next year and is considering making the part internally. After performing a capacity analysis, Redbud determined that it has sufficient unused capacity to manufacture the 18,000 parts but would need to hire a manager at an annual salary of $54,000 to oversee this production activity. Estimated production costs are determined to be as follows:

Direct material	$23
Direct labor	10
Variable overhead	5
Fixed overhead (includes manager at $4 per unit)	8
Total unit cost	$46

Required:

a. Identify the relevant costs to make this part internally.

b. Should Redbud produce the part or continue to buy it from the outside supplier?

c. What other factors are important to this decision?

The product mix decision Product A has a contribution margin of $300 per unit and requires six hours of machine time. Product B requires eight hours of machine time and provides $400 of contribution margin per unit.

Exercise 16.19
LO 2, 3

Required:
If the capacity of machine time is limited to 1,200 hours and only one product can be produced, what is the maximum amount of contribution that could be generated?

The product mix decision ABC Company produces product X, product Y, and product Z. All three products require processing on specialized finishing machines. The capacity of these machines is 1,800 hours per month. ABC Company wants to determine the product mix that should be achieved to meet the high demand for each product and provide the maximum profit. Following is information about each product:

Exercise 16.20
LO 2, 3

	Product X	Product Y	Product Z
Selling price	$150	$120	$38
Variable costs	105	60	30
Machine time per unit	3 hours	2 hours	1 hour
Monthly demand (units)	450	300	750

Required:
Determine how the 1,800 hours of machine time should be allocated to the three products to provide the most profitable product mix.

Review problem—time value of money applications An investor has asked for your help with the following time value of money applications. Use the appropriate factors from Table 6-4 or Table 6-5 to answer the following questions.

Exercise 16.21

Required:

a. What is the present value of $65,000 to be received in five years using a discount rate of 12%?

b. How much should be invested today at a return on investment of 12% compounded annually to have $65,000 in five years?

c. If the return on investment was greater than 12% compounded annually, would the amount to be invested today to have $65,000 in five years be more or less than the answer to part **b**? Explain your answer.

Exercise 16.22   **Review problem—time value of money applications** Use the appropriate factors from Table 6-4 or Table 6-5 to answer the following questions.

Required:

a. Spencer Co.'s common stock is expected to have a dividend of $5 per share for each of the next 10 years, and it is estimated that the market value per share will be $124 at the end of 10 years. If an investor requires a return on investment of 12%, what is the maximum price the investor would be willing to pay for a share of Spencer Co. common stock today?

b. Mario bought a bond with a face amount of $1,000, a stated interest rate of 8%, and a maturity date 10 years in the future for $978. The bond pays interest on an annual basis. Five years have gone by and the market interest rate is now 10%. What is the market value of the bond today?

c. Alexis purchased a U.S. Series EE savings bond for $100, and eight years later received $159.38 when the bond was redeemed. What average annual return on investment did Alexis earn over the eight years?

Exercise 16.23
LO 7   **Present value analysis—effects of estimation errors** Capital budgeting analysis involves the use of many estimates.

Required:
For each of the following estimation errors, state whether the net present value of the project will be too high or too low:

a. The investment is too high.

b. The cost of capital is too low.

c. The cash flows from the project are too high.

d. The number of years over which the project will generate cash flows is too low.

Exercise 16.24
LO 6   **Present value analysis—cost of capital** National Leasing is evaluating the cost of capital to use in its capital budgeting process. Over the recent past, the company has averaged a return on equity of 13% and a return on investment of 10%. The company can currently borrow short-term money for 7%.

Required:

a. Which of the preceding rates is most relevant to deciding the cost of capital to use? Explain your answer.

b. Without prejudice to your answer to part **a,** explain why the company might choose to use a cost of capital of 14% to evaluate capital expenditure opportunities.

Calculate NPV—compare to IRR Northern Manufacturing Ltd. is considering the investment of $85,000 in a new machine. The machine will generate cash flow of $14,000 per year for each year of its eight-year life and will have a salvage value of $9,000 at the end of its life. The company's cost of capital is 10%.

Exercise 16.25
LO 7

Required:

a. Calculate the net present value of the proposed investment. (Ignore income taxes.)

b. What will the internal rate of return on this investment be relative to the cost of capital? Explain your answer.

Calculate NPV—compare to IRR A task force of capital budgeting analysts at Morrison Ltd. collected the following data concerning the drilling and production of known petroleum reserves at an offshore location:

Exercise 16.26
LO 7, 9

Investment in rigging equipment and related personnel costs required to pump the oil	$4,900,000
Net increase in inventory and receivables associated with the drilling and production of the reserves. Assume this investment will be recovered at the end of the project	960,000
Net cash inflow from operations for the expected life of the reserves, by year:	
2019	1,600,000
2020	2,880,000
2021	1,360,000
Salvage value of machinery and equipment at the end of the well's productive life	800,000
Cost of capital	12%

Required:

a. Calculate the net present value of the proposed investment in the drilling and production operation. Assume that the investment will be made at the beginning of 2019, and the net cash inflows from operations will be received in a lump sum at the end of each year. Ignore income taxes, and round answers to the nearest $1.

b. What will the internal rate of return on this investment be relative to the cost of capital? Explain your answer.

c. Differences between estimates made by the task force and actual results would have an effect on the actual rate of return on the project. Identify the significant estimates made by the task force. For each estimate, state the effect on the actual ROI if the estimate turns out to be less than the actual amount finally achieved.

Interpretation of present value analysis and payback CarCare Garage Company is considering an investment in a new tune-up computer. The cost of the computer is $24,000. A cost analyst has calculated the discounted present value of the expected cash flows from the computer to be $26,220, based on the firm's cost of capital of 20%.

Exercise 16.27
LO 6, 7, 9

Required:

a. What is the expected return on investment of the machine, relative to 20%? Explain your answer.

b. The payback period of the investment in the machine is expected to be 4.6 years. How much weight should this measurement carry in the decision about whether or not to invest in the machine? Explain your answer.

Exercise 16.28
LO 6, 7

Interpretation of present value analysis—calculate annual cash flow Memorial Hospital is considering the acquisition of a new diagnostic scanning machine. The investment required to get the machine operational will be $1,895,000. The machine will be capable of performing 8,000 scanning procedures per year, but based on the experience of other hospitals, management estimates that the machine will be used at 75% of its capacity. The hospital's cost of capital is 10%; the machine has an estimated useful life of five years and no salvage value.

Required:

a. Assuming a constant cash flow every year, calculate the annual net cash flow required from the scanner if the IRR of the investment is to equal 10%. (*Hint:* The annual net cash flow requirement is an annuity.)

b. If the direct cash costs of operating the scanner equal 50% of the annual net cash flow requirement calculated in part **a**, what price should the hospital charge per scanning procedure in order to achieve a 10% ROI?

▇ connect Problems

All applicable Problems are available in *Connect*.

Problem 16.29
LO 2, 3

Relevant costs, special sales order—idle versus full capacity The Delmar Beverage Co. produces a premium root beer that is sold throughout its chain of restaurants in the Midwest. The company is currently producing 1,600 gallons of root beer per day, which represents 80% of its manufacturing capacity. The root beer is available to restaurant customers by the mug, in bottles, or packaged in six-packs to take home. The selling price of a gallon of root beer averages $10, and cost accounting records indicate the following manufacturing costs per gallon of root beer:

Raw materials	$3.00
Direct labor	1.50
Variable overhead	1.00
Fixed overhead	2.50
Total absorption cost	$8.00

In addition to the manufacturing costs just described, Delmar Beverage incurs an average cost of $1.00 per gallon to distribute the root beer to its restaurants.

SaveMore Inc., a chain of grocery stores, is interested in selling the premium root beer in gallon jugs throughout its stores in the St. Louis area during holiday periods and has offered to purchase root beer from Delmar Beverage at a price of $8 per gallon. SaveMore believes it could sell 200 gallons per day. If Delmar Beverage agrees to sell root beer to SaveMore, it estimates the average distribution cost will be $1.50 per gallon.

Required:

a. Identify all the relevant costs that Delmar Beverage should consider in evaluating the special sales order from SaveMore.

b. How would Delmar Beverage's daily operating income be affected by the acceptance of this offer?

c. Assume that Delmar Beverage is currently producing 2,000 gallons of root beer daily. Repeat requirements **a** and **b**.

d. Explain why your answers are different when Delmar Beverage is producing 1,600 gallons per day versus 2,000 gallons per day.

Relevant costs, special sales order—idle versus full capacity Petro Motors Inc. (PMI) produces small gasoline-powered motors for use in lawn mowers. The company has been growing steadily over the past five years and is operating at full capacity. PMI recently completed the addition of new plant and equipment at a cost of $7,800,000, thereby increasing its manufacturing capacity to 100,000 motors annually. The addition to plant and equipment will be depreciated on a straight-line basis over 10 years.

Problem 16.30
LO 2, 3

Sales of motors were 60,000 units prior to the completion of the additional capacity. Cost records indicated that manufacturing costs had totaled $60 per motor, of which $48 per motor was considered to be variable manufacturing costs. PMI has used the volume of activity at full capacity as the basis for applying fixed manufacturing overhead. The normal selling price is $80 per motor, and PMI pays a 5% commission on the sale of its motors.

LawnPro.com offered to purchase 35,000 motors at a price of $60 per unit to test the viability of distributing lawn mower replacement motors through its website. PMI would be expected to produce the motors, store them in its warehouse, and ship individual motors to LawnPro.com customers. As orders are placed directly through the LawnPro.com website, they would be forwarded instantly to PMI. No commissions will be paid on this special sales order, and freight charges will be paid by the customer purchasing a motor.

Required:

a. Calculate the cost per motor, for cost accounting purposes, after completion of the additional plant capacity.

b. Identify all the relevant costs that PMI should consider in evaluating the special sales order from LawnPro.com.

c. Should the offer from LawnPro.com be accepted? Why or why not?

d. If relevant cost analysis was not considered, is it likely that a correct special order analysis would have been made? Explain your answer.

e. Identify the key qualitative factors that PMI management should consider with respect to this special order.

f. Assume that with the additional plant capacity, sales of motors in PMI's regular market are expected to increase by $33\frac{1}{3}\%$ in the coming 12 months. Identify all the relevant costs that PMI should consider in evaluating the special sales order from LawnPro.com. Why is your answer different than in requirement **b**?

g. Assume that sales of motors in PMI's regular market are expected to increase by $33\frac{1}{3}\%$ in the coming 12 months. Should the offer from LawnPro.com be accepted? Why or why not?

Continue or discontinue a segment? MMV Inc. opened a chain of businesses several years ago that provide quick oil changes and other minor services in conjunction with a convenience operation consisting of a soup, sandwich, and snack bar. The strategy was that as customers brought autos in for oil changes, they would likely use

Problem 16.31
LO 2, 3

the convenience operation to purchase a sandwich, bowl of soup, beverage, or some other snack while they were waiting for the work to be completed on their autos. The oil change operation occupies 75% of the facility and includes three service bays. The soup, sandwich, and snack bar occupies the remaining 25%. A general manager is responsible for the entire operation, but each segment also has a manager responsible for its individual operation.

Recently, the following annual operating information for the soup, sandwich, and snack bar at one of MMV's locations caught the general manager's attention. Sales for the year were $120,000, and cost of sales (food, beverages, and snack items) are 40% of sales revenue. Operating expense information for the convenience operation follows:

Food service items (spoons, napkins, etc.)	$ 1,800
Utilities	3,600
Wages for part-time employees	24,000
Convenience operation manager's salary	33,000
General manager's salary	9,000
Advertising	10,800
Insurance	6,000
Property taxes	1,500
Food equipment depreciation	3,000
Building depreciation	7,500

While investigating these operating expenses, MMV, Inc. determines the following:

- Utilities are allocated to each segment based on square footage; however, 50% of the amount allocated to the soup, sandwich, and snack bar results from operating the food equipment.
- The general manager's salary is allocated between the segments based on estimated time spent with each operation. It is determined that 20% of the general manager's time is spent with the convenience operation.
- Advertising is allocated to each segment equally but could be reduced by $2,700 if MMV decided to advertise only the auto services.
- Insurance is allocated to each segment based on square footage, but only 25% of the amount allocated to the soup, sandwich, and snack bar results directly from its operation.
- Property taxes and building depreciation are allocated to each segment based on square footage.

Required:

a. From the preceding information, calculate the operating income from the soup, sandwich, and snack bar operation that has caught the general manager's attention.

b. Identify whether each of these operating expenses is relevant to the decision of discontinuing the soup, sandwich, and snack bar operation.

c. If MMV discontinues the soup, sandwich, and snack bar operation, how much will operating income increase or decrease for this location?

d. Should MMV continue or discontinue the soup, sandwich, and snack bar operation at this location? Consider possible opportunities for the use of this space in your response.

Continue or discontinue a segment? The segmented income statement for XYZ Company for the year ended December 31, 2019, follows:

Problem 16.32
LO 2, 3

XYZ COMPANY Segmented Income Statement For the Year Ended December 31, 2019				
	Total Company	**Product A**	**Product B**	**Product C**
Sales	$600,000	$300,000	$120,000	$180,000
Variable expenses	276,000	150,000	54,000	72,000
Contribution margin	$324,000	$150,000	$ 66,000	$108,000
Fixed expenses	282,000	164,000	46,000	72,000
Operating income	$ 42,000	$(14,000)	$ 20,000	$ 36,000

The company is concerned about the performance of product A, and you have been asked to analyze the situation and recommend to the president whether to continue or discontinue the product. During your investigation, you discover that certain fixed expenses are traceable directly to each product line as indicated here:

	Total Company	Product A	Product B	Product C
Direct fixed expenses	$102,000	$74,000	$10,000	$18,000

The remaining fixed expenses are considered to be corporatewide expenses that have been allocated to each product line based on sales revenue.

Required:

a. Prepare a relevant cost analysis for the decision to continue or discontinue product A. Comment on your analysis.

b. Assume that product A is discontinued. Prepare a segmented income statement for the remaining products. Allocate corporatewide fixed expenses as described.

c. Starting with the segmented income statement, use the information you discovered during your investigation to present a more appropriately designed segmented income statement. (*Hint:* Refer to Chapter 15.)

d. Explain to the president why the redesigned segmented income statement is more appropriate than the current one.

Calculate NPV, present value ratio, and payback Cowboy Recording Studio is considering the investment of $280,000 in a new recording equipment. It is estimated that the new equipment will generate additional cash flow of $42,000 per year for each year of its 10-year life and will have a salvage value of $30,000 at the end of its life. Cowboys's financial managers estimate that the firm's cost of capital is 10%.

Problem 16.33
LO 7, 9

Required:

a. Calculate the net present value of the investment.

b. Calculate the present value ratio of the investment.

c. What is the internal rate of return of this investment, relative to the cost of capital?
d. Calculate the payback period of the investment.

Problem 16.34
LO 7, 8, 9

Calculate NPV, present value ratio, and payback TopCap Co. is evaluating the purchase of another sewing machine that will be used to manufacture sport caps. The invoice price of the machine is $98,000. In addition, delivery and installation costs will total $5,000. The machine has the capacity to produce 12,000 dozen caps per year. Sales are forecast to increase gradually, and production volumes for each of the five years of the machine's life are expected to be as follows:

2019	3,600 dozen
2020	5,600 dozen
2021	8,500 dozen
2022	11,300 dozen
2023	12,000 dozen

The caps have a contribution margin of $5.00 per dozen. Fixed costs associated with the additional production (other than depreciation expense) will be negligible. Salvage value and the investment in working capital should be ignored. TopCap Co.'s cost of capital for this capacity expansion has been set at 16%.

Required:
a. Calculate the net present value of the proposed investment in the new sewing machine.
b. Calculate the present value ratio of the investment.
c. What is the internal rate of return of this investment relative to the cost of capital?
d. Calculate the payback period of the investment.

Problem 16.35
LO 7

Present value ratios index Information about four investment proposals is summarized here:

Proposal	Investment Required	Net Present Value
1	$50,000	$30,000
2	60,000	24,000
3	30,000	15,000
4	45,000	9,000

Required:
Calculate the present value ratio of each proposal and indicate which proposal is the most desirable investment.

Problem 16.36
LO 6

Calculate NPV—rank projects using present value ratios The following capital expenditure projects have been proposed for management's consideration at Scott Inc. for the upcoming budget year:

	Year(s)	A	B	C	D	E
				Project		
Initial investment	0	$(25,000)	$(25,000)	$(50,000)	$(50,000)	$(100,000)
Amount of net cash return	1	5,000	0	16,000	5,000	30,000
....	2	5,000	0	16,000	10,000	30,000
....	3	5,000	10,000	16,000	15,000	15,000
....	4	5,000	10,000	16,000	20,000	15,000
....	5	5,000	10,000	16,000	25,000	15,000
Per year..................	6–10	5,000	6,000	0	0	15,000
NPV (14% discount rate)		$ 1,081	$?	$?	$?	$ 2,942
Present value ratio		1.04	?	?	?	?

Required:

a. Calculate the net present value of projects B, C, and D, using 14% as the cost of capital for Scott Inc.

b. Calculate the present value ratio for projects B, C, D, and E.

c. Which projects would you recommend for investment if the cost of capital is 14% and
   1. $50,000 is available for investment?
   2. $150,000 is available for investment?
   3. $250,000 is available for investment?

d. What additional factors (beyond those considered in parts **a–c**) might influence your project rankings?

Accounting rate of return and NPV Crichton Publications uses the accounting rate of return method to evaluate proposed capital investments. The company's desired rate of return is 18%. The project being evaluated involves a new product that will have a three-year life. The investment required is $100,000, which consists of a $80,000 machine, and inventories and accounts receivable totaling $20,000. The machine will have a useful life of three years and a salvage value of $50,000. The salvage value will be received during the fourth year, and the inventories and accounts receivable related to the product also will be converted back to cash in the fourth year. Accrual accounting net income from the product will be $29,000 per year, before depreciation expense, for each of the three years. Because of the time lag between selling the product and collecting the accounts receivable, cash flows from the product will be as follows:

Problem 16.37
LO 6, 7, 10, 11

1st year	$14,000
2nd year.................................	24,000
3rd year	29,000
4th year	20,000

Required:

a. Calculate the accounting rate of return for the first year of the product. Assume straight-line depreciation. Based on this analysis, would the investment be made? Explain your answer.

b. Calculate the net present value of the product using a discount rate of 18% and assuming that cash flows occur at the end of the respective years. Based on this analysis, would the investment be made? Explain your answer.

c. Which of these two analytical approaches is the more appropriate to use? Explain your answer.

Problem 16.38
LO 7, 9, 10, 11

Accounting rate of return, payback, and NPV Tablerock Corp. is interested in reviewing its method of evaluating capital expenditure proposals using the accounting rate of return method. A recent proposal involved a $100,000 investment in a machine that had an estimated useful life of five years and an estimated salvage value of $20,000. The machine was expected to increase net income (and cash flows) before depreciation expense by $30,000 per year. The criteria for approving a new investment are that it have a rate of return of 16% and a payback period of three years or less.

Required:

a. Calculate the accounting rate of return on this investment for the first year. Assume straight-line depreciation. Based on this analysis, would the investment be made? Explain your answer.

b. Calculate the payback period for this investment. Based on this analysis, would the investment be made? Explain your answer.

c. Calculate the net present value of this investment using a cost of capital of 16%. Based on this analysis, would the investment be made? Explain your answer.

d. What recommendation would you make to the management of Tablerock Corp. about evaluating capital expenditure proposals? Support your recommendation with the appropriate rationale.

connect **Cases**

All applicable Cases are available in *Connect*.

Case 16.39
LO 7

Case study—NPV of opening a small business Jinny Buffett recently retired as a flight attendant and is interested in opening a fitness center and health spa exclusively for women in Grand Cayman, where she resides. After careful study, she is somewhat puzzled as to how to proceed. In her words, "I see my business going in one of two directions: Either I open the fitness center and health spa all at once, or I start with the health spa and hold off on the fitness center for a while. Either way, it should be a success because women on this island love to be pampered. My only concern about the fitness center is the initial cost, but if the projections look good enough, I know some investors in Phoenix who can help me get started. In any event, I plan to retire permanently in 10 years."

The following information is available:

- Jinny has identified a suitable location for her business in a new shopping center in George Town, capital of the Cayman Islands. The developer has units of 1,000 square feet and 2,500 square feet available and is willing to sell either unit for CI$150 per square foot (CI$1.00 = US$1.25). Alternatively, the space can be leased at a cost of CI$1.80 per square foot per month, on an annual basis.

- Commercial real estate values have more than doubled in Grand Cayman during the past 10 years, with no slowdown in sight. As a result, Jinny is more attracted to the purchase option because she expects the price per square foot to be CI$300 by the time she is ready to sell her unit in 10 years.

- Exercise machines and other equipment necessary to open the fitness center would cost US$50,000. In addition, US$35,000 would need to be invested in equipment related to the health spa. The useful life for all such equipment is 10 years, and the expected salvage value is not large enough to be concerned about.

- In addition, US$8,000 would need to be invested in an inventory of cosmetics and skin care products necessary to operate the health spa. This level of inventory would need to be maintained throughout the 10-year period and will be given away to loyal customers when Jinny retires permanently.

- The health spa can be operated in the 1,000-square-foot unit. Variable operating costs would include CI$0.10 per square foot per month for cleaning and CI$0.40 per square foot per month for utilities. The 2,500-square-foot unit is large enough to operate both the fitness center and health spa, and the CI$0.10 rate per square foot for cleaning would not change. However, if the 2,500-square-foot unit were used, the health spa would be located in an open loft that would need to be air-conditioned at all times. As a result, utility costs are expected to be CI$0.60 per square foot per month under this option.

- Jinny is a certified aesthetician and expects to do most of the makeovers, facials, and peels herself, but she needs a qualified assistant for the health spa. She estimates that hiring an appropriate person will cost US$25,000 per year. Likewise, for the fitness center, two full-time aerobics instructors would be hired for US$20,000 each per year, and a physical trainer would be hired for US$30,000 per year.

- Additional fixed costs include US$3,000 per year for advertising and US$4,500 per year for maintenance, insurance, and other items. These costs will be incurred without respect to the size of operations.

- Annual membership fees to the fitness center will be CI$300, and a preliminary market survey shows a demand of approximately 500 initial members. Although members tend to come and go, the net change in membership from year to year is not expected to be significant. No additional fees will be charged to fitness center members.

- Health spa fees are assessed on a user basis, although the steam room facilities are available at no charge to fitness center members. The net cash inflow from cosmetics and skin care products (after deducting the cost of inventory used and sold) is expected to be CI$8,000 per month.

- Jinny's cost of capital is 12%, and there are no taxes in the Cayman Islands.

Required:

a. Calculate the net present value in US$ of an investment in the health spa *only*, assuming that the 1,000-square-foot unit is purchased and then resold at the end of 10 years. (*Hint:* Before making your present value calculations, multiply all amounts expressed in CI$ by $1.25 to convert into US$.)

b. Calculate the net present value in US$ of an investment in the fitness center and health spa, assuming that the 2,500-square-foot unit is purchased and then resold at the end of 10 years.

c. Jinny is quite concerned about possible forecasting errors and has asked you to prepare a more conservative estimate. Repeat part **b,** assuming that the fitness center attracts only 300 members per year (rather than 500); that the net cash inflow per month from cosmetics and skin care products is only CI$6,000 per month (rather than CI$8,000 per month); and that commercial real estate values in Grand Cayman at the end of 10 years are only CI$200 per square foot (rather than CI$300 per square foot).

d. Explain why it might be in Jinny's best interest to lease (rather than purchase) the 1,000-square-foot unit if she initially decides to open the health spa only. Although no calculations are required, you should consider both quantitative and qualitative factors in your response.

e. What is your overall recommendation? Include an explanation of any additional factors that you would consider in making your recommendation. Keep in mind that Jinny has not given herself a salary in her projections. Assume that a reasonable salary would be CI$4,000 per month.

Case 16.40
LO 6, 7, 8, 9, 11

Comprehensive problem—quantitative and qualitative analysis The following data have been collected by capital budgeting analysts at Sunset Beach Inc. concerning an investment in an expansion of the company's product line. Analysts estimate that an investment of $500,000 will be required to initiate the project at the beginning of 2019. The estimated cash returns from the new product line are summarized in the following table; assume that the returns will be received in a lump sum at the end of each year:

Year	Amount of Cash Return
2019	$126,000
2020	162,000
2021	195,000
2022	144,000

The new product line will also require an investment in inventory and receivables of $80,000; this investment will become available for other purposes at the end of the project. The salvage value of machinery and equipment at the end of the product line's life is expected to be $75,000. The cost of capital used in Sunset Beach's capital budgeting analysis is 12%.

Required:

a. Calculate the net present value of the proposed investment. Ignore income taxes and round all answers to the nearest $1.

b. Calculate the present value ratio of the investment.

c. What will the internal rate of return on this investment be relative to the cost of capital? Explain your answer.

d. Calculate the payback period of the investment.

e. Based on the quantitative analysis, would you recommend that the product line expansion project be undertaken? Explain your answer.

f. Identify some qualitative factors that you would want to have considered with respect to this project before management proceeds with the investment.

Capital budget expenditure analysis: Internet assignment Annual reports provide significant information about an organization's capital budget and capital budgeting process. Campbell Soup Company provides financial reports for several years at campbellsoup.com (*All Campbell Brands → Investors → Financial Information → Annual Reports*). This exercise requires you to use Campbell's consolidated statements of cash flows, management's discussion and analysis of financial condition and results of operations, and notes to the consolidated financial statements for the most recent year presented.

Case 16.41

Campbell's

Required:

Using Campbell's most recent annual report, answer the following:

a. From Campbell's consolidated statements of cash flows:
   1. Identify the amount of cash used for capital expenditures from the Investing Activities section. How much cash was provided from the sale of capital assets?
   2. How do these amounts compare to the previous two years? Comment on the trend relative to the general cash flow position for each year.

b. Read Campbell's discussion of the "Business," and highlight the information provided about capital expenditures reported in the current year and any plans identified for next year.

c. Read Campbell's discussion of the "Risk Factors." How may the company be adversely impacted by failure to execute acquisitions and divestitures successfully?

d. Read Campbell's management's discussion and analysis of financial condition and results of operations.
   1. In the Liquidity and Capital Resources section, how were investing cash flows used or provided for capital expenditures?
   2. In the Significant Accounting Estimates section, how are fixed assets reviewed for impairment? What role does management judgment play?

e. From Campbell's notes to the consolidated financial statements, determine the following:
   1. How does Campbell's value and depreciate property, plant, and equipment?
   2. If applicable, describe Campbell's acquisitions for the year.
   3. If applicable, describe Campbell's divestitures for the year.
   4. How were Campbell's capital expenditures distributed among its business segments?

f. From Campbell's selected financial data, do the following:
   1. For the five years presented, calculate the ratio of capital expenditures to net sales.
   2. For the five years presented, calculate the ratio of net plant assets to total assets.
   3. Comment on the trends.

1. It means that the cost has been incurred, and nothing will happen to affect that cost.

2. It means that the cost is a future cost that will represent a difference between the decision alternatives, and the cost must be included in the analysis.

3. It means that as long as there is no other more profitable use of the idle capacity, any price offered that exceeds the relevant costs and provides a positive contribution margin should be accepted in the short run because it will increase current operating income.

4. It means that it is a relevant cost of making the product or component part internally because it is a cost that would not be incurred if it were purchased from outside the company.

5. It means that these expenses are irrelevant for the decision to continue or discontinue a segment of the organization because they are arbitrarily allocated to the segments—these common corporate expenses will not decrease if a segment is eliminated.

6. It means that there is a plan for making capital expenditures (i.e., investments in new plant and equipment).

7. It means that because expenditures and/or benefits are likely to extend over a period of several years, it is appropriate to recognize the time value of money when determining the economic viability of an investment.

8. It means that the present value of the future cash flows expected from the investment, discounted at an appropriate interest rate (i.e., the cost of capital), is compared to the present value of the investment—also discounted at the cost of capital if necessary because the investment is made over several periods.

9. It means that the present value of the future inflows is greater than the present value of the investment, and if this actually occurs, the rate of return on the investment will be greater than the cost of capital.

10. It means that with the net present value technique, the discount rate (cost of capital) is given so that only one set of calculations needs to be made; but with the internal rate of return method, the discount rate (actual rate of return) must be solved for, sometimes on a trial-and-error basis.

11. It means that they ignore the vital economic fact that money does have value over time and that the pattern of returns from an investment has a major effect on its real rate of return.

12. It means that the additional productive capacity of new plant and equipment will affect activity and expense levels planned in the operating budget.

Accounting—
The Future

The "Welcome" from the authors included in the preface stated that this text's broad learning objective is to enable students to achieve an understanding of the basics of financial reporting by corporations and other enterprises. We hope that this objective has been achieved. However, financial reporting challenges related to the worldwide financial reporting crisis that began in the late 1990s with Waste Management (1998) and Enron (2001) came to a head in the fall of 2008 with the continuing disclosures of financial reporting misstatements and accounting errors made by major corporations, questionable auditor oversight of the accounting and financial reporting processes, and dubious practices that rocked the mortgage industry and financial markets. The more recent LIBOR rate-fixing scandal (2012), the Toshiba accounting scandal (2015), accusations of tax and accounting fraud at Caterpillar (2017), and investigations by the SEC into the accounting practices of General Electric (2018) all serve to raise the question: "What's going on—is the material I've been learning from this text at all relevant to the real world?" The answer to that question is a resounding *yes;* accounting of the future will be built on the solid foundation presented in this text. Yet new and complex business transactions continue to appear on the horizon, and the accounting standards (both new and amended) that have been developed to deal with these complexities continue to have a gestation period of several years. Moreover, the corporate governance provisions and financial practice regulations of the Sarbanes–Oxley Act (2002) and the Dodd–Frank Wall Street Reform and Consumer Protection Act (2010) have led to a retrospective analysis of certain accounting methodologies that may not have been appropriately applied by many companies in the recent past. In light of current pressures to avoid the taint of controversy concerning any and all financial reporting matters, the accounting profession, large public accounting firms, and individual practitioners are likely to continue to face challenges—considerable, but not insurmountable—in the years to come.

The authors believe that the following seven themes will help you build a bridge to the future of accounting. These themes are presented as characteristics that accountants and users of accounting and financial statement information will encounter:

1. Having insight and integrity.

2. Having a vision for the future.

For an interesting recap of the circumstances surrounding some of the worst corporate accounting scandals of all time, visit accounting-degree.org/scandals and theguardian.com/business/2015/jul/21/the-worlds-biggest-accounting-scandals-toshiba-enron-olympus.

For a comprehensive collection of resources devoted to providing relevant information about the evolving regulatory environment under the Sarbanes–Oxley Act of 2002, visit the American Institute of CPAs website at aicpa.org, and read "A Guide to Sarbanes–Oxley" at soxlaw.com. For information relating to the implementation of the Dodd–Frank Act of 2010, see sec.gov/spotlight/dodd-frank.shtml.

FYI

3.   Competing in a global economy.

4.   Using technology effectively.

5.   Committing to lifelong learning.

6.   Becoming business partners.

7.   Turning vision into reality.

The Accounting Profession

Congress, the SEC and other regulatory agencies, and the public in general were rightly outraged by the corrupt and erroneous financial reporting and accounting practices that have drawn so much attention over the past two decades. The valuation of subprime mortgages (the mark-to-market controversy), corporate bankruptcies, executive convictions, the collapse of the auditing firm Arthur Andersen, and numerous other accounting scandals resulted from the ethical breakdown, greed, and arrogance of a very few individuals. Unfortunately, their actions affected hundreds of thousands of employees and investors—and shook the confidence of the world's equity markets. The resulting congressional hearings and legislation, criminal indictments, guilty pleas, and convictions focused an intensely bright spotlight on the accounting profession. If anything, this attention has increased and will continue to increase the demand for bright, ethical, and straight-thinking accountants, managers, and executives.

In July 2012, *The New York Times* reported Gallup poll research findings indicating that corporate misconduct no longer surprises most Americans. Only about 20 percent of Americans have much trust in banks, and 62 percent believe corruption is widespread across America. Nearly three in four Americans believe that corruption has increased over the last three years, and this raises the question: "Have corporations lost whatever ethical compass they once had?" Clearly, technical accounting issues will not become any easier to solve in the future, and seeking solutions to those issues requires competence built on a foundation of moral integrity. Evidence of sound ethical values and the ability to apply those values across economic, political, and social activities will become crucial to acceptance and recognition as a professional.

Then in February 2014, research findings released from the National Business Ethics Survey by the Ethics Resource Center (ERC) revealed that 41 percent of corporate workers surveyed observed misconduct on the job, but that was down from 55 percent in 2007. Also reported was that fewer employees (9 percent) felt pressure

THEME 1

Having insight and integrity.

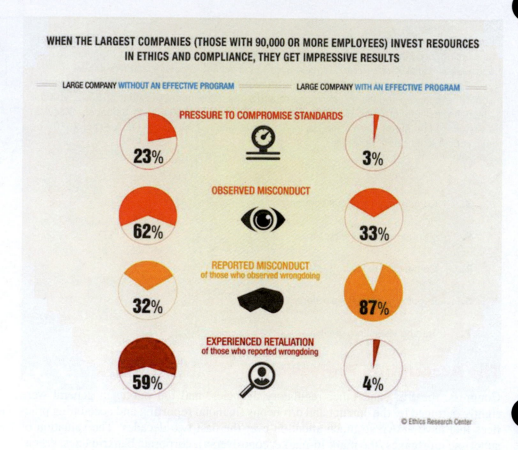

WHEN THE LARGEST COMPANIES (THOSE WITH 90,000 OR MORE EMPLOYEES) INVEST RESOURCES IN ETHICS AND COMPLIANCE, THEY GET IMPRESSIVE RESULTS

LARGE COMPANY WITHOUT AN EFFECTIVE PROGRAM   LARGE COMPANY WITH AN EFFECTIVE PROGRAM

PRESSURE TO COMPROMISE STANDARDS
23%   3%

OBSERVED MISCONDUCT
62%   33%

REPORTED MISCONDUCT
of those who observed wrongdoing
32%   87%

EXPERIENCED RETALIATION
of those who reported wrongdoing
59%   4%

© Ethics Research Center

©2018, Ethics Research Center. Used with permission of the Ethics Research Center, 2650 Park Tower Drive, Suite 802, Vienna, VA 22180, www.ethics.org.

to compromise their standards than in 2011 (13 percent). Also in 2014, the Ethics Compliance Initiative (ECI) was introduced with a mission of empowering organizations to build and sustain high-quality ethics and compliance programs with programming focused on research and best practices, networking opportunities, and certification to its membership. ECI reports that companies are working harder to build strong ethical cultures and compliance programs as illustrated in the following infographic. So, progress is being made in the right direction.

Building on a strong ethical foundation, tomorrow's accounting professionals will require enhanced skill sets to survive in a technology-driven global business economy in which their clientele will be seen as strategic business partners. The CPA designation has, since its inception, conveyed a prestigious image of technical competence and professional skill, but the CPA brand image may too narrowly define tomorrow's accounting professional. An MBA degree might provide the breadth of skills that will be required, but MBA programs typically lack the needed depth of accounting knowledge. The Certified Management Accountant (CMA) designation may come closest to testing for the broader scope of knowledge, skills, and abilities that corporate America needs in its accounting and financial professionals. To be certain, a continuing hallmark of tomorrow's accounting professional will be that services continue to be delivered with independent insight and a high degree of integrity.

Information about the CPA examination process from the American Institute of CPAs can be found at aicpa.org—see the *Become a CPA* tab. Information about the CMA examination process from the Institute of Management Accountants can be found at imanet.org—see the *CMA Certification* tab.

FYI

THEME 2

Having a vision for the future.

In 1998, the AICPA published a Vision Project report, titled "Focus on the Horizon: CPA Vision—2011 and Beyond," which proved enlightening for many accounting professionals. The Vision Project was an ongoing, professionwide initiative to understand, anticipate, and promote the requirements necessary for professional success in a new economy and to educate accounting professionals about changes. The following points summarize the CPA Vision:

Core purpose: CPAs . . . making sense of a changing and complex world.

Vision statement: CPAs are trusted professionals who enable people and organizations to shape their future. Combining insight with integrity, CPAs deliver value by

- Communicating the total picture with clarity and objectivity.
- Translating complex information into critical knowledge.
- Anticipating and creating opportunities.
- Designing pathways that transform vision into reality.

The AICPA's Vision Project identified five core competencies that are essential for CPAs to survive in the next decade: communication and leadership skills; strategic and critical thinking skills; a focus on the customer, client, and market; the ability to interpret converging information; and technological proficiency.

In 2010, as an assessment of, and extension to, the original Vision Project, the AICPA embarked on a new visioning initiative, CPA Horizons 2025, which is focused on leveraging the insights of CPAs, business leaders, regulators, thought leaders, and futurists on current and forecast trends that will affect the accounting profession operating in a technology-driven global economy. The research showed that the profession has a bright future and will need to respond quickly to ever-changing political, economic, social, technological, and regulatory environments. New insights about opportunities and challenges for CPAs and the profession over the next 15 years emerged and serve as a roadmap to mold their future. Moreover, CPAs overwhelmingly agree that the profession's core purpose, "making sense of a changing and complex world," remains relevant for today and the future.

The financial reporting breakdowns of the past two decades—caused by a relative handful of people who were responsible for major frauds, audit failures, or misapplication of generally accepted principles of accounting—underscore the need for an ethical foundation on which business practices and competencies must be built. In some ways, the future seems quite certain—CPAs must be able to analyze traditional historical data and provide forward-looking insights that create value for their client organizations and, ultimately, these organizations' shareholders. Organizations will need financial professionals who can assume leadership roles and provide guidance and support. Increasingly, CPAs will be moving out of the accounting function and into the strategic and operational areas of the business.

FYI

Information about the CPA Vision Project is available at aicpa.org/about/missionandhistory/cpavisionproject.html. The CPA Horizons 2025 Report is available for download at aicpa.org/research/cpahorizons2025/cpahorizonsreport.html.

THEME 3

Competing in a global economy.

Today's business environment is truly global in scope; the technology explosion has created a worldwide communications infrastructure that has played a major role in effectively shrinking the globe. Multinational corporations are common today and will continue to emerge as more companies seek strategic opportunities by combining with other companies as business partners to leverage their core competencies. Beyond needing people skills and the ability to perform effectively as a member of a cross-cultural team, what are the implications for an accounting professional working in a global marketplace? There will be continuing efforts toward the development of high-quality global accounting standards.

Although accounting is regarded as the language of business throughout the world, worldwide accounting rules have not existed historically. Accounting standards applied in one country may vary widely from those used in another country. Moreover, significant national differences still exist in the manner in which the accounting profession is regulated. Imagine an investor's frustration when attempting to compare the financial statements of Ford, Toyota, and Volkswagen without a clear understanding of the differences allowed in the financial reporting rules in the United States, Japan, and Germany. Or imagine the reporting costs and efforts required by a multinational corporation that operates in 100 countries and has to comply with the national accounting standards of each country. Fortunately, efforts to unify the global accounting scene are currently under way.

The International Accounting Standards Committee (IASC), replaced by the International Accounting Standards Board (IASB) in 2001, was organized in 1973 as an independent, private-sector body with the objective of harmonizing the accounting principles used by businesses and other organizations for financial reporting around the world. The objectives of the IASC, as stated in its constitution, were

1. To develop, in the public interest, a single set of high-quality, understandable, and enforceable global accounting standards that require high-quality, transparent, and *comparable* (emphasis added) information in financial statements and other financial reporting to help participants in the world's capital markets and other users make economic decisions.
2. To promote the use and rigorous application of those standards.
3. To bring about convergence of national accounting standards and international accounting standards to generate high-quality solutions.

The IASB's ability to bring convergence to the world's accounting standards has ultimately depended on the necessary acceptance of those standards by securities regulators and stock exchanges around the world, such as the Securities and Exchange Commission in the United States. The SEC endorsed the efforts of the IASC and the IASB and identified three key elements necessary for international accounting standards. The standards must

- Include a core set of accounting pronouncements that constitute a comprehensive, generally accepted basis of accounting.
- Be of high quality—they must result in comparability and transparency, and they must provide for full disclosure.
- Be rigorously interpreted and applied.

As described in Chapter 1, the IASB and the FASB have been working together since 2002 to achieve convergence of IFRS and U.S. GAAP. By November 2008, the SEC issued a roadmap for the possible adoption of IFRS standards, and in May 2011, the SEC released a more detailed proposal for the FASB to change U.S. GAAP over a number of years by incorporating individual IFRS standards into U.S. GAAP. However, the question has persisted as to whether the goal of realizing a single global accounting language could be achieved. Not discounting the significance of a basic philosophical difference about U.S. financial reporting standards based on detailed rules versus IFRS standards based on broad principles, there has been a lack of interest in accounting convergence on the part of U.S. investors and corporations because of the huge implementation cost that domestic companies and auditors would incur for changing their reporting language from U.S. GAAP to IFRS.

The SEC issued its final IFRS report findings in 2012, indicating it found little support for fully adopting IFRS standards in the United States. In addition to the United States, currently Japan and China remain as the other major capital markets who have not fully mandated IFRS adoption. IFRS is, however, permitted in the U.S. for listings by foreign companies, and as of 2017, more than 500 foreign SEC registrants use IFRS standards in their U.S. filings as illustrated in the IFRS map of Who Uses IFRS Standards? Moving forward, and as indicated in Chapter 1, it appears that the U.S. GAAP and IFRS will continue to peacefully coexist indefinitely; however, the implications are clear for today's students preparing for a career in a global economy—an understanding of and appreciation for the differences in global accounting standards is imperative.

For a current appreciation of IASB's convergence work and the status of IFRS adoptions worldwide, see the interactive, ever-evolving status and analysis of the use of IFRS standards around the world using the accompanying IFRS map, "Who Uses IFRS Standards?" (also found at ifrs.org).

Accounting and Technology

Computerized accounting systems handle much of the world's accounting today and will continue to do so in the future. Literally hundreds of inexpensive accounting systems are available, such as QuickBooks Pro and Sage 50 (formerly Peachtree), which provide fairly sophisticated transaction processing functionality to meet the basic bookkeeping needs of small businesses. At the other end of the business spectrum,

THEME 4
Using technology effectively.

For the latest IASB and IFRS developments and information about projects in progress, active research, summaries of international accounting standards, and a look at what's happening with international accounting standards around the world, see ifrs.org.

FYI

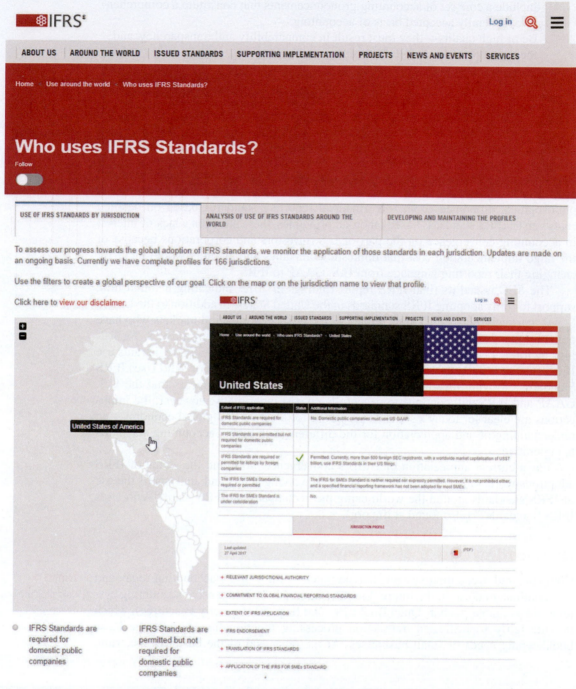

Source: ifrs.org/use-around-the-world/use-of-ifrs-standards-by-jurisdiction/#filing

enterprise-level systems, such as SAP and Oracle, provide automated solutions to support the business and accounting processes of the world's largest corporations.

Accounting was defined in Chapter 1 as a system of identifying, measuring, and communicating economic information about an entity for the purpose of making decisions and informed judgments. In its simplest form, any system is characterized by three essential flows, as illustrated here:

This systems view can be applied to the basics of accounting and illustrated as an accounting information system:

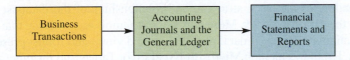

Today, and with a focus on the future, accounting has evolved into a complex, comprehensive business information system (as illustrated below)—and technology provides speed, power, accuracy, and more timely knowledge about an organization. Thus, users of such systems have a real-time window through which they can observe their organization's operations to support planning, control, and decision-making activities.

Inputs to the system have become increasingly automated as more than just the largest corporations leverage technology and the Internet by integrating their systems with the systems of their customers and vendors. Physical copies of invoices, purchase orders, receiving reports, and remittance advices have served as source documents for accounting departments of the past; this type of paperwork is increasingly becoming obsolete as physical source documents are replaced by business-to-business electronic transaction flows (i.e., computer-to-computer communications). The purchaser can scan bar codes or read radio frequency identification tags as inventory items are received and, upon verification of the purchase order by the system, authorize an electronic funds transfer providing payment to the vendor. Likewise, data collection terminals located in strategic positions throughout the manufacturing plant can provide job costing input to the system for materials used, labor costs incurred, and manufacturing overhead applied. In some cases, the data collection technology can be wired directly into operating equipment to track speed, productivity, downtime, and other important production variables. These examples of technology's role in capturing and recording business transactions clearly define an important and ever-evolving role for the accountant to play in the process of planning, analysis, design, implementation, use, and control of automated transaction processing systems.

After a business transaction has been captured by a system, it is maintained in a database—just as the general ledger provided a final resting place after transactions had been posted from the journals where they were initially recorded. *Database management systems* store data in a manner that allows users to interact with the data either through online queries or by running predefined reports. The ability to filter (cut, slice, and dice) transactions in the database into a variety of enlightening views provides a powerful tool for the business analyst and decision maker to support his or her information needs.

In the future, there will continue to be an increased emphasis on the development of user-friendly technology tools that allow financial professionals to easily retrieve data for manipulation into meaningful information. *Structured Query Language (SQL)* is the basic interface language used today to interact with databases to produce pre-defined reports or to submit ad hoc requests for information. Tasks now done effortlessly with point-and-click and drag-and-drop techniques once involved cumbersome retrieval processes requiring programmers to write detailed source code to access the database and produce the desired information. With today's technology, any user with an understanding of the basic structure and relationships of the database can access and retrieve the data effectively. Moreover, powerful tools are evolving that allow users to easily manipulate retrieved data into finely tuned views and robust presentations of information. Examples include Microsoft Excel Pivot Tables and the emerging general category of data analytics and visualization tools including Microsoft's PowerBI.

In addition to supporting internal information users, databases also provide information for external financial reporting. Most major U.S. public companies provide some type of financial disclosure through their websites. To date, however, most financial information presented on the Internet has been relatively static, consisting mostly of quarterly and annual reports presented in a manner similar to the printed annual reports that communicate an organization's financial position and results of operations. Internet-based financial reporting changes dramatically with the development of *Extensible Business Reporting Language (XBRL),* a tool that will become the digital language of all business reporting. XBRL will format financial reports (based on generally accepted accounting principles) for transport across the Internet and viewing on web browsers by public and private companies, accounting professionals, investors, researchers, financial analysts, government agencies, banks, and others. The uniformity provided by XBRL will make it much easier for a multitude of users to prepare and analyze electronic financial information. Examples include printed financial statements, filings with regulatory agencies, credit and loan information required by banks, and the ability to search and extract detailed information from different forms of financial statements.

To conceptualize how XBRL will work, think of a balance sheet presented in a spreadsheet where you might find $20,000 to be the amount of inventory as of December 31, 2019. The $20,000 amount is meaningful because you can read the column heading "December 31, 2019," and the row label "Inventory." But what happens if you extract the $20,000 amount and move it to another spreadsheet or report? Without also extracting or reentering the column heading and row label, the $20,000 amount does not convey independent meaning. With XBRL, the $20,000 amount will retain the attributes of where it belongs in the financial statements as well as its label and dates. Therefore, data can be transported into spreadsheets, databases, printed

FYI

For a complete update on XBRL development activities and other technical information about XBRL, see xbrl.org. To learn more about how XBRL works, see the list of topics under the "*What*" tab. And explore the latest news from around the XBRL world under the "*News*" tab.

reports, web pages, and more without the need to reenter attribute information. XBRL will likely be viewed as one of the most important technologies developed for financial reporting since the spreadsheet, and it should revolutionize how financial accounting information is communicated.

Data warehouses are large, refined collections of the organization's data resources—these super-databases provide high-quality, easily retrievable data, thereby allowing users to manipulate and transform data in creative ways that open new windows into an organization's operations through a vast array of data visualizations and innovative dashboards. These repositories of data visualizations—literally at one's fingertips—provide managers the data-driven insights into their operations they need to support strategic questions and direction.

Data mining technology allows organizations to search their data warehouses internally, as well as harvest other publicly available databases, to find key relationships in the data about customer patterns, market trends, and their own operating performance that provide incredible new knowledge to and about the organization—a reality that would be impossible without such technology. It's one thing to have insight and reports about the historical transactions of an organization, but the opportunities that are emerging with these "big data" technologies and strategies to become more "predictive" (predictive analytics) about what will happen in the future or more "prescriptive" (prescriptive analytics) about how to select the best decision options are opening new frontiers for those students of accounting who develop the appropriate data skills and vision for applying the technology.

Artificial intelligence (AI), the ability of machines to learn and imitate intelligent human behavior, is the next frontier for these big data strategies—and that future is here. Automated manufacturing, replacing human effort with robotics, has been occurring for several decades and it leverages the ability to program robots to perform very precise, repetitive, and continuous production steps. Newer AI applications have demonstrated the more sophisticated machine learning ability with natural language processing for responses to human questions in real time or for interpreting vast datasets of contracts or leases looking for risk or compliance concerns. AI applications are continuously evolving to further automate and streamline traditional accounting activities such as data entry and general ledger maintenance, receipts and disbursements,

To explore additional information about data analytics in accounting, and the future of big data and artificial intelligence technology, check out the following resources:

The next frontier in data analytics:
journalofaccountancy.com/issues/2016/aug/data-analytics-skills.html

The big data effect:
accaglobal.com/us/en/student/sa/features/big-data.html

How artificial intelligence is changing accounting:
journalofaccountancy.com/newsletters/2017/oct/artificial-intelligence-changing-accounting.html

How accounting firms can tap into benefits of AI:
journalofaccountancy.com/news/2018/may/how-cpa-firms-can-tap-ai-benefits-201818949.html

And for a fun and interactive AI experience, visit icaew.com/en/technical/technology/artificial-intelligence/artificial-intelligence-the-future-of-accountancy for a chat with the "AI Assistant" at the Institute of Chartered Accountants in England and Wales (ICAEW).

FYI

banking and reconciliations, payroll, taxes, and more. The opportunities for innovative solutions that address massively large and complex business challenges now seem within reach.

Students of Accounting Information

THEME 5

Committing to lifelong learning.

In today's rapidly changing business environment, business and accounting professionals must have a broad understanding of information technology and the role it plays in the 21st-century economy. It is critically important for players in this environment to understand what technology *can* and *cannot* accomplish; to possess the discipline to maintain the skills necessary to use technology to accomplish ever-changing business goals; and, finally, to integrate technology skills with leadership and communication skills to gain competitive advantages for themselves and their employers. Failure to do so will leave today's business and accounting graduates unprepared to function in a technology-driven information age. Just as robotics has replaced human effort in the manufacturing environment, so, too, will AI replace some traditional accounting functions. Accountants will clearly exist in the future, but their work and necessary skill set will be elevated by the power and opportunity provided with the technology. For certain, we must all embrace with open arms the idea of career long learning.

THEME 6

Becoming business partners.

Today's accounting students and entry-level professionals must position themselves beyond the accountant's traditional role of financial historian. Traditional number-crunching transaction work and the preparation of financial statements is now left to computers to perform. Employers of accounting professionals will need to appreciate the new roles accounting graduates can perform today and leverage their knowledge and information skills by inviting these new hires to participate in the process of defining organizational strategy. Although the *role* of accountants has changed dramatically in recent years, the *perception* of accountants (especially at lower levels of management) will take time to change because ingrained in that perception is the image of traditional scorekeepers, bean counters, watchdogs, and police. Viewed as business partners, accountants' work will be more analytical and less transactional, more decision-support oriented and less compliance oriented. In short, accountants will be more involved in running the business than ever before. These new accounting roles include financial modeling, strategic planning, business process improvement, internal consulting, financial analysis, systems implementation, information architecture, data analytics and visualizations, and organizational education. To support these changing roles of financial professionals and users of accounting information, the educational process will need to focus less on number crunching (i.e., debits and credits) and more on developing communication skills, analytical skills, interpersonal skills, and technology skills. A serious problem could occur if today's business school graduates are disconnected from the needs of organizations in the new economy.

The accountant's new role in today's technology-driven economy is that of a strategic business partner with the responsibility of developing the information needed to support the organization's *value chain functions* (discussed in Chapter 13). This new role can be illustrated as follows:

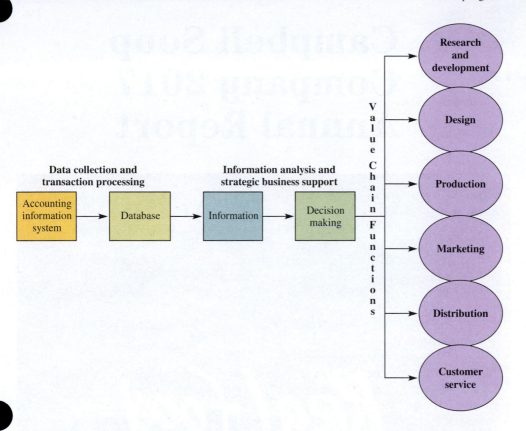

Tomorrow's accountant will play a pivotal role in enhancing long-term profitability by supporting managers at all levels within the organization's value chain in managing the resources under their control most effectively. To serve this important role, it will be essential to obtain a better understanding of the interaction between the organization's accounting information system, its information architecture and strategic decision-making needs, and each of the functional areas that are affected by strategic decision making.

Conclusion

To a large extent, what has been described as the future of accounting is already here—but not yet fully operational or widespread in application. Just as the technologies of the 20th century shaped industrial America's need for accounting information, so too will the technologies of the 21st century help to define accounting information needs in a global information age. Users of accounting information will include managers working on a team to plan, execute, and control the activities related to the entity's strategic plan. The objectives of this text have been to present a big-picture perspective of the financial statements and to show how management accounting information can be used effectively within an organization. To the extent that this epilogue provides insight into characteristics and activities of accounting professionals and future uses of accounting information technology, a further benefit has been achieved.

THEME 7
Turning vision into reality.

APPENDIX

Campbell Soup Company 2017 Annual Report

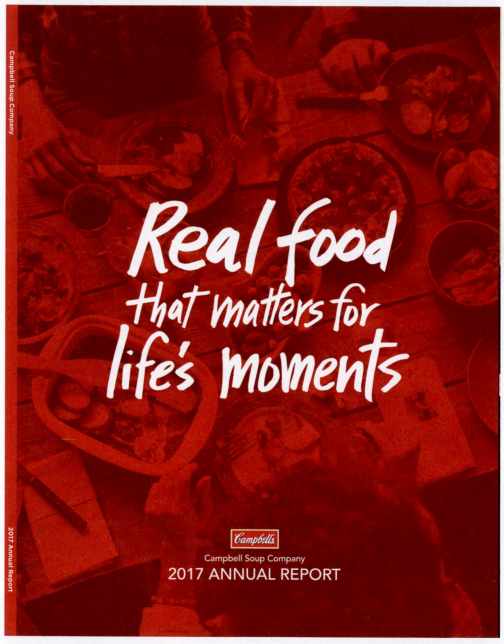

Real food that matters for life's moments

Campbell's

Campbell Soup Company

2017 ANNUAL REPORT

Courtesy of Campbell Soup Company

Fellow Shareholders,

Growth...

It has been elusive for years, as the entire food industry grapples with the seismic shifts that have altered the consumer, food and retail landscapes.

The drive to deliver sustainable, profitable top-line growth has been a consistent theme during my tenure as Campbell's CEO. Our growth strategy has been focused on two critical areas: strengthening our core business and expanding into faster-growing spaces to diversify our portfolio.

Both were necessities to address these seismic shifts: the massive changes in demographics; the evolving consumer preferences toward health and well-being, centered on fresh and real food; technological advancements reshaping the consumer shopping experience; and tumultuous socio-economic forces. These shifts have not only accelerated and converged, they have essentially reset consumer behavior. In this environment, companies and brands must differentiate themselves or risk extinction.

Over the last six years, we have made significant progress on transforming Campbell's portfolio toward faster-growing spaces, particularly health and well-being. Our commitment to health and well-being is unwavering. We chose this path because we recognized the dramatic changes taking place in our industry and that real and healthier food was better for our consumers and better for our business. Let me state it clearly and unambiguously: *Our ultimate goal is to "Be the leading health and well-being food company."*

When people look for something real to eat and something that tastes good, they are going to look for the food Campbell makes. We chose this path not because it is expedient, but because we believe it represents the future of the food industry and that it will lead to differentiated performance for our shareholders.

Denise M. Morrison
President and Chief Executive Officer

Courtesy of Campbell Soup Company

Timeline

'11 — Announced exit of operations in Russia.

'12 — Acquired Bolthouse Farms.

'13 — Acquired Plum Organics. / Acquired Kelsen Group. / Copack agreements with La Costeña & Jumex.

'14 — Sold European simple meals business. / Articulated Purpose & Growth Agenda. *Real Food that matters for life's moments.*

'15 — Significant multi-year cost savings initiative. / Major enterprise redesign & portfolio roles. / Established INTEGRATED GLOBAL SERVICES

'16 — Acquired Garden Fresh Gourmet. / Real Food Philosophy & Values. / Formed ACRE VENTURE PARTNERS / Funded habit

'17 — Partnered with CHEF'D / Raised the bar on transparency with sage project

DEFINING HEALTH AND WELL-BEING

Health and well-being means different things to different people. In fact, research shows that many consumers' beliefs around this topic simply do not align with traditional definitions. No amount of advertising or government classification will convince them otherwise. Consumers associate healthy with fresh, naturally functional and organic foods. At Campbell, we believe in putting consumers first. Understanding consumer beliefs is central to decoding the meaning of health and well-being.

Our definition begins with real food: food made with simple, recognizable and desirable ingredients from plants and animals; food crafted with care using ethical sourcing and sustainable practices; and food that is safe, delicious and available at a fair price — all three without compromise.

Real food has become a non-negotiable demand. People have simply come to expect it. Campbell is listening and taking our cues on health and well-being from consumers.

On the well-being side that means food that is engaging, comforting and provides a sense of purpose, a reward and a small moment of satisfaction or celebration. A cookie or a biscuit and a well-being product do not have to be mutually exclusive.

We are focused on delivering the benefits our consumers believe are important, including fresh and organic foods; naturally functional foods that provide energy, endurance and digestive health; and food that is relatable and tailored to individual needs through personalized nutrition.

Campbell holds an advantaged position among our peers. We exceed most other food companies in terms of the amount of vegetables and whole grains in our foods. Plus, we have a heritage of providing safe and simple foods that are affordable and accessible. We also have a powerful connection with consumers, especially families. Our brands have and will continue to play an important role in "the moments that matter" in peoples' lives.

The significant actions we have taken have helped to redefine the way people view Campbell. If consumers are looking for fresh foods, clean labels or organic offerings, they can now find it in Campbell's portfolio.

3 Campbell Soup Company

OUR GROWTH AGENDA

Our Growth Agenda is rooted in our purpose, **Real food that matters for life's moments.** We believe our four strategic imperatives will help us realize Campbell's goal of being the leading health and well-being food company and drive the greatest value for our shareholders over time.

01 REAL FOOD, TRANSPARENCY & SUSTAINABILITY

02 DIGITAL & E-COMMERCE

03 FRESH AND HEALTH & WELL-BEING

04 SNACKING

2 Campbell Soup Company

Courtesy of Campbell Soup Company

OUR GROWTH AGENDA AND FOUR STRATEGIC IMPERATIVES ARE THE ROADMAP

It is not enough to simply say what we aspire to be. We need to tell you how we will achieve it. Our growth agenda, with our purpose, ***Real food that matters for life's moments***, as a North Star, informs everything we do — from resource allocations to external development. Our four strategic imperatives provide a blueprint to become the leading health and well-being food company and to deliver improved sales growth.

1. Building Greater Trust with Consumers Through Real Food, Transparency and Sustainability

Our purpose continues to be the single most important change in our company's culture in the last few years. It has fundamentally altered the way we think, talk and act about our food.

Our purpose has led us to take principled positions about the most pressing issues facing the food industry, including transparency. At times, we have had philosophical differences with many of our peers and our trade association on important issues. As a result, we intend to withdraw from the Grocery Manufacturers Association at the end of 2017. This was not a financial decision. It was driven by our purpose and our principles.

As we strive to be the most transparent food company in the world, Campbell is partnering with the **Sage Project** to raise the bar on food transparency. Combining technology with design, the Sage Project is creating online food labels for the digital world, making information about calories, nutrition, ingredients and attributes open, accessible and easy for consumers to understand. Campbell is embracing the platform because we believe it delivers the information consumers are increasingly demanding.

These efforts complement our planned ongoing investment of $50 million over the next several years to make the kind of food that consumers are seeking and that we are proud to serve at our own tables. We are making steady progress toward our commitment to remove artificial colors and flavors from our food, while increasing the use of vegetables and whole grains and using chicken with no antibiotics. We have also completed our work to remove BPA from the lining of our soup cans in the U.S. and Canada.

2. Accelerating Digital Marketing and E-Commerce Efforts

Consumer options for how and where they buy groceries are changing rapidly. Shoppers today have immediate access to pricing, product information and reviews, literally in the palm of their hand. E-commerce is a series of tools, technologies and behaviors that, over time, build consumer expectations of convenience. It happened in entertainment. It happened in apparel. And now it is happening in food.

Today, the percentage of food sold online is in the low single digits. By 2021, we project online grocery sales to reach $66 billion annually in the U.S.[1] Over the next five years, we expect to generate $300 million of sales in this space.

To accelerate our digital and e-commerce efforts, we are building an e-commerce unit in North America to deliver the products and services our consumers demand and to drive growth, while working to scale our digital marketing capabilities. We also expect to partner with leading e-commerce companies. For example, Campbell invested $10 million and formed a strategic partnership with online meal kit company **Chef'd** to test new concepts for fresh, healthy recipes and to integrate our products into their popular meal kits. More importantly, we will gain insights from their data and analytics and participate firsthand in emerging e-commerce models.

To compete and thrive in this environment, we need to enhance our distribution capabilities to meet customer and consumer needs today and in the future. That is why we are investing in a network of distribution centers to create a more flexible distribution system to serve our e-commerce channels.

[1] *Proprietary Campbell Estimate*

Defining the future of food requires different approaches and an ecosystem of innovative partners. A prime example is the partnership we announced with Chef'd, a leading meal kit marketplace. They possess deep competencies in consumer insights, the shopper's path to purchase, digital marketing and analytics, and fulfillment capabilities. Campbell will gain valuable knowledge in emerging e-commerce trends and business models.

Campbell Soup Company **4**

> **"** We have a heritage of providing safe and simple foods that are affordable and accessible. We also have a powerful connection with consumers, especially families. Our brands have and will continue to play an important role in 'the moments that matter' in peoples' lives. **"**

3. Continuing to Diversify Campbell's Portfolio in Fresh Foods and Health and Well-Being

Campbell is a leading player in health and well-being based on the percentage of our sales from such products. We have nearly $1 billion in annual net sales from fresh products; our products provide 15 billion servings of vegetables and more than 2.4 million tons of whole grains to consumers annually; and our organic portfolio is in the top 10 in the industry and growing at double digits.[2]

Campbell's goal to lead in health and well-being is attainable. But to truly lead the industry, we will need to redouble our efforts and move with urgency to evolve our portfolio. We will continue to invest in health and well-being across the business, focusing on food with attributes such as natural, organic, functional and fresh.

[2] IRI Total US – MULO for the calendar year ending 12/31/16. CAGR based on 2013-2016

4. Increasing Campbell's Presence in the Faster-Growing Snacking Category

Consumers are continuously looking for new and better snacking solutions. Not only have the types of snacks expanded, but also the moments in which consumers look to snack across the day. Ninety percent of consumers snack multiple times a day and more than 50 percent of all U.S. eating occasions are snacks.[3]

We see an opportunity to leverage brands across our entire portfolio to participate in snacking occasions outside our cookie and baked snacks business. Our goal is to make snacks with real food ingredients accessible to all consumers, and we are pursuing an enterprise-wide snacking strategy designed to accelerate our efforts.

We plan to broaden our snacking business beyond cookies and baked snacks to include soup, mini meals and fresh snacks. This expanded snacking market is worth approximately $125 billion in the U.S. alone and growing around 3 percent.[4] We are aiming to add approximately $200 million in sales over the next five years attributable to these efforts.

[3] Hartman Group, 2014; Hartman Group, 2016
[4] BCG analysis, industry press release, IRI 2016 State of Snacking, Mintel BFY Snacks 2016

Courtesy of Campbell Soup Company

Fiscal 2017 Results

As I mentioned, the operating environment for the packaged foods industry remains challenging. Despite multiple headwinds, we delivered another year of adjusted earnings growth.* This year, sales decreased 1 percent to $7.890 billion driven by a 1 percent decline* in organic sales, reflecting lower volume and higher promotional spending. The company reported earnings per share (EPS) of $2.89. Adjusted EPS increased 3 percent to $3.04 per share, compared with $2.94 per share a year ago.*

Our Americas Simple Meals and Beverages division continued to deliver against its portfolio role with sales performance in line with the categories in which we compete and margin expansion. Global Biscuits and Snacks delivered strong profit performance. We believe the key executional issues in our C-Fresh division are largely behind us, and that this business will return to profitable growth in fiscal 2018.

We are pleased with the progress of the multi-year cost-savings program we launched in 2015. As of the end of fiscal 2017, we achieved $325 million in annual cost savings, which is a year ahead of our original expectations. As announced earlier this year, we have increased our target by $150 million and now expect to deliver $450 million in cost savings by the end of fiscal 2020. We remain committed to managing costs aggressively and reinvesting a portion of the savings back into the business in fiscal 2018 to position the company for long-term growth.

These amounts are adjusted for certain items not considered to be part of the ongoing business. For a reconciliation of non-GAAP financial measures, see page 8

The Leading Health and Well-being Food Company

Campbell is the biggest small food company, with the entrepreneurial spirit of a small company and the scale and resources of a large company. To be the leading health and well-being food company, we are leveraging the best of big and small to deliver value to our consumers, customers and shareholders.

The seismic shifts I first sensed and shared six years ago have not only accelerated and converged, they have become more urgent. Consumers no longer settle. They demand. Those companies who cannot — or choose not to — respond are running out of time, and will soon be out of luck. Like radio broadcasters who assumed TV was just a passing fancy, food companies who cannot envision their roles evolving into health and well-being food companies may very well face a similar fate. Campbell is listening to consumers and responding to their signals about health and well-being.

In closing, I want to thank our Board of Directors, the Campbell Leadership Team, our employees and our shareholders. With your ongoing support, I am confident that being the leading health and well-being food company will lead to growth rates that outperform the industry over time.

Best,

Denise M. Morrison
President and Chief Executive Officer

Chairman's Message

In fiscal 2017, Campbell Soup Company continued to live into its purpose – *Real food that matters for life's moments* – and declared its ultimate goal to "Be the leading health and well-being food company." However, it was a challenging year. The entire industry struggled to achieve top-line growth, and our ongoing effort to expand our presence in the faster-growing, on-trend packaged fresh category through Campbell Fresh fell short of expectations. Despite these challenges, Campbell was able to deliver another year of earnings growth.

Following the 2017 Annual Meeting, Charles R. Perrin will retire from the Board. Charlie has served with distinction, providing strategic counsel and outstanding leadership to management and the Board since 1999. In March 2017, we welcomed Fabiola R. Arredondo, former Yahoo! executive, founder and managing partner of Siempre Holdings and an experienced director, to the Campbell Board. The Board has also nominated Howard M. Averill, Chief Financial Officer of Time Warner Inc., for election at the 2017 Annual Meeting.

On behalf of the Campbell Board, I commend Denise and the Campbell Leadership Team for their steadfast efforts in a challenging environment. I also thank my fellow directors for their service and ongoing commitment to Campbell Soup Company. And, most importantly, I thank our shareholders for their continuing support.

Les C. Vinney
Chairman of the Board

Financial Highlights

(dollars in millions, except per share amounts)		2017		2016
Results of Operations				
Net Sales	$	7,890	$	7,961
Gross Profit	$	3,059	$	2,780
Percent of Sales		38.8%		34.9%
Earnings before interest and taxes	$	1,400	$	960
Net earnings attributable to Campbell Soup Company	$	887	$	563
Per share — diluted	$	2.89	$	1.81
Other Information				
Net cash provided by operating activities	$	1,291	$	1,491
Capital expenditures	$	338	$	341
Dividends per share	$	1.40	$	1.248

In 2017, Net earnings attributable to Campbell Soup Company included the following: a restructuring charge, related costs and administrative expenses of $37 ($0.12 per share) associated with restructuring and cost savings initiatives; gains of $116 ($0.38 per share) associated with mark-to-market adjustments for defined benefit pension and postretirement plans; impairment charges of $180 ($0.59 per share) related to the intangible assets of the Bolthouse Farms carrot and carrot ingredients reporting unit and the Garden Fresh Gourmet reporting unit; and a tax benefit and reduction to interest expense of $56 ($0.18 per share) primarily associated with the sale of intercompany notes receivable to a financial institution.

In 2016, Net earnings attributable to Campbell Soup Company included the following: a restructuring charge and administrative expenses of $49 ($0.16 per share) associated with restructuring and cost savings initiatives; losses of $200 ($0.64 per share) associated with mark-to-market adjustments for defined benefit pension and postretirement plans; an impairment charge of $127 ($0.41 per share) related to the intangible assets of the Bolthouse Farms carrot and carrot ingredients reporting unit; and a gain of $25 ($0.08 per share) associated with a settlement of a claim related to the Kelsen acquisition.

See below for a reconciliation of the impact of these items on reported results.

Reconciliation of GAAP and Non-GAAP Financial Measures

The following information is provided to reconcile certain non-GAAP financial measures disclosed in the Letter to Shareholders to reported sales and earnings results. These non-GAAP financial measures are measures of performance not defined by accounting principles generally accepted in the United States and should be considered in addition to, not in lieu of, GAAP reported measures. We believe that presenting certain non-GAAP financial measures facilitates comparison of our historical operating results and trends in our underlying operating results, and provides transparency on how we evaluate our business. For instance, we believe that organic net sales, which exclude the impact of currency, are a better indicator of our ongoing business performance. We also believe that the financial information excluding certain transactions not considered to be part of the ongoing business improves the comparability of year-to-year earnings results. Consequently, we believe that investors may be able to better understand our earnings results if these transactions are excluded from the results.

(dollars in millions)	2017	2016	% Change
Net Sales	$ 7,890	$ 7,961	-1%
Volume and Mix			-1%
Price and Sales Allowances			0%
Promotional Spending			-1%
Organic Growth			-1%
Currency			0%
Total			-1%

The sum of the individual amounts does not add due to rounding.

	2017		2016		Earnings % Change	EPS % Change
(dollars in millions, except per share amounts)	Earnings Impact	Diluted EPS Impact	Earnings Impact	Diluted EPS Impact	2017/2016	2017/2016
Net earnings attributable to Campbell Soup Company, as reported	$ 887	$ 2.89	$563	$1.81		
Restructuring charges, implementation costs and other related costs	37	0.12	49	0.16		
Pension and postretirement benefit mark-to-market adjustments	(116)	(0.38)	200	0.64		
Impairment charges	180	0.59	127	0.41		
Sale of notes	(56)	(0.18)	-	-		
Claim settlement	-	-	(25)	(0.08)		
Adjusted Net earnings attributable to Campbell Soup Company	$ 932	$ 3.04	$914	$2.94	2%	3%

BOARD OF DIRECTORS
(As of September 2017)

Les C. Vinney
Chairman of Campbell Soup Company,
Retired President and Chief Executive Officer
of STERIS Corporation

Denise M. Morrison
President and Chief Executive Officer
of Campbell Soup Company

Fabiola R. Arredondo
Founder and Managing Partner
of Siempre Holdings [2, 4]

Bennett Dorrance
Managing Director and Co-founder
of DMB Associates [2, 4]

Randall W. Larrimore
Retired President and Chief Executive Officer
of United Stationers Inc. [2, 4]

Marc B. Lautenbach
President and Chief Executive Officer
of Pitney Bowes Inc. [1, 2]

Mary Alice D. Malone
President of Iron Spring Farm, Inc. [3,4]

Sara Mathew
Retired Chairman and Chief Executive Officer
of The Dun & Bradstreet Corporation [1, 3]

Keith R. McLoughlin
Former Chief Executive Officer of AB Electrolux [2, 4]

Charles R. Perrin
Retired Chairman and Chief Executive Officer
of Avon Products, Inc. [1, 3]

Nick Shreiber
Retired President and Chief Executive Officer
of Tetra Pak Group [2, 4]

Tracey T. Travis
Executive Vice President and
Chief Financial Officer
of The Estée Lauder Companies Inc. [1, 3]

Archbold D. van Beuren
Retired Senior Vice President
of Campbell Soup Company [1, 3]

Committees

1 Audit
2 Compensation & Organization
3 Finance & Corporate Development
4 Governance

9 Campbell Soup Company

CAMPBELL LEADERSHIP TEAM
(As of September 2017)

Denise M. Morrison*
President and Chief Executive Officer

Mark R. Alexander*
President, Americas Simple Meals and Beverages

Carlos J. Barroso*
Senior Vice President, Global Research and Development
and Quality

Edward L. Carolan*
President, Campbell Fresh

Adam G. Ciongoli*
Senior Vice President and General Counsel

Anthony P. DiSilvestro*
Senior Vice President and Chief Financial Officer

Robert Furbee*
Senior Vice President, Global Supply Chain

Bethmara Kessler*
Senior Vice President, Integrated Global Services

Luca Mignini*
President, Global Biscuits and Snacks

Robert W. Morrissey*
Senior Vice President and
Chief Human Resources Officer

James Sterbenz
Senior Vice President, U.S. Sales

Emily P. Waldorf
Vice President, Corporate Strategy

*** *Executive Officers***

Courtesy of Campbell Soup Company

UNITED STATES SECURITIES AND EXCHANGE COMMISSION
Washington, D.C. 20549

Form 10-K

ANNUAL REPORT PURSUANT TO SECTION 13 OR 15(d) OF THE SECURITIES EXCHANGE ACT OF 1934

For the Fiscal Year Ended	Commission File Number
July 30, 2017	**1-3822**

CAMPBELL SOUP COMPANY

New Jersey	21-0419870
State of Incorporation	*I.R.S. Employer Identification No.*

1 Campbell Place
Camden, New Jersey 08103-1799
Principal Executive Offices
Telephone Number: (856) 342-4800
Securities registered pursuant to Section 12(b) of the Act:

Title of Each Class	Name of Each Exchange on Which Registered
Capital Stock, par value $.0375	New York Stock Exchange

Securities registered pursuant to Section 12(g) of the Act: None

Indicate by check mark if the registrant is a well-known seasoned issuer, as defined in Rule 405 of the Securities Act.☑ Yes ☐ No

Indicate by check mark if the registrant is not required to file reports pursuant to Section 13 or 15(d) of the Act. ☐ Yes ☑ No

Indicate by check mark whether the registrant: (1) has filed all reports required to be filed by Section 13 or 15(d) of the Securities Exchange Act of 1934 during the preceding 12 months (or for such shorter period that the registrant was required to file such reports), and (2) has been subject to such filing requirements for the past 90 days. ☑ Yes ☐ No

Indicate by check mark whether the registrant has submitted electronically and posted on its corporate web site, if any, every Interactive Data File required to be submitted and posted pursuant to Rule 405 of Regulation S-T during the preceding 12 months (or for such shorter period that the registrant was required to submit and post such files). ☑ Yes ☐ No

Indicate by check mark if disclosure of delinquent filers pursuant to Item 405 of Regulation S-K is not contained herein, and will not be contained, to the best of registrant's knowledge, in definitive proxy or information statements incorporated by reference in Part III of this Form 10-K or any amendment to this Form 10-K. ☐

Indicate by check mark whether the registrant is a large accelerated filer, an accelerated filer, a non-accelerated filer, a smaller reporting company or an emerging growth company. See the definitions of "large accelerated filer," "accelerated filer," "smaller reporting company," and "emerging growth company" in Rule 12b-2 of the Exchange Act.

Large accelerated filer ☑   Accelerated filer ☐

Non-accelerated filer ☐ (Do not check if a smaller reporting company)   Smaller reporting company ☐

Emerging growth company ☐

If an emerging growth company, indicate by check mark if the registrant has elected not to use the extended transition period for complying with any new or revised financial accounting standards provided pursuant to Section 13(a) of the Exchange Act. ☐

Indicate by check mark whether the registrant is a shell company (as defined in Rule 12b-2 of the Exchange Act). ☐ Yes ☑ No

As of January 27, 2017 (the last business day of the registrant's most recently completed second fiscal quarter), the aggregate market value of capital stock held by non-affiliates of the registrant was approximately $11,934,667,846. There were 300,528,501 shares of capital stock outstanding as of September 20, 2017.

Portions of the Registrant's Proxy Statement for the Annual Meeting of Shareholders to be held on November 15, 2017, are incorporated by reference into Part III.

TABLE OF CONTENTS

Issuer Purchases of Equity Securities

Period	Total Number of Shares Purchased [1]	Average Price Paid Per Share [2]	Total Number of Shares Purchased as Part of Publicly Announced Plans or Programs [3]	Approximate Dollar Value of Shares that may yet be Purchased Under the Plans or Programs ($ in Millions) [3]
5/1/17 - 5/31/17.	840,649 [4]	$58.25 [4]	783,564	$1,454
6/1/17 - 6/30/17.	305,694	$55.29	305,694	$1,437
7/3/17 - 7/28/17.	1,289,997	$51.69	1,289,997	$1,371
Total	2,436,340 [4]	$54.40 [4]	2,379,255	$1,371

[1] Shares purchased are as of the trade date.

[2] Average price paid per share is calculated on a settlement basis and excludes commission.

[3] During the fourth quarter of 2017, we had a publicly announced strategic share repurchase program. Under this program, which was announced on March 22, 2017 and effective May 1, 2017, our Board of Directors authorized the purchase of up to $1.5 billion of our stock. The program has no expiration date. Pursuant to our longstanding practice, under a separate 2017 authorization, we expect to continue purchasing shares sufficient to offset the impact of dilution from shares issued under our incentive compensation plans.

[4] Includes 57,085 shares repurchased in open-market transactions at an average price of $57.61 primarily to offset the dilutive impact to existing shareholders of issuances under stock compensation plans.

Item 6. *Selected Financial Data*

Fiscal Year (Millions, except per share amounts)	2017[1]	2016[2]	2015[3]	2014[4]	2013[5]
Summary of Operations					
Net sales	$7,890	$7,961	$8,082	$8,268	$8,052
Earnings before interest and taxes	1,400	960	1,054	1,267	1,474
Earnings before taxes	1,293	849	949	1,148	1,349
Earnings from continuing operations	887	563	666	774	934
Earnings (loss) from discontinued operations	—	—	—	81	(231)
Net earnings	887	563	666	855	703
Net earnings attributable to Campbell Soup Company	887	563	666	866	712
Financial Position					
Plant assets - net	$2,454	$2,407	$2,347	$2,318	$2,260
Total assets	7,726	7,837	8,077	8,100	8,290
Total debt	3,536	3,533	4,082	4,003	4,438
Total equity	1,645	1,533	1,377	1,602	1,192
Per Share Data					
Earnings from continuing operations attributable to Campbell Soup Company - basic	$ 2.91	$ 1.82	$ 2.13	$ 2.50	$ 3.00
Earnings from continuing operations attributable to Campbell Soup Company - assuming dilution	2.89	1.81	2.13	2.48	2.97
Net earnings attributable to Campbell Soup Company - basic	2.91	1.82	2.13	2.76	2.27
Net earnings attributable to Campbell Soup Company - assuming dilution	2.89	1.81	2.13	2.74	2.25
Dividends declared	1.40	1.248	1.248	1.248	1.16
Other Statistics					
Capital expenditures	$ 338	$ 341	$ 380	$ 347	$ 336
Weighted average shares outstanding - basic	305	309	312	314	314
Weighted average shares outstanding - assuming dilution	307	311	313	316	317

(All per share amounts below are on a diluted basis)

In March 2016, the Financial Accounting Standards Board (FASB) issued guidance that amends accounting for share-based payments, including the accounting for income taxes, forfeitures, and statutory withholding requirements, as well as classification in the statement of cash flows. We adopted the guidance in 2017. In accordance with the prospective adoption of the recognition of excess tax benefits and deficiencies in the Consolidated Statements of Earnings, we recognized a $6 million tax benefit in Taxes on earnings in 2017.

In April 2015, the FASB issued guidance that requires debt issuance costs to be presented in the balance sheet as a reduction from the carrying value of the associated debt liability, consistent with the presentation of a debt discount. We adopted the guidance in 2016 and retrospectively adjusted all prior periods.

In November 2015, the FASB issued guidance that requires deferred tax liabilities and assets to be classified as noncurrent in the balance sheet. We adopted the guidance in 2016 on a prospective basis and modified the presentation of deferred taxes in the Consolidated Balance Sheet as of July 31, 2016.

The 2014 fiscal year consisted of 53 weeks. All other periods had 52 weeks.

[1]   The 2017 earnings from continuing operations attributable to Campbell Soup Company were impacted by the following: a restructuring charge, related costs and administrative expenses of $37 million ($.12 per share) associated with restructuring and cost savings initiatives; gains of $116 million ($.38 per share) associated with mark-to-market adjustments for defined benefit pension and postretirement plans; impairment charges of $180 million ($.59 per share) related to the intangible assets of the Bolthouse Farms carrot and carrot ingredients reporting unit and the Garden Fresh Gourmet reporting unit; and a tax benefit and reduction to interest expense of $56 million ($.18 per share) primarily associated with the sale of intercompany notes receivable to a financial institution.

[2]   The 2016 earnings from continuing operations attributable to Campbell Soup Company were impacted by the following: a restructuring charge and administrative expenses of $49 million ($.16 per share) associated with restructuring and cost savings initiatives; losses of $200 million ($.64 per share) associated with mark-to-market adjustments for defined benefit pension and postretirement plans; a gain of $25 million ($.08 per share) associated with a settlement of a claim related to the Kelsen acquisition; and an impairment charge of $127 million ($.41 per share) related to the intangible assets of the Bolthouse Farms carrot and carrot ingredients reporting unit.

[3]   The 2015 earnings from continuing operations attributable to Campbell Soup Company were impacted by the following: a restructuring charge and administrative expenses of $78 million ($.25 per share) associated with restructuring and cost savings initiatives and losses of $87 million ($.28 per share) associated with mark-to-market adjustments for defined benefit pension and postretirement plans.

[4]   The 2014 earnings from continuing operations attributable to Campbell Soup Company were impacted by the following: a restructuring charge and related costs of $36 million ($.11 per share) associated with restructuring initiatives; losses of $19 million ($.06 per share) associated with mark-to-market adjustments for defined benefit pension and postretirement plans; a loss of $6 million ($.02 per share) on foreign exchange forward contracts used to hedge the proceeds from the sale of the European simple meals business; $7 million ($.02 per share) tax expense associated with the sale of the European simple meals business; and the estimated impact of the additional week of $25 million ($.08 per share). Earnings from discontinued operations included a gain of $72 million ($.23 per share) on the sale of the European simple meals business.

[5]   The 2013 earnings from continuing operations attributable to Campbell Soup Company were impacted by the following: a restructuring charge and related costs of $87 million ($.27 per share) associated with restructuring initiatives; gains of $183 million ($.58 per share) associated with mark-to-market adjustments for defined benefit pension and postretirement plans; and $7 million ($.02 per share) of transaction costs related to the acquisition of Bolthouse Farms. Earnings from discontinued operations were impacted by an impairment charge on the intangible assets of the simple meals business in Europe of $263 million ($.83 per share) and tax expense of $18 million ($.06 per share) representing taxes on the difference between the book value and tax basis of the business.

Selected Financial Data should be read in conjunction with the Notes to Consolidated Financial Statements.

Item 7. *Management's Discussion and Analysis of Financial Condition and Results of Operations*

OVERVIEW

This Management's Discussion and Analysis of Financial Condition and Results of Operations is provided as a supplement to, and should be read in conjunction with, our consolidated financial statements and the accompanying notes to the consolidated financial statements presented in "Financial Statements and Supplementary Data," as well as the information contained in "Risk Factors."

Item 8. *Financial Statements and Supplementary Data*

CAMPBELL SOUP COMPANY
<u>Consolidated Statements of Earnings</u>
(millions, except per share amounts)

	2017	2016	2015
Net sales..	$ 7,890	$ 7,961	$ 8,082
Costs and expenses			
Cost of products sold...................................	4,831	5,181	5,300
Marketing and selling expenses........................	817	893	884
Administrative expenses	488	641	601
Research and development expenses.....................	98	124	117
Other expenses / (income).............................	238	131	24
Restructuring charges..................................	18	31	102
Total costs and expenses...............................	6,490	7,001	7,028
Earnings before interest and taxes................	1,400	960	1,054
Interest expense	112	115	108
Interest income.......................................	5	4	3
Earnings before taxes.................................	1,293	849	949
Taxes on earnings.....................................	406	286	283
Net earnings	887	563	666
Less: Net earnings (loss) attributable to noncontrolling interests	—	—	—
Net earnings attributable to Campbell Soup Company	$ 887	$ 563	$ 666
Per Share — Basic			
Net earnings attributable to Campbell Soup Company	$ 2.91	$ 1.82	$ 2.13
Weighted average shares outstanding — basic	305	309	312
Per Share — Assuming Dilution			
Net earnings attributable to Campbell Soup Company	$ 2.89	$ 1.81	$ 2.13
Weighted average shares outstanding — assuming dilution	307	311	313

See accompanying Notes to Consolidated Financial Statements.

CAMPBELL SOUP COMPANY
Consolidated Statements of Comprehensive Income
(millions)

	2017			2016			2015		
	Pre-tax amount	Tax (expense) benefit	After-tax amount	Pre-tax amount	Tax (expense) benefit	After-tax amount	Pre-tax amount	Tax (expense) benefit	After-tax amount
Net earnings.			$ 887			$ 563			$ 666
Other comprehensive income (loss):									
Foreign currency translation:									
Foreign currency translation adjustments.	$ 40	$ —	40	$ 45	$ —	45	$ (312)	$ 1	(311)
Cash-flow hedges:									
Unrealized gains (losses) arising during period	19	(7)	12	(45)	16	(29)	(5)	3	(2)
Reclassification adjustment for (gains) losses included in net earnings	11	(4)	7	(9)	2	(7)	(1)	1	—
Pension and other postretirement benefits:									
Prior service credit arising during the period	12	(4)	8	93	(34)	59	—	—	—
Reclassification of prior service credit included in net earnings . . .	(25)	9	(16)	(1)	—	(1)	(2)	1	(1)
Other comprehensive income (loss).	$ 57	$ (6)	51	$ 83	$ (16)	67	$ (320)	$ 6	(314)
Total comprehensive income (loss) .			$ 938			$ 630			$ 352
Total comprehensive income (loss) attributable to noncontrolling interests.			—			3			(1)
Total comprehensive income (loss) attributable to Campbell Soup Company			$ 938			$ 627			$ 353

See accompanying Notes to Consolidated Financial Statements.

CAMPBELL SOUP COMPANY
<u>Consolidated Balance Sheets</u>
(millions, except per share amounts)

	July 30, 2017	July 31, 2016
Current assets		
Cash and cash equivalents . . . . $	**319** $	296
Accounts receivable, net	**605**	626
Inventories	**902**	940
Other current assets	**74**	46
Total current assets.	**1,900**	1,908
Plant assets, net of depreciation	**2,454**	2,407
Goodwill.	**2,115**	2,263
Other intangible assets, net of amortization	**1,118**	1,152
Other assets ($51 as of 2017 and $34 as of 2016 attributable to variable interest entity)	**139**	107
Total assets. . . . . $	**7,726** $	7,837
Current liabilities		
Short-term borrowings . . . . $	**1,037** $	1,219
Payable to suppliers and others	**666**	610
Accrued liabilities	**561**	604
Dividends payable	**111**	100
Accrued income taxes	**20**	22
Total current liabilities.	**2,395**	2,555
Long-term debt	**2,499**	2,314
Deferred taxes.	**490**	396
Other liabilities	**697**	1,039
Total liabilities.	**6,081**	6,304
Commitments and contingencies		
Campbell Soup Company shareholders' equity		
Preferred stock; authorized 40 shares; none issued	**—**	—
Capital stock, $.0375 par value; authorized 560 shares; issued 323 shares	**12**	12
Additional paid-in capital.	**359**	354
Earnings retained in the business	**2,385**	1,927
Capital stock in treasury, at cost.	**(1,066)**	(664)
Accumulated other comprehensive loss.	**(53)**	(104)
Total Campbell Soup Company shareholders' equity.	**1,637**	1,525
Noncontrolling interests	**8**	8
Total equity	**1,645**	1,533
Total liabilities and equity . . . . $	**7,726** $	7,837

See accompanying Notes to Consolidated Financial Statements.

CAMPBELL SOUP COMPANY
<u>**Consolidated Statements of Cash Flows**</u>
(millions)

	2017	2016	2015
Cash flows from operating activities:			
Net earnings . . . . $	887	$ 563	$ 666
Adjustments to reconcile net earnings to operating cash flow			
Impairment charges	212	141	6
Restructuring charges	18	31	102
Stock-based compensation	60	64	57
Pension and postretirement benefit expense (income)	(258)	317	118
Depreciation and amortization	318	308	303
Deferred income taxes	93	(30)	(49)
Other, net	18	6	15
Changes in working capital, net of acquisitions			
Accounts receivable	28	24	12
Inventories	46	59	(18)
Prepaid assets	(27)	9	10
Accounts payable and accrued liabilities	(48)	15	30
Pension fund contributions	(5)	(2)	(5)
Net receipts from hedging activities	2	44	11
Other	(53)	(58)	(52)
Net cash provided by operating activities	**1,291**	1,491	1,206
Cash flows from investing activities:			
Purchases of plant assets	(338)	(341)	(380)
Sales of plant assets	—	5	15
Business acquired, net of cash acquired	—	—	(232)
Other, net	(30)	(18)	(6)
Net cash used in investing activities	(368)	(354)	(603)
Cash flows from financing activities:			
Net short-term borrowings (repayments).	245	(762)	100
Long-term borrowings	211	215	300
Long-term repayments	(90)	—	—
Repayments of notes payable.	(400)	—	(309)
Dividends paid	(420)	(390)	(394)
Treasury stock purchases	(437)	(143)	(244)
Treasury stock issuances	2	2	9
Contributions from noncontrolling interest	—	—	9
Payments related to tax withholding for stock-based compensation	(22)	(21)	(18)
Other, net	—	—	(3)
Net cash used in financing activities	(911)	(1,099)	(550)
Effect of exchange rate changes on cash.	11	5	(32)
Net change in cash and cash equivalents	23	43	21
Cash and cash equivalents — beginning of period	296	253	232
Cash and cash equivalents — end of period . . . . $	319	$ 296	$ 253

See accompanying Notes to Consolidated Financial Statements.

CAMPBELL SOUP COMPANY

<u>Consolidated Statements of Equity</u>

(millions, except per share amounts)

	Campbell Soup Company Shareholders' Equity								
	Capital Stock								
	Issued		In Treasury						
	Shares	Amount	Shares	Amount	Additional Paid-in Capital	Earnings Retained in the Business	Accumulated Other Comprehensive Income (Loss)	Noncontrolling Interests	Total Equity
Balance at August 3, 2014....	323	$ 12	(10)	$ (356)	$ 330	$ 1,483	$ 145	$ (12)	$ 1,602
Contribution from noncontrolling interest.......								9	9
Net earnings (loss).........						666		—	666
Other comprehensive income (loss)...................							(313)	(1)	(314)
Dividends ($1.248 per share)..						(395)			(395)
Treasury stock purchased.....			(5)	(244)					(244)
Treasury stock issued under management incentive and stock option plans			2	44	9				53
Balance at August 2, 2015....	323	12	(13)	(556)	339	1,754	(168)	(4)	1,377
Contribution from noncontrolling interest.......								9	9
Net earnings (loss).........						563		—	563
Other comprehensive income (loss)...................							64	3	67
Dividends ($1.248 per share)..						(390)			(390)
Treasury stock purchased.....			(3)	(143)					(143)
Treasury stock issued under management incentive and stock option plans			1	35	15				50
Balance at July 31, 2016	323	12	(15)	(664)	354	1,927	(104)	8	1,533
Net earnings (loss)						887		—	887
Other comprehensive income (loss)....................							51	—	51
Dividends ($1.40 per share)..						(429)			(429)
Treasury stock purchased...			(8)	(437)					(437)
Treasury stock issued under management incentive and stock option plans.........			1	35	5				40
Balance at July 30, 2017	**323**	**$ 12**	**(22)**	**$ (1,066)**	**$ 359**	**$ 2,385**	**$ (53)**	**$ 8**	**$ 1,645**

See accompanying Notes to Consolidated Financial Statements.

Notes to Consolidated Financial Statements
(currency in millions, except per share amounts)

1. **Summary of Significant Accounting Policies**

In this Report, unless otherwise stated, the terms "we," "us," "our" and the "company" refer to Campbell Soup Company and its consolidated subsidiaries.

We are a manufacturer and marketer of high-quality, branded food and beverage products.

Basis of Presentation — The consolidated financial statements include our accounts and entities in which we maintain a controlling financial interest and a variable interest entity (VIE) for which we are the primary beneficiary. Intercompany transactions are eliminated in consolidation. Certain amounts in prior-year financial statements were reclassified to conform to the current-year presentation. See Note 2. Our fiscal year ends on the Sunday nearest July 31. There were 52 weeks in 2017, 2016, and 2015.

Use of Estimates — Generally accepted accounting principles require management to make estimates and assumptions that affect assets, liabilities, revenues and expenses. Actual results could differ from those estimates.

Revenue Recognition — Revenues are recognized when the earnings process is complete. This occurs when products are shipped in accordance with terms of agreements, title and risk of loss transfer to customers, collection is probable and pricing is fixed or determinable. Revenues are recognized net of provisions for returns, discounts and allowances. Certain sales promotion expenses, such as feature price discounts, in-store display incentives, cooperative advertising programs, new product introduction fees and coupon redemption costs, are classified as a reduction of sales. The recognition of costs for promotion programs involves the use of judgment related to performance and redemption estimates. Estimates are made based on historical experience and other factors. Costs are recognized either upon sale or when the incentive is offered, based on the program. Revenues are presented on a net basis for arrangements under which suppliers perform certain additional services.

Cash and Cash Equivalents — All highly liquid debt instruments purchased with a maturity of three months or less are classified as cash equivalents.

Inventories — All inventories are valued at the lower of average cost or net realizable value.

Property, Plant and Equipment — Property, plant and equipment are recorded at historical cost and are depreciated over estimated useful lives using the straight-line method. Buildings and machinery and equipment are depreciated over periods not exceeding 45 years and 20 years, respectively. Assets are evaluated for impairment when conditions indicate that the carrying value may not be recoverable. Such conditions include significant adverse changes in business climate or a plan of disposal. Repairs and maintenance are charged to expense as incurred.

Goodwill and Intangible Assets — Goodwill and intangible assets deemed to have indefinite lives are not amortized but rather are tested at least annually for impairment, or when circumstances indicate that the carrying amount of the asset may not be recoverable. Goodwill is tested for impairment at the reporting unit level. A reporting unit is an operating segment or a component of an operating segment. Goodwill is tested for impairment by either performing a qualitative evaluation or a quantitative test. The qualitative evaluation is an assessment of factors to determine whether it is more likely than not that the fair value of a reporting unit is less than its carrying amount, including goodwill. We may elect not to perform the qualitative assessment for some or all reporting units and perform a quantitative impairment test. Fair value is determined based on discounted cash flow analyses. The discounted estimates of future cash flows include significant management assumptions such as revenue growth rates, operating margins, weighted average cost of capital, and future economic and market conditions. If the carrying value of the reporting unit exceeds fair value, goodwill is considered impaired. In January 2017, the Financial Accounting Standards Board (FASB) issued revised guidance that simplifies the test for goodwill impairment, effective for fiscal years beginning after December 15, 2019, with early adoption permitted. Under the revised guidance, if a reporting unit's carrying value exceeds its fair value, an impairment charge will be recorded to reduce the reporting unit to fair value. Prior to the revised guidance, the amount of the impairment was the difference between the carrying value of the goodwill and the "implied" fair value, which was calculated as if the reporting unit had just been acquired and accounted for as a business combination.

Indefinite-lived intangible assets are tested for impairment by comparing the fair value of the asset to the carrying value. Fair value is determined based on discounted cash flow analyses that include significant management assumptions such as revenue growth rates, weighted average cost of capital, and assumed royalty rates. If the carrying value exceeds fair value, an impairment charge will be recorded to reduce the asset to fair value.

See Note 5 for information on intangible assets and impairment charges.

Derivative Financial Instruments — We use derivative financial instruments primarily for purposes of hedging exposures to fluctuations in foreign currency exchange rates, interest rates, commodities and equity-linked employee benefit obligations. We enter into these derivative contracts for periods consistent with the related underlying exposures, and the contracts do not constitute positions independent of those exposures. We do not enter into derivative contracts for speculative purposes and do not use leveraged instruments. Our derivative programs include strategies that qualify and strategies that do not qualify for hedge accounting treatment. To qualify for hedge accounting, the hedging relationship, both at inception of the hedge and on an ongoing basis, is expected to be highly effective in achieving offsetting changes in the fair value of the hedged risk during the period that the hedge is designated.

All derivatives are recognized on the balance sheet at fair value. For derivatives that qualify for hedge accounting, on the date the derivative contract is entered into, we designate the derivative as a hedge of the fair value of a recognized asset or liability or a firm commitment (fair-value hedge), a hedge of a forecasted transaction or of the variability of cash flows to be received or paid related to a recognized asset or liability (cash-flow hedge), or a hedge of a net investment in a foreign operation. Some derivatives may also be considered natural hedging instruments (changes in fair value act as economic offsets to changes in fair value of the underlying hedged item) and are not designated for hedge accounting.

Changes in the fair value of a fair-value hedge, along with the gain or loss on the underlying hedged asset or liability (including losses or gains on firm commitments), are recorded in current-period earnings. The effective portion of gains and losses on cash-flow hedges are recorded in other comprehensive income (loss), until earnings are affected by the variability of cash flows. If the hedge is no longer effective, all changes in the fair value of the derivative are included in earnings each period until the instrument matures. If a derivative is used as a hedge of a net investment in a foreign operation, its changes in fair value, to the extent effective as a hedge, are recorded in other comprehensive income (loss). Any ineffective portion of designated hedges is recognized in current-period earnings. Changes in the fair value of derivatives that are not designated for hedge accounting are recognized in current-period earnings.

Cash flows from derivative contracts are included in Net cash provided by operating activities.

Advertising Production Costs — Advertising production costs are expensed in the period that the advertisement first takes place or when a decision is made not to use an advertisement.

Research and Development Costs — The costs of research and development are expensed as incurred. Costs include expenditures for new product and manufacturing process innovation, and improvements to existing products and processes. Costs primarily consist of salaries, wages, consulting, and depreciation and maintenance of research facilities and equipment.

Income Taxes — Deferred tax assets and liabilities are recognized for the future impact of differences between the financial statement carrying amounts of assets and liabilities and their respective tax bases, as well as for operating loss and tax credit carryforwards. Deferred tax assets and liabilities are measured using enacted tax rates expected to apply to taxable income in the years in which those temporary differences are expected to be recovered or settled. The effect on deferred tax assets and liabilities of a change in tax rates is recognized in income in the period that includes the enactment date. Valuation allowances are recorded to reduce deferred tax assets when it is more likely than not that a tax benefit will not be realized.

Changes in Accounting Policy — In the first quarter of 2016, we elected to change our method of accounting for the recognition of actuarial gains and losses for defined benefit pension and postretirement plans and the calculation of expected return on pension plan assets. Historically, actuarial gains and losses associated with benefit obligations were recognized in Accumulated other comprehensive loss in the Consolidated Balance Sheets and were amortized into earnings over the remaining service life of participants to the extent that the amounts were in excess of a corridor. Under the new policy, actuarial gains and losses will be recognized immediately in our Consolidated Statements of Earnings as of the measurement date, which is our fiscal year end, or more frequently if an interim remeasurement is required. In addition, we no longer use a market-related value of plan assets, which is an average value, to determine the expected return on assets but rather use the fair value of plan assets. We believe the new policies will provide greater transparency to ongoing operating results and better reflect the impact of current market conditions on the obligations and assets. Results have been adjusted retrospectively to reflect these revisions.

2. Recent Accounting Pronouncements

In May 2014, the FASB issued revised guidance on the recognition of revenue from contracts with customers. The guidance is designed to create greater comparability for financial statement users across industries and jurisdictions. The guidance also requires enhanced disclosures. The guidance was originally effective for fiscal years, and interim periods within those years, beginning after December 15, 2016. In July 2015, the FASB decided to delay the effective date of the new revenue guidance by one year to fiscal years, and interim periods within those years, beginning after December 15, 2017. Entities will be permitted to adopt the new revenue standard early, but not before the original effective date. The guidance permits the use of either a full retrospective or modified retrospective transition method. We are currently performing a diagnostic review of our arrangements with customers across our significant businesses, including our practices of offering rebates, refunds, discounts and other price allowances, and trade and consumer promotion programs. We are evaluating our methods of estimating the amount and timing of these various forms of variable consideration. We are continuing to evaluate the impact that the new guidance will have on our consolidated financial statements, as well as which transition method we will use. We will adopt the new guidance in 2019.

In April 2015, the FASB issued guidance to clarify the accounting for fees paid by a customer in a cloud computing arrangement. The guidance is effective for fiscal years beginning after December 15, 2015, and interim periods within those years. Early adoption is permitted. The new guidance should be applied either prospectively to all arrangements entered into or materially modified after the effective date or retrospectively. In 2017, we prospectively adopted the guidance. The adoption did not have a material impact on our consolidated financial statements.

In January 2016, the FASB issued guidance that amends the recognition and measurement of financial instruments. The changes primarily affect the accounting for equity investments, financial liabilities under the fair value option, and the presentation and disclosure requirements for financial instruments. Under the new guidance, equity investments in unconsolidated entities that are not accounted for under the equity method will generally be measured at fair value through earnings. When the fair value option has been elected for financial liabilities, changes in fair value due to instrument-specific credit risk will be recognized separately in other comprehensive income. The guidance is effective for fiscal years beginning after December 15, 2017, and interim periods within those years. We are currently evaluating the impact that the new guidance will have on our consolidated financial statements.

In February 2016, the FASB issued guidance that amends accounting for leases. Under the new guidance, a lessee will recognize assets and liabilities for most leases but will recognize expenses similar to current lease accounting. The guidance is effective for fiscal years, and interim periods within those years, beginning after December 15, 2018. Early adoption is permitted. The new guidance must be adopted using a modified retrospective transition, and provides for certain practical expedients. We are currently evaluating the impact that the new guidance will have on our consolidated financial statements.

In March 2016, the FASB issued guidance that amends accounting for share-based payments, including the accounting for income taxes, forfeitures, and statutory withholding requirements, as well as classification in the statement of cash flows. The guidance is effective for fiscal years beginning after December 15, 2016, and interim periods within those years. Early adoption is permitted. We adopted the guidance in 2017. In accordance with the prospective adoption of the recognition of excess tax benefits and deficiencies in the Consolidated Statements of Earnings, we recognized a $6 tax benefit in Taxes on earnings in 2017. We elected to continue to estimate forfeitures expected to occur. In addition, we elected to adopt retrospectively the amendment to present excess tax benefits on share-based compensation as an operating activity, which resulted in a reclassification of $7 and $6 from Net cash used in financing activities to Net cash provided by operating activities in the Consolidated Statements of Cash Flows for 2016, and 2015, respectively. We also adopted retrospectively the amendment to present cash payments to tax authorities in connection with shares withheld to meet statutory tax withholding requirements as a financing activity. As a result, there was a reclassification of $21 and $18 from Net cash provided by operating activities to Net cash used in financing activities in the Consolidated Statements of Cash Flows for 2016, and 2015, respectively.

In August 2016, the FASB issued guidance on the classification of certain cash receipts and payments in the statement of cash flows. The guidance is effective for fiscal years beginning after December 15, 2017, and interim periods within those years. Early adoption is permitted. The guidance must be applied retrospectively to all periods presented but may be applied prospectively if retrospective application would be impracticable. We are currently evaluating the impact that the new guidance will have on our consolidated financial statements.

In October 2016, the FASB issued guidance on tax accounting for intra-entity asset transfers. Under current guidance, the tax effects of intra-entity asset transfers (intercompany sales) are deferred until the transferred asset is sold to a third party or otherwise recognized. The new guidance requires companies to account for the income tax effects on intercompany transfers of assets other than inventory when the transfer occurs. The new guidance is effective for fiscal years beginning after December 15, 2017, and interim periods within those years. Early adoption is permitted in the first interim period of a fiscal year. The modified retrospective approach is required upon adoption, with a cumulative-effect adjustment recorded in retained earnings as of the beginning of the period of adoption. We are currently evaluating the impact that the new guidance will have on our consolidated financial statements.

In January 2017, the FASB issued guidance that revises the definition of a business to assist entities with evaluating when a set of transferred assets and activities is a business. The guidance requires an entity to evaluate if substantially all of the fair value of the gross assets acquired is concentrated in a single identifiable asset or a group of similar identifiable assets. If this threshold is met, the set of transferred assets and activities is not a business. If it is not met, the entity then evaluates whether the set meets the requirement that a business include, at a minimum, an input and a substantive process that together significantly contribute to the ability to create outputs. The guidance is effective for fiscal years beginning after December 15, 2017, and interim periods within those years. Early adoption is permitted. We will prospectively apply the guidance to applicable transactions.

In January 2017, the FASB issued guidance that simplifies the test for goodwill impairment. Under the revised guidance, if a reporting unit's carrying amount exceeds its fair value, an entity will record an impairment charge to reduce the reporting unit to fair value. The impairment charge will be limited to the amount of goodwill allocated to that reporting unit. The revised guidance eliminates the current requirement to determine the fair value of individual assets and liabilities of a reporting unit to measure the goodwill impairment. The guidance is effective for fiscal years beginning after December 15, 2019, and interim periods within those years. Early adoption is permitted. We elected to early adopt the guidance in the fourth quarter 2017. The adoption did not have an impact on our consolidated financial statements.

In March 2017, the FASB issued guidance that improves the presentation of net periodic pension cost and net periodic postretirement benefit cost. Under the revised guidance, the service cost component of benefit cost is classified in the same line item or items as other compensation costs arising from services rendered by the pertinent employees during the period. The other components of net benefit cost (such as interest expense, return on assets, amortization of prior service credit, actuarial gains and losses, settlements and curtailments) are required to be presented in the income statement separately from the service cost component. The guidance also allows only the service cost component to be eligible for capitalization when applicable (for example, as a cost of internally manufactured inventory). The guidance should be applied retrospectively for the presentation of the service cost component and the other components of benefit cost in the income statement, and applied prospectively on and after the effective date for the capitalization of the service cost component. The guidance is effective for fiscal years beginning after December 15, 2017, and interim periods within those years. Early adoption is permitted. We plan to adopt the new guidance in the first quarter of 2018. If net periodic benefit cost was presented in accordance with the new guidance, the estimated impact on classification of expense is as follows:

Increase / (decrease) in expense	2017	2016	2015
Cost of products sold	$ 134	$ (148)	$ (42)
Marketing and selling expenses	$ 38	$ (41)	$ (12)
Administrative expenses	$ 62	$ (66)	$ (21)
Research and development expenses	$ 13	$ (19)	$ (8)
Other expenses / (income)	$ (247)	$ 274	$ 83

In May 2017, the FASB issued guidance that clarifies when changes to the terms or conditions of a share-based payment award must be accounted for as modifications. Under the new guidance, modification accounting is required only if the value, the vesting conditions, or the classification of the award (as equity or liability) changes as a result of the change in terms or conditions. The guidance is effective prospectively for fiscal years beginning after December 15, 2017. Early adoption is permitted. We will apply the guidance in evaluating future changes to terms or conditions of share-based payment awards.

In August 2017, the FASB issued guidance that amends hedge accounting. Under the new guidance, more hedging strategies will be eligible for hedge accounting and the application of hedge accounting is simplified. The new guidance amends presentation and disclosure requirements, and how effectiveness is assessed. The guidance is effective for fiscal years beginning after December 15, 2018, and interim periods within those years. Early adoption is permitted. We are currently evaluating the impact that the new guidance will have on our consolidated financial statements.

3. Acquisitions

On July 6, 2017, we entered into an agreement to acquire Pacific Foods of Oregon, Inc. (Pacific Foods) for $700, subject to customary purchase price adjustments related to the amount of Pacific Foods' cash, debt, working capital and transaction expenses. The closing of the transaction is subject to customary closing conditions and termination rights. The agreement provides that if we fail to close the transaction when all conditions to closing have been satisfied or if we are in breach of the agreement, we will be required to pay Pacific Foods a $50 termination fee. On August 21, 2017, the estate of a former Pacific Foods shareholder, Edward C. Lynch, filed a lawsuit against Pacific Foods and certain of its directors, among others, seeking in excess of $250 in damages. Because of the impediment that the lawsuit creates to closing, on September 27, 2017, we noticed Pacific Foods that it has 60 days under the terms of the agreement to resolve the issues arising from the suit if the transaction is to close. After the 60-day period, we may in our sole discretion extend the cure period or terminate the agreement. We do not believe a termination of the agreement under these circumstances will result in any termination fee payable by us.

On June 29, 2015, we completed the acquisition of the assets of Garden Fresh Gourmet for $232. Garden Fresh Gourmet is a provider of refrigerated salsa, hummus, dips and tortilla chips.

The contribution of the Garden Fresh Gourmet acquisition to Net sales and Net earnings from June 29, 2015, through August 2, 2015 was not material.

The following unaudited summary information is presented on a consolidated pro forma basis as if the Garden Fresh Gourmet acquisition had occurred on July 29, 2013:

	2015
Net sales	$ 8,174
Net earnings attributable to Campbell Soup Company	$ 668
Net earnings per share attributable to Campbell Soup Company - assuming dilution	$ 2.13

The pro forma amounts include additional interest expense on the debt issued to finance the purchase, amortization and depreciation expense based on the estimated fair value and useful lives of intangible assets and plant assets, and related tax effects. The pro forma results are not necessarily indicative of the combined results had the Garden Fresh Gourmet acquisition been completed on July 29, 2013, nor are they indicative of future combined results.

4. **Accumulated Other Comprehensive Income (Loss)**

The components of Accumulated other comprehensive income (loss) consisted of the following:

	Foreign Currency Translation Adjustments[1]	Gains (Losses) on Cash Flow Hedges[2]	Pension and Postretirement Benefit Plan Adjustments[3]	Total Accumulated Comprehensive Income (Loss)
Balance at August 3, 2014	$ 144	$ (3)	$ 4	$ 145
Other comprehensive income (loss) before reclassifications	(310)	(2)	—	(312)
Amounts reclassified from accumulated other comprehensive income (loss)	—	—	(1)	(1)
Net current-period other comprehensive income (loss)	(310)	(2)	(1)	(313)
Balance at August 2, 2015	$ (166)	$ (5)	$ 3	$ (168)
Other comprehensive income (loss) before reclassifications	42	(29)	59	72
Amounts reclassified from accumulated other comprehensive income (loss)	—	(7)	(1)	(8)
Net current-period other comprehensive income (loss)	42	(36)	58	64
Balance at July 31, 2016	$ (124)	$ (41)	$ 61	$ (104)
Other comprehensive income (loss) before reclassifications	40	12	8	60
Amounts reclassified from accumulated other comprehensive income (loss)	—	7	(16)	(9)
Net current-period other comprehensive income (loss)	40	19	(8)	51
Balance at July 30, 2017	$ (84)	$ (22)	$ 53	$ (53)

---

[1] Included a tax expense of $6 as of July 30, 2017, July 31, 2016, and August 2, 2015, and $7 as of August 3, 2014.

[2] Included a tax benefit of $12 as of July 30, 2017, $23 as of July 31, 2016, $5 as of August 2, 2015, and $1 as of August 3, 2014.

[3] Included a tax expense of $30 as of July 30, 2017, $35 as of July 31, 2016, $1 as of August 2, 2015, and $2 as of August 3, 2014.

Amounts related to noncontrolling interests were not material.

The amounts reclassified from Accumulated other comprehensive income (loss) consisted of the following:

Details about Accumulated Other Comprehensive Income (Loss) Components	2017	2016	2015	Location of (Gain) Loss Recognized in Earnings
(Gains) losses on cash flow hedges:				
Foreign exchange forward contracts	$ 6	$ (11)	$ (4)	Cost of products sold
Foreign exchange forward contracts	1	(2)	(1)	Other expenses / (income)
Forward starting interest rate swaps	4	4	4	Interest expense
Total before tax	11	(9)	(1)	
Tax expense (benefit)	(4)	2	1	
(Gain) loss, net of tax	$ 7	$ (7)	$ —	
Pension and postretirement benefit adjustments:				
Prior service credit	$ (25)	$ (1)	$ (2) [1]	
Tax expense (benefit)	9	—	1	
(Gain) loss, net of tax	$ (16)	$ (1)	$ (1)	

---

[1] This is included in the components of net periodic benefit costs (see Note 10 for additional details).

5. Goodwill and Intangible Assets

Goodwill

The following table shows the changes in the carrying amount of goodwill by business segment:

	Americas Simple Meals and Beverages	Global Biscuits and Snacks	Campbell Fresh	Total
Balance at August 2, 2015	$ 775	$ 732	$ 837	$ 2,344
Impairment charges	—	—	(106)	(106)
Foreign currency translation adjustment	—	25	—	25
Net balance at July 31, 2016[1]	$ 775	$ 757	$ 731	$ 2,263
Impairment charges	—	—	**(191)**	**(191)**
Foreign currency translation adjustment	**5**	**38**	—	**43**
Net balance at July 30, 2017[1]	$ **780**	$ **795**	$ **540**	$ **2,115**

[1]   The balance of goodwill is reflected net of accumulated impairment charges of $297 as of July 30, 2017 and $106 as of July 31, 2016, respectively.

In the fourth quarter of 2016, as part of our annual review of intangible assets, an impairment charge of $106 was recorded on goodwill for the Bolthouse Farms carrot and carrot ingredients reporting unit within the Campbell Fresh segment. In 2016, carrot performance primarily reflected the adverse impact of weather conditions on crop yields, and execution issues in response to those conditions, which led to customer dissatisfaction, a loss of business, and higher carrot costs in the second half of the year. The impairment was attributable to a decline in profitability in the second half of 2016 and a revised outlook for the business, with reduced expectations for sales, operating margins, and discounted cash flows.

During the second quarter of 2017, sales and operating profit performance for the Bolthouse Farms carrot and carrot ingredients reporting unit were well below our revised expectations due to difficulty with regaining market share lost during 2016 and higher carrot costs from the adverse impact of heavy rains on crop yields. During the quarter, we also lowered our forecast for sales and earnings for the reporting unit for the second half of 2017 based on revised market share recovery expectations and the continuing effect of unusual weather conditions on carrot costs. In addition, as part of a strategic review initiated by a new leadership team of Campbell Fresh during the second quarter, we decided to reduce emphasis on growing sales of carrot ingredients, which are a by-product of the manufacturing process, and to manage carrots sold at retail for modest sales growth consistent with the category while improving profitability. Accordingly, we reduced our expectations for recovery of retail carrot market share. As a consequence of current-year performance and the strategic review, we lowered our sales outlook for future fiscal years. We also lowered our average margin expectations due in part to cost volatility, which has been higher than expected. Based upon the business performance in the second quarter of 2017, our reduced near-term outlook, and reduced expectations for sales, operating margins and discounted cash flows, we performed an interim goodwill impairment assessment as of December 31, 2016, which resulted in a $127 impairment charge to reduce the carrying amount to $75. The updated cash flow projections include expectations that operating margins will improve from reduced levels in 2016 and 2017.

Garden Fresh Gourmet was acquired in June 2015 and is a reporting unit within the Campbell Fresh segment. During 2017, sales and operating profit performance for Garden Fresh Gourmet were well below expectations, and we lowered our outlook for the second half of 2017 due to customer losses and failure to meet product distribution goals. We expected to expand distribution of salsa beyond our concentration in the Midwest region, however this proved to be challenging as differentiated recipes are required to meet taste profiles in other parts of the country. In addition, as part of a strategic review initiated by a new leadership team of Campbell Fresh during the second quarter, we lowered our distribution and category growth expectations and, therefore, future sales outlook. Based upon the business performance in 2017, our reduced near-term outlook, and reduced expectations for sales, operating margins and discounted cash flows, we performed an interim goodwill impairment assessment on this reporting unit as of December 31, 2016, which resulted in a $64 impairment charge to reduce the carrying amount to $52. The updated cash flow projections include expectations that we will build distribution in the U.S., operating margins will expand partly driven by the benefits from further integration, and sales growth rates will exceed the company's overall sales growth rates.

The impairment charges were recorded in Other expenses / (income) in the Consolidated Statements of Earnings.

Intangible Assets

The following table sets forth balance sheet information for intangible assets, excluding goodwill, subject to amortization and intangible assets not subject to amortization:

Intangible Assets	2017	2016
Amortizable intangible assets		
Customer relationships	$ 223	$ 222
Technology	40	40
Other	35	35
Total gross amortizable intangible assets.	$ 298	$ 297
Accumulated amortization.	(92)	(72)
Total net amortizable intangible assets	$ 206	$ 225
Non-amortizable intangible assets		
Trademarks	912	927
Total net intangible assets.	$ 1,118	$ 1,152

Non-amortizable intangible assets consist of trademarks, which include *Bolthouse Farms, Pace, Plum, Kjeldsens, Garden Fresh Gourmet* and *Royal Dansk*. Other amortizable intangible assets consist of recipes, patents, trademarks and distributor relationships.

Amortization of intangible assets was $19 for 2017, $20 for 2016 and $17 for 2015. Amortization expense for the next 5 years is estimated to be $16 in 2018 and 2019, and $15 in 2020 through 2022. Asset useful lives range from 5 to 20 years.

In the fourth quarter of 2016, as part of our annual review of intangible assets, an impairment charge of $35 was recognized on the Bolthouse Farms carrot and carrot ingredients reporting unit trademark as a result of the factors previously described. Due to the factors previously described, we performed an interim impairment assessment as of December 31, 2016, which resulted in a $20 impairment charge on the trademark to reduce the carrying amount to $48.

Due to the factors previously described, we also performed an interim impairment assessment as of December 31, 2016, on the trademark in the Garden Fresh Gourmet reporting unit, which resulted in a $1 impairment charge to reduce the carrying amount to $37.

As part of our annual review of intangible assets, an impairment charge of $6 was recognized in the fourth quarter of 2015 related to minor trademarks used in the Global Biscuits and Snacks segment. The trademarks were determined to be impaired as a result of a decrease in the fair value of the brands, resulting from reduced expectations for future sales and discontinued cash flows.

The impairment charges were recorded in Other expenses / (income) in the Consolidated Statements of Earnings.

The estimates of future cash flows used in determining the fair value of goodwill and intangible assets involve significant management judgment and are based upon assumptions about expected future operating performance, economic conditions, market conditions and cost of capital. Inherent in estimating the future cash flows are uncertainties beyond our control, such as changes in capital markets. The actual cash flows could differ materially from management's estimates due to changes in business conditions, operating performance and economic conditions.

6. **Business and Geographic Segment Information**

We manage our businesses in three segments focused mainly on product categories. The segments are:

- Americas Simple Meals and Beverages segment includes the retail and food service businesses in the U.S., Canada and Latin America. The segment includes the following products: *Campbell's* condensed and ready-to-serve soups; *Swanson* broth and stocks; *Prego* pasta sauces; *Pace* Mexican sauces; *Campbell's* gravies, pasta, beans and dinner sauces; *Swanson* canned poultry; *Plum* food and snacks; *V8* juices and beverages; and *Campbell's* tomato juice;

- Global Biscuits and Snacks segment includes Pepperidge Farm cookies, crackers, bakery and frozen products in U.S. retail; Arnott's biscuits in Australia and Asia Pacific; and Kelsen cookies globally. The segment also includes the simple meals and shelf-stable beverages business in Australia and Asia Pacific; and

- Campbell Fresh segment includes Bolthouse Farms fresh carrots, carrot ingredients, refrigerated beverages and refrigerated salad dressings; Garden Fresh Gourmet salsa, hummus, dips and tortilla chips; and the U.S. refrigerated soup business.

Beginning in 2018, the business in Latin America will be managed as part of the Global Biscuits and Snacks segment.

We evaluate segment performance before interest, taxes and costs associated with restructuring activities. Unrealized gains and losses on commodity hedging activities are excluded from segment operating earnings and are recorded in Corporate as these open positions represent hedges of future purchases. Upon closing of the contracts, the realized gain or loss is transferred to segment operating earnings, which allows the segments to reflect the economic effects of the hedge without exposure to quarterly volatility of unrealized gains and losses. Only the service cost component of pension and postretirement expense is allocated to segments. All other components of expense, including interest cost, expected return on assets, amortization of prior service credits and recognized actuarial gains and losses are reflected in Corporate and not included in segment operating results. Asset information by segment is not discretely maintained for internal reporting or used in evaluating performance. Therefore, only geographic segment asset information is provided.

Our largest customer, Wal-Mart Stores, Inc. and its affiliates, accounted for approximately 20% of consolidated net sales in 2017, 2016 and 2015. All of our reportable segments sold products to Wal-Mart Stores, Inc. or its affiliates.

Net sales		2017		2016		2015
Americas Simple Meals and Beverages	$	4,325	$	4,380	$	4,483
Global Biscuits and Snacks		2,598		2,564		2,631
Campbell Fresh		967		1,017		968
Total	$	7,890	$	7,961	$	8,082

Earnings before interest and taxes		2017		2016		2015
Americas Simple Meals and Beverages	$	1,120	$	1,069	$	948
Global Biscuits and Snacks		454		422		383
Campbell Fresh		(9)		60		61
Corporate[1]		(147)		(560)		(236)
Restructuring charges[2]		(18)		(31)		(102)
Total	$	1,400	$	960	$	1,054

Depreciation and amortization		2017		2016		2015
Americas Simple Meals and Beverages	$	118	$	117	$	123
Global Biscuits and Snacks		98		96		94
Campbell Fresh		83		77		70
Corporate[3]		19		18		16
Total	$	318	$	308	$	303

Capital expenditures		2017		2016		2015
Americas Simple Meals and Beverages	$	117	$	105	$	137
Global Biscuits and Snacks		127		122		137
Campbell Fresh		47		74		82
Corporate[3]		47		40		24
Total	$	338	$	341	$	380

---

[1] Represents unallocated items. Pension and postretirement benefit mark-to-market adjustments are included in Corporate. There were gains of $178 in 2017, and losses of $313 and $138 in 2016 and 2015, respectively. Costs related to the implementation of our new organizational structure and cost savings initiatives were $40, $47 and $22 in 2017, 2016 and 2015, respectively. Impairment charges of $212 on the intangible assets of the Bolthouse Farms carrot and carrot ingredients reporting unit and the Garden Fresh Gourmet reporting unit were included in 2017 and an impairment charge of $141 on the intangible assets of the Bolthouse Farms carrot and carrot ingredients reporting unit was included in 2016. See Note 5 for information on the impairment charges. A gain of $25 from a settlement of a claim related to the Kelsen acquisition was also included in 2016.

(2)   See Note 7 for additional information.
(3)   Represents primarily corporate offices.

Our global net sales based on product categories are as follows:

	2017	2016	2015
Net sales			
Soup	$ 2,673	$ 2,690	$ 2,798
Baked snacks	2,511	2,479	2,502
Other simple meals	1,698	1,702	1,648
Beverages	1,008	1,090	1,134
Total	$ 7,890	$ 7,961	$ 8,082

Soup includes various soup, broths and stock products. Baked Snacks include cookies, crackers, biscuits and other baked products. Other simple meals include sauces, carrot products, refrigerated salad dressings, refrigerated salsa, hummus, dips and Plum foods and snacks.

Geographic Area Information

Information about operations in different geographic areas is as follows:

	2017	2016	2015
Net sales			
United States	$ 6,357	$ 6,437	$ 6,400
Australia	610	590	646
Other countries	923	934	1,036
Total	$ 7,890	$ 7,961	$ 8,082

	2017	2016	2015
Long-lived assets			
United States	$ 1,987	$ 1,967	$ 1,942
Australia	265	242	232
Other countries	202	198	173
Total	$ 2,454	$ 2,407	$ 2,347

7.   Restructuring Charges and Cost Savings Initiatives

2015 Initiatives

On January 29, 2015, we announced plans to implement a new enterprise design focused mainly on product categories. Under the new structure, which we fully implemented at the beginning of 2016, our businesses are organized in the following divisions: Americas Simple Meals and Beverages, Global Biscuits and Snacks, and Campbell Fresh.

In support of the new structure, we designed and implemented a new Integrated Global Services organization to deliver shared services across the company. We also streamlined our organizational structure, implemented an initiative to reduce overhead across the organization and are pursuing other initiatives to reduce costs and increase effectiveness, such as adopting zero-based budgeting over time. As part of these initiatives, we commenced a voluntary employee separation program available to certain U.S.-based salaried employees nearing retirement who met age, length-of-service and business unit/function criteria. A total of 471 employees elected the program. The electing employees remained with us through at least July 31, 2015, with some remaining beyond that date.

In February 2017, we announced that we are expanding these cost savings initiatives by further optimizing our supply chain network, primarily in North America, continuing to evolve our operating model to drive efficiencies, and more fully integrating our recent acquisitions. We have extended the time horizon for the initiatives from 2018 to 2020. Cost estimates for these expanded initiatives, as well as timing for certain activities, are being developed.

A summary of the restructuring charges we recorded and charges incurred in Administrative expenses and Cost of products sold related to the implementation of the new organizational structure and costs savings initiatives is as follows:

	2017	2016	2015
Restructuring charges	$ 18	$ 35	$ 102
Administrative expenses	36	47	22
Cost of products sold	4	—	—
Total pre-tax charges	$ 58	$ 82	$ 124

A summary of the pre-tax costs associated with the initiatives is as follows:

	Recognized as of July 30, 2017
Severance pay and benefits	$ 135
Asset impairment/accelerated depreciation	12
Implementation costs and other related costs	117
Total	$ 264

The total estimated pre-tax costs for actions that have been identified are approximately $380 to $420. We expect to incur substantially all of the costs through 2019. This estimate will be updated as costs for the expanded initiatives are developed.

We expect the costs for actions that have been identified to date to consist of the following: approximately $135 in severance pay and benefits; approximately $20 in asset impairment and accelerated depreciation; and approximately $225 to $265 in implementation costs and other related costs. We expect these pre-tax costs to be associated with our segments as follows: Americas Simple Meals and Beverages - approximately 30%; Global Biscuits and Snacks - approximately 38%; Campbell Fresh - approximately 4%; and Corporate - approximately 28%.

Of the aggregate $380 to $420 of pre-tax costs identified to date, we expect approximately $350 to $390 will be cash expenditures. In addition, we expect to invest approximately $180 in capital expenditures through 2019 primarily related to the construction of a network of distribution centers for our U.S. thermal plants and insourcing of manufacturing for certain simple meal products, of which we invested approximately $10 as of July 30, 2017.

A summary of the restructuring activity and related reserves associated with the initiatives at July 30, 2017, is as follows:

	Severance Pay and Benefits	Other Restructuring Costs	Non-Cash Benefits[4]	Implementation Costs and Other Related Costs[5]	Asset Impairment/ Accelerated Depreciation	Total Charges
Accrued balance at August 3, 2014	$ —	$ —				
2015 charges	87	8	7	22	—	$ 124
2015 cash payments	(1)	—				
Foreign currency translation adjustment	(1)	—				
Accrued balance at August 2, 2015[1]	$ 85	$ 8				
2016 charges	34	1	—	47	—	$ 82
2016 cash payments	(46)	(9)				
Accrued balance at July 31, 2016[2]	$ 73	$ —				
2017 charges	7	—	—	39	12	$ 58
2017 cash payments	(54)	—				
Accrued balance at July 30, 2017[3]	$ 26	$ —				

[1] Includes $45 of severance pay and benefits recorded in Other liabilities in the Consolidated Balance Sheet.
[2] Includes $17 of severance pay and benefits recorded in Other liabilities in the Consolidated Balance Sheet.
[3] Includes $2 of severance pay and benefits recorded in Other liabilities in the Consolidated Balance Sheet.
[4] Represents postretirement and pension curtailment costs. See Note 10.
[5] Includes other costs recognized as incurred that are not reflected in the restructuring reserve in the Consolidated Balance Sheet. The costs are included in Administrative expenses and Cost of products sold in the Consolidated Statements of Earnings.

Segment operating results do not include restructuring charges, implementation costs and other related costs because we evaluate segment performance excluding such charges. A summary of the pre-tax costs associated with segments is as follows:

	2017		Costs Incurred to Date
Americas Simple Meals and Beverages	$	21	$ 92
Global Biscuits and Snacks		12	78
Campbell Fresh		4	6
Corporate		21	88
Total	$	58	$ 264

2014 Initiatives

In 2014, we implemented initiatives to reduce overhead across the organization, restructure manufacturing and streamline operations for our soup and broth business in China and improve supply chain efficiency in Australia.

In 2016, we recorded a reduction to restructuring charges of $4 related to the 2014 initiatives. As of July 31, 2016, we incurred substantially all of the costs related to the 2014 initiatives. A summary of the pre-tax costs associated with the 2014 initiatives is as follows:

	Total Program[1]		Change in Estimate		Recognized as of July 31, 2016
Severance pay and benefits	$	41	$ (4)	$	37
Asset impairment		12	—		12
Other exit costs		1	—		1
Total	$	54	$ (4)	$	50

[1] Recognized as of August 2, 2015.

8. Earnings per Share (EPS)

For the periods presented in the Consolidated Statements of Earnings, the calculations of basic EPS and EPS assuming dilution vary in that the weighted average shares outstanding assuming dilution include the incremental effect of stock options and other share-based payment awards, except when such effect would be antidilutive. The earnings per share calculation for 2017 and 2016 excludes less than 1 million stock options that would have been antidilutive. There were no antidilutive stock options in 2015.

9. Noncontrolling Interests

We own a 60% controlling interest in a joint venture formed with Swire Pacific Limited to support our soup and broth business in China. We contributed cash of $14 and the joint venture partner contributed cash of $9 in 2015.

We own a 70% controlling interest in a Malaysian food products manufacturing company.

We also own a 99.8% interest in Acre Venture Partners, L.P. (Acre), a limited partnership formed to make venture capital investments in innovative new companies in food and food-related industries. See also Note 14.

The noncontrolling interests' share in the net earnings (loss) was included in Net earnings (loss) attributable to noncontrolling interests in the Consolidated Statements of Earnings. The noncontrolling interests in these entities were included in Total equity in the Consolidated Balance Sheets and Consolidated Statements of Equity.

10. Pension and Postretirement Benefits

Pension Benefits — We sponsor a number of noncontributory defined benefit pension plans to provide retirement benefits to all eligible U.S. and non-U.S. employees. The benefits provided under these plans are based primarily on years of service and compensation levels. Benefits are paid from funds previously provided to trustees and insurance companies or are paid directly by us from general funds. In 1999, we implemented significant amendments to certain U.S. pension plans. Under a new formula, retirement benefits are determined based on percentages of annual pay and age. To minimize the impact of converting to the new formula, service and earnings credit continued to accrue through the year 2014 for certain active employees participating in the plans under the old formula prior to the amendments. Employees will receive the benefit from either the new or old formula, whichever is higher. Benefits become vested upon the completion of three years of service. Effective as of January 1, 2011, our

U.S. pension plans were amended so that employees hired or rehired on or after that date and who are not covered by collective bargaining agreements will not be eligible to participate in the plans.

Postretirement Benefits — We provide postretirement benefits, including health care and life insurance, to substantially all retired U.S. employees and their dependents. We established retiree medical account benefits for eligible U.S. retirees. The accounts were intended to provide reimbursement for eligible health care expenses on a tax-favored basis. Effective as of January 1, 2011, the retirement medical program was amended to eliminate the retiree medical account benefit for employees not covered by collective bargaining agreements. To preserve the benefit for employees close to retirement age, the retiree medical account will be available to employees who were at least age 50 with at least 10 years of service as of December 31, 2010, and who satisfy the other eligibility requirements for the retiree medical program. In July 2016, the retirement medical program was amended and effective as of January 1, 2017, we no longer sponsor our own medical coverage for certain Medicare-eligible retirees. Instead, we offer these Medicare-eligible retirees access to health care coverage through a private exchange and offer a health reimbursement account to subsidize benefits for a select group of such retirees. In July 2017, the retirement medical program was once again amended and beginning on January 1, 2018, we will no longer sponsor our own medical coverage for certain Medicare-eligible retirees covered by one of our collective bargaining agreements. Instead, we will offer these Medicare-eligible retirees access to health care coverage through a private exchange and offer a health reimbursement account to subsidize benefits for a select group of such retirees.

We use the fiscal year end as the measurement date for the benefit plans.

Components of net benefit expense (income) were as follows:

	Pension		
	2017	2016	2015
Service cost	$ 26	$ 26	$ 28
Interest cost	86	98	105
Expected return on plan assets	(144)	(147)	(173)
Amortization of prior service credit	—	—	(1)
Recognized net actuarial (gain) loss	(198)	302	136
Curtailment loss	—	—	1
Net periodic benefit expense (income)	$ (230)	$ 279	$ 96

The curtailment loss of $1 in 2015 was related to a voluntary employee separation program and was included in Restructuring charges. See also Note 7.

	Postretirement		
	2017	2016	2015
Service cost	$ 1	$ 1	$ 2
Interest cost	10	15	15
Amortization of prior service credit	(25)	(1)	(1)
Recognized net actuarial (gain) loss	(14)	23	7
Curtailment loss	—	—	6
Net periodic benefit expense (income)	$ (28)	$ 38	$ 29

The curtailment loss of $6 in 2015 was related to a voluntary employee separation program and was included in Restructuring charges. See also Note 7.

The estimated prior service credit that will be amortized from Accumulated other comprehensive loss into net periodic postretirement expense during 2018 is $27. The prior service credit is primarily related to the amendments in July 2016 and July 2017.

Change in benefit obligation:

	Pension		Postretirement	
	2017	2016	2017	2016
Obligation at beginning of year	$ 2,626	$ 2,569	$ 313	$ 392
Service cost	26	26	1	1
Interest cost	86	98	10	15
Actuarial (gain) loss	(134)	210	(14)	23
Participant contributions	—	—	1	1
Plan amendments	—	—	(12)	(93)
Benefits paid	(164)	(116)	(26)	(30)
Settlements	—	(160)	—	—
Medicare subsidies	—	—	3	4
Other	(3)	(6)	—	—
Foreign currency adjustment	13	5	—	—
Benefit obligation at end of year	$ 2,450	$ 2,626	$ 276	$ 313

Change in the fair value of pension plan assets:

	2017	2016
Fair value at beginning of year	$ 2,111	$ 2,316
Actual return on plan assets	208	54
Employer contributions	5	2
Benefits paid	(154)	(106)
Settlements	—	(160)
Foreign currency adjustment	13	5
Fair value at end of year	$ 2,183	$ 2,111

Net amounts recognized in the Consolidated Balance Sheets:

	Pension		Postretirement	
	2017	2016	2017	2016
Other assets	$ 8	$ —	$ —	$ —
Accrued liabilities	14	14	29	28
Other liabilities	261	501	247	285
Net amounts recognized	$ 267	$ 515	$ 276	$ 313

Amounts recognized in accumulated other comprehensive income (loss) consist of:	Postretirement	
	2017	2016
Prior service credit	$ 83	$ 96

The change in amounts recognized in accumulated other comprehensive income (loss) associated with postretirement benefits was due to the plan amendments in July 2016 and July 2017, net of amortization.

The following table provides information for pension plans with accumulated benefit obligations in excess of plan assets:

	2017	2016
Projected benefit obligation	$ 2,270	$ 2,434
Accumulated benefit obligation	$ 2,232	$ 2,385
Fair value of plan assets	$ 1,995	$ 1,933

The accumulated benefit obligation for all pension plans was $2,399 at July 30, 2017, and $2,557 at July 31, 2016.

Weighted-average assumptions used to determine benefit obligations at the end of the year:

	Pension		Postretirement	
	2017	2016	2017	2016
Discount rate......................................	**3.74%**	3.39%	**3.45%**	3.20%
Rate of compensation increase	**3.24%**	3.25%	**3.25%**	3.25%

Weighted-average assumptions used to determine net periodic benefit cost for the years ended:

	Pension		
	2017	2016	2015
Discount rate...	**3.39%**	4.19%	4.33%
Expected return on plan assets	**7.09%**	7.35%	7.62%
Rate of compensation increase....................................	**3.25%**	3.29%	3.30%

The discount rate is established as of our fiscal year-end measurement date. In establishing the discount rate, we review published market indices of high-quality debt securities, adjusted as appropriate for duration. In addition, independent actuaries apply high-quality bond yield curves to the expected benefit payments of the plans. The expected return on plan assets is a long-term assumption based upon historical experience and expected future performance, considering our current and projected investment mix. This estimate is based on an estimate of future inflation, long-term projected real returns for each asset class, and a premium for active management.

The discount rate used to determine net periodic postretirement expense was 3.20% in 2017, and 4.00% in 2016 and 2015.

Assumed health care cost trend rates at the end of the year:

	2017	2016
Health care cost trend rate assumed for next year	**7.25%**	7.25%
Rate to which the cost trend rate is assumed to decline (ultimate trend rate)	**4.50%**	4.50%
Year that the rate reaches the ultimate trend rate.....................................	**2023**	2022

A one-percentage-point change in assumed health care costs would have the following effects on 2017 reported amounts:

	Increase	Decrease
Effect on service and interest cost	$ —	$ —
Effect on the 2017 accumulated benefit obligation	$ 3	$ (3)

Pension Plan Assets

The fundamental goal underlying the investment policy is to ensure that the assets of the plans are invested in a prudent manner to meet the obligations of the plans as these obligations come due. The primary investment objectives include providing a total return which will promote the goal of benefit security by attaining an appropriate ratio of plan assets to plan obligations, to provide for real asset growth while also tracking plan obligations, to diversify investments across and within asset classes, to reduce the impact of losses in single investments, and to follow investment practices that comply with applicable laws and regulations.

The primary policy objectives will be met by investing assets to achieve a reasonable tradeoff between return and risk relative to plan obligations. This includes investing a portion of the assets in funds selected in part to hedge the interest rate sensitivity to plan obligations.

The portfolio includes investments in the following asset classes: fixed income, equity, real estate and alternatives. Fixed income will provide a moderate expected return and partially hedge the exposure to interest rate risk of the plans' obligations. Equities are used for their high expected return. Additional asset classes are used to provide diversification.

Asset allocation is monitored on an ongoing basis relative to the established asset class targets. The interaction between plan assets and benefit obligations is periodically studied to assist in the establishment of strategic asset allocation targets. The investment policy permits variances from the targets within certain parameters. Asset rebalancing occurs when the underlying asset class allocations move outside these parameters, at which time the asset allocation is rebalanced back to the policy target weight.

Our year-end pension plan weighted-average asset allocations by category were:

	Strategic Target	2017	2016
Equity securities	47%	**48%**	51%
Debt securities	40%	**40%**	35%
Real estate and other	13%	**12%**	14%
Total	100%	**100%**	100%

Pension plan assets are categorized based on the following fair value hierarchy:

- Level 1: Observable inputs that reflect quoted prices (unadjusted) for identical assets or liabilities in active markets.

- Level 2: Inputs other than quoted prices included in Level 1 that are observable for the asset or liability through corroboration with observable market data.

- Level 3: Unobservable inputs, which are valued based on our estimates of assumptions that market participants would use in pricing the asset or liability.

The following table presents our pension plan assets by asset category at July 30, 2017, and July 31, 2016:

	Fair Value as of July 30, 2017	Fair Value Measurements at July 30, 2017 Using Fair Value Hierarchy			Fair Value as of July 31, 2016	Fair Value Measurements at July 31, 2016 Using Fair Value Hierarchy		
		Level 1	Level 2	Level 3		Level 1	Level 2	Level 3
Short-term investments....	$ 46	$ 35	$ 11	$ —	$ 43	$ 41	$ 2	$ —
Equities:								
U.S..............	338	338	—	—	349	349	—	—
Non-U.S...........	290	290	—	—	273	273	—	—
Corporate bonds:								
U.S..............	537	—	537	—	469	—	469	—
Non-U.S...........	123	—	123	—	98	—	98	—
Government and agency bonds:								
U.S..............	60	—	60	—	49	—	49	—
Non-U.S...........	31	—	31	—	29	—	29	—
Municipal bonds........	58	—	58	—	67	—	67	—
Mortgage and asset backed securities...........	8	—	8	—	7	—	7	—
Real estate...........	17	10	—	7	19	13	—	6
Hedge funds..........	38	—	—	38	45	—	—	45
Derivative assets.......	9	—	9	—	6	—	6	—
Derivative liabilities.....	(10)	—	(10)	—	(7)	—	(7)	—
Total assets at fair value...	$ 1,545	$ 673	$ 827	$ 45	$ 1,447	$ 676	$ 720	$ 51
Investments measured at net asset value:								
Short-term investments	31				20			
Commingled funds:								
Equities...........	332				309			
Fixed income	30				31			
Blended...........	86				79			
Real estate..........	84				108			
Hedge funds	103				144			
Total investments measured at net asset value:	666				691			
Other items to reconcile to fair value of plan assets..	(28)				(27)			
Total pension plan assets at fair value............	$ 2,183				$ 2,111			

Short-term investments — Investments include cash and cash equivalents, and various short-term debt instruments and short-term investment funds. Institutional short-term investment vehicles valued daily are classified as Level 1 at cost which approximates market value. Short-term debt instruments are classified at Level 2 and are valued based on bid quotations and recent trade data for identical or similar obligations. Other investments valued based upon net asset value are included as a reconciling item to the fair value table.

Equities — Common stocks and preferred stocks are classified as Level 1 and are valued using quoted market prices in active markets.

Corporate bonds — These investments are valued based on quoted market prices, yield curves and pricing models using current market rates.

Government and agency bonds — These investments are generally valued based on bid quotations and recent trade data for identical or similar obligations.

Municipal bonds — These investments are valued based on quoted market prices, yield curves and pricing models using current market rates.

Mortgage and asset backed securities — These investments are valued based on prices obtained from third party pricing sources. The prices from third party pricing sources may be based on bid quotes from dealers and recent trade data. Mortgage backed securities are traded in the over-the-counter market.

Real estate — Real estate investments consist of real estate investment trusts, property funds and limited partnerships. Real estate investment trusts are classified as Level 1 and are valued based on quoted market prices. Property funds are classified as either Level 2 or Level 3 depending upon whether liquidity is limited or there are few observable market participant transactions. Property funds are valued based on third party appraisals. Limited partnerships are valued based upon valuations provided by the general partners of the funds. The values of limited partnerships are based upon an assessment of each underlying investment, incorporating valuations that consider the evaluation of financing and sales transactions with third parties, expected cash flows, and market-based information, including comparable transactions and performance multiples among other factors. The investments are classified as Level 3 since the valuation is determined using unobservable inputs. Real estate investments valued at net asset value are included as a reconciling item to the fair value table.

Hedge funds — Hedge fund investments include hedge funds valued based upon a net asset value derived from the fair value of underlying securities. Hedge fund investments that are subject to liquidity restrictions or that are based on unobservable inputs are classified as Level 3. Hedge fund investments may include long and short positions in equity and fixed income securities, derivative instruments such as futures and options, commodities and other types of securities. Hedge fund investments valued at net asset value are included as a reconciling item to the fair value table.

Derivatives — Derivative financial instruments include forward currency contracts, futures contracts, options contracts, interest rate swaps and credit default swaps. Derivative financial instruments are classified as Level 2 and are valued based on observable market transactions or prices.

Commingled funds — Investments in commingled funds are not traded in active markets. Blended commingled funds are invested in both equities and fixed income securities. Commingled funds are valued based on the net asset values of such funds and are included as a reconciling item to the fair value table.

Other items to reconcile to fair value of plan assets included amounts due for securities sold, amounts payable for securities purchased, and other payables.

The following table summarizes the changes in fair value of Level 3 investments for the years ended July 30, 2017, and July 31, 2016:

	Real Estate		Hedge Funds		Total	
Fair value at July 31, 2016	$	6	$	45	$	51
Actual return on plan assets		1		2		3
Purchases		1		1		2
Sales		(1)		(10)		(11)
Settlements		—		—		—
Transfers out of Level 3		—		—		—
Fair value at July 30, 2017	$	7	$	38	$	45

	Real Estate		Hedge Funds		Total	
Fair value at August 2, 2015	$	6	$	39	$	45
Actual return on plan assets		1		1		2
Purchases		—		5		5
Sales		(1)		—		(1)
Settlements		—		—		—
Transfers out of Level 3		—		—		—
Fair value at July 31, 2016	$	6	$	45	$	51

The following tables present additional information about the pension plan assets valued using net asset value as a practical expedient within the fair value hierarchy table:

	2017			2016		
	Fair Value	Redemption Frequency	Redemption Notice Period Range	Fair Value	Redemption Frequency	Redemption Notice Period Range
Short-term investments	$ 31	Daily	1 Day	$ 20	Daily	1 Day
Commingled funds:						
Equities	332	Daily, Monthly	2 to 60 Days	309	Daily, Monthly	1 to 60 Days
Fixed income	30	Daily	1 Day	31	Daily	1 Day
Blended	86	Primarily Daily	1 to 20 Days	79	Primarily Daily	1 Day
Real estate funds[(1)]	84	Quarterly	45 to 90 Days	108	Primarily Quarterly	1 to 90 Days
Hedge funds[(2)]	103	Monthly	5 to 30 Days	144	Monthly, Quarterly	5 to 65 Days
Total.	$ 666			$ 691		

[(1)] Included real estate investments valued at $34 in 2016 for which a redemption queue was imposed by the investment manager increasing the redemption receipt period to up to 9 months after notice.

[(2)] Includes a fund valued at $2 in 2017 and $45 in 2016 which is being liquidated. Distributions from the fund will be received as the underlying investments are liquidated which is estimated to occur by December 31, 2017.

There were no unfunded commitments in 2017 or 2016.

No contributions are expected to be made to U.S. pension plans in 2018. We expect contributions to non-U.S. pension plans to be approximately $5 in 2018.

Estimated future benefit payments are as follows:

	Pension	Postretirement
2018	$ 175	$ 29
2019	$ 171	$ 28
2020	$ 162	$ 27
2021	$ 160	$ 25
2022	$ 161	$ 24
2023-2027.	$ 801	$ 97

The estimated future benefit payments include payments from funded and unfunded plans.

401(k) Retirement Plan — We sponsor employee savings plans that cover substantially all U.S. employees. Effective January 1, 2011, we provide a matching contribution of 100% of employee contributions up to 4% of compensation for employees who are not covered by collective bargaining agreements. Employees hired or rehired on or after January 1, 2011, who will not be eligible to participate in the defined benefit plans and who are not covered by collective bargaining agreements receive a contribution equal to 3% of compensation regardless of their participation in the 401(k) Retirement Plan. Amounts charged to Costs and expenses were $34 in 2017, $33 in 2016 and $31 in 2015.

11. Taxes on Earnings

The provision for income taxes on earnings consists of the following:

	2017	2016	2015
Income taxes:			
Currently payable:			
Federal	$ 238	$ 235	$ 246
State	39	34	31
Non-U.S.	36	47	55
	313	316	332
Deferred:			
Federal	77	(17)	(47)
State	2	—	1
Non-U.S.	14	(13)	(3)
	93	(30)	(49)
	$ 406	$ 286	$ 283

	2017	2016	2015
Earnings before income taxes:			
United States	$ 1,103	$ 705	$ 803
Non-U.S.	190	144	146
	$ 1,293	$ 849	$ 949

The following is a reconciliation of the effective income tax rate to the U.S. federal statutory income tax rate:

	2017	2016	2015
Federal statutory income tax rate.	35.0%	35.0%	35.0%
State income taxes (net of federal tax benefit).	2.1	2.7	2.2
Tax effect of international items.	(2.1)	(3.0)	(2.5)
Settlement of tax contingencies	—	—	(0.8)
Federal manufacturing deduction.	(2.1)	(3.2)	(2.9)
Goodwill impairment	3.4	4.3	—
Claim settlement.	—	(0.8)	—
Foreign exchange losses[1]	(3.9)	—	—
Other.	(1.0)	(1.3)	(1.2)
Effective income tax rate	31.4%	33.7%	29.8%

[1]   The 2017 rate was favorably impacted by a $52 benefit primarily related to the sale of intercompany notes receivable to a financial institution, which resulted in the recognition of foreign exchange losses.

Deferred tax liabilities and assets are comprised of the following:

	2017	2016
Depreciation	$ 355	$ 362
Amortization	521	541
Other	20	23
Deferred tax liabilities	896	926
Benefits and compensation	241	266
Pension benefits	98	185
Tax loss carryforwards	36	37
Capital loss carryforwards	92	88
Other	95	113
Gross deferred tax assets	562	689
Deferred tax asset valuation allowance	(120)	(118)
Deferred tax assets, net of valuation allowance	442	571
Net deferred tax liability	$ 454	$ 355

At July 30, 2017, our U.S. and non-U.S. subsidiaries had tax loss carryforwards of approximately $170. Of these carryforwards, $149 expire between 2018 and 2037, and $21 may be carried forward indefinitely. At July 30, 2017, deferred tax asset valuation allowances have been established to offset $137 of these tax loss carryforwards. Additionally, at July 30, 2017, our non-U.S. subsidiaries had capital loss carryforwards of approximately $323, which were fully offset by valuation allowances.

The net change in the deferred tax asset valuation allowance in 2017 was an increase of $2. The increase was primarily due to the impact of currency and the recognition of additional valuation allowances on tax loss carryforwards, partially offset by the expiration of tax losses. The net change in the deferred tax asset valuation allowance in 2016 was a decrease of $4. The decrease was primarily due to the expiration of tax losses, partially offset by the recognition of additional valuation allowance on tax loss carryforwards.

As of July 30, 2017, other deferred tax assets included $1 of state tax credit carryforwards related to various states that expire between 2021 and 2029. As of July 31, 2016, other deferred tax assets included $2 of state tax credit carryforwards related to various states that expire between 2018 and 2025. No valuation allowances have been established related to these deferred tax assets.

As of July 30, 2017, U.S. income taxes have not been provided on approximately $820 of undistributed earnings of non-U.S. subsidiaries, which are deemed to be permanently reinvested. It is not practical to estimate the tax liability that might be incurred if such earnings were remitted to the U.S.

A reconciliation of the activity related to unrecognized tax benefits follows:

	2017	2016	2015
Balance at beginning of year	$ 63	$ 58	$ 71
Increases related to prior-year tax positions	4	2	9
Decreases related to prior-year tax positions	—	—	—
Increases related to current-year tax positions	4	3	5
Settlements	(7)	—	(27)
Lapse of statute	—	—	—
Balance at end of year	$ 64	$ 63	$ 58

The amount of unrecognized tax benefits that, if recognized, would impact the annual effective tax rate was $43 as of July 30, 2017, $42 as of July 31, 2016, and $39 as of August 2, 2015. The total amount of unrecognized tax benefits can change due to audit settlements, tax examination activities, statute expirations and the recognition and measurement criteria under accounting for uncertainty in income taxes. We are unable to estimate what this change may be within the next 12 months, but do not believe that it will be material to the financial statements. Approximately $5 of unrecognized tax benefits, including interest and penalties, were reported in Accounts receivable in the Consolidated Balance Sheets as of July 30, 2017, and July 31, 2016.

Our accounting policy with respect to interest and penalties attributable to income taxes is to reflect any expense or benefit as a component of our income tax provision. The total amount of interest and penalties recognized in the Consolidated Statements of Earnings was $4 in 2017, $3 in 2016 and $1 in 2015. The total amount of interest and penalties recognized in the Consolidated Balance Sheets in Other liabilities was $5 as of July 30, 2017, and $6 as of July 31, 2016.

We do business internationally and, as a result, file income tax returns in the U.S. federal jurisdiction and various state and non-U.S. jurisdictions. In the normal course of business, we are subject to examination by taxing authorities throughout the world, including such major jurisdictions as the U.S., Australia, Canada and Denmark. The 2017 tax year is currently under audit by the Internal Revenue Service. In addition, several state income tax examinations are in progress for the years 1999 to 2016.

With limited exceptions, we have been audited for income tax purposes in Australia through 2010, Denmark through 2013, and in Canada through 2014.

12. Short-term Borrowings and Long-term Debt

Short-term borrowings consist of the following:

	2017	2016
Commercial paper	$ 874	$ 770
Australian note	152	—
Current portion of long-term debt	—	400
Current portion of Canadian credit facility	—	42
Variable-rate bank borrowings	10	6
Capital leases	1	2
Other[1]	—	(1)
Total short-term borrowings	$ 1,037	$ 1,219

[1] Includes unamortized net discount/premium on debt issuances and debt issuance costs.

As of July 30, 2017, the weighted-average interest rate of commercial paper, which consisted of U.S. borrowings, was 1.31%. As of July 31, 2016, the weighted-average interest rate of commercial paper, which consisted of U.S. borrowings, was 0.74%.

As of July 30, 2017, we had $1,037 of short-term borrowings due within one year, of which $874 was comprised of commercial paper borrowings. As of July 30, 2017, we issued $48 of standby letters of credit. We have a committed revolving credit facility totaling $1,850 that matures in December 2021. This U.S. facility remained unused at July 30, 2017, except for $1 of standby letters of credit that we issued under it. The U.S. facility supports our commercial paper programs and other general corporate purposes.

In June 2017, we sold an intercompany note to a financial institution of AUD $190, or $152, with an interest rate of 6.98% that matures on March 29, 2021, but is payable upon demand. Interest on the note is due semi-annually on January 23 and July 23. The net proceeds were used for general corporate purposes.

Long-term debt consists of the following:

Type	Fiscal Year of Maturity	Rate	2017		2016
Notes	2017	3.05%	$ —	$	400
Canadian credit facility	2019	Variable	**130**		215
Australian note...................................	2019	4.88%	**224**		—
Notes	2019	4.50%	**300**		300
Notes	2021	4.25%	**500**		500
Debentures	2021	8.88%	**200**		200
Notes	2023	2.50%	**450**		450
Notes	2025	3.30%	**300**		300
Notes	2043	3.80%	**400**		400
Capital leases			**7**		8
Other[1]			**(12)**		(18)
Total.			$ **2,499**	$	2,755
Less current portion[1]			**—**		441
Total long-term debt			$ **2,499**	$	2,314

---

[1]   Includes unamortized net discount/premium on debt issuances and debt issuance costs.

     In July 2016, we entered into a Canadian committed revolving credit facility that matures in July 2019. As of July 30, 2017, the total commitment under the Canadian facility was CAD $170, or $137, and we had borrowings of CAD $162, or $130, at a rate of 2.09% under this facility. The Canadian facility supports general corporate purposes.

     In June 2017, we sold an intercompany note to a financial institution of AUD $280, or $224, with an interest rate of 4.88% that matures on September 18, 2018. Interest on the note is due semi-annually on January 23 and July 23. The net proceeds were used for general corporate purposes.

     Principal amounts of long-term debt mature as follows: $654 in 2019; $1 in 2020; $700 in 2021; $1 in 2022; and a total of $1,155 in periods beyond 2022.

13. Financial Instruments

     The principal market risks to which we are exposed are changes in foreign currency exchange rates, interest rates, and commodity prices. In addition, we are exposed to equity price changes related to certain deferred compensation obligations. In order to manage these exposures, we follow established risk management policies and procedures, including the use of derivative contracts such as swaps, options, forwards and commodity futures. We enter into these derivative contracts for periods consistent with the related underlying exposures, and the contracts do not constitute positions independent of those exposures. We do not enter into derivative contracts for speculative purposes and do not use leveraged instruments. Our derivative programs include instruments that qualify and others that do not qualify for hedge accounting treatment.

Concentration of Credit Risk

     We are exposed to the risk that counterparties to derivative contracts will fail to meet their contractual obligations. To mitigate counterparty credit risk, we enter into contracts only with carefully selected, leading, credit-worthy financial institutions, and distribute contracts among several financial institutions to reduce the concentration of credit risk. We did not have credit-risk-related contingent features in our derivative instruments as of July 30, 2017, or July 31, 2016.

     We are also exposed to credit risk from our customers. During 2017, our largest customer accounted for approximately 20% of consolidated net sales. Our five largest customers accounted for approximately 39% of our consolidated net sales in 2017.

     We closely monitor credit risk associated with counterparties and customers.

Foreign Currency Exchange Risk

     We are exposed to foreign currency exchange risk related to our international operations, including non-functional currency intercompany debt and net investments in subsidiaries. We are also exposed to foreign exchange risk as a result of transactions in currencies other than the functional currency of certain subsidiaries. Principal currencies hedged include the Canadian dollar, Australian dollar and U.S. dollar. We utilize foreign exchange forward purchase and sale contracts, as well as cross-currency swaps, to hedge these exposures. The contracts are either designated as cash-flow hedging instruments or are undesignated. We hedge portions of our forecasted foreign currency transaction exposure with foreign exchange forward contracts for periods typically up to 18 months. To hedge currency exposures related to intercompany debt, we enter into foreign exchange forward purchase and sale contracts, as well as cross-currency swap contracts, for periods consistent with the underlying debt. The notional amount of foreign exchange forward contracts accounted for as cash-flow hedges was $84 at July 30, 2017, and $91 at July 31, 2016. The effective portion of the changes in fair value on these instruments is recorded in other comprehensive income (loss) and is reclassified into the Consolidated Statements of Earnings on the same line item and the same period in which the underlying hedged transaction affects earnings. The notional amount of foreign exchange forward contracts that are not designated as accounting hedges was $336 and $175 at July 30, 2017, and July 31, 2016, respectively. There were no cross-currency swap contracts outstanding as of July 30, 2017 or July 31, 2016.

Interest Rate Risk

We manage our exposure to changes in interest rates by optimizing the use of variable-rate and fixed-rate debt and by utilizing interest rate swaps in order to maintain our variable-to-total debt ratio within targeted guidelines. Receive fixed rate/pay variable rate interest rate swaps are accounted for as fair-value hedges. We manage our exposure to interest rate volatility on future debt issuances by entering into forward starting interest rate swaps to lock in the rate on the interest payments related to the anticipated debt issuances. These pay fixed rate/receive variable rate forward starting interest rate swaps are accounted for as cash-flow hedges. The effective portion of the changes in fair value on these instruments is recorded in other comprehensive income (loss) and is reclassified into the Consolidated Statements of Earnings over the life of the debt. The notional amount of outstanding forward starting interest rate swaps totaled $300 at July 30, 2017, and July 31, 2016, which relates to an anticipated debt issuance in 2018.

Commodity Price Risk

We principally use a combination of purchase orders and various short- and long-term supply arrangements in connection with the purchase of raw materials, including certain commodities and agricultural products. We also enter into commodity futures, options and swap contracts to reduce the volatility of price fluctuations of wheat, diesel fuel, soybean oil, natural gas, cocoa, aluminum, butter, corn, soybean meal and cheese, which impact the cost of raw materials. Commodity futures, options, and swap contracts are either designated as cash-flow hedging instruments or are undesignated. We hedge a portion of commodity requirements for periods typically up to 18 months. There were no commodity contracts accounted for as cash-flow hedges as of July 30, 2017, or July 31, 2016. The notional amount of commodity contracts not designated as accounting hedges was $90 at July 30, 2017, and $88 at July 31, 2016.

In 2017, we entered into a supply contract under which prices for certain raw materials are established based on anticipated volume requirements over a twelve-month period. Certain prices under the contract are based in part on certain component parts of the raw materials that are in excess of our needs or not required for our operations, thereby creating an embedded derivative requiring bifurcation. We net settle amounts due under the contract with our counterparty. The notional value is approximately $35 as of July 30, 2017. The fair value was not material as of July 30, 2017. Unrealized gains (losses) and settlements are included in Cost of products sold in our Consolidated Statements of Earnings.

Equity Price Risk

We enter into swap contracts which hedge a portion of exposures relating to certain deferred compensation obligations linked to the total return of our capital stock, the total return of the Vanguard Institutional Index, and the total return of the Vanguard Total International Stock Index. Under these contracts, we pay variable interest rates and receive from the counterparty either the total return on our capital stock; the total return of the Standard & Poor's 500 Index, which is expected to approximate the total return of the Vanguard Institutional Index; or the total return of the iShares MSCI EAFE Index, which is expected to approximate the total return of the Vanguard Total International Stock Index. These contracts were not designated as hedges for accounting purposes. We enter into these contracts for periods typically not exceeding 12 months. The notional amounts of the contracts as of July 30, 2017, and July 31, 2016, were $43 and $44, respectively.

The following table summarizes the fair value of derivative instruments on a gross basis as recorded in the Consolidated Balance Sheets as of July 30, 2017, and July 31, 2016:

	Balance Sheet Classification	2017	2016
Asset Derivatives			
Derivatives designated as hedges:			
Foreign exchange forward contracts..................	Other current assets	$ 3	$ 1
Total derivatives designated as hedges.................		$ 3	$ 1
Derivatives not designated as hedges:			
Commodity derivative contracts......................	Other current assets	$ 5	$ 3
Deferred compensation derivative contracts	Other current assets	1	1
Commodity derivative contracts......................	Other assets	1	—
Total derivatives not designated as hedges..............		$ 7	$ 4
Total asset derivatives...............................		$ 10	$ 5

	Balance Sheet Classification	2017	2016
Liability Derivatives			
Derivatives designated as hedges:			
Foreign exchange forward contracts..................	Accrued liabilities	$ 1	$ 4
Forward starting interest rate swaps...................	Accrued liabilities	22	—
Forward starting interest rate swaps...................	Other liabilities	—	44
Total derivatives designated as hedges.................		$ 23	$ 48
Derivatives not designated as hedges:			
Commodity derivative contracts......................	Accrued liabilities	$ 1	$ 4
Deferred compensation derivative contracts	Accrued liabilities	—	1
Foreign exchange forward contracts..................	Accrued liabilities	19	7
Foreign exchange forward contracts..................	Other liabilities	1	—
Total derivatives not designated as hedges..............		$ 21	$ 12
Total liability derivatives............................		$ 44	$ 60

We do not offset the fair values of derivative assets and liabilities executed with the same counterparty that are generally subject to enforceable netting agreements. However, if we were to offset and record the asset and liability balances of derivatives on a net basis, the amounts presented in the Consolidated Balance Sheets as of July 30, 2017, and July 31, 2016, would be adjusted as detailed in the following table:

	2017			2016		
Derivative Instrument	Gross Amounts Presented in the Consolidated Balance Sheet	Gross Amounts Not Offset in the Consolidated Balance Sheet Subject to Netting Agreements	Net Amount	Gross Amounts Presented in the Consolidated Balance Sheet	Gross Amounts Not Offset in the Consolidated Balance Sheet Subject to Netting Agreements	Net Amount
Total asset derivatives.......	$ 10	$ (3)	$ 7	$ 5	$ (4)	$ 1
Total liability derivatives	$ 44	$ (3)	$ 41	$ 60	$ (4)	$ 56

We do not offset fair value amounts recognized for exchange-traded commodity derivative instruments and cash margin accounts executed with the same counterparty that are subject to enforceable netting agreements. We are required to maintain cash margin accounts in connection with funding the settlement of open positions. At July 30, 2017, and July 31, 2016, a cash margin account balance of $1 and $5, respectively, was included in Other current assets in the Consolidated Balance Sheets.

The following tables show the effect of our derivative instruments designated as cash-flow hedges for the years ended July 30, 2017, July 31, 2016, and August 2, 2015 in other comprehensive income (loss) (OCI) and the Consolidated Statements of Earnings:

Derivatives Designated as Cash-Flow Hedges		Total Cash-Flow Hedge OCI Activity		
		2017	2016	2015
OCI derivative gain (loss) at beginning of year		$ (64)	$ (10)	$ (4)
Effective portion of changes in fair value recognized in OCI: .				
Foreign exchange forward contracts.		(4)	(9)	18
Forward starting interest rate swaps		23	(36)	(23)
Amount of (gain) loss reclassified from OCI to earnings:	**Location in Earnings**			
Foreign exchange forward contracts.	Cost of products sold	6	(11)	(4)
Foreign exchange forward contracts.	Other expenses / (income)	1	(2)	(1)
Forward starting interest rate swaps	Interest expense	4	4	4
OCI derivative gain (loss) at end of year		$ (34)	$ (64)	$ (10)

Based on current valuations, the amount expected to be reclassified from OCI into earnings within the next 12 months is a loss of $11. The ineffective portion and amount excluded from effectiveness testing were not material.

The following table shows the effects of our derivative instruments not designated as hedges in the Consolidated Statements of Earnings:

Derivatives not Designated as Hedges	Location of (Gain) Loss Recognized in Earnings	Amount of (Gain) Loss Recognized in Earnings on Derivatives		
		2017	2016	2015
Foreign exchange forward contracts	Cost of products sold	$ —	$ —	$ (2)
Foreign exchange forward contracts	Other expenses / (income)	14	(1)	3
Cross-currency swap contracts	Other expenses / (income)	—	2	(58)
Commodity derivative contracts	Cost of products sold	(11)	6	19
Deferred compensation derivative contracts	Administrative expenses	(3)	(6)	(7)
Total.		$ —	$ 1	$ (45)

14. Variable Interest Entity

In February 2016, we agreed to make a $125 capital commitment to Acre, a limited partnership formed to make venture capital investments in innovative new companies in food and food-related industries. Acre is managed by its general partner, Acre Ventures GP, LLC, which is independent of us. We are the sole limited partner of Acre and own a 99.8% interest. Our share of earnings (loss) is calculated according to the terms of the partnership agreement. Acre is a VIE. We have determined that we are the primary beneficiary. Therefore, we consolidate Acre and account for the third party ownership as a noncontrolling interest. Through July 30, 2017, we funded $58 of the capital commitment. Except for the remaining unfunded capital commitment of $67, we do not have obligations to provide additional financial or other support to Acre.

Acre elected the fair value option to account for qualifying investments to more appropriately reflect the value of the investments in the financial statements. The investments were $51 and $34 as of July 30, 2017, and July 31, 2016, respectively, and are included in Other assets on the Consolidated Balance Sheets. Changes in the fair values of investments for which the fair value option was elected are included in Other expenses / (income) on the Consolidated Statements of Earnings. Changes in the fair value were not material in 2017 or 2016. Current assets and liabilities of Acre were not material as of July 30, 2017, or July 31, 2016.

15. Fair Value Measurements

We categorize financial assets and liabilities based on the following fair value hierarchy:

- Level 1: Observable inputs that reflect quoted prices (unadjusted) for identical assets or liabilities in active markets.

- Level 2: Inputs other than quoted prices included in Level 1 that are observable for the asset or liability through corroboration with observable market data.

- Level 3: Unobservable inputs, which are valued based on our estimates of assumptions that market participants would use in pricing the asset or liability.

Fair value is defined as the exit price, or the amount that would be received to sell an asset or paid to transfer a liability in an orderly transaction between market participants as of the measurement date. When available, we use unadjusted quoted market prices to measure the fair value and classify such items as Level 1. If quoted market prices are not available, we base fair value upon internally developed models that use current market-based or independently sourced market parameters such as interest rates and currency rates. Included in the fair value of derivative instruments is an adjustment for credit and nonperformance risk.

Assets and Liabilities Measured at Fair Value on a Recurring Basis

The following table presents our financial assets and liabilities that are measured at fair value on a recurring basis as of July 30, 2017, and July 31, 2016, consistent with the fair value hierarchy:

	Fair Value as of July 30, 2017	Fair Value Measurements at July 30, 2017 Using Fair Value Hierarchy			Fair Value as of July 31, 2016	Fair Value Measurements at July 31, 2016 Using Fair Value Hierarchy		
		Level 1	Level 2	Level 3		Level 1	Level 2	Level 3
Assets								
Foreign exchange forward contracts[1]	$ 3	$ —	$ 3	$ —	$ 1	$ —	$ 1	$ —
Commodity derivative contracts[2]	6	6	—	—	3	2	1	—
Deferred compensation derivative contracts[3]	1	—	1	—	1	—	1	—
Fair value option investments[4]	50	—	1	49	33	—	8	25
Total assets at fair value	$ 60	$ 6	$ 5	$ 49	$ 38	$ 2	$ 11	$ 25

	Fair Value as of July 30, 2017	Fair Value Measurements at July 30, 2017 Using Fair Value Hierarchy			Fair Value as of July 31, 2016	Fair Value Measurements at July 31, 2016 Using Fair Value Hierarchy		
		Level 1	Level 2	Level 3		Level 1	Level 2	Level 3
Liabilities								
Forward starting interest rate swaps[5]	$ 22	$ —	$ 22	$ —	$ 44	$ —	$ 44	$ —
Foreign exchange forward contracts[1]	21	—	21	—	11	—	11	—
Commodity derivative contracts[2]	1	1	—	—	4	4	—	—
Deferred compensation derivative contracts[3]	—	—	—	—	1	—	1	—
Deferred compensation obligation[6]	112	112	—	—	119	119	—	—
Total liabilities at fair value	$ 156	$ 113	$ 43	$ —	$ 179	$ 123	$ 56	$ —

[1] Based on observable market transactions of spot currency rates and forward rates.

[2] Based on quoted futures exchanges and on observable prices of futures and options transactions in the marketplace.

[3] Based on LIBOR and equity index swap rates.

[4] Primarily represents investments in equity securities that are not readily marketable and are accounted for under the fair value option. The investments were funded by Acre. See Note 14 for additional information. Fair value is based on analyzing recent transactions and transactions of comparable companies, and the discounted cash flow method. In addition, allocation methods,

including the option pricing method, are used in distributing fair value among various equity holders according to rights and preferences. Changes in the fair value of investments were not material in 2017 or 2016.

(5) Based on LIBOR swap rates.

(6) Based on the fair value of the participants' investments.

Items Measured at Fair Value on a Nonrecurring Basis

In addition to assets and liabilities that are measured at fair value on a recurring basis, we are also required to measure certain items at fair value on a nonrecurring basis.

In the fourth quarter of 2017, we recognized $12 of charges, primarily asset impairment, on plant assets associated with the 2015 restructuring initiatives described in Note 7. The carrying value was reduced to estimated fair value based on expected proceeds. The carrying value was not material.

In the fourth quarter of 2016, as part of our annual review of intangible assets, we recognized an impairment charge of $106 on goodwill and $35 on a trademark of the Bolthouse Farms carrot and carrot ingredients reporting unit. During the second quarter of 2017, we performed an interim impairment assessment as of December 31, 2016, and recognized an impairment charge of $127 on goodwill and $20 on a trademark of the Bolthouse Farms carrot and carrot ingredients reporting unit.

During the second quarter of 2017, we performed an interim impairment assessment of the Garden Fresh Gourmet reporting unit as of December 31, 2016, and recognized an impairment charge of $64 on goodwill and $1 on a trademark.

Fair value was determined based on unobservable Level 3 inputs. The fair value of goodwill was determined based on discounted cash flow analyses that include significant management assumptions such as revenue growth rates, operating margins, weighted average cost of capital, and future economic and market conditions. The fair value of trademarks was determined based on discounted cash flow analyses that include significant management assumptions such as revenue growth rates, weighted average cost of capital and assumed royalty rates.

The following table presents fair value measurements of intangible assets that were recognized in the second quarter of 2017 and the fourth quarter of 2016, respectively, consistent with the fair value hierarchy:

	January 29, 2017		July 31, 2016	
	Impairment Charges	Fair Value	Impairment Charges	Fair Value
Bolthouse Farms Carrot and Carrot Ingredients				
Goodwill	$ 127	$ 75	$ 106	$ 202
Trademark	$ 20	$ 48	$ 35	$ 68
Garden Fresh Gourmet				
Goodwill	$ 64	$ 52		
Trademark	$ 1	$ 37		

See also Note 5 for additional information on the impairment charges.

Fair Value of Financial Instruments

The carrying values of cash and cash equivalents, accounts receivable, accounts payable and short-term borrowings, excluding the current portion of long-term debt, approximate fair value.

Cash equivalents of $8 at July 30, 2017, and $74 at July 31, 2016, represent fair value as these highly liquid investments have an original maturity of three months or less. Fair value of cash equivalents is based on Level 2 inputs.

The fair value of long-term debt, including the current portion of long-term debt in Short-term borrowings, was $2,582 at July 30, 2017, and $2,949 at July 31, 2016. The carrying value was $2,499 at July 30, 2017, and $2,755 at July 31, 2016. The fair value of long-term debt is principally estimated using Level 2 inputs based on quoted market prices or pricing models using current market rates.

16. Shareholders' Equity

We have authorized 560 million shares of Capital stock with $.0375 par value and 40 million shares of Preferred stock, issuable in one or more classes, with or without par as may be authorized by the Board of Directors. No Preferred stock has been issued.

Share Repurchase Programs

In March 2017, the Board authorized a new share repurchase program to purchase up to $1,500. The new program has no expiration date, but it may be suspended or discontinued at any time. Effective May 1, 2017, the new share repurchase program replaced the prior $1,000 program, which our Board approved in June 2011. In addition to these publicly announced programs, we have a separate Board authorization to purchase shares to offset the impact of dilution from shares issued under our stock compensation plans.

In 2017, we repurchased 8 million shares at a cost of $437. Of this amount, $129 was used to repurchase shares pursuant to our March 2017 publicly announced share repurchase program and $271 pursuant to our June 2011 program. Approximately $1,371 remained available under the March 2017 program as of July 30, 2017. In 2016, we repurchased 3 million shares at a cost of $143 and in 2015, we repurchased 5 million shares at a cost of $244.

17. Stock-based Compensation

In 2003, shareholders approved the 2003 Long-Term Incentive Plan, which authorized the issuance of an aggregate of 31.2 million shares to satisfy awards of stock options, stock appreciation rights, unrestricted stock, restricted stock/units (including performance restricted stock) and performance units. In 2005, shareholders approved the 2005 Long-Term Incentive Plan, which authorized the issuance of an additional 6 million shares to satisfy the same types of awards. In 2008, shareholders approved an amendment to the 2005 Long-Term Incentive Plan to increase the number of authorized shares to 10.5 million and in 2010, shareholders approved another amendment to the 2005 Long-Term Incentive Plan to increase the number of authorized shares to 17.5 million. In 2015, shareholders approved the 2015 Long-Term Incentive Plan, which authorized the issuance of 13 million shares. Approximately 6 million of these shares were shares that were currently available under the 2005 plan and were incorporated into the 2015 Plan upon approval by shareholders.

Awards under Long-Term Incentive Plans may be granted to employees and directors. Pursuant to the Long-Term Incentive Plan, we adopted a long-term incentive compensation program which provides for grants of total shareholder return (TSR) performance restricted stock/units, EPS performance restricted stock/units, strategic performance restricted stock/units, time-lapse restricted stock/units, special performance restricted stock/units and unrestricted stock. Under the program, awards of TSR performance restricted stock/units will be earned by comparing our total shareholder return during a three-year period to the respective total shareholder returns of companies in a performance peer group. Based upon our ranking in the performance peer group, a recipient of TSR performance restricted stock/units may earn a total award ranging from 0% to 200% of the initial grant. Awards of EPS performance restricted stock/units will be earned based upon our achievement of annual earnings per share goals. During the three-year vesting period, a recipient of EPS performance restricted stock/units may earn a total award of either 0% or 100% of the initial grant. Awards of the strategic performance restricted stock units were earned based upon the achievement of two key metrics, net sales and EPS growth, compared to strategic plan objectives during a three-year period. A recipient of strategic performance restricted stock units earned a total award ranging from 0% to 200% of the initial grant. Awards of time-lapse restricted stock/units will vest ratably over the three-year period. In addition, we may issue special grants of restricted stock/units to attract and retain executives which vest over various periods. Awards are generally granted annually in October.

Annual stock option grants were granted in 2017 and 2016 and were not part of the long-term incentive compensation program for 2015. Stock options are granted on a selective basis under the Long-Term Incentive Plans. The term of a stock option granted under these plans may not exceed ten years from the date of grant. Options granted in 2017 and 2016 under these plans vest ratably over a three-year period. The option price may not be less than the fair market value of a share of common stock on the date of the grant.

In 2017, we issued stock options, time-lapse restricted stock units, unrestricted stock, EPS performance restricted stock units and TSR performance restricted stock units. We did not issue strategic performance restricted stock units or special performance restricted units in 2017.

Total pre-tax stock-based compensation expense and tax-related benefits recognized in the Consolidated Statements of Earnings were as follows:

	2017	2016	2015
Total pre-tax stock-based compensation expense	$ 60	$ 64	$ 57
Tax-related benefits	$ 22	$ 24	21

The following table summarizes stock option activity as of July 30, 2017:

	Options	Weighted-Average Exercise Price	Weighted-Average Remaining Contractual Life	Aggregate Intrinsic Value
	(Options in thousands)		(In years)	
Outstanding at July 31, 2016.....................	681	$ 50.21		
Granted	489	$ 54.65		
Exercised....................................	(33)	$ 50.21		
Terminated..................................	(95)	$ 52.49		
Outstanding at July 30, 2017....................	1,042	$ 52.08	8.6	$ 2
Exercisable at July 30, 2017	194	$ 50.21	8.2	$ 1

The total intrinsic value of options exercised during 2017 was not material. During 2016 and 2015, the total intrinsic value of options exercised was $2 and $5, respectively. We measure the fair value of stock options using the Black-Scholes option pricing model. The expected term of options granted was based on the weighted average time of vesting and the end of the contractual term. We utilized this simplified method as we do not have sufficient historical exercise data to provide a reasonable basis upon which to estimate the expected term.

The assumptions and grant-date fair values for grants in 2017 and 2016 were as follows:

	2017	2016
Risk-free interest rate..	1.28%	1.68%
Expected dividend yield..	2.26%	2.46%
Expected volatility	18.64%	18.35%
Expected term..	6 years	6 years
Grant-date fair value..	$7.51	$6.86

We expense stock options on a straight-line basis over the vesting period, except for awards issued to retirement eligible participants, which we expense on an accelerated basis. As of July 30, 2017, total remaining unearned compensation related to nonvested stock options was $1, which will be amortized over the weighted-average remaining service period of 1.4 years.

The following table summarizes time-lapse restricted stock units, EPS performance restricted stock units, strategic performance restricted stock units and special performance restricted stock units as of July 30, 2017:

	Units	Weighted-Average Grant-Date Fair Value
	(Restricted stock units in thousands)	
Nonvested at July 31, 2016..	2,004	$ 45.08
Granted	586	$ 54.79
Vested..	(990)	$ 44.16
Forfeited	(379)	$ 43.87
Nonvested at July 30, 2017...	1,221	$ 50.86

We determine the fair value of time-lapse restricted stock units, EPS performance restricted stock units, strategic performance restricted stock units and special performance restricted stock units based on the quoted price of our stock at the date of grant. We expense time-lapse restricted stock units on a straight-line basis over the vesting period, except for awards issued to retirement-eligible participants, which we expense on an accelerated basis. We expense EPS performance restricted stock units on a graded-vesting basis, except for awards issued to retirement-eligible participants, which we expense on an accelerated basis. There were 155 thousand EPS performance target grants outstanding at July 30, 2017, with a weighted-average grant-date fair value of $49.89. The actual number of EPS performance restricted stock units and strategic performance restricted stock units that vest will depend on actual performance achieved. We estimate expense based on the number of awards expected to vest. In the first quarter of 2017, recipients of strategic performance restricted stock units earned 35% of the initial grants based on actual performance achieved during a three-year period ended July 31, 2016. There were no strategic performance restricted stock units outstanding at July 30, 2017.

In 2015, we issued special performance restricted stock units for which vesting was contingent upon meeting various financial goals and performance milestones to support innovation and growth initiatives. These awards vested in the first quarter of 2017 and are included in the table above. Recipients of special performance restricted stock units earned 0% of the initial grants based upon financial goals and 100% of the initial grants based upon performance milestones to support innovation and growth initiatives.

As of July 30, 2017, total remaining unearned compensation related to nonvested time-lapse restricted stock units and EPS performance restricted stock units was $22, which will be amortized over the weighted-average remaining service period of 1.6 years. The fair value of restricted stock units vested during 2017, 2016 and 2015 was $55, $44 and $56, respectively. The weighted-average grant-date fair value of the restricted stock units granted during 2016 and 2015 was $50.44 and $43.00, respectively.

The following table summarizes TSR performance restricted stock units as of July 30, 2017:

	Units	Weighted-Average Grant-Date Fair Value
	(Restricted stock units in thousands)	
Nonvested at July 31, 2016.	1,641	$ 49.13
Granted	606	$ 39.53
Vested	(251)	$ 36.26
Forfeited	(222)	$ 44.58
Nonvested at July 30, 2017.	1,774	$ 48.24

We estimated the fair value of TSR performance restricted stock units at the grant date using a Monte Carlo simulation. Assumptions used in the Monte Carlo simulation were as follows:

	2017	2016	2015
Risk-free interest rate	0.85%	0.92%	0.97%
Expected dividend yield	2.26%	2.46%	2.91%
Expected volatility	17.78%	17.25%	16.20%
Expected term	3 years	3 years	3 years

We recognize compensation expense on a straight-line basis over the service period. As of July 30, 2017, total remaining unearned compensation related to TSR performance restricted stock units was $27, which will be amortized over the weighted-average remaining service period of 1.6 years. In the first quarter of 2017, recipients of TSR performance restricted stock units earned 75% of the initial grants based upon our TSR ranking in a performance peer group during a three-year period ended July 29, 2016. In the first quarter of 2016, recipients of TSR performance restricted stock units earned 100% of the initial grants based upon our TSR ranking in a performance peer group during a three-year period ended July 31, 2015. There were no TSR performance restricted stock units scheduled to vest in 2015. The fair value of TSR performance restricted stock units vested during 2017 and 2016 was $14 and $22, respectively. The grant-date fair value of the TSR performance restricted stock units granted during 2016 and 2015 was $62.44 and $43.39, respectively. In the first quarter of 2018, recipients of TSR performance restricted stock units will receive a 125% payout based upon our TSR ranking in a performance peer group during a three-year period ended July 28, 2017.

The excess tax benefits on the exercise of stock options and vested restricted stock presented as cash flows from operating activities were $6 in 2017, $7 in 2016 and $6 in 2015. Cash received from the exercise of stock options was $2 for 2017 and 2016, and $9 for 2015, and are reflected in cash flows from financing activities in the Consolidated Statements of Cash Flows.

18. Commitments and Contingencies

Regulatory and Litigation Matters

We are involved in various pending or threatened legal or regulatory proceedings, including purported class actions, arising from the conduct of business both in the ordinary course and otherwise. Modern pleading practice in the U.S. permits considerable variation in the assertion of monetary damages or other relief. Jurisdictions may permit claimants not to specify the monetary damages sought or may permit claimants to state only that the amount sought is sufficient to invoke the jurisdiction of the trial court. In addition, jurisdictions may permit plaintiffs to allege monetary damages in amounts well exceeding reasonably possible verdicts in the jurisdiction for similar matters. This variability in pleadings, together with our actual experiences in litigating or resolving through settlement numerous claims over an extended period of time, demonstrates to us that the monetary relief which may be specified in a lawsuit or claim bears little relevance to its merits or disposition value.

Due to the unpredictable nature of litigation, the outcome of a litigation matter and the amount or range of potential loss at particular points in time is normally difficult to ascertain. Uncertainties can include how fact finders will evaluate documentary evidence and the credibility and effectiveness of witness testimony, and how trial and appellate courts will apply the law in the context of the pleadings or evidence presented, whether by motion practice, or at trial or on appeal. Disposition valuations are also subject to the uncertainty of how opposing parties and their counsel will themselves view the relevant evidence and applicable law.

We establish liabilities for litigation and regulatory loss contingencies when information related to the loss contingencies shows both that it is probable that a loss has been incurred and the amount of the loss can be reasonably estimated. It is possible that some matters could require us to pay damages or make other expenditures or establish accruals in amounts that could not be reasonably estimated as of July 30, 2017. While the potential future charges could be material in a particular quarter or annual period, based on information currently known by us, we do not believe any such charges are likely to have a material adverse effect on our consolidated results of operations or financial condition.

Operating Leases

We have certain operating lease commitments, primarily related to warehouse and office facilities, and certain equipment. Rent expense under operating lease commitments was $53 in 2017, $45 in 2016 and $48 in 2015. Future minimum annual rental payments under these operating leases as of July 30, 2017, are as follows:

2018	2019	2020	2021	2022	Thereafter
$38	$34	$30	$25	$15	$21

Other Contingencies

We guarantee approximately 2,000 bank loans made to Pepperidge Farm independent contractor distributors by third-party financial institutions for the purchase of distribution routes. The maximum potential amount of future payments under existing guarantees we could be required to make is $204. Our guarantees are indirectly secured by the distribution routes. We do not believe it is probable that we will be required to make material guarantee payments as a result of defaults on the bank loans guaranteed. The amounts recognized as of July 30, 2017, and July 31, 2016, were not material.

We have provided certain standard indemnifications in connection with divestitures, contracts and other transactions. Certain indemnifications have finite expiration dates. Liabilities recognized based on known exposures related to such matters were not material at July 30, 2017, and July 31, 2016.

19. Supplemental Financial Statement Data

Balance Sheets

	2017	2016
Accounts receivable		
Customer accounts receivable	$ 561	$ 566
Allowances	(11)	(12)
Subtotal	$ 550	$ 554
Other	55	72
	$ 605	$ 626
Inventories		
Raw materials, containers and supplies	$ 377	$ 391
Finished products	525	549
	$ 902	$ 940
Other current assets		
Fair value of derivatives	$ 9	$ 5
Other	65	41
	$ 74	$ 46
Plant assets		
Land	$ 64	$ 58
Buildings	1,553	1,488
Machinery and equipment	4,231	4,042
Projects in progress	195	176
Total cost	$ 6,043	$ 5,764
Accumulated depreciation[1]	(3,589)	(3,357)
	$ 2,454	$ 2,407
Other assets		
Investments	$ 69	$ 47
Deferred taxes	36	41
Other	34	19
	$ 139	$ 107

	2017	2016
Accrued liabilities		
Accrued compensation and benefits...	$ 241	$ 263
Fair value of derivatives..	43	16
Accrued trade and consumer promotion programs	131	130
Accrued interest..	34	35
Restructuring	24	57
Other..	88	103
	$ 561	$ 604
Other liabilities		
Pension benefits..	$ 261	$ 501
Deferred compensation[(2)]	96	100
Postretirement benefits..	247	285
Fair value of derivatives...	1	44
Unrecognized tax benefits	34	31
Restructuring	2	17
Other..	56	61
	$ 697	$ 1,039

[1] Depreciation expense was $299 in 2017, $288 in 2016 and $286 in 2015. Buildings are depreciated over periods ranging from 7 to 45 years. Machinery and equipment are depreciated over periods generally ranging from 2 to 20 years.

[2] The deferred compensation obligation represents unfunded plans maintained for the purpose of providing our directors and certain of our executives the opportunity to defer a portion of their compensation. All forms of compensation contributed to the deferred compensation plans are accounted for in accordance with the underlying program. Deferrals and our contributions are credited to an investment account in the participant's name, although no funds are actually contributed to the investment account and no investments are actually purchased. Seven investment choices are available, including: (1) a book account that tracks the total return on our stock; (2) a book account that tracks the performance of the Vanguard Institutional Index; (3) a book account that tracks the performance of the Vanguard Extended Market Index; (4) a book account that tracks the performance of the Vanguard Total International Stock Index; (5) a book account that tracks the performance of the Vanguard Total Bond Market Index; (6) a book account that tracks the performance of the Vanguard Short-Term Bond Index; and (7) a book account that tracks the BlackRock Short-Term Investment Fund. Participants can reallocate investments daily and are entitled to the gains and losses on investment funds. We recognize an amount in the Consolidated Statements of Earnings for the market appreciation/depreciation of each fund.

Statements of Earnings

Other expenses / (income)		2017		2016		2015
Amortization of intangible assets	$	19	$	20	$	17
Impairment of intangible assets[1]		212		141		6
Claim settlement[2]		—		(25)		—
Other		7		(5)		1
	$	238	$	131	$	24
Advertising and consumer promotion expense[3]	$	389	$	397	$	385
Interest expense						
Interest expense	$	114	$	118	$	111
Less: Interest capitalized		2		3		3
	$	112	$	115	$	108

---

[1] In 2017, we recognized impairment charges of $212 related to the intangible assets of the Bolthouse Farms carrot and carrot ingredients reporting unit and the Garden Fresh Gourmet reporting unit; in 2016, we recognized an impairment charge of $141 related to the intangible assets of the Bolthouse Farms carrot and carrot ingredients reporting unit; and in 2015, we recognized an impairment charge of $6 related to minor trademarks used in the Global Biscuits and Snacks segment. See also Note 5.

[2] In 2016, we recorded a gain of $25 from a settlement of a claim related to the Kelsen acquisition.

[3] Included in Marketing and selling expenses.

Statements of Cash Flows

		2017		2016		2015
Cash Flows from Operating Activities						
Other						
Benefit related payments	$	(53)	$	(55)	$	(53)
Other		—		(3)		1
	$	(53)	$	(58)	$	(52)
Other Cash Flow Information						
Interest paid	$	110	$	113	$	111
Interest received	$	5	$	4	$	3
Income taxes paid	$	320	$	325	$	333

20. Quarterly Data (unaudited)

	2017			
	First	Second	Third	Fourth
Net sales.	$ 2,202	$ 2,171	$ 1,853	$ 1,664
Gross profit	841	825	678	715
Net earnings attributable to Campbell Soup Company	292	101	176	318
Per share - basic				
Net earnings attributable to Campbell Soup Company.	.95	.33	.58	1.05
Dividends	.35	.35	.35	.35
Per share - assuming dilution				
Net earnings attributable to Campbell Soup Company.	.94	.33	.58	1.04
Market price				
High.	$ 62.30	$ 63.50	$ 64.23	$ 59.14
Low	$ 52.74	$ 52.59	$ 56.05	$ 50.62

	2017			
	First	Second	Third	Fourth
In 2017, the following charges (gains) were recorded in Net earnings attributable to Campbell Soup Company:				
Impairment charges	$ —	$ 180	$ —	$ —
Restructuring charges, implementation costs and other related costs	6	—	4	26
Pension and postretirement benefit mark-to-market adjustments	13	—	—	(129)
Sale of notes.	—	—	—	(56)
Per share - assuming dilution				
Impairment charges	—	.58	—	—
Restructuring charges, implementation costs and other related costs	.02	—	.01	.09
Pension and postretirement benefit mark-to-market adjustments	.04	—	—	(.42)
Sale of notes.	—	—	—	(.18)

	2016			
	First	Second	Third	Fourth
Net sales.	$ 2,203	$ 2,201	$ 1,870	$ 1,687
Gross profit	755	819	660	546
Net earnings (loss) attributable to Campbell Soup Company	194	265	185	(81)
Per share - basic				
Net earnings (loss) attributable to Campbell Soup Company.	.63	.85	.60	(.26)
Dividends	.312	.312	.312	.312
Per share - assuming dilution				
Net earnings (loss) attributable to Campbell Soup Company.	.62	.85	.59	(.26)
Market price				
High.	$ 52.37	$ 56.63	$ 65.48	$ 67.89
Low	$ 45.23	$ 47.77	$ 54.97	$ 59.51

	2016			
	First	Second	Third	Fourth

In 2016, the following charges (gains) were recorded in Net earnings attributable to Campbell Soup Company:

	First	Second	Third	Fourth
Impairment charge	$ —	$ —	$ —	$ 127
Restructuring charges, implementation costs and other related costs	23	10	9	7
Pension and postretirement benefit mark-to-market adjustments	80	(4)	34	90
Claim settlement	—	—	(25)	—
Per share - assuming dilution				
Impairment charge	—	—	—	.41
Restructuring charges, implementation costs and other related costs	.07	.03	.03	.02
Pension and postretirement benefit mark-to-market adjustments	.26	(.01)	.11	.29
Claim settlement	—	—	(.08)	—

In the fourth quarter of 2016, an out-of-period adjustment of $13 ($.04 per share) to increase taxes on earnings was recorded. The adjustment related to deferred tax expense that should have been provided on certain cross-currency swap contracts associated with intercompany debt. Most of the adjustment related to the third quarter of 2016. Management does not believe the adjustment is material to the consolidated financial statements for any period.

Management's Report on Internal Control Over Financial Reporting

The company's management is responsible for establishing and maintaining adequate internal control over financial reporting. Internal control over financial reporting is a process designed to provide reasonable assurance regarding the reliability of financial reporting and the preparation of financial statements for external purposes in accordance with generally accepted accounting principles in the United States of America.

The company's internal control over financial reporting includes those policies and procedures that:

- pertain to the maintenance of records that, in reasonable detail, accurately and fairly reflect the transactions and dispositions of the assets of the company;

- provide reasonable assurance that transactions are recorded as necessary to permit preparation of financial statements in accordance with generally accepted accounting principles, and that receipts and expenditures of the company are being made only in accordance with authorizations of management and Directors of the company; and

- provide reasonable assurance regarding prevention or timely detection of unauthorized acquisition, use, or disposition of the company's assets that could have a material effect on the financial statements.

Because of its inherent limitations, any system of internal control over financial reporting, no matter how well defined, may not prevent or detect misstatements. Also, projections of any evaluation of effectiveness to future periods are subject to the risk that controls may become inadequate because of changes in conditions, or that the degree of compliance with the policies or procedures may deteriorate.

The company's management assessed the effectiveness of the company's internal control over financial reporting as of July 30, 2017. In making this assessment, management used the criteria set forth by the Committee of Sponsoring Organizations of the Treadway Commission (COSO) in *Internal Control — Integrated Framework (2013)*. Based on this assessment using those criteria, management concluded that the company's internal control over financial reporting was effective as of July 30, 2017.

The effectiveness of the company's internal control over financial reporting as of July 30, 2017 has been audited by PricewaterhouseCoopers LLP, an independent registered public accounting firm, as stated in their report, which appears herein.

/s/ Denise M. Morrison
_____
Denise M. Morrison
President and Chief Executive Officer

/s/ Anthony P. DiSilvestro
_____
Anthony P. DiSilvestro
Senior Vice President and Chief Financial Officer

/s/ Stanley Polomski
_____
Stanley Polomski
Vice President and Controller
(Principal Accounting Officer)

September 27, 2017

Report of Independent Registered Public Accounting Firm

To the Shareholders and Directors of Campbell Soup Company:

In our opinion, the consolidated financial statements listed in the accompanying index appearing under Item 15(a)(1) present fairly, in all material respects, the financial position of Campbell Soup Company and its subsidiaries as of July 30, 2017 and July 31, 2016, and the results of their operations and their cash flows for each of the three years in the period ended July 30, 2017 in conformity with accounting principles generally accepted in the United States of America. In addition, in our opinion, the financial statement schedule listed in the index appearing under Item 15(a)(2) presents fairly, in all material respects, the information set forth therein when read in conjunction with the related consolidated financial statements. Also in our opinion, the Company maintained, in all material respects, effective internal control over financial reporting as of July 30, 2017, based on criteria established in *Internal Control - Integrated Framework (2013)* issued by the Committee of Sponsoring Organizations of the Treadway Commission (COSO). The Company's management is responsible for these financial statements and financial statement schedule, for maintaining effective internal control over financial reporting and for its assessment of the effectiveness of internal control over financial reporting, included in the accompanying Management's Report on Internal Control over Financial Reporting. Our responsibility is to express opinions on these financial statements, on the financial statement schedule, and on the Company's internal control over financial reporting based on our integrated audits. We conducted our audits in accordance with the standards of the Public Company Accounting Oversight Board (United States). Those standards require that we plan and perform the audits to obtain reasonable assurance about whether the financial statements are free of material misstatement and whether effective internal control over financial reporting was maintained in all material respects. Our audits of the financial statements included examining, on a test basis, evidence supporting the amounts and disclosures in the financial statements, assessing the accounting principles used and significant estimates made by management, and evaluating the overall financial statement presentation. Our audit of internal control over financial reporting included obtaining an understanding of internal control over financial reporting, assessing the risk that a material weakness exists, and testing and evaluating the design and operating effectiveness of internal control based on the assessed risk. Our audits also included performing such other procedures as we considered necessary in the circumstances. We believe that our audits provide a reasonable basis for our opinions.

A company's internal control over financial reporting is a process designed to provide reasonable assurance regarding the reliability of financial reporting and the preparation of financial statements for external purposes in accordance with generally accepted accounting principles. A company's internal control over financial reporting includes those policies and procedures that (i) pertain to the maintenance of records that, in reasonable detail, accurately and fairly reflect the transactions and dispositions of the assets of the company; (ii) provide reasonable assurance that transactions are recorded as necessary to permit preparation of financial statements in accordance with generally accepted accounting principles, and that receipts and expenditures of the company are being made only in accordance with authorizations of management and directors of the company; and (iii) provide reasonable assurance regarding prevention or timely detection of unauthorized acquisition, use, or disposition of the company's assets that could have a material effect on the financial statements.

Because of its inherent limitations, internal control over financial reporting may not prevent or detect misstatements. Also, projections of any evaluation of effectiveness to future periods are subject to the risk that controls may become inadequate because of changes in conditions, or that the degree of compliance with the policies or procedures may deteriorate.

/s/ PricewaterhouseCoopers LLP

PricewaterhouseCoopers LLP
Philadelphia, Pennsylvania

September 27, 2017

Item 9. *Changes in and Disagreements with Accountants on Accounting and Financial Disclosure*

None.

Item 9A. *Controls and Procedures*

We, under the supervision and with the participation of our management, including the President and Chief Executive Officer and the Senior Vice President and Chief Financial Officer, have evaluated the effectiveness of our disclosure controls and procedures (as such term is defined in Rules 13a-15(e) and 15d-15(e) under the Exchange Act) as of July 30, 2017 (Evaluation Date). Based on such evaluation, the President and Chief Executive Officer and the Senior Vice President and Chief Financial Officer have concluded that, as of the Evaluation Date, our disclosure controls and procedures are effective.

The annual report of management on our internal control over financial reporting is provided under "Financial Statements and Supplementary Data" on page 74. The attestation report of PricewaterhouseCoopers LLP, our independent registered public accounting firm, regarding our internal control over financial reporting is provided under "Financial Statements and Supplementary Data" on page 75.

During the fourth quarter of 2017, we replaced a financial planning and consolidation system with an upgraded version. In connection with this implementation, we modified select controls relating to financial data consolidation and financial reporting.

Except as described above, there were no changes in our internal control over financial reporting that materially affected, or were likely to materially affect, such control over financial reporting during the quarter ended July 30, 2017.

Item 9B. *Other Information*

None.

PART III

Item 10. *Directors, Executive Officers and Corporate Governance*

The sections entitled "Item 1 — Election of Directors," "Voting Securities and Principal Shareholders — Ownership of Directors and Executive Officers" and "Voting Securities and Principal Shareholders — Compliance with Section 16(a) of the Exchange Act" in our Proxy Statement for the Annual Meeting of Shareholders to be held on November 15, 2017 (the 2017 Proxy) are incorporated herein by reference. The information presented in the section entitled "Corporate Governance Policies and Practices — Board Meetings and Committees — Board Committee Structure" in the 2017 Proxy relating to the members of our Audit Committee and the Audit Committee's financial experts is incorporated herein by reference.

Certain of the information required by this Item relating to our executive officers is set forth under the heading "Executive Officers of the Company" in this Report.

We have adopted a Code of Ethics for the Chief Executive Officer and Senior Financial Officers that applies to our Chief Executive Officer, Chief Financial Officer, Controller and members of the Chief Financial Officer's financial leadership team. The Code of Ethics for the Chief Executive Officer and Senior Financial Officers is posted on our website, www.campbellsoupcompany.com (under the "About Us — Corporate Governance" caption). We intend to satisfy the disclosure requirement regarding any amendment to, or a waiver of, a provision of the Code of Ethics for the Chief Executive Officer and Senior Financial Officers by posting such information on our website.

We have also adopted a separate Code of Business Conduct and Ethics applicable to the Board of Directors, our officers and all of our employees. The Code of Business Conduct and Ethics is posted on our website, www.campbellsoupcompany.com (under the "About Us — Corporate Governance" caption). Our Corporate Governance Standards and the charters of our four standing committees of the Board of Directors can also be found at this website. Printed copies of the foregoing are available to any shareholder requesting a copy by:

- writing to Investor Relations, Campbell Soup Company, 1 Campbell Place, Camden, NJ 08103-1799;

- calling 1-800-840-2865; or

- e-mailing our Investor Relations Department at investorrelations@campbellsoup.com.

Item 11. *Executive Compensation*

The information presented in the sections entitled "Compensation Discussion and Analysis," "Executive Compensation Tables," "Corporate Governance Policies and Practices — Compensation of Directors," "Corporate Governance Policies and Practices — Board Meetings and Committees — Board Committee Structure — Compensation and Organization Committee Interlocks and Insider Participation" and "Compensation Discussion and Analysis — Compensation and Organization Committee Report" in the 2017 Proxy is incorporated herein by reference.

SIGNATURES

Pursuant to the requirements of Section 13 or 15(d) of the Securities Exchange Act of 1934, as amended, Campbell has duly caused this Report to be signed on its behalf by the undersigned, thereunto duly authorized.

September 27, 2017

CAMPBELL SOUP COMPANY

By: /s/ Anthony P. DiSilvestro
            Anthony P. DiSilvestro
       Senior Vice President and Chief Financial Officer
            (Principal Financial Officer)

Pursuant to the requirements of the Securities Exchange Act of 1934, as amended, this Report has been signed below by the following persons on behalf of Campbell and in the capacities indicated on September 27, 2017.

Signatures

/s/ Denise M. Morrison	/s/ Mary Alice D. Malone
Denise M. Morrison	Mary Alice D. Malone
President, Chief Executive Officer and Director	Director
(Principal Executive Officer)	
/s/ Anthony P. DiSilvestro	/s/ Sara Mathew
Anthony P. DiSilvestro	Sara Mathew
Senior Vice President and Chief Financial Officer	Director
(Principal Financial Officer)	
/s/ Stanley Polomski	/s/ Keith R. McLoughlin
Stanley Polomski	Keith R. McLoughlin
Vice President and Controller	Director
(Principal Accounting Officer)	
/s/ Les C. Vinney	/s/ Charles R. Perrin
Les C. Vinney	Charles R. Perrin
Chairman and Director	Director
/s/ Fabiola R. Arredondo	/s/ Nick Shreiber
Fabiola R. Arredondo	Nick Shreiber
Director	Director
/s/ Bennett Dorrance	/s/ Tracey T. Travis
Bennett Dorrance	Tracey T. Travis
Director	Director
/s/ Randall W. Larrimore	/s/ Archbold D. van Beuren
Randall W. Larrimore	Archbold D. van Beuren
Director	Director
/s/ Marc B. Lautenbach	
Marc B. Lautenbach	
Director	

CAMPBELL SOUP COMPANY
Valuation and Qualifying Accounts

For the Fiscal Years ended July 30, 2017, July 31, 2016, and August 2, 2015
(Millions)

	Balance at Beginning of Period	Charged to/ (Reduction in) Costs and Expenses	Deductions	Balance at End of Period
Fiscal year ended July 30, 2017				
Cash discount	$ 4	$ 109	$ (109)	$ 4
Bad debt reserve	3	—	(1)	2
Returns reserve[1]	5	—	—	5
Total Accounts receivable allowances	$ 12	$ 109	$ (110)	$ 11
Fiscal year ended July 31, 2016				
Cash discount	$ 5	$ 116	$ (117)	$ 4
Bad debt reserve	4	(1)	—	3
Returns reserve[1]	4	2	(1)	5
Total Accounts receivable allowances	$ 13	$ 117	$ (118)	$ 12
Fiscal year ended August 2, 2015				
Cash discount	$ 4	$ 116	$ (115)	$ 5
Bad debt reserve	3	2	(1)	4
Returns reserve[1]	5	—	(1)	4
Total Accounts receivable allowances	$ 12	$ 118	$ (117)	$ 13

[1] The returns reserve is evaluated quarterly and adjusted accordingly. During each period, returns are charged to net sales in the Consolidated Statements of Earnings as incurred. Actual returns were approximately $103 in 2017, $95 in 2016 and $105 in 2015, or less than 2% of net sales.

EXHIBIT 31(a)

CERTIFICATION PURSUANT
TO RULE 13a-14(a)

I, Denise M. Morrison, certify that:

1. I have reviewed this Annual Report on Form 10-K of Campbell Soup Company;

2. Based on my knowledge, this report does not contain any untrue statement of a material fact or omit to state a material fact necessary to make the statements made, in light of the circumstances under which such statements were made, not misleading with respect to the period covered by this report;

3. Based on my knowledge, the financial statements, and other financial information included in this report, fairly present in all material respects the financial condition, results of operations and cash flows of the registrant as of, and for, the periods presented in this report;

4. The registrant's other certifying officer(s) and I are responsible for establishing and maintaining disclosure controls and procedures (as defined in Exchange Act Rules 13a-15(e) and 15d-15(e)) and internal control over financial reporting (as defined in Exchange Act Rules 13a-15(f) and 15d-15(f)) for the registrant and have:

a) designed such disclosure controls and procedures, or caused such disclosure controls and procedures to be designed under our supervision, to ensure that material information relating to the registrant, including its consolidated subsidiaries, is made known to us by others within those entities, particularly during the period in which this report is being prepared;

b) designed such internal control over financial reporting, or caused such internal control over financial reporting to be designed under our supervision, to provide reasonable assurance regarding the reliability of financial reporting and the preparation of financial statements for external purposes in accordance with generally accepted accounting principles;

c) evaluated the effectiveness of the registrant's disclosure controls and procedures and presented in this report our conclusions about the effectiveness of the disclosure controls and procedures, as of the end of the period covered by this report based on such evaluation; and

d) disclosed in this report any change in the registrant's internal control over financial reporting that occurred during the registrant's most recent fiscal quarter (the registrant's fourth fiscal quarter in the case of an annual report) that has materially affected, or is reasonably likely to materially affect, the registrant's internal control over financial reporting; and

5. The registrant's other certifying officer(s) and I have disclosed, based on our most recent evaluation of internal control over financial reporting, to the registrant's auditors and the audit committee of the registrant's board of directors (or persons performing the equivalent functions):

a) all significant deficiencies and material weaknesses in the design or operation of internal control over financial reporting which are reasonably likely to adversely affect the registrant's ability to record, process, summarize and report financial information; and

b) any fraud, whether or not material, that involves management or other employees who have a significant role in the registrant's internal control over financial reporting.

Date: September 27, 2017

By: /s/ Denise M. Morrison
     Name: Denise M. Morrison
     Title: President and Chief Executive Officer

EXHIBIT 31(b)

**CERTIFICATION PURSUANT
TO RULE 13a-14(a)**

I, Anthony P. DiSilvestro, certify that:

1. I have reviewed this Annual Report on Form 10-K of Campbell Soup Company;

2. Based on my knowledge, this report does not contain any untrue statement of a material fact or omit to state a material fact necessary to make the statements made, in light of the circumstances under which such statements were made, not misleading with respect to the period covered by this report;

3. Based on my knowledge, the financial statements, and other financial information included in this report, fairly present in all material respects the financial condition, results of operations and cash flows of the registrant as of, and for, the periods presented in this report;

4. The registrant's other certifying officer(s) and I are responsible for establishing and maintaining disclosure controls and procedures (as defined in Exchange Act Rules 13a-15(e) and 15d-15(e)) and internal control over financial reporting (as defined in Exchange Act Rules 13a-15(f) and 15d-15(f)) for the registrant and have:

a) designed such disclosure controls and procedures, or caused such disclosure controls and procedures to be designed under our supervision, to ensure that material information relating to the registrant, including its consolidated subsidiaries, is made known to us by others within those entities, particularly during the period in which this report is being prepared;

b) designed such internal control over financial reporting, or caused such internal control over financial reporting to be designed under our supervision, to provide reasonable assurance regarding the reliability of financial reporting and the preparation of financial statements for external purposes in accordance with generally accepted accounting principles;

c) evaluated the effectiveness of the registrant's disclosure controls and procedures and presented in this report our conclusions about the effectiveness of the disclosure controls and procedures, as of the end of the period covered by this report based on such evaluation; and

d) disclosed in this report any change in the registrant's internal control over financial reporting that occurred during the registrant's most recent fiscal quarter (the registrant's fourth fiscal quarter in the case of an annual report) that has materially affected, or is reasonably likely to materially affect, the registrant's internal control over financial reporting; and

5. The registrant's other certifying officer(s) and I have disclosed, based on our most recent evaluation of internal control over financial reporting, to the registrant's auditors and the audit committee of the registrant's board of directors (or persons performing the equivalent functions):

a) all significant deficiencies and material weaknesses in the design or operation of internal control over financial reporting which are reasonably likely to adversely affect the registrant's ability to record, process, summarize and report financial information; and

b) any fraud, whether or not material, that involves management or other employees who have a significant role in the registrant's internal control over financial reporting.

Date: September 27, 2017

By: /s/ Anthony P. DiSilvestro

Name: Anthony P. DiSilvestro

Title: Senior Vice President and Chief Financial Officer

EXHIBIT 32(a)

CERTIFICATION PURSUANT TO
18 U.S.C. SECTION 1350

In connection with the Annual Report of Campbell Soup Company (the "Company") on Form 10-K for the fiscal year ended July 30, 2017 (the "Report"), I, Denise M. Morrison, President and Chief Executive Officer of the Company, hereby certify, pursuant to 18 U.S.C. Section 1350, as adopted pursuant to Section 906 of the Sarbanes-Oxley Act of 2002, that, to my knowledge:

(1) The Report fully complies with the requirements of Section 13(a) or 15(d) of the Securities Exchange Act of 1934; and

(2) The information contained in the Report fairly presents, in all material respects, the financial condition and results of operations of the Company.

Date: September 27, 2017

By: /s/ Denise M. Morrison

Name: Denise M. Morrison

Title: President and Chief Executive Officer

The foregoing certification is being furnished solely pursuant to 18 U.S.C. Section 1350 and is not being filed as part of the Report or as a separate disclosure document.

A signed original of this written statement required under Section 906 has been provided to the Company and will be retained by the Company and furnished to the Securities and Exchange Commission or its staff upon request.

EXHIBIT 32(b)

CERTIFICATION PURSUANT TO
18 U.S.C. SECTION 1350

In connection with the Annual Report of Campbell Soup Company (the "Company") on Form 10-K for the fiscal year ended July 30, 2017 (the "Report"), I, Anthony P. DiSilvestro, Senior Vice President and Chief Financial Officer of the Company, hereby certify, pursuant to 18 U.S.C. Section 1350, as adopted pursuant to Section 906 of the Sarbanes-Oxley Act of 2002, that, to my knowledge:

(1) The Report fully complies with the requirements of Section 13(a) or 15(d) of the Securities Exchange Act of 1934; and

(2) The information contained in the Report fairly presents, in all material respects, the financial condition and results of operations of the Company.

Date: September 27, 2017

By: /s/ Anthony P. DiSilvestro
     _____
     Name: Anthony P. DiSilvestro
     Title: Senior Vice President and Chief Financial
               Officer

The foregoing certification is being furnished solely pursuant to 18 U.S.C. Section 1350 and is not being filed as part of the Report or as a separate disclosure document.

A signed original of this written statement required under Section 906 has been provided to the Company and will be retained by the Company and furnished to the Securities and Exchange Commission or its staff upon request.

Shareholder Information

World Headquarters
Campbell Soup Company
1 Campbell Place, Camden, NJ 08103
(856) 342-4800
(856) 342-3878 (Fax)

Stock Exchange Listing
New York Stock Exchange Ticker Symbol: CPB

Transfer Agent and Registrar
Computershare Trust Company, N.A.
P.O. Box 505000
Louisville, KY 40233-5000
1-800-780-3203

Independent Accountants
PricewaterhouseCoopers LLP
Two Commerce Square
Suite 1700
2001 Market Street
Philadelphia, PA 19103-7042

Dividends
We have paid dividends since the company became public in 1954. Dividends are normally paid quarterly, near the end of January, April, July and October.

A dividend reinvestment plan is available to shareholders. For information about dividends or the dividend reinvestment plan, write to Dividend Reinvestment Plan Agent, Campbell Soup Company, P.O. Box 505000, Louisville, KY 40233-5000. Or call: (781) 575-2723 or 1-800-780-3203.

Annual Meeting
The Annual Meeting of Shareholders will be held on November 15, 2017 at 4:00 p.m. Eastern Time at Campbell Soup Company World Headquarters, 1 Campbell Place, Camden, NJ 08103.

Publications
For copies of the Annual Report or the SEC Form 10-K or other financial information, visit investor.campbellsoupcompany.com.

For copies of Campbell's Corporate Social Responsibility Report, write to Dave Stangis, Vice President – Corporate Responsibility and Sustainability at csr_feedback@campbellsoup.com.

Information Sources
Inquiries regarding our products may be addressed to Campbell's Consumer Response Center at the World Headquarters address or call 1-800-257-8443.

Investors and financial analysts may contact Ken Gosnell, Vice President - Finance Strategy and Investor Relations, at the World Headquarters address or call (856) 342-6081.

Media and public relations inquiries should be directed to Thomas Hushen, Associate Director, Communications, at the World Headquarters address or call (856) 342-5227.

Communications concerning share transfer, lost certificates, dividends and change of address, should be directed to Computershare Trust Company, N.A., 1-800-780-3203.

Shareholder Information Service
For the latest quarterly business results, or other information requests such as dividend dates, shareholder programs or product news, visit investor.campbellsoupcompany.com.

Campbell Brands
Product trademarks owned or licensed by Campbell Soup Company and/or its subsidiaries appearing in the narrative text of this report are italicized.

Forward-Looking Statements
Statements in this report that are not historical facts are forward-looking statements. Actual results may differ materially from those projected in the forward-looking statements. See "Cautionary Factors That May Affect Future Results" in Item 7 and "Risk Factors" in Item 1A of the SEC Form 10-K.

MIX
Paper from responsible sources
FSC® C103568

The papers utilized in the production of this Annual Report are all certified for Forest Stewardship Council® (FSC®) standards, which promote environmentally appropriate, socially beneficial and economically viable management of the world's forests. The report is printed on Explorer, manufactured with certified, nonpolluting, wind-generated electricity. This report was printed by Innovation Marketing Communications, Inc., which uses 100% renewable wind energy. Additionally, Innovation Marketing Communications, Inc. has implemented technologies and processes to substantially reduce the volatile organic compound (VOC) content of inks, coatings and solutions, and invested in equipment to capture and recycle virtually all VOC emissions from its press operations.

 Transparency. To learn more about how we make our food and the choices behind the ingredients we use, visit www.whatsinmyfood.com.

 Twitter. Follow us @CampbellSoupCo for tweets about our company and brands.

 Careers. To explore career opportunities, visit us at careers.campbellsoupcompany.com.

 Instagram. Follow us @CampbellSoupCo for stories about our company and brands.

 On the Web. Visit us at www.campbellsoupcompany.com for company news and information.

 Hungry? Visit us at www.campbellskitchen.com for mouthwatering recipes.

 Responsibility. To connect to our Corporate Social Responsibility Report, go to www.campbellcsr.com.

Index

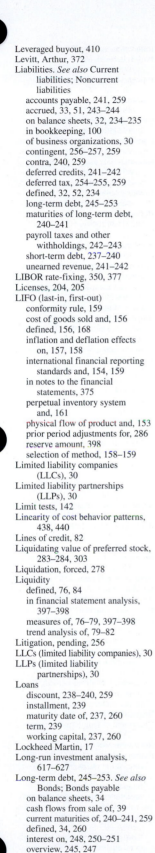